Law in Common

Law in Common

Legal Cultures in Late-Medieval England

TOM JOHNSON

OXFORD
UNIVERSITY PRESS

OXFORD
UNIVERSITY PRESS

Great Clarendon Street, Oxford, OX2 6DP,
United Kingdom

Oxford University Press is a department of the University of Oxford.
It furthers the University's objective of excellence in research, scholarship,
and education by publishing worldwide. Oxford is a registered trade mark of
Oxford University Press in the UK and in certain other countries

First Edition published in 2020

Published in the United States of America by Oxford University Press
198 Madison Avenue, New York, NY 10016, United States of America

British Library Cataloguing in Publication Data
Data available

Library of Congress Control Number: 2019941138

ISBN 978–0–19–878561–3

DOI: 10.1093/oso/9780198785613.001.0001

Acknowledgements

It is a pleasure to stand still for a moment and look back on the generosity, collegiality, and care that made the writing of this book possible. The research began as a doctoral thesis at Birkbeck, University of London, for which I received three years of funding from the Arts and Humanities Research Council. I first began to conceive of its present shape as a monograph in 2014, and subsequently during my brief time as a Junior Research Fellow at Emmanuel College in Cambridge, an opportunity for which I am grateful to the Master and Fellows there. Most of the present work, however, has been written since I took up a lectureship at the University of York in 2016. I am very lucky to find myself among such wonderful colleagues as I have here, whose friendship and camaraderie I truly value—in the seminar room, in the pub, and on the picket line. I finally completed the manuscript during my sabbatical, as a Fellow at the Davis Center for Historical Studies at Princeton University in 2018-9. There I owe thanks to the other fellows for their intellectual companionship, and to the History faculty for their hospitality.

This book was forged in archives, and I want to recognize all of the people who work at the repositories I used, whose diligence and expertise make this kind of research possible. In particular, Rosalind Caird at the Hereford Cathedral Library and Archives, Bridget Hanley and Helen Band at the Suffolk Record Offices, and Sean Cunningham at the National Archives all went beyond the call of duty. Meanwhile Jane and Terry Vosper, Ben and Ginny Johnson, and Pauline and Jon Sheffield, all generously allowed me to stay in their homes while I conducted the research. At the other end of the process, I would like to thank Ian Brookes for his diligent work in copy-editing, and my editor Catherine Steele for her great patience and help in getting the book to press.

My intellectual debts are numerous. They begin with my undergraduate tutor, Rosemary Horrox, who opened up the study of medieval England for me, insisted on the improvement of my writing, and supported me long after she had to. As it turns out, the themes of this book has not strayed so very far from the essays I wrote for her in Paper 8 many summers ago; my enduring interest in these subjects owes much to her quietly inspirational teaching. Over the course of conducting the research for the book itself, I have benefited from numerous exchanges with colleagues who have tracked down references for me, shared drafts of their work or archival sources, offered their collaboration on conferences, or made time to have a coffee and discuss a question or an idea. In this regard I would like to thank Merridee Bailey, Anna Boeles Rowland, James Bowen,

Alex Brown, Sara Butler, Frans Camphuijsen, Linda Clark, Justin Colson, Kenneth Duggan, Lawrence Duggan, Laura Flannigan, Chris Fletcher, Dan Gosling, Liz Kamali, Hannes Kleineke, Anne Lester, John Morgan, Jamie Page, Alain Pottage, Sarah Rees Jones, Samantha Sagui, Dan Smail, Chris Tomlins, Laure Verdon, Brodie Waddell, Sethina Watson, and Barbara Welke. I am grateful to each of them for their collegiality, and sorry that I do not have space here to thank them more.

I also particularly want to acknowledge three people for their intellectual friendship over many years. First, Claire Judde de la Rivière has shared her work and ideas with me since the very beginning of my PhD. Her idea of "cold politics" suffuses this book like an *acqua alta*, and I hope that it goes some way to her conception of it. Second, I am very fortunate that Sim Koole happened to come to a paper I gave in Oxford in 2012, and asked me a question so piercing that I had to seek him out afterwards; I have thoroughly enjoyed the following seven years of interrogation, and look forward to many more. Latterly, I would like to thank Carol Symes for her generosity and exactitude in reading and responding to my work. She has helped me to think in broader, more sophisticated ways about the Middle Ages, and I am proud to have her as a friend.

Many colleagues have read earlier drafts of this work, though needless to say, they are not responsible for the errors in it. My thesis examiners, Miri Rubin and Shannon McSheffrey, have consistently supported me, and first helped me to think about the project as a book; I hope that the finished version offers them some small repayment of all the good they have done me, both personally and intellectually. Chris Briggs made time to read and comment on a draft of Chapter 1, and has been unstintingly kind in his lending me his support and great expertise. Eliza Hartrich has not only indulged my questions about late-medieval towns for many years, but subsequently read a draft of Chapter 2. Her characteristically insightful comments improved it a great deal. An early draft of Chapter 3 was read by Maryanne Kowaleski; it says a lot about her that she agreed to do so even though we had never met. Her comments not only illuminated the chapter, but my conception of large parts of the book, and I am very grateful for her thoughtful response (and glad that we have, now, finally met!). At York, Mark Ormrod's comments on Chapter 7 were the model of supportive critique, saving me from many errors while helping me to see the bigger picture. And right at the end, Lena Salaymeh and Jon Connolly took time out of their fellowships to read the final draft of the Introduction and discuss it with me, offering both insight and encouragement.

Above all, I want to thank my two mentors. For close to a decade, Ian Forrest has impressed on me the ethical stakes of scholarship. He has offered support and encouragement throughout, reading and discussing this work with me countless times—including a full draft of the manuscript (and parts of it twice). If there is good in it, it probably originated with him. John Arnold, who supervised my doctoral thesis and also read the manuscript in full, has guided me through this research with great gentleness and sophistication. His ways of thinking about the past have deeply shaped this project in ways that he would be too modest to admit. I cannot thank him enough for his unwavering kindness and good humour, and for providing the model of intellectual openness to which I aspire.

Finally, I want to make some personal acknowledgements: to Tom Crewe and Tom Baker, for still making circuses with me after all these years; to Alex Patel, my oldest friend, for always sticking up for me; to my sister, Lizzie, for her good sense and resolve; and to my brother, Will, for his rambunctious wit, and for occasionally letting me win at table-tennis. None of them contributed to the substance of the book—they may stick cloths in their ears if I try to tell them anything else about "ye olde times"—but they all kept me on the level, in their different ways.

Last and most, I want to thank Erin, who sees things more clearly, and more fiercely, than anyone I know. This book grew up in the light she casts—in fact, so did I. Every day spent talking about ideas with her is a good one, and there have been many. I look forward to even more.

I offer the dedication to my parents. My mum, Nicola, taught me the care required to look for things properly, and my dad, Henry, the value of mulling them over for a while. Together they have always surrounded me with books and love. Here is the result—a book, surprise!—offered with love.

Contents

Abbreviations

Archives

AC	Arundel Castle
BIA	Borthwick Institute for Archives
BL	British Library
BLO	Bodleian Library, Oxford
BRO	Berkshire Record Office
CCCO	Corpus Christi College, Oxford
CUL	Cambridge University Library
DRO	Derbyshire Record Office
ERO	Essex Record Office
HARC	Herefordshire Archives and Records Centre
HCLA	Hereford Cathedral Library and Archives
KCC	King's College, Cambridge
LA	Lincolnshire Archives
MCO	Magdalen College, Oxford
NRO	Norfolk Record Office
NYCRO	North Yorkshire County Record Office
OHC	Oxfordshire History Centre
SROI	Suffolk Record Office, Ipswich
SROL	Suffolk Record Office, Lowestoft
TNA	The National Archives
WSHO	Wiltshire and Swindon History Office
WSRO	West Sussex Record Office
WYASL	West Yorkshire Archive Service, Leeds
YMLA	York Minster Library and Archives

Printed Primary Sources

Bracton	*Bracton on the Laws and Customs of England*, ed. G. E. Woodbine, trans., with revisions and notes, by S. E. Thorne (4 vols., Cambridge, MA, 1968–77).
CCR	*Calendar of Close Rolls* (47 vols., London, 1900–63).
CPR	*Calendar of Patent Rolls* (74 vols., London, 1891–1986).
PROME	*Parliament Rolls of Medieval England*, ed. P. Brand, S. Phillips, M. Ormrod, G. Martin, C. Given-Wilson, A. Curry, and R. Horrox (Woodbridge, 2005).
SR	*The Statutes of the Realm* (11 vols., London, 1810–28).

Secondary Sources

AHR	*American Historical Review*
Baker, *English Legal History*	Baker, J. H., *An Introduction to English Legal History* (4th edn; Oxford, 2002)
EHR	*English Historical Review*
Helmholz, *Canon Law and Ecclesiastical Jurisdiction*	Helmholz, R. H., *The Oxford History of the Laws of England, Volume 1: The Canon Law and Ecclesiastical Jurisdiction from 597 to the 1640s* (Oxford, 2004)
L&HR	*Law and History Review*
MED	*Middle English Dictionary*, ed. R. E. Lewis, et al. (Ann Arbor, MI, 1952–2001)
P&P	*Past & Present*
VCH	*Victoria County History*

Notes on Translations and Usages

All translations from Latin and French are my own, unless otherwise stated. I have included the original texts in the footnotes in those cases where unusual language was used or when I encountered more difficulty conveying the sense of the original.

I have incorporated Middle English texts in their original form, including the letters þ (thorn, equivalent to 'th') and ȝ (yogh, equivalent to 'y' or 'gh'). For the sake of intelligibility, however, I have added modern punctuation into these quotations where necessary, and in the case of particularly difficult individual words, I have added modern translations in square brackets.

Dates have been converted into the modern calendar, with years starting on January 1.

Money denominations have been left in their original forms and abbreviated according to common convention. Two halfpennies (ob.) made one pence (d.). Twelve pence made a shilling (s.); twenty shillings made a pound (£). Amounts of money were also occasionally described by contemporaries in terms of marks, which equated to two thirds of a pound (13s. 4d.).

Introduction

Here are three legal incidents from England recorded in November 1447. A shipmaster named Edmund Pottere found some driftwood—half a barrel and a small cask—floating off the Suffolk coast. He reported the items to the Hethewardmote, a local maritime law-court, and they were valued at seven pence; as was customary, he paid a fine to the court of half this amount to keep them.[1] Just over a week later in Hertfordshire, it was said that the peasant William Kene cut down a tree on his homestead which, because he was a customary tenant, was not his to cut or sell. At the next court, all of his lands were confiscated, and regranted to him under new conditions 'as a special mercy', so long as he promised to fulfil all of his tenurial obligations.[2] And a week after that, on November 29, Joan Pontisbury and five of her female neighbours went before an ecclesiastical judge in the parish church at Ludlow in Shropshire. There was gossip about town that she had stolen three kerchiefs, or head coverings, from Margaret Greve, which she vehemently denied. Thus she swore a solemn oath of innocence, and her neighbours attested to the judge that her word could be trusted.[3]

These events were all written down within about three weeks of one another in the middle of the fifteenth century. Aside from that, though, there is little that connects them together. While each concerns someone whose life otherwise went largely unrecorded, these people lived in quite different parts of the country and, it is reasonable to suppose, led quite different kinds of lives. As a respectable woman in the prosperous cloth town of Ludlow, it seems unlikely that Joan Pontisbury would have found much common ground with a rural smallholder such as William Kene, who made part of his living from freighting cartwheels to London but also held his lands 'in villeinage'; neither of them, in turn, in their landlocked settlements, can have known much of the life of someone like Edmund Pottere, master of a fishing ship and owner of a beachside cottage flooded by the sea.[4] Even the records in which these events were recorded are starkly different: Pottere's find was noted in a customary maritime court, Kene's tenancy granted in the court of an 'ancient demesne' manor of the crown, and Pontisbury's defence in an itinerant church tribunal that moved among the parishes of Hereford diocese.

[1] SROI, HD 1032/88, m. 6v. [2] TNA, SC 2/177/55, m. 11r.

[3] HARC, HD4/1/90, p. 44 [modern pagination].

[4] Pottere's scattered smallholdings comprised about five acres of land, for which he paid a small annual rent of 2s. 3d. ob., recorded in an undated rental of the Abbey of Leiston: CUL, Vanneck Box 17, I/F/1, fos. 60v, 62v.

Law in Common: Legal Cultures in Late-Medieval England. Tom Johnson, Oxford University Press (2020).

DOI: 10.1093/oso/9780198785613.001.0001

While these particularities are important to what follows, what unites these stories for the purpose of this book is that they all concern common people engaging with law through local courts. Edmund Pottere was himself one of the jury of shipmasters at Sizewell to whom local fishermen and mariners reported the things they found at sea and washed ashore, so he would have been well-used to the procedures involved in the regular valuation of these shipwrecks.[5] Joan Pontisbury, for her part, took the initiative in defending her reputation, and clearly expected to undergo this formal ritual of oath-swearing, known as compurgation, because she arrived at the church prepared, with five neighbours ready to vouch for her.[6] And William Kene, though he might have been surprised by the legalistic nature of his reprimand, ought to have known that it was on the horizon. Not only had he been ordered many times to keep the buildings on his lands in better repair (perhaps because he was extracting resources from them, such as the tree), but he was also heavily involved with the court, serving repeatedly as a homage juror, an ale-taster, and an 'affeorer', one of the two officers responsible for calculating the financial penalties meted out to tenants like him.[7]

These routine involvements with legal process must have prompted some reflection among these people about law—what it did, what it was. For Joan here, we might infer that it was an instrument, a mechanism to re-establish her reputation, or more generally, to achieve justice for a wrong. Clearly, she thought it was worth her time and effort to actively perform compurgation to clear her name, even though her accuser was never summoned to answer for defaming her. For Edmund the shipmaster, law probably looked somewhat different: his activities as a juror to the Hethewardmote were part of his more general standing in this maritime community, both marking and perpetuating his social prominence. Law, as it was constituted there in relation to shipboard discipline and maritime custom, was something that he helped to interpret and decide. And what did law mean to William, a customary tenant who was obliged to participate in the manor court as an officer, reporting offences and calculating appropriate punishments, but who also found himself subject to the sharp authority of its steward? Looking at his varied appearances in the court rolls, it is hard not to see a kind of ambivalent compliance; perhaps what law meant was neither here nor there for him—it just was.

Of course, we can only guess at the thoughts of such individuals, who lived over five centuries ago and otherwise left so little trace. But it is possible to assemble

[5] I have written about this elsewhere in Tom Johnson, 'The economics of shipwreck in late-medieval East Anglia', in *Custom and Commercialisation in English Rural Society: revisiting Tawney and Postan*, ed. J. P. Bowen and A. T. Brown (Hertford, 2016), 121–38.

[6] On compurgation, see R. H. Helmholz, 'Crime, Compurgation and the Courts of the Medieval Church', *L&HR*, 1:1 (1983), 1–26.

[7] He served annually as an affeorer from 1437, as a homage juror from 1439, and as ale-taster in 1444: TNA, SC 2/177/55, mm. 2r, 4v, 9r.

together very many of these everyday legal engagements in order to discern some patterns in the ways that common people interacted with law, and that is what I try to do in this book. An immediate challenge for such research is the sheer quantity and variety of legal institutions in late-medieval England: manorial courts, leets and tourns, borough and mayoral courts, market or 'pie-powder' courts, admiralty courts and port courts, marshland 'congregations', mining or stannary courts, Forest courts, along with a plethora of ecclesiastical courts and tribunals, many of which overlapped in a dizzying complex of institutional forms. Edmund Pottere, for example, as well as reporting to the Hethewardmote, was also subject to the jurisdiction of the manor court of Leiston, the courts of the archdeaconry of Suffolk in the diocese of Norwich, and potentially the admiralty court which sat a little way up the coast in Kessingland.[8] Most people in late-medieval England lived within the scope of multiple jurisdictions, as well as having occasional recourse to the various central courts that lay still further afield.

These jurisdictions offered quite distinct kinds of law to their suitors. The two most common tribunals in this period operated along the lines set by different legal traditions: manorial courts used a form of customary law heavily influenced by the common law of the king's courts, while lower ecclesiastical courts employed the English church's canon law, governed by provincial and diocesan legislation and local practice.[9] Other local forums drew on still more various traditions: the Forest law that grew up by prescriptive royal right and was significantly defined by the Charter of the Forest in 1217, and modified by later legislation; the loose body of maritime law and customs that were symbolized by (but bore only some relation to) the codified 'Laws of Oléron'; and the international Roman-law tradition of *lex mercatoria*, the merchant's law used in the market courts to govern trade disputes, which was granted some official status by statute but not strictly defined.[10] While 'legal pluralism', as the coexistence of multiple legal orders, is increasingly recognized as a normative state of law in past and present societies,

[8] On the archdeaconry of Suffolk, for which no judicial records survive, see Judith Middleton-Stewart, *Inward Purity and Outward Splendour: Death and Remembrance in the Deanery of Dunwich, Suffolk, 1370–1547* (Woodbridge, 2001). William Pottere, a relative of Edmund and also a shipmaster, was among a group of men who complained they had been vexed by John Chapell in the admiralty court in 1448 over the capture of a porpoise. SROI, HD 1032/88, m. 7r.

[9] On the nature of manorial customary law, see the different positions of Lloyd Bonfield, 'The Nature of Customary Law in the Manor Courts of Medieval England', *Comparative Studies in Society and History*, 31:3 (1989), 514–34 and John S. Beckerman, 'Adjudication: The Nature of Communal Judgments in a System of Customary Law', *L&HR*, 13:1 (1995), 1–22. On canon law in later medieval England, see generally Helmholz, *Canon Law and Ecclesiastical Jurisdiction*, pp. 147–236.

[10] Respectively, see *Select Pleas of the Forest*, ed. G. J. Turner, Selden Society, 13 (London, 1901); Timothy J. Runyan, 'The Roles of Oleron and the Admiralty Court in Fourteenth Century England', *The American Journal of Legal History*, 19:2 (1975), 95–111; *Lex Mercatoria and Legal Pluralism: A Late Thirteenth-Century Treatise and Its Afterlife*, ed. and transl., Mary Elizabeth Basile, Jane Fair Bestor, Daniel R. Coquillette, and Charles Donahue, Jr (Cambridge, MA, 1998).

the version of it that prevailed in fifteenth-century England was peculiarly institutional, as these traditions tended to pool in particular courts.[11]

While this pluralism is sometimes acknowledged by historians, it has rarely been scrutinized as an operative condition of law in late-medieval England, and one of the key aims of this book is to think about what it meant for people like Joan, William, and Edmund.[12] When I first began this project, I wanted to see how individuals strategically navigated between the different law-courts at their disposal, perhaps even playing one off against another.[13] Naturally, these hopes were quickly dashed on the rocks of the archives. In the first place, there survive very few concurrent sets of records for contiguous jurisdictions. I could not find, in any kind of systematic way, the same individuals acting in different courts. But I was also beginning to discern a conceptual problem: institutional pluralism was itself plural, changing according to locality. There was a substantial difference between the constellation of courts accessible in different regions; for example, the plethora of fixed courts in cities was distinct in important ways to the many itinerant tribunals that circulated through the countryside.[14] Everything seemed to be dissolving into complexity, as even the formal variety of institutions was layered upon particular local arrangements.

Yet, at the same time, reading the sources of local courts, it was hard not to be struck by similarities between them. This is true in the most basic sense that the record of almost every late-medieval secular court, whatever its jurisdiction, begins with a heading that includes the name of a place, the phrase *curia tenta ibidem*, 'court held there', and the date. Such features are a testament to the influence of handbooks on 'how to hold a court'.[15] But if they are not especially interesting in themselves, they repetitively demonstrate the way in which wider forms of cultural transmission could shape similarities in the practice of law. Indeed, we might regard the common law used in the king's courts, which by the fifteenth century had long shaped the categories and procedures of local secular jurisdictions, as one prominent such form.[16] The Hethewardmote used

[11] The literature on legal pluralism is vast. A useful introduction is Brian Z. Tamanaha, 'Understanding Legal Pluralism: Past to Present, Local to Global', *Sydney Law Review*, 30 (2008), 375–411.

[12] Though see Helen M. Jewell, *English Local Administration in the Middle Ages* (Newton Abbot, 1972).

[13] See, for example, Phillipp R. Schofield, 'Peasants and the Manor Court: Gossip and Litigation in a Suffolk Village at the Close of the Thirteenth Century', *P&P*, 159 (1998), 3–42.

[14] On the restriction of litigation outside the manor court, see Chris Briggs, 'Seigniorial control of villagers' litigation beyond the manor in later medieval England', *Historical Research*, 81:213 (2008), 399–422.

[15] For examples of such handbooks, see *The Court Baron, being precedents for use in seignorial and other local courts*, ed. Frederic William Maitland and William Paley Baildon, Selden Society, 4 (London, 1891), esp. pp. 68–79. On clerical training, see H. G. Richardson, 'An Oxford Teacher of the Fifteenth Century', *Bulletin of the John Rylands Library*, 23:2 (1939), 436–57.

[16] The best general introduction to the royal courts and common law in this period is Anthony Musson and W. M. Ormrod, *The Evolution of English Justice: Law, Politics and Society in the Fourteenth Century* (Basingstoke, 1999).

by Edmund Pottere, for example, though it tended to work within a framework of maritime rights and customs, also heard pleas of debt that resemble those heard in the court of Common Pleas at Westminster, and saw presentments for offences against the king's peace.[17] Such forms can be found across the vast array of local secular courts in late-medieval England.

But not all commonalities in the operation of law in this period can be attributed to the common law, and, I would suggest, certainly not the most interesting and important ones. For one thing, common law forms were relevant mainly to secular law, and yet ecclesiastical jurisdiction, embodied in a vast and variegated network of tribunals throughout the country, was crucial to everyday legal engagements.[18] For another, we can see many commonalities that had little to do with jurisdiction; thus local courts of all kinds, both secular and ecclesiastical, worked in flexible ways to bring about arbitrated settlements for complicated or intractable disputes.[19] And still further, there were many patterns of legal engagement that had more to do with social norms than they did with the forms of law. For example, pervasive misogynistic ideas about female speech meant that women—like Margaret Greve, Joan Pontisbury's adversary—were far more likely than men to be accused of defamation, or 'scolding', in all local courts.[20] Legal engagements in late-medieval England, while they crystallized around institutional systems of law, were also given their shape by geographical, socio-economic, and cultural patterns that emerged from everyday social life.

How can we apprehend this bewildering combination of system and locale, structure and complexity? This is a question that has confronted many historians of law and society. Most scholars working in this area now recognize that, as Shannon McSheffrey has deftly put it, 'what happened in courtrooms was not separate from "real life" but part of its texture', that is to say, law was a thoroughly 'social' phenomenon, and should be treated as such.[21] One of the great advantages of this perspective, indeed, is that it produces studies that are highly sensitive to the contingency of legal engagements, showing how they were constituted by local

[17] For pleas of debt and presentments against the peace, see e.g. SROI, HD 1032/86, mm. 1r, 4v. On the court of Common Pleas, see Margaret Hastings, *The Court of Common Pleas in Fifteenth-Century England: A study of legal administration and procedure* (2nd edn, London, 1971).

[18] Generally, see Helmholz, *Canon Law and Ecclesiastical Jurisdiction*, pp. 213–21.

[19] Almost all historiography on arbitration has focused on secular courts. For some remarks on its use in church courts, see *Lower Ecclesiastical Jurisdiction in Late-Medieval England: The Courts of the Dean and Chapter of Lincoln, 1336–1349 and the Deanery of Wisbech, 1458–1484*, ed. L. R. Poos (Oxford, 2001), pp. liv–lv. Useful insights on its more general valences can be found in Michael Clanchy, 'Law and Love in the Middle Ages', in *Disputes and Settlements: Law and Human Relations in the West*, ed. John Bossy (Cambridge, 1983), 47–67.

[20] See L. R. Poos, 'Sex, Lies, and the Church Courts of Pre-Reformation England', *Journal of Interdisciplinary History*, 25 (1995), 585–607.

[21] Shannon McSheffrey, *Marriage, Sex, and Civic Culture in Late Medieval London* (Philadelphia, 2006), p. 13.

socio-economic and cultural conditions.[22] At the same time, however, there is a risk that by regarding law and society as mutually constitutive, we make law 'too protean to be demarcated.... [and] the result is categorical collapse'.[23] This has important consequences for the histories we tell: as social historians attempting to discern flows of power within the diffuse rhythms of everyday association, we cannot let the structural force of law—with its formidable authority to command life and death—disperse into the ether and become invisible in our analyses.

My broad response to this problem, insofar as it applies to late-medieval England, has been twofold. In the first place, as a matter of historicity as much as theoretical rigour, I think it is important to attend to the neglected problem of legal pluralism with an explanation that emphasizes structure, particularly in relation to spatial organization. The thousands of law-courts may have conceived of themselves as jurisdictional islands, but they clearly operated in archipelagos, defined by their local geography and their relations with other institutions nearby. Thus urban law-courts, whether they were secular or ecclesiastical, burghal or royal, whether they drew on mercantile law or the personal authority of the mayor, tended to share distinctive features: they sat in fixed locations, they met more often and heard more business than courts elsewhere, and, given the high density of legal jurisdictions in towns and cities, they often drew ordinary litigants into jurisdictional disputes.[24] The structures of legal engagement, then, did not emanate only from a particular legal tradition, or jurisdiction, or court, then, but also from the local configuration of legal institutions.[25]

Investigating these institutional configurations—as they took shape in the countryside, towns and cities, the coast, and the forest—occupies the first half of the book.[26] As this organization suggests, it is one of my contentions that that localized social geographies exerted a strong influence on the operation of late-medieval legal systems.[27] But of course these geographies, in turn, influenced what local people wanted from their law-courts. The economies of Forest regions in

[22] A useful survey of such work can be found in Laura F. Edwards, 'Law as Social History', in *The Oxford Handbook of Legal History*, ed. Markus D. Dubber and Christopher Tomlins (Oxford, 2018), 119–34.

[23] Chris Tomlins, 'Historicism and Materiality in Legal Theory', in *Law, Theory and History: New Essays on a Neglected Dialogue*, ed. Maksymilian Del Mar and Michael Lobban (Oxford, 2016), 57–83, p. 67. The problem is explored comprehensively in Pierre Schlag, 'The dedifferentiation problem', *Continental Philosophy Review*, 42 (2009), 35–62.

[24] This is one of the main arguments set out in Chapter 2.

[25] Cf. the Foucauldian concept of the *dispositif* suggested for wider use in Alain Pottage, 'The Materiality of What?', *Journal of Law and Society*, 39:1 (2012), 167–83.

[26] By 'local' I mean 'relating to *place*' in its general sense, rather than to a specific locality, or in opposition to 'central'. For a survey of approaches to this dichotomy, see Christine Carpenter, 'Political and Geographical Space: the Geopolitics of Medieval England', in *Political Space in Pre-Industrial Europe*, ed. Beat Kümin (Farnham and Burlington, VT, 2009), 117–34.

[27] I have been influenced here by work in legal geography: see the essays in *Law and Geography*, ed. Jane Holder and Carolyn Harrison (Oxford, 2002); *Spatializing Law: An Anthropological Geography of Law in Society*, ed. Franz von Benda-Beckmann, Keebet von Benda-Beckmann, and Anne Griffiths (Farnham, 2009).

late-medieval England, as they tended to be characterized by pastoral agriculture and woodland conservation, were tied closely to the kinds of matters that ended up in court, where presentments about stray animals and illicit woodcutting, for example, were particularly prevalent.[28] This kind of symbiosis between the material landscape, socio-economic practices, and legal institutions thus helped to produce distinctive senses of law in different places—what I call 'local legal cultures'. This concept, I hope, as it draws together these different phenomena into discernible patterns, can help us to better grasp what the common people made of the tangles of local legal structures and forms with which they operated.[29]

It also directs our attention to the role of people like William, Joan, and Edmund in helping to constitute legal culture, both because their participation and cooperation with law-courts was necessary to the operation of these institutions, and also because they were involved in iterating and transmitting repertoires of socio-economic and legal practices in these locales. This is important, I think, because historians of this period—even those sympathetic to investigating the lives of non-elites—have tended to think about law as a set of structures and ideas that was generated by elites at the political centre, and concomitantly, to understand everyday legal engagements as instances in which people 'experienced' or 'became conscious' of law.[30] The concept of local legal cultures not only helps us to draw out some structural forms from the complexity of legal pluralism, but also emphasizes the ways in which these structures were perpetuated by common people themselves. Legal forms did not simply percolate downwards, but bubbled up from within associational life and its distinctive institutional engagements.

This is important, because as well as thinking about the senses of law that were generated within local legal cultures, I also want to consider the ways in which legal meaning was created within everyday life. This brings us to the second way in which I have tried to respond to the 'law and society' problem, which is to explore what I propose we call 'common legalities': widespread practices aimed at producing explicitly legal effects.[31] I will explain more precisely what I mean by this just below, but first I want to note that the ubiquity of these practices is important to

[28] On the forest economy, see Jean Birrell, 'Peasant Craftsmen in the Medieval Forest', *The Agricultural History Review*, 17:2 (1969), 91–107.

[29] The concept of 'legal culture' is often used but rarely defined in historical literature, e.g, Daniel Lord Smail, *The Consumption of Justice: Emotions, Publicity, and Legal Culture in Marseille, 1264–1423* (Ithaca, NY, 2003). It is more theorized in anthropology: e.g. Lawrence M. Friedman, 'Legal Culture and Social Development', *Law & Society Review*, 4:1 (1969), 29–44; Barbara Yngvesson, 'Inventing Law in Local Settings: Rethinking Popular Legal Culture', *The Yale Law Journal*, 98:8 [Symposium: Popular Legal Culture] (June 1989), 1689–1709; and the essays in *Using Legal Culture*, ed. David Nelken (London, 2012).

[30] Perhaps the most influential of these approaches is Anthony Musson, *Medieval Law in Context: The growth of legal consciousness from Magna Carta to the Peasants' Revolt* (Manchester, 2001).

[31] This term was pioneered by Christopher Tomlins, 'The Many Legalities of Colonization: A Manifesto of Destiny for Early American Legal History', in *The Many Legalities of Early America*, ed. Christopher L. Tomlins and Bruce H. Mann (Chapel Hill, NC, 2001), 1–20. I am using it in a slightly different way, but attempting to do some similar things with it.

my analysis, and this focus is intended to complement the localized analyses in the first half of the book. In local legal cultures we have a way to apprehend the differences between the local contexts of legal engagement, which opens up the way to see more clearly those forms of law that were produced in common. In combining these two interpretative scales, then, I am trying to conceptualize institutional pluralism and social complexity alongside the broad-based commonalities of legal engagement in fifteenth-century English society and politics.

Moving on to 'legalities', I think this concept can do useful work in helping us to understand the relationship between social life and legal institutions. Recent accounts of medieval law have aimed at 'minimalizing the structural differences between courts (and other public arenas of disputing) and the rest of social action', to use Chris Wickham's sophisticated formulation.[32] Such a perspective has been useful in directing our attention to the fluidity of law and social life. Publicly contracting to marry, for example, or rebuilding a partition wall: these were acts that took place outside of courts, and which could nonetheless have lasting legal effects, whether by establishing a marriage or establishing a property boundary. Yet at the same time, of course, these were not merely 'social' actions. They were careful, deliberative, and often legalistic performances, that explicitly appealed to legal forms.[33] What gave these actions legal force—the reason that people went to the trouble of gathering their substantial neighbours to witness a marriage proposal, or paying a surveyor to precisely measure the ground in question—was the attempt to differentiate them from the informal world of the everyday social association.

In late-medieval England, such appeals to legal form were very often oriented towards law-courts. To make this clearer, it is worth considering a single example. Guilds and religious fraternities, as voluntarist organizations, have often been understood as enforcing social control, as they regulated ethical behaviour and even dress codes among their members.[34] Crucially, though, the nature of this

[32] Chris Wickham, *Courts and Conflict in Twelfth-Century Tuscany* (Oxford, 2003), p. 306. His work stands at the apex of the 'dispute settlement' tradition in medieval legal historiography. Two early collections are: *Disputes and Settlements: Law and Human Relations in the West*, ed. John Bossy (Cambridge, 1983); *The Settlement of Disputes in Early Medieval Europe*, ed. Wendy Davies and Paul Fouracre (Cambridge, 1986). These approaches were based more or less explicitly on the 'post-processualist' approach of Simon Roberts and Simon Comaroff, *Rules and Processes: The Cultural Logic of Dispute in an African Context* (Chicago, 1981). They also tend to draw on the theory of 'habitus' outlined in Pierre Bourdieu, *Outline of a Theory of Practice*, trans. Richard Nice (Cambridge, 1977), or the more flexible heuristics of Clifford Geertz, *Local Knowledge: Further Essays in Interpretive Anthropology* (New York, 1983).

[33] I am drawing inspiration here from the critique of post-processual anthropology made in Paul Dresch, 'Introduction. Legalism, Anthropology, and History: a View from Part of Anthropology' in *Legalism: Anthropology and History*, ed. Paul Dresch and Hannah Skoda (Oxford, 2012), 1–37. See also the essays in *Legalism: Rules and Categories*, ed. Paul Dresch and Judith Scheele (Oxford, 2015).

[34] Ben R. McRee, 'Religious Gilds and the Regulation of Behavior in Late Medieval Towns', in *People, Politics and Community in the Later Middle Ages*, ed. Joel Rosenthal and Colin Richmond (Gloucester, 1987), 108–22. More generally, see Gervase Rosser, *The Art of Solidarity: Guilds in England 1250–1550* (Oxford, 2015).

control was highly legalistic: guilds made clearly articulated rules, explicitly formulated as ordinances, enforced by specified financial penalties or in the lower ecclesiastical courts.[35] After Margaret Chosell was summoned in 1429 to a church tribunal at Sedgeford in Norfolk in a dispute with the local Guild of All Saints, 'she confessed that she is a sister [of the guild], and that she has not observed their statutes'; she was thus ordered to come to an agreement with the brethren or swear her innocence.[36] The existence of such statutes shows how social associations were conceived in legal terms, but also the way in which this legality gravitated to law-courts. This kind of rule-based thinking, and the way it pooled in legal institutions, is typical of social practice and organization in late-medieval England, from marriages to almshouses to common fields.

The second half of the book, then, examines four 'common legalities', widespread practices in which we can discern an attempts to mark out law in the world. Its four chapters look respectively at how common people made law with the physical environment, in their creation and circulation of knowledge, through their deployment of vernacular English, and in their use of documents. These common legalities can be found throughout the distinctively local legal structures identified in the first half of the book: both peasants and townspeople, for example, can be seen engaging with the 'legal landscape' in similar ways, whether by conducting perambulations to mark out jurisdictional boundaries, or altering physical features in order to make them conform with new legal arrangements. In these practices, then, we can see much broader commonalities within the morass of legal pluralism in late-medieval England, and so begin to apprehend the significance of law in binding common people together in this period.

I hope that a focus on these common legalities can shine new light on the social and political history of late-medieval England, and crucially, how to understand them together. The book takes as its starting point the years around 1381: the mass revolt of this year marked a watershed in political culture, and by this time the cataclysms of the earlier fourteenth century—the collapse in population due to the Black Death in 1348–9, and the end of the 'Little Ice Age'—had broadly settled into a new socio-economic order.[37] The consequences of these two major shocks

[35] For examples of ordinances, see *English gilds: the original ordinances of more than one hundred early English gilds. . .*, ed. Joshua and Lucy Toulmin Smith, Early English Text Society, original series 40 (Oxford, 1870). The creation of the vast majority of surviving guild ordinances is complicated by the fact of their survival from the returns of 1388–9, but they do seem to have pre-existed their solicitation from the government: Caroline Barron, 'The London Middle English Guild Certificates', *Nottingham Medieval Studies*, 39 (1995), 108–45, pp. 113–4.

[36] NRO, DCN 67/6, m. 3r: 'fatetur se esse soror et quod non observaret statutas'.

[37] On the fourteenth-century ecological and economic crises, see Bruce Campbell, *The Great Transition: Climate, Disease, and Society in the Late-Medieval World* (Cambridge, 2016); also John Hatcher, 'England in the Aftermath of the Black Death', *P&P*, 144 (1996), 3–35. The literature on the 1381 is vast; for its organization and effects on political culture, see Nicholas Brooks, 'The Organization and Achievements of the Peasants of Kent and Essex in 1381', in *Studies in Medieval History Presented to R. H. C. Davis*, ed. Henry Mayr-Harting and R. I. Moore (London, 1985), 247–70; W. M. Ormrod,

rippled out over the long fifteenth century for the people I am referring to in this book, for want of a better word, as 'common'.[38] This term is not a precise category, but it has the virtue of being a contemporaneous designation that incorporates both socio-economic and political meanings, denoting the majority of the ordinary population; I include within it prosperous husbandmen and well-to-do craftsmen, the landless poor and servants, and everyone in between.[39] For the commons in general, it is well-known the instability of the fifteenth century held out new opportunities—to seek out a better standard of living, to have more say in public discourse.[40] What has received less comment is that they often pursued these opportunities through legal avenues.

Historians have long understood that these late-medieval social and political transformations had an important effect on law and regulation. As Robert Palmer argued some twenty-five years ago, royal government after the Black Death became 'intent on using the law to control society, to preserve as far as possible the status quo'; a few years later, from a different perspective, Marjorie McIntosh showed the ways in which socio-economic instability produced a growing concern with the behaviour of the poor, leading to an intensification of social control.[41] At the same time, however, there has been relatively little historiographical attention to the effects of social change on legal institutions and jurisdictional structures, which remained essentially unaffected—a curious and telling phenomenon in itself—by the drastic decline in population. While some historians have suggested that this led to a decline in the business of the manor court, for example, perhaps alongside increasing litigation in the ecclesiastical courts, we have little sense of how local constellations of institutions might have been reconfigured, or indeed, if people began to think in new ways about their relationship to law-courts in general.[42]

'The Peasants' Revolt and the Government of England', *Journal of British Studies*, 29:1 (1990), 1–30; Andrew Prescott, 'Writing about Rebellion: Using the Records of the Peasants' Revolt of 1381', *History Workshop Journal*, 45 (1998), 1–27.

---

[38] On the economic consequences, the best short survey is Christopher Dyer, 'England's Economy in the Fifteenth Century', in *The Fifteenth Century XIII: Exploring the Evidence: Commemoration, Administration and the Economy*, ed. Linda Clark (Woodbridge, 2014), 201–25. On the political consequences, see John Watts, 'The Pressure of the Public on Later Medieval Politics', in *Political Culture in Late-Medieval England*, ed. Linda Clark and Christine Carpenter (Woodbridge, 2004), 159–80.

[39] See John Watts, 'Public or Plebs: The Changing Meaning of "the Commons", 1381–1549', *in Power and Identity in the Middle Ages: Essays in Memory of Rees Davies*, ed. Huw Pryce and John Watts (Oxford, 2007), 242–60.

[40] Chris Dyer, *Standards of Living in the Later Middle Ages* (Cambridge, 1998), and, by the same author, *An Age of Transition? Economy and Society in England in the Later Middle Ages* (Oxford, 2005). On the widening of late-medieval political culture in Europe more generally, see John Watts, *The Making of Polities: Europe, 1300–1500* (Cambridge, 2009).

[41] Robert C. Palmer, *English Law in the Age of the Black Death, 1348–1381: A Transformation of Governance and Law* (Chapel Hill, NC, 1993), p. 5; Marjorie K. McIntosh, *Controlling Misbehavior in England, 1370–1600* (Cambridge, 1998).

[42] On the decline of the manor court, see Christopher Dyer, 'The English Medieval Village Community and Its Decline', *Journal of British Studies*, 33:4 (1994), 407–29; on the rise of breach of

Beyond the legal responses to these social transformations, then, I hope that the interpretative framework set out in this book can reveal changes in the ways that common people understood legal institutions. One striking example of this can be seen in the 'decline of serfdom'—the developments, after the Black Death, which saw the gradual erosion of unfree status and servile tenancies in the countryside, and the proliferation of new forms of customary landholding.[43] Yet this was not merely a decline in an amorphous social phenomenon, of course, but a change constituted in 'myriad negotiations over tenure' between lords and tenants within manor courts, of precisely the kind in which William Kene was engaged.[44] Such negotiations, I think, reflect a new sense on the part of tenants of what it was possible to do with these institutions, one that is reflected in ebullient interactions with stewards, the making of assertive by-laws, and endeavours by certain groups of jurors to use the court as a community institution, albeit a domineering one.[45] This is to say, it was these pervasive legal practices that themselves helped to bring about the widespread social transformations of this period.

This is an important theme of the book, and it had consequences not only for social relations, but also for politics. Common legalities represented crucial vectors of communication and solidarity, factors which, as many historians are beginning to emphasize, were crucial to late-medieval political culture.[46] For example, Rosamond Faith's celebrated work on the 'Great Rumour of 1377' identified over forty villages in southern and western counties in which unfree tenants attempted to secure rights for themselves by appealing to the Domesday Book, and the concept of ancient demesne.[47] We know very little about the specific mechanics of how this rumour was sustained; but it seems likely that minor lawyers, clergy, or clerks—that is, people with some legal training or practical knowledge of documentary practice—may have been involved in helping tenants see these legal manoeuvres as a route to freedom.[48] But, more than the specific exchanges of information, what is important here is that it was fundamentally a

faith litigation as an influence on manorial litigation, Chris Briggs, 'The availability of credit in the English countryside, 1400–1480', *Agricultural History Review*, 56:1 (2008), 1–24, at pp. 20–1.

43 The classic account is R. H. Hilton, *The Decline of Serfdom in Medieval England* (2nd edn., 1983).

44 Mark Bailey, *The Decline of Serfdom in Late Medieval England: From Bondage to Freedom* (Woodbridge, 2014), p. 336. More generally, see Matthew Tompkins, '"Let's Kill All the Lawyers": Did Fifteenth-Century Peasants Employ Lawyers when they Conveyed Customary Land?' in *The Fifteenth Century VI: Identity and Insurgency in the Late Middle Ages*, ed. Linda Clark (Woodbridge, 2006), 73–87.

45 I flesh out these arguments, about rural legal culture more generally, in Chapter 1.

46 On this latter point particularly, Filippo de Vivo, *Information and Communication in Venice: Rethinking Early Modern Politics* (Cambridge, 2007). More generally, see the essays in *The Voices of the People in Late Medieval Europe: Communication and Popular Politics*, ed. Jan Dumolyn, Jelle Haemers, Hipólito Rafael Oliva Herrer, and Vincent Challet (Turnhout, 2014).

47 Rosamund Faith, 'The "Great Rumour" of 1377 and Peasant Ideology', in *The English Rising of 1381*, ed. R. H. Hilton and T. H. Aston (Cambridge, 1984), 43–73.

48 Ibid., pp. 61–2. On the role of these kinds of lawyers, see Tompkins, '"Let's Kill All the Lawyers"'.

legal idea—and the practice of acting upon it—that bound these diverse people together, connecting them within a common cultural moment.

To claim that law is connective is perhaps uncontroversial. And of course, central institutions were crucial to sustaining such connections. Notions such as the 'king's peace' or the 'king's highway', for example, were used across the entirety of local secular courts in late-medieval England.[49] Common law concepts and process certainly shaped legal engagements in ways that bound people together in a broad legal culture.[50] At the same time, however, the 'network of agencies' involved in the operation of law in localities did not always correspond neatly with official structures.[51] The court of admiralty, for example, which followed procedures in the tradition of Roman law, relied heavily on highly-trained ecclesiastical personnel to conduct its business.[52] Thus for an admiralty inquiry heard at Ipswich in 1518, the admiral's sub-marshal, Robert Johnson, commissioned Richard Stone, proctor general of the Norwich consistory court to make inquiry.[53] Stone, in turn, appointed William Neve, a public notary, to hear the case; Neve's first act was to certify a citation for the defendant before the Dean of Rockland.[54] Official jurisdictional structures were always sustained by a network of interlocking cultural and institutional connections that transcended them.[55]

The social importance of such connections can be seen in action during a brief coda to the 'Great Rumour of 1377' played out in the Bishop of Winchester's manor of East Meon in Hampshire, which had not—so far as we know—been involved in the earlier movement. Twenty-three husbandmen, claimed by the episcopal administrators to owe various agricultural services 'in bondage', began to refuse to perform them in July 1448, 'affirming that they were free men and of free condition.... by colour of a certain exemplification from the book of Domesday of the said manor of East Meon, and a sinister interpretation thereof'.[56] The

[49] Both these notions, interestingly, have their roots in the early Middle Ages: see Jack K. Weber, 'The king's peace: a comparative study', *Journal of Legal History*, 10:2 (1989), 135–60; Alan Cooper, 'The Rise and Fall of the Anglo-Saxon Law of the Highway', *The Haskins Society Journal: Studies in Medieval History*, 12, ed. Stephen Morillo (Woodbridge, 2002), 39–69.

[50] Paul Hyams, 'What did Edwardian Villagers Understand by "Law"?', in *Medieval Society and the Manor Court*, ed. Zvi Razi and Richard Smith (Oxford, 1996), 69–100, pp. 80–1, 92–3.

[51] For this phrase, Michael J. Braddick, *State Formation in Early Modern England, c. 1550–1700* (Cambridge, 2000), esp. Ch. 1, 'The embodiment of the state', 11–46.

[52] See Lionel H. Laing, 'Historic Origins of Admiralty Jurisdiction in England', *Michigan Law Review*, 45:2 (1946), 163–82.

[53] SROI, SC18/40, mm. 1r–2r.

[54] For Neve's elaborate notary mark, see ibid., m. 6r. The mark is a cross, standing on a base, wherein are the words: 'Universe vie d[omi]ni m[isericord]ia et veritas'—the beginning of Psalm 24, which continues—'requirentibus testamentum eius et testimonia eius' (All the ways of the lord are mercy and truth, to those who seek his testament and testimonies).

[55] See Ian Forrest, 'The archive of the official of Stow and the "machinery" of church government in the late thirteenth century', *Historical Research*, 84:223 (2011), 1–13.

[56] This is recorded in MCO, Hilhampton 39, the bishop's exemplification of the subsequent legal proceedings, obtained in 1461. A copy of the Domesday exemplification (whether the original seized by episcopal administrators, a copy, or a further exemplification of their own) survives as Misc. 275.

bishop responded by launching legal proceedings against them, but these were inconclusive, for in 1461 they obtained another exemplification, this time from the Pipe Rolls of Henry II; the bishop, in turn, exemplified his earlier suit on a huge sheet of parchment with his enormous seal attached, perhaps intended for display.[57] While the outcome of this later dispute is unknown, its striking similarity to events two generations earlier provides a tantalizing hint of the way that a common culture of legal engagement could form and endure beyond the registration of officialdom.

Common legalities were thus crucial to the emergence of the distinctive political culture of the long fifteenth century. John Watts has argued persuasively that as the expansive government of this period brought more people into the scope of politics, so 'the commons', as both a broad constituency of people and a legitimating idea, came to take a greater prominence in public discourse.[58] As historians have long known, participation in local courts through office-holding or verdict-giving was a crucial vector of these developments.[59] But I would like to go further and suggest that a broader range of legal activities—from taking an oath to owning a document—can be understood as forming part of political life among the commons and, indeed, provide us with a heuristic for understanding of 'popular politics' in late-medieval England that proceeds from the bottom up, rather than the top down.[60] As legality gave institutional forms to the ways in which subjects understood authority and organized their associative relations, so in this period of upheaval it took on immense importance as a mode of political action; but this participation also had ambivalent long-term consequences, as it also served to restrict this range of action—a point I emphasize in the final two chapters in particular.

The two broad perspectives set out in this book—the local and the common—have been made possible by the way in which I assembled and interpreted my body of evidence. I have looked mostly at legal documents that were produced and archived locally: specifically, around a hundred different series of court rolls and books, drawn from most parts of England, from every jurisdiction that I could lay my hands on, seeking to incorporate as great a variety of material as possible.

The commons petition of 1377 which attested to the rumour also complained of the 'malicious interpretation' of the Domesday exemplifications: Faith, '"Great Rumour"', p. 44.

[57] MCO, Hilhampton 39. The pipe-roll exemplification, which notes it was pursued by three named husbandmen, survives as MCO, Misc. 164.

[58] See Watts, 'Pressure of the Public', pp. 161–2, building on Gerald Harriss, 'Political Society and the Growth of Government in Late Medieval England', *P&P*, 138 (1993), 28–57.

[59] R. B. Goheen, 'Peasant Politics? Village Community and the Crown in Fifteenth-Century England', *AHR*, 96:1 (1991), 42–62.

[60] Cf. the pioneering article by I. M. W. Harvey, 'Was there a popular politics in fifteenth-century England?', in *The McFarlane Legacy: Studies in Late Medieval Politics and Society*, ed. R. H. Britnell and A. J. Pollard (Stroud, 1996), 155–74.

While there are some particularly rich series of records where I have tried to plumb deeper, generally I have aimed for breadth rather than depth. I have not set out to explore central records in any systematic way. Even while some central courts were hearing more litigation in the fifteenth century, the overwhelming majority of common people's legal engagements took place in local institutions; there is a material reality to the claim that local law-courts heard the majority of legal business—of law—in late-medieval England.[61] To continue to privilege central records is largely to accept the view of a centralized legal system that contemporary elites wished us to have.[62] The kind of 'translocal' approach to law put forward in this book, following others elsewhere, can make visible social changes and worlds of commonality that did not originate with the state, but were produced by common people.[63]

I have also tried wherever possible to look at other kinds of legal or paralegal documents than court rolls, such as bills and petitions, depositions and testimonials, citations and summonses, deeds and contracts, notes and memoranda, among other things. These kinds of legal writing—often ephemeral and miscellaneous, and sometimes *sui generis*—are crucial to this project because of the ways in which they can supplement the official records of proceedings represented by most court rolls and books. Moreover, they tell us something significant about the textuality of late-medieval law.[64] I explore the great proliferation of 'common' legal documents in more detail in the eighth chapter, but it is important to note from the very start that they give us a much better sense of the legal writings more often produced, owned, and used by common people in late-medieval England. These writings constitute a great 'missing archive' of everyday legal documents, which have otherwise been dispersed and lost to time. But while their loss to history may be lamented, they were also significant, I think, as a contemporary social phenomenon, a crucial lineament of common legality.

Indeed, the approach of this book has involved a little rethinking of how to read legal sources. As premodern historians have long understood, legal records offer us a 'window' onto past societies, as they capture fleeting details of everyday life,

[61] On the main central courts, see Margaret Hastings, *The Court of Common Pleas in Fifteenth-Century England: A study of legal administration and procedure* (2nd edn, London, 1971); Marjorie Blatcher, *The Court of King's Bench 1450–1550: A Study in Self-help* (London, 1978); T. S. Haskett, 'The Medieval English Court of Chancery', *L&HR*, 14 (1996), 245–313.

[62] I am influenced here by the critique of common law set out in Nicholas K. Blomley, *Law, Space, and the Geographies of Power* (New York and London, 1994).

[63] See E. P. Thompson, *Customs in Common: Studies in Traditional Popular Culture* (London, 1991), pp. 10-13; the title of this book is of course a homage to his. On the concept of translocality, see Clemens Greiner and Patrick Sakdapolrak, 'Translocality: Concepts, Applications and Emerging Research Perspectives', *Geography Compass*, 7:5 (2013), 373–84. For recent works that have pursued a 'translocal' approach (without calling it that), see McIntosh, *Controlling Misbehavior*, pp. 7–11; Bailey, *Decline of Serfdom*, pp. 87–103. Thanks to Laura Flannigan for helping me to think about 'the local' in more interesting ways.

[64] I have written about this elsewhere in Tom Johnson, 'Legal Ephemera in the Ecclesiastical Courts of Late-Medieval England', *Open Library of Humanities*, 5:1 (2019), 1–27.

and hint at the still more complex social world in which people like Edmund Pottere, William Kene, and Joan Pontisbury operated: the expertise needed to recognize that some driftwood had value and was worth plucking from the sea, the boldness (or foolishness) of altering a customary homestead without permission, the humiliation of accusation and the solace of neighbourly remedy.[65] Legal records disclose these details in an offhand way, because they were subordinate to the purposes of law. Shipwrecked goods found by fishermen, and indeed the land dealings of peasants, were written down because they represented a jurisdictional right, and a revenue stream, of a local lord; insults between neighbours were recorded in service of the church's legal mission of moral correction and reconciliation.

We thus have to be cautious in using these voluble sources for social history. Firstly, there is the straightforward problem of distance between the record and everyday life: written long after the events they describe, they can seem remote from social action. We can have no idea where, or when, or how Edmund Pottere 'found' his driftwood, because these things were not relevant to the legal account.[66] Secondly, legal discourse provided a wealth of fictions for glossing social life.[67] The seizure of William Kene's lands, followed immediately by their being granted back to him on different terms, makes little sense except as a legal transaction to change his tenure; the record of course occludes the discussions that this act must have entailed. And, thirdly, we have to take account of the way that these records encoded wider cultural discourses, for example about the value and authority of female voices amplified.[68] Legal records are thus awkward sources not only because they give us partial accounts of a social world, but because they hide the ways in which they were shaped by the world they represent.

And of course, legal records were not passive witnesses to the flood of social life that rushed through the courts, but were actively involved in shaping the forms it took. They were not just stores of information, but legal acts in themselves. For some legal records this is true in a formalistic way because of their status in late-medieval court proceedings. For example, when the clerk of the court at King's

[65] For reflections on this method, see the essays in *History from Crime*, ed. Edward Muir and Guido Ruggiero, transl. Margaret A. Galluci, Corrada Biazzo Curry, and Mary M. Galluci (Baltimore, MA, 1994); *Voices from the Bench: The Narratives of Lesser Folk in Medieval Trials*, ed. Michael Goodich (Basingstoke, 2006).

[66] I have written elsewhere about this act of 'finding' and what it presupposes: Tom Johnson, 'Medieval Law and Materiality: Shipwreck, Finders, and Property on the Suffolk Coast, *c.*1380–1410', *AHR*, 120:2 (2015), 406–32.

[67] Famously, see Natalie Zemon Davis, *Fiction in the Archives: Pardon Tales and their Tellers in Sixteenth-Century France* (Stanford, CA, 1987); for late-medieval England, see the discussion in P. J. P. Goldberg, *Communal Discord, Child Abduction, and Rape in the Later Middle Ages* (Basingstoke, 2008).

[68] See Sandy Bardsley, *Venomous Tongues: Speech and Gender in Late Medieval England* (Philadelphia, 2006).

Langley wrote that William Kene now held his lands according to different terms of tenure, he was also *enacting* this change, because manorial court rolls were perhaps the most important of the authoritative writings that were consulted when someone wanted to know the terms by which a tenant held their lands.[69] But the same point is also true in a more general way, because writing was an important part of the enunciation of law in this period. Legal events in late-medieval England—courts, tribunals, inquiries, depositions, oaths, and so forth—did not take place without writing. This is not to say that writing was necessary for the transaction of legal process. But it is to say that surviving legal records, because they were a crucial aspect of law, helped to constitute the world that they describe.

I have read my sources in a way that tries to treat this as a virtue rather than a problem, by taking seriously the idea that the legal engagements recorded in court rolls were not constituted only by the scribes. I do this for two reasons. The first, more theoretical reason is that this 'surface' reading of legal records, in taking seriously what these texts purport to describe to us, does something to capture the sheer, dense legality of everyday social life of which they were a part.[70] Medieval scribes did not think they were writing fictions when they wrote that someone had 'breached faith' or 'trespassed' or been 'restored to pristine reputation': they were enunciating actions that constituted a social reality. I think it is important to recognize the facticity of these statements—in the etymological sense of a 'fact' as something that is done or made—even while we continue to probe these texts for deeper cultural meanings.[71] The second reason is simply that reading these sources in this way, I think, takes us deeper into the worlds of people whom we can otherwise perceive only dimly. I do not believe in the need to 'do justice' to my actors; people like Edmund, Joan, and William had quite enough justice in their own lifetimes. But I do believe that historians should try to write about people like them, and that the ways in which we do so are part of a longer history which is still unfolding.

[69] This is discussed further in Chapter 8. On the rolls more generally, see Zvi Razi and Richard Smith, 'The Origins of the English Manorial Court Rolls as a Written Record: A Puzzle', in *Medieval Society and the Manor Court*, ed. Razi and Smith, 36–68.

[70] Stephen Best and Sharon Marcus, 'Surface Reading: An Introduction', *Representations*, 108:1 (2009), 1–21.

[71] This point about facts is made well in Bruno Latour, *Reassembling the Social: An Introduction to Actor-Network-Theory* (Oxford, 2005), p. 90.

PART I
LOCAL LEGAL CULTURES

In the first half of this book, each chapter takes as its subject one of four local legal cultures: the rural, the urban, the maritime, and the Forest. In each case, I try to situate the distinctive kinds of legal institution we find in these places within their socio-economic contexts, before showing how people there engaged with these institutions, and the way in which these interactions generated a distinctive understanding of law—a local legal culture. Thus I suggest that rural legal culture revolved around attempts to enforce homogeneous community, urban legal culture was concerned with the spatial ordering of social relations, maritime legal culture valorized expertise as a form of legitimacy, and Forest legal culture focused upon the management of natural resources as a means of governing people. These different expectations emerged on the one hand from the quite different patterns of social life and work that we find in these localities, and on the other hand from the distinctive institutional structures that developed there; and, of course, these legal cultures subsequently fed back into the reproduction of these material and institutional structures.

As I emphasized in the introduction, local legal cultures were neither homogeneous nor disconnected from one another. Some of these localities clearly overlap with one another: much maritime legal activity took place in port towns that were no less 'towns' than they were 'ports', while Forests in late-medieval England were almost exclusively comprised of rural lands, and many of their inhabitants engaged in similar kinds of agricultural activity, and with a similar form of legal institution (in the form of seigneurial, royal, and ecclesiastical courts) as those elsewhere in the countryside. Moreover, the legal cultures in these places were not hermetically sealed off from one another, not only because they all drew on aspects of common law, parliamentary statute, and other royal institutions, but also because, as we shall see in the second half of the book, they were connected together tOugh 'common legalities', broader cultural structures of legal thought and praxis that can be seen throughout late-medieval England.

Yet the focus in the first half of the book rests upon a conviction that local legal cultures were meaningfully distinct, in ways that mattered. Townspeople, as they lived in close proximity to multiple courts which sat much more frequently and

Law in Common: Legal Cultures in Late-Medieval England. Tom Johnson, Oxford University Press (2020).

DOI: 10.1093/oso/9780198811879.001.0001

heard much more business than those in the countryside, had more opportunities to take their disputes to law, but were also often drawn into jurisdictional disputes as a result. Law, for them, was nearer, and more fraught, than it was for rural dwellers, for whom the loosening of seigneurial jurisdiction in the later fourteenth and early fifteenth centuries opened up the possibility of using the courts at their disposal to shape the community in which they lived. By contrast, the idiosyncratic institutions of the maritime legal tradition and Forest law worked in opposite directions; where maritime legal culture afforded sailors and shipmasters a large degree of control over the articulation of maritime law, the devolution of Forest law to local officers in the later Middle Ages tended to work against the ability of Forest communities to defend their customary rights. The different trajectories of local legal cultures in the fifteenth century thus had material consequences for common people, and for the ways in which they engaged with law.

Most importantly of all, local legal cultures continued to form crucial focal points of solidarity against the increasing ambitions and demands of royal government. It is an irony of legal history that the long and tangled processes by which the common law took shape in the twelfth and thirteenth centuries also helped to create the deep-rooted jurisdictional structures around which localized cultures of law would coalesce over the course of the later Middle Ages. As we shall see, common folk, whether peasant farmers, urban artisans, mariners, or Forest-dwellers, found in their local institutions a tremendous source of legitimacy for their own forms of governance; whether framed as 'custom', 'right', or 'justice', it was founded upon the authority of the locale to determine the relationship between legality and the particular forms of associative relations that characterized the locality in which they lived. To focus on local legal cultures, then, is not only to give weight to the localized forms of law that most people encountered in their everyday lives, but to show—in holding them up alongside one another—that together they gave shape to late-medieval English law as a whole.

1

Rural Legal Culture

Ordaining Community

Introduction

Legal institutions—manorial, ecclesiastical, and leet or hundred courts—were deeply embedded in rural social relations. These courts had been established as the fulcrum of villagers' legal engagement for a long time, and by the fifteenth century rural legal culture in England was characterized by a set of profound practical and ideological correspondences between law and community. In the first place, associative relations in the late-medieval countryside were constituted by a dense lattice of mutually reinforcing legal relationships; from the bargains you made to the reputation you cultivated, law provided an epistemology of rural social life. In the second place, law framed an ethical vision of rural community, which villagers attempted to create using the mechanisms available in their local courts.[1] These courts were often dominated by a relatively small, select group of richer families, and certainly the kinds of community that they wished to build and control were neither egalitarian nor inclusive.[2] Yet for all that it was hierarchical, narrow, and unrealistic, the ideal of a village united by laws served as a powerful concept for inspiring, cajoling, and enforcing action

[1] Christopher Dyer, 'The English Medieval Village Community and Its Decline', *Journal of British Studies*, 33:4 (1994), 407–29, at p. 429; cf. the critique of the unreflective use of 'community' in Christine Carpenter, 'Gentry and Community in Medieval England', *Journal of British Studies*, 33 (1994), 340–80.

[2] Phillipp R. Schofield, *Peasant and Community in Medieval England 1200–1500* (Basingstoke, 2003), p. 5. More generally, see Ian Forrest's magisterial *Trustworthy Men: How Inequality and Faith Made the Medieval Church* (Princeton, 2018), esp. pp. 129–62. The debate over the social profile of jurors is of course an old one. More communalist findings from manors in eastern England include: Edwin B. DeWindt, *Land and People in Holywell-cum-Needingworth: Structures of Tenure and Patterns of Social Organization in an East Midlands Village, 1252–1457* (Toronto, 1972); Edward Britton, *The Community of the Vill: A Study in the History of the Family and Village Life in Fourteenth-Century England* (Toronto, 1977); and, more recently, Sherri Olson, 'Jurors of the Village Court: Local Leadership before and after the Plague in Ellington, Huntingdonshire', *Journal of British Studies*, 30:3 (1991), 237–56. A sceptical critique of the methodology used in such studies can be found in Zvi Razi, 'The Toronto School's Reconstitution of Medieval Peasant Society: A Critical View', *P&P*, 85 (1979), 141–57. Useful recent interventions are Miriam Müller, 'A Divided Class? Peasants and Peasant Communities in Later Medieval England', *P&P*, supplement 2 (2007), 115–31, and Peter L. Larson, 'Village Voice or Village Oligarchy? The Jurors of the Durham Halmote Court, 1349 to 1424', *L&HR*, 28:3 (2010), 675–709.

Law in Common: Legal Cultures in Late-Medieval England. Tom Johnson, Oxford University Press (2020).

DOI: 10.1093/oso/9780198785613.001.0001

in the courts.[3] Rural legal culture was characterized by this strong emphasis on community.

The dynamics of late-medieval rural society have traditionally been understood by historians in relation to the 'decline of serfdom', as the shortage of agricultural labour after the Black Death enabled tenants to bargain away, in a piecemeal fashion, both personal villein status and the more oppressive aspects of servile tenure.[4] While these changes were undoubtedly of huge significance, I would like to suggest that the 'decline of serfdom', as our model for understanding them, is both too narrow and too negative. To begin with, it focuses our attention on just one institution, the manor, as the vehicle of institutional change, neglecting the importance of the broader constellation of rural courts, and their interconnections with one another, for the ways that rural people settled disputes and engaged with legal authority. Thus, for example, the fall in interpersonal debt litigation before manorial courts in the fifteenth century has to be understood in relation to the huge rise of 'breach of faith' litigation before the church courts.[5] One significant effect of post-plague depopulation was to create an oversupply of legal institutions, giving villagers some choice over the way that they used rural courts.

And, indeed, the notion of 'decline' is a poor fit for describing a radical transformation of social institutions that was brought about in large part from below, in thousands of microcosmic legal transactions. Late-medieval villagers did more than just erode the legal burdens of servility; they remade the legal institutions available to them, transforming the way in which they related to rural life. All courts were dependent on suitors and litigants for the profits of justice, and, to an increasing extent, for their cooperation in the execution of their mandates and the upholding of their authority. In the fifteenth century, therefore, rural institutions were under pressure to become more tractable to the needs of the people who used them. The increasing pliability of rural courts as venues for problem-solving and decision-making helped to insinuate law more closely into associative relations in the late-medieval village—and thus to deepen the ideological correspondence between law and community.

[3] This was a considerably broader enterprise than social control, for which see Marjorie K. McIntosh, *Controlling Misbehavior in England, 1370–1600* (Cambridge, 1998).

[4] The classic account is R. H. Hilton, *The Decline of Serfdom in Medieval England* (London, 1969). See also Christopher Dyer, *Lords and Peasants in a Changing Society: The Estates of the Bishopric of Worcester, 680–1540* (Cambridge, 1980), esp. pp. 264–82; E. B. Fryde, *Peasants and Landlords in Later Medieval England, c. 1380–1525* (New York, 1996); and Jane Whittle, *The Development of Agrarian Capitalism in Norfolk, 1440–1580* (Oxford, 2000), esp. pp. 28–84. Most recently, see the important work of Mark Bailey, *The Decline of Serfdom in Late Medieval England: From Bondage to Freedom* (Woodbridge, 2014).

[5] Chris Briggs, 'The availability of credit in the English countryside, 1400–1480', *Agricultural History Review*, 56:1 (2008), 1–24, pp. 19–21. For this 'market' model for understanding medieval legal culture, see Daniel Lord Smail, *The Consumption of Justice: Emotions, Publicity, and Legal Culture in Marseille, 1264–1423* (Ithaca, NY, 2003), pp. 5–19.

This chapter explores this argument in three ways. First, I set out the principal kinds of rural court available to villagers, the different kinds of legal activity they promoted, and how their logistical operations were integrated into rural life. The second section turns to look at the range of ways in which people used the courts in the course of negotiating their associative relations within the village. It argues that the rural courts were characterized by flexible and open-ended procedures which were capable of mobilizing different constituencies, both for the practical purposes of dispute settlement and as a means of legitimating their activities as a mode of building community. The third section dissects the discourses of idealized community that villagers tried to manufacture, focusing on the concepts of peace, repair, and ordaining as axes of associative relations. The conclusion, finally, returns to consider late-medieval rural legal culture in relation to our narratives of late-medieval social change.

The Logistics of Local Courts

The inhabitants of fifteenth-century rural communities used three main kinds of legal forum on a regular basis: manorial courts, hundred courts or leets (the latter often combined with manorial business), and lower ecclesiastical tribunals.[6] These three jurisdictions were technically different, and have often been studied in isolation from one another, but they interacted in a variety of ways and ought to be understood in conversation with one another.[7] Sometimes they squabbled with one another over jurisdiction, but antagonism was not the only expression of their interconnections; they might also be used in concert by villagers trying to sort out a broader problem. For example, a presentment from the leet court of Monxton (Hampshire) in 1459 complained that the rector, Thomas Sparshot, continued to keep a woman named Isabella Huchons inside his house, 'notwithstanding the correction of the ordinary and dean of that deanery hitherto ordered'.[8] From the villagers' perspective, it seems, there was a degree of fluidity between the different courts, and this was even a potential advantage in their attempts to use them to mould idealized communities.

There were, nonetheless, important differences between rural jurisdictions. The manor court, for example, has long been understood as the most important legal

[6] Helen M. Jewell, *English Local Administration in the Middle Ages* (Newton Abbot, 1972); *Lower Ecclesiastical Jurisdiction in Late Medieval England: the courts of the dean and chapter of Lincoln, 1336–1349, and the deanery of Wisbech, 1458–1485*, ed. L. R. Poos (Oxford, 2001).

[7] But see Phillipp Schofield, 'Peasants and the Manor Court: Gossip and Litigation in a Suffolk Village at the Close of the Thirteenth Century', *P&P*, 159 (1998) 3–42; Chris Briggs, 'Seigniorial control of villagers' litigation beyond the manor in later medieval England', *Historical Research*, 81:213 (2008), 399–422.

[8] KCC, MON/2, m.2r.

institution for medieval English villagers.[9] Many historians have emphasized its decline over the course of the fifteenth century, as depopulation, along with the greater mobility of rural labour, broke down the traditional triad of relationships between lord, tenants, and land which had sustained the activities of the courts.[10] It is undoubtedly true that there were fewer sessions of manorial courts in this period than there had been before, and also that they often ceased to hear very much interpersonal litigation; as Jane Whittle illustrated with one north Norfolk manor, Heveningham Bishops, the sheer volume of business in the records decreased by about half in the period between about 1450 and 1520.[11] In some places, the decline was starker still; the court of Buckland Filleigh in Devon, already little-used in the mid-1440s, was a couple of decades later little more than a copybook court, consisting almost entirely of formulaic entries that were contrived, it seems, merely to provide proof of jurisdictional continuity.[12]

At the same time, however, these changes do not necessarily amount to a wholesale 'decline'. To begin with, there are many significant exceptions—the courts of ancient demesne manors, for example, with their special legal privileges, seem to have remained extremely busy.[13] Furthermore, even in places where litigation fell away, manor courts were structurally embedded in the self-regulation of villages as agricultural communities. They remained the court of first instance when new problems needed to be confronted. Thus at Broad Chalke (Wiltshire), an apparently moribund court suddenly burst into life in 1463 to deal with a complicated dispute between the tenants, the rector, and a local tithe farmer.[14] In a similar way, the profusion of by-laws and ordinances in many fifteenth-century manorial courts bespeak an institution that was reclaimed by tenants for their own legal purposes—a point to which we shall return below.[15] Thus while some individual courts undoubtedly faded into obscurity, many others

[9] The literature is vast. Still useful is *Select Pleas in Manorial and Other Seignorial Courts*, ed. F. W. Maitland, Selden Society 2 (London, 1888); also the essays in *Medieval Society and the Manor Court*, ed. Z. Razi and R. Smith (Oxford, 1996).

[10] These arguments are summarized in Christopher Dyer, 'The Political Life of the Fifteenth-Century English Village', in *Political Culture in Late Medieval Britain*, ed. Linda Clark and Christine Carpenter, Fifteenth Century 4 (Woodbridge, 2004), 135–57, pp. 153–4.

[11] Whittle, *Agrarian Capitalism*, pp. 48–9.

[12] The remaining entries focus on fines for default of suit, brewing, and very occasional payments of heriot: CUL, MS. Add 32999, items 10, 17, 18, 20.

[13] This is true of the (generally large and commercialized) ancient demense manors I have sampled, Cookham (Berkshire), King's Langley (Hertfordshire), and Hatfield Broad Oak (Essex), respectively: BRO, D/ESK/M4–5, rolls for 1409–14; TNA, SC 2/177/48–55, rolls for 1390–1452; ERO, D/DK M1, roll for 1441–61 (a roll of 106mm). See also Marjorie Keniston McIntosh, *Autonomy and Community: The Royal Manor of Havering, 1200–1500* (Cambridge, 1986).

[14] KCC, CHA/estates2.

[15] See W. O. Ault, 'Manor Court and Parish Church in Fifteenth-Century England: A Study of Village By-Laws', *Speculum*, 42:1 (1967), 53–67; more generally, by the same author, *Open-Field Farming in Medieval England: A Study of Village By-Laws* (London, 1972).

remained enormously important as institutions of local governance throughout the fifteenth century and beyond.[16]

In many, perhaps the majority of places in fifteenth-century England, the manor court was tied closely to that held for the vill, that is, the royal administrative unit for the village, often called a leet court. In such places, the two courts were effectively combined into the same institution, and the sessions for the manor court were held twice a year to coincide with the view of frankpledge.[17] This consolidation of the two courts did not happen in the same way everywhere—some manors still held separate sessions, and more unusually still, the court for the vill might be entirely segmented, and administered through the hundred, a broader administrative division that comprised many vills.[18] Some hundred courts remained vigorous forums for civil litigation, as for example at Launditch (Norfolk), Lothingland and Mutford (Suffolk), and Warminster (Wiltshire), where the surviving rolls attest to their intense activity.[19] Elsewhere, the hundred court might still meet twice a year for a view of frankpledge during the sheriff's 'tourn' of the hundreds within his county.[20]

The lower ecclesiastical courts provided the third main kind of rural institution available to villagers. Due to differences in judicial administration between dioceses, 'village-level' ecclesiastical tribunals varied considerably.[21] In the diocese of Hereford, for example, the local church court was technically an episcopal court, with 'rural consistories' held by the bishop's ordinary in an itinerant progress through each deanery; in the large archdeaconry of Richmond (in York diocese), by contrast, the archdeacon appointed a commissary-general to perform these duties, and the archidiaconal chapters were therefore the lowest ecclesiastical

[16] Christopher Dyer, *An Age of Transition? Economy and Society in England in the Later Middle Ages* (Oxford, 2005), pp. 176, 183; on their later history, see Brodie Waddell, 'Governing England Through the Manor Courts, 1550–1850', *The Historical Journal*, 55:2 (2012), 279–315.

[17] A useful introduction is Mark Bailey, 'Manor and Leet Courts', in *The English Manor c.1200—c.1500* (Manchester, 2002), pp. 178–84. The frankpledge system was not used in the northern or far western counties: W. A. Morris, *The Frankpledge System* (London, 1910), pp. 45–55.

[18] Jewell, *English Local Administration*, pp. 42–68; see also Helen Cam, '*Manerium cum Hundredo*: the Hundred and the Hundredal Manor', in *Liberties and Communities in Medieval England: Collected Studies in Local Administration and Topography* (Cambridge, 1944), 64–90. Not all counties were divided into hundreds, and many in the north used 'wapentakes' instead; Northumberland, for example, was divided into eight wards. The hundred remained vigorous into the early-modern period: Christopher W. Brooks, *Law, Politics and Society in Early Modern England* (Cambridge, 2008), p. 265.

[19] For Launditch, see Arundel Castle, M704, mm. 1–4. The rolls of Lothingland and Mutford hundreds were bound together with rural admiralty courts for Kessingland and Kirklees (discussed in Chapter 3): SROL, 194/B1/6–9. For Warminster, see WSHO, 865/330.

[20] For example, see a sheriff's court book for Wiltshire from 1511 which records a tourn beginning in Malmesbury hundred in the north-west of the county on April 24, and then, via fifteen further assemblies held almost daily, ending in the south-easternmost hundred of Frustfield on May 10. WSHO, 190/26.

[21] Helmholz, *Canon Law and Ecclesiastical Jurisdiction*, pp. 208–21. Still useful is A. Hamilton Thompson, *The English Clergy and their Organization in the Later Middle Ages* (Oxford, 1947).

courts available in this region.[22] These jurisdictional arrangements were also more likely to change over time, as disagreements over jurisdiction or more banal processes of administrative enterprise prompted the reorganization of local church courts under different officials.[23] Among these formal divisions within the diocese, then, the countless 'peculiars' in late-medieval England which existed outside the bishop's ordinary authority begin to look less exceptional.[24]

Many peculiars were tied to secular lordships, and in some cases, their tribunals might become closely associated, in a way not so different from the common combination of leet and manorial courts. A striking example of this can be found at Ampleforth (North Yorkshire), a prebendal manor of York Minster with its own peculiar jurisdiction. During the 1450s and 1460s, its leet courts and chapter acts—both jurisdictions vested in the prebendary—were held on the same day. Remarkably, their proceedings were even recorded on opposite sides of the same pieces of parchment.[25] This amalgamation, moreover, was matched by the unusually porous boundary between the jurisdiction of the two courts. At the leet court, for example, the jurors were dubbed '*inquisitores*', a title usually reserved for the lay officers of church courts.[26] Their business was also tangled, with William Ellesslak presented for taking away tithes from a place called Nunclose in the leet of 1455.[27] Here as in some other places, the branches of secular and ecclesiastical jurisdiction were so closely entwined that they pleached together.

Even in such rather unusual fusions, however, ecclesiastical justice was different from its secular counterparts. The jurisdiction of the church courts over spiritual conduct—church attendance, the payment of tithes, and sexual misbehaviour, for example—gave their work a public, regulatory tendency, but, as we shall see, they were also an important forum for the maintenance and repair of interpersonal relations between individual parishioners.[28] Indeed, the jurisdiction they assumed over defamation in the later Middle Ages, along with their cognizance of agreements to marry and increasing claims over verbal contracts, meant that they were

[22] HARC, HD 4/1/88–99 [non-inclusive, non-sequential, court books for 1442–80]. For a detailed explanation of the archdeaconry of Richmond, see *The Records of the Medieval Ecclesiastical Courts, pt. 2: England*, ed. C. Donahue, Reports of the Working Group on Church Court Records (Berlin, 1994), pp. 105, 112.

[23] For examples of (respectively contentious and non-contentious) changing divisions of jurisdiction, see Poos, *Lower Ecclesiastical Jurisdiction*, p. xxv; *The Courts of the Archdeaconry of Buckingham, 1483–1523*, ed. E. M. Elvey, Buckinghamshire Record Society, 19 (Aylesbury, 1975) pp. xiii–xiv, xvi.

[24] R. N. Swanson, 'Peculiar Practices: The Jurisdictional Jigsaw of the Pre-Reformation Church', *Midland History*, 26 (2001), 69–95.

[25] BIA, CCP 12/Amp 3, verso [1454], CCP 12/Amp 4, verso [1456], CCP 12/Amp 5, verso [1465]. In both cases, the leet court was recorded on the recto and the chapter on the verso, although of course it is difficult to say in what order they were held (if indeed they were held as separate tribunals).

[26] On ecclesiastical *inquisitores* (normally used at visitations), see Ian Forrest, 'The Transformation of Visitation in Thirteenth-Century England', *P&P*, 221 (2013), 3–38, at pp. 9–11.

[27] BIA, CCP 12/Amp 3.

[28] See Poos, *Lower Ecclesiastical Jurisdiction*, pp. xlix–lxiv.

the principal forum for the rectification of bad words in a culture that accorded enormous power to speech acts.[29] These two aspects of ecclesiastical justice came together in the idea of the parish as a peaceful corporate community.[30] On top of the manor and the vill, then, the church courts laid a third model of legal relations on the village.

As well as these differences of jurisdiction, rural courts were also distinguished from one another by their location, regularity, and itinerancy. The vast majority of manorial courts were held within a relatively small radius of the settlements with which they were concerned. Some were more distant: suitors and jurors from six hinterland manors belonging to the Bishop of Hereford were required to travel the three or four miles into the city for his halmotes (combined manorial and leet courts), which were held in the episcopal palace next to the cathedral.[31] Did this biannual movement to the heart of the lordship inflect the tone of the proceedings? Hundred courts produced a different kind of comparative locality, often meeting at archaic open-air gathering points, such as 'Iley Oak' in Warminster hundred, or a stone somewhere in the Bishop of Ely's private hundred of North Witchford (Cambridgeshire).[32] Suitors and chief-pledges would at least have seen their counterparts from other nearby settlements fulfilling the same duties, and might have been able to compass their vill within a broader locality, which they perhaps understood as their 'country', or a smaller part of it.[33]

By contrast, for most villagers attendance at a regular session of an ecclesiastical court would have required a short journey, either to a fixed court like that at Wisbech for its deanery, or an itinerant tribunal. Nomadic courts, indeed, might drag litigants across a deanery or even further afield. Thus John Wakeman was initially accused of violation of faith (contract-breaking) at a tribunal held in the parish church of Hembsy (Norfolk) in September 1420, as part of the prior of

[29] On the church courts' takeover of defamation, see the 'Introduction' to *Select Cases on Defamation to 1600*, ed. Richard H. Helmholz, Selden Society 101 (London, 1985); on marriage, see L. R. Poos, 'The Heavy-Handed Marriage Counsellor: Regulating Marriage in Some Later-Medieval English Local Ecclesiastical-Court Jurisdictions', *The American Journal of Legal History*, 39:3 (1995), 291–309; on the proliferation of breach of faith cases in the fifteenth century, see Helmholz, *Canon Law and Ecclesiastical Jurisdiction*, pp. 229–30.

[30] Beat A. Kümin, *The Shaping of a Community: The rise and reformation of the English parish, c.1400–1560* (Aldershot, 1996); Katherine L. French, *The People of the Parish: Community Life in a Late Medieval English Diocese* (Philadelphia, 2001).

[31] The working records of the manor courts have 'Hereford palace' written in the margins, and are titled 'Halmotam ibidem tenta…': BL, Add. Ch. 27290–27310 [courts for 1469–83]. On occasion, tenants from as far away as Archenfield (some fifteen miles distant) were required to attend there: *Registrum Caroli Bothe, Episcopi Herefordensis*, ed. Arthur Thomas Bannister, Canterbury and York Society 28, (London, 1921), p. 82.

[32] On the gathering places, see K. H. Rogers, 'Warminster Hundred', in *VCH Wiltshire, Volume 8: Warminster, Westbury and Whorwellsdown Hundreds*, ed. Elizabeth Crittall (London, 1965), 1–5, p. 5; CUL, EDR/C7/29, m. 3r. This records the tourn held there in 1427, with 'Witchford stone' as the marginal place name; later courts at mm. 4r, 6r, and 11r use the same designation. While not definitive evidence, the name is not otherwise attested for the settlement or other places.

[33] On the idea of 'country', see M. L. Holford, 'Pro patriotis: 'Country', 'Countrymen' and Local Solidarities in Late Medieval England', *Parergon*, 23:1 (2006), 47–70.

Norwich Cathedral's peculiar ecclesiastical jurisdiction over his manorial estates. Wakeman was cited in Hemsby again the following May but failed to come, appearing instead in June at another of the prior's peculiars, nearby Martham, where he denied the charge; he was thus asked to appear with compurgators a week later at St. Mary in the Marsh in Norwich, some twenty miles away.[34] It is easy to imagine that this tendency was used vexatiously on occasion, both by litigants and court officials. But in the spirit of the law or not, such distances must have rendered a court's jurisdiction starkly manifest to those litigants whom it forced to travel.

Indeed, larger landlords with dispersed estates sent stewards to make the rounds of their manors in a progress that demonstrated the extent of their influence. These officials themselves covered impressive distances: in the autumn of 1455, the steward of Sir William Beauchamp (Lord St. Amand) journeyed some 125 miles in two weeks, holding seven courts for ten of his manorial possessions across Bedfordshire, Northamptonshire, and Oxfordshire.[35] Though tenants were not dragged between different manor courts, the visit of an itinerant seigneurial official on a tight schedule must have affected the courts' proceedings. Thus when a dispute broke out in 1466 between the tenants of Ringwood (Hampshire) and their lord, King's College, Cambridge, over the assize of ale, the matter was 'put in respite until the next visit of the lord's council'. Intervening records are patchy, but the same dispute, presumably sent back and forth between Cambridge and Hampshire several more times, was still rumbling on in the early 1490s.[36]

Yet if distance made negotiation more difficult, there was a strong demand from villagers for greater access to authorities. While they often complained about the summoners who did the mundane work of citation for the church courts, they might welcome the ecclesiastical dignitaries who were required to make visitation of their parish every three years.[37] These visits represented an opportunity to override local influence: a slip of paper sent forward to a Lincolnshire visitation in 1473 complained that the vicar of Worlaby had kept a concubine for six years without punishment, 'wharfore we be seke yow of your gracius lordschip þat... þei may be correkyd'.[38] Though they were relatively infrequent, visitations did draw on the work of regular ecclesiastical sessions—graphically so in the court

[34] NRO, DCN 67/2, m. 2r. St. Mary in the Marsh, no longer extant, was the parish church for the cathedral close in Norwich, and seems to have been the prior and chapter's judicial base.

[35] BL, Egerton 3540, fos. 1r–6v. See also the expenses for the steward of Willington (Derbyshire) in the mid-fifteenth century, which records the different costs of lodging and stabling in different Midlands towns: DRO, D2375M/24/2, loose sheet.

[36] KCC, RIN/6, C, recto. For the resurfacing of the dispute, see RIN/7, m. 6r. King's was of course known to contemporaries as the College of the Blessed Mary and St. Nicholas.

[37] On hostility towards summoners, low-level ecclesiastical officers, see Ian Forrest, 'The Summoner', in *Historians on Chaucer: The 'General Prologue' to the Canterbury Tales*, ed. Stephen Rigby and Alastair Minnis (Oxford, 2014), 421–42. On the rules surrounding triennial visitation, see Helmholz, *Canon Law and Ecclesiastical Jurisdiction*, pp. 219–20.

[38] LA, Vj/4, annex to fo. 21r.

book of Hartlebury peculiar in Worcestershire, where the business of the chapter was interspersed with that of the episcopal visitors.[39] The orbit of itinerant courts was thus affected by local concerns and judicial activities as well as the gravity exerted by external authorities and their representatives.[40]

Visitation was but one infrequent pulse in the legal calendar. Across all three main jurisdictions in the late-medieval countryside, major sessions tended to be held twice a year. The view of frankpledge that tended to structure the timing of leet courts was normally held biannually, once in the spring around Easter or Hocktide, and once in the autumn at Michaelmas or Martinmas.[41] The 'general' or 'full' chapters of ecclesiastical bodies (archdeaconries, deaneries, or peculiars), which technically constituted their formal tribunals, were likewise held twice (or in some places four times) a year, though, as we shall see in Chapter 2, these were more often held in towns.[42] Some manorial courts required extra time outside the leets and held one or two extra sessions a year in the intervening period at Christmas or in the early summer.[43] The court of King's Langley (Hertfordshire) was able to respond very flexibly to demand: in the period from 1436 to 1445, between two and six sessions were held each year.[44]

It is difficult to discern the effects of this periodicity on villagers' relationship to courts. For an unpaid debt, was it best to register the case at the imminent hundred court, or worth waiting to take it as a breach of faith suit at the decanal chapter some months away? Such decisions must have depended just as much on the consistency with which a court sat, about which there was sometimes genuine uncertainty—the parishioners of Uxbridge (Middlesex) wrote a letter to the Bishop of London's commissary in the late 1490s asking 'whye ye ocupye no curte this sessoun [season]'.[45] But they also depended on the elastic rhythms of rural life, set by quarterly rent-days, ploughing and harvest, micro-cycles of credit, and rumours of impending royal taxes. These cadences stretched across rural jurisdictions in different ways, from the by-laws of manorial courts that shadowed the agricultural year like a legal almanac, to the proliferation of concerns with neighbourly relations that surfaced at Easter, when parishioners taking full communion were reminded forcefully of the importance of charity.[46]

[39] See *Noble Household Management and Spiritual Discipline in Fifteenth-Century Worcestershire*, ed. James P. Toomey, Robert N. Swanson, and David Guyatt, Worcestershire Historical Society, n.s., 24 (Worcester, 2013).

[40] Cf. Forrest, 'Transformation of Visitation', pp. 27–9.

[41] Bailey, 'Manor and Leet Courts', p. 182.

[42] Jean Scammell, 'The Rural Chapter in England from the Eleventh to the Fourteenth Century', *EHR*, 86:338 (1971), 1–21.

[43] E.g. Stour Provost (Dorset): KCC, STP/6/1–7; also, Whittle, *Agrarian Capitalism*, p. 48.

[44] TNA, SC 2/177/55.

[45] LMA, DL/C/B/043/MS09064/007, fo. 29a.

[46] On by-laws, see Ault, *Open-Field Farming*, pp. 23–46. On Easter confession, charity, and legal disputes, see Tom Johnson, 'The Preconstruction of Witness Testimony: Law and Social Discourse in England before the Reformation', *L&HR*, 32:1 (2014), 127–47, pp. 129–30, 135–6.

The different courts formed part of these rural calendars, as they slotted into them.

In all their operations, indeed, these institutions were routinized in the associative lives of late-medieval villagers. Manor courts were certainly not the communal 'moots' imagined by an earlier generation of scholars, and yet, they did occasionally seem to take on the character of 'village meetings', in Christopher Dyer's phrase.[47] They were occasions for feasting: a detailed expense from Ampleforth in 1456 reveals large sums spent on ale (14d.) and bread (8d.), along with three chickens, a goose, and a lamb, at 3d. each.[48] An extra 3d. worth of ale was 'given to the *inquisitores*', and three gifts of food were received: John Wayk, Nicholas Grene, and the vicar of Ampleforth each gave a goose, and the nuns of Moxby gave a shoulder of mutton and two lambs.[49] Gifts of money and food greased the wheels even of these lowly tribunals, just as feasts on court-days may have served to foster communality and reconciliation, and to represent the corporate community—in particular its decision-makers—to itself.[50] Such a setting helps to contextualize discussions such as those that took place at Willoughby (Warwickshire) in 1481, when it was recorded that the 'common fund' (*bona communa*), totalling 52s. 4d., was to be put to the use of 'the community of the whole vill' (*communitatis tocius ville*), with the accounts returned annually at the parish church.[51]

Law-courts were thus closely integrated into the life of the village, helping to give structure and meaning to associative relations. In the fifteenth century, ties of formal jurisdiction remained—most tenants owed suit to their manorial court, after all, and lords might attempt to place restrictions on their ability to sue elsewhere. But these ties were looser, and this gave the choices of villagers between the different rural courts a greater significance in relation to the kind of community they were attempting to invoke. Just as a church court could conjure the parish as a moral community, so a leet invoked the public authority of the vill; these were meaningful cultural structures that exercised their own gravity on the way that villagers used the courts to shape and regulate their relations with their neighbours. The next section turns to examine the specific mechanisms provided by the courts for this purpose.

[47] The most infamously optimistic was, of course, George C. Homans, *English Villagers of the Thirteenth Century* (Cambridge, MA, 1941); Dyer, *Lords and Peasants*, p. 269 and also 'Political Life of the Fifteenth-Century English Village', p. 139.

[48] BIA, CCP 12/Amp 4, verso. A comparative example is from Ringwood (Hampshire): KCC, RIN/7, fo. 3v. This lists expenses made 'for the dinner of the stewards, farmers, and other incumbents [*incumbancium*]', with 9d. for bread and ale. They also ate saltfish (6d.) and oysters (1d.)—the manor was close to the south coast—along with mustard (ob.), butter (1d.); 2d. was spent on firewood.

[49] BIA, CCP 12/Amp 4, verso.

[50] See Gervase Rosser, 'Going to the Fraternity Feast: Commensality and Social Relations in Late Medieval England', *Journal of British Studies*, 33:4 (1994), 430–46.

[51] Magdalen College Oxford, 45/11, verso.

The Work of the Courts

Late-medieval rural courts were characterized by three interdependent dynamics—the flexibility of their formal operations, their ability to engage different constituencies within the village, and their capacity for legitimate enforcement—all of which facilitated the close correspondence between legal and social relations in the village. The first part of this section looks at how their flexibility in framing and resolving disputes created a spiral effect; the more they bent to accommodate litigants, the more they became wrapped up in the tangle of village relationships, and the more they had to bend. We then turn to look at how rural courts drew different groups of people into the processes of information-gathering and decision-making. This created many small, temporary alignments, but also served to broaden the social base of the courts, allowing women and poorer villagers a chance to influence proceedings. Third, we shall look at how the courts' means of enforcement—through monetary fines, seizures, and bodily punishments—served to insinuate their work ever more closely into associative life.

The vast majority of interpersonal disputes in the late-medieval countryside fell into one of two broad legal regimes: those associated with injury—to persons, reputations, or property—and those associated with broken agreements.[52] Each followed different courses through the courts. For disputes centred on injury, the difference between secular and ecclesiastical jurisdiction mattered a great deal.[53] A fifteenth-century villager whose reputation had been damaged by some shameful rebuke would only find a direct remedy in a church court, through a suit of defamation; by contrast, if he sought compensation because his crops had been trampled by a neighbour's stock, he would only get compensation from a secular court, through an action of trespass. This meant that there was no 'market' for litigation between village-level courts for disputes centred on a wrong; the only choice for a villager who did not wish to sue in the relevant court was to move vertically within the same type of jurisdiction—to the king's courts, or to those of the diocese.

'Agreement'-type disputes, by contrast, sat comfortably athwart secular and ecclesiastical jurisdiction. Debt and detinue could be framed as 'breach of faith', and vice versa, and so very similar circumstances could be litigated differently by villagers. For example, Robert Babyrstoke was attached to appear at the leet of Monxton in a plea of debt for two quarters of barley, lodged by the churchwarden there; whereas Margaret Chosell, whom we met earlier, was summoned before a

[52] A legal historian might call these 'tort' and 'contract', but here I am deliberately using broad, unloaded terminology.

[53] But cf. their shared origins: John S. Beckerman, 'Adding Insult to *Iniuria*: Affronts to Honor and the Origins of Trespass', in *On the Laws and Customs of England: Essays in Honor of Samuel E. Thorne*, ed. Morris S. Arnold, Thomas A. Green, Sally A. Scully, and Stephen D. White (Chapel Hill, NC, 1981), 159–81.

church court at Sedgeford (Norfolk), accused of breaking a promise to supply seven bushels of malt to the alderman of All Saints guild.[54] This jurisdictional fluidity meant that, leaving aside logistical considerations, plaintiffs had some choice over the forum, with consequences for the way a case might proceed. Thus Margaret Chosell was ordered to reach an agreement with the guild regarding the malt, whereas Robert Babyrstoke had some of his possessions confiscated (a jar, an iron grill, and a chest) to force him to appear at court; eventually his pledge, John at Mere, agreed to pay the debt instead. The payment of debts might thus be forced through very different routes.

With this rather freer 'market' for litigation between village-level forums, the forms of action within which disputes were framed were much more flexible. In the ecclesiastical courts, the category of 'breach of faith' was broad anyway, covering any agreement made with an oath (the courts were technically enforcing the oath, not the agreement). While the church courts had long heard such litigation, 'by the mid-fifteenth century, it had become almost a flood', in Richard Helmholz's assessment.[55] In secular courts, the two actions of debt and detinue provided remedies for the withholding of money and goods respectively, but in fact they were frequently broadened out to include other matters. For example, Joan Ely of Netherseal (Derbyshire) sued John Brocton in a plea of debt, claiming that he should have given her a bushel of rye worth 7d., and delivered some firewood or charcoal to her; neither wrong sits comfortably as a debt in the strict sense, but it is obvious that he 'owed' her, in the sense of an unperformed obligation.[56] Both secular and ecclesiastical courts, then, offered people flexible solutions to broken agreements.

This conceptual flexibility—across both regimes of dispute and the different jurisdictions—is important because of the way it blurred together legal and associative relations in the village. In taking cognizance of these murkily defined disputes, rural courts were often stretched beyond clean-cut judgments into more attenuated and open-ended processes of dispute resolution, which did not go to a final judgment by the court. This was a long-standing aspect of the courts' work, and processes to avoid judgment were institutionalized by the fifteenth century. Manorial and leet courts allowed defendants to respond to pleas by 'requesting a day for agreement', 'asking to discuss', or at King's Langley, pursuing an 'interlocution'; the manifold fines paid for a licence of agreement (*licencia concordie*) litter the margins of court rolls.[57] Likewise, though rural ecclesiastical courts often

[54] Respectively, KCC, MON/2, m. 1r; NRO, DCN 67/6, m. 3r (see also above, pp. 8-9).

[55] Helmholz, *Canon Law and Ecclesiastical Jurisdiction*, pp. 359–60.

[56] DRO, D77/2/1/5, recto.

[57] For King's Langley, see TNA, SC 2/177/55, m. 3v. (Wendover v. atte Hethe); m. 4v. (Amyot v. Keene); mm. 8r–v, 21r. (Boteler v. Multon). In this court, this word seems to have had its own technical meaning distinct from 'requesting a licence of concord'. For a quantitative analysis of licences of concord in fourteenth-century courts, see Table 4 in Chris Briggs, 'Manor Court

heard interpersonal cases as *ex officio* business, they too pushed for reconciliation between the parties, and when they achieved it used the equivalent formula 'there is peace' (*pax est*). But the strong impulse towards dispute settlement could also go beyond these regular and standardized agreements, with the courts occasionally taking a much more proactive role in resolution.[58]

Courts might intervene in complicated disputes to set up a structured arbitration. At Ringwood in the late 1450s, 'a certain matter' arose between John Notier and John Massatay concerning a house that had burned down, and it was 'declared before the steward' at the leet court. Framed awkwardly as an interpersonal plea, the parties themselves requested that the case be 'put on the wisdom' (*super discretionem*) of four nominated arbitrators, whose judgment they would abide under the large pain of £20 each. If it is instructive that they sought arbitration through the court, rather than outside it, more telling still was a clause stating that if the arbitrators could not agree, the court would nominate 'a single authority' (*unum imperium*) to make a final determination.[59] Though the case remained unresolved for several years, the court continued to take an interest in its conclusion.[60] Such an elaborate process of arbitration was rare (and the penalties involved reveal that the litigants were among the wealthier class of villagers), but the case provides a good illustration of the way that local secular courts responded to tangled disputes in open-ended ways. Indeed, such matters were jealously defended as part of their jurisdiction; at Spofforth in North Yorkshire, the court went so far as to forbid tenants from holding a 'love-ale', without 'special licence asked and obtained from the lord or his officers'.[61]

But the church courts demonstrated a possibly even greater propensity to force the resolution of disputes through arbitration. The formal dictates of canon law encouraged judges to seek settlement where possible, and some laypeople enthusiastically shared in this mandate.[62] This alignment of interests meant that the

Procedures, Debt Litigation Levels, and Rural Credit Provision in England, c.1290–c.1380', *L&HR*, 24:3 (2006), 519–58, p. 543.

[58] Their processes have been compared to the modern practice of Alternative Dispute Resolution: see Lloyd Bonfield, 'The Nature of Customary Law in the Manor Courts of Medieval England', *Comparative Studies in Society and History*, 31:3 (1989), 514–34, p. 532; cf.John S. Beckerman, 'Adjudication: The Nature of Communal Judgments in a System of Customary Law', *L&HR*, 13:1 (1995), 1–22, pp. 2–3; Phillipp Schofield, 'Peasants and the Manor Court', pp. 16–7.

[59] KCC, RIN/6, A, verso.

[60] KCC, RIN/6, D is a court from Michaelmas 1456. It includes the clause about the extra 'authority'; RIN/6, A records courts of 1460–1 (parts of the date clauses are torn away), both of which give a clearer account of the parties involved and notes the monetary penalty. There is no evidence from the interval, and the subsequent courts RIN/6, B, C (1462–4) make no mention of the matter.

[61] WSRO, PHA 7036, m. 2r. The term is *loffhale*, which is otherwise unattested; the context suggests it was similar to a 'love-day': see Michael Clanchy, 'Law and Love in the Middle Ages', in *Disputes and Settlements: Law and Human Relations in the West*, ed. John Bossy (Cambridge, 1983), 47–67. On the importance of festive drinking at court days, see fnn. 48–9 above.

[62] James A. Brundage, *Medieval Canon Law* (New York, 1995), p. 134. On the use of 'charity' by the laity to resolve disputes, see Johnson, 'Law and Social Discourse in England', pp. 135, 143–5.

church courts were adept at resolving unwieldy social conflicts. For example, at the peculiar court of Hindringham (Norfolk) in 1420, Robert Peres was accused of defaming John Coldyk, one of the lay *inquisitores* there, saying that he had stolen loaves of bread from his oven, and taken his firewood to burn.[63] John's wife denied the charge on his behalf, and he was assigned to compurgate with five oath-helpers; but later, with the help of 'interceding friends' (*mediantibus amicis*), an agreement was made for the two men and their wives, by which they were to abide under penalty of paying 40s. in alms. They also promised not to 'sustain discord or to repeat the words' under pain of further correction from the court.[64] The whole tone of the settlement—the injunction to silence, the help of friends, the threat of alms—combined an oppressive commitment to peace and charity with an interweaving of social and legal sanctions characteristic of ecclesiastical justice.

Both secular and ecclesiastical courts thus attempted to guide their constituents towards reconciliation using parameters that stretched beyond the regular procedures of the court and into the associative relationships of the village. This was clearly a product of movement in both directions, as informal settlements between individuals were also ratified by the courts through licences of agreement. But sometimes such intermeshing went even further still. Thus in 1432 at the court of Kintbury (Berkshire), where there was a strong tradition of using structured arbitrations alongside judgments, the executors of John Serne impleaded a prominent free tenant named Reginald Ramvile for 4s., which 'he has been ordered to pay them by the arbitration' of two other tenants.[65] Given that such an arbitration is not recorded anywhere in the court's otherwise comprehensive records, it is rather suggestive of the way that more involved settlements might be brought to the court for ratification and enforcement.[66] In the settlement of interpersonal disputes then, as the courts bowed to the needs of their constituents, so villagers bent their conflicts into the contours of court procedures; the result was a highly flexible set of rural institutions.

This flexibility of action carried over into the processes of information-gathering and decision-making in the rural courts. As much of the historiography has emphasized, the opportunity to report offences and give judgments before the

[63] Peres was accused in the same court of having committed adultery, but had compurgated on just one hand *de favore decani*. Coldyk had not apparently acted as an *inquisitor* before, but did hold the position again, after an interval, in 1424; at Hindringham, the offices were regularly rotated, although some men with the same family name (Lyne, Wurthy) often held them.

[64] NRO, DCN 67/2, m. 3r.

[65] BL, Add. Ch. 49228, m. 2r, court of 1432. Roger Gunter, one of the two arbitrators, had previously acted in this capacity a decade earlier: BL, Add. Ch. 49222, m. 1r. Gunter acted as affeeror in 1413 but was fined half a mark for failing to perform the office; in 1424, he appears listed as a free juror (perhaps explaining his reluctance?). He probably died soon afterwards. John Elger, the other arbitrator, only appears in this entry, though one Henry Elger acted as a free juror in 1422. BL, Add. Ch. 49218–221, 49223, 49234.

[66] Ramvile recognized the debt (and perhaps implicitly the arbitration); given the case was brought by Serne's executors, it is possible that it had been ordained by a church court: BL, Add. Ch. 49228, m. 2r.

courts tended to be restricted to small oligarchies of elite men, who co-opted these institutions for their own interests.[67] We shall look in more detail at the dynamics of the 'knowledge work' that such men performed for the courts in Chapter 6. But here I would like to highlight the small institutional fissures through which villagers who were structurally excluded from these elites could still influence and participate in the reporting of information and the process of making judgments. These mechanisms not only made the matters discussed by the courts into 'common knowledge', placing these institutions at the heart of the village's public sphere, but also allowed the courts, and the men who dominated them, to represent what they did as the common interest. Even at the same time as they systematically excluded and subordinated some people, then, the potential porousness of information reporting was part of what made the courts legitimate sites of 'community'.

It is necessary to consider information-gathering and decision-making alongside one another because of presentment, a commonly-used mechanism in manor and leet courts, which did both at once; jurors made statements of fact that were also verdicts of guilt, and their pronouncements were very rarely contested.[68] Although it had been used occasionally in manorial forums for a long time, presentment became predominant after the Black Death, correlating with both the decline of civil litigation in these forums and the burgeoning of a new flavour of moralistic social control.[69] Presentments of a slightly different nature were also used in ecclesiastical forums, as groups of laymen called *inquisitores* or *fidedigni* reported information but did not take on the role of judges, and the people whom they presented were normally able to deny their charges. As Ian Forrest has emphasized, though, these 'trustworthy men' exerted a considerable degree of influence over the shape of parochial governance, especially because in many places they were often the same men who tended to act as manorial jurors.[70]

For all that these elites were dominant in the courts, however, there were constraints on their ability to co-opt institutions for the exercise of naked

[67] Briggs, 'Manor Court Procedures', p. 544, fn. 66; for the historiography on oligarchy, see fn. 2 above. However, see also the important arguments about the way that legal structures enshrined inequality, in Forrest, *Trustworthy Men*, pp. 163–200.

[68] For a detailed discussion, see John S. Beckerman, 'Procedural Innovation and Institutional Change in Medieval English Manorial Courts', *LHR*, 10.2 (1992), pp. 236–41. For a rare case of a defendant successfully denying a presentment made against him (on procedural grounds), see KCC, RIN/5, m. 2v.

[69] Bailey, 'Manor and Leet Courts', pp. 173–5. On presentment as a mechanism of social control, see McIntosh, *Controlling Misbehavior*, pp. 8, 15, 36–9.

[70] See the analysis of this overlap in Forrest, *Trustworthy Men*, Ch. 6, 'Very Local Elites', pp. 129–62. Also Poos, *Lower Ecclesiastical Jurisdiction*, pp. lxii–iii. At Ampleforth peculiar, all but three of the twelve *inquisitores* named for the chapters of 1454, 1456, and 1465 also served as leet jurors; of these, John Sysson was named elsewhere as a tenant of Byland Abbey (as opposed to the prebend), suggesting a similar system to that at Hartlebury, in which different townships within a large parish were represented through their own *inquisitores*: BIA, CCP 12/Amp 3–5; *Noble Household Management and Spiritual Discipline*, ed. Toomey, Swanson and Guyatt, pp. 128 [Map II], 137.

power. In the first place, they were bound by oath to 'treuli enqueryn & treweli presenten', as a set of vernacular articles for fifteenth-century leet juries put it, bound 'nout [to] discoueryn [conceal] for no thing so help ȝou good & the holi doom', even against 'ȝoure felaweȝ & ȝoure owen'.[71] Such oaths created a set of ethical expectations, and occasional reports of dissent show how other villagers might hold them to account. At Yaxham (Norfolk) in 1440, it was reported that Geoffrey and John Waryn assaulted Richard Potter, a capital pledge, and shouted the following words: 'Thu & thy fellawes hedborwes [head-boroughs] of the last lete arn false forsworen harlettis, & falsly han amercied me & other; and that shal sore forthynke yow [i.e. you will regret it] alle if we lyven; and ye soten a bowte yor verdyte makyng at that day as a company of develes & nout as men.'[72] In a social world where so much power was accorded to the spoken word—and in which 'forswearing', or oath-breaking, was closely associated with masculine dishonour—behavioural codes constrained the openly deceitful use of presentment.[73]

There were also institutional checks on the way that information was reported. Many manorial courts still used a system of double presentment in the fifteenth century, in which the verdicts of the capital pledges—tithingmen from the customary tenantry—were ratified by a jury of freeholders.[74] Thus the inquest jurors of Kintbury reported in 1441 that John atte Nalde had 'made a concealment' as tithingman by not presenting a lane which his father Thomas had blocked.[75] In the church courts, the *inquisitores* worked alongside local clergy and sometimes churchwardens, creating multiple avenues for the reporting of information. Thus one of the churchwardens of Leckhampstead (Buckinghamshire) reported that the

[71] John Beckerman, 'The Articles of Presentment of a Court Leet and Court Baron, in English, c. 1400', *Bulletin of the Institute of Historical Research*, 47 (1974), 230–4, pp. 231–2. Cf. the slightly different phrase in the set preserved in *The Commonplace Book of Robert Reynes of Acle: An Edition of Tanner MS 407*, ed. Cameron Louis (London, 1980), pp. 143–4. I have not come across an oath for the lay *inquisitores* of the church courts, but there was a similar rhetoric to describe their legitimacy: for example, the offences reported to the prior of Norwich's peculiar courts were said to be 'detected by inquisitors of the village and parish, working according to the requirements of the law in that behalf': NRO, DCN 67/1a, m. 3r.

[72] TNA, KB 9/234, no. 27.

[73] Derek G. Neal, *The Masculine Self in Late-Medieval England* (Chicago, 2008), pp. 41–4. Poor witnesses before early-modern church courts might be dismissed as untrustworthy because they were more liable to bribery: Alexandra Sheppard, 'Poverty, Labour and the Language of Social Description in Early Modern England', *P&P*, 201 (2008), 51–95, at pp. 81–3. 'Forsworn' was a common insult reported in late-medieval defamation cases, see e.g. LMA, DL/C/B/043/MS09064/004, fos. 100v, 318v.

[74] On double presentment, see Beckerman, 'Procedural Innovation and Institutional Change', pp. 227–30. For a detailed description of potential variants, see Briggs, 'Manor Court Procedures', p. 546, fn. 70. Many fifteenth-century courts continued to use double presentment: see for instance MCC, 45/23 (Willoughby, Warwickshire); KCC, STP/6/1 (Stour Provost, Dorset); KCC, RIN/7, fo. 1v. (Ringwood, Hampshire).

[75] BL, Add. Ch. 49230. Both father and son regularly served as free jurors in the court. Thomas was dead within the year, and John inherited his land: Add. Ch. 49233.

other had perjured himself, falsely swearing that the churchyard was well-repaired.[76] In general, presentment created the appearance of unanimity, hiding from the court record the negotiations that must have taken place; yet this corporatist mechanism did create a space for discussion and even contestation over the production of information.

This space was important because, in both secular and ecclesiastical courts, it might be infiltrated by other villagers who wished to report information. In leet courts, if a violent offence was committed, witnesses could raise the hue in order to summon assistance; this archaic peacekeeping mechanism—which had been used disproportionately by women—was still found in a substantial minority of fifteenth-century courts, although by this time it seems more hues were raised by men.[77] Because the hue allowed anyone to report crime, it was closely regulated. For instance, in a court at Willoughby in the mid-1430s, the four capital pledges presented that the hue was raised against Elizabeth Leynor by John Toft; but the free jurors reported that in fact 'this was badly presented, because the hue was raised against John Toft'.[78] At least in the first half of the fifteenth century, the hue opened up the reporting of crime to other villagers, and thus offered a small measure of institutional balance against the domination of presentment jurors, albeit one which they themselves could work to limit.

In this way, the hue was not dissimilar to a process in the ecclesiastical courts by which individuals who were rumoured to have committed an offence could swear an oath to prove their innocence of the accusation.[79] For example, in the late 1470s Robert Sawer of Newton-in-the-Isle (Cambridgeshire) was said to be defamed of stealing some eels from the nets of Thomas Rudhale jr, and selling them to a saddler of Wisbech; he compurgated in his parish church.[80] Sawer himself may have reported this to the court in order to have the opportunity to prove his innocence, or it may have reached the court from the common report of *fama publica* (a concept I will discuss just below). Either way, this passive construction

[76] In general, see Helmholz, *Canon Law and Ecclesiastical Jurisdiction*, pp. 572–3. For summoners possibly reporting offences, see Richard Wunderli, *London Church Courts and Society on the Eve of the Reformation* (Cambridge, MA, 1981), pp. 37–8; for churchwardens reporting, see e.g. LA, Cj1, fos. 14v, 24r. For the churchwardens of Leckhamstead, see *Archdeaconry of Buckingham, 1483–523*, ed. Elvey, p. 257.

[77] Sandy Bardsley, *Venomous Tongues: Speech and Gender in Late Medieval England* (Philadelphia, 2006), pp. 75–6. Seven manors I examined were still using the hue in this period: Combe (Berkshire), Kintbury (Berkshire), Brixton Deverill (Wiltshire), Willoughby (Warwickshire), Monxton (Hampshire), King's Langley (Hertfordshire), which produced twenty-three cases between them; however, Kintbury alone produced fourteen of these. The gender balance was thirteen male to ten female hues. The latest instance I have found is from 1457 in Combe: KCC, COM/11, m. 1r.

[78] MCC, 45/13, verso.

[79] Generally, see R. H. Helmholz, 'Crime, Compurgation and the Courts of the Medieval Church', *L&HR*, 1:1 (1983), 1–26. For an example of this practice, see *Noble Household Management and Spiritual Discipline*, ed. Toomey, Swanson and Guyatt, p. 188. A relationship between hue-raising and defamation is implied, but not pursued, in Bardsley, *Venomous Tongues*, pp. 40–1.

[80] Poos, *Lower Ecclesiastical Jurisdiction*, pp. 299–300.

of a defamation case allowed the courts to draw what Ian Forrest has called 'the fault line between good and bad speech' in deciding whether allegations were to be tested or whether they were defamatory.[81] Like the hue, then, this kind of licit defamation was a speech act that allowed individuals other than the *inquisitores* and jurors to report legal information for consideration by the courts.

With this in mind, it is easy to see why the courts drew so strongly on discourses of common knowledge in their proceedings. This was most obvious in the ecclesiastical courts with the notion of *fama*, a way of talking about widely believed facts or collective judgment about a person's reputation that was known to many in the locality.[82] Thus, for example, in 1500 it was reported to a visitation at Upton, near Lincoln, that 'Agnes Yonge is a soothsayer... just as the public voice and fame bears out'.[83] And as *fama* institutionalized public knowledge in the church courts, a similar set of ideas was also a feature of secular court proceedings in a more subtle way, through the frequent appeal to a discourse of 'commonness'. There were frequent descriptions of people—bakers, brewers, quarrellers, perturbers—as 'common', alongside invocations of the 'common nuisance' caused by a blocked ditch or an unrepaired hedge; the commonness of these matters was partly a claim about their broad relevance, but also, implicitly, about the way in which information about them was generated. Like *fama*, common problems were important because they were known to everyone, and this was recognized and validated at courts.

Rural courts were thus at least notionally receptive to the concerns of a broad range of constituencies within the village. It is undoubtedly true that they worked to privilege the voices of more substantial men, the 'information brokers' of the village who tended to serve as jurors, *inquisitores*, capital pledges, officers, and churchwardens.[84] Yet the courts did also provide some institutional routes for other villagers to have their concerns addressed. The concept of *fama* was undoubtedly a legal fiction which clouded the specific channels through which information reached the church courts; but it was also a mechanism which, as Marie Kelleher has argued, 'brought stories from a broader cross-section of society into the literate, male, and adult world of the law'.[85] The strong trend towards expressing information as though it was shared in common, therefore, could cut both ways. It might give some legitimacy to the segmented interests of quite a

[81] Ian Forrest, 'Defamation, Heresy, and Late Medieval Social Life' in *Image, Text, and Church, 1380–1600: Essays for Margaret Aston*, ed. L. Clark, M. Jurkowski, and C. Richmond (Toronto, 2009), 142–61, at p. 148.

[82] Helmholz, *Canon Law and Ecclesiastical Jurisdiction*, pp. 607–9. On *fama* more generally, see the essays in *Fama: The Politics of Talk and Reputation in Medieval Europe*, ed. Thelmer Fenster and Daniel Lord Smail (Ithaca and London, 2003).

[83] LA, Vj5, fo. 7v. [84] Larson, 'The Jurors of the Durham Halmote Court', p. 681.

[85] Marie A. Kelleher, 'Law and the Maiden: *Inquisitio, fama*, and the testimony of children in Medieval Catalonia', *Viator*, 37 (2006), 351–67.

small group of 'trustworthy men', but, at the same time, it created an inducement for them to draw on common knowledge—or at least, to represent their own concerns as though they were communal—and, in so doing, to consider the 'community' whom they were supposed to represent.

In a close parallel, wider constituencies could also be drawn into decision-making processes in rural courts—both ecclesiastical and secular—through compurgation. There were some restrictions on this, especially in the church courts, where it was a frequent requirement, for example, that the 'grade' of an oath-helper would match that of the defendant—thus women testified for women, clerics for clerics, and so forth—and it was often specified that they should be 'worthy' (*honestus*).[86] Such criteria were important, and no doubt the 'worthiness' of the oath-helpers was carefully regarded by the trustworthy men who concerned themselves with the regulation of *fama*.[87] Yet within these strictures, defendants were given permission to summon what was effectively their own jury, composed of their associates. This brought people into the courts on the basis of their personal social networks with defendants, who might come from any echelon of village society. Most obviously, it permitted women to take a much more prominent role in decision-making; while in most aspects of legal life in the late-medieval countryside, women were accused, judged, and sanctioned by men, compurgation gave the impetus to groups of women.[88]

As compurgation opened the courts to a broader social base, moreover, so it drew the work of the courts closer into the associative relations of a local community. This was particularly true of the church courts. First, in *ex officio* cases in which defendants requested compurgation, ecclesiastical courts required this procedure to be announced in their local parish church before it took place, in the event that one of their co-parishioners wished to challenge it (and thus launch a fuller investigation into the alleged offence).[89] Although such challenges were rare, this process demonstrated the link between the tribunal and the locality. And, indeed, it was essential, along with the other requirements, that oath-helpers were from the same locality as the defendant: a man of Stoke Edith (Herefordshire) was held contumacious by a rural consistory judge after he 'did not purge with neighbours but with other strangers'.[90] And finally, the way in which compurgation relied on oath-swearing—in both secular and ecclesiastical

[86] For respective examples from Ampleforth, see BIA, CCP 12/Amp 3, verso; CCP 12/Amp 5, verso. I return to this point in Chapter 6, pp. 189–191.

[87] Forrest, *Trustworthy Men*, p. 83.

[88] In the couple of cases I have found from secular courts in which female defendants waged their law, no specifications were made about the qualifications for oath-helpers: BL, Add. Ch. 49222, m. 1r; TNA, SC 2/177/55, m. 8r.

[89] See Helmholz, *Canon Law and Ecclesiastical Jurisdiction*, pp. 612–3. For an instance of such a procedure, see *Archdeaconry of Buckingham, 1483–1523*, ed. Elvey, pp. 143–4.

[90] HARC, HD4/1/91, p. 139.

jurisdictions—meant that it was always closely attuned to ongoing dynamics of reputation within the village.[91]

Viewed in terms of their technical roles, relatively small groups of prominent men in the village thus tended to produce information and make decisions in the rural courts. Yet there were institutional forces acting against the use of the courts for the untrammelled hegemony of village elites. In the first place, the courts used some formal mechanisms which distributed the work involved in reporting and judging across different segments of the community. This was important not only because it brought a wider range of people into the courts, but also because it brought some semblance of legal commonality between villagers of different social stations; landless cottagers could participate in the networks of gossip that created *fama*, just as their wives could raise the hue or act as oath-helpers. This commonality may not have strongly constrained the freedom of manoeuvre of this elite, but it did create some pressure on them. The work they performed to find out information, to present 'truly', to be unanimous in judgment, or to represent common knowledge, was also the labour of maintaining their own reputations. The expectations of the people whom they regulated were what made the moral work of the courts possible, weaving it into the associative relations of the village.

For this fabric to hold together effectively, the rural courts had to be able to enforce their orders and punish those who were perceived to have transgressed. The courts had three main mechanisms at their disposal—fines, seizures of goods, and bodily punishments—but these sanctions were more often threatened than executed. This created further room for flexible negotiation at the same time as it served to legitimate the coercion or punishment that was actually carried out. Thus rather than understanding these mechanisms in relation to the courts' effectiveness, or merely as an aspect of social control, we need to consider sanctions as attempts to build ideal communities.[92] Not only did the courts exhibit considerable procedural flexibility in enforcement of their mandates, but they justified them in terms—emphasizing mercy, charity, good example, and discipline—that construed legal work in terms of moral neighbourly relations. These ideas, and their highly visible implementation, gave the courts wide legitimacy as sites for reshaping associative relations.

The most frequent sanction threatened by rural courts was the payment of fines. In secular courts, amercements were levied against specific acts of wrongdoing, and pains were used to threaten against future wrongdoing; but in fact the two were often used together. For example, at the court of West Hendred (Berkshire) in 1516, James Thykham and Emma Vynar were presented for

[91] *Select Cases in Manorial Courts 1250–1550*, ed. L. R. Poos and L. Bonfield, Selden Society 114 (London, 1998), p. lvii.

[92] For a pessimistic view of legal effectiveness, see Marjorie K. McIntosh, 'Local Change and Community Control in England, 1465–1500', *Huntington Library Quarterly*, 49:3 (1986), 219–42, p. 234; but cf. the more nuanced comments of Dyer, *Lords and Peasants*, pp. 161, 276–7.

'keeping bad rule', and amerced at 4d. each; they were ordered to desist from this behaviour under pain of 20d.[93] The lower church courts, by contrast, were technically unable to impose fines, but in practice they circumnavigated this rule, firstly by commuting punishments of public penance for money in the manner of an indulgence, and secondly by remitting punishments in exchange for payments 'in alms'.[94] Thus at Eaton (Norfolk) in March 1421, a smith who broke a contract for 8s. swore on the gospels to pay it back, half at Easter and half in August; if he did not, he would have to pay a further 20s. 'to be given to the lord Prior'.[95] In both secular and church courts monetary fines were often threatened rather than imposed, intended to remind defendants of their obligations and pressurize them into obedience.

It is clear, after all, that many payments were not enforced. Indeed, these pecuniary mechanisms must be understood within the context of the wider monetary climate in the fifteenth-century countryside, especially in relation to the large fall in the supply of bullion.[96] This has been estimated at a loss of around 3d. *per capita* in England, though such a decrease would have fallen harder on the less wealthy.[97] It is remarkable how little consideration has been given to the way that such changes might have affected legal practice; as Chris Briggs has suggested, monetary contraction may have been one of the reasons that so much manorial debt litigation went to ecclesiastical tribunals in the fifteenth century, causing a significant jurisdictional rebalancing in the process.[98] It must also have affected the payment of pains and amercements. Rather than as payments, we might understand them as the creation of a theoretical debt. Certainly, amercements were not always levied, and were sometimes explicitly withdrawn in consideration of a tenant's poverty—an allowance that echoed the practice of the church courts, who made concessions to the old, sick, and poor in their assignations of penance.[99]

Amercements were also levied strategically. Thus the tenants of Netherseal found themselves 'unjustly amerced in the court of Clifton' in 1417 after exercising their fishing rights in the River Mease; clearly the amercement was not

[93] CCCO, Bb 1/3, m. 5r.

[94] See Helmholz, *Canon Law and Ecclesiastical Jurisdiction*, pp. 624–6.

[95] NRO, DCN 67/3, m. 1r.

[96] See J. Day, 'The great bullion famine of the fifteenth century', *P&P*, 79 (1978), 3–54; more generally, John Hatcher, 'The great slump of the mid-fifteenth century', in *Progress and problems in medieval England: Essays in Honour of Edward Miller*, ed. John Hatcher and Richard Britnell (Cambridge, 1996), 237–72; also the classic essay by M. M. Postan, 'Revisions in Economic History: IX.—The Fifteenth Century', *The Economic History Review*, 9:2 (1939), 160–7.

[97] Christoper Dyer, 'England's Economy in the Fifteenth Century', in *Exploring the Evidence: Commemoration, Administration and the Economy*, The Fifteenth Century XIII, ed. Linda Clark (Woodbridge, 2014), p. 204.

[98] Briggs, 'Availability of credit', pp. 19–21.

[99] See Bailey, 'Manor and Leet Courts', pp. 176–7; for examples of these concessions in church courts, see e.g. Thompson, *English Clergy and their Organization*, pp. 220–1.

intended to garner payment, but rather to force discussion over a disputed boundary between the two lordships—and it worked, prompting counsel with the lord.[100] Amercements were also used as bargaining chips by lords in deliberations with their own tenants: John Childe of Kintbury incurred a pain of 3s. 4d. in 1448 after he failed to repair his ruined tenement, but was pardoned *ex gratia*, providing that he set aside the sum for the repairs he had neglected.[101] The remission of amercements thus represented an opportunity for the exercise of good lordship through a pecuniary kind of mercy. At Stour Provost in Dorset, a tenant named John Aleyn illicitly cut down some trees and then after they had been seized by the bailiff, took them away to sell; but he seems to have thought better of this act of defiance, and went to the manor court in 1428 to 'put himself in the lord's grace'. If his intent was to mitigate his punishment, the tactic was partially successful—a note in the rolls recorded that 'this grace has been assessed by the steward at 20d., which is levied to the use of the lord'.[102] These ideas of mercy and grace might thus provide a tool for alleviating, rather than entirely remitting, monetary fines; amercements were not blunt instruments of control, but starting points in a negotiation.

Much of the money raised through fines simply went to the authorities who ran the courts—as perquisites to the manorial lord, or to the ecclesiastical administration. Yet late-medieval villagers might also attempt to direct these payments towards local projects of improvement.[103] As Warren Ault pointed out some fifty years ago, there was a proliferation of by-laws and ordinances in rural leets during the fifteenth century which divided the proceeds of the fine equally between the lord and the church.[104] For example, the tenants of Willoughby were ordered to mend *le moatdyke* before Trinity Sunday in 1472, under pain of a shilling, with proceeds to be divided in this manner.[105] These coins may have mingled in the parish chest with payments collected by ecclesiastical tribunals: at Sedgeford in Norfolk, Richard Walsh, who confessed to working on the feast of St. Bartholomew, was threatened with a payment of 40d. for the mending of the church there if he sinned again in this way.[106] Pains, commutations, and

[100] DRO, D77/2/1/3, verso. 'Item dicunt quod omnes tenentes de Sheille solent habuerunt communem pistacionem in aqua de meys per metas de Stareslowfeld et modo amerciata sunt in curia de clifton iniuste ut dicitur Ideo tunc consuletur cum councilio [sic] domini'.

[101] BL, Add. Ch. 49235, m. 3r. Who pardoned him is not specified, but it was probably the steward; at the same court (but it should be added, nowhere else in the Kintbury rolls), the same formula was used to pardon the whole homage, who had collectively failed to repair a lane under pain of 10s.

[102] KCC, STP/7, m. 3r. 'Johannes Aleyn venit hic in curia coram Willelmo Tarent senescallo domini et ponit se in gratia domini eo quod presentatus fuit super ipsum quod . . . [etc.] . . . que gratia assessa est per dictum senescallum ad xx d quos [preceptos sunt] ei levare ad opus domini etc.'

[103] Dyer, 'Medieval Village Community and Its Decline', p. 428.

[104] Ault, 'Manor Court and Parish Church in Fifteenth-Century England', p. 53.

[105] MCO, 45/4, recto. It is possible that such payments went to the 'common fund' managed by the tenants there: see above, p. 28.

[106] NRO, DCN 67/1a, m. 2r. Commutations of penances could also be directed specifically to the church fabric, e.g. the case of William Chylde of Weobley (Herefordshire): HARC, HD94/1/88, pp. 1–3.

amercements were thus part of a highly flexible culture of sanctions, in which the lines between enforced sanction and charitable donation were blurred, helping to legitimate the courts, and their sanctions, as sites for community-building.

Not all of the courts' means of enforcement revolved around money, however; the secular courts in particular retained some sharp-edged mechanisms that allowed them to seize the goods of people who refused to attend to answer a plea (distraint), or who had repeatedly failed to perform an order (attachment). Most frequently these procedures meant that one of their animals was taken and kept in custody by the court bailiff as surety for their attendance.[107] Seizure was used for a variety of reasons and situations: John atte Helde was distrained by five sheep in 1392 because he refused to pay his customary pannage dues at Milton (Surrey); at King's Langley in 1423, the bailiff attached Thomas Barbor by two dishes worth 2s. and William Boucher by 'a chest with certain goods in it', worth 12d.; John Cornewale was distrained in Warminster hundred 'to make an agreement' concerning three pounds of wool he had taken from Richard Pykton.[108] Distraints and attachments were a quick and tangible manifestation of a court mandate.

For all this, these seizures were also open to negotiation. To begin with, goods that were taken had to be kept somewhere, and this could cause logistical problems. In the court of St. James's Priory outside Exeter, it was customary to seal distrained goods so that they could no longer be used.[109] But it was more usual to distrain animals, and these had to be put in a special enclosure, the penfold; the Durham priory estates even appointed a special official, the pinder, who was responsible for its operation.[110] Throughout England, people who considered the distraint unfair, or who needed their livestock back, might simply take them from the penfold without permission. This was not, apparently, a very serious offence, given the frequency with which it occurred and the small fines which it tended to incur; at Netherseal it was fined at just 2d. and given the vernacular name of *poundbrach*.[111] Indeed, the to and fro over the imparkment of distrained animals and their release by recalcitrant defendants, and its reporting in the courts, seems to have been one of the regular legal rhythms of rural life.

Even in more serious situations where seizures were the result of repeated contumacy, arrears, or failures to perform an order, there was some room for compromise. Thus in 1478 when John Deene was in arrears of 3s. 9d. in rent to the farmer of the manor of Ringwood, he was distrained to pay by two pewter dishes,

[107] This practice was borrowed from the common law: see Baker, *Introduction to English Legal History*, pp. 64–5; the comparison is made in Beckerman, 'Procedural Innovation and Institutional Change', p. 243.

[108] Respectively: CCCO, Ga 25/2/e; TNA, SC 2/177/54, m. 3r; WSHO, 865/330, m. 1r.

[109] KCC, SJP/1, m. 18v.

[110] B. Dodds, *Peasants and Production in the Medieval North-East: The Evidence from Tithes, 1270–1536* (Woodbridge, 2007), p. 43.

[111] DRO, D77/2/1/4, verso.

some plates, tin saucers, and a pewter pot. The court appointed arbitrators—two chosen by Deene, and two chosen by the farmer—to assess the total value the items, and they duly found them to be worth 3s.; Deene was thus given about five months to make up the remainder, under warning of further distraint.[112] This more elaborate procedure was relatively unusual, and may signify some unease over the legitimacy of the distraint (the bailiff is notable by his absence in this case).[113] The arbitrators here were not simply revealing the monetary worth of the items, but engaging in a politics of value about the worth of the goods relative to the debt, and thus about the equity of the distraint.[114] Thus while the seizure of goods was certainly a strong inducement to perform the court's orders, it did not represent the kind of 'legal plunder' that Daniel Smail has found in Mediterranean Europe, but rather acted as a kind of material negotiation.[115]

The ecclesiastical courts could not seize goods, but they did have other mechanisms to pressure and prompt action, relying, not unsuccessfully, on the rather more abstract—but no less real—threats of suspension and excommunication for those defendants who were repeatedly or deliberately contumacious.[116] The procedures of even the lower ecclesiastical tribunals meant that there was some push and pull built into these processes. For example, after Richard Colles of Dunton (Buckinghamshire) failed to appear after being cited to a tribunal at Aylesbury, he was immediately suspended by the archdeacon of Buckingham; a mandate was then sent to the curate of Whitchurch (about two miles away), giving him the power to absolve Richard, who was to attend the next court and explain why he should not be excommunicated for his contumacy.[117] The networks of church administrators thus meant that these sanctions could be quickly reversed or mitigated. As Norman Tanner and Sethina Watson have put it, 'the system did work to chasten wrongdoers, but... it required a good measure of tolerance and flexibility'.[118]

If full excommunication was more often a latent threat, local practice varied sharply, in ways that doubtless influenced the perceptions of the laity. In the

[112] KCC, RIN/7, fo. 3r.

[113] A similar case, in which a butcher forfeited his tenement and all his goods in default of rents and repairs, can be found in Woodfidley (Hampshire): KCC, FOR/8/2, 3, 5, 6r–v, 7. Here the items were said to be valued by the whole homage; in a similar case at Gayton (Lincolnshire) the presentment jurors reported the assessments, BL, MS. Egerton 3001, fo. 106v.

[114] See, in general, Arjun Appadurai, 'Introduction: commodities and the politics of value', in *The social life of things: Commodities in cultural perspective*, ed. Arjun Appadurai (Cambridge, 1986), 3–63, particularly relevant here are the comments at p. 57.

[115] See Daniel Lord Smail, *Legal Plunder: Households and Debt Collection in Late Medieval Europe* (Cambridge, MA, 2016), esp. pp. 136–80.

[116] A possible exception here is sequestration—the order to temporarily seize a party's chattels—used in civil procedure; see Helmholz, *Canon Law and Ecclesiastical Jurisdiction*, p. 345.

[117] *Courts of the Archdeaconry of Buckingham*, ed. Elvey, p. 251. This was a civil case, but the same procedure applied in *ex officio* causes.

[118] Norman Tanner and Sethina Watson, 'Least of the laity: the minimum requirements for a medieval Christian', *Journal of Medieval History*, 32 (2006), 395–423, p. 421.

peculiar of Hartlebury, for example, debtors were frequently told to make restitution (and other offenders told to do penance) under pain of excommunication; in the deanery of Wisbech, by contrast, debtors were reported and then immediately suspended from church, presumably until they paid back the money.[119] Certainly, these procedures were carefully observed by other parishioners, who derived meaning (sometimes incorrectly) from their neighbours' absences from church. Indeed, Joan Johnson of Cowley (Buckinghamshire) found herself accused of defamation after saying to John Anesely 'thow... art a strong arand theif, and therfor wer accursed [three] solemne sondeys in the chirch'.[120] The church's threats worked because, like many of their mechanisms, they drew on the heavy weight of scandal and charity, the lodestars of neighbourly relations.

As a last resort the courts would enforce bodily punishments to shame and exclude offenders from the community. In the first place, both secular and ecclesiastical courts used corporeal chastisement as a means of humiliation. The right to a view of frankpledge itself was closely associated with the *judicialia* of stocks, pillory, and tumbrel; this jurisdiction might be closely guarded by villagers themselves, as when the free jurors of Ringwood asked the farmer of the manor to make some new stocks in 1485.[121] Many places also used a cucking-stool, particularly for women accused of gossiping.[122] In the church courts, offenders were frequently enjoined to undergo public penance as a means of absolution. These penances could range from a humble barefoot procession to a full penitential flogging, but either way were located in the parish church or a nearby marketplace, in order to maximize the publicity of the punishment within the local community.[123]

Perhaps the greatest sanction available to rural secular and church courts was full exclusion from the community. In the ecclesiastical courts this was effected through excommunication, of course, which was not only a spiritual but a social sanction. In 1497 William Laburne, an excommunicant perjurer of West Ham

[119] Respectively: *Noble Household Management and Spiritual Discipline*, ed. Toomey, Swanson and Guyatt, pp. 159, 164, 174, 178–9, etc. The threat was exercised comparatively often, too, e.g. at pp. 162, 173. For Wisbech, see Poos, *Lower Ecclesiastical Jurisdiction*, pp. 337, 341, 343–5.

[120] LMA, DL/C/B/043/MS09064/007, fo. 27v.

[121] KCC, RIN/7, fo. 1v. More generally, see Mark Bailey, *The English Manor c.1200—c.1500* (Manchester, 2002), p. 183. The pillory was also closely associated with market franchises: see James Davis, 'The Cross and the Pillory: Symbolic Structures of Commercial Space in Medieval English Towns', in *Stätische Räume im Mittelalter*, ed. Susanne Shrich and Jörg Oberste (Regensburg, 2009), 241–59. On punishment more generally, see Helen Carrel, 'The ideology of punishment in late medieval English towns', *Social History*, 34:3 (2009), 301–20.

[122] Martin Ingram, '"Scolding women cucked or washed": a crisis in gender relations in early modern England?', in *Women, Crime, and the Courts in Early Modern England*, ed. Garthine Walker and Jenny Kermode (London, 1994), 48–80; for examples, see McIntosh, *Controlling Misbehavior*, p. 68.

[123] See Scammell, 'Rural Chapter', pp. 17–8; James Masschaele, 'The Public Spaces of the Marketplace in Medieval England', *Speculum*, 77:2 (2002), 383–421, at pp. 409–11. For a detailed example of such a penance from Hindringham, see NRO, DCN 67/1, m. 2r.

(Essex), warned his neighbours not to eat or drink with him, a common trope of social exclusion, 'for they have cursed me as blacke as a cole'.[124] Rural leets retained the power of banishment, and might use it to move on people who did not have strong connections to the village. Thus Thomas Cotton, a subtenant living in Kintbury, was presented for keeping a concubine, and they together being 'suspicious persons, not of good reputation' were ordered to leave his house within a week. It was further threatened that 'if they do not want to leave... then the capital pledge with the whole homage shall put them in the stocks, and keep them there until they do want to leave'.[125] The threat was apparently successful, as a marginal note recorded that Thomas had indeed 'withdrawn from the lordship'. Such punishments clearly marked out who belonged to the village community.

On the surface, the variety of tools at the disposal of rural courts for the enforcement of their orders achieved several effects: monetary fines, seizures of goods, and penances helped to raise revenue and enforce attendance at court, chastisement represented a corporeal threat to an individual's reputation, and exclusion physically removed him or her from the wider community. These sanctions were utilized as highly flexible devices, foreboding and pressurizing, rather than as blunt instruments of control; enabling the courts to become insinuated with the associative relations of the late-medieval village. It also reflected the strengthened position of rural 'consumers of the law' in the fifteenth century. Courts were in a double bind. They had to be able to enforce orders if they wished to attract villagers to litigate there, but they also had to give some consideration to defendants in order to avoid wholesale contumacy and disobedience. Enforcement through negotiation, rather than obdurate mandate, was perhaps the best way to effect this precarious balance.

The same may be said of the work performed in the courts more generally; flexibility was an essential part of rural legal culture, both a product of, and a contributing factor to, the close correspondence between legal and associative relations in rural settlements. This broad interpenetration was made possible by rural courts because of the ways in which they worked to smooth—though never level—the hierarchical relations of the late-medieval village. This is not to deny the substantial power wielded by elites there, nor to argue, indeed, that they could not manipulate the courts to achieve their own ends; rather, it is to argue that the

[124] LMA, DL/C/B/043/MS09064/007, fo. 24r. His speech—also containing the statement that he had five plums 'growyng yn myn arsehole'—was recorded in a memorandum after he was absolved, perhaps because it verged on contempt of court.

[125] BL, Add. Ch. 49234, verso: 'Item presentant quod Thomas Cotton moratur in tenemento Ricardi Smyth jr, qui quidem Thomas tenet unam concubinam et sunt persone suspectuouse et non bone fame. Ideo preceptum est dicto Ricardo quod deponat et expellat dictum Thomam cum concubina sua extra tenementum suum predictum infra septimanam proximam futuram post istam curiam. Et eciam si noluerunt removere extra tenementum predictum ac libertatem et dominium domine preceptum est decenario cum tota decena sua predictum Thomam cum concubina sua predicta ipsos in sippis ponere et illos ibidem retinere quousque voluerunt [recedere] extra libertatem'.

prevailing tides of institutions worked against outright domination. The institutional conduits for the participation of a wider range of villagers in the courts' activities meant that there were substantial pressures to act—or be seen to act—for a wider set of interests; this was a microcosm of the 'pressure of the public' that John Watts has identified in political culture more generally in this period.[126] This capacity to respond to 'the village community'—iterated in groups of compurgators, presentment jurors, suitors, or gossipers—gave the courts their legitimacy.

Community-Building in the Courts: Peace, Repair, Ordaining

What kinds of community did fifteenth-century villagers wish to build in the rural courts? This final section argues that they attempted to mould associative relations in accordance with three intersecting discourses that reflected idealized modes of community. First, the idea of 'peace' worked to conceptualize the harmonious natural condition of rural community, and to marginalize behaviours which were thought to disturb it. Second, the notion of 'repair' was used to conceive of the maintenance of the physical environment in which villagers lived; the material village—in its buildings, lanes, fields, and watercourses—provided the infrastructure of community, representing the settlement's wealth and boundaries, and creating the conditions under which harmonious associative relations could unfold. And third, villagers drew upon the idea of the 'ordaining' as a means of establishing community through the making of rules, a legalism built into associative life. In what follows, we examine each of these ideals in turn, exploring the ways in which they framed the work of rural courts in building community.

To begin with, 'peace' was a commonly encountered concept in the rural courts: in leets it meant the maintenance of the king's peace, and thus the presentment and fining of a continual succession of petty bloodsheds and assaults; in church courts, as we have seen, it was the impetus for a relentless pressure towards reconciliation.[127] In both jurisdictions, then, peace was the a priori state of being for a rural community. This idea of a 'state of peace' was central to the discourse of the leet courts, which framed crime and transgressions as taking place 'against the peace' (*contra pacem*); the work of the courts in presenting and amercing such behaviour thus reinstated the peace for the whole community. In the church courts, a similar idea was mobilized towards smaller communities. For example, after Robert Garner was said to have sown discord between Emma Pope and Leticia Garner, he claimed at a church tribunal in Hemsby that 'peace had been

[126] John L. Watts, 'The Pressure of the Public on Later Medieval Politics', in *Political Culture*, ed. Clark and Carpenter, 159–80.

[127] On the king's peace, see the useful comments in Edward Powell, *Kingship, Law, and Society: Criminal Justice in the Reign of Henry V* (Oxford, 1989), pp. 48–51; on 'peace' as a goal of the church courts, see above, pp. 31–2 in this volume.

restored' (*pacem reformatam*).[128] Peace was the *status quo ante* to which rural communities were always seeking to return.

This made peace into a normative concept which extended beyond interpersonal violence and into a broader way of imagining rural community, particularly in secular courts. John Aleyn of Stour Provost, who we met earlier, was presented in 1428 for 'hassling and threatening the tenants of the lord, so that they may not live peacefully in their tenements'.[129] 'Peace' thus inflected the enjoyment of property (a relation more noticeable in the 'peaceable possession' of the common law); villagers demanded a tenure—maintained through the courts—that allowed them to live *in* peace. This is made unusually explicit in a lengthy case against Thomasina, a servant of the vicar of Combe in Berkshire, in 1456. Presented first as a 'common quarreller, fight-picker, and scold', who had assaulted William Neell to the extent that 'he was afraid to go about his business', Thomasina then gained a reputation as an arsonist. She so threatened Thomas and Edith Havand, claiming that she would burn down their house, goods, and chattels, that they formally renounced their tenure in the manor court.[130] Peace thus encompassed more than just the prevention of violence and conflict; it was also about the building of a rural community free from unease, whose inhabitants could feel secure in their homes.

The legal logic of peace created as its corollary a cluster of concepts associated with 'disturbance'. This can often be found in manorial and leet rolls in the literal Latin *perturbatio*—thus John Wevir of Kintbury was said to keep an inn frequented by 'diverse suspect men and women, and they disturb the king's peace'.[131] It could also be said to encompass *obiurgatio* (scolding), the root of the word used to describe both John Aleyn and Thomasina, along with the less common *garrulator* (chatterer) and *barrator* (vexatious litigator). These words were frequently used in both secular and ecclesiastical courts to label myriad forms of disruptive misbehaviour, but sins of the tongue in particular.[132] Thus when Alice Causy of Hindringham defamed Nicholas and Alice Candelor as 'false thieves and usurers', it was noted, upon her failure to perform compurgation, that she had committed 'the crime of scolding [against] her neighbours'.[133] In this regard, it is

[128] NRO, DCN67/2, m. 2r.

[129] KCC, STP/7, m. 2r: '... obiurgavit et minatus est tenentes domini consimiles quod non possient pacifice morari super tenementa sua'. On Aleyn, see above, pp. 39–40.

[130] KCC, COM/11, 2, recto: 'garrulatrix altercatrix et obiurgatrix... tales minas tribuit quod circa sua negocia minime transire ausus fuit'; '... dicta Thomesina... in Editham ad tunc uxorem Thome Havand ut nuper mortuam et dictam ex magna causa timoris insultacionis et minacionis dicte Thomesine dicte Edithe elatis et factis insultis fecit mundando et incando quod tam domum qua bona et catalla ipsius Edithe et mariti sui combureret et comburere vellet...'

[131] BL, Add. Ch. 49238, m. 7r.

[132] Cf. the 'disharmony', 'disorder', and 'poverty' clusters set up (partly for quantitative purposes) in McIntosh, *Controlling Misbehavior*, pp. 9–10.

[133] NRO, DCN 67/2, m. 2r: 'crimen obiurgitatis [contra] vicinos suos'. The manuscript has a small hole between the second and fourth words, and nothing of the missing word remains, but it seems very likely to be 'contra'.

significant that such words were so frequently attached to women; peace in the late-medieval village was characterized by the absence of disturbing female voices.

As these words intersected with the aural resonances of peace (and indeed harmony), the other valences of disturbance become more pronounced; it was also a way of subsuming the interpersonal relations of the village into the discourse of 'nuisance'.[134] Thus, for example, we find another illicit innkeeper—John Massatay of Ringwood—presented for receiving 'suspect people, who commonly stay up all night in his inn, to the nuisance and disturbance (*perturbatio*) of the whole vicinity of the vill'.[135] This kind of misbehaviour might thus be framed as a kind of environmental problem, in which disturbance at once comprised the noises coming from a rowdy tavern, but also the disruption to community caused by people making such a nuisance of themselves. And indeed, vice versa, this helps to explain the way in which 'peace' might be wielded against disturbances to the village landscape: Joan de Foxle was presented at Cookham (Berkshire) because she 'stopped up a watercourse at *Wessmainlane*, 'without right, against the peace... [and] to the grave nuisance of the country'.[136] This multivalent notion of peace sat athwart legal categories, working against all kinds of moral, criminal, and environmental disturbance.

This brings us to 'repair', the second mode of community-building pursued in the rural courts, across manorial, leet, and ecclesiastical jurisdiction. For manorial courts, protecting crops from wandering livestock and ensuring that fields were properly irrigated were agricultural concerns shared by most tenant farmers, particularly in open-field regions.[137] In leet courts, the incessant orders to scour and unblock ditches and other watercourses hint at the importance of water management to village life. The maintenance of roads and paths was also important: Edward Parker was fined half a shilling by the court of King's Langley in 1423 because he had narrowed the end of *herts lane*, 'which was from old times a common way of the community'.[138] The ecclesiastical courts oversaw the upkeep of the church and churchyard, particularly at visitation, checking whether parishioners had pastured sheep in the churchyard or took away stones from the walls.[139] The management and maintenance of the village environment was central to the courts' work.

This was important because of the way that the physical world intersected with ideals of community for late-medieval villagers—a point to which we shall

[134] In towns we shall see a similar conflation of 'nuisance' with questions of moral order, but for different reasons: see Chapter 2, pp. 81–3.

[135] KCC, RIN/6, D, recto.

[136] BRO, D/ESK/M4, m. 4v: 'minus iuste et contra pacem... ad grave nocumentum patrie'.

[137] Ault, *Open-Field Farming*, pp. 40–57.

[138] TNA, SC 2/177/54, m.4r. '... que est ab antiquo communis via communitatis...' More generally, see Brian Paul Hindle, 'Roads and Tracks', in *The English Medieval Landscape*, ed. Leonard Cantor (London, 1982), 193–217.

[139] For examples of these offences respectively, DCN67/3, m. 1r.

return in Chapter 5.[140] Not only did the idea of 'nuisance' stretch to antisocial misbehaviour, but in a more positive way, nuisance could also prompt collective action in response to a common problem. At West Hendred in 1502, the leet jurors took the unusual step of presenting their own lord (Corpus Christi College, Oxford) for failing in the obligation to repair a footbridge at *le mere ende*, 'to the nuisance of the neighbours living nearby that place' (*vicinorum ibidem commorantium*).[141] Part of what made these people 'neighbours' here, rather than, say, tenants, was their shared interest in the repair of their local bridge. And indeed, the same dynamic could work on a rather greater scale, binding the community as a whole.[142] Thus even when Peter Clyffe, the farmer of King's Langley, cut down some branches overhanging a lane 'by reason of his own land', his actions were presented as 'a grave common nuisance', overriding his individual tenurial rights. A 'common nuisance' was a powerful discourse of community-building.[143]

Nuisance had an equally powerful corollary in the notion of 'repair'. Repair was not only the solution to malfunctioning infrastructure, but a kind of moral and aesthetic duty incumbent on the inhabitants of rural communities. This can be seen most clearly in relation to the fabric of the parish church, which, as we have already seen, was directly sustained by funds from the courts' mediation of disputes; the monies from alms and amercements which went to restore the church thus provided a physical manifestation of communal repair.[144] Once again, this could provide an irresistible legal logic. In a visitation of Pickworth (Lincolnshire) in 1499, the *inquisitores* complained that John Frobson and his wife Agnes did not attend church; and, moreover, that 'John does not want to contribute to the fabric of the church with the other parishioners'.[145] The two offences were different sides of the same coin in a moral universe in which, to borrow Katherine French's phrase, the church not only reflected but helped to materially constitute 'local aspirations and the shared Christian life'.[146]

The notion of repair extended also into the kinds of community fabricated in the secular courts. Anxieties about the decay and waste of the manorial estate were manifested in the leases of customary land, as tenants were enjoined to

[140] See Chapter 5, pp. 155–158.

[141] CCCO, Bb 1/19, recto. In 1513 the jurors 'petitioned the lord' (*supplicaverunt domino*) to repair the town bridge: Bb 1/3, m. 4r.

[142] In this gesture towards a whole community, it was quite different to the rhetorical framing of nuisances we find in urban legal culture, which were aimed at physically denser communities. See Chapter 2, p. 81.

[143] TNA, SC 2/177/55, m. 6v.

[144] On the space of parish churches, see French, *People of the Parish*, Ch. 5. 'Curious Windows and Great Bells: The Architecture of Community', 142–74, esp. pp. 143–5, 162–70; Beat Kümin, 'Introduction' in *Political Space in Pre-Industrial Europe*, ed. Kümin (Farnham and Burlington, VT, 2009), 5–15.

[145] LA, Vj/5, fo. 58r: 'non vult contribuere ad fabricam ecclesie cum alijs parochianis'.

[146] French, *People of the Parish*, p. 143.

'sufficiently maintain and repair' their houses and holdings. This was a visual language common to the whole legal community: when Robert Foxlow leased a ruined messuage and cottage at Bradbourne (Derbyshire), he undertook 'to repair it well according to the advice of the tenants there, on oath'.[147] The look of the manorial stock and plant was also a benchmark of lordship; tenants who saw wasted edifices also perceived a weak lord, unable to prevent the asset-stripping of his property. In 1503, Robert Coppyng was presented in the Norfolk village of Scratby for a 'stripping' (*estreppamentum*), after he tore down a large wheat barn which had been 60ft. in length. He was ordered to 'rebuild it as new, in the state it was before', a common injunction.[148] As tenants rebuilt and repaired their holdings, so they illustrated the continued vigour of seigneurial authority to conserve its property. The ideal of repair—across both secular and ecclesiastical courts—sought to build community through the conservation of the physical world.

The third and final mode of community-building was through 'ordaining'. This awkward word, though it would have been familiar to speakers of Middle English, requires some explanation.[149] It is allied to the notions of 'order' characterized by Keith Wrightson for early-modern English society; it also shares significant affinities with the ideas of 'governance' and 'rule' explored by Shannon McSheffrey, as a moral duty that linked a man's own comportment and reputation to his patriarchal control of household and the correction of moral infractions through local courts.[150] But while ordaining certainly encompassed these ideals of regulation—of bodies, behaviours, and communities—it is more akin to an ideal of regulation in itself. It is used here as a contemporary vernacular equivalent to the anthropological concept of legalism: 'a non-pretentious word for themes that include . . . an appeal to rules that are distinct from practice . . . and a disposition to address in such terms the conduct of human life'.[151] Ordaining represented the ideal that communities could make rules to organize their associative relations; that rule-making was a means of building rural community.

Ordaining can be perceived most clearly in the ordinances and by-laws that provided a common mode of ordering village life. These rules are particularly well-known to historians as means of managing agricultural practices in manorial

[147] DRO, D9392/M1, m. 1r.

[148] NRO, DCN 63/2, fo. 10r. For other examples, see e.g. King's Langley: TNA, SC 2/177/54, m. 1r, SC 2/177/55, m. 9r; or an inquisition into a building at Brackley (Northamptonshire): MCO, Brackley 209d.

[149] See *MED*, 'ordeining(e)', and 'ordeinen'.

[150] For 'order', see Keith Wrightson, 'Two concepts of order: justices, constables and jurymen in seventeenth-century England', in *An Ungovernable People: The English and their law in the seventeenth and eighteenth centuries*, ed. John Brewer and John Styles (New Brunswick, NJ, 1980), 21–46. For 'governance', see Shannon McSheffrey, *Marriage, Sex, and Civic Culture in Late Medieval London* (Philadelphia, 2003), pp. 137–63; Marjorie McIntosh, 'Finding a Language for Misconduct: Jurors in Fifteenth-Century Local Courts', in *Bodies and Disciplines: Intersections of Literature and History in Fifteenth-Century England*, ed. Barbara A. Hanawalt and David Wallace (Minneapolis, 1996), 87–122.

[151] Paul Dresch and Judith Scheele, 'Rules and Categories: an Overview', in *Legalism: Rules and Categories*, ed. Dresch and Scheele (Oxford, 2015), 1–27, p. 1.

courts, as for example at Ab Lench in Worcestershire, when three successive ordinances were made by the tenants in 1443: that everyone should confine their geese until the harvest was collected (under pain of 12d.), keep their pigs in enclosures (under 40d.), and tether their horses with a rope, especially in autumn (under 40d.).[152] Ordinances were also sometimes made in church courts, where they were directed towards the regulation of misbehavior; thus at a chapter in Ampleforth in 1456 'it was ordained and enjoined to all parishioners that none may foster, receive, or host in their house any suspect woman or women'.[153] Yet, more than setting forth specific regulations, 'ordaining' entailed the broader idealization of rules as a means of building rural community. The leet of Willoughby, for example, promulgated multiple ordinances against gambling and card-playing in the later fifteenth century; after they had been broken yet again in 1481, it was ordained that 'from now on, no one shall hold the said ordinance and provision in contempt', under pain of 3s. 4d.[154] Ordaining was understood as a social good in and of itself.

As an ideal, it was also communal. Ordinances were often represented as deriving from the common assent of the whole vill, or the whole homage. In practice, while it is highly likely that they were formulated by the trustworthy men, or even by the lord's steward, this notion of assent was more than just a trope. According to a late-medieval estate custumal, the tenants of Fountains Abbey 'shall be ready to come to the *plebiscite* when summoned', while at an ecclesiastical visitation of Helmsley and Stamford Bridge (North Yorkshire) in 1472, it was reported that 'all the parishioners there hold their *plebiscites* and other temporal ordinances in the church and churchyard', which they were warned not to do under pain.[155] These were not proto-democratic referenda, of course; the word *plebiscite* here means something like 'by-law court'.[156] Yet they do suggest a gathering in which ordinances were promulgated, and assented to by acclamation, as a means of enunciating their legitimacy among different constituencies.[157] At West Hendred in 1509, an ordinance was established by 'all the tenants [i.e. the capital pledges] aforesaid, with the assent of the lord, and the common assent of

[152] DRO, D156 M/I 1/5.

[153] BIA, CCP 12/Amp 4, verso. See also an ordinance made during a visitation at Bole in Nottinghamshire, which specified that anyone found arguing in the church or the churchyard would forfeit a pound of wax to burn before the image of the Virgin, 'if they were found culpable by four men'. YMLA, L2/3c, fo. 40v.

[154] MCO, 45/1: 'Et nichilominus ordinatum est per dictam curiam quod nullus de cetero dictum ordinacionem et provisionem contempnat...' Ordinances in subsequent years suggest this injunction was ineffective: 45/3, 45/12 [courts for 1483, 1485].

[155] For the Fountains ordinance, see Ault, *Open-Field Farming*, p. 59. Ault cites this custumal as BL, Add. Ch. 60010, but in fact he means Add. MS. 40010. For the visitation record, see YML, L2/3c, fo. 24v. On the churchyard as a space for communal gatherings, see David Dymond, 'God's Disputed Acre', *Journal of Ecclesiastical History*, 50:3 (1999), 463–97.

[156] R. E. Latham, *Revised Medieval Latin Word-List: From British and Irish Sources* (Oxford, 1980), p. 355. See the critique of such positions offered in Forrest, *Trustworthy Men*, pp. 166, 186.

[157] Dyer, 'Political Life of the Fifteenth-Century English Village', p. 142.

those congregated'.[158] Ordaining was a powerful ideal because it at once recognized the multipolar sources of authority in a rural community and represented their unity as a function of rule-making.

This connection between autonomy and community was essential within rural legal culture, which drew persistently on the discourse of custom. As several generations of medieval historians have comprehended it, custom represented a 'body of understood rules governing the rights and obligations of villeins and customary land'.[159] But regardless of the content of those rules, the way they were articulated, and so forth, in relation to the broader ideal of ordaining, the particular 'ruliness' of custom becomes much more apparent. Thus the countless agreements to hold land 'according to the custom of the manor' were not binding tenants to particular obligations (which were sometimes stated in the lease), but rather to the very notion of obeying *some* rules about the court's management of tenure, whether currently specified or yet to be articulated; and thus people like William Adams of Combe could be presented—in his case, for suing another tenant outside the lordship—because he was said to have acted 'against custom'.[160] Custom was not just about specific rules, but about the very ability of a rural settlement to ordain and articulate its own rules.

The way that ordaining brought together the idealization of rules, community, and local autonomy is nicely encapsulated by a case from Great Cressingham, in Norfolk. In 1490, the capital pledges 'ordained and made a by-law for themselves and their successors to have in perpetuity', that the lord's shepherds ought to keep his sheep off the tenants' crofts during the forty days before Martinmas, 'as such crofts ought to be reserved for the use of the tenants, to nourish their own sheep'. They specified a payment of 6s. 8d., 'for whenever the said ordinance might be broken', to be divided equally between the lord and the church. Remarkably, a note in the margin of the roll records that 'the ordinance for a by-law is void because the lord does not want to affirm it'.[161] This ordinance, which attempted to modify local custom surrounding 'shack', the system of foldcoursing widely-used in Norfolk, shows how ordaining could be used by villagers as a means of collective action against their lords. By claiming the right to ordain rules 'for their successors in perpetuity', they not only claimed a role for the court as a kind of vernacular legislature, but the authority to build a community through rules.

Along with the ideals of peace and repair, ordaining thus served as a model for the kind of associative relations that late-medieval villagers wished to build through their legal institutions. These discourses contained their own distinctive resonances, and yet they were also interwoven with one another: in a world where

[158] CCCO, Bb1/9.

[159] *Select Cases in Manorial Courts*, ed. Bonfield and Poos, p. xvii. See also *The Peasant Land Market in Medieval England*, ed. P. D. A. Harvey (Oxford, 1984).

[160] KCC, COM/12, verso.

[161] BLO, Norfolk Roll 103, m. 1v.

peace was valorized as a natural and orderly state of communal harmony, so its corollary, 'disturbance' could encompass both social misbehaviour and the kinds of environmental nuisance that the courts attempted to control; and, vice versa, the good repair of the physical world was understood as a proxy for the health of the community. Ordaining, finally, at once signified the idealized rule-boundedness of community at the same time as it undergirded and reaffirmed the essential function of the rural courts as forums for community-building. It represented a perfect community, peaceful, ordered, resplendent, and free from dissension. This unreachable ideal was the horizon towards which late-medieval rural legal culture attempted to extend, as villagers saw in law the opportunity to remould the very conditions of associative life.

Conclusion

In this chapter, I have made three interlocking arguments about rural legal culture. Firstly, I have suggested that the courts of the fifteenth-century countryside not only remained vital institutions in the face of the large-scale socio-economic changes, but actually became more closely attuned to the associative lives of the villagers who used them. In this period, rural courts became more adaptable to the needs of litigants who were more easily able to take their business elsewhere; this flexibility, in turn, led villagers to bring more tangled, complicated relations to the cognizance of the court. Secondly, I have argued that while many rural courts were certainly marshalled by elite men, they were able to represent themselves as communal institutions. Women, the landless, and the 'undeserving' poor were institutionally and socially excluded from full involvement in the work of the courts, but there were also some mechanisms—in *fama*, compurgation, the hue and cry—which could be used to highlight their concerns. Such mechanisms were important less for the influence they granted to such people, and more because of the way in which they played upon the rhetoric of corporate unity, which fed into the legitimacy of the courts as sites of community.

And indeed, the third argument I pursued here is that late-medieval rural legal culture was characterized by the idealization of 'community'. As we have seen, this was pursued through several different discourses—'peace' as a kind of harmonious accord between neighbours, 'repair' as the fabrication of a decorous physical village, and ordaining as a norm of ruliness—which represented an equitable and communal ethic of neighbourliness, aimed at the common good. In practice, of course, these discourses were often wielded in ways that reinforced the patriarchal and oligarchical tierings of village society; women who attempted to influence reputational networks could easily be reproved for making a 'disturbance', just as the poor, living in the most dilapidated tenements, were pressured to make repairs. But the ideal of community was also more than the sum of its coercive utilizations; it also provided the backbone of rural legal culture in the idea that the social relations of a rural settlement could, and indeed should, be organized *through* law.

This is significant because it helps us better understand the transitions taking place in the late-medieval countryside. The frameworks through which we tend to understand these transitions—the end of serfdom? the beginning of agrarian capitalism?—are vast, but what cannot be doubted is that law played a significant part in their unfolding. Rural legal culture was the vernacular framework through which villagers negotiated the tectonic socio-economic changes of the post-plague world. The development of customary tenure, for example, was deeply imbricated with legalistic ways of thinking, evident in its plurality of different forms—'at the will of lord', 'by the rod', 'according to the custom of the manor', or 'by copy'—among others; if such phrases suggest the presence of legally-educated men in fifteenth-century courts, then they were probably also legible to the villagers who hired them.[162] Above all, what such phrases showed was that, as Mark Bailey has put it, 'villein tenure was no longer immutable, but... could be altered through negotiation, non-cooperation or rebellion'.[163] Law was the lingua franca through which these dialogues took place.

The discourses of rural legal culture thus provided the organizing principles and expectations for the small-scale negotiations between villagers and seigneurial authorities. Thus the notion of repair framed countless new leases; Richard Broune agreed to lease a house for seven years at Bradbourne on the condition that he would rebuild it, the lord providing 'al maner tymber for to byld withal, and at þe ende of his terme [Richard] shall loeve hit tenabull'.[164] But the ideals of community might also intercede in the more fundamental relationship between lord and tenant. Thus the tenants of the manor of Meyton in Frettenham (Norfolk) petitioned their lord, the Earl of Oxford, in the late fifteenth century to complain about men who claimed to act on his behalf as stewards. They requested that the earl should force these officers to 'cessyn here malys', and thus allow the tenants 'to leve in reste and peas'.[165] The discourses of rural legal culture thus served as a buttress as villagers renegotiated the changing rural world in which they lived on their own terms.

In this sense, as I have suggested, we need to look beyond 'the decline of serfdom' as a narrative for understanding the changes in the late-medieval countryside. A considerable part of what we are seeing—in the development of

[162] Matthew Tompkins, '"Let's Kill All the Lawyers": Did Fifteenth-Century Peasants Employ Lawyers when they Conveyed Customary Land?' in *Identity and Insurgency in the Late Middle Ages*, The Fifteenth Century VI, ed. Linda Clark (Woodbridge, 2006), 73–87.

[163] Bailey, *Decline of Serfdom*, p. 318.

[164] DRO, D9392/M1, m. 3r.

[165] BLO, Norfolk Charters 109. For a full transcription of this petition and its tenurial context, see Colin Richmond, *The Paston Family in the Fifteenth Century: Ending* (Manchester, 2000), p. 204 and fn. 108.

customary tenure, the rebalancing of manorial (and other) jurisdictions, the ability of lords to enforce fines and services—is the development of the kind of self-assertive and dynamic rural legal culture that I have tried to describe in this chapter. In a world where the more aggressive demands of lordship had slackened, so the legalistic discourses cultivated in the rural courts came to take on a greater significance in framing relations between villagers and authorities. The idealized visions of community that they pursued, and the ways in which they used the courts to achieve them, tangled the language of law with their routine associative relations more than ever before. Rural legal culture in late-medieval England thus provided a means of navigating this changing and unstable world, and the new forms of authority which it brought to bear on common people's lives.

2
Urban Legal Culture
Institutional Density

Legal institutions were a pervasive feature of the late-medieval urban landscape. This helped to foster a deep association, in urban legal culture, between law and the physical space of the city. To begin with, a dense cluster of law-courts operated side by side in towns and cities. Some of these jurisdictions—the borough courts, guild assemblies—were distinctively urban, but even those that were technically similar to those found elsewhere, such as lower church courts, leets, and market courts, took different forms in urban centres, tending to meet more regularly, hear more business, and focus on different concerns. Institutional density manifested itself materially, too. Not only were these courts normally held in designated buildings or precincts, giving them a permanent physical presence, but their routine operations, carried out by hordes of officers and functionaries, were visible to townspeople throughout the city, as houses and shops were searched, offenders were arrested, and punishments were carried out in public. Townspeople lived cheek by jowl with the many legal institutions that they used.

But more than the sheer density of institutions, legal authority in towns and cities was understood—both by the people wielding it and by the urban commons—to particularly entail the governance of physical space. As Christian Liddy put it recently, 'urban politics were spatial politics'.[1] This was due in significant part to the existence of different jurisdictional territories within most late-medieval cities, with both civic governments and ecclesiastical institutions holding significant judicial franchises from the crown. This often led to disputes in the later Middle Ages as these different authorities made increasingly elaborate attempts to reconcile the rights afforded to them in royal charters and written settlements with the changing physical shape of the city.[2] In this context, the control of space was fraught with legal significance.[3] Jurisdiction was exercised in the capacity to construct, maintain, and repair parts of the built environment, and

[1] Christian Liddy, *Contesting the City: The Politics of Citizenship in English Towns, 1250–1530* (Oxford, 2017), p. 85.

[2] See Tom Johnson, 'The Tree and the Rod: Jurisdiction in Late-Medieval England', *P&P*, 237 (2017), 13–51.

[3] Lorraine Attreed, 'Urban Identity in Medieval English Towns', *Journal of Interdisciplinary History*, 32:4 (2002), 571–92. An expansion of some of these ideas can be found in Attreed, *The King's Towns: Identity and Survival in Late Medieval Boroughs* (New York, 2001), esp. Ch. 8, 'The Pursuit of Justice', 243–82.

Law in Common: Legal Cultures in Late-Medieval England. Tom Johnson, Oxford University Press (2020).

DOI: 10.1093/oso/9780198785613.001.0001

sometimes, to remove things from buildings or to tear them down.[4] The complications of territorial control in towns thus helped to produce an urban legal culture in which authority was envisioned as spatial ordering.

This chapter makes two main arguments. The first is that the density of law-courts deeply conditioned the way in which townspeople engaged with legal institutions in late-medieval towns. As Gervase Rosser has perceptively pointed out, urban historians have tended to understand jurisdictional plurality in terms of the conflicts it generated, but have given rather less consideration to its quotidian effects as a 'permanent condition' of late-medieval urban government.[5] The proximity of so many legal institutions may have made it easier for townspeople to sue in the jurisdiction best-suited to their litigation; certainly, while citizens were admonished for suing one another outside the city, there does not appear to have been any attempt to prevent intramural forum-shopping.[6] But more important than any putative consumer choice, I want to suggest, were the implications of institutional density on legal authority, as it both intensified governance and opened up the possibility of its challenge. As townspeople used different urban law-courts, they helped to constitute jurisdiction in the city, and this meant that they were routinely drawn into the relations—sometimes conflictual, sometimes cooperative, and sometimes uneasy—between different authorities.[7]

The second argument is that urban legal culture was particularly characterized by an emphasis on spatial order in associative relations. The concerns of different urban authorities with jurisdiction over space aligned closely with those of townspeople themselves; the denser concentrations of people in towns and cities, and the changing built environment of cities in the later Middle Ages, meant that workable arrangements for living close together had to be continually renegotiated.[8] As such, associative relations in urban legal culture were frequently

[4] On this idea, see Adam T. Smith, 'Archaeologies of Sovereignty', *Annual Review of Anthropology*, 40 (2011), 415–32; for a specifically urban focus see Chris Otter, 'Locating matter: the place of materiality in urban history', in *Material Powers: Cultural studies, history and the material turn*, ed. Tony Bennett and Patrick Joyce (London, 2010), 38–59.

[5] Gervase Rosser, 'Conflict and Political Community in the Medieval Town: Disputes between Clergy and Laity in Hereford', in *The Church in the Medieval Town*, ed. T. R. Slater and Gervase Rosser (Aldershot, 1998), 20–42, p. 36.

[6] On forum-shopping as a result of pluralism, see Brian Z. Tamanaha, 'Understanding Legal Pluralism: Past to Present, Local to Global', *Sydney Law Review*, 375 (2008), 375–411, at p. 389; on citizens' duty to sue in civic courts, see Eliza Hartrich, 'Rebellion and the Law in Fifteenth-Century English Towns', in *The Routledge History Handbook of Medieval Revolt*, ed. Justine Firnhaber-Baker with Dirk Schoenaers (London and New York, 2017), 189–207, esp. pp. 195–6.

[7] A similar point has been made for Italian cities (albeit with an emphasis on the structural nature of conflict) in Patrick Lantschner, 'Justice Contested and Affirmed: Jurisdiction and Conflict in Late Medieval Italian Cities', in *Legalism: Community and Justice*, ed. Fernanda Pirie and Judith Scheele (Oxford, 2014), 77–96.

[8] Generally, see John Schofield and Geoffrey Stell, 'The built environment 1300–1540', in *The Cambridge Urban History of Britain, Volume 1: 600–1540*, ed. D. M. Palliser (Cambridge, 2000), 371–93. On late-medieval change, see A. R. Bridbury, 'English Provincial Towns in the Later Middle

conceived in terms of spatial regulation. Sometimes this was explicit and straightforward, for example when neighbours demanded that waste be removed from a place of common resort.[9] But the pervasiveness of this idea meant that it also surfaced in other kinds of concern—such as sexual morality, or honest dealing—which were subsumed into a legal discourse of spatial regulation, about prostitutes blocking the streets, or markets remaining open. Spatial order, enforced by law, was foundational to the way that late-medieval townspeople imagined the legal community in which they lived.

Much of the evidence in this chapter comes from Hereford, a city in the west of England of mediocre size and importance.[10] It was a provincial economic capital in the later Middle Ages, specializing in the manufacture and marketing of wool and beef, and the site of a cathedral that stood at the centre of an ancient diocese. Though Hereford was among the twenty-five or so 'greater towns and cities' of late-medieval England identified by Jennifer Kermode, it was among the lesser of them, with a small internal area and a tax-paying population of fewer than 2,000 people in 1377.[11] Even as a 'middling' urban centre, however, it was not necessarily typical, and so I have also included material from smaller towns such as Henley-on-Thames and Marlborough, larger cities such as Salisbury and York, and the London metropolis, to reflect a broader range of urban legal experiences.[12] Although the legal culture in a market town was of course different than it was in a regional or even national capital, I would suggest that it was nonetheless driven by similar impulses, and fostered comparable dynamics in the way that people understood and related to law.[13]

Ages', *Economic History Review*, 34:1 (1981), 1–24; D. M. Palliser, 'Urban Decay Revisited', in *Towns and Townspeople in the Fifteenth Century*, ed. John A. F. Thomson (Gloucester, 1988), 1–21; Keith D. Lilley, 'Decline or decay? Urban landscapes in late-medieval England', in *Towns in Decline AD100–1600*, ed. T. R. Slater (Aldershot, 2000), 235–65.

---

[9] See Carole Rawcliffe, *Urban Bodies: Communal Health in Late Medieval English Towns and Cities* (Woodbridge, 2013), esp. Ch. 3. 'Environmental Health', 116–75.

[10] The best concise introduction to medieval Hereford remains M. D. Lobel, *Historic Towns: Maps and Plans of Towns and Cities in the British Isles with Historical Commentaries, from Earliest Times to c.1800* (2 vols., London and Oxford, 1969), i, 'Hereford'.

[11] See Jennifer Kermode, 'The Greater towns, 1300–1540', in *Cambridge Urban History*, ed. Palliser, 441–65, esp. Table 18.1: 'Characteristics of Greater Towns', pp. 442–3; on the cathedral, see Robert Swanson and David Lepine, 'The Later Middle Ages, 1268–1535', in *Hereford Cathedral: A History*, ed. Gerald Aylmer and John Tiller (London, 2000), 48–86.

[12] There is a burgeoning historiography on these 'small towns', starting with R. H. Hilton, 'Small Town Society in England before the Black Death', *P&P*, 105 (1984), 53–78. See also Christopher Dyer, 'Small places with large consequences: the importance of small towns in England, 1000–1540', *Historical Research*, 75:187 (2002), 1–24; Richard Goddard, 'Small Boroughs and the Manorial Economy: Enterprise Zones or Urban Failures?', *P&P*, 210, (2011), 3–31. On the government of York, see the essays in *The Government of Medieval York: Essays in commemoration of the 1396 royal charter*, ed. Sarah Rees Jones (York, 1997); on London, Caroline Barron, *London in the Late Middle Ages: Government and People 1200–1500* (Oxford, 2004).

[13] The very smallest towns might have had a legal culture more akin to that of the countryside, just as the largest villages (especially if they held market rights or other privileges) shared in aspects of

The chapter is structured in a similar way to the previous one. The first section of the chapter examines the logistics of urban law-courts; the range of places in which they were held, and the frequency with which they met meant that institutional density was manifested both spatially and temporally in the city. The second section explores the routine operations of urban law-courts, and the ways in which they drew townspeople into jurisdictional relations: I focus on the appointment of court officers, the scrutiny of domestic space by different jurisdictions, and the attachments of goods and arrests made by the variety of intramural authorities. The third section then turns to consider the characteristic legal matters that townspeople pursued in urban courts—relating to trade, the environment, and morality—and shows how these were infused with ideas about spatial order, as a means of organizing associative relations. The conclusion, finally, attempts to characterize urban legal culture in a broader perspective, both in terms of inter-urban relations and in comparison with rural legal culture.

The Logistics of Urban Law-Courts

This opening section sets out the principal kinds of law-court that existed in late-medieval towns and cities, discussing the physical locations in which they were held, and the frequency of their sessions. In the first place, by paying attention to the simple logistics of the different courts, I hope to show what institutional density looked like on the ground; not only were there more courts holding sessions concurrently, but they sat for longer, heard more business, and in some cases occupied the same locations. At the same time, however, I also want to emphasize here the way in which legal authorities, particularly those of the civic government and ecclesiastical institutions, were associated with their buildings and precincts. Legal jurisdiction was easily visible to late-medieval townspeople—indeed, it was often deliberately and forcibly demonstrated. This was part of what fostered the association, which we shall trace in the following sections, between the physical fabric of the city and the exercise of authority within it.

To begin with, the very walls of the city itself were legal spaces.[14] Though they had long ceased to serve a defensive purpose by the fifteenth century, they remained imposing structures: in Hereford, they were around twenty feet in height, comprising seventeen semi-circular bastions and five gatehouses.[15] They

urban legal culture. This is not the place for a debate over what constitutes 'the urban', and I intend to leave open these questions for future research.

[14] Gervase Rosser and Patricia Dennison, 'Urban culture and the Church 1300–1540', in *Cambridge Urban History*, ed. Palliser, 335–69, p. 339.

[15] *Historic Towns: Maps and Plans of Towns and Cities in the British Isles with Historical Commentaries, from Earliest Times to 1800*, ed. M. Lobel (3 vols., London and Oxford, 1969), ii, p. 5;

materialized civic jurisdiction in a few different ways, even though it actually stretched beyond the limits they marked.[16] First, they provided a stage for court sessions: in Hereford, the mayor's annual tourn for the city wards was held at each of the five gates on consecutive days.[17] Second, walls, gates, and other fortifications also doubled as prisons.[18] Indeed, the main gaol in Hereford was located in one of the gates, Bye-street, in the north-east corner of the city, where the king's justices held their sessions of gaol delivery alongside the mayor.[19] It contained nine people in the early sixteenth century.[20] And third, the physical maintenance of the walls depended on the ability of urban authorities to extract 'murage' from its citizens—or sometimes, controversially, from other inhabitants of the town.[21]

By contrast, the specialized guildhalls built by and for civic governments helped to concretize the legal privileges of citizenship. Such halls were the normal location for customary civic courts, reserved mostly to freemen.[22] In Hereford, a property by the main market called 'Bothe Hall' hosted other courts too. Given to the city in 1392 by a former mayor with the express purpose that it be used as a venue for the royal assizes and the sessions of the peace—powers that were vested in the mayor himself by 1399—the following year a royal grant mandated its use as a council chamber and town hall.[23] Uniting the performance of civic and royal

Ron Shoesmith and Richard Morriss, 'The later medieval defences', in *Hereford City Excavations*, ed. Thomas and Boucher, p. 175.

[16] Helen Carrel, 'Disputing legal privilege: civic relations with the Church in late medieval England', *Journal of Medieval History*, 35 (2009), 279–96, at p. 284.

[17] For the tourn court records, see HARC, BG11/4/1 [Tourns, 1448–1521]. On tourn jurisdiction, see Baker, *English Legal History*, p. 24.

[18] Helen Carrel, 'The ideology of punishment in late medieval English towns', *Social History*, 34:3 (2009), 301–20, p. 315.

[19] Shoesmith and Crosskey, 'Go to Gaol... In Hereford', *Transactions of the Woolhope Field Club*, 48:1 (1994), 97–139, p. 101. It was common to use gates as gaols in medieval England: Schofield and Stell, 'The built environment', p. 374. In other late-medieval cities, royal castles doubled up as prisons, but in Hereford the castle had fallen into ruin as early as the fourteenth century and, indeed, it was used as a pigsty—a poor advertisement, perhaps, for the royal authority: HARC, BG11/4/1 [1502]. On Hereford's castle, see John C. Eisel, 'The Castle Mills, Hereford', *Transactions of the Woolhope Field Club*, 50:1 (2000), p. 58; J. Duncumb, *Collections towards the History and Antiquities of the County of Hereford* (2nd edn; 8 vols; Cardiff, 1996), i, 243. On a prison break from the royal castle at Lincoln in 1420: TNA, KB9/213, no. 41.

[20] This from an unusual survival, a slip of paper listing the names of eight men (one of which was redacted) and one woman, of whom seven were from Hereford; a contemporaneous calendar of gaol delivery shows that just two of these prisoners were delivered (and that the rest of those 'delivered' were presumably bailed). HARC, BG11/8/3, [unsorted papers, Gaol Delivery], no. 1, no. 3.

[21] Attreed, *The King's Towns*, p. 256. In Hereford, the payment of murage by non-citizens was disputed: HCLA, HCA.2955b; HCLA, HCA.2960, m. 3r. The rules about the disposal of murage money were changed in 1516: HARC, BG11/19/11, ff. 209v, 211v.

[22] Schofield and Stell, 'The built environment', p. 378. On borough custom generally, see Mary Bateson, *Borough Customs*, Selden Society, 21 (London, 1906), xv–clvi; for the operation of London's customary courts, Penny Tucker, 'London's Courts of Law in the Fifteenth Century: The Litigants' Perspective', in *Communities and Courts in Britain, 1150–1900*, ed. Christopher Brooks and Michael Lobban (London, 1997), 25–41.

[23] Ian Forrest, 'The Politics of Burial in Late Medieval Hereford', *EHR*, 125:516 (2010), 1110–38, p. 1132; *CPR*, 1391–6, p. 213.

justice in one building was a clever strategy in the context of a jurisdictional dispute, at that time, over the mayor's claims to exercise a monopoly of authority within the city.[24] The Bothe Hall was also used as a freeman's prison, in which prisoners were allowed to leave the building under escort to hear Mass, or even to have dinner in the main chamber with one of their co-citizens.[25] Closed off to the majority of townspeople who did not possess the franchise, a guildhall broadcast the legal privileges afforded to citizens and, as a site for the exercise of royal jurisdictions by civic government, demonstrated the scope of their authority.

But, in fact, civic claims to govern the whole city were belied by the urban environment itself. All late-medieval towns were 'honeycombed' by the large walled precincts of urban ecclesiastical institutions, whether cathedrals, monasteries, hospitals, or sanctuaries.[26] In Hereford, the cathedral precinct alone was home to two centres of ecclesiastical authority.[27] To the east stood the Canons' Bakehouse, where the dean and chapter held their biannual leet, 'a court with a view of frankpledge for all the residents of the tenements of the dean and chapter of Hereford cathedral there within its liberty, as well as outside in the suburbs', as the heading for a 1520 session put it.[28] To the west, the bishop's palace was not only the site of his episcopal prison but also the location for his 'halmotes', courts for the tenants of his manors in the city's immediate hinterland.[29] If the walls of ecclesiastical precincts—like those of the city—did not mark the physical limits of their jurisdiction, they were clearly perceived by civic governments to represent bastions of threatening authority. Jurisdictional disputes between these

[24] On the jurisdictional dispute in Hereford, see Rosser, 'Disputes between Clergy and Laity in Hereford'. For the arbitration documents which set out the matters in dispute, see HCLA, HCA.2935 [undated arbitration of John Prophete]; HCA.2937 [dated 1409, prorogation of the arbitration]. For towns and cities obtaining jurisdiction over peace sessions, see Elisabeth G. Kimball, 'Commissions of the Peace for Urban Jurisdictions in England, 1327–1485', *Proceedings of the American Philosophical Society*, 121:6 (1977), 448–74, Appendix 1, pp. 468–71.

[25] HARC, BG11/19/11, f. 240v.

[26] Quote from Attreed, 'Urban Identity', pp. 572, 585. On sanctuaries, see Gervase Rosser, 'Sanctuary and Social Negotiation in Medieval England', in *The Cloister and the World: Essays in Medieval History in Honour of Barbara Harvey*, eds. John Blair and Brian Golding (Oxford, 1996), 57–79; Shannon McSheffrey, 'Sanctuary and the Legal Topography of Pre-Reformation London', *L&HR*, 27:3 (2009), 483–514, pp. 486–9. On cathedral precincts, N. Orme, 'Access and Exclusion: Exeter Cathedral, 1300–1540', in *Freedom of Movement in the Middle Ages: Proceedings of the 2003 Harlaxton Symposium*, ed. Peregrine Horden (Donington, 2007), 267–86.

[27] Two other ecclesiastical institutions in the city—the hospital of St. John, and the priory of Llanthony Secunda, an Augustinian house of Gloucester with large holdings on the north-west side of Hereford—also held their own 'law-days': HCLA, HCA.2962; Duncumb, *History and Antiquities of Hereford*, ii, p. 404.

[28] HCLA, R. 1146a [court for November 1520]. See also HCLA, R. 1143 [court for November 1482]; R. 1145 [court for October 1486].

[29] For the prison, see *The Register of Thomas Myllyng, Bishop of Hereford (1474–1492)*, ed. A. T. Bannister, Cantilupe Society, 23 (Hereford, 1919), iv–v. For the rolls of the halmotes, see BL, Add. Ch. 27290–310.

institutions, in Hereford and elsewhere, often hinged upon the physical enclosure and exclusivity of these precincts.[30]

Indeed, the problematic exceptionality of these precincts was compounded by the fact that they were often also the site for urban church courts.[31] The majority of towns and cities in late-medieval England were coincident with a single lower ecclesiastical jurisdiction, whether as a part of regular diocesan structures or, more commonly, as a peculiar that operated outside of the bishop's ordinary authority; in cathedral cities, of course, these courts coexisted with the judicial centres for the diocese as a whole.[32] In Hereford, the subdean of the chapter exercised peculiar jurisdiction over the city, holding his courts within the cathedral church itself. Unfortunately, the sole fifteenth-century record from this court is an effusive account of the violation of its liberties after a citizen took a horse from the canons' close, but indeed, its preservation reinforces the impression of the tight association made between urban ecclesiastical jurisdiction and these precincts.[33] In Salisbury, by contrast, the subdean rotated his chapters throughout the parish churches of the city, though he also performed judicial business from 'the judge's house'.[34] Between their large walled precincts and the knot of jurisdictions they exercised throughout the city, then, the legal presence of urban ecclesiastical institutions was highly visible.

As well as these larger buildings, open spaces in the city were important for larger, more public legal gatherings. The common grounds which urban corporations owned outside the walls, for example, were often used for court sessions. In Hereford, the city's annual 'law-day', the mayor's other leet court (after the tourn), was held in the Tollfield, just outside the city walls, while in Southampton a circular mound called Cutthorn was the customary site for the town's leet.[35] Such

[30] On the disputes over the cathedral precinct in Hereford, see Rosser, 'Disputes between Clergy and Laity in Hereford', p. 24, and HCLA, HCA.2935, HCA.2937, both relating to the arbitration of 1410. For similar disputes elsewhere: Attreed, *The King's Towns*, pp. 259, 264; F. Hill, *Medieval Lincoln*, (Cambridge, 1965), pp. 273–4, 280–5; Peter Fleming, 'Conflict and urban government in later medieval England: St Augustine's Abbey and Bristol', *Urban History*, 27:3 (2000), 325–43; Hannes Kleineke, 'Civic Ritual, Space and Conflict in Fifteenth-Century Exeter', in *Ritual and Space in the Middle Ages: Proceedings of the 2009 Harlaxton Symposium*, ed. Frances Andrews (Donington, 2011), 165–78.

[31] Schofield and Stell, 'The built environment', p. 382.

[32] As an example of ordinary authority centring on towns, Colchester was at the centre of its own archdeaconry: *The Records of the Medieval Ecclesiastical Courts, pt. 2: England*, ed. C. Donahue, Reports of the Working Group on Church Court Records (Berlin, 1994), p. 156. For some remarks on urban peculiars, see R. N. Swanson, 'Peculiar Practices: The Jurisdictional Jigsaw of the Pre-Reformation Church', *Midland History*, 26 (2001), 69–95, at pp. 72, 76. Cf. the case of Wells, a town forged within the peculiar jurisdiction of the cathedral chapter: David Gary Shaw, *The Creation of a Community: The City of Wells in the Middle Ages* (Oxford, 1993).

[33] For the case of violation of liberties, see HCLA, HCA.3209: the full *litis contestatio* is written up in fair-copy. The dean also exercised authority over clerical misconduct: *Registrum Thome Myllyng, Episcopi Herefordensis, 1474–1492*, ed. Arthur Thomas Bannister, Canterbury and York Society, 26 (London, 1921), p. iii; he evidently made visitations in the city parishes, as proceeds from these are noted in the *Valor ecclesiasticus*: Swanson and Lepine, 'The Later Middle Ages', p. 79.

[34] Mentioned in WSHO, D4/3/1 [Act-book, 1477–8], fo. 96v.

[35] This location is mentioned in HARC, BG11/3/1 [1513], loose files. For Southampton, Christian Liddy, 'Urban Enclosure Riots: Risings of The Commons in English Towns, 1480–1525', *P&P*, 226 (2015), 41–77, p. 70.

sites were not merely the physical locations for courts, however, but also part of the privileges of franchise, with their resources—water, grazing land, peat—common to the citizenry.[36] But indeed, it was the 'commonalty' of citizens, those excluded from the aldermanic governing elites, who particularly identified with these common grounds; indeed, they often occupied them in a visible demonstration of their political rights and their claim to participate in civic governance.[37] In this context, the grand ceremony of Hereford's law-day, with a congregation of citizens gathered on the Tollfield to watch the mayoral council process in their long murrey gowns and then read out the murage accounts, looks like a rather demonstrative piece of political theatre.[38]

Marketplaces also provided important open space for a variety of legal operations. To begin with, they were the sites of market and pie-powder courts.[39] These jurisdictions—which might be held by either secular or ecclesiastical authorities, or indeed both—were important because they allowed the regular transaction of commercial litigation between citizens, unenfranchised inhabitants of the town, and traders from elsewhere, according to customary law merchant, or *lex mercatoria*.[40] Markets were also important as sites of punishment. They were the normal place for the location of the pillory or stocks, often used in fact to punish offences against the market such as selling corrupted victuals.[41] And, of course, marketplaces were also used for ecclesiastical penances, not only for townspeople but also rural parishioners from the hinterland.[42] An audience was paramount; one penance ordered by the Bishop of Lincoln in 1447 included the specific order that the penitents were to walk through places in the market of Huntingdon, the nearest town to which they lived, 'where a multitude of people is present'.[43] In this variety

[36] For the citizens' common pasture rights, see TNA, STAC 1/1/19; for peat-digging, see HARC, BG11/9/11 [interfolio between ff. 176–7]. Presentments against digging or blocking the watercourses surrounding the city were common in both the law-day and tourns.

[37] Liddy, 'Urban Enclosure Riots'.

[38] HARC, BG11/9/11, f. 194v.

[39] James Davis, 'The Cross and the Pillory: Symbolic Structures of Commercial Space in Medieval English Towns', in *Stätische Räume im Mittelalter*, ed. Susanne Shrich and Jörg Oberste (Regensburg, 2009), 241–259, at p. 249.

[40] On the law merchant, see the introduction to *Lex Mercatoria and Legal Pluralism: A Late Thirteenth-Century Treatise and Its Afterlife*, ed. and transl., Mary Elizabeth Basile, Jane Fair Bestor, Daniel R. Coquillette, and Charles Donahue, Jr (Cambridge, MA, 1998), 13–188. See Charles Gross, 'The Court of Piepowder', *The Quarterly Journal of Economics*, 20:2 (1906), 231–49; and his comments in *Select Cases Concerning the Law Merchant, 1270–1638: Local Courts*, Selden Society 23, ed. Charles Gross and Hubert Hall (3 vols, London, 1908), i, pp. xiii–xxxv. More recently, see James Davis, *Medieval Market Morality: Life, Law and Ethics in the English Marketplace, 1200–1500* (Cambridge, 2012), Ch. 2, 'Regulation of the market', 137–273.

[41] James Masschaele, 'The Public Space of the Marketplace in Medieval England', *Speculum*, 77:2 (2002), 383–421, pp. 402, 405; Carrel, 'Ideology of punishment', pp. 304–5.

[42] For examples in which the penance was ordered for a city about ten miles away: NRO, DCN 67/8, m. 1r; *The Register of John Morton, Archbishop of Canterbury, 1486–1500, Volume III: Norwich* Sede Vacante, *1499*, ed. Christopher Harper-Bill, Canterbury and York Society, lxxxix (2000), p. 216.

[43] Cited in A. Hamilton Thompson, *The English Clergy and their Organization in the Later Middle Ages* (Oxford, 1947), pp. 216–18.

of legal uses, most of which presumed the existence of large and diverse crowds, marketplaces formed microcosms of the institutional density characteristic of the late-medieval city.

As a final point, it is also worth highlighting the existence of a further set of legal institutions in the form of guilds.[44] In Hereford, these were fused with civic administration early in the 1215 grant of a guild merchant, but in other provincial cities guilds more gradually insinuated themselves into municipal government.[45] Craft guilds were thus often entangled with civic institutions, and even with citizenship; William Skidmore of Hereford was expelled from the Mercers' Guild and disenfranchised 'on account of hateful words he had against the mayor' before the main civic court.[46] But the guilds also had a separate institutional existence, holding formal assemblies in their own 'comen hall', or just private inns.[47] These courts were often held four times a year, but sometimes more—the Mercers' Company of London pardoned members from attendance after agreeing that so 'many courtes and congregacions of the felyshipp . . . is tedious & grevous . . . specially for maters of no grete effect'.[48] As tedious as they may have been, though, such assemblies were crucial for the resolution of disputes among members, who were frequently enjoined against taking their quarrels to law.[49]

Urban legal institutions, then, were closely associated with the spaces that they occupied. Unlike rural settlements, late-medieval towns had a few buildings, such as gates, guildhalls, and judges' lodgings or chapter houses, that were specifically designated for the transaction of legal business or court sessions. Moreover, urban law-courts were frequently held in places—such as the common grounds used for law-days or the ecclesiastical precincts which guarded church authority—which materially represented the jurisdictions of those courts. This close association of

[44] Heather Swanson, 'The Illusion of Economic Structure: Craft Guilds in Late Medieval English Towns', *P&P*, 121 (1988), 29–48, pp. 37–8. See also Gervase Rosser, *The Art of Solidarity: Guilds in England 1250–1550* (Oxford, 2015), Ch. 5, 'Trust', 149–84.

[45] Lobel, *Historic Towns*, ii, p. 7; Ben R. McRee, 'Religious Gilds and Civic Order: The Case of Norwich in the Late Middle Ages', *Speculum*, 67:1 (1992), 69–97, pp. 72–4; Eliza Hartrich, *Politics and the Urban Sector in Fifteenth-Century England, 1413–1471* (Oxford, 2019); Richard Goddard, 'Medieval business networks: St Mary's guild and the borough court in later medieval Nottingham', *Urban History*, 40:1 (2013), 3–27.

[46] HARC, BG11/19/11, f. 186r.

[47] The pelters' guild in Norwich agreed to meet in an inn after hearing mass on 'gylde day'; the ordinances of the Exeter tailors' guild specified assemblies in 'oure comen hall'; while in Bristol the 'craftes of the Towne' were 'to go and assemble them att their halles and places accustumed' during the election of a new mayor. See *English gilds: the original ordinances of more than one hundred early English gilds . . .*, ed. Joshua and Lucy Toulmin Smith, Early English Text Society, original series, 40 (Oxford, 1870), pp. 29, 315, 420.

[48] *Acts of Court of the Mercers' Company 1453–1527*, ed. Laetitia Lyell and Frank D. Watney (Cambridge, 1936), p. 58.

[49] Ben R. McRee, 'Religious Gilds and the Regulation of Behavior in Late Medieval Towns', in *People, Politics and Community in the Later Middle Ages*, ed. Joel Rosenthal and Colin Richmond (Gloucester, 1987), 108–22, p. 113; Rosser, *The Art of Solidarity*, p. 175. For such examples from the ordinances of craft guilds (the Smiths of Chesterfield and the Tailors of Lincoln), see *English gilds*, ed. Toulmin Smiths, pp. 170, 183.

jurisdiction with the built environment made legal institutions a visible, physical presence for townspeople as they moved around the city. Yet institutional density was not only a spatial, but also a temporal quality of urban legal culture, and therefore we turn, now, to consider the timing of law-courts. In what follows, I suggest that the rhythm, frequency, and speed of court sessions in towns intensified the perception and pressures of jurisdictional plurality.

* * * *

As was the case in the countryside, there was a certain bunching of court sessions within the urban legal calendar, particularly at autumn and Easter. All of the different city fees in Hereford held their leets in autumn, though they varied slightly in their timing: the mayoral tourn was held in late August or early September (though in 1523 it was held as late as November), while the bishop's halmotes were held in early October, and the Canons' Bakehouse courts, for the dean and chapter, in late October or early November.[50] This was also the time of the second of the biannual sessions of gaol delivery, in which the mayor sat on the commission alongside the royal justices.[51] Moreover, each of these jurisdictions held another session at Easter—with the civic law-day and its elaborate processions held on Easter Sunday itself—producing an even denser grouping of sessions at this time.[52] The concurrent sittings of these leets anchored the prosecution of social and environmental regulation throughout the city at these two points in the year; but, more than this, the near-exact coincidence of their Easter sessions must have fostered a strong sense of the multiplicity of jurisdictions operating at the same time within the city.

Layered on top of these biannual leets were the quarterly peace sessions. Though they were almost always held in urban centres, these were county courts, commissioned by the crown, and they heard business that was not necessarily connected to townspeople or the civic administration.[53] In the fifteenth century, however, civic authorities throughout England secured grants to exercise this jurisdiction.[54] Large cities such as York, Newcastle, Lincoln, Norwich, and Bristol all attained county status in this period, excluding the justices and allowing them to hold their own sessions; elsewhere, the mayor simply became a justice *ex officio*.

[50] Respectively, see HARC, BG11/4/1 [1441–1537]; BL, Add. Ch. 27290–310; HCLA, R. 1143–1145.

[51] HARC, BG11/8/3 [unsorted papers, Gaol Delivery], no. 1, verso. Generally, see Alan Harding, *The Law Courts of Medieval England* (London, 1973), p. 96.

[52] For the law-days, see HARC, BG11/3/1 [1448–1557].

[53] E.g. a case heard at the Hereford sessions in 1441 called in jurors from Tyberton—about ten miles west of the city: TNA, KB9/237, m. 49. On peace sessions in general, see See *Proceedings before the Justices of the Peace in the Fourteenth and Fifteenth Centuries: Edward III to Richard III*, ed. Bertha Haven Putnam (London, 1938); J. R. Lander, *English Justices of the Peace, 1461–1509* (Gloucester, 1989).

[54] Notable exceptions to this rule were Lynn, Yarmouth, Oxford, and Cambridge—all large boroughs rather than cities—which continued to receive commissions from the crown in this period. For this and what follows, see Kimball, 'Commissions of the Peace for Urban Jurisdictions', pp. 468–71.

Indeed, the evidence from Hereford suggests that the peace sessions were styled as another kind of civic court, held, as we just saw, inside the Bothe Hall, and pertaining to the mayor's jurisdiction 'inside the precinct and liberty of the city'.[55] Nonetheless, it considerably augmented civic powers in the later Middle Ages, allowing them to make summary arrests and determinations, implement the labour laws, and use penal bonds to threaten and enforce imprisonment.[56] The spectacle of these sessions, with offenders rounded up and crowds of jurors coming in from the county, must have loomed large in the urban legal calendar.

But perhaps the most emphatic moment in the legal calendar of many towns and cities was the convening of a special court during an annual fair. The pie-powder court of the Bishop of Ely, for example, was held only for the three days of his great fair around the feast of the translation of St. Etheldreda in late October, and likewise that at Grantham was held during St. Wulfram's fair in March.[57] In practice, the lawsuits initiated before fair courts were often continued or followed up, if required, at the regular sessions of the borough courts, implying a more fluid association between these two jurisdictions.[58] Yet the temporary nature of these jurisdictions over the huge crowds that flocked to the city was clearly symbolically important to contemporaries. In Hereford, the bishop claimed jurisdiction over the entire city during his seven-day fair, with the mayor handing over his keys.[59] The yearly rhythm of urban legal culture, then, was thus anchored to events at which large numbers of people came into the city—leets, peace sessions, or indeed fairs—and crowded together in its judicial spaces.

At the same time, however, the spectacle of these gatherings was sustained by a much more regular thrum of legal business. Indeed, urban courts met far more frequently than those elsewhere. The 'three-week' hundred court in Colchester was held as often as its name suggests, and heard a huge amount of civil litigation in the fifteenth century; and even in smaller towns such as Henley-on-Thames, the

[55] HARC, BG11/17/2 [Miscellaneous Papers 1445–99], p. 25.

[56] For summary arrests and penal bonds, see HARC, BG11/19/11 [Mayor's Book, 1500–32], fos. 138r, 142v, 143r, 144r, 145r, 146v, etc.; for remarks on this more general trend, see Robert C. Palmer, *English Law in the Age of the Black Death, 1348–1381: A Transformation of Governance and Law* (Chapel Hill, NC, and London, 1993), p. 63; on the labour laws in towns, see *Justices of the Peace in the Fourteenth and Fifteenth Centuries*, ed. Putnam, pp. xxii–xxviii.

[57] For Ely, see CUL, EDR/E1/1/3, [courts for 1439–40]; for Grantham, TNA, SC 2/185/38, mm. 2r, 4r, 6r, 8r, 10r. The first couple of these are printed and translated in *Select Cases Concerning the Law Merchant*, ed. Gross and Hall, pp. 129–31. Though only a single pie-powder roll survives, the disposition of the courts in Orford (Suffolk) looks similar: SROI, HD64/1/21 [courts for 1468–9].

[58] Helen M. Jewell, *English Local Administration in the Middle Ages* (Newton Abbot, 1972), p. 134; Maryanne Kowaleski, 'The history of urban families in medieval England', *Journal of Medieval History*, 14 (1988), 47–63, p. 51. This phenomenon is attested in the records from Hereford, Grantham, and Ely mentioned in fnn 55, 57 above.

[59] Lobel, *Historic Towns*, ii, pp. 5–7. He heard pleas 'tempore nundine' at least as late as the early fifteenth century: HCLA, HCA.2936.

borough court met every third Monday to hear interpersonal suits between burgesses.[60] In Hereford, the equivalent sessions were held even more often. In the mayor's court books of the 1470s, a plea was entered on average as often as every five days for a full eleven months of the year, though there were sometimes large gaps between entries, for example around Advent and Easter, followed up by sessions held on successive days.[61] In fact, the frequency of these sessions was enshrined in a law-day ordinance of 1503, which declared that 'every freman... shall have ther court days as well upon the court day as eny other day', which suggests that while there were regularly appointed days for sessions, the convenience of entering a plea in the court at any time was a privilege of citizenship.[62]

But, in fact, we see the same high degree of frequency in urban ecclesiastical courts. These forums seem to have responded flexibly to the population size of the centre in which they were located. Thus in the small town of Wisbech, at the centre of a rural deanery in Cambridgeshire, the dean's general chapters were held just twice a year, in early summer and late autumn, though other sessions for the regular transaction of procedures were held once a month.[63] In a large city such as Salisbury, business before the subdean's peculiar court was more regularized and much more frequent, with chapters held every week, normally on Fridays.[64] And in the London metropolis, finally, the bishop's commissary court, which exercised jurisdiction throughout the city and heard many hundreds of cases each year, sat several days a week, though there was 'no obvious pattern' to the days which it met.[65] Urban church courts thus seem to have varied the number of sessions which they held on the basis of their caseload, and the speed with which they were able to get through it.

In fact, the higher incidence of secular court sessions seems to have been matched by the increased speed of their proceedings too. This was most clear in relation to the pie-powder and market courts, which not only met frequently—in Marlborough, where it functioned as the main town court, it was held every Saturday—but were also distinguished by their particular swiftness in settling

[60] R. H. Britnell, *Growth and decline in Colchester, 1300–1525* (Cambridge, 1986), pp. 24–7; for the Henley court rolls, OHC, BOR3/B2/IV/CR/2–14.

[61] HARC, BG11/2/6 [court books for 1471–2, and 1477–8]. The average gap between entries in 1471–2 was four days (median 3, standard deviation of 4), and 1471–2, six days (median 4, standard deviation of 8). In 1471–2 there is a clear gap between the middle of March and the middle of April, with Easter that year falling on March 29; in both years, no courts were held in the latter half of December nor the first week of January.

[62] HARC, BG11/19/11, fo. 150v. The plea books (BG11/2/6) also give the impression that there were set court days, as there were between one and six sessions a month when multiple pleas were entered on the same date.

[63] *Lower Ecclesiastical Jurisdiction in Late-Medieval England: The Courts of the Dean and Chapter of Lincoln, 1336–1349 and the Deanery of Wisbech, 1458–1484*, ed. L. R. Poos (Oxford, 2001), pp. xxviii–xxxii.

[64] WSHO, D4/3/1.

[65] Richard Wunderli, *London Church Courts and Society on the Eve of the Reformation* (Cambridge, MA, 1981), p. 13.

commercial litigation.[66] Indeed, in a good indication of how swiftly cases went through these courts, the scribes tended to note the hour at which a particular procedure was transacted—at the Bishop of Norwich's pie-powder, for example, Saturday sessions were held at 9 am, 3 pm, and 5 pm.[67] And, indeed, the 'law merchant' that these courts used was understood by contemporaries to hinge upon its quick procedures, which limited the number of essoins and other delays within lawsuits.[68] This seems to have worked well enough in practice: in Hereford's pie-powder court, the majority of pleas were for debts, and most of these were immediately confessed by the defendant, and settled on the same day by the promise that they would pay the sum back.[69] Such courts, with their systemic speed, exemplified the fast pace of law in the late-medieval city.

The logistics of urban law-courts helped to foster a legal world characterized by its spatial and temporal density: in the cramming together of judicial sites within the city, in the clustering of a large number of courts in the year, and in the many, rapid sessions held to transact the vast amount of legal business that townspeople brought. These arrangements were quite distinct from those in the countryside which we encountered in Chapter 1, where law-courts were closely integrated with communal life but only held at periodic intervals. In towns and cities, by contrast, the multiplicity of courts produced thinner, more numerous ties between town dwellers and urban legal institutions; though certainly citizens were attached ideologically to the civic court, like other townspeople they would have encountered a range of courts—by choice, force, or simple proximity—on a regular basis.[70] Each jurisdiction, and the way that people used it, was moulded by its shifting relations within a constellation of others. We now turn to see what this meant for townspeople in the routine operations of the courts.

Court Operations: Officers, Scrutiny, and Enforcement

The presence of different urban law-courts, often claiming jurisdiction over the same spaces in towns and cities, meant that their routine operations frequently overlapped. These overlaps took a number of different forms, sometimes producing outright disputes, but also uneasy truces, and even active cooperation; more important than any individual working arrangement is the fact that the courts operated *in relation* to one another. In this section, I look at how townspeople

[66] WSHO, G22/1/13, fos. 1–10 [67] NRO, DCN/79/11, m. 1r.

[68] *Lex Mercatoria and Legal Pluralism*, ed. and transl., Basile et al., pp. 19–20.

[69] HARC, BG11/2/6 [1439–40]. There were ninety-seven pleas this year (October to April), of which sixty-eight (70%) were for debts; proof in these cases was always by compurgation. Interestingly, in the other kinds of pleas—trespass and broken contract—where proof was by jury, defendants almost always denied the charge.

[70] On citizens' duty (or privilege) to sue litigation in civic courts, see Liddy, *Politics of Citizenship*, pp. 40–1.

negotiated these relations in their regular legal encounters, tracing three different types: first, their interactions with the hordes of officers and functionaries appointed by different law-courts; second, the intense scrutiny placed on their homes and shops by various jurisdictions; and third, the arrests of people and attachments of goods used to enforce court orders. In each case, I suggest, court operations under institutional density produced ambivalent effects for townspeople, in some ways serving to intensify legal governance while also sometimes laying it open to challenge.

To begin with, it is important to emphasize the much larger numbers of legal officers in late-medieval towns and cities. Of course, courts everywhere required such officers to give summons, make arrests, collect information, and perform other routine work, but in towns the demanding schedules of urban courts, as well as the density of institutions, meant that more such officers and functionaries operated together within a smaller area. Urban ecclesiastical courts, for example, employed a cadre of sworn lay officers known as summoners or apparitors to do the occasionally dangerous work of citing people to court.[71] In towns their activities were spatially compacted: as many as sixteen summoners operated within the square mile of the city of London in the early sixteenth century.[72] Though as a proportion of the population living there they were few, their intense activity—some of them delivered hundreds of citations a year—made them familiar and easily recognizable for Londoners, who felt that they could spot one a mile off; 'ye are but a sort of knavis', said William Somer to the summoner who cited him in 1493.[73]

Secular officers, too, were far more numerous in towns. At the annual tourn in Hereford, for example, each of the five wards chose normally around eight constables of the peace, some for the area 'inside walls' and others for 'outside walls' in the suburban vills, as well as a handful of ale-tasters. These appointments added up: in 1508, a total of fifty-seven such officers were chosen at the tourn, even before we count the twelve jurors summoned from each ward.[74] As Samantha Sagui's wonderful work on Norwich has shown, these 'mid-level' officers were drawn from a wide range of urban society, and had significant responsibilities for routine peacekeeping, the organization of the watch, and the

[71] Ian Forrest, 'The Summoner', in *Historians on Chaucer: The 'General Prologue' to the Canterbury Tales*, ed. Stephen Rigby and Alastair Minnis (Oxford, 2014), 421–42, pp. 433–5.

[72] On their wages, work, and numbers, see Richard Wunderli, 'Pre-Reformation London Summoners and the Murder of Richard Hunne', *Journal of Ecclesiastical History*, 33:2 (1982), 209–24, at pp. 212–4.

[73] LMA, DL/C/B/043/MS9064/5, fo. 141v.

[74] HARC, BG11/4/1 [1508]. Wye-bridge and Eign both chose eight constables and four ale-tasters; Widemarsh, seven constables and two ale-tasters; Bye-Street, eight constables and five ale-tasters, and St Owen's, nine constables and two ale-tasters. Generally, see Anthony Musson, 'Sub-Keepers and Constables: The Role of Local Officials in Keeping the Peace in Fourteenth-Century England', *EHR*, 117:470 (2002), 1–24.

supervision of public works.[75] All of the ecclesiastical fees in Hereford employed bailiffs of their own, as well as choosing ale-tasters for their law-days; some powerful urban ecclesiastical jurisdictions even appointed their own coroners.[76] All such officers, from the bailiffs and serjeants down to the ward constables, were required to swear oaths, and would have worn the distinctive dress allowed to them by their office; they would have been a common sight for late-medieval townspeople.[77]

And, indeed, beyond these peacekeeping officers mandated by royal jurisdictions, there were also the civic and guild officers bound up with urban government. In the civic sphere, the ideology of officership was closely associated with the status and obligations that attached to citizenship, with the franchise itself dependent on a willingness to hold civic office.[78] This was not merely a theoretical obligation in the later Middle Ages, as civic offices became more numerous and more specialized, and so drew in more members of the commonalty to participate in their execution.[79] This growth in the number of offices was partly the result of attempts by urban government to do more, as, for example, in the appointment of 'scavengers' and 'rakers' to clear away waste from the streets.[80] But it was also driven by the increased control of civic governments over craft guild structures in the post-plague labour market.[81] Guild officials—particularly the 'searchers' who were appointed for each craft—were responsible for maintaining standards and presenting offenders to the civic authorities; they were 'key mediators', as Christian Liddy has put it, from 'the town hall to the workshop and the home'.[82]

Townspeople thus lived cheek by jowl with the officers of a great plurality of jurisdictions; there was in late-medieval towns a particularly dense concentration

[75] See Samantha Sagui, 'Mid-level Officials in Fifteenth-Century Norwich', in *The Fifteenth Century 12: Society in an Age of Plague*, ed. Linda Clark and Carole Rawcliffe (Woodbridge, 2013), 101–21.

[76] For the bailiffs of the fees of the hospital of St. John and the priory of Llanthony Secunda to the north-west, respectively: HARC, BG11/8/3 [unsorted papers, Gaol Delivery], unnumbered paper; HCLA, HCA.2962. The hospital of St. Leonard's, just outside the walls of York, had the right to appoint its own coroner, and he was active (sometimes in collaboration with civic authorities) in the early fifteenth century: see YMLA, M2/6e, fos. 19r [inquest], 44v [abjuration], 45r [inquest].

[77] For example, in the Maldon town book specific oaths and provisions for livery are set out for the bailiffs, serjeants, and constables: ERO, D/B 3/1/2, fos. 14r–v. On the dress of civic government, a topic that would repay further investigation, see Stephen Rigby, 'Urban "Oligarchy" in Late Medieval England', in *Towns and Townspeople in the Fifteenth Century*, ed. John A. F. Thomson (Gloucester, 1988), 62–86, at p. 66.

[78] Liddy, *Politics of Citizenship*, pp. 29–30.

[79] McRee, 'Religious Gilds and Civic Order', p. 81.

[80] Christine L. Winters, 'The Portsoken Presentments: An Analysis of a London Ward in the 15th Century', *Transactions of the London and Middlesex Archaeological Society*, 56 (2005), 97–161, at p. 101. In London, these positions seem to have emerged from the beadle's assistants: Frank Rexroth, *Deviance and Power in Late-Medieval London*, trans. Pamela E. Selwyn (Cambridge, 2007), pp. 61–3. In Hereford, the office of 'bell-man' was responsible for both paving and raking: HARC, BG11/19/11, fos. 241r, 243v.

[81] In general, see Heather Swanson, 'The Illusion of Economic Structure: Craft Guilds in Late Medieval English Towns', *P&P*, 121 (1988), 29–48, pp. 37–8; also Rosser, *The Art of Solidarity*, pp. 149–84.

[82] Liddy, *Politics of Citizenship*, p. 151.

of men whose job it was to watch you and report what you did to legal authorities. Such men had a potentially large degree of influence over the people among whom they worked, and sometimes abused it: for example, in 1456 a trio of officers working for the Archdeacon of Colchester attempted to blackmail Alice Louthe by falsely citing her for adultery and suggesting that she would be made to undergo public purgation for the offence, which 'put her to great expense and caused many debates between her and her husband'.[83] Of course, this kind of extortion played upon the fear of townspeople that their sins—whether real or imagined—would be aired in public before their neighbours and families.[84] But it also suggests, as it clearly did for Alice Louthe's husband, that these officers were watching people very closely and so might see things that others did not. Institutional density could produce an overfamiliar form of intimacy between townspeople and the functionaries of law-courts.

It also produced problems, however, as the different urban courts attempted to square the existence of officers from various jurisdictions working within the same area. In Hereford this was a recurrent problem, which the civic and ecclesiastical authorities revisited several times during the later Middle Ages, finding several solutions. In the first place, they attempted to triangulate the appointments of officers, making the same men work for different jurisdictions. The dean and chapter had the right to appoint both a bailiff and a serjeant within their fee, and according to a later-fifteenth-century agreement, the mayor and citizens 'many tymes' had these same officers sworn as constables of the peace at the civic law-day.[85] Contrariwise, when the Bishop of Hereford appointed a bailiff for his own law-day in the city, he normally chose 'a citizen & ffreman off the seid cite' who therefore 'a certen season of the yeare hathe the hole Rule of the citie'—that is to say, a kind of 'dual citizenship' which allowed him to go where he pleased.[86] Our knowledge of these conventions, however, comes from contemporary disputes over whether they represented binding arrangements or waivable prerogatives, and there were, as we shall see, also many instances when these officers clashed.

For now, though, we turn to another effect of institutional density: the way that multiple urban jurisdictions scrutinized domestic space. As Shannon McSheffrey has shown in a wonderful article, the concern of both ecclesiastical and secular authorities to regulate marital and sexual relationships meant that the urban

[83] ERO, D/B 5 Cr68, m. 19r.

[84] See Felicity Riddy, 'Authority and Intimacy in the Late Medieval Urban Home', in *Gendering the Master Narrative: Women and Power in the Middle Ages*, ed. Mary C. Erler and Maryanne. Kowaleski (Ithaca, NY, 2003), 212–28.

[85] BLO, Herefordshire Roll 36, m. 3r. The dean and chapter claimed these officers were responsible for keeping the king's peace; the mayor and citizens claimed that they were mere rent gatherers, and that their authority for keeping the peace only came from their appointment as constables. There is evidence that the bailiffs for the fees of the bishop, the canons, and St. John's also reported to the civic law-day: HARC, BG11/17/2, no. 20.

[86] HCLA, HCA.2936.

home, far from being a private space, was open to intensive public regulation.[87] But as well as the lower church courts and ward leets making inquiry into moral offences, civic authorities were also placing increased scrutiny on the homes of townspeople in the later Middle Ages. Frank Rexroth has suggested that the fourteenth-century 'moral panics' of the aldermanic authorities in London, in particular, prompted a series of surveillance measures against an imagined 'nocturnal underworld' in the city.[88] Christian Liddy, meanwhile, has argued that the politics of the civic franchise, in the distinctive socio-economic conditions of late-medieval towns, encouraged citizens to monitor closely what their co-citizens said in the home, the workplace, and the warehouse (which for many townsmen might well occupy the same building).[89] This pervasive concern with moral order thus focused particular scrutiny upon the household as the primary unit of governance.[90]

In the first place, domestic scrutiny was routinized through the networks of male householders who watched how their neighbours behaved and produced information about them for a range of urban law-courts. The jurors of the ward courts, the manifold 'trustworthy men' of town parishes, and the aldermen of guilds and fraternities worked with one another in order to enforce a patriarchal governance within the urban household.[91] In the second place, though, the courts were proactive in rooting out offences for themselves, by conducting routine searches of houses and shops. For the policing of disorder, the officials were permitted to search houses on the thinnest of neighbourly suspicions. At St Andrew's Holborn in London, for example, Margaret Curtman had the house of Henry and Agnes Nash searched by the ward constables because a soothsayer had told her that they had stolen her clothes—apparently the constables found nothing, for she was cited to the commissary court as a common defamer.[92]

Searches were also important for trade regulation. Ale-tasters, for example, routinely intruded into homes to check upon breaches of the assize.[93] At Henley-on-Thames, they presented the wife of Thomas Spyre to the borough court

[87] Shannon McSheffrey, 'Place, Space, and Situation: Public and Private in the Making of Marriage in Late-Medieval London', *Speculum*, 79:4 (2004), 960–90.

[88] Rexroth, *Deviance and Power*, esp. pp. 27–125; for a critique, see Liddy, *Politics of Citizenship*, p. 6.

[89] Christian Liddy, 'Cultures of Surveillance in Late Medieval English Towns: The monitoring of speech and the fear of revolt', in *Handbook of Medieval Revolt*, ed. Firnhaber-Baker with Schoenaers, 311–29.

[90] Shannon McSheffrey, 'Jurors, Respectable Masculinity, and Christian Morality: A Comment on Marjorie McIntosh's *Controlling Misbehavior*', *Journal of British Studies*, 37:3 (1998), 269–78; Riddy, 'Authority and Intimacy', pp. 212–15.

[91] Shannon McSheffrey, *Marriage, Sex, and Civic Culture in Late Medieval London* (Philadelphia, 2006), p. 152; Ian Forrest, *Trustworthy Men: How Faith and Inequality Made the Medieval Church* (Princeton, 2018), pp. 215–17.

[92] LMA, DL/C/B/043/MS9064/11, fo. 158r.

[93] The bishops of Hereford also claimed the right to fine 'taverners who recuse themselves from the assize and close their doors to the ministers and bailiffs of the king': HCLA, HCA.2960.

because she was not only said to be selling ale within her house, but she also refused to let them in and test its quality.[94] Craftsmen were also required to allow the officers of their guild to enter their workshops to check their merchandise. Thus an ordinance made at the Essex town of Maldon in 1468 banned butchers from selling meat on Sunday after matins, with offenders 'to forfete all there fleysshe . . . founde in ther shoppes ther, on halffe to the tounne & that other haffe to the supervisoures of the same'; under the same penalty, they were also forbidden to 'upyn there wyndouues of there shoppes but onely the dores'.[95] Not only were such officers incentivized to carry out searches, then, but the artisans themselves were expected to make their domestic space amenable to searching.

All of this watching and searching of houses conducted for urban law-courts seems to have produced a particularly intense form of domestic governance, as different kinds of jurisdiction were concerned to investigate the same kinds of offence. Many reports in the London commissary court, for example, reference information derived from the wardmotes; in 1485, for example, a report from the parish of St Botolph's in Aldersgate that Agnes Beldon was a bawd, or madam, noted in evidence that she had been banished by the wards of Aldersgate, Faringdon, and Queenhithe, 'all for [being] a comon bawde'.[96] The close-knit reporting networks within urban neighbourhoods, then, served to intensify the courts' scrutiny of households. In a suggestive example from the Hereford tourn in 1513, John ap Richard, a juror and a constable of Eign ward, was presented and fined 3s. 4d. by the jurors of the contiguous ward of St Owens for 'entering the house of Roger Griffiths against his will'.[97] His presentment not only suggests some jurisdictional friction between wards, but also seems indicative of the more general atmosphere of domestic surveillance in late-medieval cities, where low-level officers felt emboldened to enter houses whenever they liked.

But, indeed, the fact that he was presented and fined indicates that townspeople might chafe at this level of scrutiny, and, moreover, that they could resist it through appealing to different jurisdictions. For instance, in the London parish of St James Garlickhithe in 1493, Roger Clay and Alice Pyghell were cited to the commissary court for defamation after Roger had reported to an alderman's deputy their suspicions concerning a neighbour, Anne Lowe, and the priest Thomas Bundy.[98] These salacious reports were taken seriously by the ecclesiastical authorities, as Bundy was summoned to explain himself before the Bishop of London, while Clay and Pyghell were let off with a warning. Yet it is striking that

[94] OHC, BOR3/B2/IV/CR/8, m. 3v. [95] ERO, D/B 3/1/2, fo. 12v.

[96] LMA, DL/C/B/043/MS9064/2, fo. 140r; for other cross-reporting examples from London, see Wunderli, *London Church Courts*, pp. 94–5.

[97] HARC, BG11/4/1 [1513].

[98] LMA, DL/C/B/043/MS9064/5, fo. 167v–168r. Roger had observed Anne leaning her head on Thomas's shoulder in church, while Alice had seen the two of them come out of a tavern in Cheapside, and 'he shulde goo one way and she another way'.

Roger's initial report of their information to the secular authorities was itself reported to the church courts as defamation. This was no doubt tied to local feelings about who was entitled to make such reports, but it also suggests—as did the case of Alice Louthe, above—how townspeople might use one forum to discredit accusations made against them in another.[99] The density of institutions in towns and cities, then, though it certainly piled layers of legal scrutiny upon domestic space, could also produce fissures in the legitimacy of governance.

Similar problems were manifested in the courts' attempts to enforce their orders through the arrest of goods and persons. As we saw in Chapter 1, these procedures were carried out in rural tribunals too, but in borough and market courts, with their frequent sessions and itinerant litigants, they were more common and often more elaborate. The court at Henley-on-Thames, for example, was particularly assiduous in this regard. In a typical case of 1419, Nicholas Brugges sued John North for debt, and North 'was attached by diverse goods contained in a little chest, and appraised in this court by the suitors', carefully enumerated and retained by the bailiffs.[100] Defendants could pay a small fine to have the items back, replacing them with a personal pledge; but if they failed to appear after five further sessions, then the goods were turned over to the plaintiff—thus in 1437 Thomas Lagham forfeited two pewter cooking pots, valued at 5s. 7d.[101] The correct implementation of these procedures was understood to be important; in 1429 John Couper complained that he had 'not been legitimately attached... according to the law and custom of Henley', though, as it transpired, the suitors of the court disagreed and allowed the case against him to continue.[102]

In larger towns and cities with their more numerous legal institutions, the legitimacy of attachment was also freighted with jurisdictional contention. Townspeople living within one fee could easily find themselves summoned to answer in the court of another. This provoked recurrent problems in fifteenth-century Hereford. In a dispute of 1495, the dean and chapter of the cathedral and the civic authorities complained that 'no citizens should enter the lands or fees [of the church] to make any attachments whatsoever', by long-standing agreement.[103] Accused by the civic authorities of doing precisely the same thing, the dean and chapter made an interesting assertion: they had 'never attached eny mans goods

[99] On the distinctions between 'good' defamation and 'bad' defamation, see Ian Forrest, 'Defamation, Heresy, and Late Medieval Social Life' in *Image, Text, and Church, 1380–1600: Essays for Margaret Aston*, ed. L. Clark, M. Jurkowski, and C. Richmond (Toronto, 2009), 142–61.

[100] OHC, BOR3/B2/IV/CR/2, mm. 3r. The goods included various cloths and towels (in total worth 4s. 10d.), two fur pelts (8d.), a silver powder-box (7d.), and the chest itself (8d.). We know the items were kept by the bailiffs because Brugges was one of them, and later paid a small fine (4d.) because he had failed to return the items to North after the conclusion of the suit: m. 4r.

[101] For a case where a defendant paid to have the items back, OHC, BOR3/B2/IV/CR/3, m. 1r; for Lagham, BOR3/B2/IV/CR/6, m. 1r.

[102] OHC, BOR3/B2/IV/CR/3, m. 3r. The case does not specify, unfortunately, what this law and custom concerning attachments involved.

[103] HCLA, HCA.2960.

and catells within the seid cite, but only within ther own fee for causes reasonable; and yf eny suche attachement were, it is the parties accion so greved, and not answereable to the mairs complaynt'—that is to say, it was the plaintiff's choice of forum that mattered when it came to deciding jurisdiction.[104] Routine processes of litigation could thus draw townspeople into these potentially fractious relations.

But even more than attachments and the detention of goods, arrests of persons often became particularly contentious in late-medieval towns. Arresting the wrong person, in the wrong place, or at the wrong time, had the potential to provoke jurisdictional conflict—sometimes quite deliberately so—and many late-medieval urban disputes started in this way.[105] A particularly bitter quarrel in Hereford at the turn of the fifteenth century focused on arrests.[106] The ecclesiastical authorities compiled a long list of occasions when the mayor and his officers had exceeded their jurisdiction by making arrests within the church fee: among other things, they were said to have lured tenants of the bishop's fee from their homes 'under the guise of friendship and peace, to come out into the public street, where they were arrested and taken to the king's prison'.[107] Contrariwise, they complained, when the bailiff of the bishop's fee mistook the son of Agnes Carpenter as a wandering servant and took him to the episcopal palace for judgment, the mayor sent his serjeants to threaten the bishop's officers into releasing the young man.[108] As both sides well understood, these arrests by the civic authorities were intended to demonstrate their jurisdiction over peacekeeping throughout the entire city.

Arrests did not necessarily produce conflict, however. In 1465, during the procession for St. Thomas of Cantilupe (a former bishop of Hereford and popular local saint), the mayor's serjeants arrested Robert Lesbury for pickpocketing within the cathedral precinct, and took him to the city gaol.[109] The dean, outraged by this violation of his jurisdiction, demanded the mayor hand over the prisoner; the mayor refused, claiming authority to make arrests throughout the city. But soon afterwards, in honour of the religious occasion, 'and in eschuyng of all otheir

[104] HCLA, HCA.2955b.

[105] Lorraine Attreed, 'Arbitration and the Growth of Urban Liberties in Late Medieval England', *Journal of British Studies*, 31:3 (1992), 205–35, pp. 214–5; Carrel, 'Disputing legal privilege', pp. 281–2, 286; McSheffrey, 'Legal Topography', pp. 499–500.

[106] On this dispute, see Rosser, 'Disputes between Clergy and Laity in Hereford', and fn. 26 above.

[107] HCLA, HCA.2934. The full quote is: '. . . idem maior et ballivi alium ymaginantes suam maliciam contra tenentes domini episcopi in feodo suo habitantes vadiunt ad domos suas infra dictum feodum et eos deceptorie sub colore amoris et pacis faciunt venire ad stratam publica et ibidem ipsos arrestavit et ad carceres domini regis ducunt'.

[108] HCLA, HCA.2934. Agnes Carpenter was presumably, based on this identification of her son, a widowed head of household, and perhaps a citizen (a Carpenter family was prominent in civic politics throughout the fifteenth century). But the mayor's interference was probably due to the bishop claiming (and here exercising) a power to arrest wandering servants, associated with the jurisdiction of the Justice of the Peace which the mayor had at that time recently acquired: see fnn. 20 and 44–5 above.

[109] HCLA, HCA.2945.

inconvenience', they came to an agreement, sealed by indenture, whereby the dean and chapter would keep the prisoner for three days and three nights, and then return him to the mayor.[110] This symbolic exchange reveals a consciousness of the broad audience of jurisdiction—both for the initial arrest and the prisoner exchange that resolved the dispute—that is indicative of how institutional density inflected the role of legal officers in urban legal culture. The jurisdictional pressure upon their activities meant that such agreements had to be carefully stage-managed before the townspeople on whose cooperation they depended.[111]

The significance of arrest as a signifier of jurisdiction produced different effects for late-medieval townspeople. On one hand, it made the inhabitants of both fees into pawns of jurisdictional conflict, as they were arrested, assaulted, and extorted by officers of the other. On the other hand, however, these same conflicts also laid arrests open to challenge, creating the possibility for defiance and subterfuge. That this possibility was sometimes realized is suggested in the settlement of the same dispute at Hereford in 1410, when the civic and ecclesiastical authorities agreed a battery of regulatory measures that specified 'what ought to be done about vagabonds who do many evils at night, *under colour of ecclesiastical liberties*', an issue said to be causing great discord between the inhabitants of the two fees.[112] By claiming to belong to the church fee, these people—whether indeed they were 'vagabonds' must remain an open question—were able to resist arrest by civic officers, perhaps reluctant to take a chance during the ongoing resolution of a jurisdictional dispute. The ploy, a 'weapon of the weak' that turned legal power back on itself, highlights the way that townspeople could respond creatively to living in conditions of institutional density.[113]

The routine operations of urban law-courts, as they normally involved more than one authority attempting to exercise jurisdiction within the same place as another, regularly forced townspeople to confront these conditions. This produced ambiguous effects; in many ways the multiplicity of legal operations served to intensify governance—especially in regard to the pervasive presence of legal officers, their capacity to enter homes and shops, and to make attachments and arrests—even while providing them with occasional opportunities to call its legitimacy into question. These operations present a strong contrast with those in rural legal culture examined in Chapter 1, where courts were flexible and broadly inclusive, working within the grain of rural social relations. In towns and cities, by contrast, the maintenance of watchful contact between jurisdictions

[110] A similar agreement settled a 1448 dispute in Exeter: Attreed, 'Arbitration and Liberties', p. 228.

[111] On the importance of communicating jurisdiction, see Johnson, 'Jurisdiction in Late-Medieval England', p. 48.

[112] HCLA, HCA.2951.

[113] James C. Scott, *Weapons of the Weak: Everyday Forms of Peasant Resistance* (New Haven, CT, 1985), esp. Ch. 5, 'Beyond the War of Words: Cautious Resistance and Calculated Conformity', pp. 241–303.

appears to have produced a more brittle relationship between townspeople and legal institutions, which played out on a spectrum of control and resistance. This is not to imply, however, that townspeople were merely the subjects of governance in urban legal culture. As we shall see in the following section, they also pursued their own distinctive concerns through the courts available to them.

Urban Community: Trade, Rule, Nuisance

Urban legal culture was distinguished by its emphasis on spatial order. As we have seen so far, this was manifested in the close association between different urban law-courts and the spaces they occupied in the city, but also in the way that the exercise of jurisdiction was understood to hinge upon spatial control, whether this was envisioned in relation to the whole city, a particular fee within it, and over the individual shops and houses that made it up. In this final section, we shall see how ideas about space infused the kinds of legal issue—the regulation of commerce, the management of the physical environment, and the policing of immoral behaviour—that townspeople most often brought to the courts. These kinds of business were not exclusive to cities, but the way in which they were framed through discourses of spatial order made them distinctive to urban legal culture. In what follows, I look at each of these issues in turn, focusing in particular on the ways in which they took shape through the key concepts of openness in trade, the keeping of good rule in houses, and environmental nuisance as key ideas in the regulation of associative relations in urban legal culture.

Trade matters formed a central part of urban legal culture. Townspeople used law-courts to settle disputes over merchandise, to achieve the repayment of debts, and to enforce regulations on production, monopolies, and conditions of employment. In all of these matters, the idea of openness was key to the way that people thought the market itself and the trade conducted there should work. As James Davis has written, the notion of 'the public marketplace inferred honesty, witnesses and social cooperation, while secret and hidden trade implied fraud, price-raising and other crimes because such transactions occurred outside the remit of official sanction'.[114] In particular, openness was mobilized to ensure fair trading practices, the symmetry of commercial knowledge, and creditworthiness. Part of the significance of urban legal institutions, then, lay in the collective weight they exerted on commercial relationships, staunchly pulling them into an agreeable shape.[115]

[114] Davis, *Medieval Market Morality*, p. 177.

[115] For a recent summary (and critique) of the role of institutions in creating trust in trade in a broad perspective, see Ian Forrest and Ann Haour, 'Trust in Long-Distance Relationships, 1000–1600 CE', *P&P*, 238, suppl. 'The Global Middle Ages' (2018), 191–214.

In the first place, this meant that townspeople expected trade to be conducted openly in the market. As an ordinance from Maldon put it, on market day all commerce was to be conducted within sight of the 'comonne crosse', and only within the specified trading hours: 'every man to do his beste whanne the comonne belle is ronnge'.[116] Openness provided a guarantee of common opportunity. Concomitantly, presentments against forestalling, the practice of selling outside the market, and regrating, reselling within the same market for a profit, were extremely common, particularly in regard to the sale of fish and other foodstuffs.[117] Both practices were, in part, offences against openness: forestalling took place out of the sight of market officials and other traders, while regrating, with produce resold from homes or by street-sellers, worked against the fixing of prices within the market.[118] Roger Biddyng of Yarmouth was fined as much as 40d. in 1473 for forestalling and regrating malt outside the market there, 'illicitly... and to the great prejudice' of others.[119] Trade had to be open in order to be fair.

Openness was also an important assurance of the quality of merchandise. In one remarkable case of 1440, Thomas and Joan Elbrygge were presented at Rochester, in an indictment later passed on to the royal criminal courts, for a combination of forestalling and counterfeiting. They had taken six barrels of old 'Spanish' wine, unfit for consumption, and mixed it with other wines, egg whites, and 'diverse gums and resins', in order to give it a 'pleasing appearance and delicious taste'; they then marketed their concoctions as rumneys and malmseys, 'and by this false name fraudulently counterfeited and exposed them to sale, to the grave damage and deception, and imperilling of the lives of the king's people'.[120] Keeping trade within the open market guarded against such elaborate schemes of deception, as the oversight of officials and fellow traders ensured that the quality of the goods on sale actually matched their appearance. Visibility was also important in the correction of such offences, as when defective goods were burnt publicly in the market or dishonest traders put in the pillory, to enable wide knowledge of which goods, and which people, were not to be trusted.[121]

Indeed, openness was vital for the establishment of commercial trust more generally, as urban courts provided some certainty about reputation and creditworthiness. In Hereford, for example, the mayor's court routinely registered recognizances of debt, for amounts as little as 20s., allowing creditors and debtors to set out specified repayment schedules that could be enforced, but without the

[116] ERO, D/B 3/1/2, fo. 12r. [117] Davis, *Medieval Market Morality*, pp. 323–31.

[118] See, for example, an ordinance passed in the Yorkshire town of Beverley in 1398: against *snarlers* and *haukers* wandering through the streets selling food and livestock; notably, it made an exception for those who kept 'shops in the open market'. *Beverley Town Documents*, ed. Arthur F. Leach, Selden Society 14 (London, 1900), p. 42.

[119] NRO, Y/C 4/176, fo. 15r. [120] TNA, KB9/233, no. 90.

[121] For an instance of publicly burning goods (at Henley-on-Thames in 1500), see OHC, BOR3/B2/IV/CR/14, m. 2v. On the pillory, see Davis, 'The Cross and the Pillory'.

need to conduct litigation.[122] Lower ecclesiastical courts provided a similar service through 'breach of faith' actions, allowing people to publicize and formalize existing arrangements, as well as creating a written record of the debt.[123] The Salisbury subdean's court, in particular, often took quite interventionist action in commercial matters, establishing schedules of debt repayment, and even making *ex officio* prosecutions, as against a servant named Marion Turboll, who was denounced as a 'public usurer'.[124] Both secular and ecclesiastical courts thus buttressed the normative frameworks of trade by making commerce open.

Urban legal culture was also characterized by the strict regulation of behaviour and the concern with misrule. Of course, this concern was manifested everywhere, but as Marjorie McIntosh's quantitative research into misbehaviour has suggested, it seems to have been particularly pronounced in late-medieval urban centres, with their greater extremes of inequality, and larger numbers of the immigrants, female workers, and apprentices who frequently formed the target of moral regulation.[125] Indeed, the kinds of 'antisocial behaviour'—such as fornication, gambling, night-walking, eavesdropping, and gossiping—that townspeople presented to urban law-courts were often focused on such groups precisely because they did not fit easily into the scheme of patriarchal household governance envisaged as a microcosm of civic order.[126] Building on the earlier discussion here about the scrutiny of domestic space, then, I want to turn to look at the kinds of spatial discourse that emerged in urban legal culture about the household as a site for the production and policing of morality.

To begin with, there was a persistent concern, in both secular leets held for wards and in the lower church courts, with the household as a crucible of misbehaviour. Heads of household—normally men—were expected to manage the behaviour of the other people, particularly women and servants, who lived under their rule. An ordinance of 1485 in the Essex seigneurial borough of Harwich put it in general terms: anyone who was found to 'consort, host, help, or maintain in their houses men or women of illicit and shameful governance, such as robbers, whores, thieves, and women of vile occupation', was to be fined 40d., with half given to the church and half to the lord of the manor.[127] These anxieties also found frequent expression in the charge of 'maintaining', or 'fostering' sexual misbehaviour, extremely common in both secular and ecclesiastical

[122] HARC, BG11/17/11, *passim*. [123] Forrest, *Trustworthy Men*, pp. 60–1.

[124] Respectively, WSHO, D4/3/1, mm. 11v, 10v. See also a case before the London Commissary court against a man for perjuring himself in the Guildhall regarding a debt sequestrated during testamentary litigation: LMA, DL/C/B/043/MS9064/4A, fo. 356r.

[125] Marjorie K. McIntosh, *Controlling Misbehavior in England, 1370–1600* (Cambridge, 1998), Ch. 6, 'Social ecology I: "broad response" and "no response" communities', pp. 137–69, and esp. pp. 157–61. See also the sophisticated statistical analysis of inequality and office-holding in the ecclesiastical courts, albeit for more rural communities, in Forrest, *Trustworthy Men*, pp. 144–57.

[126] McSheffrey, *Marriage, Sex, and Civic Culture*, p. 120.

[127] ERO, D/B 4/38/10, m. 1r.

forums, and known in the Hereford law-day returns for which vernacular jury presentments survive as 'bawdery holden'.[128] The house was imagined as the place where bad rule flourished and fomented, and townspeople—particularly the respectable men who reported information to the courts—attempted to redress this across the different forums available to them.

Concerns with maintaining were closely tied to the notion of 'receiving' or 'hosting' bad rule, a subtle but important spatial distinction, in which the house became misgoverned because outsiders were allowed into it. This was manifested in repeated presentments against householders like James Richardson of Marlborough, who 'received, consorted, and abetted diverse servants at night', who went to his house for 'unlawful jests', or Nicholas Hore of the church fee in Hereford, who was said to be a common curfew-breaker, hosting 'shameful people and idle vagabonds, to the nuisance of his neighbours'.[129] Similar disquiet with hosting also led to a tightening of restrictions on alehouses and other hostelries in the later Middle Ages.[130] Thus at Henley in 1458, Richard Crofte was fined 20d. for 'inn-holding without an open sign against the statute, and lodging suspect men who come to the town at night'; a few years later, in 1465, the town passed an ordinance that no one was to hold 'common and open hostelry' without a sign, under the steep penalty of 6s. 8d.[131] By publicly marking certain houses for the hosting of others, such rules also represented an attempt to prevent householders from surreptitiously or secretly receiving outsiders.

Following on from this, indeed, was the idea that external misbehaviour might infect even the well-governed houses of respectable townsmen. This found particular expression in the fear of eavesdropping, the subject of numerous presentments in late-medieval urban leets.[132] It was thought to be threatening because it represented an invasion of intimate space: as an ordinance against them from Colchester in the middle of the fifteenth century put it, eavesdroppers listened 'undyr menys wyndowes be nyght or be day to bere a wey tales or discovere ther

[128] E.g. HARC, BG11/3/1, [1513]. On harbouring and fostering in the church courts, see R. H. Helmholz, 'Harboring Sexual Offenders: Ecclesiastical Courts and Controlling Misbehavior', *Journal of British Studies*, 37:3 (1998), 258–68.

[129] Respectively: WSHO, G22/1/13, fo. 3v, translation from the unusual phrase '*illegitima joca*'; HCLA, R1145, recto (I have translated *communis vigilator* as 'curfew-breaker', rather than 'night-walker', because of the specification that he was hosting others).

[130] See Barbara Hanawalt, 'The Host, the Law, and the Ambiguous Space of Medieval London Taverns' in *Medieval Crime and Social Control*, ed. Barbara Hanawalt and David Wallace (Minneapolis, 1999), 204–23. Also useful is Margaret Aston, 'The Gentlewoman and the Tapster, or, to the pub with Colin' in *Much heaving and shoving: late-medieval gentry and their concerns*, ed. M. Aston and R. Horrox (Lavenham, 2005), 121–31. More generally, see Peter Clark, *The English Alehouse: A Social History 1200–1830* (New York, 1983); the essays in *The World of the Tavern: Public Houses in Early Modern Europe*, ed. Beat Kümin and B. A. Tlusty (Aldershot, 2002); Beat Kümin, *Drinking Matters: Public Houses and Social Exchange in Early Modern Central Europe* (Basingstoke, 2007).

[131] OHC, BOR3/B2/IV/CR/11, m. 2r; BOR3/B2/IV/CR/13, m. 3v.

[132] For the recurrence of this word, e.g. HARC, BG11/4/1 [1505].

counsel, to make debate or discencion among there neighbors'.[133] Eavesdropping was certainly bound up too, then, with scolding and gossiping, often imagined as characteristically female offences.[134] But, as the Colchester ordinance makes clear, the uncovering of intimate conversations, or making known comments that were intended only for a domestic audience, was considered inherently disruptive, an attitude which suggests that even well-ruled houses ought to be enclosed. Eavesdropping was problematic not just because external misbehaviour might corrupt domestic space, then, but because domestic behaviour might contaminate social relations outside the home.

Moving beyond the tired dichotomy of public and private, then, the problem for the legal governance of morality lay in the fluidity of intimate relations between individual households and the urban community.[135] The physically compact conditions of late-medieval cities meant that this problem had to be confronted very often indeed, as townspeople observed their neighbours' behaviour, even while they were in their own homes. Thus in 1492 John Parkyn and John Millis were summoned to the London commissary for defaming Thomas Kingislond of committing adultery with Agnes Adam; but they insisted on the veracity of their charge before the judge, with one of them saying 'I know they kept no good rule, for he enterid by a window unto her, the dur shut, and that is suspect, and I think rather for syn than for robory or eny other cause'.[136] The pair were assigned a public penance, while Thomas was warned to no longer associate with Agnes 'in suspicious places', under pain of excommunication. While the outcome is typical of the even-handed approach of the ecclesiastical courts, it suggests that the problem lay not just in the offence itself, but in the starkness of its visibility. Urban houses required close governance precisely because they were threshold spaces between intimate and associative relations, producing an often uncomfortable closeness between householders and their neighbours.

Finally, we turn to the preoccupation with environmental regulation in urban legal culture. Environmental matters were frequently pursued for their own sake in urban courts, as late-medieval townspeople sought to deal with the mountains of waste produced, the growth of polluting industries such as tanning, butchery, and smelting, and the higher incidence of plague and mortality; Carole Rawcliffe, in her comprehensive study of public health in English towns, found that environmental ordinances 'increased exponentially' after the Black Death.[137] Of course,

[133] ERO, D/B 5 R1, fo. 2v.

[134] See Sandy Bardsley, *Venomous Tongues: Speech and Gender in Late Medieval England* (Philadelphia, 2006); Karen Jones, *Gender and Petty Crime in Late Medieval England: The Local Courts in Kent, 1460–1560* (Woodbridge, 2006), 94–128.

[135] 'Intimacy' is suggested as an alternative to 'privacy' in McSheffrey, 'Place, Space, and Situation', p. 989. See also the typically incisive comments in Riddy, 'Authority and Intimacy', pp. 215–20.

[136] LMA, DL/C/B/043/MS9064/5, fo. 177v.

[137] Generally, see Rawcliffe, *Urban Bodies*, pp. 2–3 [plague], 8 [increase of ordinances], 127–8 [urban waste], 147–8 [butchers], 165–6 [fumes].

the desire for a well-ordered environment was not exclusively urban, and, as we saw in Chapter 1, it was often expressed in rural courts through a focus on the good 'repair' of the manor or the parish, as communal institutions represented by their buildings.[138] In urban legal culture, however, environmental discourse was different for a couple of reasons. First, it was more explicitly conceived in terms of 'nuisance', framing the issue in terms of individual actions that harmed others, whether neighbours or 'passers-by'.[139] In the second place, this focus on the relationship between individuals and the community meant that legal discourse about the environment often subsumed other legal concerns, about trade and morality.

Nuisance began at home, with the regulation of the spaces shared between close neighbours. As Vanessa Harding has suggested in her analysis of houses in London, 'controls in the public interest were strongest at the interface between properties', such as party walls, gardens, gutters, roofs, and indeed water supplies.[140] For example, presentments from the early sixteenth-century Aldersgate wardmote on the west side of London complained about the 'drawgths', mechanisms for drawing water, running out of people's houses, two from William Nycholson's kitchen into the town ditch, 'which noyes the kyngs pepull and the towne dyche', and others from a back alley running alongside the churchyard 'so certeyn hoolys broken owte of the same [houses] unto the baksyde of the churchyard the which hys perlowse for the church'.[141] Annoyance and danger, the calling cards of nuisance discourse, thus served to focus on the way that the actions of individual householders harmed the community: the king's people or the parish. Or, to put it more positively, the physical interfaces between townspeople constituted a social infrastructure, the maintenance of which was essential for communal living.

For similar reasons, streets formed the focus for pervasive regulation in late-medieval towns and cities, with a particular focus on keeping them free from blockages and waste.[142] This was not a claim innocent of jurisdictional politics in Hereford, where control of the streets was a sticking point in conflicts between the mayoral and ecclesiastical authorities. In a dispute of 1495, the mayor and citizens in their articles of grievance complained that officers of the dean and chapter were exercising jurisdiction 'in the open streete and high waye', rather than just over the properties of their tenants in the church fee; the civic authorities asserted 'that the comen streets and high weys... is within the seid citie [fee] and parcell of the

[138] See Chapter 1, pp. 47–48.

[139] On nuisance in common law, see Baker, *English Legal History*, pp. 422–3.

[140] Vanessa Harding, 'Space, Property, and Propriety in Urban England', *Journal of Interdisciplinary History*, 32:4 (2002), 549–69, p. 560.

[141] LMA, CLC/W/FA/005/MS01499, verso [St Ann Blackfriars].

[142] This was a statutory imperative from 1388: 12 Ric. II c. 13: *SR*, ii, pp. 59–60. More generally, see Dolly Jørgensen, 'Cooperative Sanitation: Managing Streets and Gutters in Late Medieval England and Scandinavia', *Technology and Culture*, 49:3 (2008), 547–67.

same'.[143] Indeed, town governments throughout late-medieval England made similar claims as they began to assume the responsibility for paving streets, raising money for this through a tax of 'pavage', and appointing officers for their maintenance.[144] As late-medieval civic authorities increasingly repaired the fabric of the city, indeed, so they gradually attempted to naturalize their right to govern it.[145]

In presenting a low-hanging pentice attached to a Henley-on-Thames burgage, 'a nuisance to those riding the street', then, or the throwing of filth into the king's highway in Hereford, 'to the nuisance of passers-by', leet jurors were doing some of the ideological work of civic government against its ecclesiastical rivals.[146] This work, however, was dressed up in the recurrent emphasis on the health, safety, and ease of 'passers-by' (*transeuntibus*), who were frequently conjured in such presentments as the constituency harmed by such actions. This idealization of the people flowing along city streets thus strongly resembles the discourse of 'pedestrianism' identified by Nicholas Blomley in a modern context.[147] In late-medieval cities, too, this focus on the mobility of urban community recast a range of problems—urban planning, trading practices, the disposal of waste, and even the regulation of domestic animals, in the ubiquitous presentments about pigs who wandered the streets getting in the way of passers-by—as obstructions of regulated flow, an essential quality of urban associative relations.[148]

Indeed, one of the repeated functions of environmental discourse in urban legal culture was to sublimate other concerns into questions of infrastructure. Another of the Aldersgate wardmote presentments ran against 'Antony Jenson, cobbeler foreyn, for retaylyng of bere in his housse and for castyng owte of stynkyng water to the gret noyanc of all hys neybures'; his status as an alien craftsman was apparently exacerbated by the malodorous discharges of his unlicensed brewing operation (or vice versa), creating a concoction of commercial nuisances against the urban environment.[149] In a similar mode, a 1421 presentment by a jury of St. Clement Danes, in the suburbs of London, complained that 'many pimps and suspect men come and gather around a brothel... causing insults, affrays, and discord between them and the honest and worthy men who happen to pass by there, along the king's highway... to the grave nuisance of all of the neighbours

[143] *HCLA*, HCA.2956.

[144] Rawcliffe, *Urban Bodies*, pp. 131–3; on 'paviours' in Southhampton and Nottingham, Colin Platt, *The English Medieval Town* (London, 1976), pp. 49–50.

[145] Liddy makes a similar point in respect to the 'common soil' of the city: *Politics of Citizenship*, pp. 60–1.

[146] Respectively, OHC, BOR3/B2/IV/CR/14, m. 4r; HARC, BG11/4/1 [1505].

[147] Nicholas Blomley, *Rights of Passage: Sidewalks and the Regulation of Public Flow* (Abingdon, 2011).

[148] Sixty-one separate presentments about wandering pigs are recorded in the nineteen surviving sessions of tourns (1441–1521) and law-days (1478–1520), twenty-three of which made specific reference to *transeuntibus*: HARC, BG11/3/1; BG11/4/1. It was a widespread cause of concern in English towns: Rawcliffe, *Urban Bodies*, pp. 157–60.

[149] LMA, CLC/W/FA/007/MS01501, verso [St Ann Blackfriars].

living there, and all the people passing by'.[150] Such grievances, in which instances of misrule metamorphosed into environmental nuisances, were characteristic of the way that associative relations, in urban legal culture, were conceived in terms of spatial order.[151]

It is important to emphasize, then, the fundamental fluidity of concerns about trade, morality, and the environment within urban legal culture. We can see this in any record of town leet proceedings: presentments against throwing filth in the streets, brewing ale and selling it in false measure, letting pigs wander, keeping misrule, among a litany of similar offences, all flow into one stream of invective on the membrane. This fluidity was important precisely because it was tied to the attempts of townspeople to reconfigure their social relationships through the reordering of space. In urban legal culture, forged within the dense material and institutional surrounds of late-medieval towns and cities, a host of similar concerns ran together. Building better, cleaner, more honest associative relations was thought to be possible through the building of a better city.

Conclusion

By way of conclusion, I would like to make two final points about the horizons of urban legal culture. In the first place, it is worth considering whether the profusion of formal legal institutions in towns and cities resulted in the broader circulation of formal legal knowledge among townspeople, as compared with their rural counterparts. There were undoubtedly more legal professionals, whether defined to include only people such as lawyers and notaries, or understood more capaciously to include clerks, scriveners, and summoners, and, it seems likely, more legal tracts, manuals, and documents in general circulation.[152] Of course, it is hard to know how far such specialist knowledge percolated into the lives of the average fifteenth-century townsperson. But, equally, greater opportunities to go to law in the panoply of urban courts may well have resulted in more legal experience, and concomitantly, a more intimate understanding of judicial process.

In the second place, indeed, it is also possible that townspeople had broader legal perspectives than their counterparts in the countryside. As Eliza Hartrich has highlighted, inter-urban networks were crucially important in fifteenth-century political culture, and they could create legal effects, as, for example, when

[150] TNA, KB9/216/2, no. 9.

[151] A similar point is made in Jeremy Goldberg, 'Pigs and Prostitutes: Streetwalking in Comparative Perspective', in *Young Medieval Women*, ed. Katherine J. Lewis, Noël James Menuge, and Kim M. Phillips (New York, 1999), 172–93.

[152] Generally, see E. W. Ives, *The Common Lawyers of Pre-Reformation England* (Cambridge, 1983); Nigel Ramsay, 'Scriveners and Notaries as Legal Intermediaries in Later Medieval England', in *Enterprise and Individuals in Fifteenth-Century England*, ed. Jennifer Kermode (Stroud, 1991), 118–31. On the circulation of legal texts, see Chapter 8 of this volume.

mercantile elites from civic governments across the country sought the same kinds of jurisdictional privilege from the crown, through new charters of liberties.[153] But even among more middling tradesmen, regional commercial links would have necessitated the use of other urban courts: at the Ely pie-powder, for example, we find litigants not only from nearby market towns such as March and Wisbech (15–20 miles away), but frequently from Lynn (25 miles) and London (70 miles); one case, in fact, was between two merchants from the capital.[154] Though the procedures between such courts were superficially similar, itinerant traders might have found the way in which they were enforced—such as the aggressive distraint process at Henley—to be quite different.[155] Along with local contacts and middlemen, some degree of legal savvy would have been important for navigating this world of inter-regional trade.[156]

And, indeed, even beyond this, notwithstanding the common prohibition that citizens should not sue litigation outside the civic courts, many clearly found it expedient to take their litigation to national forums, as the voluminous mercantile litigation before the courts of Common Pleas and Chancery in the fifteenth century testifies.[157] While townspeople would have needed significant economic resources to launch such litigation, it was not entirely beyond the means of common citizens. The Hereford fuller named Richard Smith, for example, felt he had nowhere else to turn but to the Council of the Marches, a royal equity tribunal for the border with Wales, after a conflict with his craft guild. Having finished thirty-two cloths, he took them to his the wardens for inspection, which they pronounced as fit to sell excepting one; but even though he agreed to withdraw it from sale, the wardens still presented him to the mayor's court, where he was amerced 7s., and put under sureties to pay the fine.[158] This seems a small amount of money upon which to take such action, but that he took it to a relatively new and rather unusual regional tribunal is suggestive of the kind of legal nous—and broader legal horizons—that even middling townspeople might acquire.

But as much these supra-local and national connections were important, urban legal culture was forged in the day-to-day rhythms of urban life in the city. It was characterized in the first place by institutional density: a large range of different law-courts, some of which were themselves distinctive to urban milieux,

[153] Eliza Hartrich, 'Charters and Inter-Urban Networks: England, 1439–1440', *EHR*, 132:555 (2017), 219–49.

[154] CUL, EDR/E1/1/3, mm. 1–7, with the case between London merchants at m. 1v.

[155] See fnn. 100–102 above.

[156] Such middlemen may lie behind the presentments for forestalling and regrating: see Maryanne Kowaleski, *Local markets and regional trade in medieval Exeter* (Cambridge, 1995), pp. 185–6; Davis, *Medieval Market Morality*, pp. 170–1, 331.

[157] See Hartrich, 'Rebellion and the Law', pp. 195–6.

[158] HARC, BG11/8/5, unnumbered. On the procedures and activities of the Council before 1525, see Caroline A. J. Skeel, *The Council in the Marches of Wales: A Study in Local Government during the Sixteenth and Seventeenth Centuries* (London, 1904), pp. 148.

concentrated within a relatively small physical area, which tended to meet more often than those elsewhere. As I have suggested, this density affected both the ways in which these courts worked, and how townspeople engaged with them. In general, it meant that people who lived in towns and cities had more choice about how to pursue legal action, whether by scorning the civic or the pie-powder court in favour of a breach of faith suit before an ecclesiastical tribunal, or by reporting an offence to this official, rather than that one (or perhaps, occasionally, by reporting it to both). But one townsperson's choice was another's coercion, in the form of a summons, or the searching of a house, or an arrest. The net effect, then, was not so much a marketplace of justice, as a high intensity of governance—and some possibilities for undermining its legitimacy.

This density was related to the emphasis on spatial ordering, in urban legal culture, as a means of conceptualizing civic community. For the various urban legal institutions, this was manifested in attempts to control the physical territory of the city, both through demonstrative jurisdictional actions such as processions or the actions of their officers, but also through building efforts, such as pavements, walls, or halls. Such attempts at territorial control sometimes aligned with the interests of townspeople—or at least, presentment jurors and minor officials—as they attempted to purify the city of pollution, both moral and physical. But I have also argued that the kind of spatial order that townspeople were interested in pursuing was strongly influenced by the material conditions of urban life, in which associative relations had to be conducted in close and constant proximity with one another. In such an environment, legal regulations often took the form of spatial regulation, creating social gridlines of sufficient width for a large population—of citizens and strangers, masters and servants, neighbours and passers-by—to live together in the city.

3

Maritime Legal Culture

Expertise and Authority

Maritime legal culture in late-medieval England was deeply shaped by the distinctive living and working conditions of the maritime world—the unpredictability of the marine environment, the great mobility of both people and their goods, and the presence of foreigners suspected to be outside of the king's allegiance. These conditions produced particular kinds of problem for legal governance. What was the right course to take in a storm to save life and property? Was that barrel found innocently at sea or taken forcibly as spoil? What really happened when that man fell overboard? Some answers to these questions could be found within the copious traditions of maritime law and custom; in practice, much of the interpretation and judgment of such matters was given over to shipmasters, as the pre-eminent and expert men of maritime communities.[1] Amidst the pervasive ambiguities of the maritime world, ideas about the authority of these men, and their crews, helped to buttress a set of complex and uncertain social relations both aboard ships and ashore.

Previous studies of maritime law in medieval Europe have given prominence to the idiosyncratic 'sea laws' that supposedly held sway across national borders, with debates focusing on untangling their origins, and the extent to which they were actually used in practice.[2] These laws were certainly important emblems of maritime legal culture, and were very occasionally invoked by courts to make jurisdictional claims, or by litigants to justify decisions that had been taken aboard ships. But as we shall see, the relevance of such laws—either as a transnational domain or a set of substantive principles—was marginal to the legal operations of maritime communities in late-medieval England. In this chapter, therefore, I focus on the relatively neglected records of local institutions of maritime governance,

[1] See Robin Ward, *The World of the Medieval Shipmaster: Law, Business and the Sea, c.1350–c.1450* (Woodbridge, 2009).

[2] For the strongest statements in favour of the use of the sea-laws, see Timothy J. Runyan, 'The Roles of Oleron and the Admiralty Court in Fourteenth Century England', *American Journal of Legal History*, 19:2 (1975), 95–111; Maryanne Kowaleski, '"Alien" Encounters in the Maritime World of Medieval England', *Medieval Encounters*, 13 (2007), 96–121; Kowaleski, 'The French of England: A Maritime *lingua franca*?', in *Language and Culture in Medieval Britain: The French of England c.1100–c.1500*, ed. Jocelyn Wogan-Browne (York, 2009), 103–17. For a strong critique of the idea of a common sea law, see Edda Frankot, *Of Laws of Ships and Shipmen: Medieval Maritime Law and its Practice in Urban Northern Europe* (Edinburgh, 2012).

Law in Common: Legal Cultures in Late-Medieval England. Tom Johnson, Oxford University Press (2020).

DOI: 10.1093/oso/9780198785613.001.0001

the courts that operated in port towns, coastal settlements, and fishing villages.[3] These courts show us how mariners, fishermen, merchants, and others actually encountered authority and envisioned law, not as a transnational superstructure, but as a set of localized relations that bound them into crew and community.[4]

As I will argue here, maritime legal culture in late-medieval England was characterized by an emphasis on nautical expertise.[5] Amidst the unpredictable and often dangerous conditions of work at sea, mariners, fishermen, shipmasters, and others conceptualized the regulation of associative relations through particular ideas about the seaworthiness of ships, skilful seamanship, and the obedience of the crew. These concepts of nautical expertise often helped to reinforce the position of shipmasters—whose expertise was officially recognized in many different ways by legal institutions—as they attempted to navigate their ships, freight the cargo of merchants, and manage a highly skilled and unusually mobile workforce; but at the same time, expertise also represented a set of broader ideals to which common mariners might also appeal. If this jurisprudence of nautical expertise often flowed within the existing channels of domination, then, it also represented a powerful discourse that bound sundry people together in the maritime community.

This chapter focuses mainly on material from East Anglia, and the coastline between the Wash and the Blackwater Estuary.[6] In the fifteenth century, this area was divided by the crown into three districts, organized around 'headports' where customs were collected: the area on the south side of the Wash was controlled by Lynn; the mainly rural stretch of coast from north Norfolk round eastwards to mid-Suffolk was under the authority of Great Yarmouth; and the area from mid-Suffolk to the northern tip of the Thames, including several small ports

[3] To my knowledge, the only dedicated study of a local maritime court is B. Schofield, 'Wreck Rolls of Leiston Abbey', in *Studies Presented to Sir Hilary Jenkinson*, ed. J. Conway Davies (London, 1957), 361–71.

[4] Of course, these social units were not distinct: see Heide Gerstenberger, 'Men Apart: The Concept of "Total Institution" and the Analysis of Seafaring', *International Journal of Maritime History*, 8:1 (1996), 173–82.

[5] Other historians have noted the importance of 'expertise' in maritime contexts more generally, see e.g. N. A. M. Rodger, 'The Naval Service of the Cinque Ports', *EHR*, 111:442 (1996), 636–51, esp. p. 644; Ward, *Medieval Shipmaster*, p. 1 and *passim*; Maryanne Kowaleski, 'The Shipmaster as Entrepreneur in Medieval England', in *Commercial Activity, Markets and Entrepreneurs in the Middle Ages: Essays in Honour of Richard Britnell*, ed. Ben Dodds and Christian D. Liddy (Woodbridge, 2011), 165–82.

[6] I have found little material relating to the Dengie Peninsula, that is, the area around Southminster, the Crouch Estuary and Foulness in Essex, which as coastal marshes were probably not densely settled. There is also relatively less material on the north Norfolk coast, as some of this is held privately and difficult or impossible to access; on what can be reconstructed from printed sources, see Jonathan Hooton, *The Glaven Ports: A Maritime History of Blakeney, Cley and Wiveton in North Norfolk* (Blakeney, 1996). Apart from these lacunae, the only major coastal settlement for which I was unable to find local records was Brightlingsea, on the tip of the Colne Estuary, which was a member of the Cinque Ports of Kent and Sussex; the best monograph on the Cinque Ports is still K. M. E. Murray, *The Constitutional History of the Cinque Ports* (Manchester, 1935).

such as Orford, Harwich, and Maldon, was under the jurisdiction of Ipswich.[7] These groupings are useful because they reveal a contemporary understanding of the way in which different kinds of maritime community, from fishing villages and estuarial settlements to port towns and major cities fitted into broader socio-economic and political systems; and indeed, together they connected with much larger maritime networks across the whole eastern coast of Britain, and beyond into the North Sea.[8] This East Anglian case study thus provides a sense of the multiplicity of maritime communities, as well as helping us trace the characteristically transnational connections of the maritime world through a local context.

I proceed first by describing this world in more detail, focusing on the environmental, socio-economic, and demographic features that made its legal culture so distinctive. The second section traces the complex development of the various maritime legal traditions—the sea laws, the customary law maritime, and the admiralty—in late-medieval England, emphasizing the wide leeway that was left to shipmasters to define and interpret law and custom. The third section turns to examine the operations of local courts in maritime communities, showing how their routine processes worked to enshrine the interests of shipmasters in relation to the operation of the fishing industry, the flow of seaborne commerce, the gathering of shipwrecked goods, and the regulation of foreign merchants. The fourth section then turns to consider the legal discourses of expertise in maritime legal culture, drawing on three case studies to look in detail at how ideals of seaworthiness, skill, and obedience were used to frame problems of authority and accountability. The conclusion, finally, considers the localized maritime legal culture I sketch here in a wider perspective, looking at the overseas legal engagements of English maritime communities.

Maritime Communities in Late-Medieval England

What made a medieval community 'maritime'? This question is more difficult to answer than it may seem.[9] In fifteenth-century England not all coastal settlements

[7] See Map 19.1 in Maryanne Kowaleski, 'Port towns: England and Wales 1300–1540', in *The Cambridge Urban History of Britain*, ed. D. M. Palliser (Cambridge, 2000), 467–94 at p. 473.

[8] On East Anglian maritime communities, see the essays in *East Anglia and its North Sea World in the Middle Ages*, ed. David Bates and Robert Liddiard (Woodbridge, 2013); David Butcher, *Medieval Lowestoft: The Origins and Growth of a Suffolk Coastal Community* (Woodbridge, 2016). On the broader east-coast community: G. V. Scammell, 'English Merchant Shipping at the End of the Middle Ages: Some East Coast Evidence', *The Economic History Review*, n.s., 13:3 (1961), 327–41; S. H. Rigby, *Medieval Grimsby: Growth and Decline* (Hull, 1993), pp. 57–61. On broader networks, see E. M. Carus-Wilson and Olive Coleman, *England's Export Trade 1275–1547* (Oxford, 1963); Dorothy Burwash, *English Merchant Shipping 1460–1540* (Newton Abbot, 1969); John D. Fudge, *Cargoes, Embargoes, and Emissaries: The Commercial and Political Interaction of England and the German Hanse 1450–1510* (Toronto, 1995).

[9] For some consideration of this problem, see Robert Van de Noort, *North Sea Archaeologies: A Maritime Biography, 10,000 BC to AD 1500* (Oxford, 2011), pp. 1–20.

comprised maritime communities, and, conversely, many maritime communities, especially ports that lay upriver from an estuary, were actually located some distance from the sea.[10] But if physical proximity does not provide an easy definition, social geography was little more determinative. Even places possessed of an indisputably 'maritime' character—such as Ipswich, a customs headport with an extensive overseas trade and a ship proudly displayed on its communal seal—contained many people, probably a majority, who rarely concerned themselves directly with the business of the sea.[11] And not everyone with maritime connections necessarily lived in a maritime community: thus in 1401 John Reve, a villein of the manor of North Fambridge—on the Crouch Estuary some ten miles from the coast—was presented at the court there for apprenticing his son into 'the craft of seamanship, across the seas, without permission'.[12] Maritime networks, then, reached into late-medieval English society in diffuse ways.

Building upon Maryanne Kowaleski's pioneering work in this area, I therefore want to suggest that three key features combined to engender 'a distinct maritime sub-culture'.[13] In the first place, if maritime communities were not always physically proximate to the sea, they were almost always environmentally entwined with it. They existed in a variety of spaces: around harbours, coves, and havens for ships, beside the arterial estuaries which brought the brackish waters inland to towns, and along the shallow beaches, sands, and saltmarshes which littered the thinly populated coastal plains.[14] They were thus forged through their adaptations to the marine environment, and the manifold dangers it posed. Storms at sea not only caused the loss of countless seafarers, but occasionally large-scale inundation that reached far inland; East Anglia was afflicted by an especially bad series of floods in the late thirteenth and early fourteenth centuries.[15] Though rather less dramatic, coastal processes of sedimentation and erosion could be just as destructive, as navigable harbours and

[10] Maryanne Kowaleski, 'The Demography of Maritime Communities in Late Medieval England', in *Town and Countryside in the Age of the Black Death: Essays in Honour of John Hatcher*, ed. Mark Bailey and Stephen Rigby (Turnhout, 2012), 87–118, pp. 91–3.

[11] See Nicholas R. Amor, *Late Medieval Ipswich: Trade and Industry* (Woodbridge, 2011), pp. 103, 164, 207.

[12] ERO, D/DMj M2, m. 1r. The rolls of North Fambridge suggest no routine connection to the maritime world among the tenants.

[13] In what follows I am referring especially to Maryanne Kowaleski, 'Peasants and the Sea in Medieval England', in *Peasants and Lords in the Medieval English Economy: Essays in Honour of Bruce M. S. Campbell*, ed. Maryanne Kowaleski, John Langdon, and Phillipp R. Schofield (Turnhout, 2015) 353–76, at p. 354.

[14] On the landscape features of the North Sea region, see David Kirby and Merja-Liisa Hinkkanen, *The Baltic and the North Seas* (London, 2000), pp. 1–15.

[15] See Mark Bailey, 'Per impetum maris: natural disaster and economic decline in eastern England, 1275–1350', in *Before the Black Death: Studies in the 'crisis' of the early fourteenth century*, ed. Bruce M. S. Campbell (Manchester, 1991), 184–208; more generally, Bruce M. S. Campbell, 'Nature as a historical protagonist: environment and society in pre-industrial England', *Economic History Review*, 63:2 (2010), 281–314, pp. 293–4.

rivers silted into mudflats, or whole settlements gradually fell away into the sea, as in the famous case of Dunwich.[16]

But as well as posing dangers, the sea also created opportunities. In the second place, then, maritime communities, both urban and rural, were characterized by an economic reliance on the sea. First and foremost, this meant fishing, an activity in which maritime communities of all sizes were involved; expeditions took place during 'fares' or seasons throughout the year, varying according to the spawning seasons and seasonal weather conditions in different waters, and more generally to the demand for fish.[17] In the fifteenth century, larger seaports from Scarborough to Dunwich harboured the larger ships necessary for year-round expeditions, with months-long voyages for Iceland cod during the summer, and shorter local expeditions during the more dangerous winter months.[18] Fishing in such places constituted a major commercial industry, with special fairs organized to sell the millions upon millions of herring that were caught off East Anglia.[19] In coastal villages, by contrast, fishermen with rather smaller craft tended to fish just offshore during the summer, to supplement a living that was otherwise maintained by farming, small-scale artisan production, and recycling or reselling the shipwrecked goods that washed up.[20]

Alongside fishing, shipping and its associated industries provided an important source of employment. While East Anglian maritime communities certainly participated within long-distance commercial networks, much shipping took place within a dense meshwork of coastal shipping. In the area around late-medieval Exeter, localized coastal trade seems to have accounted for as much as 70 per cent of shipping activity.[21] Although such data has not been compiled for East Anglia, anecdotal evidence shows a similar picture; thus, for example, we can see how ports such as Great Yarmouth, Orwell Haven (by Ipswich), and Maldon were linked together by the regular shipments of coal from Newcastle to

[16] Roland Parker, *Men of Dunwich* (St. Albans, 1980).

[17] In general, see Maryanne Kowaleski, 'The Seasonality of Fishing in Medieval Britain', in *Ecologies and Economies in Medieval and Early Modern Europe*, ed. B. G. Scott (Leiden, 2010), 117–48.

[18] Peter Heath, 'North Sea Fishing in the Fifteenth Century', *Northern History*, 3 (1968), 53–69. On Dunwich, see *The Bailiff's Minute Book of Dunwich 1404–1430*, ed. Mark Bailey, Suffolk Records Society, 34 (Woodbridge, 1992), p. 16.

[19] See Maryanne Kowaleski, 'The Commercialization of the Sea Fisheries in Medieval England and Wales', *International Journal of Maritime History*, 15 (2003), 177–231.

[20] Mark Bailey, 'Coastal Fishing off South East Suffolk in the Century After the Black Death', *Proceedings of the Suffolk Institute of Archaeology and History*, 37 (1992), 102–14, p. 112; Harold Fox, *The Evolution of the Fishing Village: Landscape and Society along the South Devon Coast, 1086–1550* (Oxford, 2001), esp. Ch. 5, 'Fishing Farmers and Cellar Settlements', pp. 107–44; Tom Johnson, 'The economics of shipwreck in late-medieval East Anglia', in *Custom and Commercialization in Rural England, c.1350–1750: Revisiting Postan and Tawney*, ed. James Bowen and Alex Brown (Hertford, 2016), 121–38, pp. 131–2.

[21] Maryanne Kowaleski, *Local markets and regional trade in medieval Exeter* (Cambridge, 1995), p. 225.

London.[22] The economic specialization of maritime communities also bred onshore connections, as in the shipbuilding industry. When the Duke of Norfolk commissioned a state-of-the-art carrack in the 1460s, it was initially constructed at Dunwich, before being floated down to Orwell Haven for completion; by 1469 the finished ship was being used to protect a fleet of fishing boats comprising men from the smaller Suffolk ports of Walberswick, Southwold, Sizewell, and Easton Bavents, among others.[23]

These economic connections produced a distinctive maritime labour market. It was characterized by high interconnectivity between maritime communities; thus men from Dunningworth, an inland Suffolk village on a navigable river, moved to settlements including Southwold, Orford, Aldeburgh, Covehithe, Yarmouth, Ipswich, and Colchester.[24] Such migration was often cyclical, due to the extra volumes of labour required to process the major catches of the fishing fares; workers might thus travel substantial distances to perform this work. In the last decade of the fifteenth century, for example, John Mathew, a mariner of Winchelsea in East Sussex, journeyed all the way to Yarmouth in Norfolk, even though he intended to stay for just five weeks 'in the tyme of fysshyng'.[25] There is good evidence too that crewing of warships, whether in the course of official naval impressment or for more questionable ventures, brought together men from different communities, as for example when fishermen from Ipswich, Woodbridge, Sizewell, and beyond took part in the seizure of two Hanse ships off the Suffolk coast in 1404.[26] Mariners, fishermen, shipbuilders, and other maritime workers seem to have represented a distinctly mobile labour force, willing and able to travel to other places for work.

These patterns of economic activity, finally, helped to contribute to the third characteristic of maritime communities, in the form of their distinctive demographic features. To begin with, it is important to remark on the way in which these may have affected gender dynamics within these communities. The patterns of offshore maritime labour, in which substantial proportions of the working male population departed for days and sometimes weeks at a time, perhaps created

[22] TNA, C 1/15/160; NRO, Y/C 4/205, m. 4r; ERO, D/B3/1/2, f. 6r. Generally, see J. B. Blake, 'The medieval coal trade of North East England: some fourteenth-century evidence', *Northern History*, 2 (1967), 1–26.

[23] BL, Add. MS. 46349, ff. 37r–43v; Judith Middleton-Stewart, '"Down to the sea in ships": decline and fall on the Suffolk coast', in *Counties and Communities: Essays on East Anglian History Presented to Hassell Smith*, ed. Carole Rawcliffe, Roger Virgoe, and Richard Wilson (Norwich, 1996), 69–83, pp. 74–5. On the ship-building industry more generally, see Ian Friel, *The good ship: ships, shipbuilding and technology in England 1200–1520* (London, 1995).

[24] Mark Bailey, *Medieval Suffolk: An Economic and Social History 1200–1500* (Woodbridge, 2007), pp. 161–2.

[25] TNA, C 1/214/66. On the massive Yarmouth fishing industry, see Anthony Saul, 'The Herring Industry at Great Yarmouth, c. 1280–c. 1400', *Norfolk Archaeology*, 38 (1981), 33–43.

[26] For the 1404 case: *CCR*, 1402–5, pp. 428–30. For naval impressment, see e.g. *CPR*, 1374–7, p. 321; *CPR*, 1401–5, p. 318; *CPR*, 1408–13, p. 425. See also Graham Cushway, *Edward III and the War at Sea: The English Navy, 1327–1377* (Woodbridge, 2011), p. 16.

more economic responsibilities for women outside of the home, and there is evidence that they played an important part in curing of fish, mending nets, and preparing tackle.[27] Moreover, the higher male mortality rate characteristic of premodern maritime communities meant that widows of mariners were often granted effective control over substantial amounts of capital—in the form of boats, tackle, and equipment—relatively early in life.[28] These features may have created a society in which women were able to exercise more economic agency, but reflections of this in the legal record are notable by their general absence.[29]

Much more striking in the documentary record, however, is the extent of the foreign-born population in maritime communities, both urban and rural.[30] As well as acting as transient workers within the flexible maritime economy, many foreign residents sought to settle.[31] Some 54 per cent of Suffolk's foreign-born population in the fifteenth century lived on the coast, for example, with coastal settlements containing on average 9 aliens, compared to an average of 1.85 for inland locations.[32] The fact that it is possible to gauge this alien population at all—through administrative and tax records in particular—is indicative of its heightened regulation by central government. After the alliance between England and Burgundy broke down in the spring of 1436, an ordinance required all Flemings resident in England to take an oath of loyalty to the crown; this was followed in 1439 with a statute compelling aliens to lodge together under the supervision of an English host, and the first plans for the alien subsidies, taxes levied on foreign-born inhabitants throughout the latter half of the century.[33] As we shall see further on, there was a persistent concern in maritime communities that such foreigners ought to be loyal and carefully supervised—and, increasingly, to pay for this privilege.[34]

The large numbers of foreign-born people in maritime communities did not merely create suspicion, however, but also rather more subtle cultural effects, particularly perceptible in language. In the late fifteenth century, the purser of the

[27] Bailey, 'Coastal Fishing', p. 107.

[28] See Sheila Sweetinburgh, 'Strategies of inheritance among Kentish fishing communities in the later Middle Ages', *History of the Family*, 11 (2006), 93–105.

[29] Kowaleski, 'Demography of Maritime Communities', pp. 88–9. For such a case from Runton and Beeston (Norfolk), see NRO, WKC 2/166 398x7, m31r: Joan Tailor took a net called a twelvescore out of another man's messuage.

[30] In general, see Maryanne Kowaleski, '"Alien" Encounters'.

[31] Higher-status aliens sometimes sought to formalize their presence through the process of denization, on which see Bart Lambert and W. Mark Ormrod, 'Friendly Foreigners: International Warfare, Resident Aliens and the Early History of Denization in England, c.1250–c.1400', *EHR*, 130: 542 (2015), 1–24. For a case of an English child of a foreign artisan successfully vindicating his nationality in late fifteenth-century Colchester: ERO, D/B 5 R2, fos. 197v–199r.

[32] Kowaleski, 'Demography of Maritime Communities', p. 106.

[33] See the essays in *Resident Aliens in Later Medieval England*, ed. Mark Ormrod, Nicola McDonald, and Craig Taylor (Turnhout, 2017), especially J. L. Bolton, 'London and the Anti-Alien Legislation of 1439–40', 33–47. This volume came from an AHRC-funded project 'England's Immigrants 1330–1550: Resident Aliens in the Late Middle Ages', which built a website that allows the subsidy data to be analysed in many ways: see https://www.englandsimmigrants.com (accessed January 21, 2019).

[34] This attitude had a longer history: Bart Lambert and W. Mark Ormrod, 'A matter of trust: the royal regulation of England's French residents during wartime, 1294–1377', *Historical Research*, 89:244 (2016), 208–26.

Bristol ship the *Trinity*, which travelled to Spain, seemed perfectly comfortable using loanwords such as *corretáge*, a brokerage fee, and *contador*, a bookkeeper, in his accounts.[35] This cosmopolitan culture was not confined to large port cities, however; the fishermen of the villages of Sizewell and Thorpe on the Suffolk coast, who collected goods washed up on their beaches or dragged up in their nets, recognized finds such as 'osmond'—Swedish iron—and 'regalbourd'—timber from Riga.[36] The distinctive occupational jargon that permeated maritime work both at sea and on land seems to have been highly amenable to such influences.[37] English mariners had regular cause to communicate with foreign counterparts among their crewmates and on vessels they encountered at sea, and it is possible that there was some kind of maritime patois with basic mutual interpretability for crews across the seas of north-western Europe.[38]

In sum, maritime communities in late-medieval England were characterized by a set of widely shared and interconnected features: their vulnerability and adaptation to the precariousness and the opportunities of the marine environment, their economic reliance on fishing, seaborne trade, and associated industries, and their peculiar demographic patterns, in particular the great degree of seasonal movement in maritime labour and the presence of a particularly large foreign-born population. These features helped to produce a maritime subculture that was at once heterogeneous and coherent, localized but highly connected and outward-looking, with a clear sense of its difference from, and value to, inland society.[39] Contoured by the unpredictability, mobility, and transnationality of living and working with the seascape, maritime communities required their own distinctive modes of law; there was, however, rather little consensus in the Middle Ages about what forms these ought to take. It is to these distinctive and contested legal traditions that we now turn.

Maritime Legal Traditions: The Rôles d'Oléron, the Law Maritime, and the Admiralty

In this section I want to focus on the three main strands of maritime legal development in the Middle Ages. The sea law known as the Rôles d'Oléron, the

[35] *The Accounts of John Balsall, Purser of the Trinity of Bristol 1480–1*, ed. T. F. Reddaway and Alwyn A. Ruddock, Camden Miscellany 23, 4th series, 7 (London, 1969), pp. 21–2.

[36] SROI, HD 371/1, mm. 1v, 11r.

[37] See William Sayers, 'Some International Nautical Etymologies', *Mariner's Mirror*, 88:4 (2002), 405–22; David Trotter, 'Oceano vox: You never know where a ship comes from. On multilingualism and language-mixing in medieval Britain', in *Aspects of Multilingualism in European Language History*, ed. Kurt Braunmüller and Gisella Ferraresi (Amsterdam, 2003), 15–34.

[38] Possibly with a matrix language of French, as suggested in Kowaleski, 'The French of England', p. 112.

[39] See, for example, Susan Rose, 'The Value of the Cinque Ports to the Crown, 1200–1500', in *Roles of the Sea in Medieval England*, ed. Richard Gorski (Woodbridge, 2012), 41–57.

'law maritime' that was used in local port courts, and the jurisdiction of the admiralty all emerged between the late thirteenth and mid-fourteenth centuries, a time when the governance of the sea took on a particular importance in the context of sustained naval conflict between England and other European powers.[40] The interaction of these different institutions was complex. While the Rôles d'Oléron and the law maritime were understood to constitute customary traditions, by the fifteenth century the admiralty claimed that they fell within its scope; meanwhile, the centralized office of the admiralty was consistently resisted both by local authorities and nationally in parliament, and yet admiralty jurisdiction was frequently exercised in port courts as a judicial franchise. In what follows, I trace each of them in turn, showing how the fluidity of these jurisdictional arrangements left open the possibility for negotiation on the ground, allowing local courts substantial leeway in articulating 'maritime custom'.

To begin with, the Rôles d'Oléron were a maritime law-code, said to be derived from a series of 'judgments of the sea' that were given on the island of Oléron, just off the coast of La Rochelle.[41] The text comprises a set of articles—the number of which varies substantially between copies—which provide general conventions for the negotiation of various nautical disputes, such as ship collision, the jettison of cargo, and discipline aboard the ship; almost all of them concerned the relationships between the shipmaster, the crew, and the merchants whose goods were being transported.[42] Though the origins of the Rôles are cloudy and much disputed among historians, the text is clearly concerned with the wine trade between Gascony, Normandy, and England, suggesting a connection with English interests; indeed, the earliest surviving manuscripts of the text come from English town books at the turn of the fourteenth century.[43] If it had a geographically specific origin, however, it was considered to have a

[40] On the development of the concept of sovereignty over the sea, see Thomas K. Heebøll-Holm, 'Law, order and plunder at sea: a comparison of England and France in the fourteenth century', *Continuity and Change*, 32:1 (2017), 37–58. On the navy generally, see Cushway, *Edward III and the War at Sea*; also useful are J. W. Sherborne, 'The Hundred Years War: the English navy: shipping and manpower 1369–1389', *P&P*, 37 (1967), 163–75; Ian Friel, 'Oars, sails and guns: The English and War at Sea, *c.*1200–*c.*1500', in *War at Sea in the Middle Ages and Renaissance*, ed. John B. Hattendorf and Richard W. Unger (Woodbridge, 2003), 69–79.

[41] The best brief introduction (placing them in a European context) is Edda Frankot, 'Medieval Maritime Law from Oléron to Wisby: Jurisdictions in the Law of the Sea', in *Communities in European history: representations, jurisdictions, conflicts*, ed. Juan Pan-Montojo and Frederik Pedersen (Pisa, 2007), 151–172, pp. 152–3.

[42] For a useful transcription, translation, and commentary of the Laws, see Ward, *Medieval Shipmaster*, Appendix 1, pp. 183–205. The original Liber Horn text consisted of twenty-four articles, but copies varied to include as many as forty-seven. For a facing translation of the Laws, (one in the Anglo-Norman and the other in Middle English), see *The Black Book of the Admiralty*, ed. T. Twiss (4 vols; London, 1871–6), i, pp. 88–131.

[43] On these early manuscript witnesses, see Maryanne Kowaleski, 'The French of England', pp. 103–5. On the contested origins of the Rôles, see fn. 2 above.

rather wider relevance, as the text was circulated throughout England, Scotland, France, and Flanders in the later Middle Ages.[44]

Perhaps more significant than the precise genealogy of the Rôles, however, are the claims that contemporaries made about it. In 1329, with England and France on the cusp of war, the English government compiled a dossier known as the *Fasciculus de Superioritate Maris* to press their claims of jurisdiction over the Channel. This included the assertion that the Rôles had been instituted by Richard I in 1189, in order 'to conserve peace and justice between people of all nations passing by the sea of England'.[45] While few historians now take this genealogy seriously, it seems to suggest that proprietorship of the Rôles constituted an impressive claim of sovereignty in the midst of foreign conflict—one that was often framed, in fact, in terms of justice and jurisdiction.[46] Indeed, a little later the French crown made its own attempt to draw on the Oléron brand, as in an *ordonnance* of 1364 Charles V of France allowed Castilian merchants to sue in the court of Harfleur according to 'the custom of the sea and the laws of Oléron'.[47] The name of Oléron was clearly thought by governments to carry some weight in the maritime world, and thus they sought to draw on its authority as their own.

Indeed, in England attempts were made to renew and revise the Rôles in the late fourteenth century in the context of reforms to the admiralty (discussed later in this chapter), but also because of changing labour relations after the Black Death, as mariners began to bargain more staunchly over their wages.[48] In 1375, a judicial commission known as the Inquisition of Queenborough was summoned to establish points of maritime custom and practice 'as they have been used in ancient times'.[49] Under the presidency of the Warden of the Cinque Ports and the Admiral of the North, a jury of shipmasters testified to eighteen articles, all of which concerned the wages and conditions of mariners; half of them, in fact,

[44] See Edda Frankot, 'Medieval Maritime Law and its Practice in the Towns of Northern Europe: a Comparison by the example of Shipwreck, Jettison and Ship Collision', PhD thesis, Aberdeen (2004), pp. 11–24; also Michel Mollat, *La Vie Quotidienne Des Gens de Mer en Atlantique IXe–XVIe siècle* (Paris, 1983), p. 87.

[45] TNA, C 47/32/19/1: 'ordinata ad conservandum pacem et justitiam inter omnes gentes nationis cuiuscunque per mare Anglie transeuntes'. For a useful summary of Anglo-French relations at this time, see John Maddicott, 'The Origins of the Hundred Years War', in *England in Europe, 1066–1453*, ed. Nigel Saul (New York, 1994), 133–43, esp. pp. 140–2.

[46] Cf. Runyan, 'The Roles of Oleron and the Admiralty Court', p. 98; Ward, *Medieval Shipmaster*, pp. 29–30.

[47] Frankot, 'Medieval Maritime Law and its Practice', p. 21, fn. 59.

[48] Maryanne Kowaleski, 'Working at Sea: Maritime Recruitment and Remuneration in Medieval England', in *Ricchezza del Mare, Ricchezza dal Mare. Secoli XIII–XVIII*, ed. Simonetta Cavaciocchi (2 vols., Florence, 2006), ii, 907–36, at p. 924. See the 1378 ordinance against mariners who deserted after taking wages for serving in the navy: *SR*, ii, p. 9 [2 Ric. II, Stat 1, c. 4]; and the petition of English shipowners in 1390 claiming that mariners, in 'close confederacy and all together', were demanding too much for wages: *PROME*, ed. Given-Wilson, vii, p. 187.

[49] Ward, *Medieval Shipmaster*, p. 23.

simply set rates of hire between London and other European ports.[50] But, interestingly, the shipmasters themselves invoked the Rôles, as they answered to the sixteenth article (concerning the right of pilotage, a fee owed to the ship's navigator) that 'they knew no better opinion or remedy than that contained in the law of Oléron'.[51] The Inquisition thus seems to represent yet another attempt to associate new measures of governance with the legitimacy of a traditional name.

Something of this legitimacy can be discerned from the fact that maritime litigants themselves invoked Oléron, in ways that bore only a tangential relation to the legal substance of its articles.[52] Thus a 1439 agreement to charter a London ship bound both parties 'according to the law of Oléron', and a judgment on an assault committed at sea before an admiralty court in 1446 was given 'according to the form of the statute of Oléron', despite the fact that the articles do not clearly contain provisions for such matters.[53] To construe the meaning of the Rôles d'Oléron in terms of its substantive rules or practical uses, then, is to misunderstand its importance. Rather, it ought to be understood in a similar manner to that which Andy Wood has suggested for custom, as having 'constituted a discursive field within which conflicts could be fought out'.[54] Shipmasters, mariners, and merchants were aware of a distinctive set of maritime legal conventions, the substance and interpretation of which was up for debate in a given dispute; but by designating these as 'the law of Oléron', they were not only making an appeal to a well-known, authoritative emblem, but also making a kind of jurisdictional claim, asserting that an issue ought to be understood within the context of maritime legal culture.

In a similar way, but far more frequently mentioned in the adjudication of maritime pleas before local courts, was the customary 'law maritime' (*lex maritima*). It bore a strong relation to the law merchant, or *lex mercatoria*, that was used in pie-powder and market courts, as we saw in Chapter 2.[55] Just as merchant pleas were heard during the hours of the market, so maritime pleas were to be

[50] *Black Book*, ed. Twiss, i, pp. 133–47. A further ten articles on the judicial privileges and duties of the admiral were added sometime after 1422: i, pp. 169–73.

[51] Ibid., p. 142: '... ne scayvent meilleur advys ne remedie mais que ce soit desoer usez et fait par manere quest contenue en le loy Doleron.'

[52] See the much cited case of Pilk c. Venere, heard in the Bristol Tolsey-court in 1339 'according to the law of Oléron, and the law of the realm'; the plaintiff posited that a shipmaster was responsible for a trespass committed by his servant, a principle that is not clear within the articles of the Oléron text. However, this case is complicated by the fact that it has survived only because it was appealed to the royal Chancery, and indeed the quoted text was interpellated in the writ. Ward has called it 'an important case without satisfactory conclusion or explanation': *Medieval Shipmaster*, p. 18. For a transcription and translation of the case, see *Select cases concerning the Law Merchant. Vol. II: Central courts, A.D. 1239–1633*, ed. Hubert Hall, Selden Society 46 (London, 1930), pp. xcv–xcvi; *Black Book*, ed. Twiss, iii, p. xii.

[53] Respectively see *CCR*, 1435–41, p. 287; *Black Book*, ed. Twiss, pp. 252–3.

[54] Andy Wood, *The Memory of the People: Custom and Popular Senses of the Past in Early Modern England* (Cambridge, 2013), p. 13. However, Oléron was emphatically distinguished from 'custom' in a Commons petition of 1402: see fn. 69 below.

[55] See Chapter 2, pp. 62, 67.

heard 'from tide to tide'; both law merchant and law maritime heard pleas between residents and strangers, used the same expedited procedures, and took the same common-law plea forms (debt, account, broken contract, trespass).[56] In one unusual case of 1314, moreover, the two laws were even considered complementary, with royal justices ordered to resolve the issue 'according to the law and custom of the realm, law merchant and maritime law, as far as they shall be necessary or useful'.[57] But while the law merchant was the subject of a learned treatise, and even officially incorporated into English law in 1353, 'law maritime' was never formally codified.[58] Its customary nature was perhaps understood to be one of its virtues, as it was cited as a means of enabling equitable justice.[59]

For all that it remained unformulated, however, the law maritime was often mentioned explicitly in the port courts of late-medieval East Anglia.[60] These courts operated in coastal settlements of all sizes, from the customary Hethewardmote of the fishing villages Sizewell and Thorpe in Suffolk, and the 'port court' at Shipden held for the Glaven ports in Norfolk, to the 'court for maritime law' in Ipswich, and the 'water court' of the major port city of Lynn.[61] In larger maritime towns, then, these designated forums for interpersonal litigation 'according to maritime law' existed among the broader array of urban jurisdictions, while in smaller settlements, maritime pleas were often integrated into manorial courts or

[56] See *Select Pleas in the Court of Admiralty*, Vol. I, ed. R. G. Marsden, Selden Society 6 (London, 1892), p. xiii; Charles Donahue, Jr, 'Medieval and Early Modern *Lex mercatoria*: An Attempt at the *probatio diabolica*', *Chicago Journal of International Law*, 5:1 (2004), 21–42. For an early use of the phrase 'tide to tide', see the 1234 customs of Wainfleet (Lincs.), in *The Medieval Lindsey Marsh: select documents*, ed. A. E. B. Owen (Woodbridge, 1996), pp. 131–4. It is worth noting, however, that these customs are recorded the Pinchbeck Register of the abbey of Bury St Edmunds, which was begun after 1333; see also the description of port courts hearing pleas tide-to-tide according to 'la ley marine', in the so-called 'Ipswich Domesday' of c.1300, which claimed to be based on a set of much older usages: *Black Book*, ed. Twiss, ii, pp. 22–3.

[57] *CPR*, 1313–17, pp. 147–8. This intriguing case also uses a 'mixed jury' of merchants and mariners.

[58] For the academic treatise, see *Lex Mercatoria and Legal Pluralism: A Late Thirteenth-Century Treatise and Its Afterlife*, ed. and transl., Mary Elizabeth Basile, Jane Fair Bestor, Daniel R. Coquillette, and Charles Donahue, Jr (Cambridge, MA, 1998); a more accessible translation can be found in Paul R. Teetor, 'England's Earliest Treatise on the Law Merchant: the Essay on Lex Mercatoria from The Little Red Book of Bristol (Circa 1280 AD)', *The American Journal of Legal History*, 6:2 (1962), 178–210. On the judicial records, see J. H. Baker, 'The Law Merchant and the Common Law Before 1700', *Cambridge Law Journal*, 38:2 (1979), p. 300, fn. 25. For the Statute of of the Staple: 27 Edw. III, stat. 2: *SR*, ii, pp. 332–43, esp. at p. 336. See also the earlier Carta Mercatoria of 1303: see Keechang Kim, *Aliens in Medieval Law: The Origins of Modern Citizenship* (Cambridge, 2000), pp. 37–40.

[59] *Select cases concerning the Law Merchant*, ed. Hall, pp. xxx–xxxi.

[60] Port courts were almost always deliberately distinguished from the market, fair, and pie-powder courts discussed in Chapter 2: in Ipswich, this division is made clear in the fifteenth-century translation of the borough's customs: BL, Add. MS. 25011, f. 3r; in Colchester, see the roll ERO, D/B5/Cr69, which has been transcribed in *Select Cases Concerning the Law Merchant, 1270–1638. Vol. I: Local Courts*, ed. C. Gross, Selden Society 23 (London, 1908), pp. 122–5. Cf. two pie-powder court sessions at Orford in 1468–9 which heard maritime pleas, though the town's leet normally incorporated maritime business: SROI, HD64/1/21.

[61] For the Hethewardmote, see B. Schofield, 'Wreck Rolls of Leiston Abbey'; for the rolls, see SROI, HD 371/1–3; HD 1032/86–8; for Shipden, see NRO, NRS 3360, 13C6 and TNA, SC 2/194/4–6; for the Ipswich court, SROI, C/2/10/3/2, p. 130, C/2/10/3/5, pp. 119–20, 398–9; and for Lynn, TNA SC 2/193/53.

leets as a part of regular sessions. Indeed, it is important to emphasize that the law maritime was often blurred together with other conventions in these courts, as, for example, when three local mariners were presented at the Colchester local admiralty court for using dragnets in the Colne Estuary 'against the law maritime, and that of England'.[62] The 'law maritime' in these local courts, then, was less a body of substantive rules than a way of appealing—not unlike references to the law of Oléron—to a set of expectations and conventions in relation to maritime pleas.

In the later fourteenth century, however, the English government made attempts to bring the 'law maritime' under tighter control through the institution of the admiralty. Before 1350, admirals were naval officials whose duties related largely to administrative and military affairs, though sometimes they had been required to hold inquisitions or to act in a judicial capacity in delegated tribunals.[63] But during the 1350s the admiralty accrued much wider judicial powers, and no later than 1360 seems to have established its own court.[64] As early as 1361, it was defending its jurisdiction against royal justices, demanding in a case of piracy that 'felonies, trespasses and wrongs committed at sea should be brought before the king's admirals and terminated according to the law maritime'.[65] This bullishness continued over several decades, as the admiralty began to claim jurisdiction over interpersonal pleas between merchants and mariners, threatening grave punishments for those who tried to have maritime cases heard at common law.[66] But its jurisdiction was far from clear, as the crown continued to issue commissions to redress piracy claims to royal justices and, of course, in 1375 attempted to codify maritime law and custom in the Inquisition of Queenborough.[67]

Concern over the extent of admiralty jurisdiction came to a head in the parliaments of 1390 and 1391, when the Commons complained that the admiral was overreaching his jurisdiction, and demanded a clarification of his powers. In the latter case, the king responded that while the admiral should have no jurisdiction over matters 'touching the body of the counties, whether at land or at sea', nor cognizance of shipwreck, he was empowered to hear criminal offences committed

[62] ERO, D/B 5/R2, f. 215r.

[63] Ward, *Medieval Shipmaster*, pp. 29–36; see also the earlier office, 'the keeper of the coast': see R. G. Marsden, 'The Vice-Admirals of the Coast', *EHR*, 22:87 (1907), 468–77, pp. 470–1.

[64] *Select Pleas in the Court of Admiralty*, ed. Marsden, pp. xiv–xliii.

[65] *CCR*, 1360–4, p. 265.

[66] For example, *CCR*, 1364–9, p. 458; also *Black Book*, ed. Twiss, i, pp. 68–9 [articles 20 and 21]; pp. 82–3 [article 35]. This evidence, which Twiss tentatively dates to 1360–9, is suspect, and seems to be a compilation of older material with additions that were designed to appear old (but betray themselves by anachronism): see ibid., pp. xxxii–xxxiv, xliv–xlvi. In the context of this jurisdictional conflict, it seems possible to read this confusion as the product of a deliberate campaign of obfuscation aimed at a maximalist assertion of the admiralty's powers.

[67] Ward, *Medieval Shipmaster*, p. 38. These commissions, interestingly, instructed royal justices to follow maritime law, in ways that would not prejudice the office of admiralty. On the Inquisition of Queenborough, see fn. 49 above.

at sea, and as far inland as the first bridge of a navigable river.[68] But the Commons, having gone that far, sought to capitalize further; in the parliament of September 1402, they requested that the admirals ought to 'exercise their laws solely according to the law of Oléron and the ancient laws of the sea, and by the law of England, and not by custom, nor by any other manner'.[69] Testament though it is to the continued allure of the name of Oléron, this particular request was denied by the king. Arguments over admiralty jurisdiction thus rattled on through the first decade of the fifteenth century, with further complaints in 1410 that the admiral was hearing pleas outside his powers, and forcing people to travel to his court in Southwark.[70]

It is from this time, in fact, that we have the first working records of the central admiralty court, during the office of Thomas Beaufort (Admiral of the North and West from 1408), and it seems to have been extensive.[71] As well as the 'principal court' (*curia principalis*) held at a quay in Southwark, the admiralty had deputies operating throughout the south coast, and another permanent court at a quay in Bristol.[72] The central admiralty court heard pleas 'touching the maritime law', in cases of trespass, broken contract, debt, and detention of chattels, drawing extensively upon the highly technical procedural apparatus of Roman law.[73] This resulted in a reliance on notaries and other ecclesiastical officials with the requisite expertise in civilian procedures and forms; thus the proctor general of the Norwich Consistory was commissioned to undertake an admiralty inquiry, and he in turn appointed a public notary to conduct the hearing.[74] As well as civil pleas, the admiralty also investigated criminal matters at sea, such as shipboard

[68] *PROME*, iii, p. 291: '. . . quereles, et toutes autres choses faitz ou sourdantz deinz les corps de countees, sibien par terre come par eawe . . . la court de l'admiralle eit nulle manere conissance'; 15 Ric. II. c. 5. See also 14 Ric. II c. 3; *SR*, ii, pp. 77–9.

[69] *PROME*, iii, pp. 472, 498.

[70] Ibid., p. 641. These complaints were related in part to the admiralty of John Holand, the Earl of Huntingdon: see Ward, *Medieval Shipmaster*, pp. 39–41.

[71] On Beaufort: *CPR*, 1405–8, p. 467. The text of the commission specifically mentions the earlier statutory restrictions on the admiral's jurisdiction. Beaufort had been admiral of the west since 1403; see *Select Pleas in the Court of Admiralty*, ed. Marsden, p. li. Evidence for the workings of the administration has survived only because it was copied into a formulary in the mid-fifteenth century: *Black Book*, ed. Twiss, i, Appendix 1, pp. 347–92; they are contained in BL, Cotton Vespasian B. 22, ff. 64–90. The first documents in the set are not dated, and omit the full names of people and places, as a formulary; some of the later documents, however, are dated to the period between 1410 and 1412.

[72] See *Black Book*, ed. Twiss, i, Appendix 1, pp. 347–53 [Southwark and south coast]; pp. 359–60 [a session held at Bristol].

[73] For the pleas, see respectively, ibid., pp. 348–9, 350, 350–1, 351. On the civil procedure, see Ward, *Medieval Shipmaster*, pp. 28, 30, 35. For examples of civil procedure from Beaufort's time, see *Black Book*, ed. Twiss, i, pp. 351, 362 [citations]; 366–8 [letters of proxy for proctors]; 373 [notarial attestation]. This association of admiralty procedure with civil law stretches back into the muddy waters of the mid-fourteenth century: see L. H. Laing 'Historic Origins of Admiralty Jurisdiction in England', *Michigan Law Review*, 45:2 (1946), 163–182.

[74] SROI, SC18/40, mm. 1r–2r. For the elaborate notarial mark of William Neve (beloved grammar-school teacher of Matthew Parker, the future archbishop of Canterbury), see m. 6r.

discipline and piracy, both *ex officio* and under specific commissions from the crown, throughout the fifteenth century.[75]

At the same time, however, another means of avoiding the admiralty was found, as port towns began to secure exemption from the interference of the admiral in their charters of liberties from the crown.[76] This privilege, in fact, was widely interpreted as according the right to hold their own admiralty courts; records from Ipswich, Dunwich, and Colchester in the later fifteenth century show these tribunals in action, concerned with the public and criminal side of admiralty business, with interpersonal pleas according to maritime law reserved to their port courts.[77] The admiral's deputies continued to hold regular sessions in some localities, but they did so in places without the strong liberties necessary to fend off such jurisdictional claims; interestingly, in both the small port of Shipden in Norfolk, and in the hundred of Kessingland in Suffolk, these sessions provided a forum not only for criminal business, but also for interpersonal pleas heard according to law maritime.[78] Admiralty jurisdiction, therefore, seems to have achieved some local purchase when it was farther removed from the central admiralty administration.

These different traditions of maritime law in late-medieval England thus developed in complex interrelation to one another, with frequent contestations over the extent of their role in maritime governance. This had two important consequences. In the first place, it left open the possibility of challenging the jurisdiction of legal institutions that claimed to use these traditions. This was particularly the case with the interference of the central office of admiralty in local maritime pleas, but was also occasionally manifested through appeals, to the royal

[75] Crown-commissioned inquiries into maritime affairs were directed to the admiral and his officials, but also to local authorities E.g. SROI, C/2/6/2; *CPR*, 1467–77, p. 605; *Black Book*, ed. Twiss, i, pp. 362–5; N. A. M. Rodger, *The Safeguard of the Sea: A Naval History of Britain, Vol. I, 660–1649* (London, 1997), p. 149; Ward, *Medieval Shipmaster*, pp. 33–40.

[76] Marsden, 'Vice-Admirals', p. 472. Bristol, Boston, Dartmouth, Grimsby, Hull, Lyme Regis, Newcastle, Poole, Southampton, Tynemouth, and Weymouth all did the same. For an example of a landowner obtaining similar exemption, see the grant to Margaret, the king's consort, in *CPR*, 1452–61, pp. 115–6. Colchester copied many of these statutes, alongside its charters, into its civic books: ERO, D/B 5 R1, fos. 21r–22r; D/B 5 R2, fos. 16r, 21r–v, 26r.

[77] Respectively: [Ipswich] SROI, C/2/10/3/6, p. 140; C/2/10/3/7, p.18; C/2/10/3/8, pp. 391, 394; [Dunwich] BL, Add. Ch. 40733; [Colchester] ERO, D/B5/R2, ff. 213r–217r. It should be noted, however, that earlier in the fifteenth century, Colchester seems to have exercised some admiralty rights through its borough leet court: e.g. ERO, D/B5/Cr69, m. 20r. Yarmouth, Orford, and Harwich, like Colchester, evidently exercised admiralty-type rights within their borough courts. See respectively: [Yarmouth] NRO, Y/C 4/161–223; [Orford] SROI, HD64/1/12–29; [Harwich] ERO, D/B4/38/7–11. Marsden notes that explicit grants of admiralty jurisdiction were made to Yarmouth, Dartmouth, and Rochester: *Select Pleas in the Court of Admiralty*, ed. Marsden, pp. xiii–xiv.

[78] For sessions from Shipden, see *Black Book*, ed. Twiss, i, pp. 246–75. Though the jurisdictional divide is not clear, Shipden also held a port court in the early fifteenth century: NRO, NRS 3360, 13C6; TNA, SC 2/194/4–6. The admiralty courts at Kessingland, a royal hundred, were under the jurisdiction of the 'admiral of the lord king' (curia admiralius domini regis), and bound together with the rolls of the hundred court there. See SROL, 194/B1/6–9; also, David Butcher, *Lowestoft, 1550–1750: Development and Change in a Suffolk Coastal Town* (Woodbridge, 2008).

Chancery or the admiralty, against the decisions of local port courts when they made judgments according to maritime law.[79] In the second place, it meant that the scope and logic of what contemporaries understood by maritime law and custom—whether it went by the name of 'Oléron', the provisions of admiralty jurisdiction, or the customary 'law maritime'—was open to considerable interpretation. As we shall see in the following section, this scope left plenty of leeway for shipmasters to pursue their own agendas within the local institutions of maritime governance.

Shipmasters in the Local Courts: Fishing, Wreck, Trade, and Foreigners

Local courts in maritime communities took many different forms, including customary port courts, admiralty tribunals, as well as both urban and rural leets that exercised different maritime jurisdictions. Despite this formal variation, however, they tended to focus on very similar concerns: the control of fishing, the administration of shipwreck, the regulation of trade, and the governance of foreign-born residents. These concerns, of course, reflected the distinctive socio-economic characteristics of maritime communities that we examined in the first section of this chapter. But, as we shall see in what follows, the way in which these issues were pursued in the courts often helped to enshrine the particular interests of shipmasters, who, as the paradigmatic experts of the maritime world, were accorded particular prominence in the operation of the courts, in reporting information, in policing the traffic of goods and people, and in making judgments in disputes.

Shipmasters did not represent a coherent class or occupational group. Some owned their own vessels as small-scale entrepreneurs, while others worked for hire at the behest of shipowners; some were manifestly part of a social and political elite, while others seem to have been particularly experienced mariners who traded on their skills and contacts.[80] But, regardless of this relative socio-economic diversity, they were given an utterly crucial role in the administration of law; as Maryanne Kowaleski has written, 'no other occupational group was so often recognised or relied upon by the crown and parliament for their informed

[79] For complaints of interference, see the complaint of a Yarmouth man impleaded before the admiral: NRO, Y/C 4/223, m. 13r; a shipmaster of Thorpe (Suffolk) presented for vexatiously suing his fellows in the admiral's court: SROI, HD 1032/87, m. 7r. For appeals out of local maritime courts, see Pilk c. Venere (fn. 52 above): *Select cases concerning the Law Merchant*, ed. Hall, pp. xcv–xcvi; in a case of 1383 a defendant in a maritime court in Padstow (Cornwall) insisted that only 'the court or jurisdiction of the admiralty' was competent to hear his case: TNA, KB 27/491, m. 51r–v.

[80] Generally, see Ward, *Medieval Shipmaster*, pp. 48–68; also *Minute Book of Dunwich*, ed. Bailey, p. 18.

expertise as were shipmasters'.[81] The same might well be said of their role within the maritime courts, where they were required to report catches, shipwrecks, and discipline aboard ships, and to judge in pleas before the tribunals. In return, they were given licence to interpret maritime law and custom in ways that benefited their own interests—as commercial fishermen, as employers of crews, and as agents in the coastal shipping trade.

To begin with, the ecology of maritime landscapes represented a major source of concern before the local courts, which were utilized to protect the interests of professional seafarers in several different ways. In the first place, access to maritime resources was restricted through the control of space. The mid-fifteenth-century treatise *De Officio Admirallitatis* asserted that, at least for the purpose of building fish-weirs, 'the saltwater ought to be common to all'.[82] Though there were substantial profits to be made from such weirs and other devices, this idea of commonality—much like the idea of the 'common street' that we encountered in Chapter 2—was used to justify restrictive regulations.[83] Thus, for example, the jury of Colchester admiralty court presented the Abbot of St. John's for blocking the Colne Estuary with 'stakes and palisades of oak in the town's waters, between Last Hill and the crane there on both sides of the channel... so that mariners with their ships and boats have not been able to pass the aforesaid place without grave danger'.[84] Drawing on this idea of the 'common' river, then, maritime juries attempted to claim it for their own uses above others.

The right to exploit fishing resources was subject to similar protectionist impulses, which were manifested in the courts very frequently in a concern to preserve fish populations.[85] Such concern was based upon an ecological sensibility that if juvenile fish—known in the records as 'fry' or 'broods'—were caught before they could reproduce, then the sustainability of fish stocks would be imperilled.[86] This idea was often used as a justification for punishing the use of dragnets and other bottom-trawling devices, as they were understood to destroy the brood; at the Yarmouth leet, a remarkable range of specialized vocabulary was employed in presentments against 'grangyngnetts', 'nawestelnetts', 'groundnettes', 'settenetts', 'seynes', and simply, 'illicit nets' in the Yare.[87] Such methods tended to be used by small-scale fishers or those who practised it as a by-employment in estuarial rivers, harbours, and other inland waters; in the 1370s, it was even claimed that

[81] Kowaleski, 'Shipmaster as Entrepreneur', p. 181.

[82] *Black Book*, ed. Twiss, i, pp. 233–4.

[83] Bailey, *Medieval Suffolk*, p. 155. See Chapter 2, pp. 81–2.

[84] ERO, D/B5/R2, f. 213r. The clashes between the Colchester civic authorities and the abbey frequently centred on its water-mills: see Richard Britnell, *Growth and decline in Colchester, 1300–1525* (Cambridge, 1986), pp. 20–1, 30–1; ERO, D/B5/R2, ff. 45v–46v, 67r–75v [compilations of presentments against the Abbot].

[85] Bailey, 'Coastal Fishing', pp. 109–10; Fox, *Fishing Village*, pp. 47–83.

[86] Kowaleski, 'Seasonality of Fishing', p. 132.

[87] NRO, Y//C 4/161, m16r; Y/C 4/167, m. 21r; Y/C 4/170, m. 20r; Y/C 4/175, m. 14r; Y/C 4/178, m. 16r.

agricultural labourers were turning to fishing in this manner because it offered lucrative wages.[88]

In a similar way, maritime courts also worked to restrict customary rights to the mussels and oysters that could be gleaned from tidal inlets.[89] As a bill from a jurisdictional dispute over an area near the Blyth Estuary in Suffolk rehearsed in the middle of the fifteenth century: 'it hath ever be used that whanne ony such fortune of muskelys happed to bedde in ony parte of the seid port [men of many nearby towns]...have used to come theder & fecch of them & bere them a wey...which haue ben & yet is to the grette comfort & releff of the kyngs pore pepill'.[90] In the local courts, however, such practices were routinely fined; thus men of Fingringhoe, Arlesford, and Rowhedge, on the Colne Estuary in Essex, were repeatedly presented at Colchester for 'dragging for oysters in the common river, at an inappropriate time'.[91] At Orford in 1461 the leet even made an 'ordinance and statute' to ban dredging for oysters or other fish, unless outside 'the latitude of the golden noble', a local place name which delimited the harbour—in essence restricting local fishing to those who had seaworthy boats.[92] Through appeals to the preservation of fish stocks, then, local courts attempted to control the access of poor people to maritime resources.

Responsibility for the regulation of sea fishing, by contrast, was left to the shipmaster of each boat, who was required to report his haul for taxation within various 'dole' systems. Calculated *pro rata* according to the size of the catch and the annual price of fish, at Dunwich the town dole was worth as much as £10 a year to the corporation's finances in the early fifteenth century, and at Yarmouth anyone who failed to pay was to be imprisoned until they did.[93] These dole systems were administered by men prominent in the fishing industry; at Walberswick, for example, the tithe on fish known as 'Christ's dole', was apprised by churchwardens who themselves both owned and captained fishing boats.[94] Shipmasters were also responsible for reporting those parts of the catch which could not be sold: animals classed as 'royal fish', such as whales, porpoises, dolphins, sturgeon, and conger eels, formed part of the royal prerogative, and had to be rendered—normally to local lords who held this right as a franchise. At Sizewell

[88] Bailey, 'Coastal Fishing', p. 110.

[89] On the gleaning right: Wood, *Memory of the People*, pp. 7, 13.

[90] SROI, HA30/369/394, m. 3r. The dispute is discussed in detail in Tom Johnson, 'The Tree and the Rod: Jurisdiction in Medieval England', *P&P*, 237 (2017), 13–51.

[91] ERO, D/B 5 Cr67, mm. 2r, D/B 5 Cr70, m. 2r, D/B 5 Cr71, m. 2r. Different species of fish spawn at different times: Kowaleski, 'Seasonality of Fishing', pp. 118–9.

[92] SROI, HD64/1/14, verso.

[93] *Minute Book of Dunwich*, ed. Bailey, p. 15; NRO, Y/C 4/205, m. 4v.

[94] Four of the five 'churchreeves' named for 1450–1 appear subsequently in the accounts as shipowners (their boats captained by others), and three of them as shipmasters in their own right: SROI, FC185/E1/1, pp. 1–8 [modern pagination]; see also Middleton-Stewart, '"Down to the sea in ships"', pp. 75–6.

and Thorpe in Suffolk, some fifty porpoises were caught in the period 1443–80, and had to be rendered to the lord in exchange for a set quantity of wheat.[95] These animals were both valuable and prestigious, and fishermen who ignored the custom were subject to steep fines from the jury of shipmasters that comprised the local court.[96]

As well as fish, the sea also provided maritime communities with goods that were shipwrecked or jettisoned and hauled up in nets or discovered on beaches. The finding of 'flotsam' (floating debris), 'jetsam' (jettisoned goods), and 'lagan' (sunken goods hauled up in nets) at sea was tightly regulated.[97] As with royal fish, the right to these wrecks was technically a royal prerogative, but in most places by the fifteenth century it was a franchise held locally by coastal landowners and other jurisdictions, and exercised through manorial, civic, admiralty, and port courts.[98] In almost every late-medieval East Anglian court that exercised this right, the person who found the thing in question had to report it to the jury of shipmasters in the court—or, at Scratby in north Norfolk, an official known as the 'searcher of wrecks'.[99] The jurors assessed the value of the item, and the finder then paid a fine of half of its value in order to keep it.[100] As I have argued elsewhere, these processes for the collection and registration of shipwreck created a distinctive legal regime centred around the idea of 'finding', which gave the courts—and the shipmasters in particular—the power to establish apparently ownerless objects as legitimate pieces of property.[101]

[95] Johnson, 'The economics of shipwreck', p. 134–7. The custom was that the captor received either four or eight bushels, depending on whether the porpoise was found at land or sea. See also Fox, *Fishing Village*, p. 53.

[96] For porpoises given as gifts: one to John Hopton from the churchwardens of Walberswick, in Colin Richmond, *John Hopton: A Fifteenth Century Suffolk Gentleman* (Cambridge, 1981), p. 145; another was given to Jack Cade by the corporation of Lydd, I. M. W. Harvey, *Jack Cade's Rebellion of 1450* (Oxford, 1991), p. 88; see also Bailey, 'Coastal Fishing', pp. 77–8. For a 1390 presentment for failing to present a porpoise: SROI, HD 371/1, m. 11v.

[97] See Rose Melikan, 'Shippers, salvors, and sovereigns: Competing interests in the medieval law of Shipwreck', *The Journal of Legal History*, 11:2 (1990), 163–82.

[98] Respectively, examples can be found in: [manorial courts] Foulness (Essex): ERO, D/DK M136; Blythburgh and Walberswick (Suffolk): SROI, HA30/314/19c, HA30/314/19d/1–21, HA 30/369/390; Felixstowe, Trimley, and Walton (Suffolk): SROI, HA119/30/3/17, mm. 3r, 12r. Runton and Beeston (Norfolk): NRO, WKC 2/166 398x7; Scratby and Hemsby (Norfolk): NRO, DCN 63/2; [civic courts] Great Yarmouth: NRO, Y/C 4/176, mm.4r–v; Y/C 4/205, m.13v; Dunwich: BL, Add. Ch. 40733; Orford: SROI, HD64/1/12–21, 23, 25, 26, 28; Harwich: D/B 4/38/8, mm. 1v, 6v, 7r; [admiralty] Colchester: ERO, D/B5/R2, fos. 213r–217v; Kirkley and Kessingland, SROL, 194/B1/6–9; [port] Shipden: NRO, NRS 3360, 13C6, m. 8r.

[99] NRO, DCN 63/2, m. 11r.

[100] An exception is from Lincolnshire, where the earlier records of the manor of Ingoldmells do not mention any profit for the finder: *The Court Rolls of the Manor of Ingoldmells*, ed. W. O. Massingberd (London, 1902), *passim*. This may have resulted in the large numbers of presentments there for carrying off wreck: pp. 22, 24, 55, 58, 59, 67. In the later Middle Ages, the practice of the court or the manner of recording wreck may have changed: in 1436 reference is made to the costs of the finders: p. 272.

[101] Tom Johnson, 'Medieval Law and Materiality: Shipwreck, Finders, and Property on the Suffolk Coast, *c.*1380–1410', *AHR*, 120:2 (2015), 407–32.

This legitimacy was tested, occasionally, by the claims of individuals who survived the wreck of their ships, came to land, and sought to claim back their goods, as in 1451 when the *George* of Danzig was wrecked on the north Norfolk coast, and the owner, John Roredans, secured an inquisition from the admiral's deputy there.[102] Such incidents, along with the financial perquisites that courts took from the profits of wreck, made it important for local courts to keep close control of salvaging; thus John Travasse, who found an 'oyster dragge' in Orford's port, was reprimanded for setting a bad example to others after he sold it without permission, and two men of Beeston (Norfolk) were fined 6d. each as 'common perambulators on the seashore and removing wreck from there'.[103] These suspicions were not always misplaced in an economy that relied heavily on borrowing, recycling, repair, and reuse, and the legal boundaries between these practices had to be carefully negotiated; William Drawton of Harwich was fined a shilling in 1452 after he took 'a panel from an old ship lying on the mudbanks'.[104]

Indeed, the operation of wreck rights also allowed the lines between illicit theft and acts of salvage to become blurred. In 1380 two shipmasters of Sizewell, John Ode and Thomas de Carleton, 'found and captured' a whole ship, worth a mark (13s. 4d.), which they duly reported to the customary port court there, the Hethewardmote. They claimed that the ship had been 'floating, as it had been abandoned by alien enemies', and that with the help of some others they had brought it to land at Sizewell. Soon afterwards, however, two other men named John Tasel and Roger del Hel claimed that the ship was theirs, and rather than waiting for a judgment, they led a large crowd of people to storm the shipyard, took the ship, and removed it to another port at Minsmere, just outside the jurisdiction of the court.[105] The circumstances of the claims are hazy, of course, but this was the problem with a property regime centred around 'finding': once some doubts had been created around the ownership of the vessel, the best legal claim was the one that could be backed by immediate force and a jury of shipmasters willing to testify to the legitimacy of the prize.

The economy of shipwreck depended on broader patterns of seaborne trade, which generated its own legal issues. In the first place, the local maritime courts seem to have remained important for the suing of interpersonal litigation throughout the later Middle Ages. Much like the pie-powder courts of which they were close cousins, these forums offered itinerant traders the opportunity to

[102] *CPR*, 1446–52, pp. 440–1. The deputy, Brian Stapleton, was ordered to return the goods to John 'pursuant to the statute of 27 Edward III', which provided for a fee for the salvagers; see Melikan, 'Shippers, salvors, and sovereigns', pp. 175–6. For similar cases, see *CPR*, 1429–36, p. 201; *CPR*, 1441–6, p. 270.

[103] SROI, HD64/1/14, recto; NRO, WKC 2/58 394x5, mm. 19v, 20v.

[104] ERO, D/B 4/38/8, m. 7v. A very similar case also survives from the admiralty court at Kessingland: SROL, 194/B1/7, m. 1r.

[105] Johnson, 'Medieval Law and Materiality', p. 421.

achieve the quick enforcement of debts and contracts, tried before a jury of shipmasters.[106] But if they offered a speedy and specialist form of justice, they were nonetheless serious tribunals; cases might involve large sums, and merchants sometimes hired attorneys to represent their interests there.[107] Such expertise was valuable. In a 1434 case before the Ipswich maritime law court, the defendant in a plea for a £20 debt, John Noble, successfully demurred by pointing out that the plaintiff, in his plea, had never specified the place in which it was to be repaid; the court agreed that this invalidated the plea, and discharged Noble, while holding the plaintiff in mercy for a false claim.[108] This legalistic adherence to the form of a plea suggests an unusually proceduralist sense of the 'law maritime' in this particular court.

As well as the extensive bureaucratic infrastructure used in head-ports for the collection of royal customs on overseas trade, local courts also took on a regulatory role in overseeing customary duties and tolls that were charged by civic authorities in port towns.[109] Customs at Lynn, for example, were levied not just according to the types or value of merchandise freighted, but also the size of the ships themselves: the officials were to take 5d. from ships with a draught of up to 1¾ fathoms, 6d. for up to 2¾ fathoms, and 12d. for 3 fathoms and above.[110] Long must have been the arguments on the docks over a quarter-fathom (18 inches) in choppy waters. As such tolls were established locally, they seem to have been particularly resented by merchants, who complained of their arbitrary nature.[111] Certainly, the water-bailiffs who were charged with collecting them did not face an easy task. Serving in this role at Yarmouth in early April of 1503, a local shipmaster by the name of Richard Hosteler was setting out to a Newcastle master 'what of right he shuld paie for mesurage of colys' when a scrivener named William Garrs interrupted with his dagger drawn, asserting with 'many riotous & disputous wurdes' that no measurage was owed.[112]

More common than outright confrontation, however, were suspicions of evasion. The water-bailiffs of Maldon, for example, often took action—even confiscating an

[106] See p. 67 above.

[107] E.g. a 1499 case from Ipswich: SROI, C/2/10/3/5, p. 119, and a 1469 case from Orford (though heard in its pie-powder court, it involved an agreement to freight a ship): SROI, HD64/1/21.

[108] SROI, C/2/5/1/1, recto.

[109] On royal customs, see Kowaleski, 'Port towns', pp. 472–3; for local customs evidence, Olive Coleman, 'Trade and Prosperity in the Fifteenth Century: Some Aspects of the Trade of Southampton', *Economic History Review*, 16:1 (1963), 9–22.

[110] NRO, KL/C7/4, p. 98. The payments in question were for the wages of the customs officials. A fathom is about six feet.

[111] For example, in 1518 the mariners of the small but growing settlement at Aldeburgh petitioned Chancery claiming that 'unlawefull tolls & importunate exaccions' levied at Newcastle 'hath so impoverysshed yor seid poure tenants [that they] shall nott be abyll to defend the seid towne... from the kyngs enemys'. TNA, C 1/458/5.

[112] NRO, Y/C 4/205, m. 4v. This story was recorded as a report to the Peace Session there. Garrs's role is not clear, but given the nature of the dispute, it seems possible that he was acting as legal counsel for the Newcastle shipmaster.

entire shipment of sea-coals—when merchants attempted to bypass the port there in favour of the wharves at the nearby village of Heybridge.[113] Local officers were also charged with the detection of smuggling. An inquest held at Ipswich in May 1438 found that a Dutch shipmaster named Joceus Cosyn had colluded with two local merchants to unload six fardels of wool worth 40 marks into a storehouse, break them into twelve small bundles, and then lade them on an outbound ship without being cocketed by the customs searchers; after they were caught in the act by one of the civic officers, they quickly sailed up the Orwell Estuary to a quay by the village of Woolverstone, allowing them to spirit away the goods and 'defraud the lord king of his customs', with the help of the manorial lord there.[114] Though the inquest jurors noted that the village quay was within Ipswich's liberties, it shows the potential problems that maritime hinterlands might represent to ports.[115]

It also illustrates the particular suspicion to which foreign merchants like Cosyn were subject in maritime communities.[116] Many local courts followed the parliamentary legislation of 1404, revisited at the request of the Commons in 1432 and 1439, that required alien merchants to lodge with English hosts.[117] But at the small Essex port of Harwich, in particular, distrust of foreigners seems to have been endemic. In 1446 the town made its own ordinance forbidding aliens from hosting foreigners [*extraneorum*], under the penalty of 40s., after two resident Dutchmen were caught hosting unregistered aliens who had gone out after curfew, and Derek Barber, an alien, was said to have 'uncovered the counsel of the town and the country to aliens, against the peace'.[118] This concern that foreign-born residents posed a threat to security seems to have endured throughout the decade, as in 1456 Adam Palmer was fined the large sum of 6s. 8d. because 'he showed our French enemies the secret way to safely lead their ship to our port of Orwell'; the same year, a crowd of women were fined after they chased a group of 'Esttyrlyng' merchants out of the town.[119]

While the demonization of aliens thus seems to have had a basis in popular feeling, then, it also accorded with the widespread impulse among local port authorities to regulate the commercial activities of aliens.[120] Foreign merchants

[113] ERO, D/B 3/1/2, fo. 6r. And a similar case on fo. 6v, with a 'hy fine' charged on measurage.

[114] SROI, C/2/6/2. Joceus's nationality is not noted, but he is said to be from a place called 'Outdraught Hardwareught' (presumably Utrecht-Harderwijk). If he was taxed as an alien, he would have faced a subsidy of 60s. per sack of wool: Carus-Wilson and Coleman, *England's Export Trade*, Appendix 3, pp. 194–6.

[115] Harold Fox, 'Two Devon Estuaries in the Middle Ages: Fisheries, Ports, Fortifications and Places of Worship', *Landscapes*, 8:1 (2007), p. 46.

[116] See fnn. 29–33 above.

[117] *PROME*, ed. Given-Wilson, iii, 543; iv, 402; tr-v, 24. See fn. 33 above.

[118] ERO, D/B4/38/8, m. 4r. [119] Ibid., m. 11r.

[120] See Alwyn A. Ruddock, 'Alien Merchants in Southampton in the Later Middle Ages', *EHR*, 61:239 (1946), 1–17; Wendy Childs, 'Irish Merchants and Seamen in Late-Medieval England', *Irish Historical Studies*, 32:125 (2000), 22–43.

not only faced considerably higher local duties—at Dunwich they paid a levy of 8d., as well as a higher rate of portage for their ships—but also much tighter supervision. At Maldon, they were required to hand over their lead-line, the instrument used to sound depths in shallow waters and avoid running aground.[121] There was also suspicion that foreigners were evading the dues they owed; at Colchester in 1458, Peter Skynner and Agnes Petrisson, both noted as aliens, were fined 20s. each after they were said to have 'received the goods and merchandise of alien merchants secretly in their houses, and kept them hidden there so that the collectors of customs and subsidies of the king at Ipswich would not be able to have view of them'.[122] While there is also some evidence that foreign merchants and mariners used the local maritime courts for their own litigation, the overall picture is one of mistrustful and punitive regulation, underscored by both rising nationalist sentiment and the commercial interests of English mariners and merchants.[123]

In sum, local courts in maritime communities, as they dealt with issues associated with fishing, wreck, and trade, generally worked to secure the interests of shipmasters. They protected the commercial fishermen on whose taxes many secular and ecclesiastical authorities relied at the expense of small-scale coastal fishers; they enforced the property rights of the shipmasters who claimed to find shipwrecked goods at sea; and they enabled the regulation of merchants, enforcing contracts and taking tolls from coastal shipping. All this was made possible by some distinctive mechanisms in the maritime courts—the systems of accounting and auditing fish catches, the presentation of wrecks, and the appointment of officers such as the water-bailiff. But most of all, legal responsibilities in these communities were vested in the shipmasters, who were relied upon to report information and make judgments in a host of different situations before the courts. As we shall see in what follows, this was also translated into the broader discourse of expertise that characterized maritime legal culture.

A Jurisprudence of Expertise: Seaworthiness, Skill, Obedience

In this final section, I want to explore in more detail the way in which seamen conceptualized law through recourse to ideas about nautical expertise. Ideals about the seaworthiness of ships, the skill of mariners, and the obedience of the

[121] For Dunwich's tariffs: BL, Add. Ch. 40740; for Maldon, ERO, D/B 3/1/2, fo. 15r.

[122] ERO, D/B 5 Cr69, m. 13r.

[123] On aliens using port courts, see e.g. at Shipden in Norfolk: NRO, NRS 3360, 13C6, m. 8r; and at Ipswich maritime, SROI, C/2/10/3/2, p. 130 [Jacobus Dwyland]; C/2/10/3/5, p. 598 [D. Hesteman, 'gubernator Islandie']; more generally, see Kowaleski, '"Alien" Encounters', pp. 111–12. On English identity, see Andrea Ruddick, *English Identity and Political Culture in the Fourteenth Century* (Cambridge, 2013).

crews were used to respond to the range of legal problems that were encountered during the course of work at sea; in what follows we look at three case studies of particularly detailed sources that show how these ideals framed expectations about, and legal negotiations over, covenant, accountability, and authority. As we shall see, this jurisprudence of expertise often served the interests of ship-owners and shipmasters, as navigators, entrepreneurs, and employers. But it is important to emphasize that their interests were also, sometimes, those of their crew, whether in attempting to save a sinking ship or defending a long-standing employer. While the idea of nautical expertise thus helped to reinforce existing hierarchies, then, it nonetheless provided all seafarers with a way of conceptualizing law, and was thus central to wider maritime legal culture.

To begin with, I want to look at how the seaworthiness of ships was used to frame expectations about contracts by focusing on a case from a petition to Chancery from the last decade of the fifteenth century.[124] Thomas Boweman, a mariner and small-time fish merchant of Cromer in Norfolk, secured the services of a shipmaster named Robert Shene to convey him with a shipment of ling and cod from Blakeney to Lynn. They encountered a storm on the way, however, and the ship proved less than seaworthy: the sails were blown off, the keel sprang a leak, and 'all that wer in the saide kele were in grete peril and in poynt of perishing'. Shene then called Boweman to take the helm, 'bicause he cowde gode skill', and he managed to direct the ship ashore, upon which it grounded and fell apart, causing the loss of the cargo. Far from accepting liability however, Shene launched an action of trespass against Boweman in the nearby port court at Cley, and packed the jury; Boweman thus petitioned for a writ of *certiorari*, in order to subject the case to review by the chancellor, according to equity.

Just as the petition provides an interesting example of the options available to merchants who felt they were ill-served by the port courts, it is also provides a great amount of detail about the material qualities of the ship, and shows the way in which they came to serve as the locus of the dispute, both for Boweman and—so far as we can see through a hostile report—for Shene too. To begin with, Boweman claimed that Shene had 'made promise and warantized that hys said kele . . . cabull and sailes of the same [ship] were sufficient, strong, and able'; this appears to have been an oral agreement, or simply a minimum expectation, for he makes no mention of charter-party, the form of written contract sometimes used for maritime freight arrangements.[125] As they encountered the storm, the foresail 'was blowen awaie into the see for rotenisse and feblenesse', the keel begin to leak, and 'the mayne saile for olde and febleness brake on sondre in many pecis and blew into the see'; as they came to shore, the 'kele cam with the shore and there for olde

[124] TNA, C 1/188/8. The petition can be dated to 1493–1500 on the basis of the Chancellor to whom it is addressed. The quotes that follow are from this document.

[125] Ibid.; Ward, *Medieval Shipmaster*, pp. 81–2.

and feblenesse brake on sonder'.[126] Boweman thus placed an exceedingly strong emphasis on the deterioration of the ship, a material instantiation of Shene's contract breach.

Shene, for his part, claimed that the breaking up of the ship was Boweman's fault. His suit of trespass in the Cley port court, for £20 worth of damages, asserted that during the storm, Boweman had taken the helm by force, usurping Shene's role as 'maister mariner'; in particular, he alleged that Boweman's 'violence and demeanor' in piloting the ship had caused the keel to become 'so distressed that she was utterly lost in the haven'.[127] Interestingly, Shene here seems to have been deploying ideas of skill and obedience, to which we shall turn just below, as means of framing Boweman's accountability. In the face of such allegations, Boweman reinforced his own claim with an appeal to common opinion. As he put it, 'all this trouble came for lake of gode sailes and taklyng, as the mariners that were in the saide kele, and many other that wer upon the londe seyng this grete jeparde, woll recorde and testifie'. This represents a remarkable invocation of maritime expertise: not only does it imply that seaworthiness could be judged by the consensus of the crew, but also that they would know better than the shipmaster himself, and his peers in the port court, who, as Boweman contended, 'no thing knowe of the mater'.

While Boweman, Shene, and the rest of the crew lived to tell the tale, not every seafarer was so lucky, and this brings us to the next case study, focusing on the ideal of skill. On the last Thursday of Lent in 1518, two young mariners named Richard Astill and William Shorte were in a small boat on the Orwell Estuary in Suffolk at low tide, dragging for oysters in the shallow waters. It was a miserable, stormy day, the wind blustering so loudly that it was difficult to hear, and their boat had been blown over into the middle of the channel. As they set their dragnets once more, they noticed that a very large ship was approaching them at speed. The sailors in the ship, the *John Evangelist* of Harwich, were shouting to Richard and William to get out of the way—the channel was too narrow, and the winds too strong for their vessel to change course. William called to Richard to cut the rope to the dragnets, which were anchoring their boat in the middle of the channel. Richard looked up, but made no move, and now it was too late: the *John Evangelist* smashed into the boat, throwing the two men into the brackish waters. William was quickly pulled out by Thomas Branston, who was close at hand in another oyster boat, and lived to tell the tale; Richard Astill was drowned.

It is possible to write this story in such detail, more than five hundred years later, because these events were the subject of an admiralty inquiry taken in March

[126] TNA, C 1/188/8.

[127] Ibid. This reconstruction of Shene's reasoning has of course been taken from Boweman's characterization of it, a task made more difficult by damage to this portion of the document. However, the sense seems correct.

1518 by a public notary named William Neve. It asked 'whether this ship, belonging to Edward Redde, had provided the cause of Richard's death at that place and time?'[128] This was an important point to establish. If it could be shown that the *John Evangelist* was the 'object that moved towards', or caused Astill's death, then it would be forfeit to the admiral as deodand.[129] On the other hand, if Astill was responsible for his own death, Redde, a shipmaster who had only recently acquired the *John Evangelist*, could keep the ship.[130] But the case was also part of a larger dispute between the admiral and the corporation of Ipswich over jurisdiction in the River Orwell, which had been rumbling since the 1490s.[131] The town had lost one of the charters that exempted it from the admiral's intervention, and while its bailiffs continued to hold admiralty pleas as late as 1513, they were vulnerable to interference.[132] They were indeed consulted in the early stages of the 1518 inquiry, and though they cooperated with Neve, they lost no time in procuring a new charter from the king. Confirmed in March 1519, it detailed their admiralty powers and explicitly defined the boundaries of their maritime jurisdiction.[133]

In these complicated circumstances, the depositions of the mariners who were called to testify to Neve's inquiry take on a particular significance. Every single one of them attested that Astill's death was his own fault, due to a critical lack of skill. In the first place, Shorte and Astill had failed to take due precautions. Hugh Page, who had been dragging oysters not fifteen fathoms away, described how they 'had not festenyd there dragge rope at þe ynde off þe boote as oþer ded, for iff they had adoen so, þe bootte shuld alyen rygth in the streme'; as it was, 'the said bootte ded lye overqwarte þe streme, wiche causyd more perill than shuld an happyd iff þe bootte had alyen rygth'.[134] Once again, an appeal to the common opinion of the maritime community—by doing 'as others did'—was used as a means of explaining legal liability, with Astill failing to make his boat lie 'right'. Another onlooker from the shore, a mariner named John Swettman, agreed, suggesting that 'iff þei had be wyesse, with a litell labor... as þei mygth a doon

[128] SROI, SC18/40, m. 1r.

[129] On deodand, see R. F. Hunnisett, *The Medieval Coroner* (Cambridge, 1961), pp. 31–4. On the admiralty's claim of deodands, see *Black Book*, ed. Twiss, p. 242; see also Ward, *Medieval Shipmaster*, p. 42.

[130] SROI, SC18/40: all of the witnesses in the inquiry say that they had known the ship itself for longer than they had known Redde, and several of them had only known him for a year, perhaps suggesting that he was a relative newcomer to the maritime community around Orwell Haven.

[131] BL, Add. MS. 10358, fo. 39r.: a memorandum from August 1493, recording an incident in which the Earl of Oxford, then admiral of England, had arrested a Breton ship in the Orwell port, breaching the town's liberties. The bailiffs responded by sending a copy of their charter to the earl, who responded that he would be 'frendely to them in this poynt'.

[132] SROI, C/2/10/3/8, p. 394 [modern foliation]; *Ipswich Borough Archives 1255–1835. A Catalogue*, ed. David Allen (Woodbridge, 2000), p. 8.

[133] SROI, C/1/1/20.

[134] SROI, SC18/40, m. 4r.

right weele, þe bootte and men had been saff'.[135] Their lack of wisdom, their failure to know what the right thing to do was, was the cause of Richard's death.

All of the witnesses testifying to the inquiry, indeed, emphasized their own expertise—not in hindsight, but in how they made decisions at the time—as way of justifying this explanation. Thomas Branston, who had also been dragging for oysters in his own boat, recalled how he had perceived the *John Evangelist* when it was some two or three miles away, and 'so continually had þe shippe in syete'; he noted that once it reached a place called Pin Mill, 'þe wyend was att sowth sowth weste and blewe myche . . . and tempeste rosse þat tyme more and more', and the river 'was iij quarter ebbyng water and more and still fallyng'; and that the great ship, approaching on the leeshore, 'halyd to wyend ward and so kepte þe beeste off þe chanell, as was the beeste course and right course for þe shippes waye'.[136] Branston's own awareness of these adverse weather conditions, his cautious regard of the approaching ship, and his analysis of where it was heading thus fed into his explanation of liability. All properly expert mariners, whether they were on the ship or not, ought to have seen and known its 'right course', which Astill 'mygth [have] awoyded with oon tryllyng off an oore'.

As a final point, it is also worth noting the way in which this idea of skill melded with that of obedience to frame authority in the course of everyday relations on the river. All of the eyewitnesses to the crash emphasized that the crew on the *John Evangelist* had called to Astill and Shorte, exhorting them to move. John Jamys, one of the mariners on the ship recalled that he 'and oþer off his cumpany made proclamation and callyd un to them', saying things like '"þe shippe will nott weie [shift]!", "Att þe reverens off god, make waye!" and "Be ware off þe shippe!"; and "Kytt yowr dragge rope, and iff it cooste a noble ye shalbe payed for itt, for we muste nedys kepe þe chanell"'.[137] Such phrases not only highlighted, once more, that the larger ship's course was the 'right' one, but their very utterance implied the authority of its mariners to give commands to Astill and Shorte, who, as Jamys said, 'made noe waye for þe shippe as oþer boots dedd'. Failure to heed these commands—to obey what common maritime expertise demanded—was what led to Astill's death. Thus, as Jamys emphasized, the collision happened 'withowt any viciuys defaute, saffe in þe defaute off þe said William and Richard'—a crucial default of skill.

While the depositions to the Astill inquiry offer an unprecedented degree of detail, such sentiments seem to have been common. Maritime juries in inquests into deaths at sea routinely blamed mariners who had died for their lack of skill. Three cases from the Ipswich admiralty court, heard just a few years before, accounted in similar ways for the deaths of men aboard Ipswich ships: John Paret, a merchant in the *James* died at Langerpoint, at the tip of the Orwell

[135] Ibid., mm. 4r–5r. [136] Ibid., mm. 3r.

[137] Ibid., m. 3r. This quote is from a continuous passage of text; I have simply inserted punctuation.

Estuary, after his oar snagged in the water and took him overboard; William Orkeneyman, on board the *Andrew* on its way to Iceland, 'fell out of the ship on account of his negligence'; while John Jenewey, in the *Anne* on the way to Zealand, was said to have fallen out of the ship by his own 'improvidence', that is to say, his lack of foresight.[138] Such verdicts were certainly useful for the owners of ships, who were excused the heavy penalties that would have been due as deodand. Yet while the mariners and shipmasters who served on these juries were defending the interests of capital, they did so in ways—emphasizing the negligence, improvidence, the 'default' of wisdom, the failure to do what was right—that worked to enshrine the unanimity of nautical expertise, and their status as experts.

Finally, we turn to the ideal of obedience and the way in which it was used to frame the authority of shipmasters. Here, I want to look at a brief case study from an admiralty session held at Shipden in the spring of 1446. John Well, a shipmaster of Cromer, had been captaining a small ship or 'farcost' that was lying at anchor on the high seas. For some unspecified reason he ordered that William Barker, one of the crew, ought to be held in the hull, and he was left there for three days without access to food, water, or treatment. In this cold, damp confinement his feet became gangrenous and later had to be amputated. The presenting jury affirmed that Well's actions, in necessitating this amputation, constituted a 'mayhem'—a mutilation—which was said to be an offence 'against the maritime laws, the Statute of Oleron, and a bad example to others'. However, the judge in the court, having examined the crew, found that Barker's injuries and maiming were not the fault of John Well, 'and this is verified by the majority of the mariners who were in the ship at that time of Lent, according to the form of the statute of Oléron'.[139]

This case is unusual not only in showing something of the exercise of the shipmaster's quasi-judicial authority aboard a ship, but also in its relatively exact allusion to the laws of Oléron. The laws do in fact mention the removal of a limb (albeit, a fist) as a potential punishment for striking a shipmaster, and indeed, the investigation of mayhems was identified in the Inquisition of Queenborough and in subsequent rulings on the jurisdiction of the admiralty.[140] While the presentment does not make clear the precise nature of Barker's disobedience, the description of him being 'thrown' into the hull, and 'detained' there, strongly suggests that he had defied his master Well in some way.[141] Cases of disobedience were commonly punished in the admiralty courts. To take three presentments from the local admiralty court at Kirkley in the early sixteenth century: Orto Johnson 'was inobedient to Robert Coleyns, shipmaster, on the shore'; Robert Spurling and

[138] SROI, C/2/10/3/8, p. 394.

[139] *Black Book*, ed. Twiss, pp. 252–3.

[140] Ward, *Medieval Shipmaster*, pp. 187, 197–8 [Oléron], pp. 213–4 [Queenborough]; *PROME*, iii, p. 291.

[141] *Black Book*, ed. Twiss, pp. 252–3.

John Jacobson were fined 3s. 4d. each for committing an assault on their shipmaster; and Robert, a servant of John Hykks, 'did not want to obey Robert Hutton, master, in a ship in the northern regions'.[142] The court, of course, was composed of a jury of shipmasters.

But while the shipmaster undoubtedly carried a great deal of authority on board his ship, his power was not absolute. In a one of the articles of inquiry laid out in the treatise *De Officio Admirallitatis*, the obedience of the crew was explicitly linked to the rulership of the shipmaster; admiralty courts were to inquire into 'those mariners or sailors who are rebels against their captains or masters on the sea, and conversely, whether those same captains and masters treat them well... according to the provisions of the statute of Olleron'.[143] Once more, Oléron was held up as a symbol, but not just of the power of the shipmaster, but as a potential recourse for the crew. And, indeed, while the judgment went against Barker, it was emphatically based on the eyewitness testimony of the crew, and their understanding of the provisions of the laws of Oléron—clearly, they regarded his punishment to have been legitimate. While Barker's treatment thus makes clear the harsh extent of the shipmaster's power over life and limb, it is also a powerful example of the way that it was subject to supervision by the expert testimony of mariners.

Nautical expertise, then, in its various guises, thus provided a way in which mariners, shipmasters, and merchants conceptualized the legal problems thrown up by the unpredictable and dangerous conditions of working at sea. In many ways, the ideals of expertise were used to justify the particular commercial and legal interests of merchants, in comprising a set of reasonable expectations for contracts, for shipmasters, in preserving their authority over the ship, and for shipowners, by limiting their liabilities. Yet, as we have seen, the notion of expertise also carried resonance for a much wider constituency of seafarers, as a set of idealized associative relations within maritime legal culture. In this ambivalence, indeed, expertise was a characteristic form of legitimate knowledge, which we shall examine in Chapter 5. Rooted in vernacular understandings of knowledge, expertise at once enabled legal institutions to extract information from the maritime community at the same time as it allowed mariners and others to remould the authority of the courts for their own purposes.

Conclusion

Maritime legal culture in late-medieval England was characterized by its emphasis on nautical expertise. This idea had its genesis in the distinctive legal traditions of

[142] Respectively, SROL, 194/B1/7, m. 2v, 3r.

[143] *Black Book*, ed. Twiss, pp. 229–30.

the laws of Oléron, the law maritime, and the admiralty, which afforded maritime communities the right to interpret and decide their own affairs. This was reinforced in the practice of local maritime courts, in which shipmasters in particular were permitted to report information and make decisions within the distinctive environmental, socio-economic, and demographic conditions of the communities they sought to govern. And, as we have just seen, it was fully elaborated in the way that seafarers interpreted and judged the legal problems with which they were confronted during the course of their work at sea. Ultimately, nautical expertise was a way of creating trust in maritime relationships—trust in the seaworthiness of the vessel, trust that mariners knew how to handle ships, trust that agreements would be upheld, and trust in the authority of the shipmaster.

As a final point, here, I would like to consider the limits of expertise as a means of creating trust within the broader horizons of the maritime world, as East Anglian mariners engaged with authorities outside England, in the North Sea and beyond.[144] Edda Frankot's research into the practice of maritime law across this region in the later Middle Ages suggests that English mariners would have encountered very similar legal cultures, generated from the common expertise required within medieval maritime societies: 'as the courts consisted of men with experience in trade and shipping, verdicts would be based on their practical knowledge of these subjects'.[145] Yet for all that expertise was important in local legal engagements, it seems to have been of limited utility in negotiating long-distance relationships within the constantly shifting international relations of fifteenth-century Europe; mariners and merchants had to use different legal forms to navigate the ongoing cycles of reprisals carried out through trade that were enabled, and sometimes encouraged, by sovereign powers.[146]

To begin with, authorities routinely mandated attacks on the merchant shipping of hostile nations, as in 1436 when the English crown granted royal licences to shipmen to 'resist the king's enemies', and to keep whatever they managed to take.[147] On the other hand, authorities were under pressure to deliver justice to wronged merchants; the issuance of letters of marque allowed them to seize property from the piratical merchants (or their co-citizens) who had taken from them, as restitution for their losses.[148] Whatever the benefits of this policy, it also caused a proliferation of claims in Chancery by foreign merchants from friendly

[144] See Ian Forrest and Anne Haour, 'Trust in Long-Distance Relationships 1000–1600 CE', in *P&P*, 238, suppl. 13 (2018), 190–213.

[145] Frankot, 'Medieval Maritime Law and its Practice', p. 197.

[146] See Marcus Pitcaithly, 'Piracy and Anglo-Hanseatic Relations, 1385–1420', in *Roles of the Sea*, ed. Gorski, 125–45.

[147] Fudge, *Cargoes, Embargoes, and Emissaries*, pp. 12–3.

[148] See Bryan D. Dick, '"Framing Piracy": restitution at sea in the later Middle Ages', unpublished PhD thesis, University of Glasgow, (2010), pp. 84–147. Such letters were ratified in admiralty courts; for examples, see *Documents relating to Law and Custom of the Sea*, ed. R. G. Marsden (2 vols; London, 1915), i, pp. 149, 152, 159, 190.

powers who had been wrongly despoiled of their goods.[149] And, finally, princes granted 'safe-conducts' to favoured foreign shippers and merchants—or those who were willing to pay for them—which notionally protected them from attack by ships under their authority; in England the court of admiralty was sometimes called to investigate 'diverse spoliations, robberies, and infractions of safe-conducts of the king and truces between the king and foreign princes by certain pirates at sea'.[150] None of this is to suggest that the late-medieval seas were 'lawless', but rather that seafarers were forced to hedge their bets and put their trust in many different kinds legal institution.[151]

These transnational engagements with sovereign authorities generated a different kind of legal discourse, focused on rather broader legal concepts. In the first place, maritime communities might appeal to ideas of natural justice. For example, in 1463 news reached the city council of Lynn that seven of their merchants had been imprisoned in Bremen, in a pit sixty feet underground, so it was said, in retaliation for a perceived wrong. The council wrote a letter to their counterparts in Bremen requesting their release, which was copied into their memorandum book.[152] It began in the conventional language of diplomacy, emphasizing the continual friendship between the citizens and councils of the towns, and the advantages their relationship had conferred. But taking a more strident tone, the writer noted that the damages and injuries had been done by 'other persons', and so the Lynn merchants had been imprisoned 'against justice and law, which do not wish anyone to be punished for an unconnected transgression, and so we request your discretion, probity, and friendship'.[153] This language of *amiticia*, combined with a broader appeal to equity and conscience, thus aimed at a set of common legal principles that could sustain the bilateral bonds of trust required for maritime trade.

Yet, as a final point, it is important to emphasize that the legal cosmopolitanism of English maritime communities was embedded in their localized institutions of governance. As a concluding example, I want to look at a remarkable petition sent by the bailiffs of Dunwich to the Admiral of France in 1472, which shows how this combination might work in practice. The petition opens with the claim that it was written on behalf of 'alle the maystyrs, marynerys of schyppys, as well to ffysshere men as marchawntys applying to the see for here trewe purchas and levyng that welyn sewyn to have them that wonyn up

[149] From 1453 the Chancellor was to hear such claims, though clearly his jurisdiction was not exclusive of that of the admiral: *Select Pleas in the Court of Admiralty*, ed. Marsden, pp. liv–v.

[150] *CPR*, 1467–77, p. 525.

[151] For the notion of the medieval seas as 'lawless': Rodger, *The Safeguard of the Sea*, p. 78. For a critique of this pervasive discourse, Philip E. Steinberg, *The Social Construction of the Ocean* (Cambridge, 2001), Ch. 1, pp. 8–38.

[152] NRO, KL/C7/4, p. 173 [modern pagination].

[153] Ibid.: 'contra iusticiam et legem que non vult aliquem puniri pro transgressione aliena hac de causa vestram discrecionem probitatem et amiticiam requirimus'.

on the coostys wyth inne the cownte'.[154] This broad invocation of maritime community was aimed at maximizing the sense of dissatisfaction, as they complained to the admiral that the guarantees which he had granted to them, the 'saff cundytts on trust undyr yowr promys', had been broken by 'dyvers schyppys of werre & men that wern undyr yowr obeysawns'. Listing at length some seven robberies at sea—including one incident in which a French shipmaster pretended to be Scottish in order to lure English fishermen close enough to rob them of some £55 worth of saltfish—they employed language of deception and betrayal that emphasized the trust that had been broken between them.

Written to a French royal institution in vernacular English, this petition encapsulates the way in which maritime legal culture in late-medieval England stretched between the local and the transnational. The bailiffs emphasized that the detailed accounts of piracy, recounted down to the cruel minutiae of a captain named Janyn Skarnet deliberately pouring away the English sailors' beer, came from a trustworthy and legitimate source, the shipmasters themselves: 'and dewly they han been examynyd to infoormyn us of the very trewthe, and ther up on they madyn here othys, and infoormyd us, ech mayster be hym self'. The very truth, of course, could only be garnered from an examination of these men, testifying under oath about what happened. Requiring 'a dew remedye and restytucyon be maad', they concluded with a threat: 'ellys, sere, we may nowgth, ner xull nowgth, doryn trustyn ony saff cundytts heer aftyr in tyme comyng'.[155] Emphasizing the necessity of trust in these long-distance relationships spoke to a broader maritime language of law, perhaps, but it ultimately rooted that trust in the credence and authority of shipmasters, the prime exponents of maritime legal culture.

[154] BL, Add. Ch. 40683. [155] Ibid.

4

Forest Legal Culture

Accounting for Vert and Venison

Forests in late-medieval England were large areas of land that had been designated as royal hunting reserves under the Norman and Angevin kings. Although many Forests included tracts of woodland and even denser forest, they were not wholly wooded, and often encompassed swathes of upland moor, marshes, and fens, as well as arable and pastoral farmland.[1] The royal Forest was a vague geographical jurisdiction—including not only crown lands, but also those of other lords—that was constituted by the operation of Forest law there, with its characteristic restrictions on rural dwellers, aimed at preserving the 'vert and venison', the greenwood habitat and the game animals within it. To live in an area designated as Forest, however, was not merely to be subject to an extra layer of legal restrictions, but also to possess a distinctive legal identity as a 'comuner of the forest', as a vernacular bill of 1476 put it, with a special connection to the crown and a set of customary rights to wood and pasture.[2] In these tightly controlled hunting landscapes, then, Forest legal culture worked to frame the fragile balance between rights and regulation in the management of natural resources.

Historiographical attention to the royal Forest as a legal institution has tended to focus on the development of its idiosyncratic law, or on the Forest eyres of the thirteenth and fourteenth centuries, the great judicial and administrative endeavours undertaken to regulate the Forests during what one commentator has called 'the Forest system at its height'.[3] Relatively little attention, however, has been devoted to the late-medieval Forests; indeed, the prevailing consensus has been that Forest administration after the end of the reign of Edward I was in a state of 'weakness', 'decline', 'decay', 'chaos', or 'desuetude'.[4]

[1] Throughout this chapter, I use the capitalized 'Forest' to refer to a particular legal institution (e.g. Sherwood Forest) or to the institution as a whole (e.g. the royal Forests), and the uncapitalized 'forest' to refer geographically to a large wooded region, as in modern usage.

[2] Quote from TNA, DL 39/2/7, m. 3r. On Forest law the pre-eminent account is still G. J. Turner, 'Introduction: The Forests in the Thirteenth Century,' in *Select Pleas of the Forest*, ed. G. J. Turner, Selden Society 13 (London, 1901), ix–cxxxiv. On the connection between the Forests and the crown, see Richard Almond and A. J. Pollard, 'The Yeomanry of Robin Hood and Social Terminology in Fifteenth-Century England', *P&P*, 170 (2001), 52–77.

[3] For the quote: Charles R. Young, *The Royal Forests of Medieval England* (Philadelphia, 1979), Ch. 5. 'The Forest System at Its Height: Law and Administration', pp. 74–113.

[4] Quotes respectively from Charles Petit-Dutaillis, *Studies and notes supplementary to Stubbs' Constitutional history*, transl. W. T. Waugh (3 vols, Manchester, 1908–15), ii, p. 244; Young, *Royal*

Law in Common: Legal Cultures in Late-Medieval England. Tom Johnson, Oxford University Press (2020).

DOI: 10.1093/oso/9780198785613.001.0001

With no Forest eyres after 1358, and the last comprehensive royal review of the Forests held in 1377, the fifteenth century, in this aspect as so many others, has been understood as a period of retrenchment and deterioration in Forest governance.[5] In this narrative, it was not until the advent of the Tudors that order was restored, with a flurry of Forest eyres held under Henry VII from 1488 onwards as part of a more general attempt to restore the royal prerogative.[6]

As I have argued elsewhere, this historiographical story about the decline of late-medieval Forest justice and administration is not only mistaken, but also misses the wood for the trees, so to speak.[7] First, the crown did continue to exercise some form of indirect control over the Forests both through the commissions of inquiries, the returns for which have not tended to survive to the present day, and also the centralized appointment of Forest officers. Second, to focus solely on central institutions is to miss the structural significance of local institutions in the governance of the Forests, which continued unabated through the fifteenth century. And third, the key development in the later Middle Ages was not the retrenchment of the royal Forest, but the expansion of Forest legal culture—in its characteristic officers, procedures, and concerns—to other tribunals, normally in places where there were seigneurial hunting parks, a point to which we shall return later in this chapter.[8] In order to understand properly the significance of the late-medieval Forests for legal culture, then, we need to look beyond their bounds.

As I shall argue in this chapter, Forest legal culture in late-medieval England revolved around the management of the 'vert and venison', the rhetorical pairing of woodland resources and deer that formed the central concern of Forest law. This emphasis on management was built into the very structures of the local courts that drew on this legal tradition, which often served more as mechanisms of

Forests, p. 149; Raymond Grant, *The Royal Forests of England* (Stroud, 1991), esp. Ch. 9, 'The Decline of the Forests, 1377–1485', at pp. 170–1; S. A. Mileson, *Parks in Medieval England* (Oxford, 2009), p. 141; John Langton, 'Medieval Forests and Chases: Another Realm?', in *Forests and Chases of Medieval England and Wales, c. 1000 to c.1500*, ed. John Langton and Graham Jones (Oxford, 2010), 14–35, at p. 20.

[5] On the Forest eyres, see D. Crook, 'The Records of Forest Eyres in the Public Record Office, 1179 to 1670', *Journal of the Society of Archivists*, 17:2 (1996), 183–93.

[6] Generally, see R. B. Manning, *Hunters and Poachers: A Social and Cultural History of Unlawful Hunting in England, 1485–1640* (Oxford, 1993). On the revival of the royal prerogative, see Harold Garrett-Goodyear, 'The Tudor Revival of Quo Warranto and Local Contributions to State Building', in *On the Laws and Customs of England: Essays in Honor of Samuel E. Thorne*, ed. Morris S. Arnold, Thomas A. Green, Sally A. Scully, and Stephen D. White (Chapel Hill, NC, 1981), 231–95.

[7] Tom Johnson, 'The Redistribution of Forest Law and Administration in Fifteenth-Century England', in *Fifteenth-Century England XV*, ed. Linda Clark (Woodbridge, 2018), 93–108.

[8] See I. M. W. Harvey, 'Poaching and Sedition in Fifteenth-Century England', in *Lordship and Learning: Studies in Memory of Trevor Aston*, ed. Ralph Evans (Woodbridge, 2004), 169–82. The Statute of Merton (1236) and the Statute of Westminster I (1275) both prohibited trespassing in parks. An act against commoners keeping dogs (previously an offence only in Forest law) was passed in 1390: 13 Ric II Stat. 1, c. 13. A later act against unlawful hunting was passed in the first Tudor parliament: 1 Hen. VII, c. 7.

financial accounting than as tribunals for the resolution of disputes or the enactment of justice; it was intensified by the concerns of the specialist local officers—such as foresters, woodwards, and verderers—who were often paid in kind with timber and venison, and who were obliged to account for the way in which they cultivated and used these resources. The inhabitants of Forests, although they possessed significant customary rights, were thus faced with a legal regime that offered relatively little scope for the kind of idealized community-building that characterized other areas of the late-medieval countryside. Forest legal culture was not built around associative relations between people but, rather, the allocation and usage of natural resources. As we shall see, this worked to make law revolve around claims about the most judicious methods of conserving the Forest, a plane of argument that was tilted against tenants.

This chapter proceeds in the same manner as the one which preceded it. First, we turn to examine the kinds of landscape and economy typically comprised by Forests and seigneurial parks. The second section then sets out the main institutions of this legal regime. As well as showing the ways in which local and royal courts combined in the management of the Forests themselves, I also explain how these institutions came to permeate more widely. With these points established, we turn in the third section to consider the characteristic procedures of Forest governance; as I shall argue, there is a blurring between many of these processes and methods for accounting the resources provided by Forests and parks, in the form of wood, pasture, and game. The fourth section then turns to the characteristic discourses of Forest legal culture, focusing upon ideas about enclosure, preservation, and warrant that were used by both officers and tenants to frame contestations over the legitimate management of resources. The conclusion, finally, considers the relationship of Forest legal culture to the others discussed in the first part of this book.

Forest Landscapes and Economies

The total area covered by Forests and chases in medieval England—a question that much exercised an earlier generation of historians—is not precisely known.[9] More recently, two scholars have characterized Forests as constituting 'half our historical geography', in the course of a project which has identified and mapped nearly a thousand Forests and chases in England and Wales.[10] That is an exaggeration,

[9] See Margaret Ley Bazeley, 'The Extent of English Forest in the Thirteenth Century', *Transactions of the Royal Historical Society*, 4th ser., 4 (1921), 140–72; Elizabeth Cox Wright, 'Common Law in the Thirteenth-Century English Royal Forest', *Speculum*, 3:2 (1928), 166–91.

[10] John Langton and Graham Jones, 'Deconstructing and reconstructing the Forests: Some Preliminary Matters', in *Forests and Chases*, ed. Langton and Jones, 1–13, p. 3. For the project website, see http://info.sjc.ox.ac.uk/forests/ (accessed February 12, 2016).

but it hints at the wide potential remit of Forest jurisdiction, which was probably at its maximum extent before 1204.[11] Over the next century, the area covered by royal Forests was successively reduced due to baronial pressure on the crown.[12] At the same time, however, the reach of Forest jurisdiction expanded in the later Middle Ages, as its concepts and procedures spread to other kinds of local court; as legal institutions, the significance of the Forests cannot be reduced to their land mass. To conceive of them as homogeneous blocs of territory, laid out on a map, is thus often to flatten out the diversity of different landscapes and economies that were drawn into Forest legal culture.[13]

With these caveats in mind, it is nonetheless true that Forests, and lands that were drawn into Forest legal culture, often exhibited certain physical traits. In the first place, they frequently included large tracts of moorland and open pastures; and in the second place, they probably contained larger and more numerous areas of woodland.[14] Both of these features can be explained by the fact that such places were often more sparsely populated and less well-suited to arable farming.[15] The lands that became Forests may thus have been deemed useful mainly as hunting grounds during the critical period of Forest designation in the century after the Norman Conquest.[16] Subsequently, Forest law served to reinforce these landscape differences, by inhibiting (if never completely preventing) the cutting down of trees at the same time as other woodlands were being cleared for arable agriculture, and by restricting land use and settlement more generally in order to enable hunting.[17] There was thus some symbiosis between the legal Forest and the geographical forest.

[11] This was the year in which the entire counties of Essex, Devon, and Cornwall (among other tracts) were disafforested by King John, though all of them retained substantial Forests within their bounds. Bazeley, 'Extent of English Forest', p. 148.

[12] See Young, *Royal Forests*, Ch. 4, 'The Forest Becomes a Political Issue', pp. 60–73; Ch. 7, 'Political and Constitutional Struggles, 1258–1327', pp. 135–48.

[13] For maps of the Forest, see *Forests and Chases*, ed. Langton and Jones, Fig. 1, p. 1; Bazeley, 'Extent of English Forest', pp. 140–1; Young, *Royal Forests*, pp. 152–3.

[14] On moorlands, see Angus J. L. Winchester, 'Vaccaries and Agistment: Upland Medieval Forests as Grazing Grounds', in *Forests and Chases*, ed. Langton and Jones, 109–24; on pastures, see Andrew Watkins, 'Cattle Grazing in the Forest of Arden in the Later Middle Ages, *Agricultural History Review*, 37:1 (1989), 12–25; on woodlands, see Oliver Rackham, *Ancient Woodland: Its History, Vegetation and Uses in England* (London, 1980).

[15] Grant, *The Royal Forests*, pp. 5–7.

[16] There is consensus that the Normans introduced the legal concept of the Forest to England, but there were undoubtedly royal hunting parks in Anglo-Saxon England: see Della Hooke, 'Pre-Conquest Woodland: Its Distribution and Usage', *Agricultural History Review*, 37:2 (1989), 113–29, pp. 122–3, 125–6. Cf. Chris Wickham, 'European Forests in the Early Middle Ages: Landscape and Land Clearance', *Settimane di Studio del Centro Italiano di Studi Sull'alto Medioevo*, 37:2 (1990), 479–545.

[17] This is the conclusion of a recent case study: Richard Jones and Mark Page, 'Characterizing rural settlement and landscape: Whittlewood Forest in the middle ages', *Medieval Archaeology*, 47 (2003), 53–83. See also Tom Williamson, *Shaping Medieval Landscapes: Settlement, Society, Environment* (Macclesfield, 2003), p. 59. On hunting in Forests, see Richard Almond, 'The Forest as Hunting Ground', in *Forests and Chases*, ed. Langton and Jones, 68–80.

Indeed, similar connections can be perceived in microcosm in the hundreds of seigneurial hunting parks that were constructed throughout medieval England, many of them within areas of royal Forest.[18] Regardless of the geographical features they shared in common—and often they seem to have coincided with woodland cover, higher ground, and poorer quality soils—the way that parks were delimited and managed significantly shaped their physical layout and land use.[19] 'At its very essence a medieval park had a dual purpose: it kept game in and people out,' Oliver Creighton has written.[20] Parks were indeed physically enclosed by earth banks, hedges, fences, walls, and sometimes with elaborate deer-leaps, making them difficult to enter and exit.[21] Within these enclosures, there were often areas of managed woodland and 'launds' (grazing lawns); in some parks there were also fishponds, rabbit warrens, and even areas of arable land.[22] Parks thus contained dense concentrations of the resources—woods, game, livestock—that the Forest courts, and other local legal institutions were concerned to regulate, distribute, and protect.

On the other hand, much afforested land was neither wooded nor intensively managed. In the north-east and south-west of England in particular, the major Forests were comprised of extensive, open moorlands.[23] The upland moors of north Yorkshire, in the royal Forest of Pickering and the Bishop of Durham's Forest of Allertonshire, were exploited for large-scale sheep rearing by both monastic and secular lords, the former often employing the grange system developed by Cistercian houses.[24] The use of these vaccaries (for cows) and bercaries (for sheep) required relatively little labour, with settlements comprising small hamlets of between four and twelve households.[25] In the summer, some of these upland communities were briefly augmented by lowland villagers who drove their sheep up on to the moors of the northern Forests, living in shiels (temporary huts) while their animals pastured.[26] In the royal Forest of Dartmoor, by contrast, this kind of intercommoning agreement gave way in the later Middle Ages to a system

[18] It has been estimated based on documentary evidence that there were 1,900 parks in existence in the Middle Ages, and quite possibly more that went undocumented: Leonard Cantor, 'Forests, Chases, Parks and Warrens', in *The English Medieval Landscape*, ed. Cantor (London, 1982), p. 81.

[19] Mileson, *Parks in Medieval England*, pp. 2–3, 48–58.

[20] Oliver H. Creighton, *Designs Upon the Land: Elite Landscapes of the Middle Ages* (Woodbridge, 2009), p. 123.

[21] Stephen Moorhouse, 'The Medieval Parks of Yorkshire: Function, Contents and Chronology', in *The Medieval Park: New Perspectives*, ed. Robert Liddiard (Macclesfield, 2007), 99–127, pp. 104–5.

[22] Mileson, *Parks in Medieval England*, p. 64.

[23] Grant, *The Royal Forests*, p. 5; cf. Angus J. L. Winchester, 'Dividing Lines in a Moorland Landscape: Territorial Boundaries in Upland England', *Landscapes*, 2 (2000), 16–32, pp. 18–19.

[24] A. J. Pollard, *North-Eastern England During the Wars of the Roses: Lay Society, War, and Politics 1450–1500* (Oxford, 1990), pp. 35–7.

[25] Winchester, 'Vaccaries and Agistment', p. 116.

[26] Winchester, 'Dividing Lines in a Moorland Landscape', p. 18.

of direct management, in which moorland tenants took over the droving and pasturing of lowland cattle.[27]

These moorland landscapes were not used solely for pastoral agriculture. First, as hunting Forests, the moorlands were shared year-round with the king's deer: in the Forest of Pickering it was reported at the beginning of the sixteenth century that 'the said dere shulde resoorte [among] . . . all the moores in commen for the kinggs tenants'.[28] Secondly, whilst moors were largely open, they did of course also contain crofts and other smallholdings, hived off for arable farming during the agrarian expansion of the thirteenth century.[29] And third, the moorland Forests were also important as centres of quarrying and mining. Parts of the North Riding of Yorkshire, and indeed swathes of the West Riding, produced quantities of iron, lead, coal, slate, and clay, for use both in local industry and export.[30] Dartmoor, Exmoor, and the High Peak in Derbyshire were all technically royal Forests, but in the later Middle Ages they were administered by the Duchy of Lancaster and do not seem to have hosted any kind of Forest courts, but rather stannary courts devoted to the regulation of their extensive tin- and lead-mining industries.[31]

But other Forests, too, often sustained industrial economies through their extensive tracts of woodland.[32] Timber, as well as providing raw materials for woodcutters and woodworkers, enabled the large-scale production of charcoal, which in turn fostered the artisanal manufacture of glass, pottery, and iron.[33] Thus, for example, a royal surveyor sent to Ashdown Forest in Sussex in the late fifteenth century, having dutifully recorded the wages of the court officers and the customs of the tenants there, was clearly more impressed with the bloom smithies.[34] He noted that the water-powered mills at Newbridge could make 24 tons of iron per year at a production cost of £4 8s. 4d.; 'yf the tonne be solde at forge it is comenly solde for £5, somtyme £6, so comenly clere . . . by the yere at

[27] See Harold Fox, *Dartmoor's Alluring Uplands: Transhumance and Pastoral Management in the Middle Ages*, ed. Matthew Tompkins and Christopher Dyer (Exeter, 2012).

[28] TNA, DL 39/3/28B, m. 2r.

[29] See Christopher Dyer, 'Conflict in the landscape: the enclosure movement in England, 1220–1349', *Landscape History*, 28:1 (2006), 21–33, pp. 23–4.

[30] On the North Riding, see J. Linda Drury, 'Durham palatinate forest law and administration, especially in Weardale up to 1440', *Archaeologica Aeliana*, 5th ser., 6 (1978), 87–105, p. 89; on the West Riding, Moorhouse, 'The Medieval Parks of Yorkshire', p. 123.

[31] On the mining communities, see the debate started by Ian Blanchard, 'The Miner and Agricultural Community in Late Medieval England', *Agricultural History Review*, 20 (1970), 96–106; continued by John Hatcher, 'Myths, Miners, and Agricultural Communities', *Agricultural History Review*, 22 (1974), 54–61; Ian Blanchard, 'The Miner and Agricultural Community in Late Medieval England', *Agricultural History Review*, 22 (1974), 65–7. Neither writer remarks on the fact that these areas were afforested.

[32] Jean Birrell, 'The Medieval English Forest', *Journal of Forest History*, 24:2 (1980), 78–85, pp. 81–2; Angus J. L. Winchester, *Landscape and Society in Medieval Cumbria* (Edinburgh, 1987), pp. 103–4.

[33] Jean Birrell, 'Peasant Craftsmen in the Medieval Forest', *Agricultural History Review*, 17:2 (1969), 91–107.

[34] On this production method in medieval Forests, see Glenn Foard, 'Medieval Woodland, Agriculture and Industry in Rockingham Forest, Northamptonshire', *Medieval Archaeology*, 45:1 (2001), 41–95, pp. 73–8.

lest £20 or at lest 40 marks'.[35] As well as iron, the production of charcoal also helped to stoke the tile- and brick-making industries in Forests with good supplies of clay; Merevale Abbey in the Forest of Arden fired as many as 40,000 tiles and bricks at its kiln in Pinwall in 1499.[36]

Such enterprises of course required large capital expenditure, but woodland economies also sustained distinctive forms of small-scale production. Many parks produced wood for sale through the practice of coppicing; it was possible to cultivate short, thin sticks for firewood by coppicing a tree every year, while longer cycles of five to seven years could generate larger beams for timber—both rhythms can be seen in the accounts of some late-medieval estates.[37] There is evidence too for the use of grafting in the fifteenth century, in the fruit orchards that often formed an important embellishment of seigneurial parks.[38] Wood also produced a variety of resources for tenants. A number of presentments in the Forest courts show women making lye (wood ashes mixed with water and left to evaporate) as a detergent or bleaching agent for cloth, presumably for household use.[39] As we shall see, coppices also provided wood for fuel and building, which were often distributed through customary rights called 'housebote', 'ploughbote', 'cartbote', or 'wenbote', rights claimed by tenants for building and repairing their tenements and certain tools.[40]

As well as timber, woodlands served as shelters for the stocks of deer and other game that provided the *raison d'etre* for Forests. Far from the idealized 'wild beasts' of chivalric literature, most deer in late-medieval England were half-domesticated, confined within parks and nurtured by keepers.[41] Indeed, they had to be carefully managed: leaving aside their potential capture by poachers, both fallow and red deer were vulnerable to murrains, which seem to have plagued the late-medieval Forests.[42] At the Forest of Salcey in Northamptonshire, for

[35] TNA, E 32/197, quote from p. 6 [modern pagination]. He also noted that the price of iron had fallen recently, and that the margins of the business were tight—'if it be not well folowed cannot prevaill'.

[36] Andrew Watkins, 'Landowners and Their Estates in the Forest of Arden in the Fifteenth Century', *Agricultural History Review*, 45:1 (1997), 18–33, p. 26.

[37] Mileson, *Parks in Medieval England*, p. 69.

[38] For the grafting of walnut- and apple-trees, see a case in *Yorkshire Star Chamber Proceedings*, ed. William Brown (Yorkshire Archaeological Society Record Series, 41, 1909), p. 17; also Watkins, 'Forest of Arden in the Fifteenth Century', p. 24.

[39] For example, a presentment at Borrowby in the Forest of Allertonshire charged three unnamed women (listed as wives of tenants) as 'whiteners of cloth whereby they destroy the lord's wood'; their activities prompted a general ordinance against this practice, under pain of 40d. NYRCO, ZBD/1/52/12, m. 5r.

[40] Jean Birrell, 'Common Rights in the Medieval Forest: Disputes and Conflicts in the Thirteenth Century', *P&P*, 11 (1987), 22–49, pp. 34–5.

[41] Creighton, *Elite Landscapes of the Middle Ages*, p. 149. On the wildness of the game more generally, see William Perry Marvin, *Hunting Law and Ritual in Medieval English Literature* (Cambridge, 2006), esp. Ch. 2, 'Bloodsport and the Symbolic Order of the Forest', 46–81.

[42] Jean Birrell, 'Deer and Deer Farming in Medieval England', *Agricultural History Review*, 40:2 (1992), pp. 121–2. As she points out, the word 'murrain' covered a multitude of ailments, and notes 'wyppys' (deer-warts?) and 'rotte' (foot-rot) from a 1515 document. See also the remarks on deer

example, over the first five years of the reign of Henry VII, thirty deer died of murrain in 1485, twenty in 1486, eighteen in 1487, fourteen in 1488 and fifteen in 1489; a total of ninety-seven in a few short years.[43] Deer also required careful protection over the winter, whether by planning or the special dispensation of wood resources. Thus at Needwood Chase (Lancashire) in 1440–1, as much as seven acres of pasture was retained for deer hay, and at Weybridge (Northamptonshire) in the early sixteenth century the steward felled extra browsing-wood 'this last hard wynter, for the salvacion of the kyngs game'.[44]

Of course, such efforts were thought to be worth their while because deer were a valuable commodity. In the first place, they formed the object of the *hunt à force* (on horseback, with hounds) and its attendant rituals of aristocratic solidarity.[45] Though such hunts required the kinds of large open spaces that were more typical of the royal Forests, the construction of deer-coursing runs in parks, along with the hunting of smaller game such as hares, partridges, and pheasants, opened up this socially prestigious pastime to a broader class of gentlemen.[46] In the second place, as we shall see in the next section, the hunting of such animals produced a highly-esteemed type of meat that could be conspicuously consumed and distributed within patronage networks. Thus, for example, Henry VI granted a buck from Sapley Forest in Huntingdonshire to the provost and fellows of his new foundation of King's College in June 1453, and Sir Brian Sandford, the warden of Pickering Forest, gave a doe to his servant John Walker for his wedding feast in 1491.[47] While the keeping of deer and other game, and the maintenance of parks for their sustenance, was hardly economical, the investment was repaid in the cultural capital that that they accrued for their owners.[48]

With such prestigious prizes, it is perhaps little surprise that poaching was so widespread in the later Middle Ages.[49] In reality, though, it was probably not the

morality and management in Richard Thomas, 'Chasing the Ideal? Ritualism, Pragmatism and the Later Medieval Hunt in England', in *Breaking and Shaping Beastly Bodies: Animals as Material Culture in the Middle Ages*, ed. Aleksander Pluskowski (Oxford, 2007), 125–48, pp. 142, 144.

[43] TNA, DL 39/2/7, m. 3r.

[44] Respectively: Birrell, 'Deer and Deer Farming', p. 118; TNA, DL 39/2/4, m. 4r.

[45] The classic article remains Marcelle Thiébaux, 'Hunting in the Middle Ages', *Speculum*, 42:2 (1967), 260–74; on its representation in literature, Susan Crane, 'Ritual Aspects of the Hunt à Force', in *Engaging with Nature: Essays on the Natural World in Medieval and Early Modern Europe*, ed. Barbara A. Hanawalt and Lisa J. Kiser (Notre Dame, 2008), 63–84.

[46] Smaller game were sometimes known as 'beasts of the chase': see Marvin, *Hunting Law and Ritual*, pp. 108ff; see also Naomi Sykes, 'Animal Bones and Animal Parks', in *Medieval Park*, ed. Liddiard, 49–62, p. 53. On deer-coursing, see Christopher Taylor, 'Ravensdale Park, Derbyshire, and medieval deer coursing', *Landscape History*, 26:1 (2004), 37–57.

[47] Respectively: TNA, DL 39/2/7, m. 3r; DL 39/3/16, rot. 1, m. 4r. See also Manning, *Hunters and Poachers*, pp. 9–13.

[48] Mileson, *Parks in Medieval England*, pp. 46–7.

[49] Generally, see Jean Birrell, 'Who Poached the King's Deer? A Study in Thirteenth Century Crime', *Midland History*, 7 (1982), 9–25.

casually glamorous activity of the Robin Hood ballads.[50] The logistics of both licit and illicit seigneurial hunting depended on Forest workers who acted as guides, servants, and abettors in the capture of animals; for example, an indictment of the 1470s from Waltham Forest (Essex) recorded that a buck had been killed 'by certeyn felesship' harboured by John Stokker, a labourer of Lambourne.[51] Forest inhabitants not only assisted others, though, but clearly took the opportunity to hunt for themselves, putting their local knowledge to use with their dogs, nets, and the oft-cited but rarely-specified 'engines'—probably snares of various kinds—to catch and kill deer and other game.[52] In the majority of individual cases it is difficult to assess whether such poaching was for sport or meat, though these need not have been mutually exclusive motivations.[53] Like the hard-fought rights to use woods and pastures, the occasional taste of illicit venison offered a privilege that perhaps did something to offset the restrictions of living within a Forest or an imparked manor.

Such activities certainly chime with a more general impression of Forest communities as independent and assertive, linked, perhaps, to their unburdened tenancies on assarted grounds and their physical remoteness from the ties of seigneurial power.[54] Certainly, some Forests were closely associated with rebellion and sedition: the men of Galtres waged a campaign of violent intimidation against St. Mary's Abbey in York over pasture rights in 1433 and again in the 1460s and 1470s.[55] Much like the maritime communities we examined in Chapter 3, the inhabitants of late-medieval Forests were vigorous in their defence of special customary rights and possessed of a strong local identity, which set them apart from the rest of the realm.[56] Thus the *communitates* of the Forest of Dean accused of attacking Severn grain-barges in the 1430s were described as a 'wild people (close and adjacent to Wales), and the whole community of the Forest... cares nothing for the law, its officers, or its procedures'.[57] From the perspective of the Common Pleas at Westminster, where this suit was lodged, it might have seemed

[50] Certainly this is the case in the *Gest*: 'But alway went good Robyn... / And alway slewe the kynges dere / And welt them at his wyll.' J. C. Holt, *Robin Hood* (London, rev. edn., 1989), pp. 21–2.

[51] TNA, DL 39/2/10, no. 12.

[52] E.g. DL 39/2/13 [Surrey Eyre of 1488], mm. 5v–6r. See also Jean Birrell, 'Peasant deer poachers in the medieval forest', in *Progress and problems in medieval England: Essays in Honour of Edward Miller*, ed. Richard Britnell and John Hatcher (Cambridge, 1996), 68–88, esp. pp. 74–5. More recently, see the interesting archaeological argument for the consumption of venison by non-elites in the Middle Ages: Naomi Sykes, 'Taking Sides: The Social Life of Venison in Medieval England', in *Animals as Material Culture*, ed. Pluskowski, 149–60.

[53] Harvey, 'Poaching and Sedition', pp. 171–3.

[54] Winchester, *Medieval Cumbria*, pp. 63–4, 134–5.

[55] TNA, SC 8/140/6996 [a parliamentary petition by the abbot requesting inquiry in the 1420s]; C 49/21/22 [for the judgment—given in favour of the abbot]; C 1/43/32 [the 1460s–70s petition].

[56] Almond and Pollard, 'Robin Hood and Social Terminology', p. 72–3.

[57] TNA, CP40/688, rots. 113r–117r [suits by Tewkesbury merchants, also in 1433]; see also CP40/818, rots. 305–8 [similar suits pleaded in 1466]. Thanks are due to Dr Hannes Kleineke for his generosity in directing me to these disputes, and supplying me with the references.

so. But a closer inspection of local Forests reveals a culture steeped in law and its institutions—it is to these that we now turn.

Forest Law in the Later Middle Ages: Local Courts, Officers, and Eyres

Forest law in fifteenth-century England operated at three institutional levels. Locally, the customary courts of the royal Forest—along with those local courts outside it that borrowed aspects of Forest law—generally served to regulate pasture, prevent trespasses against the woods, and prosecute poaching. Second, these courts were often supervised by a cadre of officers, many of whom were appointed by commissions from the crown; these prestigious posts were often fiercely contested, which meant that such officers often kept meticulous accounts to guard against accusations of mismanagement. Third, while regular centralized supervision of the royal Forests waned after the end of the reign of Edward III, in the later fifteenth century some efforts were made to rejuvenate central Forest administration. In what follows we examine each of these levels in turn, proceeding from the customary Forest courts and the diffusion of their procedures to other local courts, to the appointment of officers, and finally to the revival of the Forest eyres in the later fifteenth century. As we shall see throughout, the way in which Forest law was managed, and the chains of bureaucracy that existed between its institutions, created a strong emphasis on accountability, by which I mean both the quantification of Forest resources and the pressure to audit them.

To begin with, the precise name, jurisdiction, and powers of a local Forest court depended on wider patterns of lordship and custom.[58] In many Forests, this local court was referred to as a 'swannimote'.[59] This title probably refers to the function of these courts in regulating the pasture of 'swine' in the woods; though this is only a very partial description of these courts' activities, such an etymology does speak to the courts' recurrent concern with the accounting of resources.[60] Indeed, the term 'swannimote' was used widely across English Forests, from Sparsholt (Hampshire) to Weybridge to Pickering.[61] Other courts had different names according to their administration. For example, in the Forests held as part of the estates of the Duchy of Lancaster, such as Duffield Frith (Derbyshire) and Needwood Chase, local courts were referred to as 'woodmotes'; though the name

[58] John Langton, 'Medieval Forests and Chases: Another Realm?', in *Forests and Chases*, ed. Langton and Jones, pp. 26–7.

[59] A handful of courts from the north and north-west used the term 'swainmote' instead; the metathesis may simply be based on regional pronunciation. For examples, see TNA, DL 39/2/8, m. 1r. (Wharmore, Lancashire); Drury, 'Durham palatinate forest law and administration', p. 100.

[60] On the etymology (and the word's mixed usage), see Turner, 'Introduction', pp. xxix–xxx.

[61] Respectively: TNA, DL 39/2/10, no. 29; DL 39/2/4, no. 11; DL 39/2/2, m. 1r.–2v.

might imply a preoccupation with the vert of the Forest, their business in fact resembles those of the swannimotes elsewhere.[62] Alternatively, the 'forestmotes' of the Bishop of Durham in Allertonshire might have been so termed to emphasize their status as palatinate 'Forests'—a term normally reserved for royal possessions.[63]

Alongside these customary 'motes', there also in some places continued to exist a Forest jurisdiction known as the 'court of attachments' (*curia attachiamentis*). Such courts are understood to have been mandated by the Forest Charter in 1217, which ordered that Forest officers should meet every forty days to present trespasses and compel offenders to appear at the next Forest court, in a system that was theoretically integrated with the Forest eyre.[64] In practice, however, even in the late thirteenth century these courts did not always maintain this special function, and in many places they seem to have been interchangeable with swannimotes.[65] Nonetheless, by the fifteenth century, some courts of attachment do seem to have developed a more specific jurisdiction, becoming associated in particular with vert trespasses.[66] More specifically, where records survive, they were the forum for the payment of small, routine fines for the taking of wood: thus at the frequent itinerant courts in the Forest of Galtres in the early 1460s, most suitors paid up to a shilling for taking cartloads of branches, while others, such as William Wody of Shipton, were fined for trespassing on the royal launds.[67]

While the records of courts of attachment have rarely survived on their own, this jurisdiction was often interpellated in the proceedings of local seigneurial courts.[68] The appearance of such 'attachments' in manorial courts is part of a wider trend in the later Middle Ages whereby local courts heard what look like 'Forest pleas', appointed officers such as foresters and parkers, and used some of the terms and procedures associated with the Forest courts. These associations developed for a couple of different reasons. In the first place, as Isobel Harvey has argued, the statute of 1390 which forbade artificers, labourers, and indeed anyone with lands worth less than 40s. a year from keeping greyhounds marked 'a radical

[62] TNA, DL 39/2/1–2 [Duffield]; DL 30/110/1646, DL 30/110/1652, DL 30/111/1666 [Needwood].

[63] NYRCO, ZBD 50/15, m. 1v; ZBD 50/18, m. 4v; ZBD 51/2, m 3v; ZBD 51/5, m. 3r; ZBD 51/9, m. 1v; ZBD 51/12, m. 1r; ZBD 51/14, m. 4v; ZBD 51/27, m. 1r–2v. Private seigneurial Forests were often known as 'chases' instead, although there does not seem to be any substantive legal distinction between the two, as has often been thought: see Turner, 'Introduction', pp. cix–cxv.

[64] See the lengthy discussion in Charles R. Young, 'The Forest Eyre in England during the Thirteenth Century', *American Journal of Legal History*, 18:4 (1974), pp. 323–6.

[65] Turner, 'Introduction', pp. xxxvi–xxxvii.

[66] Ibid., pp. xxx–xxxi; Grant, *The Royal Forests*, pp. 37, 171; TNA, DL 39/2/2. Although cf. the oath taken by officers of the swannimote, which specifically associates the courts of attachment with pig pasturing: TNA, WARD 2/60/234/145.

[67] TNA, SC 2/211/43, m. 1v.

[68] For 'wood attachments' in Forest courts, see, for example, TNA, DL 39/2/2, mm. 1r–v (Pickering woodmote); NYCRO, ZBD 51/5, 9, 11, 14, 27, etc. (Allertonshire Forestmotes). For the wood attachments in manorial courts, see, for example: NYCRO, ZFL/111, mm. 8r, 15r (Ingleby Arncliffe, for free tenants only); WSRO, PHA 7036, mm. 1r, 2v, PHA 7037, recto, PHA 7038, m. 1r, etc. (Spofforth); WYASL, WYL163/568, mm. 3v, 4v, 5v, 6r, etc. (Middleham Honour).

change in the law of hunting'.[69] Not only did it make poachers of many peasant hunters, but it also meant that poaching could be presented in a range of secular jurisdictions.[70] Lords with parks seized the opportunity to prosecute offences against their game through their own courts; at Walberswick in Suffolk, John Herpyngham was presented in late 1497 for keeping a greyhound, 'and does not have the lands or tenements to maintain one, against the form of the statute'. He was fined the apparently arbitrary but by no means negligible sum of 3s. 4d.[71]

The prosecution of Forest-type offences in local courts was also linked to the obtaining of royal grants of free warren and licences to impark; indeed this was dramatically clear at Walberswick, where a rash of poaching prosecutions followed shortly after the lord's attainment of free warren in 1404.[72] Although parks and warrens were technically distinct from one another, both privileges became an important accoutrement of lordship over the course of the thirteenth and fourteenth centuries; as Stephen Mileson has shown, moreover, such grants and licences were most often sought (or asserted) by lords with possessions in or close to the bounds of the royal Forest.[73] But wherever they were located, they often seem to have been interpreted as conferring forms of Forest jurisdiction. For example at Lord Latymer's imparked manor of Danby in North Yorkshire, in the Forest of Pickering, the views of frankpledge included sections for wood attachments, 'agistment in the forest', a manorial officer known as the 'receiver of the forest', and even expenses for the conducting of a 'regard', a historic procedure of Forest law discussed later on.[74]

Forest legal culture, then, came to extend an influence outside the boundaries of the royal Forests into the many seigneurial parks of late-medieval England. Interestingly, there is even a sense that Forest law itself was no longer considered as the sole dominion of the crown. Thus, in 1518, Charles Bothe, Bishop of Hereford, complained that one of his more substantial tenants had established

[69] Harvey, 'Poaching and Sedition', p. 174. The statute of 1390 (13 Ric. II Stat. 1 c. 13) represented quite a turnaround from the (rejected) petition of the Commons in 1372 that complained of great impoverishment and damage to crops caused by the inability of commoners to hunt in Forests and purlieus: *PROME*, v, p. 265. The 1390 statute against dogs expanded upon a very similar prohibition in Forest law: Turner, 'Introduction', pp. xii, xxi.

[70] The statute provided for the regulation of the offence by Justices of the Peace. Certainly, the king's courts prosecuted this offence: a Hertfordshire indictment of 1409 against the butcher John Hurre was sent to the King's Bench, quoting the statute almost to the letter: TNA, KB9/197/1, 10.

[71] SROI, HA30/312/200, m. 14v. This was presumably a mercy for not pursuing further action; at the court of Netherseal in Derbyshire in 1438, two men were presented for 'keeping greyhounds against the statute', and the bailiff was instructed to pursue writs against them: DRO, D77/2/1/7, recto.

[72] See Colin Richmond, *John Hopton: A Fifteenth Century Suffolk Gentleman* (Cambridge, 1981), p. 8. For the offences, see SROI, HA30/314/19d/1–21, mm. 1r, 3r, 5r, 6r, 8r, 9r, 10r, 11r; HA 30/369/412, m. 2v.

[73] Mileson, *Parks in Medieval England*, pp. 124–6, including Fig.18. This relationship had been postulated in Turner, 'Introduction', p. cxvi.

[74] On Danby's status as a park, see L. M. Cantor, *The Medieval Parks of England: A Gazetteer* (Loughborough, 1983), pp. 88–9; Pollard, *North-Eastern England*, p. 37. For mention of this officer, NYRCO, ZAL 1/1/10, m. 1r.

their own park, 'to the let and distubaunce of his game, contrarye to the statute of the forest'.[75] By the time he was writing, the claim that Forest law belonged as much to lords as to the king was clearly not far-fetched; of course, they had just as much desire to protect their woods and game, and they had paid to acquire the right to do so legally. Words, concepts, and procedures traditionally associated with the Forests, then, such as 'vert', 'wild beasts' (*feras*), 'housebote', pannage, and wood attachments, seeped into the discourse of local courts, carrying Forest legal culture—and particularly its concern with managing and accounting for resources of pasture, wood, and game—beyond the Forests themselves.[76]

This diffusion of Forest legal culture took place at the same time as a more general trend away from centralized Forest administration.[77] In the later fourteenth and fifteenth centuries, the crown supervised Forests in three main ways. In the first place, judicial commissions were issued to local royal officials or Forest officers to investigate offences committed in specific Forests, on an ad-hoc basis—a long-standing judicial practice that had existed alongside the eyres.[78] In the second place, the royal Chancery continued to send out regular orders for 'regards' to be held for individual Forests, once again maintaining an older administrative exercise that had been used as early as the twelfth century, and was clearly entrenched by the time of the Forest Charter of 1217.[79] Officers called regarders were ordered by the crown to investigate the state of a Forest and whether crown rights had been infringed, according to a set of articles, in preparation for the coming of the Forest eyre justices.[80] Even though no Forest eyres were actually held in the period between the 1350s and 1460s, regards were ordered regularly for the Forest of Sherwood, and also occasionally for the Forests of Galtres, Inglewood, Pickering, Rockingham, and Rutland.[81]

[75] *Registrum Caroli Bothe, Episcopi Herefordensis*, ed. Arthur Thomas Bannister, Canterbury and York Society, 28 (London, 1921), p. 48.

[76] E.g. '*feras infra parcum*' at the Neville manor of Spofforth (Yorkshire) in 1499: WSRO, PHA 7042, recto. On the concept of *feras* more generally, see Marvin, *Hunting Law and Ritual*, p. 60. 'Housebote' was included in an *inter vivos* land transfer at Wootton Wawen (Warwickshire), which was never afforested: KCC, WOW/176, m. 2r. Pannage can be identified widely: see Birrell, 'Common Rights in the Medieval Forest', pp. 25, 37–8, 40.

[77] See Johnson, 'Redistribution of Forest Law'.

[78] For an early example, see *CPR*, 1281–92, p. 398: a commission from Edward I 'to enquire and do justice' regarding trespasses against vert and venison in the Forest of Feckenham. Of course, this practice coincided with the decline of both the general and Forest eyres: see Anthony Musson, *Public Order and Law Enforcement: The Local Administration of Criminal Justice 1294–1350* (Woodbridge, 1996), pp. 11–33. For fifteenth century commissions, see e.g. *CPR*, 1413–16, pp. 113, 413; *CPR*, 1416–22, pp. 79, 389; *CPR*, 1436–41, p. 86; CPR, 1461–7, p. 102.

[79] Turner, 'Introduction', p. lxxv. The regard, and the officers known as regarders were mentioned explicitly in the Charter in capita 5–7.

[80] Grant, *The Royal Forests*, pp. 43–6, 170.

[81] For Sherwood, *CCR*, 1422–9, pp. 69, 260, 471; *CCR*, 1429–35, pp. 192, 364; *CCR*, 1435–41, p. 478; *CCR*, 1441–7, pp. 221, 472; *CCR*, 1447–54, pp. 111, 450; *CCR*, 1455–60, p. 179. For Galtres: *CCR*, 1422–9, pp. 69, 471; *CCR*, 1435–41, p. 284. For Inglewood, *CCR*, 1429–35, p. 215; *CCR*, 1435–41, p. 284. For Pickering *CCR*, 1422–9, p. 471, *CCR*, 1429–35, p. 364. For Rockingham *CCR*, 1422–9, p. 343. For Rutland: *CCR*, 1447–54, p. 256; *CCR*, 1455–60, p. 311.

Unfortunately, almost none of the returns for these commissions have survived, but it is clear from local records that the duties of regarders varied from Forest to Forest.[82] At Pickering in 1408, two regarders were fined for failing to appear at a swannimote, implying a regular local presence; at Rockingham in the 1480s—albeit after a period of substantial reform in the Forest administration—they appear in their more traditional role as external auditors; at a Surrey session their role was not obviously distinguished from the verderers, who were responsible for the day-to-day regulation of the woods; and at West Bere (Hampshire) they received timber and venison as part of their perquisites, like the other salaried officers.[83] That contemporaries considered regarders to be part of Forest administration cannot be in doubt, but their technical responsibilities seem to have percolated through local arrangements. While the crown retained the aspiration and some of the infrastructure of centralized supervision of the Forests throughout the later Middle Ages, the day-to-day administration of the Forests was generally localized.

Indeed, this can be seen most clearly in the increasing use of individual appointments to other Forest offices in the later fourteenth and fifteenth centuries. Most notably, the crown began to appoint a 'master forester' or warden to take charge of the overall supervision of a Forest, and also verderers, who were responsible for the day-to-day management of the forest administration.[84] These senior offices were generally given to high-ranking knights and gentry who were in favour with the king, but they were not ceremonial roles; those who failed to carry out their duties properly were often replaced, as for example in 1436 when a new verderer was required for the Forest of Windsor because the occupant, Thomas Bulloke, was said to be 'too much occupied with his own business to have leisure for exercise of that office'.[85] These men, in turn, were charged with

[82] I have only come across one such return, for the Forest of Rockingham, preserved among the 'Ancient Indictments' of the King's Bench: TNA, KB 9/233, no. 71. Interestingly, no commission for it is preserved, at least among the printed editions of the close and patent rolls.

[83] Pickering: TNA, DL 39/2/2, m. 1v; Rockingham (a unique survival of a late-medieval regarder's roll): TNA, DL 39/2/14; Surrey: TNA, DL 39/2/18, mm. 1v, 4r. West Bere: TNA, DL 39/2/10, nos. 25, 26.

[84] The earliest reference I have found to 'master forester' as a royal office is 1360: *CPR*, 1358–61, p. 472 (a pardon and grant to William, Baron Greystock, who had assumed the office without licence). There are many, much older grants giving 'custody' or 'keeping' of royal Forests. Like other royal offices, some of these became associated with particular families—such as the Hastings family for Pickering, the Sturmy family for Savernake (Wiltshire), and the Lisle family for Chute (Hampshire)—and were passed down as part of an estate: see Johnson, 'Redistribution of Forest Law', p. 98, fn. 30. The practice of appointing verderers seems to have been a new policy under Edward I, as it was introduced from the beginning of his reign, and had never happened under Henry III. See *CCR*, 1272–9, p. 12.

[85] For the quoted case: *CCR*, 1435–41, p. 27. Other verderers were replaced due to death, age, sickness, or for failing to live in or near the Forest; one man was accused of illiteracy. For examples of sickness and age as a reason for replacement: *CCR*, 1422–9, p. 170, *CCR*, 1429–35, p. 154, *CCR*, 1435–41, p. 81. For not living nearby: *CCR*, 1422–9, p. 361, *CCR*, 1429–35, pp. 4, 12, 263, 272–3, *CCR*, 1435–41, p. 81. For lack of leisure: *CCR*, 1422–9, p. 166, *CCR*, 1429–35, pp. 3, 4, *CCR*, 1435–41, pp. 27, 144; for the case of illiteracy, see *CCR*, 1442–7, p. 97.

appointing and managing a cadre of officers responsible for policing and maintaining the Forest on the ground: the rangers and walkers who patrolled the parks and launds, the woodwards who supervised the conservation and allocation of wood, and, more generally, foresters, who might do both.[86]

Such Forest appointments, in addition to the stipends they offered, were prestigious. In addition to the healthy stipends attached to them, officers received specified quantities of timber and venison as perquisites, which could be conspicuously consumed or given as gifts within patronage networks.[87] Even outside of the royal Forests in imparked manors, where 'foresters' or parkers were often appointed as part of the more general manorial administration, the control which these offices afforded over wood and game seems to have represented a considerable benefit of the job.[88] But the desirability of these offices also meant that their holders were frequently challenged by others, particularly if it could be argued that they were illicitly taking too many perquisites and failing to conserve the Forest.[89] Melding with the traditional concerns of Forest law with the preservation of the 'vert and venison', these circumstances gave rise to a discourse of accountability in the administration of Forests and parks that strongly pressurized these officers to account for the disposal of their resources—the practical consequences of which we shall see in the next section.[90]

For now, it is worth noting the way in which this logic was given new impetus by more regular supervision of the Forests in the second half of the fifteenth century. Although this has traditionally been attributed to an administrative initiative of Henry VII, there is some evidence to suggest that it was underway during the 1460s and 1470s, when Henry Bourchier was the Chief Justice of the

[86] E.g. for foresters, walkers, and rangers (all paid the same wages) at Ashdown Forest, see TNA, E 32/197, mm. 1r–2r; at Waltham, each 'bailiwick' of the Forest was supposed to be served by one 'riding forester', four foresters, and a woodward—there were concerns in the 1480s about the use of deputies and residency: DL 39/2/22, m. 3v; at Pickering in the 1400s, woodwards were appointed for each vill in the Forest: DL 39/2/2, m. 1r. Some Forests also appointed *agistatores*, responsible for maintaining pasture and pannage: e.g. at Bere in Hampshire, DL 39/2/10, no. 21, or Windsor, DL 39/2/15, no. 11.

[87] For the stipends attached to these offices, which could amount to as much as £10 per year, see e.g. *CPR*, 1422–9, p. 5; *CPR*, 1436–41, pp. 63, 78.

[88] For foresters appointed in imparked manors, see e.g. Coverham, NYCRO, ZDX, m. 3r; Ingleby Arncliffe, ZFL 110, m. 1r, Kettlewell, WYASL, WYL163/568, m. 1r; Healaugh Park, WSRO, PHA 6970, m. 1r.

[89] Consider, for example, the thirty-year struggle over the Forest of Sapley and Weybridge, the custodianship of which was an appurtenance of the manor of Wolley (Huntingdonshire). Held in 1462 by John Tiptoft, who was executed during the readeption, its subsequent descent and regranting provoked a lengthy lawsuit before the king's council learned in the law in the late 1480s; on the legal proceedings between Gerard Stukeley and Sir Thomas Lovell, and associated evidence, are bundled in TNA, DL 39/2/4. Generally, see Johnson, 'Redistribution of Forest Law', pp. 98–9.

[90] From the second half of the fourteenth century, grants of Forest offices began to include specific provisos that the officer would preserve the vert and venison: see *CPR*, 1350–4, p. 5. This sense continues sporadically thereafter: see *CPR*, 1370–4, p. 249, *CPR*, 1377–81, p. 591, *CPR*, 1385–9, pp. 211, 428 (the latter grant including the explicit proviso 'that he abide therein [in the Forest of Galtres] in person and keep the vert and venison'); *CPR*, 1436–41, p. 367, *CPR*, 1461–7, p. 13. On the integrity of foresters, see also generally Birrell, 'Deer and Deer Farming', pp. 121–2.

Forests south of the Trent.[91] However, the Forest eyres launched from 1487 onwards certainly represented a new scale of activity, even if these efforts dissipated after a few intense years.[92] For example, the material from a single eyre, held at Windsor on August 4, 1488, fills two separate files, including nearly fifty separate items of varying shape, size, and judicial purpose, which were later compiled into a final fair copy.[93] The eyres also archived older local documents; in some places, such as the Forest of Salcey, earlier swannimote rolls only survive because they were copied by the eyre clerks.[94] The eyres thus represented a remarkable administrative endeavour, attempting both to assess the recent governance of the Forests and working to reform them.

They were supposed to work, as their thirteenth-century predecessors had, by sending Forest justices to counties to hold sessions for the conviction and punishment of previously presented offenders.[95] In practice, reimplementing such an ancient system was complicated, and proceedings appear to have been rather more flexible.[96] At Waltham Forest, for example, fresh indictments were made ahead of the sessions in the summer of 1489, while at Salisbury, there was some confusion over jurisdiction; two men implicated in the catching of swans had their fines respited 'until the justices may be advised whether the inquests for these trespasses ought to be held before the said justices, or not'.[97] Most eyres heard a range of Forest business, but, with a couple of exceptions, the agenda was often dictated by the Forest juries themselves.[98] While they still revolved around the traditional concerns with the protection of the 'vert and venison', therefore, the

[91] The earliest evidence is an 'eyre' (a grand title for what was in fact a brief session to warrant a claim to the keepership of the Forest of Stowood and Shotover): TNA, DL 39/2/5. Likewise, another so-called eyre from 1477 was just an exemplification of a claim made by Sir John Seymour to lands in Savernake Forest (Wiltshire): TNA, E 146/2/37. Other business associated with Bourchier can be found in *The Black Book of Southampton*, ed. A. B. Wallis Chapman, Southampton Record Society, 12 (3 vols: Southampton, 1912–15), iii, pp. 140–5. My thanks to Linda Clark for this reference.

[92] Generally, see Grant, *The Royal Forests*, pp. 181–3; Crook, 'Records of Forest Eyres', p. 188; Johnson, 'Redistribution of Forest Law', pp. 99–100. On later efforts at Forest administration under Henry VII, see for example, at Whaddon Chase in Buckinghamshire and at Windsor respectively: TNA, DL 39/3/19; DL/39/3/23. Tellingly, perhaps, neither is construed as an 'eyre'. The last effort to employ the eyre system was somewhat half-hearted: in 1538 Thomas Cromwell, as Chief Justice of the Forests North of the Trent, ordered the compilation of the *Liber Negro*, a book that compiled some administrative information related to a few northern Forests; in spite of the fact that a couple of these items were titled 'eyres', they did not constitute Forest eyres properly speaking, either in form or function. TNA, E 36/77, ff. 1r, 9r.

[93] This was the eyre for the Forests of Berkshire. For the two miscellaneous bundles, see TNA, DL 39/2/15, 16; for the fair copy, see DL 39/2/17.

[94] TNA, DL 39/2/7, mm. 5r–7r (copies of swannimote rolls for 1476–83).

[95] On the workings of the older system, see Young, *Royal Forests*, Ch. 3, 'The Angevin System at Work', pp. 33–59.

[96] It is clear that they wished to get the details right, as a precedent roll and a formulary of Forest writs were compiled at this time: respectively, TNA, DL 39/3/30; DL 39/4/3.

[97] Respectively, TNA, DL 39/2/22, mm. 1r–9r; TNA, DL 39/2/20, m. 4r.

[98] Many of the sessions included lengthy (and largely redundant) processes for 'claims of liberties', in which local lords and monastic houses presented evidences of title for lands within the Forest: e.g. at Bernwood Forest (in both Buckinghamshire and Oxfordshire) in 1489: TNA, E 146/1/10, mm. 9–15.

eyres also provide an excellent view into the ways that late-medieval Forest communities understood Forest law, and attempted to repurpose some of its key ideas in the pursuit of their own concerns.

Overall, the institutions of Forest governance in late-medieval England worked to produce a legal culture focused upon the management of forest landscapes. Concern with the 'vert and venison' had always lain at the heart of Forest law, and this was continued through the courts of attachment that regulated wood-cutting, or the regards that reviewed the Forests every three years. But this tendency was given new impetuses and magnified by the ways in which Forest administration was redistributed during the later fourteenth and fifteenth centuries. On the one hand, the dispersal of Forest jurisdictions to local courts enabled lords to adopt its procedures for the management of their own parks and warrens; and on the other, the devolution of the administration of royal Forests to local officers, and the concomitant competition for the patronage and perquisites these positions offered, created a pressure on them to account for the woods, pasture, and game at their disposal. In the following section, we turn to look at the ways in which this emphasis on accountability infused the routine operation of institutions in Forest legal culture.

Forest Courts and Accountability: Wood, Pasture, and Game

Forest institutions in late-medieval England worked to figure wood, pasture, and game as scarce and fragile natural resources that had to be carefully managed and regulated. Brushwood, branches, and timber were sorted into different categories that dictated who could use them and how; pastures in open moorlands and woodlands were marked, divided, and enclosed in order to control access to common rights; and game animals themselves—not only deer, but also foxes, hares, and a variety of gamebirds—were protected and delimited in order to preserve legitimate hunting and prevent illicit poaching. This concern with nature as a resource was driven, as I have been emphasizing, by the desire of Forest officers to both exploit and account for their perquisites. This fed into the way that local Forest courts worked on a routine basis, less as institutions for the settlement of disputes or the upholding of justice, but as tribunals for the rendering of account. In what follows, we shall see this in the way that these courts worked to classify, quantify, and restrict forest resources, producing a legal culture that was founded upon a rationale of accountable management.

In the first place, the classification of the resources within forests and parks was essential to imagining them as commodities that could then be quantified and allocated. To begin with, wood was divided between different species: oak, for example, was highly valued as building timber for large structures, and the right to take a certain number of oaks per year was specifically included as part of the privileges of Forest officials, while it was only rarely granted by them to Forest tenants in order to make repairs to their tenements.[99] Similarly, holly was supposed to be reserved as winter fodder for deer; at Carlton-in-Coverdale, John Rider was fined after he 'stripped the leaves off holly trees for the grazing of his animals in winter, without licence'.[100] By demarcating different kinds of wood for different uses, then, the woodwards and foresters of the local courts were able to enrol the rights of the tenantry within their management of the Forest. Indeed, at Borrowby in the Forest of Allertonshire, an ordinance was passed against cutting the roots of any tree, with crab-apples and birches singled out for special protection—'except in Ellerbeck, where the trees are defective and weak'.[101] Customary rights were upheld, then, by limiting them to inferior resources.

Indeed, such concerns also applied to the parts of trees tenants were permitted to take. When it came to the collection of wood, for example, Forest tenants who claimed the right of firebote were often restricted to windfall or dead wood that had been blown out of the trees naturally, while the taking of greenwood was forbidden; of course, as Jean Birrell has pointed out, the lines between these categories were open to negotiation in practice.[102] While they mostly used the 'branches', presumably for firewood, there are also frequent references in Forest courts to 'stubs' (stumps), 'rynds' (bark), and 'boghes' (boughs).[103] These parts of trees had quite different uses: stumps were burnt as fuel, bark could be used for tanning and cordwaining, and boughs could be used for construction.[104] And for woodwards and foresters concerned with the sustainability of wood resources through careful coppicing and grafting, particular attention was paid to the cutting of young or small trees, as when William Rymor was fined at Brompton in Allertonshire for 'cutting a young ash in his garden without licence'. Such careful classification of resources in local courts, then, was justified in relation to the preservation of the Forest.

Game animals, too, were carefully classified. An inquisition into the management of the Forest of Pickering in the early sixteenth century, after a lengthy dispute between two claimants to the office of master forester there, produced reams of documentation from both sides over alleged abuses in illicit taking of wood and game.[105] In the course of enumerating the theft of venison, no fewer

[99] For oaks granted as perquisites, see e.g. NYCRO, ZBD/1/52/3, m. 3v; TNA, DL 39/3/11, m. 3r; DL 39/3/16, Rot. 5, m. 1r.

[100] WYASL, 163/568, m. 3r.

[101] NYRCO, ZBD/1/52/12, m. 4v.

[102] Birrell, 'Common Rights in the Medieval Forest', p. 31, also fn. 33 there.

[103] Respectively: WSRO, PHA 7035, annex 1 (Spofforth); DL 30/487/2, m. 7r (Knaresborough); DL 39/3/11, m. 3r (Scholes, in the Honour of Pontefract).

[104] Birrell, 'Peasant Craftsmen', p. 103, mentions bark used thus in the thirteenth century.

[105] On the dispute, see Robert Bell Turton, *The Honor and Forest of Pickering*, North Riding Record Society, n.s., 1 (London, 1894), pp. xxiv–xxvi; documents from the dispute are printed at pp. 167–204. They also survive in TNA, DL 39/3/16, 26, 27, 28A, 28B.

than fourteen different terms were used to designate deer of various kinds, including not only the more obvious distinctions between red and fallow deer, and male and female animals, but also their ages—a 'tegg' being a two-year-old fallow doe, for example, and a 'broket' a male red deer of the same age—distinctions that were important in the culture of hunting.[106] The capacity for such specificity not only demonstrated the officers' detailed knowledge of the state of the Forest, but also their expertise in distinguishing different objects of prey; in the context of this contestation over the competent management of the vert and venison, perhaps such language was supposed to signal their fluency with the courtly discourses of the chase.[107]

Indeed, the differentiation of game was part of what sorted hunters from criminal poachers. John Lokwood of Scarth, a notorious poacher on the Osmotherley moors in the 1480s, was presented at an Allertonshire Forestmote for chasing 'all the deer that happened to be . . . on the moors and in the woods and fields, and also lesser game such as roe-deer, foxes, and hares, as well as the grazing animals of the tenants . . . to the grave damage both of the lord and of the tenants'.[108] Part of the ire directed at him here seems to have lain in his undirected, wanton chasing of any animal that he stumbled across, which not only disturbed the broader landscape, but which clearly differentiated his pursuit from that of a legitimate hunter. Moreover, the notion that some kinds of animals ought to be classified as 'game', and thus reserved for the plates of the aristocracy, seems to underlie the disdain that can be detected in some poaching presentments. For example when Robert Thornton and William Lewte were caught hunting partridges with 'nets and devices' in the fields of Linton near the river Wharfe, the bailiff was ordered to carry out a cruelly ironic punishment, confining the poachers in the stocks, and retaining their hunting equipment for the use of the lord.[109] There was little doubt here over who had the privilege to take and eat such birds.

The routine operations of these institutions also worked to quantify these commodities, both as a means of assessing the state of the park or Forest and also as a means of controlling the exercise of customary rights. In the customary swannimotes of the Forest, for example, tenants often possessed the right to fatten their pigs over the winter on the beechmast, chestnuts, and acorns that amassed on the woodland floor, a right known as pannage.[110] In most places, they paid a fixed rate per animal for this right, but the precise amount was fixed by local custom. For example at the Forest of Galtres in the early 1460s, tenants paid a

[106] These terms are tabulated in Turton, *Forest of Pickering*, pp. 139–40.

[107] On the connections between hunting law and literature, see Marvin, *Hunting Law and Ritual.*

[108] NYCRO, ZBD/1/52/12, m. 1r. Lokwood was presented for poaching two years later in the manorial court of nearby Ingleby Arnecliffe: NYRCO, ZFL/111, m. 4r.

[109] WSRO, PHA 7036, m. 2v.

[110] Birrell, 'Common Rights in the Medieval Forest', p. 38.

penny for a pig and a half-penny for a piglet; in 1461, with nineteen people paying for 52 pigs and 110 piglets, this brought in a small revenue of 8s. 11d.[111] By contrast, at the Forest of Salcey about a decade later, a more complex system prevailed, with tenants paying 4d. for a sow or a boar, 3d. for a 'pig', and 1d. for a 'shotling', a weaned piglet.[112] While in the court record these processes look highly repetitive and bureaucratic, for tenants who owned and pannaged different numbers and kinds of animals, they must have represented an important opportunity to enunciate their customary rights.[113]

Similar processes characterized the courts of attachment that regulated the collection of wood in Forests and parks. For example, in the honour of Middleham with its large complex of parks, two consecutive courts in 1449 and 1450 recorded 'attachments for cutting greenwood': in each year about sixty people were presented, paying small fines of between 1d. and 3d., and the lists of names and payments in the two courts were almost identical.[114] The regularity of the lists, along with other internal features of the evidence, thus gives the appearance of a standardized system of payments for wood arranged by household, allowing the collation of information about the use of these resources.[115] Why, then, did these courts frame routine payments as infractions?[116] A suggestive clue lies in the records of nearby West Tanfield, where the long list of 'tenants at will attached for cutting greenwood', each of whom paid just a token 1d. fine, was appended with the formulaic phrase that 'each individually puts himself in the lord's mercy'.[117] This formal structure of infraction and mercy—even for routine fines—may have been a way of signalling that the tenantry did not have the right to this wood by either custom or prescription, and reserving the capacity of the officers to halt such collection when they saw fit.

And, of course, as well as pasture and wood, the courts also kept track of the king's deer, diligently reporting any that had been found dead. At a swannimote in the Forest of Sapley and Weybridge, for example, in 1455 the jury reported 'by true estimation the deer that died of murrain since the last session', as well as the

[111] TNA, SC 2/211/43, m. 1r.

[112] TNA, DL 39/2/7, m. 6r. Interestingly, payments differed between the different woods (some of which were available for pannage all year around, others only for winter).

[113] Tellingly, the Galtres records (TNA, SC 2/211/43) have been labelled in the archive catalogue as a set of 'accounts'; while they certainly resemble accounts, the documents themselves are headed as 'courts', and contain a little legal business.

[114] WYASL, WYL163/568, m. 2r–v. On the Middleham parks, see Moorhouse, 'The Medieval Parks of Yorkshire', p. 103.

[115] The lists are somewhat redacted, suggesting that the scribe was working from a pre-existing list of tenants; moreover, just five of the people in the first list, and four in the second, were women; a low overall proportion, but roughly what would be expected if each name was a head of household. WYASL, WYL163/568, m. 2r–v.

[116] This was a routine practice in other kinds of court, too, e.g. for breaches of the assize of bread and ale: James Davis, 'Baking for the common good: a reassessment of the assize of bread in Medieval England', *Economic History Review*, 57:3 (2004), 465–502, pp. 488–9.

[117] NYRCO, ZJX 3/1/62, m. 1r.

fawns that had been killed by foxes and other vermin, perhaps as part of an attempt to project future stock numbers.[118] At some courts, these reports bear a resemblance to coroners' inquests, as foresters speculated on the way in which deer had been killed; at Bernwood Forest, a fawn found dead was said to have 'been hit in the neck by a catapult', another had died of murrain, and a third deer was found dead by *le ferr hegge*, 'but they do not know how it came to its death'.[119] Such detailed reviews not only allowed officers to keep track of deer stocks, but also to account for their management of the Forest should their position be challenged.[120] These routine modes of quantifying the commodities of game, pasture, and wood, then, transformed the local Forest courts into tribunals of accounting.

The local courts also sought to place tight restrictions on the ways in which Forest tenants used the landscape and its resources. In the first place, when it came to pasture, tight limits were placed on the kinds of animal that could be put in certain places; for example, there were repeated bans against keeping goats (which strip the bases of trees and eventually destroy them), and they were often explicitly excluded from Forest pasture rights.[121] The courts also attempted to intervene in the calendrical cycles of transhumance by upholding 'fence month', preventing pasture within Forests and parks the two weeks either side of Midsummer, when does were fawning.[122] Restrictions were even placed on the way in which tenants drove their animals. For example, when John Lofthous of Bedale was presented at Crakehall in 1449 for taking some sixty sheep to Bedale Park without licence, there seems to have been a particular concern over his use of dogs that chased and bit the animals, causing one of them to die; while at Soureby, in Allertonshire, a pain of 4d. was imposed on any tenant who drove their cattle on horseback beyond a place called *keldgate*, where they were required instead to go by foot.[123] For Forest tenants, the enjoyment of customary rights was hedged all around by regulation.

In a similar vein, Forest courts also regulated tenants' working animals in order to exclude the possibility of their use for hunting. The Forest Charter had ordained that any dogs kept within the bounds of the Forest ought to be expeditated or 'lawed'—that is, that they had their dewclaws removed, effectively preventing

[118] TNA, DL 39/2/4, mm. 11r, 12r. See Birrell, 'Deer and Deer Farming', pp. 115–7.

[119] TNA, E 146/1/10, rot. 6, m. 2v.

[120] This was the case at Sapley and Weybridge, for example: see fn. 89 above.

[121] Goats were specifically excluded from the pasture rights of the rector of Winterslow (Wiltshire) in the Forest of Clarendon: TNA, DL 39/2/20, annex 6; however, cf. their specific inclusion (indicating, conversely, its exceptionality) among the Forest rights of the Abbot of Notley in the Forest of Bernwood: TNA, E 146/1/10, m. 5r. For bans, e.g. at Osmotherley (North Yorkshire), see NYCRO, ZBD 51/27, m. 1r; ZDX, m. 19r.

[122] E.g. at Pickering: TNA, DL 39/2/2; Salcey, DL 39/2/7, m. 7r; verso; Osmotherley, NYCRO, ZBD/1/52/12, m. 9v. Promising to uphold fence month was part of the oath of the swannimote, preserved in a late-medieval version in TNA, WARD 2/60/234/145. See also Turner, 'Introduction', p. xxvi; Birrell, 'Deer and Deer Farming', p. 114.

[123] Respectively, WYASL, WYL163/568, TNA, SC 2/211/92, m. 3r.

them from fast running—and this practice seems to have endured into the fifteenth century.[124] For example, at Windsor Forest in the 1480s, Thomas Stevyns of Frimley was fined the high price of 3s. 4d. for keeping an unlawed mastiff, while at Clewer Park, William at Lee was reported to have three such dogs, with the pointed note that he 'does not have lands worth 40s.', a reference to the statute of 1390.[125] For the tenants of pastoral forest landscapes, who relied upon dogs for herding and guarding livestock, this requirement must have represented yet another burdensome restriction enforced by the local cadre of officers. At Hatfield Chase in 1456, Thomas Wayte was attached after his dogs 'devoured three of the lord's wild beasts in the park, after the warning given to him by the parker'; even with this vindication, such warnings hint at the grinding regularity of Forest regulations, and the resentment they must have produced among the tenantry.[126]

Indeed, some local officers went further than warnings, and instead enshrined their diktats into by-laws, as we can see in a series of ordinances made at the Forestmote of Osmotherley in February 1482:[127]

> It is enjoyed to all tenants who keep cattle inside the lordship or common, that they must move them before the feast of the Finding of the Holy Cross [3 May] under pain of 12d.
>
> And that anyone who takes any beast into *lez Clak* shall lose to the lord 3d. each time
>
> And that anyone who commits any trespass in the woods of the lord shall lose to the lord 12d.
>
> . . . And that no one shall cut hedges called *Beldbusks*, or any oak, or any other tree growing on the moor or between *lez acregarth*, for the defence of cattle for the time being, or shall lose each time 2d.

While it was not uncommon, of course, for local courts to make ordinances in this manner, in the Forests they were rarely made with any reference to the 'common assent' of the tenantry; rather, they seem to have been conceived solely as a set of financial penalties—or perhaps even a price-list—for routine access to wood and pasture.[128] Such ordinances were both a symptom and a cause of a legal culture that revolved around accounting.

For the tenants of Forests and imparked manors, the local courts and orders of their officers thus presented a series of choices that boiled down to how much

[124] Turner, 'Introduction', pp. xii, xxi.

[125] Respectively, TNA, DL 39/2/13, m. 5v; DL 39/2/15, no. 17v. On the statute see fn. 69 above.

[126] WYASL, WYL160/205/77, m. 2r. '. . . canes dicti Thome iugulaverunt tres feras domini infra parcum post premunicionem ei datum per parcarium'.

[127] NYCRO, ZBD 51/27, m. 1r.

[128] On the making of ordinances in other rural courts, see Chapter 1, pp. 49–51.

money they wished to pay at the next court session. Did you want to take wood? How much? And what kind? Did you wish to keep a dog? To pasture pigs? How many? And where? This rationale of accounting pervaded the operation of the fifteenth-century Forest institutions, as it had their predecessors; Turner wrote of the thirteenth-century Forest eyre that it 'was almost as much a financial assembly as a court of law'.[129] What was new, however, in the later Middle Ages, was the devolution of Forest administration to the officers in both Forests and within imparked manors; acquisitive agents of local power, concerned to account for their prudent management of resources, they ran the local courts in such a way as to extract as many perquisites and profits, rendering the customary rights of the tenants as a cost to be restricted as far as possible. Yet even within this constrictive legal discourse of management, there were openings for tenants to make their own claims about the governance of the Forest, and it is to these ideas that we now turn.

Forest Management: Enclosure, Preservation, and Warrant

In the final section of this chapter, I want to explore the way in which discourses for the management of resources were constructed within Forest legal culture. As I shall argue, although these discourses were forged within the rationale of accountability that dominated Forest governance, they were nevertheless open to reinterpretation by Forest communities, who were able to transform them in order to assert legal claims about the distribution of resources. In the first place, we look at the idea of enclosure, portrayed as both a positive measure to protect parks and game, but also as a depredation of custom; second, the notion of preservation, which was both marshalled against the customary rights of the tenantry and repurposed by them to forward their own interests; and third, we turn to the system of warrants which structured ideas about the legitimate allocation and distribution of resources. These contestations over the management of Forests and parks were fought out on the terms set by the officers. While Forest tenants were sometimes able to deploy these ideas for their own ends, therefore, they were ultimately ensnared within a legal discourse that privileged the putative needs of the vert and venison above their own.

To begin with, the enclosure of land was particularly fraught in Forest legal culture. In the first place, the woodland and pastoral upland landscapes which Forests often comprised were particularly vulnerable to what Christopher Dyer has called 'the enclosure movement of the thirteenth century', when the expansion of cultivation, the reclamation of wastes, and the creation of seigneurial hunting

[129] Turner, 'Introduction', p. lx.

parks led to a wave of enclosures of what had been common lands, as well as localized protests against them.[130] And indeed, in the second place, while Forest territories were not physically bounded, the parks within them—like parks everywhere—certainly were, with a combination of fences, walls, ditches, mounds, and palisades, with 'deer leaps' that allowed the animals to get in, but not to escape.[131] Significant investment was made in maintaining these physical boundaries: at Hatfield Chase, an official called the *palaciator* was appointed (and fined for failing to carry out his duties), while at Ingleby Arncliffe there was held a 'view of reparations to the stone walls, pales, hedges, and ditches of the park', with the total costs of repairs estimated at 74s. 6d.[132] Enclosure thus represented an expensive project of Forest lordship, concretizing authority through control of the landscape.

The idea of enclosure, reinforced by these physical limits, was thus routinely used to exclude tenants from accessing woodland resources.[133] At Knaresborough Forest, for example, the court rolls are strewn with presentments against those who were said to have 'broken the park pale', or who had committed a 'common trespass' within it, more often than not as a precursor to illicit woodcutting or the pannaging of pigs 'without licence'.[134] In some cases, people even sought to use the wood from the pale itself, as when Robert Martyn, a labourer of Salisbury, was indicted at a Forest eyre for taking away 'four *palebordys de le parke pale*' at Clarendon, and assaulting the forester's servant who tried to stop him.[135] Yet there is also a sense that the pale was there to prevent the mobility of tenants within imparked landscapes more generally, as for example when James Sutherome was fined 4d. 'for breaking the park pale at Bilton and making his common way there'.[136] Beyond the desire to control access to brushwood and mast-forage, then, the enclosure of parks aimed to 'prevent the forms of physical movement associated with the commoning economy'—stopping tenants from going where they pleased without the supervision of the officers.[137]

The inhabitants of Forests and imparked manors, for their part, clearly conceived of enclosure as an affront to their common rights and resisted it in a

[130] Dyer, 'Conflict in the landscape', pp. 21–2; also Birrell, 'Common Rights in the Medieval Forest', p. 22.

[131] Creighton, *Elite Landscapes of the Middle Ages*, p. 128; see also John Langton, 'Forest fences: enclosures in a pre-enclosure landscape', *Landscape History*, 35:1 (2014), 5–30. Though Forests were not bounded, their bounds were certainly known precisely to contemporaries: see the report of the jurors at Whaddon Chase in Buckinghamshire: TNA, DL 39/3/19, m. 3r.

[132] Respectively, WYASL, WYL 160/205/55, m. 1v, NYRCO, ZFL/110, m. 13v. See also reparations at the parks of Altofts and Rounday in West Yorkshire: TNA, DL 39/3/11, mm. 2r, 4r.

[133] On the importance of access in rural landscapes more generally, see Stephen Mileson, 'Openness and Closure in the Later Medieval Village', *P&P*, 234 (2017), 3–37.

[134] E.g. TNA, DL 30/487/2, m. 7r, DL 30/487/3, m. 5r.

[135] TNA, DL 39/2/20, m. 7v. [136] TNA, DL 30/487/4, m. 1r.

[137] Nicholas Blomley, 'Making Private Property: Enclosure, Common Right and the Work of Hedges', *Rural History* 18:1 (2007), 1–21, p. 5.

number of ways. In the first place, they attempted to destroy its physical barriers, such as walls, fences, and hedgerows. Sometimes, individuals appear to have acted alone, as when Thomas Whythyngham of Spofforth set fire to an oak tree that formed part of the pale boundary in 1472, apparently in order to create an opening into the park.[138] More often, however, the destruction of the pale was a demonstrative action performed by tenants acting together in groups. In the late 1460s, during the course of a long-running dispute over common pasture rights between men of the Forest of Galtres and St. Mary's Abbey in York, some three or four hundred men came to the abbey just after midnight, it was claimed, and 'hewe and breke adoun' its enclosures, 'showted and cryed and shot arows there at mennes doorres'.[139] This campaign was clearly intended to intimidate, but like many other such performative demolitions of park pales and other enclosures in the later fifteenth century, it also sought to physically erase the legal claims to divide and delimit woodland landscapes.[140]

As well as direct actions aimed at delegitimizing enclosure, however, Forest communities also pursued such claims through legal channels. The Forest Charter had forbidden assartment, purprestures, or encroachments on crown demesnes—in defence of the king's rights rather than those of his tenants—and this was seized upon by Forest communities to combat enclosures.[141] At the Forest eyre at Bernwood, for example, there seems to have been a coordinated effort against Sir William Rede, the chief keeper of the Forest there. The vills of Brill and Boarstall, as well as the twelve free jurors of the Forest, all made near-identical presentments complaining that Rede had enclosed a coppice at Pans Hill for seven years, 'to the grete anoysaunce of the kyngs dere', and insisted that this enclosure 'owith to be braked up now'.[142] Interestingly, such presentments never seem to have featured in the routine operations of the Forest courts, where such complaints may well have fallen upon deaf ears among seigneurial officers; yet they were a recurrent feature of presentments to the eyres in the 1480s, suggesting the way in which these once-in-a-lifetime judicial events were seized upon by Forest communities eager to air their grievances to external justices.[143]

[138] WSRO, PHA 7034, m. 1r.

[139] TNA, C 1/43/32. For the earlier dispute, see fn. 55 above.

[140] R. W. Hoyle, 'Thomas Lord Darcy and the Rothwell Tenants, c.1526–1534, *The Yorkshire Archaeological Journal*, 63 (1991), 85–107; Briony McDonagh, 'Making and Breaking Property: Negotiating Enclosure and Common Rights in Sixteenth-Century England', *History Workshop Journal*, 76 (2013), 32–56; Marvin, *Hunting Law and Ritual*, pp. 158–73; Mileson, *Parks in Medieval England*, pp. 154–5. For an example of the late 1490s, in which Miles Wilstrop's park, orchards, and rabbit warrens were destroyed by his enemies, see *Yorkshire Star Chamber Proceedings*, ed. William Brown, Yorkshire Archaeological Society Record Series, 41 (Leeds, 1909), pp. 15–19.

[141] The same provision was carried into both the 'Customs of the Forest', and the 'Articles of Regard', later orders on Forest procedure: see Turner, 'Introduction', pp. xxxvii–xxxviii, lxxvi–lxxvii, cxxxv–cxxxvii.

[142] TNA, E 146/1/10, mm. 1, 2, 4, 5. Quotes taken from the free jurors' presentment.

[143] For other examples, see TNA, DL 39/2/13, m. 4r, annex 16 [Windsor]; DL 39/2/23, m. 10r [Waltham]; DL 39/3/19, m. 3r [Whaddon Chase].

We can see precisely what was at stake in such appeals in a petition made by the tenants and inhabitants of six townships 'adionynge to the kings forest' of Knaresborough in the early sixteenth century to the Chancellor of the Duchy of Lancaster, who was responsible for overseeing the Forest. They complained that they had long paid money to the king's receivers there to have pasture rights 'in all grounds within the seid forest not inclosed nor inpayled', at any time of year, 'unto nau late that the kyngs auditor & other the kyngs officers hath commaunded the seide grounde to be diched & qwikked so þat yor seid besechers can not use & haue the seide comen as other ther antecessors hath used afore theym, to ther gret hurt & impoverysshyng'.[144] In this appeal, the kind of enclosure that was routinely enforced and justified by local officers as a means of restricting access to woodland resources was thus refigured as an affront to long-standing usage (though not, interestingly, custom).[145] The idea of enclosure thus contained a tension between different claims about how Forests and parks ought to be managed—on the basis of exclusion, or on the basis of preservation.

This brings us, indeed, to the idea of preservation as another pervasive concept within Forest legal culture. Not unlike the ideal of 'repair' that we examined in Chapter 1, through which rural people were hassled and encouraged to maintain the physical fabric of the village, preservation represented a way of imagining the upkeep of Forests and parks as physical spaces.[146] At the same time, however, it contained different valences. Preservation was more closely linked to the naturalness of the Forest environment; at the heart of these landscapes, after all, were the *ferae domini regis*, the 'wild beasts of the lord king', the notional wildness of which was an essential fiction of hunting.[147] And, more than this, the preservation of the Forest was a key idea in the struggles amongst the gentry for its lucrative offices. As part of a challenge laid against the tenure of John Hastings, Master Forester of Pickering in 1495, Richard Cholmley caused to be compiled a list of his supposed misdeeds, headed: 'Memorandum that thise be the damages, distrucciones, hurtes and wastes doon by John Hastyngs Esquier . . . in the groves and undirwoods of the forest of pykering . . . to the great and utter destruccion of the same'.[148] This idea of preservation formed a key pillar of this discourse of accountability, and was used to frame a variety of contestations over rights and legitimacy.

[144] TNA, DL 39/4/9. The document can be dated to the period between 1505 and 1509 because it was addressed to Richard Empson, who was Chancellor of the Duchy of Lancaster between these dates. The six towns were Clint, Ripley, Ferrensby, Plompton, Follifoot, and North Timble.

[145] It is noteworthy that they paid for these pasture rights: see pp. 136–7 above.

[146] See pp. 47–9 above.

[147] The wildness of the hunted animal is an essential aspect of hunting across many different cultures: see Matt Cartmill, *A View to a Death in the Morning: Hunting and Nature through History* (Cambridge, MA, 1993), pp. 29–30. According to *Bracton*, they were *res nullius* until they were caught (*Bracton*, trans. Thorne, ii, p. 42); in practice, of course, they belonged to the king, as contemporary phrases like that quoted from the rolls of Hatfield Chase make clear: WYASL, WYL160/205/107, m. 2v.

[148] TNA, DL 39/3/16, m. 1r. On this dispute, see Johnson, 'Redistribution of Forest Law', p. 93.

In the first place, the idea that the Forest ought to be preserved filtered down into the regular management of Forest tenants. This can be seen most frequently in the notion that Forests or parks were being 'destroyed' by the unlicensed taking of wood. Thus two women at Kettlewell were presented by the forester for having 'broken and uprooted the hedges of the East Hay... to the true destruction of the underwood there'; as elsewhere in England, the idea of 'hedge-breaking' was a common way of criminalizing poor women who drew on such resources for fuel.[149] But in Forest legal culture, the sharp-edged custodianship of the officers applied much more broadly, and extended also to the manner in which wood was taken. At Knaresborough in 1471, Robert Lister and his daughter were said to have 'lacerated' the wood and taken it away; the next year, John and Robert Sporett were presented for 'uprooting the hedges and other wood there'.[150] Underlying this extravagant rhetoric was the idea that the preservation of woodland depended on careful and sustainable management; a discourse that was manifestly used to control and supervise the activities of the tenantry.

Indeed, this same idea of 'destruction' was also used to frame prosecutions of illicit hunting. Those who were poaching for sport or food were routinely said to have 'destroyed' the king's game; and, indeed, the idea of 'destruction' seems to lie behind more malicious endeavours too. For example, at 1488 at Hatfield Chase, information from James Anton and John Grayve, keepers of the king's deer, reported that a large crowd of men came with dogs and gave chase to a herd of around a hundred deer, 'and by their chase drowned many of the deer in the river Trent, such that the herd of the king's beasts were destroyed and ruined, in great contempt of the king'.[151] Such deliberate mass destruction of deer was rare, of course, but, like the tearing down of park pales, it struck to the heart of seigneurial (or in this case, royal) authority. To destroy the game was to destroy the very material of the Forest: at Waltham in 1470, a wax-chandler of London was indicted for killing two does 'without warrant or licence, against the assize of the Forest, to the grave destruction of the Forest'.[152] Amidst the prevalent association of poaching with political sedition in the fifteenth century which Isobel Harvey has emphasized, such rhetoric begins to take on a more authoritarian aspect.[153]

Yet precisely this notional concern with the welfare of the king's deer, and its elision with the preservation of the Forest, opened up opportunities for Forest communities to foreground their own interests. In a striking example from the eyre of Windsor Forest in 1487, the jurors of Chobham presented that the Abbot

[149] WYASL, WYL163/568, m. 1v; Marjorie K. McIntosh, *Controlling Misbehavior in England, 1370–1600* (Cambridge, 1998), pp. 9–10, 86.
[150] Respectively, TNA, DL 30/487/2, m. 7v, DL 30/487/3, m. 5v.
[151] WYASL, WYL 160/205/107, m. 2v.
[152] TNA, DL 39/2/10, no. 9.
[153] Harvey, 'Poaching and Sedition'.

of Chertsey owed customarily to repair a local bridge at Washford.[154] The bridge, they claimed,

> would commonly be crossed by the foresters, verderers, regarders, bailiffs, and other of the king's ministers for the Forest, as well as by horses, carts, and other men crossing. [But] the same bridge now . . . is totally ruined and broken and has been for the last six years. And so everyone wishing to cross there goes around another way through the Forest, not only to the nuisance of the country and the Forest, but also to the destruction of the pasture of the king's game there.

Through this inventive juxtaposition, the jurors were able to link a local problem with an intransigent lord to the wider issue of the preservation of the Forest: not only were the king's officers prevented from carrying out their routine duties in monitoring the Forest, but the very sustenance of the king's game was imperilled. The idea of preservation, much like that of enclosure, though it was often marshalled against the rights of Forest inhabitants, could also be repurposed to defend their interests.

Finally, I want to turn to the notion of 'warrant' that was used to frame the legitimate allocation of resources in Forest legal culture. As noted in the previous two sections, the perquisites which attached to Forest offices allowed their holders to access both timber and venison, which were often distributed within patronage networks.[155] Such distribution depended on the notion that such gifts were warranted by the authority of the crown. In some Forests this was literally true, with orders coming from the royal family directly; among the evidences preserved at Sapley and Weybridge are copies of letters sent by the Queen (Margaret of Anjou), charging the master forester there to deliver bucks to a 'welebelovid servant, John Stephen', and another to John Prysot, chief judge of the Common Pleas.[156] But the notion of warrant was also attached to the authority of Forest officers themselves to take their due perquisites and distribute them locally, and so it came to suffuse local governance too, framing contestations over the legitimate allocation of forest resources.

Most straightforwardly, the idea that Forest resources had to be warranted placed them at the discretion of officers, and penalized those tenants who failed to ask their permission. Thus in a typical report to a 1483 swannimote in Windsor Forest, the deputy forester, William Hodde, presented that Hugh Askyn had cut some four oaks 'without licence or warrant'.[157] Such notes were felt necessary even in presentments against poachers; Thomas Brende, a husbandman, was indicted by the foresters at a Bernwood swannimote for killing a hare with three

[154] TNA, DL 39/2/13, m. 4r, annex 7.
[155] See pp. 125, 131–2 above.
[156] TNA, DL 39/2/4, no. 11, verso.
[157] TNA, DL 39/2/15, no. 16.

greyhounds, 'against the statute of the Forest, where he has neither warrant nor tenure'.[158] At the level of local governance, this idea of warrant often thus enshrined the authority of Forest officers to allocate resources in the way that they thought best; in one remarkable instance at the Forest of Rockingham, the chief keepers, John de Welles and Guido Watson, warranted the slaughter of some sixteen bucks and twenty-eight does between 1486 and 1489, 'to distribute the venison among the gentry of the country, for the better security and utility of the Forest'.[159] The implication seems to be that the preservation of the Forest could be achieved by bribing potential poachers; even such bald inducement could be reframed as an authenticated claim.

But warrants were not just for the gentry; the same ideas influenced the allocation of wood (never, of course, venison) to the Forest tenantry. Thus in the regard of the woods at Pontefract in 1492 diverse accounts of where the timber and firewood had been distributed included notes where the 'master steward' had warranted deliveries made as gifts or repairs alongside those that were taken as part of customary rights, as for example when William Nettylton took twelve oaks and saplings 'for wayn & plogh boote', and another eight for 'makynge of shepefolds'.[160] Customary rights, as we have seen throughout, were held in sufferance—in fact, they were not truly conceived as rights within local patronage networks. Concomitantly, Forest tenants were forbidden from redistributing the wood for themselves, particularly for profit. Thus at the Forest of Knaresborough, John Skerow was fined in 1461 for 'taking wood outside Oakden and selling it outside the lordship, without licence', while a couple of years later William Watir was presented by the forester in 1464 for cutting, in total, eighty cartloads of trees and branches, and 'selling them for his own use'.[161] The idea of warrant thus delegitimized uses that fell outside the aristocratic gift economy of Forest legal culture.

At the same time, however, Forest communities themselves also appealed to the idea of the warrant as a means of defending their own interests. In particular, they seem to have kept a close eye on which local hunters had obtained permission, and which had not. In a vernacular indictment again to the Waltham Forest eyre, four men and the reeve of Chingford Hatch reported their neighbour John Craythorne, who had 'diverse and many tymes hunteth withinne þe kyngs forest of Waltham without licence or warrant, to þe grete hurte & undoing of þe conyes [rabbits] within þe said forrest, and þat he hath used þis rule iij yeres . . . fully bifor this present sessyons'.[162] It is not hard to perceive a local grudge under this

[158] TNA, E 146/1/10, m. 1r.

[159] TNA, DL 39/2/14, mm. 2r: '. . . et venacionem inde ceperunt et asportaverunt ad distribuendum inter generosos patrie ibidem pro maiore securitate et utilitate dicte foreste'.

[160] TNA, DL 39/3/11, m. 4r.

[161] TNA, DL 30/487/2, m. 7r; DL 30/487/3, m. 5v. Part of Watir's offence evidently consisted in the locations from which he had taken wood, which were noted meticulously in the presentment.

[162] TNA, DL 39/2/10, no. 2.

indictment—it may simply have been the brazenness of Craythorne's 'bad rule', but it may be that his open hunting was endangering more careful poaching operations.[163] While the idea that Forest resources ought to be warranted by local officers was thus often used as a means of destabilizing the rights of Forest inhabitants, then, it provided a broader means of constructing legitimacy that they might employ for themselves.

The concern within Forests and parks with the management of natural resources, coupled to the strained role of gentry officers as both local overseers and accountable agents of seigneurial property rights, produced an elitist and bureaucratic legal regime, in which ordinary tenants were afforded relatively little space to exercise their rights: the needs of the Forest, of the vert and venison, were routinely placed above them. Yet even within this airless legal culture, they found room to manoeuvre, transforming ideas about enclosure, preservation, and warrant—so often used as justifications for restricting and weakening their claims on resources—into means of challenging the authority of the officers and buttressing their interests. Each of these ideas, as we have seen, provided a frame for contestations over legitimacy; in Forest legal culture, so manifestly lacking a discourse of justice, this concern with the legitimate allocation of woodland resources stood in for a vision of associative relations.

Conclusion

This chapter has argued that Forest legal culture was principally characterized by a concern with the supervision and control of woodland resources, the 'vert and venison'. As Michael Power put it, 'the idea of audit shapes... conceptions of the problems for which it is the solution', and the same might be said of the style of accountable management we find in the fifteenth-century Forests; framed as delicately balanced environments that would naturally degrade without careful management, they demanded a system of warrants, the physical delimitations of enclosure, and an ideology of preservation.[164] The tools for this rationale were there in the traditional dictates of Forest law, but they were aggravated by the redistribution of Forest administration and jurisdiction that took place in the later Middle Ages; as we have just seen, there were opportunities for Forest tenants to draw upon this legal discourse of management to pursue their own ends, even if ultimately it was used against their interests. By way of conclusion here, I would like to consider briefly the relative distinctiveness of Forest legal culture compared with the others discussed in the first half of this book.

[163] My thanks to Ian Forrest for this suggestion.
[164] Michael Power, *The Audit Society: Rituals of Verification* (Oxford, 1997), p. 7.

To begin with, it is worth highlighting the extent to which Forest communities considered themselves to be set apart from others by virtue of their special customary rights. Thus at Knaresborough in 1462, the Forest jurors presented that they were being asked to pay more in taxes; when they refused, 'the king's officers had taken arrests inside the lordship, against the custom of the Forest, because they say they are accustomed to pay no more than 5d., from time immemorial, and now they have to pay 3s. 4d.'[165] The custom of the Forest was not, of course, a well-defined code so much as a sense of legal privilege, one that gave such communities a special identity. Such privileges were felt most sharply, perhaps, at their boundaries. In the Forest of Salcey, it was reported in the 1490 that a place called Hawney was being claimed as a purlieu—an area of land that had been disafforested.[166] The Forest jurors complained: 'we say [it] is forest grounde, to the wyche all purley men saith nay for they sey it is their purlue and so they use it styll'.[167] As so often with these sources, it is difficult to penetrate what lay behind such appellations; more salient is the way in which they commanded the loyalty of common people, enrolling them in the maintenance of constitutional structures.

While I have been emphasizing the dispersal of Forest legal culture beyond the royal Forests then, there were limits to this; tenants of imparked manors, who might find themselves subject to no fewer restrictions on their access to the resources of parks and warrens, had no special status. As elsewhere in the late-medieval countryside, they were notionally protected by manorial customs, and even this might be used against them; at the manor of Ingleby Arncliffe in 1461 Thomas Rotor was fined 6d. by the forester after he was found 'often inside the woods taking greenwood and cut-wood every day, carrying it with three servants against custom, and the pain that was previously imposed on him'.[168] We can still see much of rural legal culture in the Ingleby rolls, as in other imparked manors, as tenants used the courts to resolve disputes, make by-laws (though, as we have seen, these were also closer to the control of parkers), and uphold order. Yet noteworthy by its absence in these courts is the sense that law provided a means of imagining community. Living with the bureaucratic rigidity of Forest legal culture, but without recourse to the privileged legal identity of the communities of the royal Forest, the tenants of imparked manors had the worst of both worlds.

In other ways, Forest legal culture bears more resemblance to that of the maritime world we examined in Chapter 3. As in maritime legal culture, there was in the Forests a distinctive form of expertise that was enrolled in ideas about

[165] TNA, DL 30/487/3, m. 5r.

[166] On disafforementment, see Bazeley, 'Extent of English Forest', with a map of Salcey at p. 160. A useful technical discussion on disafforestment is Turner, 'Introduction', pp. ciii–cx. The purlieus—rarely mentioned in fifteenth-century sources—became more important in the early-modern period. See Manning, *Hunters and Poachers*, Ch. 4, 'The Purlieu Men and the Ancient Constitution', 83–108.

[167] TNA, DL 39/2/7, m. 3r.

[168] NYCRO, ZFL 110, m. 1r.

legitimacy; yet in the Forest legal culture, this specialist knowledge, about the sustainability of woodland and deer populations, was located much more firmly with a class of elite administrators than was the case in the maritime world. While, as we saw, shipmasters often took a leading role in the articulation of nautical expertise, as a discourse of legal justification it at least gestured to a broader *mētis*, or vernacular cunning, among the seafaring population.[169] In Forest legal culture, by contrast, expertise—like so much else—was conceived of as a possession of the elite, linked to the aristocratic culture of hunting and the gentry officers' management of wood and game resources.[170] The inhabitants of Forest communities of course possessed expertise, but it was subversive—expressed in park-breaking, wood-stealing, and poaching—rather than celebrated within Forest legal culture.

We might say, then, that late-medieval Forest legal culture was distinctive in a set of familiar ways. Forged within a relatively distinctive landscape and economy, it coalesced around a set of laws and customs in the late twelfth and early thirteenth centuries, which in turn developed, in the later Middle Ages, into an idiosyncratic legal tradition with its own institutions and identity. At the same time, however, Forest legal culture was peculiarly oppressive, both because it continued to bear the imprint of sovereign power that lay at the heart of Forest law, and also because of the particular way in which it developed in the fourteenth and fifteenth centuries. For the inhabitants of the Forest as for the tenants of imparked manors who came to feel some of its weight, Forest legal culture offered no means of conceiving community, or an idealized form of associative relations, or indeed a vision of justice. Rather, with its fundamental concern with the welfare of the 'vert and venison', it offered merely a self-contained ideology of resource management. With this discourse, as with so much else, Forest tenants could only make do and mend.

[169] On the concept of *mētis*, see James C. Scott, *Seeing Like a State: Why Certain Schemes to Improve the Human Condition Have Failed* (New Haven, CT, 1998), pp. 315–6.

[170] See Marvin, *Hunting Law and Ritual*, pp. 82–130.

PART II
COMMON LEGALITIES

In this second half of the book, we turn to look at four broader patterns in the ways that common people engaged with law—what I have suggested we call 'common legalities'. In what follows, we examine the ways in which people conceptualized law through the material landscape, their participation in the production of knowledge for legal institutions, the growing use of the English language in fifteenth-century law, and finally the proliferation of legal documents that non-elites came to possess in this period. It is vital to stress at the outset that these four patterns of legality are perceptible across the variety of local legal cultures that we examined in the first half of the book; indeed, I would stress that they become fully visible only through comparative attention to these different local contexts. While in each case the reasons for their wide cultural valence were different, they all illustrate the ways in which legality was sustained from below through the actions of the commons.

At the same time, however, these common legalities were not all of the same kind. Chapter 5, with its focus on 'the legal landscape', addresses a form of meaning-making with exceedingly deep roots, one found across the premodern world. While many landscape practices—in marking property boundaries, establishing rights of way, or perambulating territory—were embedded in long cultural continuities, I emphasize that material change in fifteenth-century England meant that the relationship between law and the physical world often had to be reiterated and renegotiated. In a different way, Chapter 6 also addresses a continuity in legal engagement, as we examine the ways in which people contributed to the making of legitimate knowledge. Acts such as witnessing, rendering jury verdicts, or contributing to *fama* ('public fame') were long-standing and relatively stable institutions in fifteenth-century England, across different local legal cultures. My purpose, then, is not to provide an account of change so much as a heuristic—the 'economy of legitimate knowledge'—to better understand what was at stake in these common legal engagements; though, as we shall see, they came to take on new significance in the fifteenth century, with the increasing openness of public discourse.

Law in Common: Legal Cultures in Late-Medieval England. Tom Johnson, Oxford University Press (2020).

DOI: 10.1093/oso/9780198811879.001.0002

This brings us to chapters 7 and 8, both of which explore the emergence of new common legalities in this context. Chapter 7 addresses the growth of English as a 'legal vernacular' in the later Middle Ages, overtaking Anglo-Norman French and making ever more incursions into Latin documentation. I argue that though the capacity to engage with law in their own language opened up some new possibilities for the ordinary population, the use of English also came with the price of increased legal scrutiny. Very closely linked to this change was the proliferation of legal writings, which forms the subject of Chapter 8. I suggest here that the later fourteenth and fifteenth centuries underwent a 'documentary revolution', as the vast majority of the population in England came to possess legal documents. Yet while these documents provided common people with new means of creating trust, guaranteeing authenticity, and accessing authorities, they also created new burdens of expectation, as institutions came to demand the production of documents as a standard mode of proving claims. Even as these changes were generated from below, then, they ultimately served to bind common people ever more tightly to legal authority.

Common legalities are important to the aim of this book because they help us to understand widespread practices of legal engagement in this period in ways that go beyond the framework of 'centre' and 'locality'. While the central institutions of royal government and common law certainly feature in what follows, and can even be seen to have provided some of the conceptual frameworks for these practices, they were not determinative; looking athwart different local contexts and jurisdictions we can see more clearly the complex system of social and cultural practices that helped to make law what it was in fifteenth-century England. And, indeed, by attending to the formation of legal culture 'from below', I think we can cast some new light on current debates about political culture in the later Middle Ages. The growth of government in this period was undoubtedly important in bringing more and more people into the ambit of politics; but I would also suggest that in common legalities, as a broadly shared sense of what law meant and what it could do, we can see that the common people met the government halfway.

5
The Legal Landscape

Introduction

As we saw in the first half of this book, local landscapes played a crucial role in the way that legality was articulated. In the first place, they sustained forms of socio-economic activity that shaped specific forms of legal engagement; we saw this particularly in the maritime world, where seaborne trade created the necessity for regimes of shipboard governance, and in Forests and parks, where access to woodland resources was carefully regulated. Moreover, we saw how the characteristics of local landscapes also formed part of the imaginary of local legal cultures, as for example in the notion that good 'repair' ought to be an object of community-building in the countryside, and in attempts to bring spatial order to the built environment in towns and cities. But while these local legal cultures produced distinctive discourses about the landscapes in which they were situated, there were also similarities in the ways that common people in late-medieval England engaged with law through the material world. In this chapter, I want to focus on the landscape as one of the most pervasive media of legality, shaping the ways in which common folk practised and conceived of law.

Law had a physical presence in the landscape of late-medieval England. Legal ideas did not consist merely in words and writings, but were constituted in their concrete manifestations in the material environment; this was the terrain upon which they were articulated, contested, and resolved. People whose lives were lived so close to the land understood these regimes of signification intuitively.[1] They knew the places in which they dwelt and worked were replete with different legal claims, some so well established by generations of institutional or customary arrangements that they formed part of the architecture of the everyday, while others remained latent in the slowly changing land, ready to become problematic if a stream were diverted, or new buildings were constructed. The existence of such claims imbued everyday mobilities with legal significance: people had to watch their step, moving through the world in ways that accorded with some claims while contesting others—droving cattle through a particular field, moving a boundary stone to its 'proper' place, fishing at a certain point on the river—in a legal language that was broadly comprehensible. The late-medieval landscape

[1] See the comments in Barbara Bender, 'Introduction: Landscape—Meaning and Action', in *Landscape: Politics and Perspectives*, ed. Bender (Oxford, 1993), 1–17.

Law in Common: Legal Cultures in Late-Medieval England. Tom Johnson, Oxford University Press (2020).

DOI: 10.1093/oso/9780198785613.001.0001

represented a large surface on which non-elites could make their own legal inscriptions.

Medieval historians have long analysed law in spatial terms, with a particular focus on the legal categorization of certain spaces, such as taverns, urban houses, sanctuaries, and the effects of these categories on social practice.[2] As I seek to build on this foundational work, I also make two points of departure. First, this scholarship has been almost exclusively urban in focus. Yet, as we have seen, space was crucially important in other legal cultures too, and it is important that we understand the broader commonalities in the spatiality of law throughout premodern England.[3] Second, much work on medieval legal spaces has reflected a 'top-down' conception of legal meaning, as though authority were straightforwardly mapped onto territory.[4] Yet the legal landscape, as it was worked and reworked by the commons, actually provides an exemplary instance of the way in which non-elites systematically sustained the operation of law. The landscape required constant labour to give it the appearance of stability; we thus need to place much more focus on the people who were actually getting their hands dirty to support or subvert regimes of legal meaning.

The chapter is divided into three parts. The first investigates the ways in which common people were prompted by law-courts to produce knowledge about the legal landscape, through practices of perambulation, the holding of views, the determination of bounds, and the names they gave to the land; the co-constitution of this knowledge is vital for understanding the ways in which people made legal statements *through* the landscape, which forms the subject of the second section. Here, we examine the many ways they did this, through their everyday movements in and interactions with the physical world, and analyse what was at stake in these variously pointed, neglectful, and undeliberative interventions. The third

[2] Respectively, see Barbara A. Hanawalt, 'The Host, the Law, and the Ambiguous Space of Medieval London Taverns', in *Medieval Crime and Social Control*, ed. Hanawalt and David Wallace (Minneapolis, 1999), 204–23; Vanessa Harding, 'Space, Property, and Propriety in Urban England', *Journal of Interdisciplinary History*, 32:4 (2002); Shannon McSheffrey, 'Sanctuary and the Legal Topography of Pre-Reformation London', *L&HR*, 27:3 (2009), 483–514. For early approaches to space in medieval legal history, see Barbara H. Rosenwein, *Negotiating Space: Power, Restraint, and Privileges of Immunity in Early Medieval Europe* (Manchester, 1999); the essays in *Medieval Practices of Space*, ed. Barbara Hanawalt and Michal Kobialka (Minneapolis, 2000); Daniel Lord Smail, *Imaginary Cartographies: Possession and Identity in Late Medieval Marseille* (Ithaca, NY, 2000).

[3] For work on law and custom in rural spaces, see Nicola Whyte, *Inhabiting the Landscape: Place, Custom and Memory, 1500–1800* (Oxford, 2009); also Nicholas Blomley, 'Making Private Property: Enclosure, Common Right and the Work of Hedges', *Rural History* 18:1 (2007), 1–21; Briony McDonagh, 'Making and Breaking Property: Negotiating Enclosure and Common Rights in Sixteenth-Century England', *History Workshop Journal*, 76 (2013); and the work on rural space in particular in French historiography, with essays in *L'espace rural au Moyen Âge, Portugal, Espagne, France (XIIe–XIVe siècle): Mélanges en l'honneur de Robert Durand*, ed. Monique Bourin and Stéphane Boisellier (Rennes, 2002); *Écritures de l'espace social: Melanges d'histoire medieval offerts à Monique Bourin*, ed. D. Boisseuil, P. Chastang, L. Feller et J. Morsel (Paris, 2010).

[4] I have argued against such a view in Tom Johnson, 'The Tree and the Rod: Jurisdiction in Late-Medieval England', *P&P*, 237 (2017), 13–51; see also Rab Houston, 'People, Space, and Law in Late Medieval and Early Modern Britain and Ireland', *P&P*, 230 (2016), 47–89.

section, finally, considers the broader ecology of legal action, by looking at cases in which environmental change interrupted the legal landscape; such instances show up the complex interconnections between legal and ecological order, and the ways in which contemporaries in the later Middle Ages conceived of the relationship between authority and the natural world. The conclusion attempts to place the arguments of this chapter in a broader historiographical perspective.

Knowing the Legal Landscape: Perambulating, Viewing, Bounding, Naming

Across late-medieval England, the landscape was understood to be an object of legal knowledge best articulated by local people—especially by older, trustworthy men.[5] While judges and law officers framed this knowledge through the kinds of questions that they asked, it was local jurors and witnesses who provided it, their answers suffused in their own assumptions about the ways in which landscapes could be known. Produced in the interaction between official inquiries and vernacular responses, then, the legal landscape was a form of hybrid knowledge; in what follows, I try to do justice to this hybridity by exploring four common ways in which this knowledge was articulated. First, we look at the perambulations conducted to mark out and demonstrate jurisdiction; second, to the conscious 'viewing' of the land, which privileged its visuality; third, to 'bounding', the separation of land into discrete parcels; and fourth, to the naming of landscape features as a means of evoking a broader community of legal knowledge. In each case, I show how these different practices of knowing, stimulated by but not reducible to official processes, produced different landscape legalities, setting up the terms on which people might confirm, negotiate, or interrupt it.

The act of perambulation—the circumnavigation of a piece of territory in order to articulate its boundaries—was a widespread and long-standing practice in premodern Europe in general, and across the range of late-medieval English jurisdictions in particular.[6] In the first place, the celebration of Rogation had long included ritual processions related to the local landscape, and certainly by the fifteenth century involved the 'beating of the bounds', the ritual circuit of parish boundaries; although these have often been interpreted in relation to religious practice, they could take on a legal meaning in the context of disputes over chapel

[5] See Ian Forrest, *Trustworthy Men: How Inequality and Faith Made the Medieval Church* (Princeton, NJ, 2018), Ch. 12, 'The Material Church', pp. 285–306; Bronach C. Kane, *Popular Memory and Gender in Medieval England: Men, Women and Testimony in the Church Courts, c. 1200–1500* (Woodbridge, 2019).

[6] See, for example, in Chris Wickham, *Courts and Conflict in Twelfth-Century Tuscany* (Oxford, 2003), pp. 143–4; Matthew H. Hammond, 'Assemblies and Writing of Administrative Documents in the Central Medieval Kingdom of the Scots', in *Medieval Legal Process: Physical, Spoken and Written Performance in the Middle Ages*, ed. Marco Mostert and P. S. Barnwell (Turnhout, 2011), 123–46.

burial rights or tithes.[7] In a similarly ceremonial way, annually 'riding the franchise' in towns and cities formed an important demonstration of the boundaries of late-medieval civic jurisdiction, especially given the persistent worries about its encroachment by other institutions.[8] Perambulation was also institutionalized as a key feature of late-medieval Forest administration, as it had been since the time of the Forest Charter, serving as an opportunity to present new assarts and purprestures.[9] Across a range of jurisdictional contexts, then, perambulation was a pervasive practice of knowing the legal landscape.

Perambulation was crucially bound up with movement. When called upon to testify to the bounds of the parish, for example, witnesses to ecclesiastical tribunals almost always remembered them in sequential order, clearly articulating a journey that they themselves had undertaken. Thus, in a dispute heard in the episcopal consistory court at York in 1406, William Page, a fifty-year-old parishioner from Newton-on-Ouse, rehearsed the boundaries there as follows: 'the said parish is separated from the parish of Alne in the north part by a hedge, called in the vernacular *yeltongarth*, which extends to a place called *Lynton riddyng*, and from there the parish extends along the river Ouse on the western part, and from there to the bridge of Beningborough on the south part, and from there to the eastern limit with Beningborough . . . to a stream in the Forest [of Galtres] called *le flete*, and so from there to a certain bridge called *Tollertonbryg*, and from there to a certain place called *Lynton Ker*, and thence back to the said hedge *le yeltongarth*, where it first began'.[10] As a form of landscape knowledge, perambulations thus

[7] Ronald Hutton, *The Rise and Fall of Merry England: The Ritual Year 1400–1700* (Oxford, 2001), pp. 34–5. Useful comments on rogation processions in early medieval Europe can be found in Carol Neuman de Vegvar, 'Converting the Anglo-Saxon Landscape: Crosses and their Audiences', in *Text, Image, Interpretation: Studies in Anglo-Saxon Literature and its Insular Context in Honour of Éamonn Ó Carragáin*, ed. Alistair Minnis and Jane Roberts (Turnhout, 2007), 407–29, pp. 414ff. Rogation processions of parish boundaries have more often been treated by early-modern historians: Steve Hindle, 'Beating the Bounds of the Parish: Order, Memory, and Identity in the English Local Community, c. 1500–1700', in *Defining Community in Early Modern Europe*, ed. Karen E. Spierling and Michael J. Halvorson (Aldershot, 2008), 205–27; Alexandra Walsham, *The Reformation of the Landscape: Religion, Identity, and Memory in early Modern Britain and Ireland* (Oxford, 2011), pp. 252–60. On the articulation of parish boundaries in disputes over burial rights, see Ian Forrest, 'The Politics of Burial in Late Medieval Hereford', *EHR*, 125:516 (2010), 1110–38, at p. 1129, fn. 82; and on the explicit mention of rogation processions in (later) tithe disputes, Paula Simpson, 'Custom and Conflict: Disputes over Tithe in the Diocese of Canterbury, 1501–1600', unpublished PhD, University of Kent (1997), pp. 34–52.

[8] Christian D. Liddy, *Contesting the City: The Politics of Citizenship in English Towns, 1250–1530* (Oxford, 2017), pp. 68–72, quote at p. 69.

[9] On the institution of perambulation, see *Select Pleas of the Forest*, ed. G. J. Turner, Selden Society 13 (London, 1901), pp. ciii–cvi; for a fifteenth-century example, a perambulation of the Forest of Rockingham, see TNA, KB 9/233, no. 71.

[10] BIA, CP.F.25, depositions, m. 1r. The dispute concerned tithes of *silva cedua* ('woods-to-be-felled'), which were owed on trees aged twenty years or more; fourteenth-century legislative wrangles between ecclesiastical councils and parliament over the definition resulted in 'some of the most improbable and contentious distinctions found in any part of English law': Helmholz, *Canon Law and Ecclesiastical Jurisdiction*, p. 449. My thanks to Dan Gosling for alerting me to these thorny issues.

relied upon the serialization of the memorialized landscape features that formed boundaries, which were linked together through processual movement.

The ritual performance of perambulation was thus extremely important in the demonstration of jurisdiction. Staying in York, it was reported in 1482 that 'certan persons of [Galtres] forest, to the nombyr of [60] persons, hawe used to cum in to the owt gateys of the Cite to make thar perambulacon in the averer [harvest] tym and yf tha found not opyn the gayts of the garth tha wold brek them opyn', a custom which the civic authorities took it upon themselves to refuse thereafter.[11] While the city clearly regarded such an intrusion as a threat to its own jurisdiction, it is a telling recognition of the forceful determination of perambulators to follow their route. Disrupting them, concomitantly, represented a grave challenge to authority. Thus at the manor Walberswick in 1435, after he was alleged to have appropriated part of the common lands by planting hedges, Roger Newman was fined a shilling for calling the capital pledges 'false and perjured', and for having 'interrupted the capital pledges during the perambulation'.[12] His offence clearly involved not only the denigration of their honesty, therefore, but also the disruption of the mobile production of knowledge which formed the very basis of the court's jurisdiction.

This knowledge was insured by the repetitive nature of perambulations, and yet as spatial performances, they were not completely rigid. At Ipswich in 1519, after a minor jurisdictional disagreement with the Admiral, the burgesses sought a clarification of their boundaries 'and that a perambulation of the jurisdiction ought to be taken and made'.[13] The text of this perambulation strongly resembles one that had been copied earlier in the fifteenth century, but it also shows how the jurors updated their knowledge of the legal landscape as they went along. Most often they did this by making reference to the new tenants or owners of a piece of land to which the boundary was adjacent, such as a lane 'by the gate sumtyme [belonging to] olde Roger Parnelle, nowe Elizabeth Bacen, widow'; but they also

[11] *York Civic Records*, vol. 1, ed. Angelo Raine, Yorkshire Archaeological Society Record Series XCVIII (York, 1939), p. 63.

[12] SROI, HA30/314/19d/1–21, m. 3v. Five years later, the jurors were ordered 'to make scrutiny and leet perambulation of this manor': HA30/312/194, m. 21r; in the 1490s, two capital pledges were fined because they 'did not want to make perambulation with the others': HA30/312/200, m. 22r.

[13] This is rehearsed in the *inspeximus* of a charter of Edward IV: SROI, C 1/1/20. This was almost certainly a response to the admiralty inquisition held at Shotley in 1518 into the death of the mariner Richard Astill, on which see Chapter 3 of this volume, pp. 110–111. There is some slightly earlier evidence suggesting that Ipswich's admiralty jurisdiction was vulnerable. A memorandum of 1493 in the town's register book records how the Earl of Oxford, then Admiral of England, arrested a Breton ship from the Orwell; in response, the town bailiffs sent the charter of their liberties to Hedingham Castle. After it was read to him, the Earl gave the intriguing response, 'comaund me to the bailleffs of yippiswich and sey to them I wyll be frendely to them in this poynt and in all other conteyned in your chartyr, and do for them therynne as a burgeays and as oon of you.' BL, Add. MS. 30158, fo. 39r. The fact that the burgesses did not show their charter in 1518, as they had done twenty-five years earlier, suggests that perhaps they had lost it—the original is indeed now missing: *Ipswich Borough Archives, 1255–1835: A Catalogue*, ed. David Allen, Suffolk Record Society, 43 (2000), p. 8.

noted the way the landscape had changed—proceeding at one point 'unto an hawthorn that stoode in the high waie ther nowe cut downe'—and new place names, as when they went 'unto Albisborn Deyry, nowe called Pondis Hall'.[14] As perambulations worked by continually reinscribing the legal landscape, then, they could smoothly incorporate its changes; though their encirclement evoked the idea of coherent territories, as a form of knowledge they were crucially constituted by movement.

This brings us to the second mode of producing landscape knowledge, the 'views' which emphasized the visuality of terrain.[15] Formalized views were conducted in a range of institutional contexts in fifteenth-century England. Probably the most long-standing and prevalent was the manorial survey, in which officials summoned a jury to testify to the lands and rents of a given manor. Although these surveys did not always proceed from a visual inspection, the high turnover of land in post-plague England, and the concomitant changes to holdings, meant that it was more often necessary to view the land itself.[16] Views also formed a part of more regular administration in both town and country, as jurors—and sometimes specialist craftsmen such as masons—were occasionally summoned to examine buildings and lands under dispute.[17] Finally, in ecclesiastical jurisdiction, physical inspections of the church fabric and its cemetery were routine aspects of visitation, at which both the rector and the trustworthy men of the parish (as the parties responsible for the maintenance of the chancel and the nave respectively) had the opportunity to make their case for repairs.[18] Views and surveys were thus one of the most widespread modes of generating knowledge about the legal landscape.

As Irus Braverman has suggested, legal regimes often privilege the visuality of territory because it seems to provide a neutral way of establishing a legal claim, merely confirming what is manifest to everyone.[19] Witnesses before the church courts routinely appealed to their sight as a means of justifying their pronouncements. William Page, whom we saw above giving testimony in a tithe dispute at Newton-on-Ouse, said that he could testify to the truth of the articles put to him

[14] SROI, C1/1/21. The earlier text is recorded in the town's register book, BL, Add. MS. 30158.

[15] Generally, see Kate Giles, 'Seeing and Believing: Visuality and Space in Pre-Modern England', *World Archaeology*, 39:1 (2007), 105–21.

[16] See Mark Bailey, *The English Manor, c.1200–1500* (Manchester, 2002), Ch. 2, 'Manorial Surveys, Extents, and Rentals', pp. 21–95; on later techniques, see Andrew McRae, 'To Know One's Own: Estate Surveying and the Representation of the Land in Early Modern England', *Huntington Library Quarterly*, 56:4 (1993), 333–57. See also the essays in *Local Maps and Plans from Medieval England*, ed. R. A. Skelton and P. D. A. Harvey (Oxford, 1986).

[17] See, for example, the *London Assize of Nuisance, 1301–1431: A Calendar*, ed. Helena M. Chew and William Kellaway, London Record Society, 10 (London, 1973). On the use of specialists, see Forrest, *Trustworthy Men*, pp. 138–9.

[18] See Ian Forrest, 'The Transformation of Visitation in Thirteenth-Century England', *P&P*, 221 (2013), 3–38, p. 28.

[19] Irus Braverman, 'Hidden in Plain View: Legal Geography from a Visual Perspective', *Law, Culture and the Humanities*, 7:2 (2010), 173–86.

'because since the age of discretion, he knew and saw' the collection of tithes had taken place in a particular manner; the elision of seeing and knowing, common in such depositions, is telling.[20] This, indeed, formed part of the legitimacy of the view as a tool for resolving disputes. At the manorial court of Kintbury in 1478, a combined jury of twelve freemen and the customary homage reported that a hedge marking the boundary between two manors had been 'put outside of its right course . . . by a space of 6 feet and more, and this is plainly apparent by the metes and bounds put there from ancient times'.[21] With the borders plain and apparent to anyone who had eyes, it was perhaps harder to believe that disruptions of the legal landscape were the result of mere neglect.

Yet at the same time as legal views aimed to establish the obviousness of the claims they confirmed, they of course actually worked to reduce the complex, and sometimes contradictory meanings given to the terrain, replacing them with a single vision of the legal landscape.[22] Thus, for example, at Ingleby Arncliffe in North Yorkshire, a court of 1480 recorded 'a view of reparations to the stone walls of the park pale, of the hedges and ditches'.[23] The manorial jury reported on a total of 700 rods (around 3.5km) of the boundaries, divided into seven unequal sections, apportioned each part a value and named the landowner or tenant who was legally responsible for its repair. In focusing only on repairs, tenure, and obligations, this view drastically flattened the complexity of this landscape; the court rolls reveal a much more complicated picture, characteristic of imparked manors, in which tenants were engaged in the ongoing negotiation of access to woodland, through a range of fines, pains, customary rights, and gifts.[24] While this was particularly pronounced within the bureaucratic legal regime of Forest legal culture, views everywhere worked to reduce and fix the legal landscape.

Indeed, there are sometimes suggestions that the fixity provided by views was undesirable. For example, jurors at the manor of Barton-le-Clay in Bedfordshire in 1454 had to be ordered under pain to 'view the headland that Walter Wodeward appropriated to himself, and then to give a verdict at the next court', implying some

[20] BIA, CP.F.25, depositions, m. 1r. A witness in another church cause swore upon an issue 'as longe as I have these ij eeys to see', pointing to his eyes as he said this, suggesting the depth of embodied feeling that attached to the epistemology of sight; for the example, see Tom Johnson, 'The Preconstruction of Witness Testimony: Law and Social Discourse in England before the Reformation', *L&HR*, 32:1 (2014), 127–47, p. 129.

[21] BL, Add. Ch. 49238, m. 1r.

[22] A point made very well by legal geographers: see Nicholas Blomley, 'Simplification is complicated: property, nature, and the rivers of law', *Environment and Planning A*, 40 (2008), 1825–42; Marianna Valverde, 'Seeing Like a City: The Dialectic of Modern and Premodern Ways of Seeing in Urban Governance', *Law & Society Review*, 45:2 (2011), 277–312. These theorists all took inspiration from James C. Scott, *Seeing Like A State: How Certain Schemes to Improve the Human Condition Have Failed* (New Haven, CT, 1998).

[23] NYRCO, ZFL 110, m. 13v. A similar view of the park at Hatfield Broad Oak (Essex) in 1441 was presented as a 'perambulation': ERO, D/DK M1, m. 4v.

[24] See Chapter 4, pp. 134–40.

reticence in determining this issue.[25] The imposition of a definitive set of legal meanings on the landscape even prompted attacks on those carrying out the view. This may have been the motive behind Roger Newman's disturbance of the perambulation at Walberswick, and it was explicitly identified as the reason behind an assault on Richard Covesby in 1433, when he was menaced by men of the fenland village of Moulton in Lincolnshire as he attempted to survey (*desurvoier*) some ditches there on behalf of the Abbot of Crowland.[26] Contemporaries knew that views were not simple acts of clarification but involved the production of potentially contentious perspectives. There thus lay a tension in viewing as a mode of knowing the legal landscape, between the objectivity accorded to sight as a mode of knowledge and the multiplicity of viewpoints that might be taken.

Closely linked to the use of views was the practice of bounding. This involved both the physical work of erecting barriers or markers in the landscape and also the conceptual work of perceiving the landscape as a set of discrete parcels, each of which contained specific rights and obligations. Indeed, it is clear that much land was not physically bounded, perhaps particularly in regions of open-field farming.[27] But it was certainly conceptually bounded by legal claims to particular pieces of land. For example, an inquisition was held in 1453 into the tithes owed on a large piece of arable called 'Smalelond' in Herefordshire, which was farmed by the inhabitants of three separate parishes. Those from Church Withington reported that 11 acres belonged to the glebe of the rectory, of which 7½ acres were farmed by Agnes Genettes and the rest by Agnes Deme; another 148 acres belonged to the glebe of the prebendary, but these were divided into individually leased parcels of between 3 and 12 acres in size. Finally, they said, there was one acre called 'Cecil-long-acre', the tithes of which pertained to the chapter of Hereford Cathedral. The other vills asked about the tithes owing on Smalelond were similarly precise.[28] Locals clearly saw clear-cut rights in such open fields.

Nonetheless, bounding was sometimes resisted, or performed reluctantly. In the Bishop of Hereford's manor of Hampton, in 1477, the whole tenantry was put in mercy for 20s. because 'they did not put down limits and stakes between the [lands of the] demesne and the tenants, and between the tenants themselves, whether free or customary, as they were ordered to do by the [feast of the] Lord's Ascension at the latest'. They were ordered to make the bounds by the following

[25] BL, Add. Ch. 34322, recto. The area of land in question was probably quite small; Walter was presented at the same court for appropriating nine feet of land from the tenement of William Lynne in Shelland, on the estate of Ramsey Abbey.

[26] TNA, C 1/12/53. This area of Lincolnshire had been embanked in the early thirteenth century and there were strong obligations on local communities to continue to repair and scour the channels: see H. E. Hallam, *Settlement and Society: a study of the early agrarian history of south Lincolnshire* (Cambridge, 1965), esp. pp. 26–9.

[27] The classic study is Warren O. Ault, *Open-Field Husbandry and the Village Community: A Study of Agrarian By-laws in Medieval England* (Philadelphia, 1965). See also Trevor Rowley, 'Medieval Field Systems', in *The English Medieval Landscape*, ed. Leonard Cantor (London, 1982), 25–55.

[28] HCLA, HCA 244.

Christmas or suffer an even heavier penalty of 40s., and eventually they did so.[29] No doubt the time and labour required to make these boundaries physical was begrudged, but the conceptual work of bounding was also potentially fraught. In 1429 the free tenants of Kintbury asked for an adjournment 'in order to discuss and return a verdict on the metes and bounds' between the demesne lands of their own lord, the Prioress of Nuneaton, and those of the Prioress of Amesbury. The recess was granted and the next summer they reported that 'according to the court of the lady of this manor, [the bounds are] from the steps and footpath leading to the church up to the mill of Kintbury'.[30] Such a cautious approach suggests the riskiness of setting bounds where a happy imprecision had prevailed. In making the legal landscape more certain, bounding might force uncomfortable claims to surface.

But it was not always enough merely to note and name the bounds; sometimes it was important to physically delimit the land itself. An arbitration made in 1479 between two hostile neighbours, the Yorkshire gentlemen Richard Clarvaux and Roland Place, ordered them to 'sufficiently fence or make to be fenced with dike, qwykfalle, pale, or heege, the bounds of there severell grounds, pasturs and medowes; and theyn from thenfurth so kepe and upholde [them] so þat the catall belongyng them or any their tenants come not in to everich oþers grounds through defaute of closure'.[31] It seems that tensions had built up as the tenants' cattle had wandered across the boundaries of the lands, whereupon they had been distrained and impounded by the others. It is significant that the dispute lay not in the location of the boundaries, but rather in the fact that they were routinely traversed by wandering cattle—a point to which we shall return in a moment. In fifteenth-century England, good neighbours made good fences; as a practice of knowing the legal landscape, bounding was constituted not simply in the heuristic for dividing claims to the terrain, but also in the tangibility of physical partition.

Fourthly and finally, I want to look at vernacular names as a mode of producing knowledge about the legal landscape.[32] Unlike perambulations or views, there was of course no legal procedure such as 'naming', yet we find vernacular place names in almost every kind of legal document in late-medieval England. There is also good evidence to suggest that we ought to understand these not just as pre-given appellations, but as the product of processes of deliberative and enunciative naming among certain individuals or communities. Even people who lived in the same locale might know the same features by different names. To take a small example, the parish boundaries of Newton-on-Ouse, mentioned above, comprised a stream along its southern border; while Robert Elysson knew the whole thing as

[29] BL, Add. Ch. 27305, recto; Add. Ch. 27306, recto. A similar order was made at Catton in North Yorkshire in April 1477: WSRO, PHA 6914, m. 4v.

[30] BL, Add. Ch. 49226, mm. 2r–v. [31] NYCRO, ZQH 1, f. 155v.

[32] I have written about the strategy of naming in Johnson, 'Jurisdiction in Late-Medieval England', pp. 40–1.

'Bayneton Beck', both Hugo Wartre and Thomas Fyssher separated it into 'Bayneton Beck' and 'Ayquodsdyke', and John Colyngham referred to it as 'the stream at the end of the garden of Robert Bayneton'.[33] Such small variations were unimportant in this particular context, but they nonetheless carried legal connotations, as holding a piece of land abutting a watercourse carried with it certain duties.[34] It mattered, then, whether the stream's name was a generic toponym or a signal of proprietorial interests and obligations.

Indeed, the names given to rural places came to take on a particular significance in the context of the post-plague land market, as the rapid turnover of holdings meant that it was harder to keep track of tenants and their lands and obligations. At Withyham in East Sussex, where there appears to have been a severe breakdown of trust between the farmer of the manor and the tenants, the beadle was ordered to distrain William Warner to do fealty for his lands, but was unable to because 'it is unknown by him where those lands... do lie'; it was left to an inquisition of the tenants to tell him that Warner held a meadow called (ironically?) Bedellmeed, previously in the tenure of William Vaghan, for which he paid 3d. ob. annually.[35] In the vernacular names of lands, manorial tenants had their own means of knowing the legal landscape, which in rare cases such as this they were able to wield as specialist local knowledge. But names were also used as a tool of seigneurial administrators to ensure that tenures corresponded to existing written records in rentals; thus, for example, it was recorded at a manor court in Milton that Henry Basset claimed 'two virgates of land called *Clement Elys*', apparently in reference to its previous tenant.[36] Control over names thus subtly inflected the balance of power in tenurial negotiations.

As a final point, indeed, it is important to highlight how naming could form the basis of more explicit legal conflicts. In a dispute between Sir Roger Swillington and the borough of Dunwich in the late fourteenth and early fifteenth century, a crucial point of contention was the ownership and jurisdiction over an area of marshy land that had once formed the town's harbour, before it filled with silt and sand.[37] At the request of the burgesses, the disputed land—a place called 'Oldehaven' and a marsh called 'Kingsholme'—was seized into the king's hands in 1400 pending an inquiry into its ownership.[38] The subsequent inquisition, as well as confirming Swillington's claims more generally, found that this marshland 'ought not to be called *Kyngesholme*, but that name is newly put upon it by the

[33] BIA, CP.F.25, depositions, mm. 1r–4r.

[34] Generally, see Joshua Getzler, *A History of Water Rights at Common Law* (Oxford, 2004).

[35] KCC, WIT/17, m. 4r.

[36] CCCO, Ga/25/4/1. Manorial administrators for Corpus Christi College, Oxford, were clearly using such rentals to conduct court business: at a court a couple of years later, they reeled off the names of no fewer than seven previous tenants of a croft, the rent of which was in arrears: Ga/25/5/a.

[37] I write about this dispute in more detail in Johnson, 'Jurisdiction in Late-Medieval England', pp. 30–3.

[38] *CCR*, 1399–1402, pp. 160–1.

men of Dunwich'; instead, it was said to comprise three pieces of land called Lenaldesmersshe', 'Middelmersshe', and 'Chirchemersshe'.[39] The Dunwich burgesses, who had persistently appealed to the crown on the basis of their royal charter and fee farm, had renamed the land for the king, while Swillington, and perhaps his tenants, insisted that it remained as discrete blocks of marshland with specific customary associations.[40] Names were potent means of marking jurisdiction because they evoked the idea of widespread, uncontested knowledge of the legal landscape.[41]

In sum, these different modes of producing knowledge about the legal landscape all privileged certain kinds of claim at the expense of others. The practice of perambulation, as it repetitively circled the same boundaries, adapted fluidly to the changing landscape while helping to elide such change; the holding of views, as they emphasized the visual aspects of the landscape, often served to fix them; the determination of bounds elicited the production of both conceptual and physical parcels of land; and, as we have just seen, processes of naming gestured towards wider communities of knowledge. While each of these practices was to some degree prompted by official action, they also relied on witnesses, jurors, tenants, and others to articulate legal claims in the landscape. This co-production of the legal landscape was significant not only because, as we shall see in Chapter 6, it is typical of the formation of legitimate knowledge, but also, for more immediate purposes, because these epistemologies set the terms of engagement for the legal landscape, as people sought to make legal interventions through the ways that they moved through, interpreted, and transformed the landscape itself. It is to these interventions that we now turn.

Interventions in the Legal Landscape

That people in late-medieval England perceived legal meaning in the landscape is clear. But they did not merely stand and stare; they travelled around, moving earth

[39] *CCR*, 1405–9, p. 337. Whilst the 'church' and 'middle' references are fairly clear, it is obscure who or what 'lenald' was.

[40] SROI, HA30/314/19d/1–21, m. 6r. The tenurial situation was probably even more complicated than that. The 1405 agreement had referred to a part of the disputed land as rented by Peter Helmet, and a clause was inserted specifically to protect the rights of this parcel. Peter Helmet was mayor of Dunwich several times in the early 1400s, and the Helmet family had been prominent in local politics for several generations: see Thomas Gardiner, *An Historical Account of Dunwich* (London, 1754), pp. 73–9. A 1439 grant of a piece of marshland there adjacent to that of 'a certain Peter Helmet' (by then presumably dead) was made to William Bollyaunt to hold 'by the rod at the will of the lord'. SROI, HA30/312/194, m. 19r.

[41] For a similar case: an arbitration over common pasture, from Dunstable and its surrounding villages in 1475, noted *inter alia* that a standing cross that served as a boundary marker 'is named *White Crosse* and not *Porte Crosse*', see *Bedfordshire Notes and Queries, Vol. III*, ed. Frederic Augustus Blaydes (Bedford, 1893), pp. 291–6 (quote at p. 293).

and produce and possessions, altering the material world in ways both small and large, disturbing settled legal arrangements as they went. Some landscape alterations clearly represented deliberate legal interventions, as when in 1505 the citizens of Hereford processed solemnly out of the city to mow the grass on a piece of land that they claimed as their common, in the face of opposition from the dean and chapter of the cathedral.[42] When historians have considered such actions—demonstrative acts of hedge-breaking, grazing, or mass ploughings, for example—it has often been within the context of the enclosure of common land in early-modern England.[43] As we have seen, though, particularly in Chapter 4 in relation to the enclosure of seigneurial parks, the conducting of disputes *through* the landscape had a much longer history throughout the Middle Ages, and was part of the way in which ordinary tenants attempted to resist enclosures from as early as the thirteenth century.[44]

Yet, in the broader scheme of premodern socio-political relations, this kind of showpiece action and counteraction was relatively rare. More often, interventions in the landscape took place at much smaller scales of material politics, through negligent, inconsiderate, or makeshift alterations which shifted slightly outside the grooves of legal norms, like the meandering 'desire paths' that cut corners from established walkways. In what follows, we first turn to look at how movements—of people, animals, and objects—were understood to disrupt and unsettle the legal landscape, and second at how quotidian alterations to the physical world, such as digging, building, and repairing, instantiated and challenged legal claims. Of course, such everyday interventions in the legal landscape could still become focal points for both domination and resistance. But once we begin to account for the prevalence of such interventions, across a range of jurisdictional and environmental contexts, they begin to take on a new significance; the complex of ways in which people were entwined with the material world in everyday life comes to seem one of the most important and pervasive means by which legality was produced in late-medieval England.[45]

To begin with, we can see how even everyday movements were understood to conform to or change the legal landscape. Rural footpaths, for example, did not

[42] TNA, STAC1/1/19; Gervase Rosser, 'Conflict and Political Community in the Medieval Town: Disputes between Clergy and Laity in Hereford', in *The Church in the Medieval Town*, ed. T. R. Slater and Gervase Rosser (Aldershot, 1998), 20–42, p. 34.

[43] McDonagh, 'Making and Breaking Property'; Blomley, 'Making Private Property'; also R. W. Hoyle, 'Thomas Lord Darcy and the Rothwell Tenants, c.1526–1534, *The Yorkshire Archaeological Journal*, 63 (1991), 85–107; and, in an urban context, Christian Liddy, 'Urban Enclosure Riots: Risings of the Commons in English Towns, 1480–1525', *P&P*, 226 (2015), 41–77.

[44] See Marjorie McIntosh, *Controlling Misbehavior in England, 1370–1600* (Cambridge, 1998), pp. 84–8; Chris Dyer, 'Conflict in the landscape: the enclosure movement in England, 1220–1349', *Landscape History*, 28:1 (2006), 21–33.

[45] I am influenced here by Jane Bennett, *Vibrant Matter: a political ecology of things* (London and Durham, NC, 2010), and Tim Ingold, 'Toward an Ecology of Materials', *Annual Review of Anthropology*, 41 (2012), 427–42.

represent immutably fixed routes, but rather offered suggestions for movement that existed in tangled relation with rights of way. These suggestions might be ignored: thus four men were presented at Wootton Wawen (Warwickshire) in 1453 for 'unjustly making a way at *le Pryoresorcheyard*', or a couple of years later at Combe (Hampshire), William Dennamme and Henry William were fined 3d. each for breaking a hedgerow at *Nynoke*, and 'making a way there, continuing all the way here, with their carts'.[46] While such offences seem to have partly consisted in damaging hedges, they also hinged on the potentiality of the new routes created by these actions. A common way might quickly become difficult to dislodge from the landscape. Even small-scale, one-off movements opened up space for future transgressions. But if impassable roads or circuitous routes sometimes swayed people to venture new ways and face the consequences, so established rights of way must have exerted a gravity over movement—silent in the court rolls—which kept most people, most of the time, on the straight and narrow.

The built environment structured different kinds of legal movement. If roads and streets were far more impervious to the establishment of new ways, they were nonetheless supposed to constrain certain kinds of movement, as can be discerned in the frequent presentments for night-walking and vagabondage across late-medieval England.[47] These offences have rightly been understood by historians within the context of social control; a typical presentment against Joan Bodeham of Westwood (Suffolk) in 1498 identified her as not only as 'a common wanderer (*perambulatrix*) around her neighbours' houses at night time', but also as a 'common scold with her neighbours', for which she was fined a shilling.[48] Concerns about the untrustworthy behaviour of women, servants, and the poor were thus crystallized around a suspicion of wandering and rambling; this was understood to correlate with disorderly conduct not only because it took place outside of patriarchal households, but also because such aimless movement was the inverse of the idealized urban flow which, as we saw in Chapter 2, civic authorities aimed to foster in city streets.[49]

Legal landscapes of all kinds were thus unsettled by the illicit movement of people. But of course, in a predominantly agricultural economy, it was not only people who might move. The roaming, wandering, and roving of animals over pastures—most often pigs, cows, horses, and sheep, but also sometimes geese and goats too—raised particular problems for regulation. In the first place, this was because pasture rights lay right at the juncture of economy and society: they

[46] Respectively KCC, WOW/176, m. 6r; COM/10, recto.

[47] On both offences, see McIntosh, *Controlling Misbehavior*, pp. 64–7 [night-walking]; 88–93 [vagabondage].

[48] SROI, HA30/312/200, m. 14r.

[49] See p. 82 of this volume; also Jeremy Goldberg, 'Pigs and Prostitutes: Streetwalking in Comparative Perspective', in *Young Medieval Women*, ed. Katherine J. Lewis, Noël James Menuge, and Kim M. Phillips (New York, 1999), 172–93.

were not only a valuable resource but across late-medieval England signified enfranchisement with a community, whether for urban citizens, manorial tenants, or Forest inhabitants.[50] This relationship came under increasing strain during the fifteenth century, when the trend towards pastoral farming meant that rights to grazing land became a valuable commodity, which people were willing to sell or lease.[51] Thus in 1504 the vicar of Northallerton was presented for 'having among his sheep diverse sheep of diverse signs, as it is supposed from the flocks of strangers, taken by the vicar to agist on the moor for his own profit'.[52] Such transactions were problematic because they uncoupled the use of the pasture from obligations to the community who regulated it.

Indeed, pasture rights were understood in starkly material terms, as illicitly pastured animals were understood to 'overburden', 'occupy', or 'oppress' the common lands, their simple presence damaging the landscape. Pasture was conceived of as a limited resource, the conservation of which was held in delicate balance by the customary legal regime. For example, at West Hendred in 1509 it was reported that the whole tenantry made an ordinance that 'from now on no one shall overburden, in English "*surcharge*", either the whole common, or any part of it, with more animals than the quantity to which their tenure entitles them, under pain of 6s. 8d.'[53] This conception, moreover, meant that the straightforward movement of animals was understood to constitute a claim of rights. Thus at Combe in 1455, four husbandmen were presented because their animals were said to have 'trampled and destroyed the lord's pasture between *Stony Crosse* and *Wodemere*, for a space of about two acres, claiming that pasture there as their own pasture'.[54] In the legal landscape, simply keeping animals in a particular place was understood as a statement, whether it concorded with expectations and affirmed membership of a community, or stood out as a discordant note against such normative claims.

Yet animals might also intervene in this landscape without any direction from humans, and this caused a different set of problems. Thus a presentment at a Forestmote in Northallerton in 1493 ordained 'that any tenants having disruptive cattle (*catalla irracionabilia*), which break or destroy the hedges and branches of the lord, or others, ought to move them as they have been warned by the official

[50] Respectively, see Liddy, 'Urban Enclosure Riots', pp. 51–4; Jean Birrell, 'Common Rights in the Medieval Forest: Disputes and Conflicts in the Thirteenth Century', *P&P*, 11 (1987), 22–49; Christopher Dyer, *Lords and Peasants in a Changing Society: The Estates of the Bishopric of Worcester, 680–1540* (Cambridge, 1980), p. 369.

[51] Christopher Dyer, *Standards of living in the later Middle Ages: Social change in England, c.1200–1520* (Cambridge, 1989), pp. 131–44.

[52] NYRCO, ZBD/1/52/27, m. 2v. At Shelwick in Herefordshire, the whole tenantry was put in mercy for 40d., lest any of them conceded any of their common pasture to outsiders: BL, Add. Ch. 27300, recto.

[53] CCCO, Bb 1/3. 1509, recto. [54] KCC, COM/10, recto.

under pain of 3s. 4d.'[55] Such animals were themselves understood as 'disorderly', upsetting the *ratio* that was supposed to underlie common grazing. This same idea also inflected responses to animal movements elsewhere, for example in the pervasive presentments against pigs wandering through both urban and rural streets, or in the cattle which sometimes roamed into villages. Six inhabitants of Wells in Norfolk were presented at the court there in 1448 because their cows were 'roaming in the streets and doing damage to the gardens of diverse of their neighbours, and destroying their crops, all because they did not want to put them in the custody of the common dairy of Wells'.[56] Beasts had to be constrained; left to wantonly wander, they showed up the brittleness of the legal landscape, and the regimes of common rights that were supposed to undergird the management of pasture.

As well as people and animals, the placement and movement of physical things formed an important aspect of the legal landscape.[57] As I have written elsewhere, the shipwrecked objects that washed up randomly on late-medieval coastlines confronted the fishermen who found them with a series of legal duties: these items had to be reported to the local court, valued by a jury of shipmasters, and a fine paid on their worth before the finders were allowed to keep them. Only after the proper procedures had been performed could such shipwrecked goods become legitimate pieces of property.[58] But these processes were not confined to this coastal milieu. Such problematic objects haunted medieval English law, from the deodands demanded by coroner's inquests to the leaking gutters and tumbledown party walls that were scrutinized by the Assize of Nuisance.[59] When such objects suddenly ceased to fulfil the role expected of them—by no longer existing in good repair, killing somebody, or failing to have an obvious owner—it was up to legal processes to restore them to the background status of an everyday thing.

Some objects were tied closely to the legal landscape. Boundary stones, for example, particularly prevalent in moorland areas, were often moved by people hoping to gain pastoral territory from neighbouring settlements.[60] For example, in 1496 men of Aldborough in North Yorkshire successfully obtained an order from the local tourn court that the tenants of nearby Arkendale ought to show evidence

[55] NYRCO, ZBD/1/52/12, m. 6r. The same phrase was often used at swannimotes (for pigs, too) in the Forest of Bowland, in Lancashire: TNA, DL 39/2/8, mm. 2r, 5r, 6r.

[56] AC, M878, m. 1r.

[57] On the problems with trying to distinguish between landscape and objects, see Tim Ingold, 'Materials against materiality', *Archaeological Dialogues*, 14:1 (2007), 1–16.

[58] Tom Johnson, 'Medieval Law and Materiality: Shipwrecks, Finders, and Property on the Suffolk Coast, ca. 1380–1410', *AHR*, 120:2 (2015), 407–32.

[59] R. F. Hunnisett, *The Medieval Coroner* (Cambridge, 1961), pp. 32–4; *London Assize of Nuisance*, ed. Chew and Kellaway.

[60] For examples from North Yorkshire: Sessay, TNA, SC 2/211/94, m. 1r; Ampleforth, BIA, CCP 12/Amp 6, recto; Bellerby, NYCRO, ZDX, mm. 18v, 20r; and Ross-on-Wye (Herefordshire), HCLA, AM33/3, m. 2r.

for their right to common sheep on Minskip Moor, which lay between the two vills.[61] Two years later Robert Thomson launched a private trespass suit against John Pudsay for removing a 'merestone' from the south of Minskip Moor. Pudsay demurred, answering that 'the whole vill of Arkendale had been excommunicated in the chapel of Arkendale on account of that stone, and he had heard this excommunication; [but while] he recognizes himself to be one of those who removed that stone, he says it was not a merestone'.[62] Of course, if the stone had had no significance at all, there would have been little reason for Pudsay and his neighbours to remove it; rather, it was 'not a merestone' because it did not accord with the *real* boundaries, as the men of Arkendale saw them—a statement which shows up the depth of the connection between such objects and the legal landscape.

Indeed, all kinds of customary render relied on the proper placement of material things within the landscape. An Essex dairy farmer named John Barle was called before the Bishop of London's consistory court to explain a dispute with his vicar in 1492, after they disagreed over the form of his tithe payments. According to Barle, he was long accustomed to pay 4d. in tithes for each of his cows, annually at Michaelmas (September 29); but the vicar had recently demanded instead 'according to ancient custom [that he] would have the milk of the cows at every tenth day'. For sixth months Barle had obliged with this demand, bringing either milk in pitchers or cheese, and leaving it in the church porch—a customary place for transactions, often designated as the site for the disposal of willed legacies or the payment of other kinds of debt.[63] But very often, Barle alleged, the vicar failed to collect these tithes; and so the milk was knocked over and lapped up by dogs, the cheese was gnawed by mice, or the produce was stolen.[64] This case shows in wonderful detail the dynamism of the legal landscape as it was constituted by movements of people, animals, and things; in these same flows we can see the great legal vulnerabilities of this material world, and the precariousness of its proper ordering.

Turning from these fleeting movements, I would now like to look at everyday changes to the physical form of the legal landscape. Many common socio-economic practices depended on such alterations, and so routinely trod the edges of dispute. To begin with, digging to obtain materials such as peat, gravel,

[61] TNA, DL 30/489/10, m. 1r.

[62] TNA, DL 30/487/10, m. 2v: '... dicit quod villatus de Erkindeyn excommunicatus pro predicto petro in capella de Erkynden et dictus Johannus audivit predictum excommunicationem et ille cognovit se de unius illorum qui removerant petrum ibidem et dixit et [sic] non fuerit mereston, et ad declarandam predictam declaracionem et hoc petit ut inquiritur'. As can be seen, the Latin text is less than clear; however, the case is more interesting for the (disputed) facts it reveals than the precise course of legal procedure undertaken here.

[63] David Postles, 'Micro-spaces: church porches in pre-modern England', *Journal of Historical Geography*, 33 (2007), 749–69, esp. pp. 760–3.

[64] LMA, DL/C/A/001/MS09065, fos. 98v–99r. These folios are damaged and parts of the text are obscure; it is unclear which parish John Barle lived in.

and clay for domestic use and small-scale production was carefully controlled in a range of contexts.[65] Inhabitants who did not hold land and outsiders were fined for digging without licence, while those who possessed common rights to dig were prevented from digging excessively, beyond what was permitted by custom.[66] Those who dug also had a responsibility to leave the land in a good state of repair. Maud Man of Litcham in Norfolk, testifying about customary rights of common there in the early fifteenth century, recalled that once upon a time an outsider who came to the village late one evening had fallen 'in a pit newe graven [newly dug] & was in point to a perichid; & whan þat straunge man kam in to Lucham he pleynyd hym of his disese [complained of his injury] ... & what man of Lucham hadde þat pit graven & nout stoppid it aȝen & he was mercied [fined] grevousli in Lucham cort'.[67] Digging in the legal landscape could uncover all kinds of claims.

Digging was also important for the maintenance of the land. One of the most common types of presentment in late-medieval England was the order to 'scour', unblock, and repair ditches, dykes, and drains, or the fining of those who had failed to do so. Such orders were given with slightly distinctive inflections depending on their context. Within settlements, both urban and rural, they were often framed in terms of the social harm caused by overflowing gutters and sewers; thus Richard Flamell was presented in 1481 at Willoughby for 'permitting an unscoured ditch in his close ... to overflow with water and flood the king's highway, to the grave nuisance' of his neighbours.[68] But in the countryside more generally, such floods could have more serious consequences for agricultural production. In fenland areas in particular, rural tenants owed digging boonworks to protect the land from flooding, controlled through 'marshland congregations'. One such tribunal, held on the borders of Norfolk and Cambridgeshire in 1483, ordered the fenland vills of Walsoken and Emneth to 'sufficiently dig forty sewers

[65] Of course, there were specific legal arrangements for digging industrial products such as tin, silver, and coal, in the stannaries of the south-west and the free miner areas of the Peak District: on their relation to agricultural communities, see the debate between Ian Blanchard, 'The Miner and the Agricultural Community in Late Medieval England', *Agricultural History Review*, 20:2 (1972), 93–106; John Hatcher, 'Myths, Miners, and Agricultural Communities', 54–61, and Ian Blanchard, 'Stannator Fabulosus', 62–74, both in *Agricultural History Review*, 22:1 (1974).

[66] For example, John Wynter in 1505 for digging on Hayes Heath in Runton (Norfolk) 'without title or licence': NRO, WKC 2/166 398x7, m. 32r; or George Armestrang of Ampleforth for 'digging *interisidia* on the more against the custom of the prebend' in 1465: BIA CCP 12/Amp 5, recto. But these rights could also be legitimately purchased by outsiders, as at Kintbury in 1438 when William Lodelaw and John de Anyngton paid the lord 2s. each to dig for clay there for two years: BL, Add. Ch. 49229, m. 1v.

[67] NRO, KIM 1/9/6, m. 2r. At the leet court of Harwich in 1456, all tenants were enjoined under pain of 20s. to sufficiently fence their sewers and drains at Dovercourt on account of their 'danger to horses and men': ERO, D/B 4/38/8, m. 11r.

[68] MCO, 45/11, recto. For urban contexts, see Dolly Jørgensen, 'Cooperative Sanitation: Managing Streets and Gutters in Late Medieval England and Scandinavia', *Technology and Culture*, 49:3 (2008), 547–67. See also David Hall, 'The drainage of arable land in medieval England', in *Water Management in the English Landscape: Field, Marsh and Meadow*, ed. Hadrian Cook and Tom Williamson (Edinburgh, 1999), 28–40.

called 'Shoveloads' under pain of 100s.[69] Rural water management involved large-scale cooperation that had to be legally impelled.

The social importance of such continuous, legally-ordered digging to direct and stem the flow of water in such areas became starkly visible in its absence. At a royal inquest held at Wisbech in 1439 into the sewers that drained the fens of northern Cambridgeshire, it was reported that Thomas Floore of Ockham had failed to repair the ditches lying around his twenty-four acres of land there. According to the jury, this defect of just thirty feet worth of gutters had caused the flooding of over 10,000 acres of land in and around the town, belonging to hundreds of other people.[70] If this was likely an exaggeration, both in terms of the numbers affected and the directness of Floore's liability, his indictment exposes the potential consequences of neglect, and the difficulty of coordinating digging. Even outside of fenlands, the pervasiveness of dykes and ditches meant that ordinances for water regulation were common; at Ampleforth in 1465, it was ordered that everyone should 'emend and clean the courses of water called *watersewers*, and ensure that they keep their accustomed routes'.[71] This work that ensured the water followed its 'right' course was both legal and material, binding people in their communal obligations.[72]

This work did not only take place through digging, however, but through active construction. In Colchester, an arbitration agreement of *c.*1488 between two townsmen, John Whitefoote and William Blakborne, copied down into the town's register, shows how these same concerns might pervade the built environment too. A panel of four 'lande-lokers' was appointed to resolve a dispute over the gutters that carried water across the men's tenements in the parish of St. Runwald.[73] For his part, Blakborne was ordered to repair a leaden gutter thirty-one feet long, which would run the length of the church and deposit the water where it met the high street; Whitefoote was ordered to make a new lead gutter, specified at twelve feet and two inches, 'and the water that fallyth in to the seid gutter shal voyde and falle upon the grownd of the foreseid Willm Blakborne as it hath don be old tymys pasyd and so . . . shall have his cors thorow whitefots yerde as it hath done be old tymys passyd'.[74] Even as the urban landscape was remade, then, it was important that water should follow its customary routes. Everywhere in late-medieval England, the channelling of water was also about the

[69] NRO, BL/DR/2/1, f. 2v–3r. This book was made in the later sixteenth century, but seems to have incorporated these earlier courts as a formulary for correct procedure. Records of 'sewer congregations' survive from south Lincolnshire around the late fifteenth century, and were also held much earlier: see *The Medieval Lindsey Marsh: Selected Documents*, ed. A. E. B. Owen (Woodbridge, 1996).

[70] TNA, C 47/7/5/19, m. 2v.

[71] BIA, CCP 12/Amp 5, recto.

[72] The phrase 'rectus cursus' was frequently used to describe water routes: e.g. at Willoughby: MCO, 45/21, 45/22.

[73] ERO, D/B 5 R2, fo. 92r.

[74] A similar arbitration from Cambridge of 1476, in which one of the arbitrators is identified as a mason, survives as BLO, Cambridgeshire Ch. 34.

channelling of neighbourly relations, its flows materializing the obligations they held to one another.

Building works more generally represented an important mode of quotidian intervention in the legal landscape. New constructions, of course, could cause significant disruptions to established legal claims. In 1517, Richard Nevile, a vintner of Hereford admitted before the mayor to beginning the construction of a suburban building that had not only damaged the city walls, but also enclosed common land. In an act of submission, he was bound over for £40 to abide the judgment of the civic authorities; after 'ponderynge the comyn wele & laudable custome of the seid citie', they ordered him to remove 'all maner of tymber stakes, thornes, & stones from the seid comyn grounde & never fromhensforth to inclose the same but suffer it to lye to thuse of the commons'.[75] If this emphatic rhetorical assertion of 'commonness' is notable for the way it was girded by the fashionable concept of the 'commonweal', its material aims were also significant.[76] Nevile was not only ordered to take away the stakes and stones that probably comprised the foundations of his new structure, but also to maintain the damaged section of the city walls for the rest of his life, a continuous reminder of his encroachment and the collective ideal of citizenship.[77]

A similar set of concerns found different expression in rural contexts. If permission for a new building had not been sought from the lord or their steward, it was more often considered as an encroachment on custom. Thus at the Forest of Knaresborough in 1462, John Person was presented for building an enclosure next to his house 'where tenants of the lord king by right ought to customarily have common with their sheep at the open time yearly since time out of mind'.[78] Even quite small additional structures were seen as impositions that detracted from the enjoyment of common customary rights. At the court of Askrigg in May 1449, Matthew Ketilwell was presented for 'raising and newly making a certain stone wall on the king's highway at the Beck Gate, lying perpendicular in the highway so that it is stopped up, and no inhabitant of the village is able to travel, nor to cart grass, hay, or firewood there'.[79] Erecting this new structure had clearly interfered with use of the road, but the carting of grass, hay, and firewood was not generic bucolic detail; it referred to the specific material disruption of the kinds of customary right that the tenants there enjoyed. Unpermitted new buildings physically upset the working of a rural landscape replete with custom.

[75] HARC, BG11/19/11, ff. 218v–219r.

[76] On the use of this rhetoric, see John Watts, 'Public or Plebs: The Changing Meaning of "the Commons", 1381–1549', in *Power and Identity in the Middle Ages: Essays in Memory of Rees Davies*, ed. Huw Pryce and John Watts (Oxford, 2007), 242–60, esp. at p. 257. In Hereford, it seems to have been a buzzword: in 1518 the citizens and commons sent a bill to the law-day requesting the increase of entry fines to the franchise for the good of the commonwealth: HARC, BG11/3/1 [1518].

[77] See Liddy, *Politics of Citizenship*, pp. 60–4.

[78] TNA, DL 30/487/3, m. 5r. [79] NYCRO, ZDX, m. 10r.

Old buildings, too, formed part of that same customary landscape, as the maintenance and even rebuilding of long-standing structures constituted tenurial obligations in late-medieval manorial courts. In April 1412 John Swuylor of Milton agreed to lease an acre of land called *le Spyche*, for ninety-nine years; along with standard customary obligations and an annual rent of 24d., it was stated that 'he shall build a house for his living-place before Michaelmas, that is to say, in 1413', and if he failed to do so, the lord could re-enter.[80] The lord of the manor might help tenants to maintain and rebuild structures by providing building materials. At Spofforth, an annex attached to the court rolls for the year 1474 records the grants of lumber made to tenants from the lord's demesne woods. Richard Typlyng got some elder trees 'to make a chaumbre flue in his kylne house'; William Yreve received the same 'to beyld a chaumbyr ende'; and John Guysburght, the parson, received fuelwood along with 'tymbyr to beyld his bakows [bakehouse or back-house] of. x. postes'.[81] It is clear that manorial officials, jurors, and other local notables did especially well out of the lord's largesse.[82] The building and maintenance of structures helped to concretize seigneurial authority within the manor.

Correspondingly, tumbledown buildings and poorly repaired houses represented a visible deterioration of this authority, the aesthetics of an unobliging tenantry. This may help to explain the tides of presentments ordering tenants to repair 'ruined' houses in late-medieval manorial courts. This drive to repair, as we saw in the Chapter 1, was certainly an ideal of rural community, but it was also strongly shaped by an understanding of the manor as heritable property, the damage of which represented a long-term reduction in its value. Thus a tenement and half-virgate named *Fowlers* was seized from Thomas Mill at West Hendred in 1489 'because he has committed excessive waste, to the disinheritance of the lord'.[83] Such presentments were also tied up with an understanding of the built environment that bound up the material condition of houses with legal claims. Thus at Brackley (Northamptonshire) in 1380, John Draper and his wife Benedicta made a written agreement with the lord to lease a holding called *le Blakhall*, on the condition that they would fix it up within six years; but they fell into arrears and the building was abandoned, and by 1402, the new lord had asked twelve local men to explain the situation in a letter testimonial. After rehearsing the terms of the contract and the sequence of events, the witnesses said that they

[80] CCCO, Ga 25/3/a, m. 1r.

[81] WSRO, PHA 7035, annex 1.

[82] Ibid: John Bekerton, who got timber to mend his oxen-house, was a regular manorial juror; William Thornton, who received timber to mend his house and build a pigsty, was a constable; the bailiff and foresters received fuelwood; and Thomas Middleton received five trees 'by virtue of a warrant'. A roll of a 'view' of the woods on the Duchy of Lancaster estate of Pontefract survives from 1492, and shows much the same phenomenon: TNA, DL 39/3/11. Such grants are particularly significant in light of the growing material differentiation between the peasantry in the later fifteenth century: Forrest, *Trustworthy Men*, pp. 227–8.

[83] CCCO, Bb 1/9, recto. He had also failed to pay his rent, which undoubtedly exacerbated the issue.

'diligently inspected the house, both inside and outside', and found that several of the rooms, including one called the *le longchamber*, had been without a roof for the past ten years, and that it 'was so defective that without a new timber frame it could not be repaired'. Interpreting the building alongside the contract, they concluded that 'the agreement plainly allowed [the lord] to reenter' the property, and to hold it again 'in its former state'.[84] Even after so many years, this idealized 'former state' was the background against which all landscape change was imagined, and the foundation of legitimacy upon which all demands to repair, remodel, or rebuild were constructed.

Indeed, the idea of a stable landscape was crucial for projections of legal authority everywhere. In a dispute of *c.*1495 between the mayor of Hereford and the dean and chapter of the cathedral there, one of the central points of contention lay in the jurisdiction of the civic authorities over commercial and domestic premises within the parts of the 'church fee' in the city.[85] The dean and chapter complained that not only was the mayor demanding fines and tolls from its tenant shopkeepers, but also that 'whereas there be stalles, pentisis and other signes of crafts-menne dwelling within the church fee, the maire of the said citie wold by his autorite compelle the parties to put theme downe, in derogacione'.[86] The dean's claims over that part of the city depended in part on these visible signs of urban trade, which expressed the capitular jurisdiction over these properties and the businesses they contained. The city authorities, by removing them, aimed to demonstrate their authority over commercial regulation matters throughout the whole city, and in the process, no doubt, warned people off taking tenancies with the chapter. Jurisdiction in late-medieval England lay in this power over the very means of signification in the legal landscape.[87]

In sum, then, interventions in the legal landscape took a great many forms. As we saw in the first part of this section, even the fleeting movements of humans, animals, and objects across the land relied upon a delicately balanced legal kinetics, in which people were expected to know the 'right' way to go, and even subtle divergences were closely monitored and corrected; and in the second half of this section we have seen how quotidian modifications to the physical terrain through digging and ditching, building and taking down, were understood as

[84] MCO, Brackley 209d. John and Benedicta had long since died, but the witnesses said that she had tried to grant the holding to her brother; the testimony is clearly designed to uphold the lord's claim. Interestingly, a near-exact copy of the letter—dated a year later, and with a different set of witnesses, said to have made their testimony before the steward of the manor—survives as Brackley 114. Presumably it is this latter detail that explains the reproduction.

[85] On these disputes, see Rosser, 'Conflict and Political Community', and pp. 73, 81 in this volume.

[86] HCLA, HCA 2960, m. 5r.

[87] On the signification of the medieval city, see Michael Camille, 'Signs of the City: Place, Power, and Public Fantasy in Medieval Paris', in *Medieval Practices of Space*, ed. Hanawalt and Kobialka, 1–36; on the importance of communicating jurisdiction, Johnson, 'Jurisdiction in Late-Medieval England', pp. 16–17.

actions that reordered the diverse legal claims present in the landscape, or even interfered with its ability to signify such claims. In their routine interactions with the material world, then, there lay the possibility for common people to challenge or subtly deflect legal authorities, pressing their own interpretations instead. Yet, at the same time, too great a focus on such actions risks neglecting the dynamism of the landscape itself, its subtle flexures and responses to the rhythms of everyday work, which bound human agency in a tighter cast than we might imagine. The very tangible materiality of law in late-medieval England meant that it lay partly beyond the jurisdiction of man.

Nature as a Legal Protagonist

The physical landscape, like its meanings, is neither static nor unchanging; it may change rapidly and unexpectedly even without human action. In our own age of burgeoning environmental catastrophe, the idea of nature as a 'historical protagonist', in Bruce Campbell's phrase, is perhaps less surprising.[88] It is of course very difficult to ascribe to the material environment complete determinative agency over people's lives, just as it is a fallacy to see all landscape change as man-made. But as a raft of recent work in the humanities has highlighted, the very boundaries that are set between 'natural' and 'human' are historically contingent and subject to negotiation.[89] And indeed, in legal contexts more particularly, deciding what change is 'natural' and what change is 'human' is also about deciding who is answerable to what.[90] In the unstable and—it sometimes seemed to contemporaries—capriciously changeable landscape of late-medieval England, claims about which changes were natural and which were human were thus also claims about accountability, rights, and jurisdiction. In this final section, I want to use three case studies to develop this point in more detail, showing how environmental change could both disrupt and settle prevailing legal order.

To begin with, I would like to look at an example that frames legal issues around the idea of 'decay'. As we saw with Forest legal culture in Chapter 4, the conceptualization of natural resources as fragile and potentially wastable helped to justify the strict regulation of ways that Forest tenants could access and use them.[91] In a similar manner, the concept of decay was deployed as means of legitimating claims about the man-made landscape.[92] In 1487, a memorandum

[88] Bruce M. S. Campbell, 'Nature as historical protagonist: environment and society in pre-industrial England', *Economic History Review*, 63:2 (2010), 281–314.

[89] In general, see Bruno Latour, *We Have Never Been Modern*, trans. Catherine Porter (Cambridge, MA, 1993).

[90] David Delaney, *Law and Nature* (Cambridge, 2003), p. 45.

[91] See Chapter 4, pp. 144–5.

[92] On the use of this concept in ecclesiastical administration, see Forrest, *Trustworthy Men*, pp. 292–3.

from the town book of the small Essex borough of Maldon noted that 'the brygge... callid fulbrygge was... in decaye bothe in stone werke & also in wodyng & pylyng'. This decay, of course, necessitated repairs, so the bailiffs asked the chamberlains 'to take & to felle as moche wode as was growing in the common stretis & lanes of the bourgh'.[93] As they set about this task, they began to stack up the accumulated timber; but in a lane bordering the lands of the Abbey of Beeleigh, a substantial landowner in the area, the abbot's men attempted to carry away the wood that had been felled, in a demonstrative denial of the borough's rights there.[94] However, a crowd of townsmen assembled to ward them off, and so 'the abbot hadde there never a stykk & his cartis went home ageyn idill'.

This incident provoked a broader jurisdictional dispute between the town and abbey. It went to arbitration by Robert Plomer, a Justice of the Peace, and John Berdfeld, the auditor of the Earl of Essex; though Maldon possessed a royal charter and an urban government, it was a seigneurial borough, split between two manors.[95] After a perambulation of the boundaries was undertaken, and evidences of title shown to the arbitrators, it was decided that the lane from which the timber had been taken 'was a bounde of the towne & comen for the town afforn the abbey of Byleigh was an abbey'. That is to say, the townsmen had the older, better claim to this lane, and so had the right to take the wood from all the streets of the town, including those that bordered the abbey lands; 'so the abbot & his conseill were peacid'.[96] In a gesture of goodwill, the chamberlains allowed the abbot to re-fence the borders along the road to prevent his cattle from escaping. As part of the settlement, however, the town council agreed to let the abbot build fences on his side of the lane.

Of course, this protracted entry in the town's book was mainly about establishing a legal precedent—the borough prevailed and this helped to establish a more general settlement over the jurisdictional boundaries in Maldon. Yet it also contains an illuminating conception of the boundaries between human and natural agency. To begin with, the dispute was framed as the product of the 'decay' of a man-made structure, the bridge. But, of course, the solution pursued by the civic authorities—gathering wood from the trees in the lanes bordering the town—was far from obvious; indeed, it was a calculated assertion of their common

[93] ERO, D/B 3/1/2, f. 39r.

[94] R. C. Fowler, 'The Abbey of Beeleigh by Maldon', in *VCH Essex Volume II*, ed. William Page (London, 1907), pp. 172, 175.

[95] One manor was owned by the Bourchier Earls of Essex, and the other by the Earls of Oxford (though neither Earl was lord of the town in the late fifteenth century). Plomer was also Chief Steward to Henry Bourchier; clearly the Earls of Essex were considered impartial 'good lords' in this dispute. See Paul R. Cavill, *The English Parliaments of Henry VII 1485–1504* (Oxford, 2009), pp. 126–7.

[96] ERO, D/B 3/1/2, f. 39r.

rights there.[97] The rationale of 'decay' obfuscated the townsmen's culpability in provoking the dispute by taking 'as much wood' as they could from the streets. Their victory, in this narrative, rested on the idea that changes to the material city—the decay of its infrastructure, the right to fell trees, the building of boundary fences—existed along a single plane of action, working at each stage to naturalize civic authority over the urban landscape.[98] Decay and waste were not neutral descriptions of material condition, then, but represented ways of drawing the boundaries of the 'natural' so as to incorporate the necessity of legal regulation.

Turning now to our second case study, we can also see how natural change was not only used to justify legal interventions, but also their absence. In March 1518 the mayor of Norwich, the prior of the Cathedral Convent there, and their large retinues all 'went out all toyeders at the north gate of the seid cite' into its hinterland, in a surveying procession that aimed to establish their respective jurisdictions.[99] The two parties had a long history of territorial disputes in and around Norwich, and these had recently become violent.[100] In 1516, the Justices of Assize demanded a resolution to outstanding claims, and just over a year later the settlement was begun through this collective itinerary of the city's hinterland. The procession set out towards the villages Lakenham and Eaton, where the citizens claimed pasture rights. The draft text which records its progress sutures a narrative of the perambulation with a more straightforward survey, with the parties pointing out topographical boundary markers such as rivers, crosses, highways, and ditches, and laying claims to the lands between, some of which were corroborated by witness statements—made 'by dyuers olde men of the seid cite, and also by dyuers tenants of the seid priore'—or written evidence.

As the procession reached Eaton, they 'vewed & sawe a pasture grounde lyeng by the seide syde [of Eaton] on the est parte & at the wode ende on the north parte yn Eyton'. Everyone agreed that the citizens had always used this pasture as common, even in its arable parts during harvest time, despite the fact that the manor was a part of the priory estates. Indeed, an agreement of 1205 had established these boundaries over three centuries before.[101] But something had

[97] Ibid. This is suggested by the appendage of an otherwise irrelevant note at the end of the memorandum, explaining that ten years before this dispute (i.e. around 1477) the town chamberlains had 'fellde there & caryed aweye pacifically viij lodis of wode for the repayryng & wodyng of the strete a lytill este benethe seynt peters chirche'.

[98] A similar point is made in relation to the 'common soil' of towns in Liddy, *Politics of Citizenship*, p. 60.

[99] NRO, DCN 63/2, court books for 1503–8 and 1524 onwards. See NRO, DCN 89/7, for the arbitration text, this quote, and those that follow.

[100] On the broader background to these disputes, see Lorraine Attreed, 'Urban Identity in Medieval English Towns', *Journal of Interdisciplinary History*, 32:4 (2002), 571–592, at pp. 581–5; on the early sixteenth-century disputes, see *The Records of the City of Norwich*, ed. William Hudson and John Tingey (2 vols., Norwich and London, 1906–10), ii, pp. cxxxvii–cxxxix, including a plate depicting the decorated initial on the ratified agreement of 1524.

[101] *Records of the City of Norwich*, ed. Hudson and Tingey, vol. ii, pp. 212–4.

clearly changed in that time. The mayor and aldermen alleged that the area of this common pasture, bounded by the prior's woodland, had shrunk: the 'grounde there, as the seid wode growth, was taken oute of the seid comyn... & nowe is a wode'. That is to say, the woods bordering the common land had expanded, decreasing the size of the pasture. They produced a witness named Walter Talls to corroborate this allegation. He said 'that he sawe his fader ere the seid grounde & sett it with acarns aboute [fifty] yers past & more, & that he helped geder the accorns to sett the seid grounde withall'.[102] Thus over half a century, growing from the acorns he and his father had planted, a column of oak trees had made its slow advance onto the citizens' commons.

Much is left unsaid in this draft text. The arbitration was not agreed formally until 1525, when it was finally established by two royal charters, a delay explained by the huge reluctance of the citizenry to abrogate their cherished rights of common in Eaton and Lakenham.[103] But abrogate they did, in exchange for eighty acres of land elsewhere and a large annual due of £13 6s. 8d.[104] This exchange is significant, because it shows that the priory's claims to these lands, though they contradicted written evidence, seem to have hardened merely through the growth of the oak trees themselves, a remarkable demonstration of the legal power of material change, but also of the tensions at the heart of the city's case. Rights of all kinds, of property, of jurisdiction, of custom, had to be exercised continuously in order to hold up in law, and the physical landscape provided a crucial support to such exercises.[105] While Walter Talls's testimony created a useful point of origin for this change, it also exposed the half-century during which this wood had slowly grown into the commons, and the neglect of the citizens in exercising their rights over the pasture. This conceptualization of landscape change worked to obfuscate such negligence, establishing their ownership over the ground below.

Turning to our third case study, a similarly slow—but much more momentous—kind of natural change took place on the Suffolk coast over the course of the Middle Ages. During the late thirteenth and fourteenth centuries, the town of Dunwich was severely afflicted by storms and by coastal avulsion, with two consequences. First, the town itself was slowly falling into the sea, as the small cliff on which it stood was gradually undermined by waves and occasional storm surges; second, the mouth of its harbour—the source of its wealth through tolls and taxes—was silting up, making it impossible for ships to pass there,

102 NRO, DCN 89/7.

103 *Records of the City of Norwich*, ed. Hudson and Tingey, vol. i, p. cx. For abstracts of these charters, see vol. i, pp. 43–4 (items XXVI and XXVII).

104 Norman Tanner, *The Church in Late Medieval Norwich, 1370–1532* (Toronto, 1984), pp. 153–4.

105 In English law, see Baker, *English Legal History*, p. 57; more generally, see Wickham, *Courts and Conflict*, pp. 283–4.

and so for the town to sustain its revenues.[106] In 1390, the town's trouble was compounded by the reopening of a long-standing dispute with Roger Swillington, the lord of Blythburgh. With Dunwich's harbour unfit for shipping, the fishing village of Walberswick, which lay within the lordship, served as a haven for this stretch of coast, harbouring both local fishing boats and merchant ships from further afield, a further detriment to the town's jurisdiction and its revenue collection. So began a set of legal disputes over the jurisdictional boundaries between town and lordship that would last, intermittently, for over eighty years.[107]

The complexity of these disputes was compounded by the continual shifting of the sands, gravel, and stones between the harbours of Walberswick and Dunwich, and the passage of the estuarial rivers. By 1405, after royal proclamations had been issued, law-suits entered into, and violence between the two parties, an arbitration settled the conflict in favour of Swillington, deciding that the new land formed by the silting up of Dunwich's harbour belonged to the lordship, not the town. This document set a new boundary between the two parties at the midpoint of the 'new haven' of Walberswick, adding an extraordinary clause:

> Also bothe parties graunten þat ȝef it so befalle þat the forsaid newe haven þat nowe is, be stoppyd be rage of the see or be ony other aventure, & breke up on another parte, þat thane the place where the forsaid newe haven is ate Walberswyks þat now is, shal be a fulle bounde for evermore betwene bothe parties.[108]

That is to say, if further coastal accretion or storms shifted the coastline once more, then the boundary established in the 1405 indenture ought nonetheless to remain. The 'rage of the sea' was a rendering of the Latin phrase *impetum maris*, which had been used in earlier legal settlements relating to Dunwich to explain the changing landscape; here, it was used to force a settlement in the face of ongoing environmental change, transferring the disharmony of the dispute onto the natural world.[109]

This unusual provision soon proved to have been prudent. Over the next thirty years, the new haven of Walberswick, like that of Dunwich before it, had begun to silt up, becoming 'soo feble and schold [shallow] & sonds & groundes soo growen in the stremys therof that no schip may seylen in no comyn owte'.[110] By 1435, the new lord of Blythburgh, Sir John Hopton, and the burgesses of Dunwich had

[106] On these processes, see Mark Bailey, '*Per impetum maris*: natural disaster and economic decline in eastern England, 1275–1350', in *Before the Black Death: Studies in the 'crisis' of the early fourteenth century*, ed. Bruce M. S. Campbell (Manchester, 1991), 184–208, at pp. 195–7.

[107] I discuss this dispute in detail in Johnson, 'Jurisdiction in Late-Medieval England', pp. 26–30.

[108] SROI, HA30/369/327.

[109] This Latin phrase was used in a 1332 royal inquisition into Dunwich: SROI, HD 1538/208/3. It was also used elsewhere: see Bailey, 'Per Impetum Maris', pp. 192, 194, 200.

[110] SROI, HA30/50/22/27.2 (1).

agreed a solution to this problem: a new shipping channel would be cut on the north side of the boundary between the lordship and the town. Much about this episode remains unclear, and it is doubtful that the channel was ever made.[111] But the text written in 1435 which provided for this agreement is revealing. Whoever drafted the text had read very thoroughly the documents from the earlier disputes, particularly that of 1405, and produced a careful narrative account rehearsing what had happened. It started by stating simply that 'in olde tyme ther was an hauene rennyng under the town of Donewich', before noting that it 'was, be castyng et werkyng of the see, stopped & distroyed, and sithen an newe haue brake owt of þe see' at Walberswick.[112] The rage of the sea, it seems, had been transmuted into a more diligent 'working'.

This was significant in the context of the new shipping channel, which was controversial. First, it was to be cut on Hopton's land, north of the boundary dividing the lordship and the town, and he was keen to emphasize that it was to be made because of his 'goodnesse & for the effectuell love that he haith to his neybouris' and constituted no kind of legal precedent. Second, it was essential that the new channel, by creating a new water-crossing in this marshy landscape, did not interfere with the territorial boundaries between lordship and town in respect to those established in the 1405 composition. The solution to this was a clever and rather self-conscious legal distinction between environmental and man-made change: 'the newe hauene that is made be mannis hand is nought... the bounde... in as moche as it is not made be fortune of þe casting of the gravell as the compocyssion wills'.[113] That is to say, the earlier arbitration was interpreted to have provided for changed boundaries should the river move again; the 1435 licence made sure that the boundary remained in place because it was not the 'the rage of the sea', but 'man's hand' intervening in the environment.[114]

This distinction between the unpredictable 'rage of the sea' and the directed application of 'man's hand' was the central preoccupation of the 1435 licence. It represents a creative response to an unusual problem, demonstrating emphatically how distinctions between natural and human environmental change were intimately bound up with conceptions of accountability. Indeed, it also looked forward to potential future problems caused by landscape change, and further provisions

[111] Colin Richmond, *John Hopton: A Fifteenth Century Suffolk Gentleman* (Cambridge, 1981), p. 153. The balance of evidence suggests it was not: a further dispute in the 1460s between Hopton and Dunwich produced a huge amount of documentation about the boundaries, none of which mentioned a channel. See SROI, HA30/369/335; HA30/369/394; HA30/312/87.

[112] SROI, HA30/50/22/27.2 (1). [113] Ibid.

[114] This seems, strictly speaking, to have been an unnecessary precaution for two reasons. Firstly, the 1405 indenture does not limit environmental change to 'the rage of the sea', but includes change from 'ony other aventure', which implies very broad criteria. Secondly, it specified that if the water moves, the haven at Walberswick 'that now is' shall be a boundary forever. [SROI, HA30/369/327.] The fact that the lawyers in 1435 tiptoed around the indenture, then, is suggestive. Either it was unclear and they misunderstood it, or they felt that it was unclear and applied a deliberately blunt logic to its provisions in order to simplify it.

were made 'incasfortune that the same feble hauene [at Walberswick] weyll frie and growe to gravell & ston as other places be þe see [have] don'.[115] These clauses thus present yet more ways of theorizing landscape change, introducing the idea that the grounds might spontaneously generate themselves, like hatching fish fry, and also suggesting that it was possible to infer this from what had happened elsewhere in 'other places by the sea'. Finally, the licence proposed some solutions should these projected changes take place. To begin with, a tree was to be planted to 'bere record of the... true bounde'. But even this was not secure, and so to voyden trouble & travers that may falle in cas wer the rages of the see put down the tree or ells it were remeved or putte down be mannys hand', the boundaries were also measured, and the distance of 209 rods was recorded in the text.[116]

This dispute provides a remarkable instance of the way that shifting the boundaries between natural and human action carried legal implications. The 1405 arbitration and the 1435 licence that followed both framed the dispute as having been caused by the sea, which had disrupted an orderly legal landscape; a highly convenient fiction in the context of a settlement. Yet the multiple concepts that were developed throughout these documents to explain what the sea had done suggest rather more ambiguity: was the sea raging, working, or casting, or was the land growing? Each of these ideas conjured a different relationship between the human and the natural world. While the sea's 'rage' created hapless victims, when it 'worked' it could be counterbalanced with 'man's hand'; and if it would simply and unstoppably cause the 'growth' of land, then it could be opposed through the cultivation of a natural marker, a tree, that would grow with the landscape, and in the measurement of the ground itself. The conceptual boundaries established here between human and natural agency, then, came to correspond with the modes of dispute resolution that the parties envisaged; we can see, in these documents, the subtlety of the ways in which contemporaries imagined and worked within the legal landscape.

Overall, then, each of these three case studies presents an instance of environmental change—a rotting bridge, a growing copse, a silting harbour—that was understood to provoke a reorganization of the legal boundaries which these sites had hitherto supported. They show, in the first place, the fact that the landscape in late-medieval England was always in a state of slow but constant unfolding, both systemically, for example in the shift towards pastoral agriculture, and also microcosmically, through the gradual ways in which people altered the physical world; the legal consequences of this relentless change, likewise, had to be continually renegotiated, a point to which I shall return shortly. But in the second place, these examples have also shown that the conceptualization of environmental change was always bound up with ideas about rights, accountability,

[115] SROI, HA30/50/22/27.2 (1). [116] Ibid.

and jurisdiction. As David Delaney has written, 'control over the meaning of "nature" translates into control over the things thus naturalized, which, in turn, translates into control over people'.[117] Even as we recognize nature as a legal protagonist in late-medieval England, then, we must not lose sight of the roles it was given to perform, the ways in which could be commandeered to achieve an illusion of stability amidst the flux.

Conclusion

This chapter has argued that we need to place the landscape much closer to the centre of how we understand everyday engagements with law in late-medieval England. As we have seen, people were routinely expected to articulate knowledge about the legal landscape—through perambulations, views, boundaries, and names—in order to clarify claims or settle disputes. And, more than this, in their quotidian working lives common people had to understand the lie of the land, as they moved around, drove animals, dug channels, maintained buildings, and erected new structures. The legal meaning immanent in these ecological complexes of people, animals, and objects allowed people to make deliberate interventions in the landscape, but it also entangled them in a delicate web of potential disputes. Concomitantly, environmental change on a larger scale involved more complicated renegotiations of legal responsibility; phenomena such as coastal accretion, rotting timbers, and growing woodlands all raised difficult questions about who, and what, was accountable for conflicts, and, moreover, the best ways to resolve them.

There are three main conclusions I want to draw out from this chapter. The first links back to one of the overall arguments of the book, which is that our conceptualization of legal engagement in late-medieval England must look beyond historiographical models that emphasize ordinary 'consciousness' of law as a purely psychological or cultural phenomenon. As we have seen here, law was a physically proximate presence for people living in fifteenth-century England.[118] The tangibility of legal practice in the material world suggests a world in which 'knowledge' or 'awareness' of law was more pervasive; authority was something that could be seen and touched—in the walls of the lord's deer park, the boundary stone out on the moor, the tithes placed in the barn. As the archaeologist Adam T. Smith has suggested, the physical world was 'instrumental in shaping the

[117] Delaney, *Law and Nature*, p. 45.

[118] See Paul Hyams, 'What did Edwardian Villagers Understand by "Law"?', in *Medieval Society and the Manor Court*, ed. Zvi Razi and Richard Smith (Oxford, 1996), 69–100; Anthony Musson, *Medieval Law in Context: The growth of legal consciousness from Magna Carta to the Peasants' Revolt* (Manchester, 2001).

experience, perception, and imagination of authorization and subjection'.[119] We must begin to think, then, about the ways in which material infrastructures shaped subjects in ways that pay heed to the depth of their entanglement with law, without foreclosing the possibilities of resistance.

The second conclusion I want to draw out here concerns the meanings that people attributed to the landscape in late-medieval England. It is a commonplace among historians of the premodern landscape that it was a 'palimpsest' of meaning, as layers of custom, memory, or religious significance accreted on top of one another over generations of cultural change.[120] Implicit in this terminology, I think, is the idea that the landscape was a source of constancy beneath a world of shifting human affairs, and that it was thus particularly suitable for the long-term thesaurization of meaning in oral societies. There is some truth to this: people clearly saw correspondences between the well-established physical footpath and the conceptual right of way, or the long-standing customary placement of a stone and the true boundary that it marked. The notion of an orderly past landscape, indeed, provided an important foil for the conceptualization of disruptive change, which, as we have seen, could be summoned at convenient moments in the course of disputes.

At the same time, however, these historiographical conceptions of the premodern landscape as a vehicle of memory and custom are too narrow. In the first place, they neglect contemporary anxieties about the capacity of the landscape to continually connote legal meaning; people worried that trees marking boundaries might be cut down or blown over, or that 'merestones' might be moved. Legal meaning was always difficult to fix in place, always potentially transitory, and required recurrent effort to preserve. The legal landscape required constant labour, whether in the physical digging or hauling or building that brought the physical world back into line with the conceptual one, or in the ideational work of perambulations, views, and depositions that affirmed and reinforced its legal meanings. We shall look in more detail at the work that went into the production of this kind of 'legitimate knowledge'. But, more than this, to explain the hermeneutics of premodern landscapes solely in terms of memory misses the extent to which people looked *forwards* through the land: to the future inheritance of manorial property, to the changing boundaries wrought by shifting sands, to a new way made where none had been before. The landscape was also a way that people stretched the limits of authority, using it to imagine the world anew.

Thirdly and finally, the subtle shifting flux of the landscape and its meanings, momentary attempts to pin them down to one another also represented

[119] Adam T. Smith, 'Archaeologies of Sovereignty', *Annual Review of Anthropology*, 40 (2011), 415–32, at pp. 423–4.

[120] Whyte, *Inhabiting the Landscape*, p. 9; Giles, 'Visuality and Space in Pre-Modern England', p. 115. But see the discussion of palimpsest as a cliché in Walsham, *The Reformation of the Landscape*, pp. 6–7.

explanations of the boundaries between human and natural action. At the heart of Cosgrove's influential work is the notion that the word 'landscape', though we tend to use it in a straightforward way (as I have here), is a concept that performs ideological work, representing an 'imagined relationship with nature'.[121] There was no 'landscape' in premodern England, and we will do well to remember that it was the land as much as the law that was being constructed during contestations and negotiations over the meanings that it might hold.[122] In shifting relation to one another, legality was assembled from material concepts such as growth and decay at the same time that the landscape was built from legal components such as common pasture, cottages held in customary tenure, or the king's highway. At moments of dispute, the boundaries between law and the landscape could be redrawn, retracing the lines of power that lay between the people who lived between them.

[121] Denis E. Cosgrove, *Social Formation and Symbolic Landscape* (London and Sydney, 1984).

[122] Of course, there was also literally no word 'landscape' in English before the middle of the sixteenth century, though that is not the point here.

6
The Economy of Legitimate Knowledge

Introduction

Legal institutions throughout late-medieval England relied systematically on common people to provide knowledge about diverse matters: what crime had taken place, what the relevant custom was, and as we saw in Chapter 5, where the boundaries lay and who was to maintain them. In a straightforward way, this information was needed for various purposes of governance, ensuring that criminals were punished, dues collected, and matters settled. The principal procedures by which legal institutions collected this information—juries, witnesses, and *fama* or 'common opinion'—developed over the course of the twelfth and thirteenth centuries, and remained important well into early modernity (and beyond).[1] Yet if these mechanisms of knowledge were old in the later Middle Ages they took on a new significance in an era in which people were beginning to demand more from the institutions that governed them. Legal institutions not only had an interest in securing knowledge that was authentic and truthful for the purposes of justice and government, therefore, but also in affirming knowledge that would convince the people whom they sought to command, and secure their assent.

People who rendered up their information and knowledge to the courts were well aware of their role in these processes. For example, as many historians have recognized, witnesses before the church courts were capable of shaping their testimony in ways that—while cajoled and cosseted by canon law procedures—served their own purposes, or those of their friends and patrons.[2] But through other mechanisms too, people were occasionally able to use the opportunities provided by institutional demands for information to guide legal proceedings

[1] On earlier developments, see James Masschaele, *Jury, State and Society in Medieval England* (New York, 2008); Ian Forrest, 'The Transformation of Visitation in Thirteenth-Century England', *P&P*, 221 (2013), 3–38; John S. Beckerman, 'Procedural Innovation and Institutional Change in Medieval English Manorial Courts', *L&HR*, 10:2 (1992), 197–252. A useful introduction to these issues can be found in the first chapter of Anthony Musson and W. M. Ormrod, *The Evolution of English Justice: Law, Politics and Society in the Fourteenth Century* (Basingstoke, 1999). For a longer perspective on the jury in particular, see the essays in *Twelve Good Men and True: The Criminal Trial Jury in England, 1200–1800*, ed. J. S. Cockburn and Thomas A. Green (Princeton, NJ, 1988).

[2] See Robert N. Swanson, '"... et examinatus dicit ...": Oral and Personal History in the Records of English Ecclesiastical Courts', in *Voices from the Bench: Narratives of Lesser Folk in Medieval Trial*, ed. Michael Goodich (Basingstoke, 2006), 203–26; Jeremy Goldberg, *Communal Discord, Child Abduction, and Rape in the Later Middle Ages* (Basingstoke, 2008); Tom Johnson, 'The Preconstruction of Witness Testimony: Law and Social Discourse in England before the Reformation', *L&HR*, 32:1 (2014), 127–47.

Law in Common: Legal Cultures in Late-Medieval England. Tom Johnson, Oxford University Press (2020).

DOI: 10.1093/oso/9780198785613.001.0001

towards their own aims. We saw in Chapter 4 the jurors of Chobham, in Surrey, who took the occasion afforded by a visiting Forest eyre to complain—in language that emphasized the grave damage to the king's game—that their lord, the Abbot of Chertsey, had failed to repair a bridge for six years.[3] As institutions asked people to report, judge, and value for the purposes of governance, then, those who performed this work requested, in return, some effective responses to their local problems. The institutional demand for knowledge, in short, opened up a space of negotiation in which common people were able to exert some pressure on the terms of their own governance.[4]

The procedures that framed these negotiations were flexible, and this made them resilient in the face of the obstacles that commonly arose. On the one hand, the courts had procedures that allowed them to accept awkward forms of knowledge such as rumours or impartial witnesses; on the other hand, the people who were summoned knew how to frame knowledge in various ways to emphasize its credibility and trustworthiness, making it more amenable to the courts. There were, of course, also rare occasions in which negotiations might break down altogether, as presentment jurors concealed some relevant titbit from the steward, or the *inquisitores* at an ecclesiastical visitation taciturnly replied 'all is well' to the inquiries. Viewing such transactions of information between courts and their constituents in aggregate, we can begin to perceive the operation of a whole economy of legitimate knowledge.

This chapter begins by looking at the three main ways in which knowledge was framed before the courts, in the concepts of *fama*, testimony, and verdict. I suggest that there was a basic correspondence between these official concepts and the kinds of knowledge that common people understood to be legitimate, which relied on the locality, credibility, and manifest qualities of information; this created a platform upon which the work of producing and transacting knowledge could be negotiated. The second section examines the kinds of 'knowledge work' that legal institutions asked people to perform, from the mnemonic labour of remembering to the deliberative tasks of evaluating and inquiring. I argue that the laboriousness of this work—emphasized, for example, through the rhetoric of diligence—helped to legitimate the knowledge it produced. The third section then turns to look at what people wanted from their negotiations over knowledge. Supplying information was a way for people to establish their credibility, to belong to an influential group, and to perform an ethical duty; it could also be a powerful stimulus for collective action, and to effect material change to living conditions, rents and dues, and local infrastructure.

[3] TNA, DL 39/2/13, no. 5; see Chapter 4, pp. 144–5.

[4] John Watts, 'The Pressure of the Public on Later Medieval Politics', in *The Fifteenth Century IV: Political Culture in Late Medieval Britain*, ed. Linda Clark and Christine Carpenter (Woodbridge, 2004), 159–80.

Throughout each of these sections we shall see the close entwinement between local courts and the communities that used them. As people supplied information to courts, so they also took information from them, using their verdicts and the testimonies given there as credible sources of knowledge which they might use themselves—which might in turn feed once again into the work of the courts. This chapter considers these spirals of information through the anachronistic heuristic of economy and work because it helps, I think, to identify discrete phases in these cycles that can be more carefully scrutinized. At the same time, it draws our attention to the ways that people found out information from legal institutions, and how such communications affected the way that those institutions operated.[5] The conclusion, then, briefly explores how legitimate knowledge was circulated beyond courts themselves. Such channels of communication tell us not only about how individuals understood law, but also about how the expectations of a public may have helped to shape the kinds of knowledge that legal institutions produced.

Legitimate Knowledge: Jurors, *Fama*, and Witnesses

By the fifteenth century, there were three main concepts through which knowledge was introduced into legal institutions: the 'true statement' of jurors given in a verdict, the public opinion encapsulated by the notion of *fama*, and the specialist or eyewitness knowledge that was obtainable through witness testimony. These concepts derived from relatively distinct legal traditions that framed knowledge with rather different goals in mind—the Roman law idea of *fama*, for example, was not understood to be conclusive proof of anything, but rather served as a whiff of suspicion that might provoke a prosecution, whereas the verdict, as its etymology implies, was supposed to present a 'true statement' about some matter or another.[6] Yet, despite their formal differences, these concepts shared some key qualities in the way that they framed information: good knowledge was local, distinctive to and representative of a particular place, it was discerned—that is, carefully and expertly picked out—by credible people, and it was manifest, obvious to any neutral observer. These criteria stretched across

[5] This is a central theme of Ian Forrest, *The Detection of Heresy in Late Medieval England* (Oxford, 2005), esp. Ch. 5, pp. 113–42.

[6] The best legal discussion on *fama* can be found in Helmholz, *Canon Law and Ecclesiastical Jurisdiction*, pp. 331–6, 570–3, 607–12. See also Richard M. Fraher, 'Conviction According to Conscience: The Medieval Jurists' Debate concerning Judicial Discretion and the Law of Proof', *L&HR*, 7:1 (1989), 23–88; R. H. Helmholz, *The Ius Commune in England: Four Studies* (Oxford, 2001), Ch. 2, pp. 82–134. Good discussions of the social significance of *fama* can be found in *Fama: The politics of talk and reputation in medieval Europe*, ed. Thelma Fenster and Daniel Lord Smail (Ithaca, NY, 2003); Marie A. Kelleher, 'Law and the Maiden: *Inquisitio*, *fama*, and the testimony of children in Medieval Catalonia', *Viator* (2006), 351–67.

the different concepts and the jurisdictions in which they were deployed, facilitating a broad understanding of what made knowledge legitimate.

This understanding was not restricted to professional legal thought, however. Indeed, these qualities of localness, credibility, and manifestness were important precisely because they were readily intelligible to the people who used the courts, translating into vernacular understandings of what made knowledge legitimate and trustworthy. Common folk in late-medieval England trusted knowledge that was local to their own street or parish, that was reported by honest and credible people, and which was openly and commonly known; they resorted to such explanations when they repeated gossip, insulted their neighbours, or justified themselves in other contexts. These frameworks of legitimacy were thus shared widely throughout late-medieval society, both inside and outside of legal institutions; they were not merely indicative of the close cultural entwinement of local law-courts and the communities that used them, but also crucial to the negotiations that took place over information. Common understandings of how knowledge became legitimate created the platform for transactions over the labour required to produce it, and its compensation.

To begin with, legitimate knowledge had to be local. This was a deep-rooted idea in both the common-law and Roman canon-law traditions, and it was central to the notions of *fama*, testimony, and verdict, which were closely bound together before the late twelfth century. As Mike Macnair has argued, the roots of the jury lie in the combination of these three concepts, as early jurors were understood as witnesses to local reputation, or *fama*.[7] A comparably indistinct combination of sworn inquests and eyewitnesses seems to have characterized the practice of early church courts in England.[8] Over the course of the thirteenth century, both royal and ecclesiastical courts came to work out more precise, and distinctive procedures as officials grappled with the problem of how to trust local information.[9] Canon law distinguished more clearly between *fama* as a way of accessing report of a locality without according it any probative force, and sworn witness testimony as a kind of proof that was closely scrutinized for local bias; the Angevin common law, by contrast, lumped all these functions together into the jury, as both a fact-gathering and decision-making institution.[10] Local knowledge was built into the foundations of medieval English legal institutions.

[7] Mike Macnair, 'Vicinage and the Antecedents of the Jury', *L&HR*, 17:3 (1999), 537–99.

[8] Charles Donahue, Jr, 'Proof by Witnesses in the Church Courts of Medieval England: An Imperfect Reception of the Learned Law', in *On the Laws and Customs of England: Essays in Honor of Samuel E. Thorne*, ed. Morris S. Arnold, Thomas A. Green, Sally A. Scully, and Stephen D. White (Chapel Hill, NC, 1981), 127–58; Helmholz, *Canon Law and Ecclesiastical Jurisdiction*, pp. 338–9.

[9] Forrest, 'Transformation of Visitation', pp. 13–4.

[10] S. F. C. Milsom, 'Law and Fact in Legal Development', *University of Toronto Law Journal*, 17:1 (1967), 1–19; Raoul C. van Caenegem, 'Reflexions on Rational and Irrational Modes of Proof in Medieval Europe', *Tijdschrift voor Rechtsgeschiedenis*, 58 (1990), 263–79; Beckerman, 'Procedural Innovation and Institutional Change'.

In late-medieval practice, of course, the particular locale represented in courts varied significantly. In the royal courts of gaol delivery, which extended across whole counties, it was often difficult for the sheriffs who empanelled jurors to find sufficient willing free men from the 'neighbourhood' (*visnetus*) in which an offence had been committed, though, as Edward Powell has shown, they do seem to have made an effort to secure at least one man from the relevant hundred.[11] Local courts were able to aim closer than this. In hundreds themselves, as indeed larger manors, courts received information from different townships within the precinct of their jurisdiction, a practice also used in the peculiar ecclesiastical court for the very large parish of Hartlebury.[12] In towns, local knowledge for secular purposes was often figured through the ward, which was often related—both by obligations of murage, and perhaps the more intangible sense of neighbourhood—to a city gate.[13] Church courts and visitations naturally relied on the parish as a discrete unit of locality, both for the purposes of placing witnesses who testified in instance suits, and also for assessing where *fama* came from. Local knowledge, then, tended to be institutionalized through units of vill, manor, ward, and parish.

Common people seem to have framed legitimate knowledge in similarly local terms. For example, in 1491 Lewis Taylor was cited to the London commissary for accusing Alice Grey of adultery and saying that 'all Themys Strete didde wondir on hir'—referring perhaps to the specific street or the ward that bore its name.[14] Interestingly, though, jurors often mentioned the parish as the defining unit of locality; thus the inquest for the Surrey Forest eyre reported an offence 'in the parish of Egham within the king's Forest of Windsor'.[15] Witnesses may also have tailored their understandings of local knowledge by jurisdiction: deponents before the church courts, asked to locate *fama*, of course routinely used the parish as a frame of reference, but in a 1517 inquiry at Ipswich (discussed in detail in Chapter 3), witnesses described the *fama* about Richard Astill's death as

[11] Edward Powell, 'Jury Trial at Gaol Delivery in the Late Middle Ages: The Midland Circuit, 1400–1429', in *Twelve Good Men and True*, ed. Cockburn and Green, 78–116, at pp. 83–8.

[12] For a large manor (including a small town) that took its capital pledges from different settlements therein, see Hatfield Broad Oak (Essex): ERO, D/DK M1, m. 13r [court for 1443, including the places Colwell Street, Broad Street, Woodrow, Bush End Manwood End]. For Hartlebury, see *Noble Household Management and Spiritual Discipline in Fifteenth-Century Worcestershire*, ed. James P. Toomey, Robert N. Swanson, and David Guyatt, Worcestershire Historical Society, n.s., 24 (Worcester, 2013), pp. 167–8.

[13] On wards generally, see Jennifer Kermode, 'The Greater towns, 1300–1540', in *The Cambridge Urban History of Britain Volume 1: 600–1540*, ed. D. M. Palliser (Cambridge, 2000), 441–65, at pp. 456–7; cf. the cross-fertilization of ward with other forms of urban governance, explored in Shannon McSheffrey, *Marriage, Sex, and Civic Culture in Late Medieval London* (Philadelphia, 2006), pp. 150–63.

[14] LMA, DL/C/B/043/MS9064/11, fo. 211r.

[15] TNA, DL 39/2/13, 6, m. 1r. There are many similar examples of the parish being used as the frame of reference for the King's Bench indictments, e.g. KB9/215/1, no. 3; KB9/216/2, no. 9; KB9/225, nos. 7, 14, etc.

circulating throughout 'the vills of Woolverstone and Shotley, and other nearby and neighbouring places'.[16] But if it is difficult to discern any preferred institutional unit through which people conceptualized local knowledge, what cannot be doubted is that the locality of knowledge—whether in the street, the parish, the vill—was central to its legitimacy.

But who was to speak on behalf of the local? To be legitimate, knowledge needed to be reported by credible local men, who, as we saw in the first half of this book, were often the members of rather narrow, oligarchic elites.[17] But, as Ian Forrest has shown in his remarkable new book, there were two other important factors that determined the status of 'trustworthy men': in the first place, local socio-economic conditions and stratification seem to have had some influence on the extent to which office-holding was dominated by this elite or rotated more evenly; and in the second place, he points out, office-holding itself, as it brought such men into contact with authorities, was itself a contributory factor to the formation of elites.[18] These credible people were also expected to act out their credibility within widely understood intellectual and ethical parameters; specifically, they were expected to be both discerning and honest. These qualities undoubtedly applied to the trustworthy men as they jostled for position, but they were also applied to other people who might contribute to *fama* or bear witness. The legitimacy of the knowledge produced through these mechanisms depended on it.

Formal procedures and criteria used in local courts emphasized the credibility of the people who gave them information. In the church courts, for example, *fama publica* had to be believed by creditable people, the 'good and serious men' of the parish, in order to provoke compurgation.[19] While testimony in ecclesiastical suits might be taken from anyone, exceptions could be made to witnesses along the lines encapsulated in a legal tag: 'condition, gender, age, discretion, reputation, fortune, and truthfulness'.[20] Such challenges were not uncommon. John Waldron, a sawyer who testified before the London consistory court in 1491, was said to be unreliable on the basis of his poverty, perjury, and sexual immorality, characterizations backed up by well-known stories about him.[21] Secular courts, by contrast, did not police the reputations of jurors so formally, tending instead to emphasize property qualifications.[22] But jurors were certainly supposed to be trustworthy,

[16] SROI, SC18/40, m. 3r. See Chapter 3, pp. 110–111.

[17] See pp. 33–6, 68–71, 101–2 in this volume.

[18] Ian Forrest, *Trustworthy Men: How Inequality and Faith Made the Medieval Church* (Princeton, NJ, 2018), esp. Ch. 6, pp. 129–62.

[19] Forrest, *Detection of Heresy*, p. 71. The same was true of its use in the royal courts, in the inquisitions *de bono, gestu et fama* to establish the reputations of people arrested on suspicion of felony: see J. B. Post, 'Jury Lists and Juries in the Late Fourteenth Century', in *Twelve Good Men and True*, ed. Cockburn and Green, 65–77, at pp. 75–6.

[20] Helmholz, *Canon Law and Ecclesiastical Jurisdiction*, p. 340.

[21] McSheffrey, *Marriage, Sex, and Civic Culture*, p. 178.

[22] For example, in many manorial courts with view of frankpledge, in distinguishing juries of customary and free tenants: Beckerman, 'Procedural Innovation and Institutional Change', pp. 229ff.

and it was a grave offence to accuse them of bad faith; thus Robert Legget of Lynn was fined 4s. in 1455 for 'saying before the people that the jurors of the four leets were dishonest for giving their verdict against him'.[23] Legitimate knowledge was thus bound up in the trustworthiness of the people who produced it.

The people who rendered information to courts also had to be wise and discerning. Discretion was essential to medieval notions of justice and, indeed, this terminology was routinely used to describe ecclesiastical judges and the men who made up urban governments.[24] It also dissipated into information-gathering mechanisms of the local courts. Thus a 1426 tithe agreement from Beoley (Worcestershire) was not only arbitrated by a *discretus*, John Tymes, but also drew on the testimony of five *discretis viris*.[25] Similar language was used in secular courts too: an ordinance at the leet of Willoughby in 1481 ordered that no one was to put their cattle in the common for longer than their portion, as it was assigned to them 'by six or seven of the most discerning men of this lordship'.[26] Discernment was needed because so much knowledge also involved interpretation; as we saw in Chapter 3, for example, the shipmasters who served as jurors in the maritime courts were trusted to determine the difference in value between two otherwise indistinguishable items of shipwreck.[27] Discerning informants ensured that the courts did not receive an indiscriminate flood of information, and, moreover, subtly imparted their trustworthy expertise in the form of legal facts. Legitimate knowledge was discerned, not spewed.

The people who used the courts seem to have largely shared these concerns about the qualities of the people who produced knowledge. Concerns over trustworthiness and discernment came together in the vernacular concept of 'honesty'. Alice Pyghell, who we met in Chapter 2, defamed her parish priest of committing adultery with a woman named Anne Lowe, saying: 'I, a honest woman, saw [them] . . . suspecyously in taverns . . . and a honest of this paryshe saide yff . . . Thomas had lykyd . . . they shuld never depert.'[28] She was repeating

See also the qualifications of jurors for the royal courts: Masschaele, *Jury, State and Society*, pp. 155–6, 195–7.

[23] See J. S. Beckerman, 'The articles of presentment of a court leet and court baron, in English, c.1400', *Bulletin of the Institute of Historical Research*, 47 (1974), 230–4, at p. 231. For the example, NRO, Y/C 4/161, m. 16r.

[24] For ecclesiastical judges, see Fraher, 'Conviction According to Conscience', esp. pp. 55–60; for urban government, James Tait, *The Medieval English Borough* (Manchester, 1936) 306–7. See also some interesting comments on this theme by Penny Tucker, 'London's Courts of Law in the Fifteenth Century: The Litigants' Perspective', in *Communities and Courts in Britain, 1150–1900*, ed. Christopher Brooks and Michael Lobban (London and Rio Grande, 1997), p. 40.

[25] KCC, WOW/215. Two of these men were vicars, and another was described as a squire (*armiger*).

[26] MCC, 45/1: 'Et quod nullam pasturat sive ponat catalla sua in communi quousque limitatur eidem . . . per sex vel septem de discretioribus istius dominij.'

[27] See Chapter 3, pp. 104–5. More generally, see Tom Johnson, 'Medieval Law and Materiality: Shipwrecks, Finders, and Property on the Suffolk Coast, *ca.* 1380–1410', *AHR*, 120:2 (2015), 407–32.

[28] See Chapter 2, pp. 72–73. LMA, DL/C/B/043/MS9064/5, fos. 167v–168r.

gossip, perhaps, but a discourse of 'honesty' clearly framed her perspective upon this social world. Status as an honest person was thus tied to the ability to perceive moral infractions, but it was about more than silent moralism; honesty was about acting upon what you saw, constituting a dutiful participation in governance. Thus, for example, it was reported that 'all the onest persones of the towne' went with the bailiffs of Maldon to walk their boundaries during their dispute with the Abbey of Beeleigh.[29] As a value that could be easily translated into the world of the courts, honesty comprised both the respectability and responsibility that people wanted from those who produced legitimate knowledge.

Yet if legitimate knowledge was produced through the careful discernment of these honest, upstanding people, it was also supposed to be manifest. This was linked to what Daniel Smail has dubbed the 'legal culture of publicity' that prevailed in medieval Europe, in which lawfulness was closely associated with openness.[30] But manifestness, as a quality of legitimate knowledge, was also bound up in the idea of truth as something that was plain to everyone. This was a key aspect of *fama*. Although it was certainly judged and reported by discerning, honest parishioners, it was also common knowledge. For example, Thomas Heylar was cited to a chapter in Salisbury in 1477 for the offence of disturbing services in his parish church, 'because it had been ~~proved~~ denounced and declared [to be] notorious and public by the relation and testimony of trustworthy men of the same parish of this crime'.[31] The scribal redaction is telling; there seems to have been some conceptual slippage between 'proof' that something had happened, and its declaration of notoriety by the relation of trustworthy men.[32] While the channels of publicity were controlled by credible men, therefore, it was important that legitimate knowledge was thought to be known to all.

Manifestness was not just a social quality, however, indicating that information was widely known; it was also a quasi-divine quality, that associated legitimate knowledge with the kind of absolute truth that was (or would be) tested by God.[33] Jurors before secular courts swore an oath on the Gospels to present offences 'wythoutt anny conceylmentt hade so helpe me god & haly dame & by thys boke'.[34] It might be made even more explicit in testimonies: witnesses testifying to the descent of the manor of Casthorpe in Lincolnshire in 1470 were said to speak 'of our owne conscience, and as we shall aunswer afore all myghty god on þe

[29] ERO, D/B 3/1/2, fo. 39r.

[30] Daniel Lord Smail, *The Consumption of Justice: Emotions, Publicity, and Legal Culture in Marseille, 1264–1423* (Ithaca, NY, and London, 2003), pp. 211–3.

[31] WSHC, D4/3/1, m. 21r. The case thereafter became procedurally complicated, as a promotor of the cause is introduced, though Heylor was put to compurgate on eight hands.

[32] On *notorium*, see Fraher, 'Conviction According to Conscience', pp. 39–44.

[33] Cf. the theological qualities of *fides* explored in Forrest, *Trustworthy Men*, Ch. 1, pp. 15–32.

[34] TNA, WARD 2/60/234/145. This is an oath to be repeated by swannimote jurors, written in the early sixteenth century.

day of jugement'.[35] And, beyond these theological qualities, the idea of manifest knowledge was also latched onto the language of custom. Thus, for example, in an unusual vernacular 'confession' made at the manor court of Milton in 1505, John Reynold testified that a certain place was part of the manor there, 'and so hit hath bene callid and seid seync he was born and before, as he shall awnshere before god'.[36] Manifest knowledge was thus legitimate because of the way in which it paired the mundane observations of the human eye with the probative authority of the divine.[37]

When common people talked about the manifest qualities of legitimate knowledge, they made similar associations. In a vernacular bill submitted to the visitation of Lincoln and Stow deaneries in 1473, an informant wrote to the visitors that a man named Thyrston Fayreclogh had owed 26s. 8d. to the church for many years, but that the churchwardens 'chan newyr get yd howt off his handys, and god know as they haue gret need ther to want for renewing off ther bellis'.[38] A parochial scandal was linked to what was supposedly common knowledge about the need for repair through this device. But there was often a rather sharper edge to the idea of manifestness in vernacular understandings of legitimate knowledge. For example, John Warde of the parish of St. Nicholas Shambles in London was cited to the commissary in 1490 for accusing his neighbour Alice Merys of murdering her husband, adding 'knowyst not thow, that menne know the wel inough?'[39] His jibe not only suggested that Merys was ignorant of her own reputation, but also that this alleged shameful secret was open and notorious in the community. His words tapped into the idea that the manifestness of knowledge carried power, especially to humiliate and degrade.

Altogether, then, legitimate knowledge was understood to comprise several key qualities: a close tie to the locale which it concerned, the credibility and discernment of the people who produced it, and the manifestness of the information. These broad ideas formed part of the key mechanisms—*fama*, jury verdict, and testimony—through which local courts gathered and received information in late-medieval England, but they were also closely bound up with the ways that common people seem to have thought about what made knowledge legitimate. Vernacular understandings were inflected in different ways from the formal principles of the courts—for example, in emphasizing the 'honesty' of jurors at the expense of discretion—but they were not fundamentally different; these two cultural systems, the learned law and the law of the street, interacted in such routine ways that it is hardly surprising that they were mutually influential. These

[35] Bodleian, Lincolnshire Charter 1. [36] CCCO, Ga/25/5/d.

[37] This point gives the replacement of the so-called 'irrational proofs' in common law with the jury a somewhat different complexion, a point made in Paul Hyams, 'Trial by Ordeal: The Key to Proof in the Early Common Law', in *Laws and Customs of England*, ed. Arnold, Green, Scully, and White, 90–126, at p. 118.

[38] LA, Vj/4, fo. 17r. [39] LMA, DL/C/B/043/MS9064/4, fo. 164r.

conceptualizations of knowledge shared by people and the courts they used, therefore, facilitated the easy and systematic exchange between the two. Courts could ask laypeople to perform the work of generating information, and expect to get in return some intelligible, credible, and above all legitimate knowledge.

Knowledge Work

Legal institutions required four main kinds of knowledge work—watching, remembering, valuing, and inquiring—from the people whom they commanded as suitors, jurors, and other constituents. These activities are not generally understood as work; while historians have noted the hassle, cost, and general 'burden' of jury service, less attention has been given to the labour involved in generating a verdict, for example.[40] Yet there are a few reasons to consider the work that went into the production of knowledge. First, this terminology helps to highlight the transactional quality of the activities, with knowledge work compensated by the opportunities it provided for petition and redress. Second, as with other types of work, different kinds of labour were apportioned to specific people, and, moreover, the performance of certain kinds of knowledge work also distinguished certain people as authoritative officers, for example, or trustworthy parishioners.[41] Third, the idea of 'knowledge work' directs our attention to the fact that information did not simply appear in the courts—it was manufactured by deliberate practices of inquiry, investigation, and solicitation. Legitimate knowledge was made, in short, and in its claims to authenticity and credibility, it bore the imprints of its making.

To begin with, the work of watching was a routine part of the upkeep of peace and order, and required the deployment of specialist officers. All towns and vills were required by the Statute of Winchester (1285) to set constables of the peace to keep watch at night, but some were more proactive still.[42] Maritime communities in particular employed a range of different forms of surveillance, from the customs searchers in headports who ensured that goods were cocketed to the *vagantores* or *scrutatores* who reported shipwrecks along the coast.[43] Concern about seaborne attacks even led the authorities at Lynn to make a highly detailed ordinance in 1457, setting out the requirements for the watch: watchers had to be over twenty-one years old, 'sufficiently prepared, by inspection of the constable', and ready to

[40] Anthony Musson, *Medieval Law in Context: The growth of legal consciousness from Magna Carta to the Peasants' Revolt* (Manchester, 2001), p. 112; Masschaele, *Jury, State and Society*, p. 200.

[41] Forrest, 'Transformation of Visitation', pp. 21–2.

[42] A. J. Musson, 'Sub-Keepers and Constables: The Role of Local Officials in Keeping the Peace in Fourteenth-Century England', *EHR*, 117:470 (2002), 1–24, at p. 21.

[43] Johnson, 'Medieval Law and Materiality', p. 420, fn. 75.

stay up from the evening high tide to that in the morning, when they could go to Mass.[44] In the Forests, too, officials took a proactive role in discovering crime; the foresters in Weybridge in 1448 searched the house of a labourer named Thomas Walton, and found buck-stalls (fences for trapping deer) which he had used to kill a doe.[45] The work of watching was mostly reserved to court officers, or those whom they deputed: people who watched, or searched, or roamed without official authority were presented as eavesdroppers, night-walkers, and 'common perambulators'.[46]

Indeed, watching work was also expected of the wider community of adult men through the ancient system of frankpledge, in which every man over the age of twelve was sworn into mutual surety with ten others into a group called a tithing, each of whom watched over the behaviour of the others. While it has been posited that this system collapsed in rural society after the Black Death due to heightened mobility and depopulation, some studies have found that it was more resilient, adapting to local circumstances.[47] Where it was retained, it was clearly thought to be a useful method of social control. At Willoughby in Warwickshire, for example, there was clearly a local perception of moral crisis in the late fifteenth century, with repeated presentments against servants who were gambling, drinking, and staying out late, and, concomitantly, the prosecution of those who remained outside tithing was severe.[48] And indeed, tithing seems to have remained important in towns, as for example at Hereford, where the tourn court continued to enforce frankpledge through the 1520s; here and elsewhere, membership of the tithing—and watching more generally—formed an important aspect of masculine respectability for urban heads of household.[49]

But apart from frankpledge as an institutionalized form of watching, it was also understood as a widespread moral duty among neighbours. For example, in 1503 in the parish of All Hallows-by-the-Tower in London, Henry Waterman accused Martina Lokynden of sexual immorality, saying 'strong hore thou wer jappid in the chair in thyn owne howse... and I saw on the moro [two] men commyng out of thi howse which had [been] with the all night'.[50] Such close watching was

[44] NRO, KL/C7/4, p. 94.

[45] TNA, DL 39/2/4, m. 13r.

[46] Quote from a presentment at Runton (Norfolk) against a man who walked the seashore looking for wrecks to take away: NRO, WKC 2/166 398x7, m. 19v. On night-walkers and eavesdroppers, see Marjorie McIntosh, *Controlling Misbehavior in England, 1370–1600* (Cambridge, 1998), pp. 65–7.

[47] See D. A. Crowley, 'The Later History of Frankpledge', *Bulletin of the Institute of Historical Research*, 48:117 (1975), 1–15; L. R. Poos, *A Rural Society after the Black Death: Essex 1350–1525* (Cambridge, 1991), pp. 91–2. A more sceptical case is put by Phillipp R. Schofield, 'The Late Medieval View of Frankpledge and the Tithing System: An Essex Case Study', in *Medieval Society and the Manor Court*, ed. Zvi Razi and Richard Smith (Oxford, 1996), 408–39.

[48] MCO, 45/1, 4, 12, 23.

[49] Christian D. Liddy, 'Cultures of Surveillance in Late Medieval English Towns: The monitoring of speech and the fear of revolt', in *The Routledge History Handbook of Medieval Revolt*, ed. Justine Firnhaber-Baker with Dirk Schoenaers (London and New York, 2017), 311–29, at pp. 313–4. For Hereford's tourn courts, see HARC, BG11/4/1 [Tourns, 1448–1521].

[50] LMA, DL/C/B/043/MS9064/9, 56v.

perhaps facilitated by the cramped living conditions of late-medieval cities; as I suggested in Chapter 2, the tight governance of urban households can partly be explained by anxiousness over the way in which they blurred the boundaries between intimate and associative relations.[51] Yet if watching was intensified in towns, it was still important in the countryside, as we can see in the manifold presentments against night-walking, eavesdropping, and misbehaviour in general; how else could it be known that John Broune of Ringwood 'lived suspiciously'?[52] Local courts thrived off the constant deliberative knowledge work of watching one's neighbours.

By contrast, the work of valuing, most often necessary in secular courts, was more differentiated.[53] The valuation of tenements and lands, or repairs to them, for example, was always assessed by the whole homage, as the custodians of customary tenure.[54] By contrast, for the assessment of damages in interpersonal litigation and presentments, local courts relied on special officers known as affeerors; a set of leet presentment articles from Peterborough asserts that there ought to be four of them, although in rural courts there were normally two.[55] As Anne DeWindt found in her study of the small town of Ramsey (Cambridgeshire), men who acted as affeerors were very often also serving jurors, and at Kintbury in Berkshire they seem to have acted in concert with the reeve.[56] Indeed, in the more specialized milieu of maritime courts, we saw that the shipmasters who served as jurors also provided values for the shipwrecks that were registered there.[57] Across the board, then, the kinds of worthy men who held office and acted as jurors were expected to be able to recognize and assess worth themselves.[58]

But if these men were trusted to know worth, their knowledge work was still subjective. The shipmasters at Sizewell and Thorpe in Suffolk, for example, in the course of providing nearly one thousand valuations for shipwrecks over the century *c.*1380–*c.*1480, showed some pronounced tendencies: their valuations strongly favoured even numbers, clung to coin denominations such as shillings,

[51] See Chapter 2, p. 80.

[52] KCC, RIN/7, fo. 2v. It is interesting to speculate whether the more centrally located and visually striking houses of the richer peasantry made it easier for them to monitor one another's behaviour: see Stephen Mileson, 'Openness and Closure in the Later Medieval Village', *P&P*, 234 (2017), 3–37.

[53] On the use of local representatives in financial administration for the church, see Forrest, *Trustworthy Men*, Ch. 11, pp. 267–84.

[54] Examples: Broad Chalke (Wiltshire), KCC, CHA/estates3; Stour Provost (Dorset), KCC, STP/4, m. 5r; Willoughby (Warwickshire), MCC, 45/4.

[55] Mary Bateson, 'The English and the Latin Versions of a Peterborough Court Leet, 1461', *EHR*, 19:75 (1904), 526–8; Mark Bailey, *The English Manor, c.1300–c.1500* (Manchester, 2002), pp. 171, 176.

[56] Anne Reiber DeWindt, 'Local Government in a Small Town: A Medieval Leet Jury and Its Constituents', *Albion: A Quarterly Journal Concerned with British Studies*, 23:4 (1991), 627–54, at p. 654 [Appendix II]; BL, Add. Ch. 49220–1.

[57] Tom Johnson, 'The economics of shipwreck in late-medieval East Anglia', in *Custom and Commercialisation in Rural England, c.1350–1750: Revisiting Tawney and Postan*, ed. James Bowen and Alex Brown (Hertford, 2016), 121–38.

[58] On the judgment of worth and its role in determining reputation, see Alexandra Sheppard, *Accounting for Oneself: Worth, Status and the Social Order in Early Modern England* (Oxford, 2015).

and were far more discriminating for items worth less than two shillings.[59] But if these mental habits seem harmless, they could have bite in more contentious circumstances. At Gayton (Lincolnshire) in 1501 the homage jurors were asked to assess some goods distrained from Richard Carter for unpaid agistment dues. They appraised ten of his household items—including some brass pots, a candlestick holder, a spit, and a whetstone—and valued them at 7s 10d, exactly the amount that Carter owed.[60] Yet if assessments of worth were slanted, official process at least gave them an aura of legitimacy—defendants in Kintbury frequently 'put themselves on the appraisal of the court' in order to mitigate the damages they owed a plaintiff.[61] Valuing was not simply about recognizing worth, then, but also carefully calibrating it in a way that was at once credible and equitable.

Some kinds of knowledge needed by the courts were rather more intangible. Most crucially, they often needed people to remember things. This mnemonic labour underpinned the whole system of custom, as, in Andy Wood's characterization, 'a sense of the past that legitimated claims to rights, space and resources in the present'.[62] The routine gestures towards custom in the manorial court were clearly undertaken by the adult men who acted as tithingmen and jurors, and, indeed, their typically long tenures in office would have given them a good operational knowledge of standard practice.[63] Still, there were some matters that eluded them. At King's Langley in 1438, the homage were ordered 'to better inquire into all and singular matters which are not at present in the memory of these same men of the homage, in order to make and render a true verdict at the next court to be held there'.[64] The elision of memory with truth here, in the work of 'making' the verdict, provides an excellent illustration of the way that mnemonic labour was demanded by legal institutions in order to create a kind of authentic remembered knowledge.

Indeed, precisely because homage jurors were focused on more quotidian and operational aspects of custom, in the kinds of focused disputes over traditional practice which took place outside the manor court, the work of memory was often given over to elderly villagers.[65] In 1416 six parishioners of Brenchley (Kent),

[59] From data based on the following rolls: SROI, HD 371/1 [1377–97]; HD 371/2 [1398–1409]; HD 1032/86 [1422–9]; HD 1032/87 [1432–5]; HD 1032/88 [1436–82]. Database explained in more detail in Johnson, 'Economics of shipwreck', pp. 123–6.

[60] BL, MS Egerton 3001, fo. 106v.

[61] E.g. BL, Add. Ch. 49225, m. 2v, Add. Ch. 49229, mm. 1r, 3r, 3v.

[62] Andy Wood, *The Memory of the People: Custom and Popular Senses of the Past in Early Modern England* (Cambridge, 2013), p. ix.

[63] *Select Cases in Manorial Courts 1250–1550*, ed. L. R. Poos and Lloyd Bonfield, Selden Society 114 (London, 1998), p. xxxiv.

[64] TNA, SC 2/177/55, m. 3r. 'Die datum est prenominato homagio ad melius inquirendo de omnibus et singulis materijs non ad presens in memoria ipsorum hominum homagiatum ut verum veredictum faciunt et dabunt ad proximam curiam ibidem tenenda...'

[65] Ages were often exaggerated: see Forrest, *Trustworthy Men*, p. 135.

'beynge of the age the leeste of us of thre skore wynter and one, and [the most] seniore of us, [four] skore wynter', made deposition as to the descent of the manor because, as their attestation put it, 'we ben men of grete age'.[66] This emphasis on age might even mitigate gendered hierarchy. Of the twelve witnesses summoned to rehearse the claims of the vill of Litcham (Norfolk) to a piece of common ground in the early fifteenth century, three were women; one, Amy of Ridone, was said to be 100 years old—which of course simply meant 'very old'—and testified, like the others, to the pasturing of beasts and the digging of the gravel pits, 'and of manie oþere thyngs rehersid aforn'.[67] In these showpiece acts of recollection, the aged bodies that bore the memories thus helped to substantiate the old knowledge that they claimed to bring forth.

In the course of disputes over tithe customs, ecclesiastical courts also drew particularly on older people for memories, but otherwise the kind of mnemonic labour they demanded was of a rather different kind.[68] To begin with, witnesses were introduced into court by one of the parties to the dispute, and while the safeguards against bias were occasionally exercised, it is clear from their testimonies that most witnesses were partisan; but church courts tended to take many depositions and then weigh or discount their value, rather than refusing to admit certain witnesses *prima facie*.[69] The social range of people who acted as witnesses for the ecclesiastical courts was thus much wider than, say, those who acted as homage jurors. But the kind of knowledge work they were asked to do was different. Testifying to articles in the libel which had been hashed out by the advocates of the litigating parties, witnesses were not asked to remember in free form, but rather to recount fairly recent events within a structure that might be made tighter or looser by their willingness to expand or the examiner's prodding questions.[70] The burden of credibility was thus borne more by the procedures of the courts than the narrative labour of the witnesses themselves.

Finally, we turn to the knowledge work of 'inquiring' into rights and facts; we have already seen a species of such work in Chapter 5 in the 'views' and boundary-making events which were required to clarify the legal landscape.[71] But we must add to such tasks a broad variety of deliberative decision-making that jurors, *inquisitores*, and other trustworthy men were required to perform. As John Beckerman has written, 'finding the truth could be an arduous task. Medieval juries had to weigh evidence and consider the statements, testimony, and opinions of others to supplement their personal knowledge.'[72] Inquiring was distinct in

[66] BL, Add. Ch. 36522. [67] NRO, KIM 1/9/16, m. 2r.

[68] On tithe disputes, see Bronach Kane, 'Custom, Memory and Knowledge in the Medieval English Church Courts', in *Clergy, Church and Society in England and Wales, 1200–1800*, ed. Rosemary Hayes and Bill Sheils (York, 2014), 61–81.

[69] Helmholz, *Canon Law and Ecclesiastical Jurisdiction*, pp. 338–40.

[70] See Goldberg, *Communal Discord*, pp. 40–1. [71] See Chapter 5, pp. 158–160.

[72] Beckerman, 'Procedural Innovation and Institutional Change', p. 220.

important ways from the kind of dispute settlements in which such men also participated in the local courts, through both informal arbitration or the adjudication of pleas, which were explicitly conducted through determination—that is, considered negotiation over the settlement.[73] Inquiring, by contrast, figured the issue at hand as a matter in which there was a single right answer, which the jurors would uncover through inquiry. It operated, therefore, on the basis of a different jurisprudential ideal. Where settlement looked forward to a future of peace between parties, 'inquiring' looked backwards to uncover the truth.

Inquiring, like viewing and valuing, was an explicitly laborious form of knowledge work. Jurors were expected by stewards, officials, and judges to work hard on their verdicts. They were charged, as were the homage at Ringwood over the rents and services owed for a parcel of land, to 'diligently inquire', or, like the jurors at Milton (Surrey) who drew a blank after being charged to ascertain a heriot, 'to better inquire'.[74] These orders, if they had to be repeated, might be coupled with pains or other threats, and, as we shall see in more detail later in the chapter, the courts' refusal to accept claims of ignorance in response to inquiries was a key battleground in the negotiations over knowledge. This was because inquiry was not just a matter of finding truth, of course, but a matter of making it. For example, at the vill of Mockley in Warwickshire, the capital pledge William Hobbeday asserted that John Dalton, the vicar of nearby Wootton Wawen, had taken a parcel of 18 yards of Kersey wool, and then left the lordship 'suspiciously at night'; whether he had been taken as a felon, Hobbeday did not know, and he was ordered 'to better inquire before the next court'.[75] Here, as elsewhere, the work of inquiry was what created facts out of suspicion, turning something that was common knowledge into manifest truth.

In sum, local legal institutions of all kinds demanded several types of knowledge work from their constituents. While these methods sometimes overlapped, they tended to generate different kinds of knowledge—valuations produced monetary figures where remembering customs produced decisions—and, moreover, to establish its authenticity in different ways, whether emphasizing the special expertise of the people who produced it, or relying on the credibility of the trustworthy men who tended to perform such duties for the courts. But, as we have seen, other people might become involved when other cultural structures—such as advanced age, suspicion, or publicity—were perceived to be more important for establishing trust in knowledge. Yet more important even than the particular kinds of person who produced knowledge was the fact that all of these activities were understood and enacted as a kind of labour. The discourses associated with diligence, scrutiny, and inquiry (among others) were part of a legality in which knowledge was explicitly *made* through work, and the very

[73] See Chapter 1, pp. 30–2. [74] KCC, RIN/5, m. 4r; CCCO, Ga/25/5/b, recto.
[75] KCC, WOW/176, m. 4r. Mockley was a vill, sometime submanor of Wootton Wawen.

processes of this work—these careful, deliberative, pensive labours—were what made such knowledge legitimate.

Negotiating Knowledge

Knowledge work took time, it could cause consternation and disagreement, and it might be stressful; pronouncing a verdict that turned out to be false, or stumbling from an agreed line when giving testimony might result in reputational damage or financial penalties. So why did people agree to do such work? First, they stood to gain in terms of their reputation, status, and dealings; acting as a juror, witness, or officer provided individuals with the opportunity to pursue personal grievances, to jostle with rivals, and to gain and preserve their status in the local community.[76] Second, providing knowledge and judgment—speaking the truth, bearing witness, emphasizing charitable relations—was also an ethical duty. This ethic could be self-serving, but that does not mean it was not earnestly felt, and it gave people a powerful justification for rendering information to the local courts.[77] And third, knowledge work enabled people to achieve material aims—the lowering of rents, the preservation of customs, the repair of communal infrastructure through collective action; it offered opportunities for grievances to be aired, and justice to be demanded.

These three potential benefits of course could overlap. An upstanding villager who served as an *inquisitor* for the local ecclesiastical court might perniciously pursue a personal dispute with his neighbour by reporting him, all the while considering his actions to be justified, even incumbent on him, from his moral duty to report his suspicions about sin; likewise, collective action might be mobilized in ways that materially benefited a powerful individual while serving the aims of a community that gained from their employment or patronage—such was the case for the community of mariners who testified to protect the shipowner Edward Redde in the 1517 inquiry at Ipswich mentioned in Chapter 3.[78] Motivations are always hard to fathom, especially half a millennium after the event for a group of people whose lives were so scantly documented. But it is possible to explore the cultural structures through which their knowledge work was justified, and the ways in which they negotiated its value. In what follows, we look at each of these three main reasons—ethics, the pursuit of status, and collective action—that people performed knowledge work, followed by an examination of the reasons that such negotiations broke down.

[76] Forrest, *Trustworthy Men*, esp. Ch. 7, pp. 163–200.
[77] For a different view on this tangle of interests; see ibid., pp. 196–9.
[78] See fn. 16 above, and Chapter 3, pp. 110–111.

To begin with, the performance of knowledge work for the courts carried its own virtue. An inquest into a ruined building in Brackley (Northamptonshire), recorded in a charter in 1402, claimed the jurors had given their verdict 'because it is pious and meritorious to present true testimony for all'.[79] This was a trope, of course, but that does not mean that it was without significance to contemporaries. William Neve, the public notary who was commissioned to hear the 1517 Ipswich inquiry, chose for his notarial mark a cross on a base inscribed with the beginning of a passage from Psalm 25: 'All the paths of the Lord are mercy and truth unto such as keep his covenant and his testimonies.'[80] For a professional record-maker, it was an apposite slogan. Greater elaboration on the same theme, particularly in the vernacular, even carries the ring of a sermon, as in a vernacular testimonial letter from York which declared 'it is both nedeful, medful & meritory to bere trewe wittenes & to recorde þe treuth of every thynge þat stondeth in doute'.[81] Quite apart from the ethical injunctions against false witness and perjury, then, there was also a discourse that emphasized the positive spiritual benefits of knowledge work. Telling the truth was its own reward.

Of course, there were also rather less virtuous reasons for bearing witness; the opportunity to feed courts with information was firmly grasped by local elites who were eager to pursue and preserve authority. Historians have long perceived a 'village aristocracy' who dominated the juries of manorial and leet courts, considering them to have been engaged in competitive struggles both to gain local power and to exert it over their social inferiors.[82] With such pervasive institutional and socio-economic dominance, however, it is crucial to understand how knowledge work in particular related to status competition.[83] The first and most immediate point to make is that some kinds of work such as watching, appraising, and inquiring—those that required discernment and deliberation—were bound up with the performance of such status. As Shannon McSheffrey has pointed out for the London wardmotes, 'jurors' activities were part and parcel of respectable

[79] MCO, Brackley 209. The first part of the charter recorded a term-of-life lease, in 1381, to John and Benedicta Draper, of a tenement called *le Blakhalle*, which they promised to repair within six years; by the time of the inquest, John had died, and the rent was in arrears.

[80] Psalm 25:10 (translation from the King James Bible); SROI, SC18/40, m. 5r: 'Universe vie domini misericordia et veritas [requirentibus testamentum eius et testimonia eius]'.

[81] *A Volume of English Miscellanies illustrating the History and Language of the Northern Counties of England*, ed. J. Raine, Surtees Society, 85 (Durham, 1890), p. 39.

[82] More recently on this question, see Sherri Olson, 'Jurors of the Village Court: Local Leadership before and after the Plague in Ellington, Huntingdonshire', *Journal of British Studies*, 30:3 (1991), 237–56; Miriam Müller, 'A Divided Class? Peasants and Peasant Communities in Later Medieval England', *P&P*, supplement 2 (2007), 115–31; Peter L. Larson, 'Village Voice or Village Oligarchy? The Jurors of the Durham Halmote Court, 1349 to 1424', *L&HR*, 28:3 (2010), 675–709.

[83] For some (slightly earlier) examples of status competition among office-holders, see Forrest, 'Transformation of Visitation', pp. 31–3.

men's exercise of authority over their dependents', both inside and outside their households.[84] The determinative moralism of this knowledge work enabled such men to perform this 'respectable masculinity'.

This authority came with its burdens, however. Due to the fortunate survival of some letters from early-fifteenth-century Berkshire, we can see something of these liabilities in the travails of Thomas Walyngton, a man of problematically middling status, who was pressured from both above and below as he attempted to negotiate the knowledge work that was required of him.[85] Walyngton's family had long held a small estate in the manor of Balsdon that had traditionally comprised free lands, but in the wake of the Black Death his father, Adam, had obtained a croft that he held initially at will and later 'by indenture' for the term of his life.[86] Yet Walyngton was evidently a well-connected man who considered himself to be of some social stature, an opinion that provoked trouble with the lord of the manor at Balsdon, William Derell. In a petition to Walter, Lord Hungerford, Walyngton complained that he was 'yturment in evrywyse' by Derell, who had ordered him to serve as a tithingman there, 'þe wech ys noutt lawfull', Walyngton claimed, because he paid 2s. annually to evade homage and suit of court.[87]

Yet at the same time as he attempted to assert himself against sheriffs and wrote to a lord asking for his assistance, Walyngton was also subject to the pressure of other substantial villagers who may have considered themselves his equals. In 1413, he was twice cited to the leet court of nearby Kintbury to show title to his lands, and to respond for 'the many trespasses' he had committed on the commons there with his beasts.[88] One of the two stewards at this court was William Coventre, whom Walyngton would claim, in another letter to Hungerford written around this time (this one, interestingly, in Anglo-Norman French), had ousted him from his common meadows.[89] As Walyngton disdained to act as a 'trustworthy man' at the level of the manor, then, he was also deprived of the capacity to assert his rights there; instead he resorted to petitioning superiors, in order to go

[84] Shannon McSheffrey, 'Jurors, Respectable Masculinity, and Christian Morality: A Comment on Marjorie McIntosh's *Controlling Misbehavior*', *Journal of British Studies*, 37:3 (1998), p. 272.

[85] I call Walyngton 'middling' because his status is interestingly ambiguous. The Wallington family had held a small estate in Kintbury since the early thirteenth century, and this was increased in 1343 by Thomas's grandfather, Robert de Wallington; the estate was later regarded to have formed part of a manor called Balsdon. Thomas and his wife Alice sold whatever was left of it in 1447–8, and it subsequently passed to William Waynflete, whereupon it formed part of the endowment of Magdalen College, Oxford. See Harold J. E. Peake, 'Kintbury', in *VCH Berkshire: Volume 4*, ed. William Page and P. H. Ditchfield (London, 1924), pp. 205–17.

[86] Adam Walyngton did homage for these lands in 1360 and 1372: see TNA, SC 2/153/55, mm. 1r–v, 3r.

[87] MCO, Letters 31. Derell was lord of the manor of Balsdon via his wife, Elizabeth, until 1429, when he sold it to Walter, Lord Hungerford.

[88] BL, Add. Ch. 49218, recto and verso.

[89] MCO, Beenham, 164. This letter refers to 'Sir Walter Hungerford'; if this appellation is significant, the letter can be dated between 1399 and 1418, the time between his knighting and his elevation to a barony.

over the heads of this class of local officers. Such a strategy is suggestive of the way in which the use of different legal forms was not simply bound up with access or resources, but also with contemporary perceptions of the prestige which attached to them.[90]

Around the same time, Walyngton successfully petitioned the Justices of the Peace of Berkshire to have a man named Roger Gunter bound over to keep the peace, after he had threatened Walyngton with maiming.[91] The context of this threat is unclear, but Gunter was a member of a prominent Kintbury family, a fixture among the free jurors in the leet there, where he had also served as affeeror.[92] Along with the other jurymen, he continued to pursue Walyngton throughout the 1420s for trespasses on the Kintbury common, until in 1428 they landed him with the substantial fine of 40d., and threatened a harsher penalty still.[93] Overall, then, Walyngton's travails are suggestive of the double-bind presented by respectable masculinity at this level. While his impressive patronage meant that he could aspire to hundredal or county-level trustworthiness, he was still easily ensnared in village politics; and as he disdained to perform knowledge work at that level, an archetypal oligarchic leet juror like Roger Gunter was able to manoeuvre against him. The opportunities for status and advancement provided by knowledge work, then, were fraught with the complexities of local institutions and their politics.

Whatever these complexities, however, they were not necessarily restricted to the class of trustworthy men. For instance, acting as a witness to the church courts, though it was often knowledge work performed by the prosperous, credible men whose testimony would be most valuable to litigants, was also open to other kinds of people.[94] In a tangled defamation case from Littlebury (Essex) heard in the London consistory in 1510, four witnesses testified for the plaintiff; the first two, Thomas Barker and John Felstede were husbandmen, but their testimony was followed by that of two labourers, George Bruk and George Parker.[95] Social status does not tell the full story here, though, as both Barker and Parker were members of a local manorial jury; indeed, the case hinged on the fact that one of their fellow

[90] As a rhetorical form, of course, petitioning often emphasized differences in status at the same time as attempting to build affinity through good lordship: see Gwilym Dodd, 'Writing Wrongs: The Drafting of Supplications to the Crown in Later Fourteenth-Century England', *Medium Ævum*, 80:2 (2011), 217–46.

[91] MCO, Beenham 40. This is a writ from the JPs to the bailiff of Hungerford liberty. The writ is undated, but must have been created between 1408 and 1417, because it was sent by Sir Thomas de la Pole, who was included on the 1408 commission but not on the next one, in 1417: *CPR*, 1408–13, p. 479; *CPR*, 1416–22, p. 449. Walter Hungerford, Walyngton's patron, was on both commissions.

[92] BL, Add. Ch. 49218, recto. His subsequent appearances in the rolls are manifold: see e.g. BL, Add. Ch. 49223, 49224, mm. 1r–v, 2r, 49225, mm. 1–4r. His father, John Gunter, had also held two acres of land in Balsdon in the 1370s: TNA, SC 2/153/55, m. 2r.

[93] BL, Add. Ch. 49225, m. 2v.

[94] P. J. P. Goldberg, 'Fiction in the archives: the York cause papers as a source for later medieval social history', *Continuity & Change*, 12:3 (1997), 425–45, at pp. 431–2.

[95] LMA, DL/C/206, fos. 31v–36v.

jurors had committed perjury, and the court had failed to act on this once it became known. The credibility they gained from testifying, then, was subject to its own ongoing negotiations; as Alexandra Sheppard has suggested, the act of witnessing 'is likely to have *informed* processes of identity-making rather than simply recorded them'.[96] If the social capital of knowledge work was sometimes shared more widely, then, it also necessitated a navigation of complex risks.

In rare cases, otherwise disenfranchised groups might also seize control of knowledge work in a bid to signal their own moral status. Women acting alone might not have had the requisite authority to report information to local institutions, but working together they could be highly effective; a violent assault by four men on another at King's Langley in 1453 was brought to the court after no fewer than twenty women were said to have 'justly raised the hue' on them.[97] And in a remarkable incident from a church court held in Buckingham in the early sixteenth century, we can see an even larger group of women commandeering knowledge of *fama*. The case is worth quoting at length.[98]

> Agnes Yve, wife of Thomas Yve, is detected as a common defamer of her neighbours, calling diverse honest women 'whores' and many other scandalous words, and sowing discord among the said parishioners. Agnes appeared with many other honest women of the aforesaid parish, to the number of forty women, with all of them together and each of them separately having better acquaintance of Agnes; they affirmed the *fama* that Agnes is a common defamer before the judge sitting for this tribunal. And because Agnes Yve is not able to compurgate herself upon this detection and *fama*, therefore the judge declares her convicted and orders her to swear an oath to undertake penance, in the manner and form as follows, viz., that she shall immediately ask forgiveness from the parishioners in a penitential manner and from henceforth she shall never use such scandalous words.

[96] Sheppard, *Accounting for Oneself*, pp. 23–4; her emphasis.

[97] TNA, SC 2/177/55, m. 19r.

[98] *The Courts of the Archdeaconry of Buckingham 1483–1523*, ed. E. M. Elvey, Buckinghamshire Record Society, 19 (Aylesbury, 1975), p. 313: 'Agnes Yve uxor Thome Yve alias Clement detecta quod est communis diffamatrix vicinorum suorum vocando diversas honestas mulieres meretrices ac multa alia verba scandalos ac seminando discordias inter parochianas predictos. Comparuit dicta Agnes ac multe alie honeste mulieres parochie predicte usque ad numerum xl[ta] mulierum eiusdem Agnetis noticiam meliorem habentes que omnes coniunctim et unaqueque separatim coram judice pro tribunali sedenti affirmauerunt famam predictam et quod predicta Agnes Ive est communis diffamatrix... Et quia prefata Agnes Yve non potuit se purgare super deteccione et fama predictis ideo judex reputauit ipsam conuictam et onerauit ipsam iure iurando ad penitenciam peragere modo et forma modo et forma sequentibus, viz. quod immediate petat veniam et a parochianis modo penitentis et quod amodo non utet talibus verbis scandalosis... ' Interestingly, Agnes had been named two weeks earlier as the accomplice of Thomas Neele, who was cited for adultery, 'as it more plainly appears from detections made by the parishioners there, set out in a certain bill [in quadam billa porrecta]'. Ibid., pp. 306–7.

This relatively terse and apparently procedural entry glosses what seems to have been an extraordinary scene, in which a crowd of women frogmarched their unloved neighbour straight to court, and demanded that action be taken against her. Yet their forceful intervention was not portrayed as rowdy or unlawful; rather, it was granted the authentic status of *fama*. It is a remarkable instance of the occasional fissures that ruptured the misogynistic hegemony of late-medieval legality, as such women, with their 'better acquaintance' of the matter at hand, might seize the opportunity to perform knowledge work for themselves. Not only were they thus able to coerce Agnes into submission, but in obtaining the recognition of the court they legitimated their position as 'honest women' who were sometimes permitted to act as a moral force in parochial life.

Indeed, this case also shows how the performance of knowledge work could also mobilize action aimed at extracting concessions from figures of authority. Such moments were relatively rare, of course, and, as we shall see in what follows, they often tended to focus on what seem with hindsight like relatively minor concerns: the maintenance of infrastructure, the provision of spiritual services, and the definition of customs and dues. Of course, for contemporaries, these matters were hardly trivial, and, what is more, in a society as unequal as that of fifteenth-century England, they clearly provided a horizon of expectations for what could be reasonably demanded. Yet, at the same time, it is telling that even within the confines of demands made through legal institutions, reports that actively or implicitly questioned a figure of authority were still—for the most part—cushioned by legalistic justifications emphasizing that some kind of obligation was not being met. Even while knowledge work offered opportunities to speak some truth to power, then, such reports had to be crafted in the right way.

To begin with, as we saw in a number of different contexts through the first half of the book, people expected secular legal authorities to maintain roads and bridges, and were willing to use local institutions to demand this.[99] In one instance, the jurors of Milton even presented their own lord at the view of frankpledge for failing to repair a footbridge at *le mere ende*, apparently to some avail; through one of their biannual opportunities to liaise with their distant ecclesiastical lord via the court steward, the jurors were thus able to ameliorate a piece of local infrastructure at seigneurial expense.[100] More unusual tribunals offered further opportunities still, as we can see with indictments sent to the Court of the Verge, an itinerant tribunal under the jurisdiction of the royal marshal, which heard pleas from within a twelve-mile radius of the king's household.[101] In 1440, presented with the king's ear to complain about 'all manner of treasons, felonies, trespasses, nuisances', what did the jurors from Iver in

[99] See Chapter 1, pp. 47–8; Chapter 2, pp. 81–2. [100] CCCO, Bb 1/19.

[101] See W. R. Jones, 'The Court of the Verge: The Jurisdiction of the Steward and Marshal of the Household in Later Medieval England', *Journal of British Studies*, 10:1 (1970), 1–29.

Buckinghamshire report? That the highway between Iver and Drayton often flooded because of a ruinous wharf, which the Dean of St. Paul's Cathedral customarily maintained, but had failed to repair since 1428.[102] Such concerns were not glamorous, perhaps, but they were important to local communities; through such knowledge work, they could hold lords to account.

Similarly, the *inquisitores* who spoke for the parish had a keen sense of the obligations owed to them by ecclesiastical institutions, and a mechanism, in visitation, that enabled them to complain to superior authorities.[103] These included understandable frustrations with rectors like William Strynger of Witherley (Leicestershire), who had another rectory in Kent and who, his parishioners complained, was 'not resident, nor discrete, nor sufficient'.[104] But concerns might also take on more knotty problems of local administration involving the revenue of a benefice; a presentment made at Bole (Nottinghamshire) in 1472 to the visitors from York Minster that the vicar there was 'not suitably endowed', implies some sympathy with his situation alongside frustration with the capitular management.[105] Some reports were blunter still in their requests: three parishioners of Rauceby, testifying to a visitation of Lincoln and Stow deaneries in 1500, declared that 'they are accustomed to have a secular [priest as] vicar, [so] they request that from now on, monastics not be admitted'.[106] Such a statement not only illustrates the extent to which the respectable laity might attempt to take charge of the spiritual health of the wider community, but also the way in which they grabbed the opportunities of visitation with both hands.

In fact, more routine complaints about spiritual provision might also be made through the secular courts, pursuing similar goals in different ways. For example, manorial jurors might use lands—such as the glebe or other parcels belonging to the rectory—to highlight ecclesiastical duties that were not being fulfilled. Thus the tenants of the honour of Coverham presented, in 1443, that the rector of Spennithorne ought to find a chaplain for three days, specified as Monday, Wednesday, and Friday, before detailing the entitlements of the rectory with regard to the pasturing of ewes.[107] This move looks calculated to exert the pressure of seigneurial authority on the local clergy, reminding them of their spiritual obligations and the fact that, as members of the agricultural community, they were reliant on the goodwill of the manorial jurors. Indeed, such jurors were comfortable pursuing clergy more directly. The assertive moralism of fifteenth-century leets certainly extended to misbehaving chaplains like Robert Humfrey of

[102] TNA, KB 9/230A, no. 65.

[103] From as early as the 1270s, bishops sought knowledge from parishioners about their clergy: see Forrest, 'Transformation of Visitation', p. 13; *Trustworthy Men*, pp. 309–10.

[104] LA, Vj/3, fo. 6v. [105] YML, fo. 40v.

[106] LA, Vj/5, fo. 77v: '... parochiani ibidem dicunt quod solebant habere vicarium secularem petunt quod deinceps non admittantur religiosi'.

[107] NYCRO, ZDX, m. 3r.

Wootton Wawen, who was presented twice in 1454, first for brawling, and also for being a 'common *nyghte walker* and frequenting the house of John Pryory at dishonest times', for which he was fined a total of 3s.[108] If ecclesiastical authorities were unable or unwilling to act, knowledge work could be used flexibly across jurisdictions to pursue such clergy.

As well as checking the obligations owed to them by authorities, knowledge workers also acted to defend and define their own obligations as tenants and parishioners. This was particularly true for the jurors of manorial courts, who had to regularly pronounce on a 'core' of custom but were also occasionally confronted with an unusual situation that demanded they draw from its 'periphery'.[109] Of course, part of this work was deciding what constituted an unusual situation. For example, when Joan Whyng, a widow of Ringwood, died seised of half a cottage in the winter of 1487, the bailiff followed standard procedure and identified the heriot, a tenant's 'best beast or chattel' that was owed as a death duty owed to the lord—in her case a four-gallon cauldron. But when this was reported to the court, the homage came and said that the 'the heriot for the half-cottage ought not to be demanded by the lord, because Joan was not a tenant'.[110] This was evidently news to the steward, given that the property in question carried a rent of 12d. per year, and that William Cokkes had paid a hefty fine to the lord for its reversion a decade previously; the jurors were ordered to inquire into the custom of the lordship.[111] Such interpretations of custom did not go unchallenged, therefore, but they might enable jurors to question the kinds of seigneurial due that lingered after the Black Death—perhaps especially if they were felt to be unnecessary or unfair in particular cases.[112]

Indeed, custom could become a battleground for rather more fraught engagements between tenants and manorial authorities. At Withyham in Sussex, for example, the entry of a new farmer of the manor, John Hardwick, prompted several incidents with the tenantry that focused on their knowledge of custom. At Hardwick's first court in 1434, three tenants refused to acknowledge that they owed services; questioned, they replied that they had owed none during the time when the Prior of Hastings had owned the manor. This claim was put to the beadle and tenants, 'who considered it to be true'.[113] The following year, Robert Leveregge made a similar refusal, on the basis that he had owed no services when the manor had been in the possession of the crown—perhaps a hint that the

[108] KCC, WOW/176m, m. 5r.

[109] This useful model of custom is suggested in *Select Cases in Manorial Courts 1250–1550*, ed. L. R. Poos and Lloyd Bonfield, Selden Society 114 (London, 1998), p. xxxiv.

[110] KCC, RIN/7, fo. 3r.

[111] For the reversion, ibid. (this was copied from the earlier entry, the roll for which has not survived).

[112] On the durability of heriots, which were not a mark of unfree status, see Mark Bailey, *The Decline of Serfdom in Late Medieval England: From Bondage to Freedom* (Woodbridge, 2014), pp. 52–3.

[113] WIT/17, m. 1r.

tenants considered it to be ancient demesne, and thus free of all services.[114] In the second court of that year, the tenants complained that a new rental had been compiled which had omitted certain lands and rents, and so they wished to see 'the ancient rental'.[115] And at the next court, a large missing rent was decided by the farmer, steward, and council without consultation of the homage; a move that seems to have provoked Robert Leveregge to utter some 'malicious, hateful words [which] threatened both the steward and the court', for which he was fined half a mark.[116]

This rancorous dispute was eventually settled in a remarkably simple way, as the manor was regranted by the crown as part of a pension given to Sir James Fenys, who seems to have brought in his own administrative staff, who were quickly able to get the tenants onside.[117] But while the court rolls are only allusive about the precise nature of the disagreement with Hardwick, it does seem to have comprised a battle over the tenants' knowledge of custom. This was a pressing issue in the fifteenth-century countryside, where many demesne farmers were attempting to squeeze out profits within rather tight margins, but without the full apparatus of seigneurial force possessed by lords.[118] As Hardwick found out to his cost, demesne farmers were particularly vulnerable to the knowledge work of an assertive tenantry, because of the disruption caused to the institutional knowledge of the court—the production of the new rental at Withyham is indicative—which might have normally served to buttress the more defensive claims made by the homage regarding the rents and services they owed. Drawing on Andy Wood's characterization, we might thus say that custom was an 'epistemic' form of knowledge work, as it was at the centre of negotiations over the interpretative frameworks that ought to be used to determine rights and obligations between lords and their tenants.[119]

But if relations with authorities became even more acrimonious, they had a couple of final resorts. In the first place, if reporters felt that they were not being listened to, then the implicit contract of knowledge work was being undermined. In an unusual case reported to a Lincolnshire visitation in 1500, some thirteen parishioners of an unnamed settlement in the marshlands of the south-east of the county made the following report: 'they have nothing to detect because Thomas Porter, dean of Holland, sat and held a court . . . and all their detections . . . went

[114] Ibid., m. 2r. On the claim of ancient demesne as a mode of peasant resistance, see Rosamund Faith, 'The "Great Rumour" of 1377 and Peasant Ideology', in *The English Rising of 1381*, ed. R. H. Hilton and T. H. Aston (Cambridge, 1984), 43–73.

[115] WIT/17, m. 3r. [116] Ibid., m. 4r.

[117] Ibid., mm. 6r–7v. The handwriting of the rolls changes radically with the change in ownership, suggesting at least a new scribe; the tenants quickly performed homage to Fenys, and, as far as the rolls show, there was no further acrimony.

[118] See Christopher Dyer, 'The Political Life of the Fifteenth-Century English Village', in *Political Culture in Late Medieval Britain*, ed. Clark and Carpenter, 135–57, at p. 146.

[119] Wood, *Memory of the People*, p. 14.

before him'.[120] But clearly they had not been impressed with the outcome of these sessions, and used the visitation to complain directly to his superiors: 'Many crimes were detected at that time, and before the official in that court. But nothing may be corrected subsequently except with money [as commutation]. Therefore, it seems that no one here has done public penance, unless they were a pauper.'[121] If offenders could simply buy their way out of doing penance, the parishioners were saying, there was no point in their detecting crime to the ecclesiastical officials who came to hold courts.[122] Tribunals were not enough—if this group of trustworthy men were to do knowledge work, they wanted the full course of law in exchange.

But, in fact, knowledge workers might also simply refuse to give any response whatsoever. They might do this in rather dramatic ways: at a view of frankpledge held at Whitstones and Wick in Worcestershire in 1450, the free jurors were said to have come 'armed in a warlike manner' and declared that they would not render any verdict; ordered to come again the next day, they attended again but would not say anything.[123] If such open refusal was rare, reports of *omnia bene*, 'all is well', are very frequent in late-medieval court records. Some of these, perhaps, were genuine statements that peace and harmony reigned within a community. But some clearly glossed a more complicated reality. For instance, the episcopal visitation book for Lincolnshire in 1473 records a simple *omnia bene* from the four *inquisitores* for the parish of Linwood. Yet an ephemeral document headed 'Lynnewode', preserved haphazardly within the book, noted a number of weighty matters for detection: a very large amount of money owed to the church, a debt preventing the purchase of new bells and a chalice, and a man who was in the habit of beating his father and mother.[124] Of course, it is impossible to know who wrote these memoranda—a good guess might be a rival group of trustworthy men.[125] But regardless of who wrote them, they demonstrate that the taciturn official report was hiding something: to say *omnia bene*, to give nothing away, was its own kind of statement.

Perhaps, indeed, we should begin to read reports of *omnia bene* rather differently. The five townships reporting to a Northallerton halmote, for example, look as though they were protesting too much when they declared, in 1480, '*omnia bene*, and all the pains and by-laws made and ordained hitherto are being observed

[120] Vj/5, fo. 48v. The precise location of the place is unknown because this visitation book is badly damaged and the margin where the place name would be is missing.

[121] Ibid. 'Sed nulla propterea sit correctio nisi pecunaria. Quia non erat visum hic quod aliquis hic publice penituit nisi pauperinus fuerit'.

[122] The case also shows up the blurry boundaries between visitation as both a legal and a pastoral event: Forrest, 'Transformation of Visitation', pp. 8–9.

[123] Christopher Dyer, *Lords and Peasants in a Changing Society: The Estates of the Bishopric of Worcester, 680–1540* (Cambridge, 1980), pp. 278–9.

[124] LA, Vj/4, fos. 16v–17r.

[125] On such documents and their role in understanding the church courts, see Tom Johnson, 'Legal Ephemera in the Ecclesiastical Courts of Late-Medieval England', *Open Library of Humanities*, 5:1 (2019), 1–27.

well, and they have nothing else to present'.[126] Where does power lie in such an interaction? To paraphrase James Scott, such reports seem, on the one hand, 'to pay a symbolic due to the officially constituted order' by recognizing the right of the courts to ask for information.[127] But on the other hand, by refusing to give any information, a report of *omnia bene* denied the possibility of an unwanted intervention in affairs over which the local trustworthy men wanted to take the lead, or, indeed, an embarrassing snub from authorities who took no action after hearing their reports. Back in the muddy waters of motivations, perhaps the most important point is that knowledge workers were able to withdraw their labour. In this formulaic phrase, late-medieval court rolls reveal thousands of microcosmic strike actions, as the benefits of rendering information to the courts were rejected in favour of a strategy that was not written down, and has been lost to time.

Overall, then, as it framed the encounter between people and the local courts, the transaction of knowledge work, and the cultural capital it afforded to the people who performed it, stimulated a series of complex institutional dynamics. The most common mechanisms of reporting ensured that the virtue of bearing witness and speaking the truth was distributed narrowly among small groups of men, reinforcing the kind of respectable masculine credibility that was bound up with routine moral governance.[128] Only rarely were other groups—such as the groups of women who explicitly gathered themselves into the 'moral majority' requisite for *fama*—able to seize such work, and the credibility it brought, for themselves. And people spent the social capital they earned through knowledge work in various ways, by pursuing individual grievances with enemies, or trying to manoeuvre themselves into a superior position; they might also attempt to act on behalf of a collective against the interests of an authority, to have a bridge repaired or lower customary dues. And, as we have just seen, they might even symbolically destroy any capital they gained through knowledge work by refusing to say anything at all. The demand that people perform knowledge work, then, might even serve as a powerful stimulus for collective organization against the very institutions that made such demands.

Conclusion

In this chapter, I have set out the closely intertwined relationships created in the communication of information between common people and their local

[126] NYCRO, ZBD/1/52/3, m. 3r. Elsewhere, gnomic phrases suggest a more complex understanding of *omnia bene*: at a hundred court in Witchford, the four men and bailiff of Chatteris said that 'they do not know what to say to any article which has been put to them. But all is well.' CUL, EDR/C7/34, m. 3v.

[127] James C. Scott, *Weapons of the Weak: Everyday Forms of Peasant Resistance* (New Haven, CT, 1985), p. 283.

[128] See Forrest, *Trustworthy Men*, pp. 229–33.

law-courts in terms of the 'economy' of legitimate knowledge, a framing which highlights, variously, the labour that went into the production of knowledge, the values that were ascribed to the legitimacy of such knowledge, and the kinds of negotiated transaction that its production could create. I have argued that there was a correspondence between legal and vernacular understandings of what made knowledge legitimate, which allowed the courts to demand information, and people to provide it, at a basic level of parity. From there, we saw how these demands were met through the performance of different kinds of 'knowledge work'—from the labour involved in reaching a jury verdict to the effort of remembering—and the rhetoric of diligence and inquiry that the courts fostered. In the last section, finally, I showed how people leveraged their knowledge in aid of particular goals, and, moreover, the 'recessions' that periodically affected this economy if the people expected to provide knowledge felt that there was some deficit of legitimacy in the institution for which they were working.

Considering these complex and multifaceted dynamics as an economy that produced legitimate knowledge, I would like to suggest here, by way of conclusion, three ways in which this commodity circulated and held value beyond the immediate context of the local courts in which it was routinely enunciated. In the first place, most obviously, this knowledge helped to sustain the operations of the wider legal systems that webbed throughout the late-medieval English polity. This was a straightforward function of ecclesiastical visitations, which drew direct lines between the parish and diocese, but it was also implicit in the potential for an indictment before some local secular court—most commonly a view of frank-pledge—to find its way to the royal courts at Westminster.[129] For example, after John Rolf stole two horses said to be worth 46s. 8d. from Thomas Smyth at King's Langley, the offence was reported as a felony at the next leet there on the June 1, 1440; a royal writ dated to June 8 certified that Rolf was in the Marshalsea prison in London, and requested a copy of the indictment, which was duly sent and filed.[130] The occasional alignment of these local and national operations helped to sustain the idea often invoked in the rhetoric of such tribunals, that the twelve sworn jurors were indeed testifying *pro rege*.[131]

Legitimate knowledge could also circulate laterally between different legal jurisdictions. This was certainly true locally; as we saw in Chapter 1, for example, the leet jurors of Monxton in Hampshire complained about the behaviour of

[129] After 1461, however, sheriffs were required to send all indictments straight to the Justices of the Peace, without conducting any process: see *Proceedings before the Justices of the Peace in the Fourteenth and Fifteenth Centuries: Edward III to Richard III*, ed. Bertha Haven Putnam (London, 1938), p. xxxvii.

[130] The roll is TNA, SC2/277/55, m. 5r; the writ is TNA, KB9/232/89, the copy of the indictment is KB9/232/90. The copy differs from the original in omitting his alias, John Basset (the leet roll notes that he was a bastard son of Thomas Rolf).

[131] To take a selection of various local courts at which this phrase was used: the view of frankpledge at the manor of Buckland Filleigh, CUL, MS Add. 3299, items 13–15; the courts of Witchford hundred, CUL, EDR/C7/29, m. 11v; the borough court of Marlborough, WSHC, G22/1/13, fo. 2v.

the rector there, Thomas Sparshot, after he continued to live with a woman 'notwithstanding the correction of the ordinary' of the deanery.[132] But legitimate knowledge might also be deliberately passed across national jurisdictions, too, as for example with the 'criminous clerks' who were convicted before lay judges and then handed over to the ecclesiastical authorities for punishment.[133] Certainly not all locally generated legitimate knowledge was straightforwardly accepted by the higher courts; indeed, the Chancery had a special writ, that of *certiorari*, which allowed losing defendants to challenge the verdicts of lower courts on the basis of procedural error; as we saw in Chapter 3, this was a powerful weapon against courts, such as those in the maritime world, whose precise jurisdiction was open to question.[134] Yet among the vast mass of information produced in local courts in fifteenth-century England, such formal objections were rare, a testament to the legitimacy of the knowledge produced there.

Legitimate knowledge also circulated outside of legal systems, however, and bled into political discourse more generally.[135] In this world of rapidly circulating rumours, 'wonderful bills', anonymous letters and memoranda of tidings, royal proclamations and seditious libels, knowledge ratified by courts formed part of the currency of regular news.[136] Thus Agnes Paston wrote to her son John around 1451 that she had spoken to a man at the village of Paston, who informed her that a wall had been built across the procession-way there, and 'men hopyd that the wall chuld be broke doun a-geyn'. This popular annoyance had been reflected judicially, for 'he seyd that I was amercyid for stoppyng of the seyd wey att the last generall court', though he did not know for how much.[137] When village elites expressed their dissatisfaction by amercing their own lord, then, this was understood as a sign that something needed to be done. The legitimate knowledge produced by local courts thus filtered up into the world of the governing classes, helping to sustain the connections between the commons and the late-medieval polity, with its multiple loci of power.

But in the third place, finally, such information was above all a local commodity, recirculated among the same communities who helped to create it. People

132 KCC, MON/2, m. 2r; Chapter 1, p. 21.

133 A. K. McHardy, 'Church Courts and Criminous Clerks in the Later Middle Ages', in *Medieval Ecclesiastical Studies in honour of Dorothy M. Owen*, ed. M. J. Franklin and Christopher Harper-Bill (Woodbridge, 1995), 165–83.

134 On *certiorari*, see Baker, *English Legal History*, pp. 48–50. It has been suggested that cases on *certiorari* 'almost invariably' resulted in acquittals: J. B. Post, 'Crime in later medieval England: some historiographical limitations', *Continuity and Change*, 2:2 (1987), 211–24, pp. 214–5. On *certiorari* in maritime courts, see Chapter 3, pp. 101, 109.

135 See Colin Richmond, 'Hand and Mouth: Information gathering and use in England in the later middle ages', *Journal of Historical Sociology*, 1:3 (1988), 233–52.

136 Wendy Scase, '"Strange and Wonderful Bills": Bill-Casting and Political Discourse in Late Medieval England', in *New Medieval Literatures*, 2, ed. Rita Copeland, David A. Lawton, and Wendy Scase (Oxford, 1998), 225–47.

137 Norman Davis, *Paston Letters and Papers of the Fifteenth Century* (3 vols., Oxford, 1971–6), i, p. 34.

reused the legitimate knowledge produced by courts in a variety of ways. Many late-medieval Londoners, for example, can be seen to have insulted their neighbours with reference to the judgments of the wardmotes; Elizabeth Baret said to Anna Wylkynson, 'thow wer indyted owte of the ward when thow wer [a] maiden, for prests resorting unto the'.[138] Judicial information also became a part of communal narratives about customary rights: Thomas Bulwere of Litcham remembered that his father, Edmond, had been amerced half a shilling in the manor court there for covering over some clay pits used by the whole community—he had seen him give the money to the hayward, Jon Skynnere.[139] Upon the grit of thousands of such transactions were laid the foundations of common legalities, guaranteeing the legitimacy of law. As Stephen Shapin and Simon Schaffer have put it, 'whenever groups of people come to agree about what knowledge is, they have practically and provisionally solved the problem of how to array and order themselves'.[140] Legitimate knowledge, a co-creation of the local courts and the people that used them, allowed for such ordering—from the bottom up.

[138] LMA, DL/C/B/043/MS9064/8, 303v. [139] NRO, KIM 1/9/16, m. 1r.

[140] Steven Shapin and Simon Schaffer, *Leviathan and the Air-Pump: Hobbes, Boyle, and the Experimental Life* (new edn; Princeton, NJ, 2011), p. xlix.

7

Legal English and the Vernacularization of Law

Introduction

One autumn in the 1520s, a young apprentice named John Bedowe was languishing in prison in Hereford's Bye-street gate for some unspecified offence against his master. By his own account, he was a 'pore fatherles and motherless chylde', but he had acquired the ability to write in English. Somehow, while still in gaol, he managed to get a hold of some paper and a quill, and began to write for his freedom. The first of his letters to the mayor of Hereford pleads that as a young man, he was not able to find anyone to stand his bail, to act as bond for his 'good a-berrynge'. So he asked for the mayor's grace in helping him obtain release, and promised to leave the city for as long as his master should live; he complains, finally, that he is 'i-famyche for mete, allmost', and asks, as he does throughout the letter, for the mayor to be a good master to him, 'now ore never'.[1] This remarkable piece of evidence not only shows a humble member of late-medieval society adept in the formal techniques of letter-writing—the letter ends with the formulaic phrase, 'no more to yow at thys tyme but Ihu have [you] yn hys keppynge'—but is also steeped in the petitionary discourse of charity, good mastership, and grace as a means of obtaining a remedy outside the formal dictates of law.

Bedowe was not granted his wish—at least not immediately—for it seems that he composed another letter soon afterwards.[2] Rather more direct in tone, this letter simply asked that the mayor might 'loke apone' the activities of Hugh Cotlare, another inmate in the Bye-street gate gaol. Signed by Bedowe and six other prisoners, the letter reported that Cotlare was threatening to impeach the mayor 'of hy tresson, & of mordore & of extiorsyone', and to give evidence against him and the other ruling citizens to the royal authorities; moreover, he planned to escape the prison 'with hys sottoll lawe & falsete', and was ready to kill anyone who stood in his way. Of course, implicit in the report of this information, which the seven signatories promised they would be willing to 'testyfy a fore maystor meyere', was that they were faithful men, looking out for the public good, and willing to comply with the authorities. While there is one brief insinuation of

[1] HARC, BG/11/17/3, item 4. [2] Ibid., item 5.

Law in Common: Legal Cultures in Late-Medieval England. Tom Johnson, Oxford University Press (2020).

DOI: 10.1093/oso/9780198785613.001.0001

petition—the prisoners 'pray' that the mayor might investigate Cotlare 'yn the reverrens of Gode'—the letter is otherwise forthright, a style which further underlines the trustworthiness of the informants. Indeed, had it not been made by a panel of suspected felons, the letter is not so far removed from the indictments composed by jurors for the Hereford law-days.[3]

We do not know what became of Bedowe and his fellow prisoners.[4] Yet these unusual documents cast some light on the vernacular legal discourse that had emerged in England over the course of the fifteenth century. While much in the petition belongs, naturally, to the broad tradition of 'plaint literature' identified by Wendy Scase, the particular expressions on which it draws are illustrative of the rich vocabulary of legal concepts that materialized in English during this period.[5] Bedowe did not describe himself as a humble petitioner, but as a 'true yonge man', a self-designation that gestured more widely to his law-worthiness; he did not merely ask for grace, but suggested that he should be banished, rather than imprisoned.[6] This idiomatic legal register could bring together formal concepts from law—in impeachment, ward, treason, murder and extortion—alongside colloquial expressions, such as the relation of Hugh Cotlare's remark that he was free to kill someone as 'e wolde honge hymselffe twysse'.[7] These letters, then, illustrate how a flexible and authoritative written English had become available to legal discourse, at once accessible to people like Bedowe and legitimate in the eyes of institutions and officials.

This chapter explores the growing use of English as a written 'legal vernacular' over the course of the fifteenth century, and sets out three main arguments.[8] The first is that we can only understand the emergence of vernacular writing in legal discourse by looking to the local contexts of legal production. Hitherto, historians have tended to focus on the emergence of English within the records of central government, and as such have tended to omit the great variety of local documents

[3] See Chapter 2, See below, p. 253.

[4] While Hereford's civic archives are relatively rich for this period, Bedowe does not appear elsewhere. A document headed 'The names of the presoners in bystretegate', dated to late 1518, does record the presence of a Thomas Apowell, the same name as one of the signatories to the second letter: HARC, BG 11/8/3. While this is a common name in this region, it is plausible that the same man might still be in prison two years later, if the letter was indeed composed—as suggested by a modern archival note—in 1520.

[5] Wendy Scase, *Literature and Complaint in England, 1272–1553* (Oxford, 2007).

[6] On 'true men', see Derek G. Neal, *The Masculine Self in Late-Medieval England* (Chicago, 2008), pp. 42ff.

[7] HARC, BG/11/17/3, item 5. The expression is equivalent to 'might as well be hanged for a sheep as a lamb'.

[8] My concern is solely with English, rather than Anglo-Norman or the Celtic vernaculars—Welsh, Irish, and Cornish—that were spoken in the English realm and dominions at this time. Generally, see R. R. Davies, 'The Peoples of Britain and Ireland, 1100–1400: IV Language and Historical Mythology', *Transactions of the Royal Historical Society*, 6th ser., 7 (1997), 1–24, and for contemporary governmental attitudes to these languages, see Gillian Brennan, 'Language and nationality: the role of policy towards Celtic languages in the consolidation of Tudor power', *Nations and Nationalism*, 7:3 (2001), 317–38.

that used English during this period; once we include them in a corpus of vernacularization, the overall picture begins to look different. The legal vernacular did not simply grow upwards and outwards from the royal Chancery, but emerged through a series of complex and staggered changes in the practices of local clerks, administrators, scriveners, and, indeed, literate common folk such as John Bedowe. While the proliferation of vernacular documentation was certainly related to the tacit acceptance and partial adoption of English in royal government writing, we must understand it within the broader context of a widespread and popular usage of the legal vernacular. Vernacularization was not one but a series of processes, driven from below as well as above.

With this in mind, it is important to remember the limits of vernacularization. Latin was the hegemonic language of legal record throughout England in 1500 as it had been in 1400 and 1300 before that. While Anglo-Norman French ceded some ground to English, it retained its cachet as a language for the texts used by professional lawyers (who, of course, also spoke it), among other things.[9] The emergence of English as a legal vernacular did not take hold uniformly across late-medieval society, and so we need to think more carefully about the specific kinds of discursive values that it held. The second argument here, then, is that as a legal language English worked as a signifier of authenticity, a mode of signalling fidelity to real speech, and as a way of gesturing towards wider audiences or publics. By focusing on the specific ways in which the legal vernacular was deployed (and, by implication, the value which remained in the use of Latin and to a lesser extent French), we can get a better sense of what it meant to contemporaries during these processes of vernacularization.

This brings us to my third argument, which is that the growing significance granted to English as a legal language affected common people in late-medieval England in ambivalent ways. While people were able to use a vernacular legal register in strategic ways, as John Bedowe's two letters so vividly demonstrate, in doing so they were also drawn more tightly into the remit of institutional authority. Thus, for example, the use of the vernacular to transcribe the voices of such people is indicative at once of the growing weight that was given to their speech, but also of attempts by both ecclesiastical and secular legal authorities to monitor and control it. While in some ways the processes of vernacularization we see in the fifteenth century thus seem to follow a trajectory towards a more inclusive public discourse, as the 'common tongue' spoken by the majority of the populace became a language appropriate for expressing ideas about legitimacy, it was ultimately constrained by the relatively limited modes in which English was allowed to be legal.

[9] See Paul Brand, 'The languages of the law in later medieval England', in *Multilingualism in Later Medieval Britain*, ed. D. A. Trotter (Cambridge, 2000), 63–76.

In making this argument, I want to re-examine recent claims about the roles that non-elites were able to adopt in public discourse in late-medieval European polities.[10] As John Watts has argued recently, the predominant ideological concepts of fifteenth-century English politics were 'open to deployment by the humbler members of society', and this suggests the existence of a 'common public language' of political discourse.[11] While I certainly agree that such a language existed and was deployed by non-elites, the dynamics at work in the vernacularization of legal language expose the extent to which the terms of this discourse remained outside of their control; indeed, the very 'commonness' of this language may actually have worked to mask the inequalities of power that underlay such participation. While people like John Bedowe were certainly able to deploy the legal English to make rhetorical appeals to vernacular forms of authenticity and legitimacy, therefore, the success of such appeals was ultimately at the discretion of authorities. English emerged as a legal language within certain constraints, then, and vernacularization represents a case study of the restrictions, as much as the opportunities, that such common discourse presented to the commons.

This chapter proceeds first by tracing the emergence of the vernacular in legal writings in England from the second half of the fourteenth century onwards. I suggest that we need to broaden our perspective of vernacularization to include locally produced documentation; in doing so, we can see that the vernacularization of law followed different trajectories across a variety of documentary contexts. Having established the limits of vernacularity, I turn in the second section to consider the values that were attributed to English as a language of legal communication. By looking at the kinds of document in which English came to be used by scribes in the later Middle Ages, I suggest that it was considered particularly effective for evoking the qualities of orality, authenticity, and publicity. The third section considers the effects of vernacularization for the mass of common people in their legal engagements. While the emergence of legal English in some ways signifies the extent to which the vernacular 'voice of the people' came to matter in fifteenth-century England, I argue that its effects were not wholly positive for those people. The conclusion, finally, considers these issues in relation to debates about the late-medieval public sphere.

[10] For work in this vein, see *The Voices of the People in Late Medieval Europe: Communication and Popular Politics*, ed. Jan Dumolyn, Jelle Haemers, Hipólito Rafael Oliva Herrer, and Vincent Challet (Turnhout, 2014); *La Comunidad Medieval Como Esfera Pública*, ed. Hipólito Rafael Oliva Herrer, Vincent Challet, Jan Dumolyn, María Antonia Carmona Ruiz (Seville, 2014).

[11] John Watts, 'Popular Voices in England's Wars of the Roses, *c.* 1445–*c.*1485', in *Voices of the People*, ed. Dumolyn, Haemers, Herrer, and Challet, 107–22, at pp. 115–6.

The Vernacularization of Law

In 1380, almost all legal documentation produced in England was written in Latin, or, occasionally, Anglo-Norman French, and a century and a half later this was still true. Yet beneath this seemingly stable surface were the currents of a momentous change, as English came to be used—and in some cases, even preferred—as a language for some kinds of legal document. The vernacularization of law in the long fifteenth century was significant not because it was overwhelming or conclusive, then, but because it represented a turning of the tides of common legalities, a gradual volte-face against several centuries of tradition.[12] Like all such cultural shifts, it was complex and diffuse. Therefore I suggest that we trace the presence and proliferation of vernacularity in different genres of documentary production: first, in the records of local courts and their proceedings; second, in the locally produced extracurial documents, such as settlements or petitions; and third, in the records of centrally directed legal systems, both ecclesiastical and secular. While these processes were certainly linked (sometimes explicitly by contemporaries), examining them separately in this way better shows the limited contexts in which English emerged as a written legal language.

Vernacularity in medieval England has provoked much critical discussion in the last two decades. While no scholar would now subscribe to the idea of the 'triumph of English' in the later Middle Ages, there is a broad consensus that this was a period of critical change in the uses and meanings of vernacular languages in England.[13] In the first place, historians have shown the great complexity (and partiality) of the developments surrounding the increased use of English in royal government records in the later fourteenth and early fifteenth centuries, systematically revising J. H. Fisher's older thesis that central government was responsible for the diffusion and standardization of Middle English.[14] In the second place, in a parallel move, literary scholars have deconstructed the idea that there was a single English form of 'vernacularity', which was inherently oral, demotic, and diametrically opposed to Latin (or French).[15] Such discussions have revealed that

[12] On this transformation in elite English legal discourse, see Sebastian Sobecki, *Unwritten Verities: The Making of England's Vernacular Legal Culture, 1463–1549* (Notre Dame, IN, 2016).

[13] For the 'triumph' narrative, see Basil Cottle, *The Triumph of English 1350–1400* (London, 1969). For a range of recent work, see the essays in *Vernacularity in England and Wales, c. 1300–1550*, ed. Elizabeth Salter and Helen Wicker, Utrecht Studies in Medieval Literacy, 17 (Turnhout, 2011).

[14] On this narrative, see J. H. Fisher, *The Emergence of Standard English* (Lexington, KY, 1996). For more recent work that has helped to revise it, see W. M. Ormrod, 'The Use of English: Language, Law, and Political Culture in Fourteenth-Century England', *Speculum*, 78:3 (2003), 750–87; Gwilym Dodd, 'The Spread of English in the Records of Central Government, 1400–1430', in *Vernacularity in England and Wales*, ed. Salter and Wicker, 225–66; Christopher Fletcher, 'Langue et nation en Angleterre à la fin du Moyen Âge', *Révue française d'histoire des idées politiques*, 36 (2012), 233–52.

[15] See the essays in *The idea of the vernacular: An anthology of Middle English literary theory, 1280–1520*, ed. Ruth Evans, Andrew Taylor, Nicholas Watson and Jocelyn Wogan-Browne (University Park, PA, 1999); *The Vulgar Tongue: Medieval and Postmedieval Vernacularity*, ed. Fiona Somerset and Nicholas Watson (University Park, PA, 2003).

vernacularity is not an essential quality of any language, but rather describes its (usually inferior) relation to other languages. In order to apprehend the meaning of English as a vernacular, therefore, we have to understand the broader 'language ecology' in this period, and the interconnectedness of linguistic change.[16]

In what follows, I try to build on this work in two ways, each of which entails taking a broader perspective of vernacularization. In the first place, as Gillian Draper has suggested, we need to look at a wider range of contexts for late-medieval documentary production in which the English vernacular came to be used.[17] In the course of dismantling the triumphalist narratives that bound up the emergence of English with the royal state, recent work has nonetheless tended to retain this focus on central institutions.[18] Yet, as we shall see in what follows, processes of vernacularization were also taking place locally in late-medieval England, from the records of urban legal authorities to the commissioning of English petitions by rural communities. In the second place, moreover, once we begin to look to these local contexts of documentary production, we can see more clearly the interrelations between English and other languages within different genres of legal writing, and, accordingly, the different trajectories that they followed. Such a perspective, then, reveals the complexities—and limitations—that were at work in the vernacularization of law.

To begin with, it is important to attend to the long continuity in the use of the vernacular within local court records of all kinds. English (and to a lesser degree French) terms were used in these records (and other associated documents, such as accounts) almost from the time that their proceedings began to be written down in the early thirteenth century.[19] These vernacular terms were almost always nouns, used of course for people and places, but also for officials, buildings, objects, animals, and customs.[20] In regard to customs, indeed, there is an even greater continuity buried in the use of such vernacular terms, as many Old English words, such as *soc* and *wite*, *-penny* and *-bote*, were retained within the deep cultural structures of local law.[21] While it is easy to dismiss this form of

[16] On 'language ecology', see Tim William Machan, *English in the Middle Ages* (Oxford, 2003), pp. 9ff.

[17] G. M. Draper, 'Writing English, French and Latin in the Fifteenth Century: A Regional Perspective', in *Fifteenth-Century VII: Conflicts, Consequences and the Crown in the Late Middle Ages*, ed. Linda Clark (Woodbridge, 2007), 213–26.

[18] See Dodd, 'The Spread of English'.

[19] See the dates in the list compiled by J. R. Hulbert, 'English in Manorial Documents of the Thirteenth and Fourteenth Centuries', *Modern Philology*, 34:1 (1936), 37–61, p. 40ff. On French in manorial documentation, see Richard Ingham, 'Mixing Languages on the Manor', *Medium Ævum*, 78:1 (2009), 80–98, p. 85; Laura Wright, 'Mixed-Language Accounts as Sources for Linguistic Analysis', in *Multilingualism in Medieval Britain (c.1066–1520)*, ed. Judith A. Jefferson and Ad Putter (Turnhout, 2013), 123–36.

[20] Respectively, e.g.: 'le thethyngman', BL, Add. Ch. 49222, m. 5v; 'le shoppe', BL, Add. Ch. 49243, m. 3v; 'I wodchoke pot precij ij d', KCC, FOR/8/2; 'I equo bay', KCC, BRD/5/9; KCC, MON/2; 'cum housbote et haybote'.

[21] On the importance of 'wite' in Anglo-Saxon law, see Tom Lambert, *Law and Order in Anglo-Saxon England* (Oxford, 2017), pp. 59–60.

vernacularity as evidence of poor Latinity on the part of the clerks who made such records, Andrew Butcher has rightly pointed out that they were deliberate textual choices, conditioned both by scribal tradition and immediate communicative purposes.[22] These infinitesimal and localized instances of vernacularity thus held cultural significance precisely because they operated within a 'matrix language' of Latin, and so both reflected and perpetuated ideas about the significance of English in the legal record.[23]

We can see this more clearly when we turn to consider the different trajectories of vernacularization within local legal cultures. In the countryside, manorial court rolls proved to be deeply stable in their limited use of English across the later Middle Ages. Despite this general stability, the second half of the fifteenth century did see an intensification of the use of English in this context, sometimes creating the kind of 'macaronic' texts familiar to literary scholars.[24] Thus, for example, at Bradbourne in Derbyshire in the late 1470s we find several presentments that mixed English and Latin, such as 'Item Thomas Parker that he hath taken shepe contrari to the burlay [by-law] in misericordia domini'.[25] These instances are relatively rare, though, and may be linked to changes in the format of such documentation, as it came to include notes, memoranda, and other ephemeral texts—along with the increased survival of such materials—in a trend also perceptible in the rural church courts.[26] While the hold of Latin was thus gradually loosened—a trend that continued into the sixteenth century and beyond—vernacularization on the whole was limited in rural legal culture, perhaps because of the way that limited vernacularity was entrenched in the language ecology of manorial documentation.[27]

This existed in stark contrast to urban legal culture, where English came to be used very frequently in legal records of all kinds over the course of the later Middle Ages but along very different trajectories. In the first place, Anglo-Norman had long been important to civic documentary culture, and continued to be used for a

[22] See Andrew Butcher, 'Textual Production and Vernacular Behaviour: Locating a Fifteenth-Century Administrative Book', in *Vernacularity in England and Wales*, ed. Salter and Wicker, 295–323.

[23] This useful idea is from Ingham, 'Mixing Languages on the Manor', pp. 83–4.

[24] Machan, *English in the Middle Ages*, pp. 103–4.

[25] DRO, D9392/M1, m. 3r.

[26] On these (often vernacular) ecclesiastical legal ephemera, see Tom Johnson, 'Legal Ephemera in the Ecclesiastical Courts of Late-Medieval England', *Open Library of Humanities*, 5:1 (2019), 1–27. The changing format of manorial documents, shifting from rolls to books in this period, is an interesting and unexplored topic. Books seem to have offered the potential for different textual practices: for example, the court book of the manor of Gayton (Lincolnshire), 1482–1517, was used as a kind of legal commonplace book, with various texts related to manorial business (such as letters, arbitrations, contracts, and ordinances) copied in English: see BL, MS Egerton 3001, fos. 26v, 32r, 118v–119v, 147r, 205v, 236v.

[27] For manorial courts in the early modern period, see Brodie Waddell, 'Governing England Through the Manor Courts, 1550–1850', *The Historical Journal*, 55:2 (2012), 279–315. He does not discuss the language of these documents, but provides many quotes in the vernacular through pp. 287–92.

variety of legal purposes, from custumals to ordinances and mandates, throughout the fourteenth and early fifteenth centuries, and perhaps especially in port towns, where French was more likely to be widely spoken and known.[28] Over the course of the fifteenth century, however, this space for vernacularity increasingly came to be occupied by English, at the same time as the kinds of legal documentation produced by town governments was becoming more extensive and miscellaneous, to include registers and books devoted to the recording of general memoranda, council minutes, letters, and a variety of other kinds of documents—many of them in the vernacular.[29] It is hard not to see this clear process as related to the distinctive pressures of civic politics, as the governing authorities increasingly found themselves having to justify and publicize their decisions to a broad constituency of citizens.[30]

Vernacularization in urban legal culture not only started from a different point, then, because of the widespread use of Anglo-Norman, but also saw legal English become much more pervasive than in the countryside. Indeed, in some places it even came to displace Latin as a language of court records. At Hereford, for example, the earliest surviving copy of law-day proceedings, from 1478, is written almost entirely in English, with just the date and heading recorded in Latin.[31] Interestingly, some later proceedings continued to use English while others switched back to Latin (the practice seems to have varied by ward); we find a similar phenomenon in the mayoral and pie-powder courts of the borough of Marlborough, where some experimentation with more extensive uses of English in 1502 had disappeared by the time of the next surviving roll of 1515.[32] But if the use of English for urban court proceedings was not a conclusive switch, the many contemporaneous English bills of indictment to the Hereford tourns indicate the direction of travel in the later fifteenth century.[33] English became predominant as a legal language in urban legal culture as perhaps nowhere else.

Differences between local traditions of documentary production, then, were crucially important in determining the trajectories of vernacularization. But they were not the only forces at play, as becomes clear when we turn to the production

[28] Generally, see Richard Britnell, 'Uses of French Language in Medieval English Towns', in *Language and Culture in Medieval Britain: The French of England c.1100–c.1500*, ed. Jocelyn Wogan-Browne (York, 2009) , 81–9, and on maritime towns, Maryanne Kowaleski, 'The French of England: A Maritime *lingua franca*?', in ibid., 103–17. French was possibly even used as a language of pleading in civic courts during the late thirteenth and fourteenth centuries, in emulation of the common law: Ormrod, 'The Use of English', p. 766.

[29] For examples, see *The Red Paper Book of Colchester*, ed. W. G. Benham (Colchester, 1902); *The York House Books 1461–1490*, ed. L. C. Attreed (2 vols., Stroud, 1991); *The First General Entry Book of the City of Salisbury 1387–1452*, ed. D. R. Carr, Wiltshire Record Society 54 (Trowbridge, 2001).

[30] Generally, see Christian D. Liddy, *Contesting the City: The Politics of Citizenship in English Towns, 1250–1530* (Oxford, 2017), Ch. 6, pp. 165–205. He does not discuss vernacularity per se, but includes several examples in which such use of English was clearly important.

[31] HARC, BG11/3/1 [1478].

[32] WSHC, G22/1/12, fos. 2r, 3v; G22/1/13, fos. 1r–10v.

[33] HARC, BG11/4/1 [1509, 1513].

of extracurial documents, such as property deeds, affidavits, releases, arbitrations, letters testimonial, wills, and a variety of other stand-alone legal writings.[34] Of course, many such records continued to be written in Latin beyond the end of the Middle Ages. For example, among the muniments of Hereford cathedral, which stretch back to before the Conquest, there are just six items written in English before 1475, of which all but one (a defeasance on a bond) were memoranda; yet between 1475 and 1530, we find some sixteen documents (of which six were bonds, grants, or leases) written in English.[35] But if this was hardly a revolution, it is worth remembering that these muniments were created for an ecclesiastical establishment with a strong sense of its perpetuity and a broader cultural attachment to Latin. Even the most conservative institutions began, in the late fifteenth century, to create and archive documents—even those important to the establishment of their rights—that were written in English.

The petition, as another important genre of localized documentary production—and one traditionally associated with vernacularity—underwent a very different transition to the use of English.[36] Through the thirteenth and fourteenth centuries petitions were almost always written in French, but relatively suddenly, by the standards of cultural change, came to be mostly written in English during the first half of the fifteenth century. In a quantitative analysis, Gwilym Dodd found a 'tipping point' in the use of English for three kinds of petition sent to parliament and Chancery in the 1430s and 1440s.[37] Certainly, by the time other conciliar equity courts were established later in the fifteenth century, there was little question that they would receive supplications in English.[38] As Dodd has stressed elsewhere, it is important to understand these developments within their wider institutional frameworks: Latin remained the predominant language of record for both institutions, and French was still used for the parliament rolls.[39] Yet such petitions were not, for the most part, produced within royal government, but by petitioners elsewhere.[40]

[34] See the collection of Middle English documents published in Lorenz Morsbach, *Mittelenglische Originalurkunden von der Chaucer-zeit bis zur mitte des XV. Jahrhunderts* (Heidelberg, 1923).

[35] *Hereford Cathedral Muniments*, v; vi, pp. 1247–82. Up to 1477 (an arbitrary division in the catalogues, but useful as a heuristic), there were several dozen documents written in French, and, surprisingly, two written around 1500 (petitions). For an idea of sample size, there are eighty-five documents surviving from 1477–1530.

[36] See Scase, *Literature and Complaint*, Ch. 1, pp. 5–41.

[37] Gwilym Dodd, 'The Rise of English, the Decline of French: Supplications to the English Crown, c. 1420-1450', *Speculum*, 86:1 (2011), 117–50, pp. 122–5. The timing was slightly staggered: private petitions to parliament tipped to English in 1436, petitions to the Chamberlain in 1439, and common petitions to parliament in 1445. While it is not possible to date Chancery bills with much accuracy, a similar shift appears to have taken place in their composition during the 1430s: ibid., p. 123.

[38] See Baker, *English Legal History*, pp. 117–9.

[39] Dodd, 'The Spread of English', pp. 234, 246.

[40] This thorny issue is discussed in Dodd, 'The Rise of English, the Decline of French', pp. 120–1. It is worth nothing that private parliamentary petitions were often produced by people who were connected to royal government or the king's household: see ibid., appendix [unpaginated]. More

This is not, however, to downplay the influence of the practice of royal government on the changing patterns of documentary practice in the localities. In the first place, there may be a kernel of truth in the significance that has traditionally been afforded to the famous Statute of Pleading of 1362, which specified that the proceedings of both royal and seigneurial courts ought to be conducted in English.[41] As Mark Ormrod has shown, the motives behind this legislation were complicated: not only did it serve as a piece of 'gesture politics' by Edward III in the midst of the Hundred Years War, it was also a jurisdictional gambit, a way of reinforcing the role of the landed classes on the nascent commissions of the peace, against the influence of the professional Westminster judiciary, and their specialist Law French.[42] Yet, for all this, it is worth wondering whether the statute may have had unintended consequences. Announced alongside a general pardon and festivities to mark Edward III's fiftieth birthday, it signalled to a wide audience that English was to be regarded as a language of law.[43] While it is certainly not a monocausal explanation of vernacularization, then, it may have propagated the idea, in the later fourteenth century, that English writing could carry authority.[44]

At the very least, it is striking that many of the earliest instances of English being used for certain genres of documentation survive from the couple of decades after the promulgation of the statute. For example, one of the earliest known documents written in English, an account of dealings between Thomas Gylys and Robert Wanstallen, survives from around 1371; another, a small indenture recording the receipt of a delivery of animals and agricultural equipment to a manorial bailiff, from 1377.[45] While neither of these documents were strictly 'legal', but rather served immediate communicative functions as memoranda, both described legal transactions using an English language of law. From soon afterwards, in the 1380s, however, more straightforwardly legal documents written in English do survive: the oldest proved wills written in English, what is often regarded as the earliest English petition to parliament, by the Mercers' Company of London in

generally, see T. S. Haskett, 'County Lawyers? The Composers of English Chancery Bills', in *The Life of the Law: Proceedings of the Tenth British Legal History Conference*, ed. P. Birks (London, 1993), 9–23.

[41] 36 Edw. III c. 15: *SR*, i, 375–6. The statute applied only to the oral pleading of courts, and not to legal and governmental documentation, which manifestly remained in Latin, and in some cases, varieties of French: see W. Rothwell, 'English and French in England after 1362', *English Studies*, 82:6 (2001), 539–59.

[42] Ormrod, 'The Use of English', pp. 763–73. On Law French, see Brand, 'Languages of the law'.

[43] A similar point is made in Dodd, 'The Spread of English', p. 255.

[44] Of course, this was precisely the same period in which an influential group of writers and court poets with connections to royal government were self-consciously fashioning a canon of Middle English literature: see Jeremy Catto, 'Written English: The Making of the Language 1370–1400', *P&P*, 179 (2003), 24–59.

[45] Respectively, BL, Harley Ch. 78. D. 3, noted in H. Flasdieck, *Mittelenglische Originalurkunden (1405–1430)* (Heidelberg, 1926); BL, Harley Ch. 55 B 45; Morsbach, *Mittelenglische Originalurkunden*, no. 2.

1388, and the smattering of English returns that were made by local guilds in response to the royal inquest of 1388–9.[46] While the survival of such documents is of course accidental to some degree, it does seem to hint at a rising tide of English documentary production in this period.

And indeed, further encouragement for the production of documents in English came from the practice of royal government. This was made explicit in the famous decision of the London Brewers' Guild in 1422 to use English for its own records, which made reference to the practice of Henry V in causing his 'letters missive' to be made in 'the common idiom'—though they wrote this in Latin.[47] Historians have long seen this switch to English in royal signet letters from 1417, along with the growing use of English in parliamentary documentation, as key signposts of vernacularization, but, as Gwilym Dodd has pointed out, it is important to understand these changes within the context of wider administrative reforms, as well as to distinguish between the use of the vernacular in the political discourse of parliament, which was increasingly common, and its use in official documentation, which was still rare.[48] It was not until later in the fifteenth century, with the issuance of proclamation texts in English under Edward IV, and the recording of statutes in English from the reign of Richard III, that its role as an appropriate language for government became entrenched.[49]

Indeed, as a final point, the vernacularization of legal documents produced within central legal systems was both slow and restricted in comparison with those produced elsewhere. The records of the royal courts of King's Bench and Common Pleas were kept almost exclusively in Latin throughout the fifteenth century and beyond, with two exceptions: the appeals of 'approvers'—felons who made fulsome confessions naming accomplices in a bid to save themselves—taken by coroners were sometimes recorded in English, as were the vernacular words of those accused of 'treasonable speech', on which I shall say more later in this chapter.[50] It is noteworthy that in both instances English was used to convey putative speech acts; in the church courts, too, we find similar islands of oral vernacularity in the sea of Latinate legal writings, as over the course of the later

[46] These examples are heralded as augurs of 'triumph' in Cottle, *The Triumph of English*, p. 17. For a detailed discussion of the 1388 Mercers' petition to Parliament and its many complexities, see Scase, *Literature and Complaint*, pp. 65–82. On the inquest into guilds, see Gervase Rosser, *The Art of Solidarity: Guilds in England 1250–1550* (Oxford, 2015), pp. 64–5.

[47] Ormrod, 'The Use of English', pp. 784–5. It is noteworthy that contemporaneously, other guilds in London were using a mixture of English and French: see W. Rothwell, 'Sugar and Spice and All Things Nice: From Oriental Bazar to English Cloister in Anglo-French', *The Modern Language Review*, 100, supplement (2005), 38–50, p. 38.

[48] Dodd, 'The Spread of English', pp. 228, 234.

[49] On proclamation texts, see Charles Ross, 'Rumour, Propaganda and Popular Opinion during the Wars of the Roses', in *Patronage, the Crown and the Provinces in Later Medieval England*, ed. Ralph A. Griffiths (Gloucester, 1981), pp. 15–32; on the switch to English statutes, see *SR*, ii, p. 494.

[50] For a famous vernacular approver's appeal, see Margaret Aston, 'A Kent Approver of 1440', *Bulletin of the Institute of Historical Research*, 36:93 (1963), 82–90.

fifteenth century many dioceses began to record witness depositions for instance causes in English.[51] While both secular and ecclesiastical legal systems did begin to admit English documents more in the administration of their operations—in bishops' registers, for example, or the materials assembled for the fifteenth-century Forest eyres—on the whole they remained resistant to vernacularization.[52]

In sum, then, the vernacularization of law was not one, but a series of processes that followed different trajectories across a range of legal writings. The causes of vernacularization were thus numerous, varying substantially not only in different local contexts of documentary production—urban and rural court records providing an obvious contrast, as we saw—but also in response to the requirements of specific institutions. Yet despite the specificities of each of these processes, it is also possible to discern some wider trends in the chronology of vernacularization across late-medieval England. The first key transition for the use of legal English occurred in the last two decades of the fourteenth century, when throughout the country people began to produce many kinds of extracurial documents in English, a trend which continued slowly across the later Middle Ages; there was also a subtler movement in the second half of the fifteenth century towards the use of English in official documentation, both in some kinds of court record and in the communications of the royal government.

Indeed, there were also patterns in the way that vernacularization occurred across genres of legal writing. Where Latin was used as a matrix language, particularly for court proceedings, it remained largely impervious to vernacularization; the limited use of English we find in such records, even if it slightly increased across the fifteenth century, may be understood as part of the further development of an administrative language that had always been macaronic to some degree. On the other hand, English made real inroads into genres of documentation which had traditionally been kept in French, most notably in the case of petitions.[53] Though it is clear that different documentary traditions and contexts shaped the way in which vernacularization occurred, therefore, it is also clear that these processes were mutually influential—sometimes explicitly so for contemporaries—and so furthered the use of legal English as a kind of viral

[51] Jeremy Goldberg, *Communal Discord, Child Abduction, and Rape in the Later Middle Ages* (Basingstoke, 2008), pp. 35–6. There is a great need for work on the extent, chronology, and significance of the use of vernacular in ecclesiastical depositions. It is important to note that many legal ephemera presented to visitations or produced for other church courts were written in the vernacular: see Johnson, 'Legal Ephemera', e.g. at pp. 9–10, 13–4, 19–20.

[52] For example, see the English documents (several of them being petitions or pleadings before equity courts) copied in the register of Charles Bothe, bishop of Hereford in the early sixteenth century, see Arthur Thomas Bannister, *Registrum Caroli Bothe, Episcopi Herefordensis*, Canterbury and York Society, 28 (London, 1921), pp. 5, 35, 45–54, 61–3, 78–9, 82–3, 85, 132–3, 151, 254, 302. In the Forest eyres, bills of indictment, records of Forest boundaries, and miscellaneous notes and memoranda were sometimes recorded in English, but the language of record for the proceedings remained in Latin: see Chapter 4, pp. 132–4.

[53] Dodd, 'The Spread of English', p. 228.

cultural change, spreading from point to point. In order to understand the significance of this change, we turn now to examine some of the reasons that English was considered valuable as a language of law.

The Value of English as a Language of Law

The use of English as a language of legal composition was a choice. As we have seen, Latin remained the hegemonic language of legal discourse throughout this period, and French was available as an alternative vernacular in some instances. Thus when a scribe used English, it was not usually from ignorance of Latin, nor, it seems likely, from boredom.[54] On the contrary, the decision to use English in a legal document arguably required more mental effort and deliberation, because to write law in the vernacular was also to venture outside of the prescribed forms that were available in Latin. This choice was particularly acute given that a scribe was frequently creating documents that were intended to impart influence, to persuade, or provoke. The use of English thus not only had to be safe and benign—that is, it would not invalidate a deed, for example—but would ideally be rhetorically valuable, adding something to the power of the text. And indeed, when we look at the kinds of documentary context in which late-medieval scribes used English, I suggest that its chief value lay in its capacity to communicate orality, authenticity, and publicity; in what follows, we examine each of these qualities in turn.

To begin with, there was a deep association between English and orality in late-medieval legal practice. As William Shareshull, Chief Justice of the King's Bench, was said to have put it in 1355, 'Latin was a formal language to put in writs, and English was the speech of laymen'.[55] Yet, despite this binary, the vernacular 'speech of laymen' was also in this period becoming a matter of concern for legal writings. As we shall see in the next section of this chapter, the growing attention to deviant speech by various legal authorities in the later Middle Ages meant that it was increasingly transcribed in the original language in which it was spoken. But, as I want to emphasize here, English was also used by scribes to insinuate orality in legal documents for rhetorical purposes. Perhaps the most prosaic example of this phenomenon is the widespread use of the word 'vocatur' (Latin: 'it is called') as a means of introducing an English place name: 'a meadow

[54] The latter is an explanation suggested for the appearance of the vernacular in the deposition of a heretic, in Steven Justice, 'Inquisition, Speech, and Writing: A Case from Late-Medieval Norwich', *Representations*, 48 (1994), 1–29, p. 8.

[55] Y. B. 29 Edw. III, Lib. Ass. 33, fo. 164r [Seipp number: 1355.211ass]. Accessed through David Seipp, *An Index and Paraphrase of Printed Year Book Reports, 1268–1535* [http://www.bu.edu/law/faculty-scholarship/legal-history-the-year-books/].

called *Bedellmeed*'; 'the lord's water called *le Myllenpond*'; 'land on the hill called *Berewykeshull*'.[56] Thousands of such gestures to orality littered late-medieval court rolls, thus helping to sustain the divide that Shareshull mentioned between the formal matrix of Latin and the world of lay speech.

Alongside these routinized evocations of the oral world, late-medieval scribes also often used English to convey formal speech acts.[57] We can see this explicitly, on occasion, when vernacular bills of indictment introduced the jurors' presentments as 'we say that...', a form used in a few such files of the fifteenth-century Forest eyres, for example.[58] More widespread was the use of English in the surviving texts of oaths taken by jurors, officials, and others, which in the fifteenth century were nearly always copied in the vernacular.[59] Even articles of presentment for the jury of leet and manorial courts, traditionally recorded in Latin or sometimes in French, were translated into English in this period; one surviving text specifically references the oath it was designed to induce, with the invocation to 'treuli presenten alle the articules of this court of the weche ȝe schul been charged, so help ȝou good & the holi doom'.[60] Writing such texts in English, of course, was designed to ensure the adherence to the precise form of words in a verbal oath.[61] English was not just a means of referring to vernacular speech that took place outside of legal settings, therefore, but a tool to fix and regularize legal speech acts.

Finally, English was often used in order to rhetorically evoke oral statements, even when it is clear that the actual vernacular words transcribed on the document probably bear only a very loose relationship to words that were spoken. This is made explicit in an unusual return to a royal inquisition on the Isle of Wight in 1466 into the wreckage of a Genoese carrack called the *Santa Maria*; while the text began in formulaic Latin, the collective statement of the six squires who served as jurors was rendered 'in the form that follows, in

[56] Respectively, KCC, WIT/17, m. 4r [Withyham]; MON/2, m. 1v [Monxton]; CHA/estates1, m. 9r [Broad Chalke]. This construction was also used more occasionally to introduce other English words, such as those for animals, objects, or customs.

[57] Cf. the comments in Scase, *Literature and Complaint*, p. 40.

[58] See, for example, the files presented at Northamptonshire in 1476: TNA, DL 39/2/7, m. 3r; or the presentments to Waltham Forest in 1488–9, DL 39/2/22, m. 1r. Other vernacular presentments used the form 'we present' (which was still, of course, an oral declaration): e.g. for some of the surviving London wardmotes: LMA, CLC/W/FA/005/MS01499, MS01501.

[59] For example, the oath of swannimote jurors, TNA, WARD 2/60/234/145; the oaths of urban officials at Maldon, ERO, D/B 3/1/2, 14r; the form of abjuration for a felon in the red paper book of Colchester, D/B 5 R2, fo. 42v. Interestingly, the earlier compilation known as the red parchment book in Colchester includes instructions for the officers of the lawhundred in English, but oaths for officers in both English and French: respectively D/B 5 R1, fos. 2r–v, 23v.

[60] See John Beckerman, 'The Articles of Presentment of a Court Leet and Court Baron, in English, c. 1400,' *Bulletin of the Institute of Historical Research*, 47 (1974): 230–4, p. 233.

[61] It has been suggested that the royal government began to issue royal proclamations with a vernacular text for precisely this purpose: James A. Doig, 'Political Propaganda and Royal Proclamations in Late Medieval England', *Historical Research*, 71:176 (1998), 253–80, pp. 264–5.

English words'.[62] The length of this vernacular statement, the frequent interlineations, and at last the statement that the jurors had 'putte to ther sealles' to the inquisition rather belie its claim to represent a transcription of speech. But, in fact, the invocation of orality was a common rhetorical strategy for vernacular testimonial documents. For example, the formal attestation made by six aged inhabitants of Brenchley in 1416, which we saw in Chapter 6, maintained the first-person plural throughout: 'we beynge of the age the leeste of us of thre skore wynter', 'we knoynge & neghtbors beyinge', 'we seyne to helpe us gode and halydame'.[63] This latter phrase may indicate that, just like an oath text, such documents were designed to be read aloud.

But the putative orality of vernacular testimonials might also have served other rhetorical purposes. For example, in an English certification made by the tenants of Newton Solney (Derbyshire) in 1476, a certain claim was dismissed because 'we seyn that no men harde ner knew [of it] nor non off owre ancestres afore us'.[64] The use of English did not just refer to the authorized orality of the witnesses' sworn deposition, therefore, but also alluded to the broader world of vernacular oral transmission that helped to constitute customary rights; a document in English could claim to be closer to that world, and thus to the faithful recording of custom. Such valences seem more pronounced, perhaps, when we compare English testimonials to their Latin equivalents; one from Brackley (Northamptonshire) in 1402, for instance, was written almost entirely in the third person, and made no allusion to the voices or perspective of the witnesses whatsoever.[65] Of course, it was only slightly more removed from the speech of witnesses than vernacular testimonials; yet in deploying English in such documents, scribes were able to highlight the trust mechanisms—sworn oaths, made by aged, male jurors—that were associated with legal speech acts.

English was also used to rhetorically signify publicity in legal writings. This had a couple of different inflections. In the first place, as we saw just above, English certainly came to be understood, in the later Middle Ages, as the proper language for the elaboration of custom, as a widely shared set of traditions. A striking

[62] TNA, C 145/322, no. 13, m. 1r, '. . . qui dicit super sacramentum suum predictum in forma qua sequitur in anglicis verbis videlicet . . .'

[63] BL, Add. Ch. 36522; above, Chapter 6, pp. 196–7. This document is noted in Flasdieck, *Mittelenglische Originalurkunden* [no. V]. The same device is used, and a similar effect achieved, by the vernacular 'chirographs' appended to the sentences against the lollards of Norwich diocese in 1428–31: see *Heresy Trials in the Diocese of Norwich 1428–31*, ed. Norman Tanner, Camden Society, 4th ser., 20 (London, 1977), pp. 57–9 [abjuration of John Skylly], 81–2 [John Kyngent], 85–6 [Richard Fleccher], etc. Justice, 'Inquisition, Speech, and Writing', pp. 12–3, does not distinguish these texts of abjuration and the depositions contained in the same volume, which I would suggest bear quite different relationships to speech acts.

[64] DRO, D5236/4/42.

[65] MCO, Brackley 209d. This is a testimonial concerning the dilapidated state of a manorial building. The only first-person verb used is *innotescimus*, 'we have learned by experience', which can be disregarded: it was so formulaic as to give its name to a kind of document (i.e. the *inspeximus*), and it was used merely to introduce an otherwise disembodied narrative of events.

instance of this can be found in an arbitration award made in 1507 between Wilton Abbey and King's College, Cambridge, concerning the disposition of tithes in the manor of Broad Chalke in Wiltshire. The document, made by the notary public William Stubbe, is written in exquisite Latin, but when it came to describe the practices 'used from antiquity, according to custom, for a long time', it breaks into English: the parson should 'take every [third] weke the yere I cartelode of... underwode', that on each of Easter, Ascension, and Pentecost he should receive a cheese, that he was entitled to 250 sheep on the south pasture and 100 wethers on the east, and that he should till 'with the freemen at the day of the plowbede... and he shall take for that custome as other free men doth take'.[66] More than just signalling the orality of these customs, the use of English here seems designed to convey that they were widely known and agreed upon among the local inhabitants.

English did not just represent the language of the commons, however, but was also understood to publicize legal communications. This was of course linked to wider trends in the vernacularization of public discourse from the later fourteenth century, perhaps best symbolized by the famous 'rebel letters' of 1381; one thing that can be said for certain about their myriad meanings is that contemporaries understood their vernacularity to be significant.[67] As written communications in English entailed the idea of wide circulation, to write a legal document in English was to gesture at a broad reception. This may be another reason that we increasingly find letters testimonial written in the vernacular. While their conventional rhetorical opening—'be it known to all Christian people who see or hear these present letters'—was borrowed from Latin, in English it entailed a much wider potential audience, crucial for documents that were attempting to establish public knowledge of matters such as ancestry or reputation.[68] The use of English as a public language had an 'authenticating quality': not only did it conjure associations of fidelity, but it suggested that the document had been laid open to wide public scrutiny, and that there was nothing to hide.[69]

Indeed, as a final point, legal English also signified authenticity more generally. Thus it was increasingly used as a language for arbitrations more generally in the later Middle Ages. In such contexts, English signalled that an honest attempt was

[66] KCC, CHA/33, the initial quote is translated from 'ab antique et iuxta consuetudine a longo tempore usitat'. This 'plough-bede' was probably a communal boonwork, perhaps accompanied by drinking—'plough-scot' or 'plow-bene' was such an obligation, while a 'bede-ale' was a drinking party.

[67] See Stephen Justice, *Writing and Rebellion: England in 1381* (Berkeley, CA, 1994), pp. 30–1. On an earlier set of vernacular documents in politics, see Henry III's letters, discussed in Machan, *English in the Middle Ages*, pp. 21–69.

[68] For letters testimonial proving English ancestry, see, for example, *A Volume of English Miscellanies illustrating the History and Language of the Northern Counties of England*, ed. J. Raine, Surtees Society, 85 (Durham, 1890), pp. 35ff. For one certifying good reputation, see ERO, D/B 5 R2 [Colchester Red Paper Book], fos. 198r–199r, a copy of a testimonial letter made in 1493 by citizens of Colchester on behalf of Thomas Parker, 'in salvation of his good name'.

[69] Dodd, 'The Spread of English', p. 236.

being made to come to an agreement, by working around the formulae of Latinate legalese that such settlements were attempting to avoid. Thus, for example, two squires of Richmondshire concluded a bitter boundary dispute in 1478 with a finicky arbitration document, including the provision that Richard Clairvaux and his wife should 'sitt in þere parishe churche chaunsell on the southside in such placis as he and hys ancestres and þeire wyffys hertofor have allweys used to sitte and none oþer wysse'; another provision specified that if his dogs ran outside of his lands while chasing after a hare, then he should not follow them, but try to call them back—but his rival, Roland Place, should only 'rebuke þame and no noder hurt ne damage do þame'.[70] Such a document might just as well have been written in Latin, of course, but in English it signalled a closeness to the nitty-gritty details of the negotiations that had produced it.

In a similar way, the authenticity of English was part of what made it so effective as a language of petitioning in the later Middle Ages, because it allowed a close rendition of the substance of the matter at hand that was unhindered by legal formulae.[71] Of course, rubrics for formal English writing—whether in letters, petitions, or other texts—developed as it came to be more widely adopted, partly under the influence of the *ars dictaminis* tradition; one authority has gone so far as to remark that 'even the casual reader of late medieval English correspondence can see that the letters are almost exclusively formulaic'.[72] If that is perhaps true in a formalistic sense, it disregards the extent to which English offered clerical writers a new vocabulary for legal expression. As Wendy Scase has recently argued, there lies an alternative tradition in the experiments in the 'literature of clamour' in the later fourteenth century, when many Middle English writers attempted to give creative voice to extrajudicial plaint, in both literary modes and in actual supplications.[73] The point of all this, for our purposes here, is that even if English developed its own conventions, its flexibility meant that it could function as a more authentic transcription of a plaintiff's intent.

To give an illustration of this, we can turn to the letters of Thomas Walyngton, which I examined in some detail in Chapter 6.[74] In the first two decades of the fifteenth century, he wrote (or caused to be written) two petitions to Walter, Lord Hungerford, one in French, and another in English, and a comparison of the two is instructive. The French petition is vanishingly short, comprising just sixty-three words, conforms tightly to dictaminial formulae, and makes a simple request:

[70] The document was copied into Richard Clairvaux's cartulary: NYCRO, ZQH 1, fos. 155r–156v.

[71] Dodd, 'The Spread of English', p. 236.

[72] Malcolm Richardson, 'The *Dictamen* and its Influence on Fifteenth-Century English Prose', *Rhetorica: A Journal of the History of Rhetoric*, 2:3 (1984), 207–26, at p. 214; see also, by the same author, 'The Fading Influence of the Medieval *Ars Dictaminis* in England After 1400', *Rhetorica: A Journal of the History of Rhetoric*, 19:2 (2001), 225–47.

[73] Scase, *Literature and Complaint*, Ch. 5, pp. 170–86. This is a concise summary that does not do full justice to the complex and multilayered argument she presents.

[74] See Chapter 6, pp. 201–2.

'he is maliciously asked to pay "housebote" in his common meadow lands in the franchise of Hungerford, may it please you to grant the said supplicant your good counsel'.[75] His English petition, sent some time later, is not only over five times longer, but shows much greater ease of expression. While it also follows conventional forms of address and salutation, these are far more elaborate, going into great detail in its expression of humility, obeisance, and loyalty.[76] And, moreover, Walyngton found far greater latitude to explain his problem in the vernacular: he wrote of being 'manesset' (menaced), 'never yfayne' (not happy), 'a pressid', and 'yturment in evrywyse' by his enemy William Derrell, who 'say þat he nell [kneel] for no man'.[77] As a legal language, English allowed colloquial expressions such as these to coexist with formal conventions, within an expressive and authentic language of plaint.

In sum, English had a number of particular qualities as a legal language, which enabled scribes to achieve rhetorical effects, most of them bound up with the idea of English as the language of the 'common people'. As I have suggested here, English evoked orality, and thus came to be used to transcribe and ordain legal speech acts, and also to suggest that vernacular legal documents were tied to such speech acts. Its oral associations, moreover, gave it a public quality, allowing scribes to suggest that legal documents written in English were widely known, and that they provided a close representation of common knowledge on matters such as custom. And finally, as we have just seen, English also provided a more authentic language for law, as its flexibility both signified a willingness to work beyond formulaic constraints, and also offered more creative possibilities for legal expression. Of course, for all these qualities, there remained things that English could not do—it never became a 'language for writs' in the later Middle Ages. Yet across the documentary contexts in which it was used, English held legal value because of its associations with the commons; we now turn to look at the consequences of this for the common themselves.

The Common People's Language

Of course, English people had for a long time spoken about law in their own language. Paul Hyams is surely right that late-thirteenth- and early-fourteenth-century villagers, long inured in the workings of legal institutions, had their own

[75] MCO, Beenham 164. '...come ele est tourtousement hozebota de sez communes pratis terres deinz les fraunches de Hungerford... plese a vous de graunter a le dit suppliant vostre bone consaill'. 'Housebote' was a common Forest right, to take windfall from the lord's woods, for which a small annual fine was paid—the issue here is probably that it was a mark of customary tenure, and Walyngton considered himself of higher status.

[76] MCO, Letters 31. It is worth quoting in full: 'Reverent & worchepful Lord with al humilite of hertt ye recomend me un to ȝow Thomas Walynton ȝowr dovoett beedman Wyllingg & desyringg to here of ȝowr welfare & prosperite for þe wech y praye everydaye as y am grettly bownd þer to and god quitt ȝow gracyus lorde wer y ne suffyce & ever gracyus lord I putt my governawns holly on ȝow as myn tryst ys in ȝow.'

[77] Ibid.

'vernacular conceptions of what is right and just' which fed into their understandings of law.[78] What changed, over the course of the later Middle Ages, was the cultural significance of the vernacular: if English was still 'þe comoun peplis langage', as the bishop Reginald Pecock put it in the early fifteenth century, then it was also becoming widely accepted as a written language through which legal concepts might be legitimately framed.[79] In what follows, I try to apprehend the effects of this for common people, in ways that map roughly onto the values of legal English that we examined in the previous section. First, I examine the increasing legal attention that was paid to vernacular speech; we then turn to the use of English as a language for the transcription of custom; and finally, to English as a language of plaint. Overall, I suggest that the effects of vernacularization were ambivalent; while it undoubtedly opened up new possibilities for the way that common people engaged with legal authorities, it also opened up new mechanisms of control.

To begin with, the way in which various legal institutions apprehended speech acts was changing in late-medieval England. In the first place, as Richard Helmholz has written, 'spoken words gave rise to the great majority of causes that came before the English ecclesiastical courts during the later Middle Ages'.[80] While the overwhelming mass of these vernacular words were never written down in that language, it became increasingly common for church courts in this period to transcribe English phrases that look tantalizingly like 'real' speech acts, though such transcriptions were often appended with the formula 'or words to that effect'.[81] The reasons for these new recording practices may well lie in doctrinal changes. In particular, the growing trend for alleged defamatory words to be transcribed in English may well relate to subtle transformations during the fifteenth century to the legal criteria for defamation, which made it more important to record precisely the speech in question.[82] The 'shamefoll tales' that ordinary

[78] Paul Hyams, 'What did Edwardian Villagers Understand by "Law"?', in *Medieval Society and the Manor Court*, ed. Zvi Razi and Richard Smith (Oxford, 1996), 69–100, p. 92.

[79] See Sarah James, '"Langagis, whose reules ben not writen": Pecock and the Uses of the Vernacular', in *Vernacularity in England and Wales*, ed. Salter and Wicker, 101–17, pp. 103, 106, 110.

[80] Helmholz, *Canon Law and Ecclesiastical Jurisdiction*, p. 565.

[81] This phrase, 'in anglicis dicendo verba subscripta seu alia eis in effectu consimilia', was common, e.g. in a case before the London commissary in 1471: LMA, DL/C/B/043/MS9064/2, fo. 27v. On the methodological issues at work in such testimonies, see Tom Johnson, 'The Preconstruction of Witness Testimony: Law and Social Discourse in England before the Reformation', *L&HR*, 32:1 (2014), 127–47.

[82] There are two considerations here. First, Helmholz has suggested that 'from at least the middle of the fifteenth century' the criterion for the imputation of a specific crime (e.g. "you stole this sheep from me") was breaking down, allowing plaintiffs to allege general defamations (e.g. "you are a thief"). Second, particularly in the later fifteenth century, the legal opinion emerged that defamation in the church courts ought to be restricted to the imputation of spiritual crimes (e.g. adultery), and that the imputation of secular crimes (e.g. theft) were a matter for the royal courts; this shift appears to have been the basis for the development of the common-law action of slander in the early sixteenth century. These two observations come from R. H. Helmholz, *Select Cases on Defamation to 1600*, Selden Society 101 (London, 1985), pp. xxix–xxx and xliii–xlv.

parishioners found themselves hauled before the courts for repeating, then, were increasingly transcribed in vernacular form.[83]

A similar trend, albeit one that emerged earlier and for different reasons, can be seen in the secular courts. From around the turn of the fifteenth century, the Statute of Treasons of 1352 came to be understood to have comprised 'treason by words'; thus there began a raft of cases in the royal criminal courts focused on words spoken against the king.[84] Over the course of the fifteenth century, such seditious language was more often recorded in English.[85] This scrutiny of speech was certainly driven by the fractious political atmosphere: the perceived fragility of the Lancastrian regime, the apparent threat of Lollardy to the English Church, and of course a piercing memory of the events of 1381 meant that secular authorities of all kinds, via their networks of officers, paid increasingly close attention to what common people were saying.[86] Yet it is important to note also the concurrence of important changes in the regulation of speech in local secular courts, as the late fourteenth century saw the decline of the hue and cry as a mechanism of communal policing and the rise of 'scolding' presentments.[87] This parallel deserves further attention, but, as Samantha Sagui has suggested in her study of the hue in later medieval Norwich, there are compelling connections to be found between changes in social organization, political culture, and the policing of words.[88]

All in all, anxieties about how to control deviant speech thus became a hallmark of late-medieval English legal culture.[89] The vernacularity of that speech was important. In the first place, as I have been suggesting, there is a connection between the tightening regulation of speech and the increasing—if not universal—transcription

[83] This phrase was uttered by the Londoner Alice Salter, who in 1492 was said to have defamed Katerina Burton of bad governance [est mali regiminis], saying 'and thow summyn me to the court I shall tell the shamefoll tale by the as may be thought'. LMA, DL/C/B/043/MS9064/5, fo. 159v.

[84] See the discussion in J. G. Bellamy, *The Law of Treason in the Later Middle Ages* (Cambridge, 1970), pp. 107–8, 116–18; also Paul Strohm, *England's Empty Throne: Usurpation and the Language of Legitimation 1399–1422* (New Haven, CT, 1998), pp. 25–7.

[85] Generally, see Helen Wicker, 'The Politics of Vernacular Speech: Cases of Treasonable Language, c.1440–1453', in *Vernacularity in England and Wales*, ed. Salter and Wicker, 171–97.

[86] Generally, see Simon Walker, 'Rumour, Sedition and Popular Protest in the Reign of Henry IV', *P&P*, 166 (2000), 31–65. For lollardy, see Margaret Aston, 'Lollardy and Sedition 1381–1431', *P&P*, 17 (1960), 1–44; for towns, Christopher Fletcher, 'News, Noise, and the Nature of Politics in Late Medieval English Provincial Towns', *Journal of British Studies*, 56 (2017), 250–72; Christian D. Liddy, 'Cultures of Surveillance in Late Medieval English Towns: The monitoring of speech and the fear of revolt', in *The Routledge History Handbook of Medieval Revolt*, ed. Justine Firnhaber-Baker with Dirk Schoenaers (London and New York, 2017), 311–29. Similar trends are perceptible elsewhere in Europe: see Jan Dumolyn and Jelle Haemers, '"A Bad Chicken was Brooding": Subversive Speech in Late Medieval Flanders', *P&P*, 214 (2012), 45–86.

[87] Sandy Bardsley, *Venomous Tongues: Speech and Gender in Late Medieval England* (Philadelphia, 2006), Ch. 3, pp. 69–89.

[88] Samantha Sagui, 'The hue and cry in medieval English towns', *Historical Research*, 87:236 (2014), 179–93.

[89] For a broader perspective on deviant speech in medieval culture, see the essays in *The Hands of the Tongue: Essays on Deviant Speech*, ed. Edwin D. Craun (Kalamazoo, MI, 2007).

of speech in English.[90] But the cases in which officials (and scribes) did use English in their reports were often those in which precision was deemed important. In a febrile political atmosphere, it was important to decipher cryptic vernacular allusions or popular witticisms, as with the chaplain who compared Henry IV to a *haysugge*, or hedge-sparrow, or the Dutchman who said Henry VI 'lokyd more lyke a childe than a man', and that he would replace the emblem of a ship on the coinage with than of a sheep.[91] And at the level of local social relations, church courts frequently had to determine whether, for example, it was defamatory to say things such as 'thy husband may sing coko a Friday', as Joan Bulwyk did of Margaret Mendam in the London parish of St Mary Aldermanbury.[92] Even while erratically deployed, the use of English to record vernacular speech was ultimately a technology of legal control.[93]

The impulses behind its deployment become very clear in some instances. For example, an inquiry was made in 1460 into whether a writ of arrest was delivered to Thomas Bowgelmaker, after his master, Simon Tabeler, accosted the royal sub-bailiff who had brought it. Tabeler's angry words were recorded in English ('Thou shall not arrest hym here, and yif thou wylt hym arrest I shall sle the here with my daggar'), but the official's response to him was recorded in Latin ('If you do not permit me to have the aforesaid Thomas Bowgelmaker and you do not wish to obey the arrest, I will return [a response to the writ] that you committed a rescue [i.e. a forcible obstruction]'). In turn, Simon replied, 'I set not a halfpennyworth of ale be the, do thi worst.'[94] Such a bizarrely bilingual rendering of this conversation is only comprehensible if we understand the vernacular provided a deliberative documentary mode of surveilling illicit speech, rather than some kind of 'fissure' or parapraxis in the text.[95] Just as significant is the figuration of the legal official's words in Latin, drawing a stark contrast between the Latinate weight of authority that lay behind an official's oral commands and the voluble colloquialisms of the common voice. The increasing use of the vernacular to record speech in such contexts was inextricably related to attempts to monitor and discipline such voices.

[90] Colloquial insults or subversive words were still sometimes translated into Latin throughout the fifteenth century. For example, a Norfolk scribe in 1417 went to the trouble of translating a defamation defendant's plea that they had said something like "I cannot piss holy water like you can" (fatebatur se dixisse alia verba seu consimilia, "ego nescio mingere aquam benedictam veluti tu scis"): NRO, DCN67/1, m. 3r.

[91] Respectively, TNA, KB 27/582, m. 3v; KB 9/262, no 2. The first example is discussed in Walker, 'Rumour and Sedition', p. 35; the latter (which was a trope) in Wicker, 'Politics of Vernacular Speech', pp. 193–5.

[92] Joan successfully compurgated against the charge: LMA, DL/C/B/043/MS9064/5, fo. 10r.

[93] There is also an analogue here with the idea that descriptions of sexual abuse in ecclesiastical depositions ought to be understood as voyeuristic, even pornographic texts, suggested in Goldberg, *Communal Discord*, pp. 110–11.

[94] TNA, KB 9/291, no. 73: the Latin is 'nisi tu permittas me habere prefatum Thomam Bowgemaker et arrestum predictum obedire volueris ego retornabo super te rescursum in hac parte'.

[95] On such notions, see Justice, *Writing and Rebellion*, p. 7.

This is not to suggest that all these developments were unequivocally negative for the common subjects of legal authority. For those people who were summoned to make formal legal depositions before the church courts and in some other contexts, for example, the increasing tendency for testimonies to be recorded in English also offered some opportunities to shape the terms of debate; as I have argued elsewhere, witnesses were not only keenly partisan in the way that they testified for one side or another, but were also adept in manipulating the specific conceptual language that emerged from these disputes.[96] It does not seem a stretch to suggest that the recording of their depositions in English enhanced their ability to sway these cases—a point to which we shall return to just below in relation to the articulation of custom. Yet such opportunities were relatively rare in late-medieval England, and insofar as such vernacular transcriptions were still subject to the scrutiny and judgment of ecclesiastical officials, they seem to be the exception that proves the rule. The growing use of English to record deviant speech undoubtedly indicates, as Helen Wicker has put it, 'the fact that the voices that spoke them could no longer be overlooked'.[97] But, as I have been suggesting here, such supervision was ultimately a means of coercive legal authority.

Turning to the second point, the use of the vernacular as a language of custom was similarly ambivalent for common people, albeit for quite different reasons. To begin with, it does seem possible that the transcription of customs in English offered certain tenants (older, more 'trustworthy', male tenants, of course) the opportunity to dictate the form in which they were expressed, and, consequently, to shape some of the rules and obligations which were to govern their agricultural community.[98] We can see something like this at work in an unusual roll of vernacular depositions relating to a piece of common land, or 'lings', at Litcham in Norfolk, surviving from the first decades of the fifteenth century.[99] Although the roll itself gives no explanation of why these twelve depositions—from nine old men and three elderly women who had grown up in the village—were taken, it is clear from their substance that they were produced within the context of a challenge to the exclusive rights of Litcham tenants to the use of the lings, against

[96] Johnson, 'Preconstruction of Witness Testimony', pp. 143–5.

[97] Wicker, 'Politics of Vernacular Speech', p. 196.

[98] On the knowledge work of generating custom, see Chapter 6, pp. 206–7. A similar point has been made about custumals in particular, in Andy Wood, *The Memory of the People: Custom and Popular Senses of the Past in Early Modern England* (Cambridge, 2013), pp. 59–60.

[99] NRO, KIM 1/9/16. This document is discussed in Philippa Maddern, 'Imagining the Unchanging Land: East Anglians Represent their Landscape, 1350–1500', in *Medieval East Anglia*, ed. Christopher Harper-Bill (Norwich, 2005), 52–67, at pp. 66–7. She dates the document to the 1420s. A date of around this time is likely; the will of one of the witnesses, Thomas Bulwer, was proved in 1429. By this time he was half-rector of Narborough, some twelve miles distant from Litcham, but had a nephew who still lived there. NRO, NCC will register 'Surflete', fo. 52r.

the claims of people from the neighbouring settlements of Mileham, Beeston, and Kempston.[100]

The vernacularity of these depositions is complex. The document is in some ways highly formulaic. Witnesses were clearly asked to testify to specific subjects, which were indexed with small labels sewn on to the side of the roll—'pasturyng', 'of turvis', 'drying of ffysh'—and after every statement that they enjoyed a right on the lings was appended the phrase 'without the letting of any man'.[101] Yet the vernacularity of the depositions also seems to have permitted some slippage between these conventional images of commoning with looser affirmations. For example, William Boter dutifully spoke about digging gravel and clay, flacks and turves, the distraint of foreign cattle, and common boundaries, before saying that he 'saugh diverse times & often pleyes pleyed up on þe fornseyd lyngs, made be þo men of Lucham, þat is to seyne steraclis [pageants], schetyngs [archery], wrestlyngs, renning for þe spere, rennyng at þe fotbal for kaks [cakes], with owten lettyng of ani man'.[102] Many of the other witnesses recalled such festivities. But if it was thus understood as a conventional image, in this colloquial English it also seems to capture a more indistinct sense of common ownership rooted in a vernacular sense of place, rather than a purely legalistic rehearsal of rights—and indeed, the way in which these two ways of understanding the lings co-existed in the minds of the witnesses.

The transcription of these customs in English, while it was undoubtedly part of a broader rhetorical strategy aimed at signifying the legitimacy of the claims that were being made, allowed the witnesses a greater degree of action in formulating the terms of the dispute. We can see similar dynamics at work in other vernacular attestations, such as the English 'statutes' made at Wymeswold in Leicestershire, roughly contemporary with those of Litcham.[103] While this document had a far more normative purpose in setting out by-laws for the common fields there, its vernacularity enabled a far more expansive sense of the practical workings of these customs; thus it was specified that gleaners were not to 'bere hom no scheves of no mannes bot if they be given hem well and truly'.[104] These words 'well and truly'—which, tellingly, were later redacted—reveal something of the moral economy that took place out in the harvest fields, and the pragmatics of the negotiations between the marginal poor (for whom the vernacular, of course, did little) and the customary tenantry. Such documents, even as they deployed English to emphasize

[100] The otherwise blank verso of the roll contains what looks like a contemporary archival memorandum: 'Md that all the deposiscons expressed with ynne this Rolle be conteyned in a nother gret rolle beryng this signe', which was 'Lucham', written across the top half of a cross.

[101] NRO, KIM 1/9/16, m. 1r, next to the statements of Thomas Bulwer.

[102] Ibid., m. 2r.

[103] *Report on the manuscripts of Lord Middleton, preserved at Wollaton hall, Nottinghamshire*, ed. William Henry Stevenson, Historical Manuscripts Commission (Hereford, 1911) , 106–9.

[104] Ibid., p. 108.

the authenticity of custom, thus do seem to have more closely captured its vernacular logic.

Of course, most enunciations of custom in the fifteenth century were still written in Latin. It is telling that when English did break through in this context, as for example in the court rolls of Bradbourne, mentioned earlier in this chapter, it was clearly associated with the making and breaking of by-laws, suggesting once again this connection between vernacularity and custom.[105] Yet such instances, along with the kinds of document made at Litcham and Wymeswold, were exceedingly rare within the broader field of late-medieval by-laws and customary declarations; but, in fact, in their exceptionality they provide some light by which we can see more clearly the stakes of the linguistic conservatism in manorial court rolls.[106] In a world in which it had become thinkable (and in some contentious cases even desirable) to write customs in the vernacular, the continued and repetitive denial of this possibility in these rolls seems more concrete. This is not to say it was a deliberate tendency on the part of manorial scribes; on the contrary, it is an instance of the way that convenience, training, and tradition can absorb and deflect the possibility of social change. While the vernacularization of custom might have opened up some opportunities for tenants, then, its effects were constrained by the authoritative weight of the Latin matrix language in manorial documentation.

Turning to the final point, perhaps the clearest benefits of the use of English for common people can be discerned in the emergence of a vernacular language of petitioning. Much attention has been paid to the petitions sent to the equitable jurisdiction of the Chancellor (and to a lesser extent, the bills presented to parliament), but here I want to focus on those produced for local courts. We shall look at these documents in more detail in Chapter 8, where I focus on their qualities as a media technology, but here I would like to consider their linguistic functions.[107] Local petitions, as they came to be written in English, permitted a particularly flexible form of legal communication; while it could draw from the deep well of vernacular discourse about law and right, it was also highly tolerant of neologisms, and of concepts borrowed from Latin and French.[108] While it is undoubtedly true, as we have seen, that English petitions developed their own genre conventions within which petitioners had to work, the possibility of using the vernacular still offered a particularly plastic language to craft legitimate plaint.

[105] DRO, D9392/M1, mm. 3r–4r. On a smaller scale, the words '*anglice* surchard' were inserted into a by-law against overcommoning at West Hendred (Berkshire) in 1509: CCCO, Bb 1/3.

[106] As does the translation of older Latin custumals into English during the fifteenth century: see e.g. P. Woods, 'The Parsonage, or Rectory Manor of Godalming, and a Fourteenth-Century Custumal Thereof', *Surrey Archaeological Collections*, 22 (1909), 12–36.

[107] See Chapter 8, For the qualities of petitions as media, see below, pp. 253–4.

[108] A similar remark has been made in relation to post-Conquest Latin: from Catto, 'Written English', p. 33.

To begin with, the proliferation of bills sent to ecclesiastical judges ahead of late-medieval parochial visitations often used the vernacular in clever ways, blurring the boundaries between the reporting of information and the solicitation of remedy. For example, a bill sent to visiting judges by the parish notables of Worlaby (Lincolnshire) in 1473 was formulated as a petition, beginning 'Reverent and worschypfull lorde, with all our service as lawly as we can to your worthy lyves'.[109] It then reverts to the gossipy reports found in all visitation bills, with the 'knawlege' that the vicar there was keeping a concubine, which had gone unpunished for more than six years. But it ends as a petition, with an explicit request: 'we beseke yow of your gracius lordschip that ... thei may be correktyd'. Clearly, these parishioners saw the petition as the best genre in which to construct this complaint about the morality of their priest. The vernacular allowed them to play upon the Latinate language of 'correction' at the same time as invoking the petitionary discourse of good lordship that made it possible to make an explicit request of the official. Legal English could fuse genres of legal communication, enabling the laity to shape ecclesiastical procedures to their own purposes.

This facility was put to good use outside of institutional contexts, too, enabling common people to claim the authority of legal expertise in their own language. For example, a vernacular petition sent in 1485 by tenants in Frettenham, in Norfolk, to their lord, the Duke of Gloucester, issues a number of grievances against the misdeeds of local officials in the manorial court, and asks the duke for justice. Complaining that a man named Thomas Whyte had distrained their cattle for the payment of undue taxes, 'the seid pore tenantes were fayne to sue replegidre to have here catell, to there gret costes ... wheche trubeles and vexacones putte þe seyd tenantes to there finiall destruccon, withowte the better remedy may be had by your good & gracious lordshep'.[110] The use of the tropes of plaint—the 'poor tenants', the 'gracious lord', and the hope of remedy—was entirely conventional, of course, but in the vernacular they also bracket a distinctive legal idea when the tenants mention their reluctance to sue replevin ('replegidre') as a way of claiming back their cattle.[111]

We should not be surprised, of course, that the tenants were aware of this most common of common-law writs.[112] Yet by naming it in English, the technical vocabulary of law was seamlessly incorporated into a supplication that also drew on rather less technical, vernacular terms, such as 'trouble' and 'vexation', as a means of conveying the great injustice to which the tenants had been subjected. They were thus able to depict themselves as serious petitioners, cognizant of the legal avenues that might have been open to them, without seeming—as

[109] LA, Vj/4, annex to fo. 21r. [110] OBL, Norfolk Charters 109.

[111] On replevin, see David J. Seipp, 'The Concept of Property in the Early Common Law', *L&HR*, 12:1 (1994), 29–91, at pp. 58–60.

[112] Anthony Musson, *Medieval Law in Context: The growth of legal consciousness from Magna Carta to the Peasants' Revolt* (Manchester, 2001), p. 101.

they might have done had their petition been written in Latin or French—so well-versed in the ways of law that their claims of poverty, and their request for assistance, seemed false. Like John Bedowe's petitions to the mayor of Hereford, with which this chapter began, the use of the vernacular as a language of petitioning enabled people to creatively combine different registers of legal discourse—pulling at both popular notions of justice and official notions of correct procedure—to great rhetorical effect.

In sum, the growing legitimacy of English as a legal language in the later Middle Ages had ambivalent effects for common people; the different documentary contexts of vernacularization were crucial to the kinds of possibility it opened up in their engagements with law. As we have seen, the use of the vernacular to monitor and record speech, while it undoubtedly signalled the increasing authority of the popular voice, was ultimately a mode of legal control. And while transcriptions of custom in English did offer some tenants more opportunity to modulate its recorded forms, these were relatively rare within the context of manorial documentary production, which remained resolutely bound to Latinate forms. It is only in petitions that we can perceive more straightforward benefits to the utilization of a legal English, as it offered the flexibility to hold together the technicalities of legal discourse with more creative explorations of vernacular conceptions of right. The effects of vernacularization, then, the possibilities and constraints it entailed, were closely bound to the documentary forms and surfaces which they provided for vernacularity.

Conclusion

This chapter has argued that the fifteenth century saw the emergence of the English vernacular as a widely accepted language of legal expression. I made three broad arguments. The first was that we need to nuance our understanding of the 'vernacularization' of law. There is little doubt that by 1500 the vernacular was used far more often, and in a much greater variety of documentation that it had been a century earlier. This shift has often been seen from the perspective of the political centre, but, as I have endeavoured to show here, we may better understand it through attention to the local contexts of documentary production. Such a heuristic not only shows the breadth of the uses of English throughout late-medieval society, but also highlights the significance of vernacularity as a quality of writing, even in kinds of documentation which remained Latinate throughout the Middle Ages. Conceptualizing the vernacularization of law as a more diffuse and stuttering cultural process enables us to better capture the significance of the forms in which it emerged.

This leads us, indeed, to look for its causes elsewhere than the changing practices of central institutions. Certainly, part of the explanation for the increasing use of the vernacular in law must be related to a wider shift in the uses of written English in the second half of the fourteenth century, as it was enshrined as a national language of literature and perhaps more importantly, a viable 'everyday' scribal mode. The latter development has not been given sufficient attention, and indeed more investigation of early 'business English' would pay large dividends for our understanding of this cultural shift.[113] Yet within the realm of law, as I have suggested here, we must also look to the changing values attributed to the vernacular. English came to signify certain qualities—orality, authenticity, and publicity—at the same time that the monitoring of speech, the authenticity of custom, and petition as a form of legal plaint were becoming increasingly important. Such developments were co-constitutive; the vernacularization of law was both a cause and an effect of cultural change.

And indeed, as I have been suggesting, the emergence of the legal vernacular was entangled with the broadening social base of participation in later medieval politics. As John Watts has compellingly shown, political culture in this period encompassed the engagement of a large and often ill-defined 'commons', not just in staged insurgencies or beneath the wings of aristocratic struggles, but as an essential condition of its operation and discourse.[114] While I wholeheartedly agree with these arguments, I also think that it is important to think about the limits of this fifteenth-century political culture, and the emergence of English as a legal language is a useful heuristic for this. In the first place, as I have been arguing here, vernacularization was not a straightforward correlate of a more open public discourse; rather, English was granted legitimacy on certain terms, within certain and restricted forms. While the vernacularization of law does, I think, reflect real changes in the balance of power in late-medieval society towards the commons—albeit in enormously complex and diffuse ways—the ways in which it was institutionalized stymied its more radical potential.

And, indeed, as a final point I would like to make a more speculative suggestion about the role of vernacular communication in public discourse. In his influential work on sixteenth-century Venice, Filippo di Vivo asked of the *popolo*: 'Is it possible to say that, barred from political action, they participated in political communication? Was communication, in fact, itself a form of political action?'[115] This question is an extremely useful lens through which to consider

[113] Catto, 'Written English', p. 37 asserts that 'business English' appears a generation after Chaucer.

[114] Watts, 'Popular Voices'; and, by the same author, 'The Pressure of the Public on Later Medieval Politics', in *Fifteenth Century IV: Political Culture in Late Medieval Britain*, ed. Linda Clark and Christine Carpenter (Woodbridge, 2004), 159–80; and 'Public or Plebs: The Changing Meaning of 'the Commons', 1381–1549', in *Power and Identity in the Middle Ages: Essays in Memory of Rees Davies*, ed. Huw Pryce and John Watts, (Oxford, 2007), 242–60. But cf. the more pessimistic view presented in Ian Forrest and Vincent Challent, 'The masses', in *Government and Political Life in England and France, c.1300–c.1500*, ed. Christopher Fletcher, Jean-Philippe Genet, and John Watts (Cambridge, 2015), 279–316.

[115] Filippo de Vivo, *Information and Communication in Venice: Rethinking Early Modern Politics* (Oxford, 2007), p. 2.

the current historiography on premodern political culture, which tends to extrapolate 'political action' among the commons from the top down, within the terms set for it by elites.[116] But if we can begin to understand everyday vernacular communications—not just those 'political' moments at which someone called the king a hedge-sparrow—as part of public discourse in fifteenth-century England, I think its political culture would begin to look rather different. Attention to this vernacular world of everyday communications would reveal its 'cold politics': forms of organization among the commons—such as church-ales, common funds, and perhaps even playing football for cakes—which did not translate into straightforwardly 'political' action. It is here, at the very margins of public discourse, that we might find the most interesting effects of the vernacularization of authority.

[116] Movements have been made in this direction by Fletcher, 'News, Noise, and the Nature of Politics'; Liddy, *Politics of Citizenship*, ch. 5, 125–64. I survey some of this historiography in Tom Johnson, 'News and Networks', in *A Cultural History of Media in the Middle Ages*, ed. Carol Symes (forthcoming).

8
Common Legal Documents

Introduction

Late-medieval England was a world awash with humdrum legal writings: from the huge, variegated mass of parchment and paper associated with manorial documentation and church administration to the great hordes of private legal instruments recording contracts, conveying property, and sealing agreements, and still rarer oddments. All such archival survivals hint at the 'lost archive' of routinely produced and discarded legal documents. These writings, though, are not mere witnesses to a vanished world; as Shannon McSheffrey has put it, documents themselves 'must also be understood as agents in the historical process'.[1] Written objects were not simply an after-effect of law, but essential to its contemporary functions and meanings. This chapter explores 'common' documents—those legal writings frequently encountered by common people, owned by them, or even commissioned or made by them—to consider how they could inflect our understanding of late-medieval law.

I make three main arguments. The first is that late-medieval England underwent a documentary revolution, as the vast majority of the population came to possess legal writings for themselves. There were many dynamics to this transformation: some were straightforward continuations of the earlier cultural transition 'from memory to written record' so memorably described by Michael Clanchy; others derived from new impulses within post-plague society, such as the tumultuous land market, and the growing ambition of government.[2] Historians have long noticed the apparent increase of writing in fifteenth-century England, but there have been few attempts to understand its significance, outside of the basic relationship that has been posited between literacy and social advancement.[3] Yet by focusing on the huge expansion of legal documents among the commons, we can move away from the problematic heuristic of 'literacy',

[1] Shannon McSheffrey, 'Detective Fiction in the Archives: Court Records and the Uses of Law in Late Medieval England', *History Workshop Journal*, 65 (2008), 65–78, p. 66.

[2] Michael Clanchy, *From Memory to Written Record: England 1066–1307* (2nd ed., Oxford, 1993).

[3] C. L. Kingsford, *Prejudice and Promise in XVth Century England: The Ford Lectures 1923–4* (Oxford, 1925); F. R. H. DuBoulay, *An Age of Ambition: English Society in the late Middle Ages* (London, 1970); Michael J. Bennett, 'Education and Advancement', in *Fifteenth-Century Attitudes: Perceptions of Society in Late Medieval England*, ed. Rosemary Horrox (Cambridge, 1994), 76–96.

Law in Common: Legal Cultures in Late-Medieval England. Tom Johnson, Oxford University Press (2020).

DOI: 10.1093/oso/9780198785613.001.0001

towards a more textured understanding of the relationship between writing and socio-political relations in the Middle Ages.[4]

This brings me to my second argument, which is that the late-medieval documentary revolution enabled many more people to do things with writing. While they had long encountered legal writings passively—hearing charters read aloud, seeing the compilation of court records, or swearing oaths on the gospels, for example—in the later Middle Ages their ownership of documents also enabled them to pursue their own legal aims.[5] This can be seen particularly in the proliferation of supplicatory writings that directly requested justice from remote authorities, but more generally in the ways that people used various documents in creative attempts to circumvent, cajole, or manipulate court processes.[6] New uses of writing, moreover, changed socio-legal relations, as non-elites banded together to commission elaborate legal documents, or families kept archives to defend their property rights. In some ways, then, the increased ownership of documents, both individually and collectively, gave such people more agency in their legal dealings.

My third argument, however, is that this rising tide of documents in the later Middle Ages served ultimately to constrain their flexibility of legal action. Documents subtly bound people to legal institutions in new ways. Indentured leases, testimonial letters, or financial certificates may have opened up a new route into the storehouse of legal authority, but they required people to make a series of small concessions in their subscription to institutional forms. Like the 'terms and conditions' to which we absent-mindedly agree online, legal writing implicitly set up technical rules of engagement that governed the play of interactions between common people and the local law-courts that they used.[7] While they now possessed some wherewithal in this engagement, they were little match for the late-medieval institutions built on mountains of parchment and paper, which could store and use documents in far more powerful ways. More people may have held more documents, but their documents came to hold them.

The first part of the chapter sets out the broader trajectories of the increase in writings in late-medieval England, as a crucial context for the arguments

[4] On the problems of defining 'literacy' for the Middle Ages, see Franz H. Bäuml, 'Varieties and Consequences of Medieval Literacy and Illiteracy', *Speculum*, 55:2 (1980), 237–65; C. F. Briggs, 'Literacy, reading, and writing in the medieval West', *Journal of Medieval History*, 26 (2000), 397–420; Leidulf Melve, 'Mapping Public Debates along the Oral–Literate Continuum (1100–1300)', *Along the Oral–Written Continuum: Types of Texts, Relations and their Implications*, ed. Slavica Rankovic, Leidulf Melve, and Else Mundal (Turnhout, 2010), 73–100.

[5] Clanchy, *From Memory to Written Record*, pp. 44–80, 96–100. More broadly, see Adam J. Kosto, *Making Agreements in Medieval Catalonia: Power, Order, and the Written Word, 1000–1200* (Cambridge, 2001), pp. 268–94.

[6] See the essays in *Medieval Petitions: Grace and Grievance*, ed. W. Mark Ormrod, Gwilym Dodd, and Anthony Musson (York, 2009).

[7] My thanks to Sethina Watson for this metaphor, and helping me think this issue through. A similar argument has been made in relation to modern 'cost-benefit analysis': see Andrea Mennicken and Peter Miller, 'Accounting, Territorialization and Power', *Foucault Studies*, 13 (2012), 4–24.

presented here about law. The second section looks in more detail at the vectors of 'documentary revolution' after the Black Death, with a particular focus on the appearance of copyhold tenure, the rise of identificatory documents, and the proliferation of bills. The third section considers the opportunities these writings presented to non-elites, and considers the strategies that went into their formulation and presentation. The fourth section shows how everyday engagements with law became increasingly ensnared within processes and objects of writing, from the summonses that brought people to court to the documents which they were expected to bring with them, and the consequences of this. The conclusion, finally, considers the broader implications of these arguments for how we should understand the 'peculiar movement' by which law's 'transfer of force' took place in the late Middle Ages.[8]

The Production of Writing in Late-Medieval England

In order to understand why the documentary revolution came about, we need to look at some of the broader changes in the production of writing in late-medieval England. There is a broad historiographical consensus, following the work of Clanchy, that the twelfth and thirteenth centuries witnessed a huge proliferation of writing, driven largely by bureaucracy.[9] Yet, with the exception of some piecemeal work on scriveners, there is no such paradigm to explain how these developments continued in the later Middle Ages.[10] As I shall briefly suggest here, the proliferation of bureaucratic writing endured, but it was intensified by new developments in governmental culture, and a set of new material conditions in the production of writing. In particular, the increasing numbers of writers along with the proliferation of paper made clerical writing much cheaper to produce, and much more widespread. These were crucial conditions for the documentary revolution described in the next section.

One of the most important continuities between the central and later Middle Ages is the persistent escalation of bureaucratic writing. This certainly took place in royal government: while the 'geometrical progression' of documentary increase did not endure, there still survive roughly four times as many documents from the fourteenth century as from the thirteenth.[11] There was also a great proliferation in

[8] Bruno Latour, *The Making of Law: An Ethnography of the Conseil d'État*, trans. Marina Brilman and Alain Pottage (Cambridge, 2010), p. 143.

[9] Though cf. the argument, against Clanchy, for an even earlier such transition in England, in Nicholas Karn, 'Information and its retrieval', in *A Social History of England, 900–1200*, ed. Julia Crick and Elisabeth Van Houts (Cambridge, 2011), 373–80.

[10] On scriveners, see Kitrina Bevan, 'Clerks and Scriveners: Legal Literacy and Access to Justice in Late Medieval England', unpublished PhD thesis, University of Exeter (2013).

[11] For the idea of 'geometrical progression': Clanchy, *From Memory to Written Record*, p. 58. A very crude sense of this later-medieval increase can be gained by looking at the numbers of documents

ecclesiastical record-making and record-keeping in this period, particularly in diocesan administration.[12] For both secular and church governments, the reason for this increase in documentation is straightforward: they were attempting to do more.[13] Major foreign wars required new scales and methods of taxation and provisions for defence, which brought more people into the scope and exercise of government, and binding them up with new modes of peacekeeping; meanwhile, the programme of pastoral reform pursued by the late-medieval church involved ever closer scrutiny and discipline of the laity.[14] Many of the processes that underlay all this government, following what were by this time well-entrenched imperatives of bureaucratic accountability, were written.[15]

This expansive bureaucracy was not confined strictly to governmental institutions, however. Precisely the same processes of expansion served to disperse governmental agency to officers in the localities, from the powerful gentlemen who filled county offices and served as justices of the peace, down to the constables and jurymen of the village, and the 'trustworthy men' who acted for the parish.[16] All of these men made, used, and kept written records in ways that well exceeded the bounds of the 'pragmatic literacy' required by their official responsibilities.[17] We have known for a long time how deeply fifteenth-century English gentry lived in a world of writing, in their vast letter collections, literary commissions, and

preserved in governmental departments in TNA: in Exchequer, the rough figures are 8,500 from the thirteenth century, 34,000 from the fourteenth; for the Chancery, the figures are 13,000 and 59,000 respectively.

[12] Some sense of this increase can be gained in David M. Smith, *Guide to Bishops' Registers of England and Wales: A Survey from the Middle Ages to the Abolition of Episcopacy in 1646* (London, 1981), and *The Records of the Medieval Ecclesiastical Courts Part II: England*, ed. Charles Donahue (Berlin, 1994).

[13] On royal government, see Gerald Harriss, 'Political Society and the Growth of Government in Late Medieval England', *P&P*, 138 (1993), 28–57; W. M. Ormrod, *Political Life in Medieval England, 1300–1450* (Basingstoke, 1995). For similar developments in the church, see Ian Forrest, *The Detection of Heresy in Late-Medieval England* (Oxford, 2006).

[14] The classic version of this 'war state' thesis is put in Richard W. Kaeuper, *War, Justice, and Public Order: England and France in the Later Middle Ages* (Oxford, 1988); a compelling critique and revision can be found in John Watts, *The Making of Polities: Europe, 1300–1500* (Cambridge, 2009). For the consequences of pastoral reform, see Norman Tanner and Sethina Watson, 'Least of the laity: the minimum requirements for a medieval Christian', *Journal of Medieval History*, 32 (2006), 395–423.

[15] See John Sabapathy, *Officers and Accountability in Medieval England 1170–1300* (Oxford, 2014).

[16] On gentry officers, see Christine Carpenter, *Locality and Polity: A Study of Warwickshire Landed Society, 1401–1499* (Cambridge, 1992); generally on constables, Anthony Musson, *Public Order and Law Enforcement: The Local Administration of Criminal Justice 1294–1350* (Woodbridge, 1996); on jurors, James Masschaele, *Jury, State, and Society in Medieval England* (New York, 2008); on local church administrators, Ian Forrest, *Trustworthy Men: How Inequality and Faith Made the Medieval Church* (Princeton, NJ, 2018).

[17] This term originated in M. B. Parkes, 'The literacy of the laity', in *Scribes, scripts, and readers: studies in the communication, presentation, and dissemination of medieval texts* (London, 1991), 275–97; more generally, see Helen Lacey, 'Pragmatic Literacy and Political Consciousness in Later Medieval England', *Cahiers électroniques d'histoire textuelle du LaMOP*, 5 [issue: L'écriture pragmatique. Un concept d'histoire médiévale à l'échelle européenne] (2012), 38–70.

bureaucratic responsibilities, and the ways in which these different textualities intersected.[18] Yet, with the exception of Steven Justice's path-breaking work on modes of rural literacy, the extent to which this same density of writing penetrated local governance is yet to be fully appreciated.[19]

The personal book of Robert Reynes, for example, probably compiled over the last couple of decades of the fifteenth century, is a remarkable example of how 'official' writing in the village spurred and intersected with a more pervasive culture of collecting information.[20] The son of a carpenter from the village of Acle in Norfolk, we know very little about Reynes's life other than from the material he assembled in his book. We know that he was a churchwarden in the mid-1470s, and an alderman of the parish guild of St Edmund in the late 1490s, because he transcribed their accounts. It seems likely that he was a reeve for the manor, because he also copied in a rental, among other court documents. Yet he also clearly collected information that interested him personally, such as a note of historic fires in Acle, a list of guns that Venice had sent to the Ottoman crusade, and many medical charms and recipes. Local administrators like Reynes produced written information along several different axes of institutional authority, then, and writing saturated their lives on a new scale.

If the survival of his book was unusual, Reynes himself was not. Far more people in the later fourteenth and fifteenth centuries possessed the ability to read, and perhaps write, because of a great expansion in the provision of literate education. In a quantitative study of schools founded in late-medieval York diocese, Jo Moran discovered a growth in the number of parish 'reading' or 'song' schools, with an appreciable take-off in numbers after 1350, and an even greater proliferation after 1400.[21] These kinds of school taught children to read, write, and make accounts—such skills were specifically mentioned in the curricula of village elementary schools in rural Yorkshire in the late fifteenth century—as the foundations for clerical training.[22] This period also saw the foundation of more grammar schools, which taught the advanced Latin required for further study, and the establishment of institutions, particularly in Oxford and London, that were devoted specifically to quasi-legal 'business' training, in matters such as land conveyancing.[23]

[18] A good summary of this can be found in Colin Richmond, 'Hand and Mouth: Information gathering and use in England in the later middle ages', *Journal of Historical Sociology*, 1.3 (1988), 233–52.

[19] See Steven Justice, *Writing and Rebellion: England in 1381* (Berkeley, CA, 1994).

[20] *The Commonplace Book of Robert Reynes of Acle: An Edition of Tanner MS 407*, ed. Cameron Louis (London, 1980).

[21] Jo Ann Hoeppner Moran, *The Growth of English Schooling 1340–1548: Learning, Literacy, and Laicization in Pre-Reformation York Diocese* (Princeton, NJ, 1985), Ch. 4, 92–122, esp. 'Chart 1', on p. 118.

[22] Ibid., p. 50.

[23] H. G. Richardson, 'An Oxford Teacher of the Fifteenth Century', *Bulletin of the John Rylands Library*, 23:2 (1939), 436–57; Janice Gordon Richter, 'Education and association: the bureaucrat in the reign of Henry VI', *Journal of Medieval History*, 12 (1986), 81–9; Caroline Barron, 'The Expansion of Education in Fifteenth-Century London', in *The Cloister and the World: Essays in Medieval History in Honour of Barbara Harvey*, ed. John Blair and Brian Golding (Oxford, 1996).

These developments in education appear to have resulted in a surfeit of clerical workers in late-medieval England. Contemporaries themselves certainly perceived such an increase. When the 'writers of court hand' constituted themselves as a London guild in 1373, the preamble to their ordinances noted that various people 'who call themselves scriveners [*escryveyns*] and undertake to make wills, charters and all other things touching the said craft' were not only ignorant of the city's distinctive legal customs, but were 'also less skilled than the scriveners . . . who for a long time have been versed in their craft'.[24] Alongside the well-known rise in the numbers of ordained clergy in this period, and the relative scarcity of beneficed positions for them to fill, these flailing attempts to create and maintain a monopoly over documentary writing in the city imply an abundance of unregulated clerical labour.[25]

Even outside of the capital, 'scrivener' emerges clearly as a distinctive and widespread occupational identity in the later Middle Ages.[26] The activities of one such nameless professional operating in Bury St Edmunds during the early 1460s can be discerned from his register; a single folio records an apprenticeship contract, a recognizance of debt, a property grant, a receipt of payment, a will, and a house sale, among other things.[27] The volume of his work suggests that individual items were not expensive.[28] Technical legal writing required for ecclesiastical litigation was probably more dear—at between 8d. and 12d. for a citation, or 14d. for a witness deposition—whereas humdrum written process in an urban court, such as having a plea entered (4d.) or noting the appointment of an attorney (2d.), cost very little.[29] But most striking is that from the later fourteenth century many governmental institutions stopped retaining scriveners and started paying them piecemeal, creating a 'gig economy' which created incentives to take on as many jobs as they could manage.[30]

[24] *Scriveners' Company Common Paper 1357–1628 with a Continuation to 1678*, ed. Francis W. Steer, London Record Society (London, 1968), p. 2. Cf. the excoriating criticism of this edition in Richard Firth Green, 'The Early History of the Scriveners' Company Common Paper and its So-Called "Oaths"', in *Middle English Texts in Transition: A Festschrift dedicated to Toshiyuki Takamiya on his 70th birthday*, ed. Simon Horobin and Linne R. Mooney (Woodbridge, 2014), 1–20.

[25] On rising numbers of clergy, see Moran, *Growth of English Schooling*, pp. 123–49.

[26] Nigel Ramsay, 'Scriveners and Notaries as Legal Intermediaries in Later Medieval England', in *Enterprise and Individuals in Fifteenth-Century England*, ed. Jennifer Kermode (Stroud, 1991), 118–31.

[27] A. E. B. Owen, 'A Scrivener's Notebook from Bury St Edmunds', *Archives*, 14:61 (1979), 16–22, at p. 18. The manuscript is CUL, Add. MS. 7318 [fos. 59r–v].

[28] Rather more is known about scribal labour in literary production, the costs of which varied considerably: see Erik Kwakkel, 'Commercial organization and economic innovation', in *The Production of Books in England 1350–1500*, ed. Alexandra Gillespie and Daniel Wakelin (Cambridge, 2011), 173–91.

[29] For the cost of ecclesiastical citations (via a Lincoln proctor's bill of 1439), see Dorothy Owen, *The Medieval Canon Law: Teaching, Literature and Transmission* (Cambridge, 1990), pp. 28–9; for the witness deposition (albeit by a very skilled scribe, William Ebesham): A. I. Doyle, 'The Work of a Late Fifteenth-Century English Scribe, William Ebesham', *Bulletin of the John Rylands Library*, 39:2 (1957), 298–325, p. 300; for the town court costs (in Bristol), see Bevan, 'Clerks and Scriveners', pp. 108–9.

[30] Ramsay, 'Scriveners and Notaries', p. 121.

This cheaper labour was also made possible by changes to the nature of scribal production. A distinctive cursive script known as 'anglicana' had been used in England from the thirteenth century onwards for both literary and bureaucratic purposes, as an alternative to the elaborate Gothic 'textura'.[31] But from the middle of the fourteenth century, English scribes began to imitate styles of cursive found in continental Europe; these experiments developed into the distinctive script we now call 'secretary' hand.[32] Secretary, as its modern appellation indicates, quickly took hold as the script of choice for bureaucratic writings of all kinds (and to a lesser extent in the production of literary manuscripts), because it was much quicker to write. This, in turn, served to reduce the amount of time that scribes spent working on a writing project and, in turn, cut the cost of scribal labour in general.

Just as important, if not more so, was the growing use of paper in England. Prior to 1300 almost all permanent writing in England was conducted on parchment, made from stretched and treated animal skins.[33] From the middle of the fourteenth century onwards, however, paper from France and Italy began to be imported on a large scale by town governments, religious institutions, and central government for record-keeping purposes.[34] One of the major advantages of paper, mass-produced from recycled rags in water-powered mills that could produce as many as 2000 sheets every day, was its cheapness.[35] As early as 1400, paper was around eight times as cheap to buy as parchment; by the middle of the fifteenth century its cost had halved, and would halve again by 1500.[36] While paper was not used for all late-medieval administration, it was easily accessible and very widely used.

Altogether, then, these transformations, mainly in later-fourteenth-century England, enabled the considerable increase of writing that characterized late-medieval legality. The growth of governance brought more people to participate in written administration and to do so in more active ways, the expansion of education meant that there were more people able to write, and changes in the organization of scribal labour and the technology of manuscript production made

[31] A good overview in Erik Kwakkel, 'Decoding the material book: cultural residue in medieval manuscripts', in *The Medieval Manuscript Book: Cultural Approaches*, ed. Michael Johnston and Michael Van Dussen (Cambridge, 2015), 60–76, pp. 62, 68–9.

[32] Daniel Wakelin, 'Writing the Words', in *The Production of Books*, ed. Gillespie and Wakelin, 34–58, p. 42.

[33] Though cf. the widespread use of wax tablets for draft writing: Clanchy, *From Memory to Written Record*, p. 145; Michelle P. Brown, 'The Role of the Wax Tablet in Medieval Literacy: A reconsideration in light of a recent find from York', *The British Library Journal*, 20:1 (1994), 1–16.

[34] Orietta Da Rold, 'Materials', in *The Production of Books*, ed. Gillespie and Wakelin, 12–33, p. 24. For a more general survey on paper-making in Europe, Lothar Müller, *White Magic: The Age of Paper*, transl. Jessica Spengler (Cambridge, 2014), pp. 22–51.

[35] Timothy Barrett, 'Parchment, Paper, and Artisanal Research Techniques', in *Scraped, Stroked, and Bound: Materially Engaged Readings of Medieval Manuscripts*, ed. Jonathan Wilcox (Turnhout, 2013), 115–127, p. 117; Pamela Robinson, 'The format of books: books, booklets and rolls', in *The Cambridge History of the Book in Britain, Volume 2, 1100–1400*, ed. Nigel J. Morgan and Rodney M. Thomson (Cambridge, 2008), 41–54, p. 48.

[36] R. J. Lyall, 'Materials: the paper revolution', in *Book Production and Publishing in Britain*, ed. Jeremy Griffiths and Derek Pearsall (Cambridge, 1989), 11–29, p. 11.

such writings much cheaper to produce. That these changes were related is clear; how they were related is much harder to say, and indeed considerably more research is needed on the material and cultural production of non-literary writing in late-medieval England. But, regardless of what caused these shifts and which was determinative, this broader proliferation of clerical writing was undoubtedly crucial in underpinning the documentary revolution of this period, to which we now turn.

Vectors of Documentary Revolution

This 'documentary revolution' was a distinct transformation, representing above all a kind of change in material culture, as more people in England began to possess legal documents of their own. This was a revolutionary change because it involved a massification of writing technology within medieval society, and because it both represented and perpetuated significant changes in social and political organization, about which I shall say more in subsequent sections of this chapter. Here, though, I want to look at the three main vectors by which legal documents became objects of common ownership: first, the development of copyhold tenure, second, the drive towards identification and certification in a more mobile society, and third, the emergence of the bill as a legal medium. These changes followed quite different trajectories, driven by demographic, socio-economic, and legal phenomena, but they nonetheless converged to cause the creation of common legal documents on a vast scale.

The most important of these changes, affecting the most people, was the development of copyhold tenure. This is a subject that has long engaged historians interested in the 'decline of serfdom' in the period after the Black Death.[37] The decisive fall in the value of rural land in England after around 1380 led landlords to experiment with new forms of manorial lease designed to lure tenants, which in turn provoked significant upheaval to socio-economic structures such as tenure, personal freedom, and the land market.[38] Debates have centred on how and when

[37] Most recently, see Mark Bailey, *The Decline of Serfdom in Late Medieval England: From Bondage to Freedom* (Woodbridge, 2014).

[38] For an overview, see Christoper Dyer, 'England's Economy in the Fifteenth Century', in *The Fifteenth Century XIII: Exploring the Evidence: Commemoration, Administration and the Economy*, ed. Linda Clark (Woodbridge, 2014), 201–25. On the debate over villeinage and the 'seigneurial reaction', see Christopher Dyer, 'Villeins, Bondmen, Neifs, and Serfs: New Serfdom in England, *c.* 1200–1600', in *Forms of Servitude in Northern and Central Europe: Decline, Resistance, and Expansion*, ed. Paul Freedman and Monique Bourin, Medieval Texts and Cultures of Northern Europe, 9 (Turnhout, 2005), 419–35; Mark Bailey, 'The Myth of the "Seigniorial Reaction" in England after the Black Death', in *Peasants and Lords in the Medieval English Economy: Essays in Honour of Bruce M. S. Campbell*, ed. Maryanne Kowaleski, John Langdon, and Phillipp R. Schofield (Turnhout, 2015), 147–72. On the land market, see the essays in *The Peasant Land Market in Medieval England*, ed. P. D. A. Harvey (Oxford, 1984).

'copyhold tenure' (of the kind later formalized in common law during the sixteenth century) first emerged and, more recently, on the degree of tenurial security afforded to late-medieval tenants; there is now a broad consensus that in both cases localized factors were determinative.[39] There was nonetheless a broader pattern throughout England, as peasants began to request copies of the manorial court roll which recorded their entry into tenure. This emerged as one of the most pervasive trends of the late-medieval countryside.[40] Crucially, it was a kind of legal change that emerged 'from below'.

In post-plague society, then, the holders of customary land began to commission and keep their own property deeds on a vast scale.[41] This represents a remarkable transformation in the ownership of legal documents. Yet the very nature of this change, in dispersing such documents among the peasantry, has mitigated against the preservation of its material evidence. Most of these documents, sometimes only valid for a few years according to the term of the lease, were probably stored in the homes of the peasants who asked for them, and survive only rarely within institutional repositories.[42] Countless such copies have been lost to time; doubtless many were used as kindling. Those which do survive in modern archives—often relating to the same piece of land, threaded together with string or collected into files—were made by the generation of rentiers who began to buy up rural land in the later fifteenth and sixteenth centuries as evidence of continuous title.[43] The huge expansion that materialized in the form of these peasant-owned copies, then, was relatively short-lived, and constituted in ephemeral documents that, if they survived at all, were broadly dispersed.

The impact of this change, though, was momentous. Customary tenures covered just under half of all land in England, and in the flux of the post-plague land market, many more people came to lease it.[44] There is some evidence, too,

[39] A succinct summary of these debates can be found in Matthew Tompkins, 'Peasant Society in a Midlands Manor, Great Horwood 1400–1600', unpublished PhD thesis, University of Leicester (2006), pp. 4–5.

[40] Bailey, *Decline of Serfdom*, pp. 25–6.

[41] Peasant deeds had existed before, such as the *cartae nativorum* of Peterborough Abbey: Clanchy, *From Memory to Written Record*, p. 50, though the creation of these records was extremely distinctive: see Paul R. Hyams, 'The Origins of a Peasant Land Market in England', *The Economic History Review*, 23:1 (1970), 18–31. The practice of taking copies emerged in some places before 1400: see Rosamond Faith, 'Berkshire: Fourteenth and Fifteenth Centuries', in Harvey, *Land Market*, 106–77.

[42] See the forty seigneurial copies from the Suffolk manor of Staverton, noted in Bailey, *Decline of Serfdom*, pp. 221, fn. 73; SROI, HD1538/357/13–29, 36–59.

[43] Christopher Dyer, 'The Agrarian Problem, 1440–1520', in *Landlords and Tenants in Britain, 1440–1660: Tawney's Agrarian Problem Revisited*, ed. J. Whittle (Woodbridge, 2013), 19–34, and Harold Garrett-Goodyear, 'Common Law and Manor Courts: Lords, Copyholders and Doing Justice in Early Tudor England', in *Landlords and Tenants*, ed. Whittle, 35–51. For examples of such copies, see, for example, the eight copies, beginning with a lease in 1408, from the Suffolk manor of Ufford, held together on a parchment lace: SROI, HD1538/424/2–10; or the file of copies made for the manor of Yoxford: SROI, HA 30/369/307.

[44] There was extensive regional variation in the distribution and extent of customary and freehold land: see B. M. S. Campbell, 'The Agrarian Problem in the Early Fourteenth Century', *P&P*, 188 (2005),

that the growing use of copies spurred freeholders to present their charters for registration in court. The emergence of copyhold copies thus thronged the documentary ecosystem of the manorial courts, as the principal tribunals of rural life, and created a new source of institutional memory.[45] Copies enabled late-medieval peasants to secure their rights relative to their lord with writings that enshrined the precise conditions of their tenure. But such opportunities were bought at the cost of new obligations: as possession of copy become an increasingly important proof of customary tenure, so the onus was placed on tenants to preserve documents as evidence of title. As we shall see in the following sections, while the proliferation of copies after the Black Death afforded peasants some parity with their legal institutions, it also created new implicit duties.

For now, I want to turn to the second vector of the late-medieval documentary revolution, the proliferation of documents for identification and verification. The widespread emergence of this form was part of a broader cultural shift throughout late-medieval Europe in which identification became a routine mode of governance.[46] In England more particularly, we can see that this shift was the result, in a number of different ways, from the population crisis after the Black Death. The plague prompted a drastic shortage in labour and, concomitantly, waves of migration among artisanal and agricultural workers, who moved to find better wages, more advantageous conditions of employment, and cheaper land.[47] The demand for labour meant that the mobility of non-elites—both within England and, as new research is showing, from continental Europe too—became endemic within late-medieval English society.[48]

3–70; for the later period, Margaret Yates, 'The market in freehold land, 1300–1509: the evidence of feet of fines', *Economic History Review*, 66:2 (2013), 579–600.

---

[45] Bailey, *Decline of Serfdom*, pp. 292–3.

[46] Valentin Groebner, *Who Are You? Identification, Deception, and Surveillance in Early Modern Europe*, trans. Mark Kyburz and John Peck (New York, 2007).

[47] See Bailey, *Decline of Serfdom*, pp. 78–9. While sceptical of its role as an aspect of 'seigneurial reaction', Bailey accepts that there was an increase in serf migration. See also Chris Dyer and Simon A. C. Penn, 'Wages and Earnings in Late Medieval England: Evidence from the Enforcement of the Labour Laws', *Economic History Review*, n. s., 43:3 (1990), 356–76, pp. 363–5; Peter McClure, 'Patterns of Migration in the Late Middle Ages: The Evidence of English Place-Name Surnames', *Economic History Review*, n.s., 32:2 (1979), 167–82.

[48] The classic J. Ambrose Raftis, *Tenure and Mobility: Studies in the Social History of the Medieval English Village* (Toronto, 1964); Christopher Dyer, *Lords and Peasants in a Changing Society: The Estates of the Bishopric of Worcester, 680–1540* (Cambridge, 1980), esp. 244–63; Zvi Razi, *Life, marriage and death in a medieval parish: Economy, society and demography in Halesowen 1270–1400* (Cambridge, 1980), pp. 117–24; Marjorie McIntosh, *Autonomy and Community: The Royal Manor of Havering, 1200–1500* (Cambridge, 1986), pp. 221–3; P. J. P. Goldberg, *Women, Work, and Life Cycle in a Medieval Economy: Women and Work in Yorkshire c. 1300–1520* (Oxford, 1990), pp. 280–304; E. B. Fryde, *Peasants and Landlords in Later Medieval England* (Stroud, 1996), pp. 116–7, 142–3. On exogenous migration, see Milan Pajic and Bart Lambert, 'Immigration and the Common Profit: Native Cloth Workers, Flemish Exiles, and Royal Policy in Fourteenth-Century London', *Journal of British Studies*, 55:4 (2016), 633–57; the essays in *Resident Aliens in Later Medieval England*, ed. Mark Ormrod, Nicola McDonald, and Craig Taylor (Turnhout, 2017).

This had diffuse effects on governance, as authorities attempted to keep track of this movement through writing, and a number of longer-term trends towards written verification crystallized in this period. In the church courts, for example, the use of certificatory writings became fully routinized in the later Middle Ages; lay defendants were expected to be able to prove their assertions about the taking of confession or the undergoing of penance with their own documents. And in the maritime world, as we saw in Chapter 3, the raft of documentary technologies used to regulate overseas mercantile trade—in safe conducts, passports, and customs cockets—became much more pervasive in the fifteenth century, required not just of large commercial shippers but also by coastal fishermen.[49] In general, mobility was perceived as a problem for late-medieval governance, and documents, as a well-established mode of identification, naturally proliferated in attempts to control it.

But there were also more specific governmental endeavours in this period that created new kinds of common legal document specifically for this purpose. The drastic legislative attempts to tighten labour law and wage controls in 1349 and 1351 had largely failed.[50] But in the later fourteenth century, as Robert Palmer has argued, the governing classes came to perceive unregulated labour as a severe threat to the established socio-economic hierarchy.[51] Thus an unsuccessful petition to the Commons in 1376 complained that 'labourers and artisans', by their 'ingenuity' and 'great malice' had managed to avoid the penalties of the earlier legislation, because 'as soon as their masters accuse them of bad service or pay them... [they] flee and suddenly run away from their employment'.[52] After a few such false starts, action was taken in 1388 with the Statute of Cambridge: all labourers travelling to look for work were ordered to carry a 'letter patent' or 'letter testimonial' explaining 'the cause of his going, and the time of his return'; any wandering labourer found without one was to be put in the stocks or returned whence they came for punishment.[53]

[49] See Chapter 3, pp. 116–17.

[50] The classic account, essentially still standing, is Bertha Putnam, *The Enforcement of the Statutes of Labourers During the First Decade after the Black Death, 1349–1359* (New York, 1908). A useful calendar of this legislation is printed in Elaine Clark, 'Medieval Labor Law and English Local Courts', *American Journal of Legal History*, 27:4 (1983), 330–53, pp. 349–53. See also Chris Given-Wilson, 'The Problem of Labour in the Context of English Government, c. 1350–1450', in *The Problem of Labour in Fourteenth Century England*, ed. James Bothwell, P. J. P. Goldberg and W. M. Ormrod (York, 2000), 85–100. On earlier attempts to control mobility, for example in the Statute of Winchester (1285), see Henry Summerson, 'The Enforcement of the Statute of Winchester, 1285–1327', *Journal of Legal History*, 13:3 (1992), 232–50.

[51] Robert C. Palmer, *English Law in the Age of the Black Death, 1348–1381: A Transformation of Governance and Law* (Chapel Hill, NC, 1993); on taking these perceptions seriously as economic indicators, see John Hatcher, 'England in the Aftermath of the Black Death', *P&P*, 144 (1994), 3–35.

[52] *PROME*, ii, 340.

[53] 12 Ric. II, c. 3; *SR*, ii, p. 56. The records of this parliament do not survive among the parliament rolls, and therefore only the version on the statute roll, and contemporary chronicle accounts (which differ in some small particulars) preserve its text: see J. A. Tuck, 'The Cambridge Parliament, 1388', *EHR*, 84:331 (1969), 225–43, at p. 228.

The documentary apparatus for this scheme was carefully elaborated. Testimonial letters were to cost no more than a penny for workers to procure, a very low price for a legal instrument, which in turn suggests that they were intended to be widely and easily available.[54] And special seals, marked with the name of the locality where the worker had obtained his letter, were to be used to certify the documents, and to guard against fraud. Although scarcely any of these cheap and ephemeral documents have survived, we know that local authorities diligently undertook to produce them, because several such seal matrices have survived.[55] While most show a remarkable uniformity of design, that for Flaxwell hundred in Lincolnshire was inscribed with the additional text 'PRO SERVIS—'for servants', suggesting that there was a degree of local initiative in elaborating the mechanisms of verification.[56] This new legislation, then, did not merely ramp up controls on labour, but represented a step change in the documentary governance of workers.[57]

But as momentous as these changes were, the intent of the Statute expanded beyond merely the control of labour, and signalled the royal government's attempt to keep control of mobility in general. Specific provisions were made for wandering mendicants who travelled under licence in order to beg for alms, or pilgrims who were visiting a distant holy site: they too were ordered carry letters testimonial to identify themselves, lest they be suspected as vagabonds or mobile workers.[58] The logic of documentary identification thus provoked a kind of ripple effect, as carrying papers became essential for travel lest the suspicions of local communities and their legal officials were provoked. In the context of the mass mobility of late-medieval English society, this served once again to swell the number of legal documents possessed by common people, as they moved for family, work, or devotion. While the Statute of Cambridge was an essential intervention by the state, then, its effects continued to proliferate and gain momentum from more diffuse institutions of local governance.

The third vector of documentary revolution, the development of the bill genre, represented a longer cultural change that took place over the course of the later Middle Ages. As Wendy Scase has brilliantly argued, this period saw the emergence of 'complaint' as a mode of engaging with authority which sat athwart legal,

[54] On the cost of documents, see Ramsay, 'Scriveners and Notaries', pp. 125–6.

[55] Albert Way, 'Notices of the king's seals for passes given to Labourers and Servants, in accordance with the Statute passed at the Parliament of Cambridge, Sept. 12 Richard II. A. D. 1388', in *Antiquarian Communications: being papers presented at the meetings of the Cambridge Antiquarian Society* (London, 1859), 280–6.

[56] Weston S. Walford and Albert Way, 'Examples of medieval seals', *Archaeological Journal*, 11 (1854), 367–80, pp. 378–9.

[57] Many people were presented for moving between jurisdictions in order to receive higher wages or better terms of employment against the statute: Bertha Putnam, *Proceedings before the Justices of the Peace in the Fourteenth and Fifteenth Centuries: Edward III to Richard III* (London, 1938), pp. 130, 216, 224–5, 349, 358–60, 367, 374, 391, 448.

[58] 12 Ric. II, c. 7–8; *SR*, ii, p. 58.

literary, and political discourse.[59] Bills were the paradigmatic documentary genre of this discourse, used to supply information, persuade and petition, and to request remedy. And the effects of this broader cultural shift were felt early on in formal legal processes, for example in the development of 'procedure by bill' in the royal courts during the thirteenth century, the bills of indictment that crowded the criminal side of the court of King's Bench, and the mounting petitions sent to the royal Chancery as a site of equity jurisdiction.[60] At the same time however, the bill spilled over the boundaries of these formal confines to become one of the most pervasive formats of document more generally in late-medieval England.

Bills are difficult to define precisely, but I use the word here to single out two characteristics, one material and one functional.[61] In the first place, the word 'bill' almost always referred to a single sheet or slip of paper, small and portable. They were also normally made of paper, or more occasionally, from the cheap off-cuts trimmed from the edges of parchment skins.[62] These qualities of size, format, and material were certainly part of what contemporaries understood by the word 'bill'; the word connects the dozens of small slips produced for the Hereford law-day with the more substantial production of a 'bill indented' used to record a contract at Monxton in 1459, or the rather elaborate petitionary documents formally presented to authorities with the insurrectionary bills posted in public, demanding justice.[63] While such writings were clearly put to very different purposes, they were united by their use of this small, portable, relatively cheap, often ephemeral format—qualities which made bills highly accessible and easily distributable.

In the second place, whatever the specific purpose of their creation, bills almost always stood in supplementary relation to the procedures of the legal system in which they were produced. Bills were the cables through which so much legal information travelled, from the memo on the offences of parishioners of Barkby sent ahead to the visitation of Lincolnshire in 1413, to the small slips used by the farmer of Pontefract manor to record the names of tenants who had illicitly cut

[59] Wendy Scase, *Literature and Complaint in England, 1272–1553* (Oxford, 2007).

[60] On procedure by bill, J. H. Baker, *An Introduction to English Legal History* (4th edn., Oxford, 2002), pp. 40–4; on bills of indictment, John G. Bellamy, *Criminal Law and Society in Late Medieval and Tudor England* (Gloucester, 1984), pp. 90–114; on the composition of Chancery petitions, see Timothy S. Haskett, 'Country Lawyers? The Composers of English Chancery Bills', in *The Life of the Law: Proceedings of the Tenth British Legal History Conference*, ed. P. Birks (London, 1993), 9–23.

[61] The *MED* (q.v., 'bille (n)'), lists six distinct documentary meanings: (1) a formal document; (2) a formal plea or charge; (3) a formal written petition; (4) a written agreement or contract; (5) a statement or record; (6) a personal letter, message, or note.

[62] On the production of these off-cuts, see Kwakkel, 'Commercial organization and economic innovation', pp. 186–7. One example (also remarkable as an early instance of vernacular documentation) is BL, Harleian Charter 78. D. 3., an account of transactions between Robert Wanstallen and Thomas Gylys, c. 1371.

[63] For the bills submitted to the Hereford law-day, see HARC, BG/11/3/1. For the 'bill indented', KCC, MON/15. On the various quality of Chancery bills, see Haskett, 'Country Lawyers?'. On public bills, see Wendy Scase, '"Strange and Wonderful Bills": Bill-Casting and Political Discourse in Late Medieval England', in *New Medieval Literatures* 2, ed. Rita Copeland, David Lawton, and Wendy Scase (Oxford, 1998), 225–47.

saplings from *Alderrhagh* wood in 1492.[64] Little bills like these existed on the same spectrum as the elaborate petitions which flooded Chancery in the fifteenth century.[65] Bills gave material form to all that was untidy and human about legal systems, allowing memos, nudges, and favours to seep into its operations, smoothing its strictness and easing its flexibility—they can be found almost everywhere in late-medieval court records, rising on the tide of legal and administrative writing.

The documentary revolution that I have sketched out here was the product of diffuse socio-economic, governmental, and cultural change. Some impetuses were generated more from above—the royal government and ecclesiastical authorities wished to make more people prove their identities—while others, such as the drive towards the making of manorial copies, seem to have been demanded from below; and these different motors of change no doubt interacted in complex ways, as more people were drawn into the uses and benefits of writing. Yet more important, for my concerns here, than the causes of this revolution were its social and political effects on everyday life in late-medieval England. By 1450 almost everyone in common society, from wandering beggars and itinerant labourers through to manorial tenants, churchwardens, and reeves, might be expected to possess and use documents in a way that simply had not been true a century earlier. This represented a radical shift in popular material culture, as documents—physical artefacts of rights and obligations—came to form a part of how people conducted their legal lives. It is to such activities that we now turn.

The Opportunities of Writing: Legitimacy, Access, and Authority

Common legal documents opened up various opportunities for those common people who now counted them among their possessions. In essence, they allowed individuals and communities to draw from the deep reserves of cultural authority accorded to writing; this can be seen, for example, in the way that people wielded documents as symbols of legitimacy. But, more than this, as these writings gave a readily available material form to law, so they also offered people the opportunity to manipulate it, whether by changing the physical documents themselves, or by using writing to change the tone of their legal interactions. The proliferation of common legal documents thus enabled people to negotiate with one another—and with the legal institutions to which they were subject—in ways that had not previously been possible. In what follows, I consider what people used documents

[64] For a bill from the visitation, see LA, Vj/3, fo. 2a; for its wider context, see Forrest, *Detection of Heresy*, pp. 208ff. For the Pontefract wood payments, see WSRO, PHA 7033, m. 2v.

[65] Haskett, 'Country Lawyers?'.

to do, how they understood the legitimacy they conveyed, and, finally, the ways in which writing was used to make demands of legal authorities.

To begin with, it is worth noting the quotidian nature of the agreements and deals that people thought it necessary to record. So far as we can tell, the pervasive lending of money and goods that characterized everyday economic exchange in both town and countryside remained oral in the later Middle Ages, as people used the well-established legal mechanisms to register petty debts in the records of ecclesiastical and manorial courts when they needed to collect.[66] Written agreements only tended to be made for larger sums of money.[67] Yet if legal documents were not made for trivial reasons, nor were they exceptional. The memoranda recorded in the notebook of the Bury St Edmunds scrivener mentioned above reveal a kind of life-cycle of legal events that would have been conducted in writing for an average townsman: an indenture for an apprenticeship, a lease or sale for a property, a contract with a builder to enlarge a house, a grant in trusteeship, a testament and its appendices.[68] Such personal landmarks, involving larger commitments of time, capital, and property, were thought necessary to record.

Understandably, then, people placed a good deal of value on the legal documents which they owned. This can be seen in the first instance in the pains they took to store them—among the things stolen in 1461 from the house of Martin Mayn, a prosperous husbandman from Cotleigh in Devon, were 'two boxes of writings and charters', an arrangement which, though it was unsuccessful in this instance, suggests an attempt to secure them safely.[69] But as well as seeking to preserve their documents in general, there is some evidence that people valued certain pieces of writing in particular. In a remarkable case before the manorial court of Kintbury in 1418, Margaret Alisaundre claimed a virgate of customary land upon the death of her husband William; she paid a large fine of half a mark which covered the fee for her admission to his holding, but also 'for her name to be written down on the same copy by which her husband had held'.[70] Though she

[66] See Chris Briggs, 'Manor Court Procedures, Debt Litigation Levels, and Rural Credit Provision in England, c. 1290–c.1380', *L&HR*, 24:3 (2006), 519–58.

[67] For instance, of the sixty-eight debt pleas heard at the pie-powder court of Hereford in the year 1439–40, three included mention of a 'written obligation' or a 'written indenture' that proved the debt. The average value of debt litigation in this jurisdiction was generally low, with a median of just over 7s., but the three debts recorded in writing were valued at £40 (the highest-amount plea in the court that year), 100s., and 60s. respectively: HARC, BG11/2/6 [court book for 1439–40], written contracts at pp. 2, 5, 10 [modern pagination].

[68] Owen, 'A Scrivener's Notebook', p. 18. The word 'townsman' is deliberately gendered; women were far less likely to be apprenticed or involved in property transactions, though of course they did make wills.

[69] KCC, SJP/1, m. 1, annex. For some discussion of the roles of chests in bourgeois medieval households, see Katherine Wilson, 'The household inventory as urban "theatre" in late medieval Burgundy', *Social History*, 40:3 (2015), 335–59, pp. 347–50.

[70] BL, Add. Ch. 49221, verso: '. . . fecit finem cum domina ut possit tenere totam illam terram . . . et in eadem copia per quam vir suus tenuit nomine eius imponebatur'. By 1454, the holding was in the hands of a prominent Kintbury family, the Walronds: Add. Ch. 49237, m. 3v.

could clearly have afforded a new copy of her lease, she chose to have the old one altered, suggesting a particular attachment to this piece of parchment or paper.

Reusing a copy in this way made it into a peculiar kind of legal heirloom, giving an affective material presence to the inheritance claims made upon customary tenures. But such attempts to thesaurize the rights of inheritance in specific pieces of writing could also cause problems. For example, in 1488 at the court of Ringwood, John Chyng asked to be admitted to the tenure of a cottage 'by virtue of a certain copy shown in court', which had been created a decade earlier. However, the clerk noted that the admission could not go ahead: 'complaint is made because the said copy is suspicious, and the name of the said John has been scratched—therefore inquiry shall be made of the court rolls'.[71] Perhaps this was a deliberate fraud, or perhaps someone had simply attempted to update their copy in the manner of Margaret Alisaundre. Either way, such manipulation highlights the way that people's attachment to particular documents could actually run against the bureaucratic logic of the courts.

It also suggests that these kinds of legal documents diffused a kind of visual literacy among the commons. As Steven Justice has argued, late-medieval peasants could engage in 'minimally literate' ways with the legal documents they owned, for example by recognizing their own names or those of their lands, without having to comprehend them fully as texts.[72] And indeed, this visual relationship to written material is illuminated through the two predominant technologies of verification for stand-alone documents. First, personal seals, a part of everyday material culture as early as the thirteenth century, were deployed by a wide range of people in the later Middle Ages.[73] However, their ubiquity also seems to have caused some anxiety about their authenticity. The widow of a Norwich burgess, for example, managed to persuade the civic authorities there to co-seal a testimonial letter she commissioned in a matter concerning the administration of her father's will in 1436, 'as my sele is not openli knowen'.[74] Her seal, depicting the Virgin, is indeed utterly generic, yet it is telling that she thought it should be appended alongside the more renowned sign of the institution. Such practices suggest a powerful and widespread cultural association between legal agency and seals.[75] Second, in another well-established practice, people used the material qualities of the written surface as a technology of trust. Probably the most common method to guard against fraud was the creation of 'indented' documents or chirographs: the text of an agreement was written out twice on the same sheet, and then cut in half

[71] KCC, RIN/7, fo. 7r. [72] Justice, *Writing and Rebellion*, pp. 34–5.

[73] On seal use, see Clanchy, *From Memory to Written Record*, pp. 309–17.

[74] ERO, D/DCm Z18/9. The letter provides notification of her intent to the executor of her father's will regarding the annual rents of two properties in Norwich, which she wished to pass on to her own son.

[75] In general, see Brigitte Bedos-Rezak, *When Ego was Imago: Signs of Identity in the Middle Ages* (Leiden, 2011).

using a zigzag pattern, ensuring that only the true halves would match up.[76] These technologies were used for routine transactions: one vernacular 'bille endented' of 1459 records an agreement that Gylbert Smyth should repair two barns and a sheephouse at Monxton in Hampshire, taking 33s. 4d. as an allowance; another, from Wirksworth in Derbyshire, that Robert Vernon and Thomas Heype would take over the lands of Amy Man in exchange for building her 'a lytyll howse at the ȝate that sche myght dwelle in hur lyfe', along with half an orchard, firewood, and pasture for her cow—this document was also sealed by Vernon.[77] The diffusion of common legal documents, therefore, enabled people to deploy the widespread understandings of legitimacy that attached to the material forms of writing.

At the same time, of course, this opened up the potential for fraud. Indeed, forgery appears to have been common in late-medieval England—perhaps connected to the abundance of unregulated scribal labour discussed above—and was practised by people who saw in documents the potential to make a quick buck.[78] Thus in 1438 a group of two tailors, a yeoman, and a 'chop-church' managed to extort around 40s. in money and gifts from the inhabitants of Westminster by carrying 'forged bills made in the manner of indictments, which they showed to diverse people, affirming that they had been indicted, when [in fact] they had not'.[79] A near identical case from a few years earlier, involving two husbandmen of Acton and Ealing extorting money in the same way, included a general monition against 'any false marks, or made-up indictments, aimed at terrorizing the king's people', a phrase that captures nicely the symbolic weight that people attached to such official documents, a point I shall discuss more in the conclusion to this chapter.[80]

As a final argument here, however, I want to look at the ways in which common documents could open up different kinds of access to legal authority. To begin with, visitation, as 'a record-centred event', may have been an especially opportune moment for parishioners to make the most of writing as a mode of legal communication with the church courts.[81] In one remarkable instance of 1472, for example, the visitors for the dean and chapter of York Minster recorded that the inhabitants of Haxby 'have shown a certain schedule containing certain

[76] See the discussion of elaborate indentures used by the Bristol town clerks in Bevan, 'Clerks and Scriveners', p. 136.

[77] Respectively, KCC, MON/15; DRO, D258/26/11/2.

[78] It was perceived as a problem: the Commons successfully petitioned for a statute to allow the trespass writs to be made for crimes of forgery in 1419: 7 Hen. V, c. 2: *PROME*, iv, p. 121; *SR*, ii, p. 202. More generally, see Nigel Ramsay, 'Forgery and the rise of the London Scriveners' Company', in *Fakes and frauds: varieties of deception in print and manuscript*, ed. Robin Myers and Michael Harris (Winchester, 1989), 99–108.

[79] TNA, KB 9/230B, no. 22. A 'chop-church' was one who dealt in ecclesiastical benefices, in this case perhaps suggesting an existing reputation for dishonesty.

[80] TNA, KB9/216/2, no. 8.

[81] Ian Forrest, 'The Survival of Medieval Visitation Records', *Archives (The Journal of the British Records Association)*, 38:125 (2017), 1–10, p. 10.

petitions . . . which is attached to this folio'.[82] Fortunately, this document is still there in the visitation book, written out on paper in a tidy hand, though interestingly, it is annotated with a number of corrections and redactions.[83] Still, it is undoubtedly a petition, beginning as follows: 'Compleynes lamentablie to god almyghti and to yowre tender compassion & pities under hym . . . the pouere inhabitants of the tounship of Haxby'.[84] This description of the petitioners was significant, because the township was divided between the prebendal parishes of Strensall (two miles away) and Driffield (some twenty miles away), and was thus served by a chapel of convenience.

As they rehearsed, the poor inhabitants, 'so constreyned with grete povete', could no longer afford to maintain a priest there, 'without help socor and releve of the prebendaries and vicares'. Therefore, they requested that the small tithes that they paid to the prebendaries and vicars of Strensall and Driffield might be diverted so 'that we myght have a prest . . . at oure chapel to minister unto us divine services and other sacraments acordyng to our licences', referring to their licence to have such services at the chapel.[85] While the visitors gave no definite answer to the request, they did make a note on the verso of the petition that 'the parishioners say that the share of both prebends . . . comes to about 20 marks', suggesting both that they took the petition seriously, and also that the parishioners had successfully managed to lodge their own framing of the issue at the centre of inquiries.[86] Among the hordes of parochial bills sent ahead to visitation in this period, then, it would seem that the act of performatively presenting a piece of writing in this manner was a particularly effective method for catching the attention of the authorities.

Written communications, as opposed to those conducted orally in open court, also offered people the opportunity to appeal over the heads of the local officials who held these tribunals, to the authorities on whose behalf they held them. This was particularly important when those officials were thought to be corrupt. An example I discussed in Chapter 7, an English petition by the tenants of Frettenham (Norfolk) to their lord, the Earl of Oxford, is a case in point.[87] The manor had been leased to four different farmers in a short period, and as a result, they had been accosted by several different men claiming jurisdiction of the court there. They asked that he might 'vowche saffe to sende your wrytynge to eche of these gentyllmen that vexen the seid pore tenantes, that thei . . . mowen cessyn here

[82] YMLA, L2/3c, fo. 15v.

[83] YMLA, L2/3c, fo. 15v, annex. The substantive redaction, notably, relates to the specific tithes apportioned to the prebendary (corn, wool, lambs) and those to the vicar (cow, calf, and foal—initially misattributed to the prebendary—and hemp, flax, pigs, geese, and hens). I have written about the material qualities of this and other ephemeral documents in more detail in Tom Johnson, 'Legal Ephemera in the Ecclesiastical Courts of Late-Medieval England', *Open Library of Humanities*, 5:1 (2019), 1–27.

[84] YMLA, L2/3c, fo. 15v., annex.

[85] Ibid.

[86] Ibid., verso.

[87] See Chapter 7, p. 237.

malys [may cease their malice] & late the tenantes leve in reste'.[88] They also requested that he might 'sende sum other indifferent gentylman of yoris' to collect their rents, thus effectively asking him to replace his steward. Such a bold request was only possible through writing, both because of its logistical requirements, in attempting to bypass local officials, and because the genre conventions of supplicatory writing opened up a way to directly ask things of powerful lords.

For all this, though, it is important to emphasize that these kinds of elaborate and demonstrative uses of persuasive writing coexisted with rather informal written communications between non-elites and legal authorities. Though such writings were probably widespread, they have only rarely survived.[89] To conclude this section, therefore, I want to turn finally to a particularly detailed case study which not only captures this kind of routine written communication, but, more remarkably, shows the kind of success it could achieve. The document in question, sent by an unidentified group of parishioners from Uxbridge, in the deanery of Middlesex, to the commissary of the Bishop of London, probably ought to be classified as a letter. Signed allusively 'by your levers [faithful] of Woxebrygge', writing on the verso entreated that 'this byll be delyverid... in haste', implying some urgency.[90] Moreover, the use of the concluding phrase 'no mor to you at this tyme', though formulaic, may hint at a regular correspondence.

They were writing to complain about Robert Bukeland, one of the summoners for the commissary court—lay officials who carried mandates and citations to defendants on behalf of the ecclesiastical authorities.[91] The parishioners alleged that he had not only brought two misgoverned women into the parish, but also falsely cited a number of parishioners, including even Agnes Grene, who 'hath bene of good gydynge honeste levynge conversacion & rule [all] days of her lyffe'.[92] After a raft of condemnation against Bukeland's 'bauderye', the Uxbridge parishioners were extraordinarily bold in their demand: 'where upon, put hym to his purgacion amonge his neyghbers'. Less a request than an order, this incitement to force a process of compurgation embodies a remarkable claim to determine *publica fama* as the common opinion of the parish.[93] But for all that, it seems to have worked.

Bukeland had been the main summoner for the parishes west of London since about February 1496, with 'B' or 'R Buk' noted in the margin for the cases he

[88] BLO, Norfolk Charters 109. [89] See Johnson, 'Legal ephemera', pp. 5–7.

[90] LMA, DL/C/B/043/MS09064/007, fo. 29r.

[91] On summoners, see Ian Forrest, 'The Summoner', in *Historians on Chaucer: The 'General Prologue' to the Canterbury Tales*, ed. Stephen Rigby and Alastair Minnis (Oxford, 2014), 421–42, pp. 436–8. More generally, see Richard Wunderli, 'Pre-Reformation London Summoners and the Murder of Richard Hunne', *Journal of Ecclesiastical History*, 33:2 (1982), 209–24.

[92] LMA, DL/C/B/043/MS09064/007, fo. 29r.

[93] On the use of *fama* in criminal cases before the church courts, see R. H. Helmholz, 'Crime, Compurgation and the Courts of the Medieval Church', *L&HR*, 1:1 (1983), 1–26.

brought back to the court.[94] Soon afterwards, in March, his wife was reported as a common scold in Uxbridge; but it was her victims who were required to purge themselves of her allegations against them, while Robert had her continued absence from court excused.[95] In late August, the commissary court book records that Bukeland had peremptorily cited no fewer than ten people, from Chelsea, Uxbridge, Acton, Staines, and Isleworth.[96] The purpose of this entry is not entirely clear—peremptory citation refers to a legitimate procedure, rather than implying any condemnation—and, in fact, the next four entries in the court book, though extremely brief, were also Bukeland's work.[97] But among the list of people he had cited was Agnes Grene of Uxbridge, whose plight was to inspire the letter, and after this date Bukeland completely disappears from the records.[98] It would seem that the parishioners got their wish that he be removed.

This letter, preserved by chance among the folios of the commissary's register, provides a remarkable example of the way that people might use common documents to harness legal authority. If it did not fit very snugly within the procedural conventions of legal process, it proved an exceptionally well-judged intervention. Against his peremptory citations brought against them, they demanded that he should be tested by the social and oral proof of compurgation, a sworn denial; against his formulaic Latinate letters of citation, they issued an informal, vernacular 'bill', written as a letter; against his individual caprice in handing out multiple citations for pecuniary gain, they used writing to represent themselves as a parochial community united by a shared sense of morality and justice. Their petition, therefore, not only manifested the neighbourliness which they claimed against Bukeland's individualistic corruption, but also instantiated an authentic legitimacy that stood in stark opposition to his legalistic citations—a strategy which apparently won them the sympathy of the commissary.

Ultimately, then, the diffusion of common documents helped to redefine the terms of written authority by opening up the power of legal writings to a much broader constituency of people. In particular, as I have suggested here, the possession of legal writings by non-elites opened up new, more participatory interactions with legality, as they kept documents at home, preserved them as heirlooms, used them to record major transactions, commissioned them to solve common problems, to tell legal authorities what they wanted, to persuade them to

[94] LMA, DL/C/B/043/MS09064/007, fos. 11r–v, 13r, 20v, 21v, 23v, 26r, 27v. Before this time, London's western hinterland had been served by a summoner named 'Bray': fos. 3r–v, 6r, 7v–8r.

[95] Ibid., 12v. That she was reported at all suggests that the 'faithful parishioners' had previously managed to send information to the commissary without Bukeland's involvement.

[96] Ibid., fo. 26v.

[97] See Helmholz, *Canon Law and Ecclesiastical Jurisdiction*, pp. 317–21.

[98] The next time the commissary began receiving cases from these parishes in January 1497, a summoner with the initial 'C' reported Rose Barat as a bawd: LMA, DL/C/B/043/MS09064/007, fos. 36r, 37r. This man was soon replaced by someone else with the initial 'N', who remained at least until August 1497: Ibid., fos. 37v–38r, 39r, 40r, 46r, 47v, 51r.

act on their behalf. At the same time, however, the greater access and manoeuvrability that documents afforded in relation to law and authority was defined in terms that were ultimately fixed by legal institutions. And, indeed, the role of local courts in verifying, archiving, and enforcing documents tied people more closely to bureaucratic processes beyond their control. It is to this process that we now turn.

Documents, Institutions, and Verification

Local courts in the later Middle Ages were occasions for the compilation and exhibition of writing. This had been the case for some time. At the turn of the thirteenth century, larger institutions were beginning to keep written lists of those men in tithing; just a generation later the first written proceedings of manorial courts were made, perhaps in a bid to lure free tenants away from the *curia regis*, with its written rolls.[99] By the turn of the fourteenth century, the practice of making records of local courts had become very widespread indeed, and was by this time normal practice across royal, seigneurial, and ecclesiastical jurisdictions.[100] As John Beckerman has suggested, 'the record of the court rolls... gradually replaced the testimony of the suitors and the sworn inquest as the ultimate authority about what had occurred in court'.[101] Court rolls thus formed an essential medium of the legal power of local courts, as well as a common representation of authority more generally.[102]

The increase of documents in the later Middle Ages transformed again these associations, changing the meanings of writing in local courts. On one hand, as we saw in the previous section, the widespread ownership of legal documents among the broader populace afforded them some degree of parity with the institutions

[99] Clanchy, *From Memory to Written Record*, p. 97; R. M. Smith, 'Some Thoughts on "Hereditary" and "Proprietary" Rights in Land under Customary Law in Thirteenth and Fourteenth Century England', *L&HR*, 1:1 (1983), 95–128, p. 97; Zvi Razi and Richard M. Smith, 'The Origins of the English Manorial Court Rolls as a Written Record: A Puzzle', in *Medieval Society and the Manor Court*, ed. Razi and Smith (Oxford, 1996), 36–68.

[100] On estate records, see P. D. A. Harvey, 'English Estate Records, 1250–1330', in *Pragmatic Literacy, East and West, 1200–1300*, ed. Richard Britnell (Woodbridge, 1997), 107–18. For records of the county court, which seem to have developed rather earlier, see Robert Palmer, *The County Courts of Medieval England, 1150–1350* (Princeton, NJ, 1982), pp. 38–40, 46–7, 156ff. Ecclesiastical records followed a different trajectory but enter at the same point; their proceedings were recorded from an early date, but local tribunals were not held regularly until the end of the thirteenth century: see Robert Swanson, 'Universis Christi Fidelibus: the Church and its Records', in *Pragmatic Literacy*, ed. Britnell, 147–64, p. 153; R. H. Helmholz, 'Local Ecclesiastical Courts in England', in *The History of Courts and Procedure in Medieval Canon Law*, ed. Wilfried Hartmann and Kenneth Pennington (Washington, DC, 2016), 344–91, p. 350.

[101] John S. Beckerman, 'Procedural Innovation and Institutional Change in Medieval English Manorial Courts', *L&HR*, 10:2 (1992), 197–252, p. 224.

[102] Justice, *Writing and Rebellion*, pp. 46–52.

that they used, which no longer possessed a monopoly on access to legal record. On the other hand, however, the documentary revolution also created burdensome new expectations; as people were increasingly supposed to possess their own documents, so any failure to do so could become problematic. This began to change the emphasis of court business in several different ways: they came to focus more and more upon the display of writings, upon the processing of written information, and upon the scrutiny of documents. In considering all three of these developments, we shall see how the heightened levels of document ownership bound people more closely within the regimes of verification used by the courts.

To begin with, late-medieval institutions began to require the exhibition of documents as evidence. This was particularly pronounced in manorial courts. As we saw earlier in this chapter, tenants began to request a copy of the part of the court-roll which recorded their entry into tenure, thus acquiring what Mark Bailey has called 'a quasi-legal document, which could be (and was) subsequently produced in the manorial court as proof of title to the land'.[103] These documents quickly became part of the routine of the transfer of customary land. Thus when Walter Chapton died in 1420 possessed of a four-acre customary holding, his wife Matilda and son William claimed the reversion as his joint tenants, 'for which they have shown a copy of the enrolment [*copiam irrotulacionis*] of the court'.[104]

By the later fifteenth century, these copies had become all but indispensable. At the halmote for Burton in Herefordshire in 1474, for example, in three unrelated land transfers the steward made an order 'to let the copy be seen' so that the transactions could be completed; in the third of these cases, it was noted that Thomas Walker was holding 'without permission or copy', and his lands were seized from him.[105] The possession of a written copy was rapidly becoming the *sine qua non* for customary tenure. This tended to disperse the responsibility of reproducing the court's proceedings and customs, as the court's rolls, rentals, and surveys were no longer the sole records of what had happened. At West Hendred in 1509, a proclamation was made that anyone who held or sublet land within the manor was to obtain licence for their tenure at the next court, and the whole homage was ordered to come and show the lord 'their copies and evidences'.[106]

Such demands could be a powerful tool for lords to suppress extravagant demands from the tenantry. Striking evidence of this comes from the Berkshire manor of Kintbury in 1468, apparently in response to the tenants' claim that the manor was ancient demesne (and, concomitantly, that they were not obliged to make certain customary payments):[107]

[103] Bailey, *Decline of Serfdom*, p. 21. [104] KCC, RIN/5, m. 5r.

[105] BL, Add. Ch. 27300, recto. [106] CCCO, Bb 1/3, recto.

[107] On ancient demesne, see Rosamund Faith, 'The "Great Rumour" of 1377 and Peasant Ideology', in *The English Rising of 1381*, ed. R. H. Hilton and T. H. Aston (Cambridge, 1984), 43–73.

> Order is given to all tenants to show the charters and copies by which they claim to hold from the lady, and by what services and customs [are] in the writings which they claim to hold by *ancent de mayn*, and this under the pain of forfeiting their tenure and lands, before the next court.[108]

The routinization of displaying copies in manorial courts thus changed their operation of customary law. The enunciation of custom and the tenurial arrangements which it permitted became less an exercise of creative negotiation, and instead turned into the exhibition (and perhaps comparison) of documents—an exercise that the authorities who held the courts were rather more likely to win. This is not to say that written copies froze custom, but rather that they transformed its mediation, in ways that affected power relations. Battles over custom came to be fought out in writing, a medium which created strategic vulnerabilities for tenants engaging with legal institutions that created and managed substantial archives.

In other institutional contexts, however, people were asked to display documents not to establish their rights, but rather to prove their claims. This was particularly true in the lower church courts, which routinely asked defendants to produce written certificates to corroborate their assertions, for example to prove that they were married to the person they were living with, or to show that they had undergone confession.[109] They might even be asked to bring writings demonstrating judicial process had taken place. When Edmund Lymbermier of Holme Street, just outside Norwich, was cited before the capitular courts for adultery with a woman named Agnes in March 1431, he confessed to the sin, but protested that he had already been punished for it. The judge responded by giving him two weeks to show his 'letter of correction', testifying to his penance. Agnes fared less well, as it was noted that 'she did not exhibit a letter of correction and is therefore enjoined to do penance'.[110] The demand for certificates and other legal writings thus shifted the burden of verification off the courts and onto the people whom they disciplined.

This burden of verification stretched into all kinds of local legal settings. Numerous inhabitants of York in the 1470s and 1480s felt it necessary to obtain letters testimonial recording that they had been born on the 'right' side of the Scottish border.[111] And indeed, written identification was thoroughly routine for

[108] BL, Add. Ch. 49238, m. 9r. 'Pena data est omnibus tenentibus ad ostendum cartas et copias per quod clamant tenere de domina et per quas servicias et consuetudines in scriptis qua clamant tenere per ancent de mayn et hoc sub pena cuiuslibet eorum forisfactur tenure sue [sic] et terrarum etc erga proxima curia.' A very similar order was also made in Add. Ch. 49241, m. 1r.

[109] For the request of a certificate to prove marriage, see NRO, DCN 67/8, m. 2r. For the request of a certificate 'or token' of confession, see Tom Johnson, 'The Preconstruction of Witness Testimony: Law and Social Discourse in England before the Reformation', *L&HR*, 32:1 (2014), 127–47, p. 130.

[110] NRO, DCN 67/8, m. 1r.

[111] See the eight letters enrolled in the York registers in *A Volume of English Miscellanies illustrating the History and Language of the Northern Counties of England*, ed. J. Raine, Surtees Society, 85 (Durham, 1890), 35–40. More generally, see J. A. F. Thomson, 'Scots in England in the Fifteenth Century', *Scottish Historical Review*, 79:207 (2000), 1–16.

those who regularly crossed jurisdictional boundaries. Thus Pieter Johnes, 'an honest man and master of a small ship called the *Jesus*', carried a small sealed certificate to the tiny port of Blakeney in Norfolk from the Flemish town of Veere in 1479 to show his entitlement to customs privileges.[112] Legal identification generated more documents, moreover, as it was verified. This can be gleaned in the travails of another shipmaster, Thomas Sutton. Taking a hundred quarters of grain from Norfolk to Essex in the *Thomas*, he unloaded first at Harwich, and received 'a certain writing made by the inhabitants', certifying that he would not take the grain out of the realm; this writing was subsequently checked by the bailiffs of Colchester after he unloaded at the port of New Hithe there, and enrolled in their accounts.[113] Certificatory writings demanded their own certification, creating an ever-increasing spiral of material demanded and processed in such local jurisdictions.

The business of courts thus came increasingly to focus on the scrutiny of documents. This could cause problems for the people expected to supply documents to this network. For example, in the manor of Stour Provost in 1420, John Clyntefeld was distrained to show his title to three closes of pasture and a small piece of land, as a preliminary procedure, it seems, to a rival claim from Stephen Gascoigne, who claimed it by hereditary right of his wife. Clyntefeld accordingly showed 'a certain copy of the court here, held during the time when John Aston was steward', some thirty-four years previously. The court inspected the copy, which indeed showed title to one of the closes, but noted that 'as to the other closes, and the little piece of land, it says nor shows anything', and so the matter was put to counsel.[114] Whether or not Clyntefeld's deception was wilful, it shows the kind of gap that might open up between memory and written record, and the importance of the role of the court—or, in this instance, a seigneurial official—as an arbiter of documentary proof.

One way of getting around such problems was for courts to act as written repositories, registering deeds, bonds, and other private instruments. At Hereford, in a way that was common for urban jurisdictions, the mayor's court kept detailed records of bonds for debts, good behaviour, or some other obligation.[115] Manorial courts were also used for such enrolments: John Twinton, who held just a cottage and curtilage at Ringwood, paid no heriot when he died in 1451 'because of an agreement made with the steward, and enrolled in the record of the last court', which, unfortunately, has not survived.[116] While such enrolments

[112] TNA, E 122/195/3, no. 9. [113] ERO, D/B 5 R2, fo. 118v–119r.

[114] KCC, STP/4, m. 3r. [115] HARC, BG11/17/11, *passim*.

[116] KCC, RIN/5, m. 2r. A view of frankpledge for the previous year in fact survives in the same roll at m. 5r (the membranes are out of date sequence suggesting it was bound much later), but it is badly damaged; in any case, it does not seem to contain any such agreement. It is quite possible that the surviving rolls are (partial) copies, in a sinister instance of how seigneurial control of the archive might enable selective editing of customary rights and dues.

undoubtedly enabled tenants to benefit from the durability and stability of institutional archives, it also put them at their mercy for accessing their writings. Thus in 1472 the parishioners of Knaresborough complained to ecclesiastical visitors that the prebendary, who also held secular jurisdiction there, was concealing the rolls of his court 'to the great prejudice of the tenants'.[117] To deposit or enrol documents with an institutional authority was thus also to place oneself at their discretion.

Local courts not only registered writings in their own archives, however, but might also create them at the request of suitors, as two testimonial letters made in the Colchester moothall demonstrate. The first was created in 1493 for Richard Johnson, the son of an immigrant goldsmith, who had been 'reputed and takyn as a person aliegn and strange not born within realme of Ynglond'; the town's bailiffs testified that he had been born there, and so ought 'to have his liberte as anynglisman off byrth'.[118] The second letter testified not to the birth, but to the general reputation of Thomas Parker, 'a trew and wel disposed yoman', who had been defamed of some unspecified crime. He had asked the bailiffs 'to sertifie our parfyte knowlich of his demeanyng in wryting under our seall in salvacion of his good name'.[119] These are unusual survivals—both were enrolled in the town's memorandum book—but they show a world in which the maintenance of personal reputation was no longer purely oral; and now that it was proved through writing, it was much more closely tied up with legal institutions.

In sum, the widespread ownership of legal documents entangled people in recursive cycles of documentary authority, processes ultimately controlled by local courts. Issued with documents to prove who they were, what actions they had taken, or what rights they claimed, so, in turn, they were expected to be able to produce these documents before legal authorities, in order that they could be checked and verified. And as more documents were issued, more of the burden of making oneself identifiable, claiming rights, and pushing back on dues was shifted onto the individual. This had two major effects. In the first place, it exposed individuals to new risks: using the wrong document, letting it get scratched, damaged, lost, or stolen, opened up new possibilities for legal error and one-upmanship. In the second place, ironically, these risks made them ever more reliant on courts to display, verify, enrol, and process documents, and to produce yet more of them. As documents brought the forms of law into common possession, so they subtly formed more biddable subjects for legal authorities.

117 YMLA, L2/3c, fo. 20r.

118 ERO, D/B 5 R2, fos. 197v–199r. On such questions of nationality and birth, see Andrea Ruddick, *English Identity and Political Culture in the Fourteenth Century* (Cambridge, 2013), p. 102.

119 ERO, D/B 5 R2, fos. 199r–200r.

Conclusion

The media theorist Cornelia Vismann has written that 'the erratic side of the law—the administrative operations, the transmission medium itself—remains a blind spot of legal history'.[120] In this chapter, I have tried to show how a revolution in the numbers and diffusion of legal documents, as a type of media technology, changed the contours of common legalities in late-medieval England. As I have suggested, writings ushered in opportunities for common people to access and use legitimacy in ways that had not previously been possible; but at the same time, these documentary media came packaged with new kinds of commitments to the law-courts that produced and processed them. Even as documents seemed to disperse access to law among a broader range of people, then, they also brought these people more firmly under the control of legal institutions.

All of these arguments are based on the notion that the materiality, as much as the textuality, of legal writings was vital to their historical significance.[121] And indeed, documents in medieval Europe had meanings to contemporaries not just as texts, but as *things*, which were handled, pored over, demonstratively displayed, or destroyed. Historians have long recognized that this created important symbolic functions for texts. As Carol Symes has written of twelfth-century Arras, 'the gesture, the posture, the sound, and the spoken word were the powerful discursive modes through which writing was publicized', and this remained true into the later Middle Ages.[122] Writing was present in every stage of public legal processes, from the proclamation of new parliamentary statutes to the widespread practice of touching the gospels during pervasive oath-swearing ceremonies. Such demonstrative use of legal writing to signify authority remained extremely important in late-medieval England, even as documents became ubiquitous.

Understood alongside the proliferation of writing which I have been describing, the continued weight of written law suggests that people felt the total burden of legality grow heavier in late-medieval England. If this seems fanciful, it is worth remembering the fear that official writing, in particular, could inspire. A corrupt summoner in Colchester, acting on behalf of the London commissary-general, managed to extort a shilling from Christina Howell, by 'telling her that she had been detected and accused of diverse crimes, namely adultery, and that *she was written in the commissary's book*'.[123] The idea that their sins were written down in

[120] Cornelia Vismann, *Files: Law and Media Technology*, trans. G. Winthrop-Young (Stanford, 2008), p. 75.

[121] Simon Franklin, *Writing, Society and Culture in Early Rus, c.950–1300* (Cambridge, 2002), pp. 3–4.

[122] Carol Symes, 'Out in the Open, in Arras: Sightlines, Soundscapes, and the Shaping of a Medieval Public Sphere', in *Cities, Texts and Social Networks, 400–1500: Experiences and Perceptions of Medieval Urban Space*, ed. Caroline Goodson, Anne E. Lester, and Carol Symes (Farnham, 2010), 279–303, p. 287.

[123] ERO, D/B 5 Cr67, m. 19v. 'dicendo quod ipsa fuit detecta et accusata de diversis criminibus videlicet de crimine adulterij coram commissario predicto et in libro eiusdem commissarij scripto'. The indictment goes on to emphasize that in fact no such accusation existed in the book.

a book somewhere had a powerful resonance for the late-medieval laity told often to keep Judgment in mind. Indeed, writings were often used in the course of earthly judgments. William Morgan was put in the stocks at Hereford with 'a paper about his head with diverse words within' in 1513 for uttering treasonous words, a mode of discipline also used frequently by the London ward-motes.[124] Such punishments assumed a link between writing and publicity, but they also forced offenders to embody such exposure.

Late-medieval people felt writing in their bones. When the summoner Thomas Kyrkman went to the London parish of St. Botulph's Bishopsgate in 1514 to deliver a citation against Richard Tyller, he was met with a stream of abuse by the defendant: 'Thou bawdy knave and that bawdy courte thou com froo, thou haddest as gode not haue broght writing against my norse as thou dist'.[125] To be cited was to have 'writing brought against you' (and your arse), a fully embodied process of sexual humiliation. Concomitantly, fantasies of revenge often involved the physical consumption of documents. It is easy to feel sorry for Thomas Ginford and Thomas Talbot, who, as they attempted to serve a writ of subpoena on a widow of Bildeston in Suffolk, were attacked by her neighbours, made to kneel, and forced to 'eete the writte, bothe wex and parchement'.[126] Pieces of parchment and paper thus performed affective work as physical objects bearing the law's power to wound, shame, and command in deeply corporeal ways.

The proliferation of documents that took place in late-medieval England should not be imagined, then, as a mere snowstorm of fluttering papers, but as a cumulative, constraining force that constituted legal authority. Indeed, we need to think about the way that premodern law was sustained by a huge quantity of textual work: by the officials who verified and archived writings, by the people who carried them around and presented them in court, by the scriveners who prepared them, scraping clean and inscribing the parchment, or cutting the paper correctly into strips—all the way back to the proto-industrial processes that made possible the manufacture of all these materials. 'The power of law, like that of a chain, is exactly as strong as its weakest link and we can only detect this link by following the chain link after link, without omitting a single one.'[127] If we think of the investment of materials and labour that lay behind the penny testimonial letter

[124] HARC, BG11/17/3 [Miscellaneous Papers, 1513–93], no. 3, fo. 3. On punishments in the ward-motes, see Martin Ingram, '"Popular" and "Official" Justice: Punishing Sexual Offenders in Tudor London', in *Legalism: Community and Justice*, ed. Fernanda Pirie and Judith Scheele (Oxford, 2014), 201–26, at pp. 215–17.

[125] LMA, DL/C/B/043/MS09064/011, fo. 127r. The orthography of 'my norse' is as written; this was common in Middle English writing, where 'an initial n- is often attached to words beginning with a vowel', but does not always necessarily signify a phonetic: *MED*, q.v. (n- (prosthetic.)).

[126] TNA, C 1/15/197. On the widespread violence against summoners, see Forrest, 'The Summoner', pp. 436–8.

[127] Latour, *The Making of Law*, p. 75.

of each labourer in late-medieval England, the force of so flimsy a thing as a document—the force of premodern law—becomes more readily visible.

The distribution of documents among a wider segment of the population in the later Middle Ages, then, also represented a redistribution of governmental force. In this sense, the famous tactical destruction of seigneurial archives in the rising of 1381, when 'the seizure and destruction of documents happened wherever rebellion did', appears more like a relic, the last customary vandalism against the 'growth of government' that had proceeded on a tidal wave of writing.[128] Two generations later, no one in Cade's revolt of 1450 seems to have thought of burning archival documents—on the contrary, they set about producing them: the rebel leaders employed scriveners, secretaries, and couriers, and commissioned written bills and petitions, drawing heavily on legal language, in order to put out their message as widely and as authoritatively as possible.[129] Even as they rebelled, the late-medieval commons were co-opted in sustaining the media-technology used to bind them to governmental norms. The dissipation of documents had hedged them all about with written authority: in the writings that filled chests in the houses of husbandmen, that weighed down the pockets of travelling labourers, there lay the materials of a deeply percolated legality.

[128] Justice, *Writing and Rebellion*, p. 40; Gerald Harriss, 'Growth of Government', p. 57.

[129] I. M. W. Harvey, *Jack Cade's rebellion of 1450* (Oxford, 1991), pp. 75–6, 80–1. Copies of three main bills can be found in the appendices, pp. 186–91. On the legal language of these bills, see Theron Westervelt, 'Manifestoes for Rebellion in Late-Fifteenth-Century England', in *Political Society in Later Medieval England: A Festschrift for Christine Carpenter*, ed. Benjamin Thompson and John L. Watts (Woodbridge, 2015), 184–98.

Conclusion

Towards a Common Constitution

This book has tried to give a sense of the great variety of common people's legal engagements in late-medieval England at the same time as drawing them together into broader structures. In the first half of the book, we saw how localized clusters of environmental, socio-economic, and institutional forms could combine to produce distinctive senses of what law was, and what it could do; in the second half of the book, we surveyed 'common legalities' that penetrated across these local legal cultures, constituted in widespread practices of legal engagement. These two different heuristics have hopefully complemented one another: while the majority of these engagements took place locally, within the institutions that were most readily available to common people, I have endeavoured to show that there were also significant commonalities across local contexts in ways that are not reducible to national or central institutional structures. Law in late-medieval England was something made in common.

Law looks different once we think about its structures as effects of widespread praxes. It was not just a mechanistic instrument of order, nor a discourse used manipulatively to justify existing arrangements of power and hierarchy, though it was certainly these things; it was also a pervasive means through which common people understood their relationships to one another. Law was thus a way in which they built a meaningful associational life—in short, it was part of a constitution, in the old sense, that bound people together in a shared understanding of governance. In this concluding section, I want to reflect on this 'common constitution' in fifteenth-century England, with a particular focus on the political implications of the model of law I have set out in this book. First I suggest some ways in which legality could intersect with the recent historiography of late-medieval political culture; second, I argue that law can help to connect the social and political history of this period.

In the past few years, historians have begun to advocate for a rather broader understanding of fifteenth-century politics, emphasizing the role of people other than the king and the circle of elite aristocrats in shaping policy. As Gerald Harriss stated over a quarter of a century ago, late-medieval 'government became something in which subjects were involved, something they learned to manipulate,

Law in Common: Legal Cultures in Late-Medieval England. Tom Johnson, Oxford University Press (2020).

DOI: 10.1093/oso/9780198785613.001.0001

criticize and even change'.[1] And, in the intervening years, more depth and detail has been added to his picture, such as on the role of urban politics in fostering such engagements, on the ways in which non-elites could participate in political action both locally and nationally, and, more recently, on the media of news, rumour, and information in allowing a broader public to take part in and help to shape political discourse.[2] Yet while there is a general agreement that a more broadly participatory political culture formed in the later Middle Ages, we have still tended to accord primacy to traditional modes of 'politics'. If we now accept that more people had a stake in, and might have influenced, elite political institutions or actors, there have been relatively fewer attempts to consider the kinds of politics they participated in 'elsewhere', away from the political centre.

Legal engagements, I would suggest, were one of the key ways in which non-elites built this politics of the elsewhere. The local institutions through which they made law were fulcrums for collective organization, decision-making, and dispute resolution within this quotidian scale of politics. The ideas that these institutions framed, both locally through distinctive forms of expertise and senses of right, and more broadly through conceptions of legality and justice, were bound into a broader ethic of associational life. Law was not, of course, the only plane on which this politics took place, nor was it a mode in which all non-elites could take part on an equal basis. Women, of course, but also the indigent poor and foreigners, were systematically excluded from active participation in local law-courts; indeed, their political marginality was significantly constituted by this exclusion from these institutions. But for all that we must qualify its reach and possibilities, law and legal institutions were nonetheless one of the most important ways in which common people negotiated and conceptualized their associational relationships.

In the kinds of legal structure built from below, therefore, we can perceive a political culture along the lines described by John Watts as 'a common acceptance of certain principles and practices and made real by a necessary deference to these

[1] Gerald Harriss, 'Political Society and the Growth of Government in Late Medieval England', *P&P*, 138 (1993), 28–57.

[2] On urban political culture, see Lorraine Attreed, *The King's Towns: Identity and Survival in Late Medieval Boroughs* (New York, 2001); more recently, Christian D. Liddy, *Contesting the City: The Politics of Citizenship in English Towns, 1250–1530* (Oxford, 2017). On popular politics, I. M. W. Harvey, 'Was there a popular politics in fifteenth-century England?', in *The McFarlane Legacy: Studies in Late Medieval Politics and Society*, ed. R. H. Britnell and A. J. Pollard (Stroud, 1996), 155–74; Christopher Dyer, 'The Political Life of the Fifteenth-Century English Village', in *The Fifteenth Century IV: Political Culture in Late Medieval Britain*, ed. Linda Clark and Christine Carpenter (Woodbridge, 2004), 135–57. On rumour and propaganda, see James A. Doig, 'Political Propaganda and Royal Proclamations in Late Medieval England', *Historical Research*, 71:176 (1998), 253–80; Simon Walker, 'Rumour, Sedition and Popular Protest in the Reign of Henry IV', *P&P*, 166 (2000), 31–65, and more recently, Christopher Fletcher, 'News, Noise, and the Nature of Politics in Late Medieval English Provincial Towns', *Journal of British Studies*, 56 (2017), 250–72.

in public statements and other behaviour'.[3] But I would suggest that we also need to think more carefully about *whose* actions we consider to be political, and *by whom* they were accepted as such, and, therefore, the range of 'principles and practices' that we include within the scope of politics. Most historians would now accept that the politics of the village and the politics of parliament were connected to one another.[4] But even as we have begun to concede a greater role in late-medieval politics to non-elites, we have been too hesitant, perhaps, to think beyond the modes and concepts of elite politics—of hierarchy, retinues, authority, policy—that we have inherited. Bringing ordinary people into late-medieval politics, then, also means accepting that they might not have acted in ways that look—or were represented as—'political' in the traditional ways in which this sphere of action has been understood within late-medieval historiography.

In order to properly understand the growth of late-medieval government, then, I think we need to move beyond simply expanding the places in which we look for politics, but also open up the kinds of conceptual links we are willing to make as historians. For example, we might consider the chain of associations between the conceptualizations of 'common' that we find in local courts—such as the common street, the common river, or the common baker—and the kind of 'common' we find within elite political discourse, such as 'commonweal' and the 'commons'. These concepts bore an analogous relation, such that the craftsman who condemned the blockage of a city street because it ought to be 'common' might apprehend in similar terms, for example, the Duke of York's claims to rule in the name of the commonweal.[5] This is not to say that such discursive connections were in any way straightforward or mechanistic, but rather that if we are to take seriously the idea of broader political culture in the later Middle Ages, then we need to look even for these more attenuated networks. The leet court was part of what gave parliament its authority, the by-law was part of what gave the statute its force; such connections were what made the constitution common.

In a similar way, we need to expand our sense of *how* government happened in this period. As Christine Carpenter has noted recently, there seems to be gap between the vast ambitions of the late-medieval English government—'policing, taxing and making its law available right down to village level'—and what it could practically achieve with the systems of communications, surveillance, and control

[3] John Watts, 'Conclusion', in *The End of the Middle Ages? England in the Fifteenth and Sixteenth Centuries*, ed. Watts (Stroud, 1998), 263–70, p. 266.

[4] R. B. Goheen, 'Peasant Politics? Village Community and the Crown in Fifteenth-Century England', *AHR*, 96:1 (1991), 42–62.

[5] See John Watts, 'Public or Plebs: The Changing Meaning of "the Commons", 1381–1549', in *Power and Identity in the Middle Ages: Essays in Memory of Rees Davies*, ed. Huw Pryce and John Watts (Oxford, 2007), 242–60, pp. 251–2.

at its disposal.[6] Yet this distance between centre and locality quickly melts away once we begin to conceive of the legal structures that were built upwards, overlapping and interlacing with those that reached down from the centre: some routes, such as the composition of a collective petition, could take people directly from the village to the Chancery, while others, such as the information constituted by inquest juries, might have to go through several stages of local and regional processing; others still, such as the ordinance passed at a decanal chapter, sat athwart the realm of 'politics' traditionally conceived. The tangled edifice of legal culture, in other words, provided an infrastructure for the more expansive aims of late-medieval government.

At the same time, however, it was precisely the nature of that infrastructure which also disrupted the flow of governmental power. Common legalities, as I have argued, involved more than just the reception of commands and the manipulation of legal ideas; they were also constituted in landscapes, performances, and physical objects. The successful transmission of government thus depended on a host of phenomena which were well beyond its strict control: in the local roads maintained by leet presentments, in the material endurance of a testimonial letter or writ upon contact with its angry recipient, in the audience's reaction to the proclamation of a new statute. These were the true grounds of the late-medieval polity, the power of which was a great deal more diffuse than we have tended to understand it. Government here was not just a system of political relationships—however broadly we conceive that—but a system of things, too.[7] Common legalities played an essential role in gathering these things together into categories as property, rights, or jurisdiction, and so providing a plane on which negotiation and action could take place.

If a broader conception of legal culture permits a more holistic understanding of late-medieval political culture, I hope that it may also work to show the ways it connects with the social history of this period. Moves in this direction took place, to some extent, in the historiography of early-modern England, through the work of Keith Wrightson, Andy Wood, Steve Hindle, and others.[8] Late-medievalists would profit from engaging in a similar conversation, and in doing so, might be able to significantly revise our chronology and conceptualization of premodern social and political change. As Isobel Harvey pointed out some two decades ago,

[6] Christine Carpenter, 'Political and Geographical Space: The Geopolitics of Medieval England', in *Political Space in Pre-industrial Europe*, ed. Beat Kümin (Farnham and Burlington, VT, 2009), 117–34, p. 118.

[7] See the essays in *Material Powers: Cultural studies, history and the material turn*, ed. Tony Bennett and Patrick Joyce (London, 2010).

[8] *The Experience of Authority in Early Modern England*, ed. Paul Griffiths, Adam Fox, and Steve Hindle (Basingstoke, 1996); Andy Wood, *The Politics of Social Conflict: The Peak Country, 1520–1770* (Cambridge, 1999); Steve Hindle, *The State and Social Change in Early Modern England, c. 1550–1640* (Basingstoke, 2000); Keith Wrightson, 'The "Decline of Neighbourliness" Revisited', in *Local Identities in Late Medieval and Early Modern England*, ed. Norman L. Jones and Daniel Woolf (Basingstoke, 2007), 19–49.

'much of the explanation for the changed political atmosphere of the fifteenth century lies in the fact that the populace lived in a world so different economically and socially from that of their forebears in the fourteenth century'.[9] With the notable exception of Marjorie McIntosh, few historians have attempted to frame these pervasive connections between socio-economic and political transformation, or how they impacted what came later.[10]

This is because for a long time the social history of the later Middle Ages has been conceptualized in relation to decline: in the stagnated population and economic slump of the fifteenth century, the erosion of the village community that is said to have taken place in this period, and, most importantly of all for late-medieval England, in the 'decline of serfdom' after the Black Death.[11] Mark Bailey's magisterial work on this latter subject has significantly challenged some of components of this narrative, but if anything, has re-emphasized its essential premise.[12] Yet the problem with the notion of serfdom's 'decline' is that it foregrounds the erosion of the old order, rather than the emergence of something new; it thus highlights the waning of elite authority at the expense of the increasing power of the commons. What we are seeing—and this is clear with law as with much else—is more complex than simply the deterioration of old structures of power, but rather their transformation.

The onus, then, cannot only be on political historians finding 'the political' within the ordinary contexts of late-medieval society; it must also lie in the way that we understand the scope of that society itself, and its capacity to change the frame of the political. Much social history in the past three decades has illuminated the 'cold politics' of countless ordinary domains: the power relationships inherent and constituted in gender dynamics and discourses, in the regular spaces of associational life, in the quotidian organization of the village, the town, the guild, and the parish.[13] Yet this immensely rich understanding of these relationships and discourses has remained curiously segmented from the kind of power that political historians discuss; and, more importantly still, these conversations have not really influenced the kinds of 'culture' from which political culture has

[9] Harvey, 'Was there a popular politics?', p. 158.

[10] See Marjorie Keniston McIntosh, *Controlling Misbehavior in England, 1370–1600* (Cambridge, 1998), which located the roots of early-modern social and cultural change in the later Middle Ages.

[11] On the depressed economy, John Hatcher, 'The great slump of the mid-fifteenth century', in *Progress and problems in medieval England: essays in honour of Edward Miller*, ed. John Hatcher and Richard Britnell (Cambridge, 1996), 237–72; on village community, Christopher Dyer, 'The English Medieval Village Community and Its Decline', *Journal of British Studies*, 33:4 (1994), 407–29; on the decline of serfdom, the classic account is R. H. Hilton, *The Decline of Serfdom in Medieval England* (London, 1969); also Christopher Dyer, 'Villeins, Bondmen, Neifs, and Serfs: New Serfdom in England, c. 1200–1600' in *Forms of Servitude in Northern and Central Europe: Decline, Resistance, and Expansion*, ed. Paul Freedman and Monique Bourin (Turnhout, 2005), 419–35.

[12] Mark Bailey, *The Decline of Serfdom in Late Medieval England: From Bondage to Freedom* (Woodbridge, 2014). For a summary of his arguments, pp. 307–37.

[13] My thanks to Claire Judde de la Rivière for sharing her ideas about 'cold politics' in premodern Europe, a topic on which, along with Chris Fletcher, we have organized various workshops.

been constructed in more recent historiography. It is vital that social historians begin to insert themselves in this conversation: to explain how the tectonic socio-economic and cultural shock of the late fourteenth century remodelled the late-medieval polity.[14]

In this book, particularly in the last two chapters, I have suggested some of the places in which we might trace such a transformation. The documentary revolution of the fifteenth century, in particular, highlights these connections between the traditional domains of social and economic history—in copyhold and tenurial arrangements, itinerant workers and labour laws—and those of the political, in the power relationships that were constituted and transmuted through these new documentary forms. But this was just one trajectory within a broad sweep of late-medieval social transformation; we must also look to processes of agrarian change, to the rebalancing of gender relations, to the changing spatial relationships of rural life, to new kinds of building and domesticity, to the development of popular religion (and of course heresy), to new understandings of work and labour, and many more things besides. We need to understand how these social, cultural, and material rearrangements of post-plague England connected to the changing shape and capacities of late-medieval government, that is, to think about how, in the long fifteenth century, 'the commons' was constituted.

Legality was one of the key vectors of this constitution because of the way in which it threaded institutional power into the intimate spaces of associational life. If we may take one final example, in 1524 Joan Combes was said to have seen her neighbour and personal enemy Elizabeth Wakefield standing outside her house in the parish of St Albans Wood Street. She reacted furiously just at the sight of her, calling her a thief, a heretic, and a traitor; Elizabeth responded calmly, 'when ye haue spoken i-nowghe mastres, I pray you take ye home'. This just infuriated Joan further, as she cried, 'Nay by godds body! I wyll stand here in spight of thy tethe, for yt ys the kings high way.'[15] These words were rearticulated by a third woman, a witness named Joan Cocks, a fletcher's wife originally from County Durham. Her testimony bring us into a world in which legality—the claim to simply stand in this particular place here, which was also the 'king's highway'—helped to constitute social relations, and so gave it a politics that at once originated in and transcended the everyday.

These common constitutions, the structures of power assembled from within the materials that made up common lives were what made possible the kind of ambitious institutional government of late-medieval England. They were also what—over the course of the late fourteenth and fifteenth centuries at least—helped to thwart it, as individuals called down the power of the king's peace onto

[14] For a top-down framing of this problem, see Robert C. Palmer, *English Law in the Age of the Black Death, 1348–1381: A Transformation of Governance and Law* (Chapel Hill, NC, and London, 1993).

[15] LMA, DL/C/207, f. 10r. For the rest of the depositions see ff. 15v, 23v, 24v–25r.

their enemies, manorial tenants composed bylaws against the will of the steward, or parishioners acted collectively against the extortions of a corrupt summoner. Neither the concept of law itself, nor its local institutions, offered any radical solutions to the injustices and inequalities of late-medieval society. But in these everyday moments when it was repurposed, when the lateral bonds of associational justice withstood the violence of hierarchy, we can see, constituted but fleetingly, the true capacious force of law made amidst the commons.

Bibliography

1. Primary Sources: Unpublished

Arundel, Arundel Castle (AC)

M702–4	Court rolls of Litcham hundred
M878	Court rolls of Wells and Warham

Cambridge, King's College (KCC)

BIG/117	Court rolls of Biggin
BRD/4–7	Court rolls of Brixton Deverill
CHA/estates1–4	Court rolls of Broad Chalke
CHA/31–4	Papers connected to a tithe dispute at Broad Chalke
COM/10–12	Court rolls of Combe
FOR/8/1–9	Court rolls of Woodfidley
HER/1	Court rolls of Archenfield
MON/1–2	Court rolls of Monxton
MON/15	Indenture for house repairs at Monxton
RIN/5–7	Court rolls of Ringwood
RIN/50	Custumal of Ringwood
SJP/1	Court rolls of St. James's Priory, Exeter
SJP/135, 166	Inquisitions in St James's Priory court leet
SJP/169	Notes on costs of holding court
STP/4–6	Court rolls of Stour Provost
WIT/17–19	Court rolls of Withyham
WOW/176	Court rolls of Wootton Wawen
WOW/27, 46–7, 597	Various documents connected to Wootton Wawen
WOW/35, 215	Writings relating to tithes at Wootton Wawen and Beoley

Cambridge, University Library (CUL)

MS Add. 3299	Court rolls and other financial papers for Buckland Filleigh
EDR/E1/1/3, 5, 8	Court rolls of the liberty of Ely

Chelmsford, Essex Record Office (ERO)

D/B 3/1/1–2	Composite books of Maldon
D/B 4	Court rolls of Harwich
D/B 5	Cr Borough court rolls of Colchester
D/B 5/R1	Red Parchment Book of Colchester
D/B 5/R2	Red Paper Book of Colchester
D/DCm Z18/9	Testimonial letter of Christina Brasier
D/D K/M136	Accounts of Foulness
D/DMj M2	Court rolls of North Fambridge

Chichester, West Sussex Record Office (WSRO)

PHA 6914–16	Court rolls of Catton
PHA 6970	Court roll of Tadcaster and Healeagh
PHA 7033–43	Court rolls of Spofforth

Chippenham, Wiltshire and Swindon History Office (WSHO)

192/26	Court book of the Sheriff of Wiltshire's tourn
865/330	Court rolls of Warminster Hundred
1300/83	Forest eyre of Savernake
1720263	Petition to the Duke of Gloucester
D4/3/1	Act book of the subdean of Salisbury Cathedral
G22/1/12–14	Court rolls of Marlborough
G25/1/20	Court roll of Wilton

Hereford, Herefordshire Archives and Records Centre (HARC)

AM33/3	Court rolls of Hereford Palace
BG11/2/6–7	Pleas, rolls, and files of the mayor's court in Hereford
BG/11/3/1	Rolls and files for law-days in Hereford
BG/11/4/1	Rolls and files for tourns in Hereford
BG/11/8/3	Rolls and files for gaol delivery in Hereford
BG/11/8/5, 6, 8	Miscellaneous papers from the city of Hereford
BG/11/17/1	Customs of the city of Hereford
BG/11/17/2–3	Miscellaneous papers from the city of Hereford
BG/11/17/11	Court book of the mayor of Hereford
BG/11/28	Miscellaneous papers
BG/11/29	Council of the Marches of Wales, Letters and Petitions
HD4/1/1	Act book of instance causes for Hereford diocese
HD4/1/88–110	Act books of 'rural consistories' for Hereford diocese

Hereford Cathedral Library and Archives (HCLA)

HCA130–HCA3209	Deeds, documents, and legal papers concerning the dean and chapter of Hereford
R1121, 1143–6, 1146a	Court rolls of Hereford Palace and the Canons' Bakehouse

Ipswich, Suffolk Record Office, Ipswich (SROI)

C1/1/8	Indenture concerning behaviour aboard ships at Ipswich
C/1/1/20	Royal charter to Ipswich
C1/1/21	Inspeximus of the bounds of Ipswich
C/1/8/4	Royal charter to Ipswich
C/2/6/1	Inquisition into piracy
C/2/6/2	Inquisition into piracy
C/2/10/3/2	Composite court book of Ipswich
HA30/312, 314	Court rolls of Westwood, Blythburgh, and Walberswick
HD64/1/12–29	Court rolls of Orford
SC18/40	Proceedings of an Admiralty inquisition

Leeds, West Yorkshire Archive Service (WYASL)

WYL160/205/55, 68, 76–7, 98, 107	Court rolls of Hatfield Chase
WYL163/158	Court rolls of Kettlewell

Lincoln, Lincolnshire Archives (LA)

Cj/1	Act book of the prebendary of Buckingham
Vj/0	Visitation book for the city of Leicester
Vj/3	Visitation book for Leicestershire and Huntingdonshire
Vj/4	Visitation book for Lincoln and Stow deaneries
Vj/5	Visitation book for Lincoln deanery

London, British Library (BL)

Add. Ch. 23173	Lease of game in Bedington
Add. Ch. 27290–310	Court rolls of Hereford Palace
Add. Ch. 34322, 34370	Court rolls of Barton-le-Clay
Add. Ch. 36522	Attestation of the inhabitants of Brenchley
Add. Ch. 40683	Petition to the French admiral from the bailiffs of Dunwich
Add. Ch. 40727–40740	Court rolls and other documents relating to Dunwich
Add. Ch. 49218–49328	Court rolls of Kintbury
Add. MS 36905	Custumal of Kintbury
Add. MS 46349	Accompt and Memorandum Book of Sir John Howard
MS Egerton 2540	Court book for the manors of William Beauchamp
MS Egerton 3001	Court book of Gayton

London, The National Archives (TNA)

C 1	Court of Chancery, Early Proceedings
C 49/21/22	Proceedings in a dispute between convent of St Mary, York, and the men of the Forest of Galtres
DL 30/128/1931, 1940–1	Court rolls of Pickering
DL 30/486/11–13	Court rolls of Knaresborough
DL 30/487/1–8	Court rolls of Knaresborough
DL 30/487/8, 10, 13	Court rolls of Aldborough
DL 30/489/2	Court rolls of Roecliff
DL 30/489/12	Court rolls of Knaresborough
DL 39/2/1	Court rolls of Duffield Frith
DL 39/2/2	Court rolls of Pickering
DL 39/2/4	Swannimote court rolls for the Forest of Weybridge and Sapley
DL 39/2/7	File of Forest proceedings for Northamptonshire
DL 39/2/8	Swannimote court rolls for Wharmore
DL 39/2/10	File of bills of indictment for Waltham Forest
DL 39/2/11	File of Forest pleas for Essex and Hampshire
DL 39/2/13	File of the Forest Eyre for Windsor
DL 39/2/14	Regarders' roll of Rockingham Forest
DL 39/2/15–18	Files and rolls of the Forest Eyre for Surrey and Windsor
DL 39/2/19–20	File of the Forest Eyre for Wiltshire
DL 39/2/21	Roll of convictions for Waltham Forest
DL 39/2/22	Roll of presentments for Waltham Forest
DL 39/2/23–4	Files of the Waltham Forest Eyre
DL 39/3/11	Roll of a view of the woods at Pontefract
DL 39/3/16, 26–7, 28A–B	Files and rolls relating to dispute at Pickering Forest

DL 39/3/23	Roll of presentments for Whaddon Chase
DL 39/3/29	Enrolment of a plea concerning Knaresborough Forest
DL 39/4/8	Calendar of indictments for the Forest Eyre of Surrey
E 32/197	Survey of the Forest of Ashdown
E 32/335	Bounds of Cliff Forest
E 146/1/10	File of the Forest Eyre at Bernwood
E 146/2/36–8	Perambulations and other documents relating to Savernake Forest
E 146/3/22	AOrder concerning wastes in Feckenham and Savernake Forests
KB 9	Court of King's Bench: Crown Side: Indictment Files
MPC 1/56	Map of Inclesmoor
REQ 2	Court of Requests
SC 2/153/55	Court rolls of Balston
SC 2/168/13	Court rolls of Plymton
SC 2/177/54–5	Court rolls of King's Langley
SC 2/193/53	Court rolls of King's Lynn Stapleware 'Water' and pie-powder
SC 2/211/43	Court rolls of Galtres Forest
SC 2/211/92, 94	Court rolls of Northallerton
SC 2/285/38–9	Court rolls of Grantham pie-powder
SC 8	Special Collections: Ancient Petitions
WARD 2/60/234/145	Oath of the Swannimote

Lowestoft, Suffolk Record Office, Lowestoft (SROL)

193/C4/1	Rental of the lands of Thomas Rosebury
194/B1	Admiralty and half-hundred court rolls for Kirkley and Kessingland
491/2/1	Borough ordinances of Southwold

Matlock, Derbyshire Record Office (DRO)

D77/2/1/1–14	Court rolls of Netherseal
D156/M/I1/6	Court roll of Ab Lench
D258/26/11/2	Testimonial letter of Robert Vernon
D939Z/M1	Court rolls of Bradbourne
D2375/110/21/1–2	Court rolls of Foremark
D2375M/24/2	Court rolls of Willington
D5236/4/42	Certificate by the tenants of Newton Solney

Northallerton, North Yorkshire County Record Office (NYRCO)

ZBD 1/50/15, 18	Court rolls of Osmotherley
ZBD 1/51/1–2, 5, 9, 12, 14, 27	Court rolls of Osmotherley
ZBD 1/52/3, 12, 27	Court rolls of Osmotherley
ZDX	Court rolls of Coverham
ZFL 110–11	Court rolls of Ingleby Arncliffe
ZQH 1	Cartulary of Richard Clarvaux

Norwich, Norfolk Record Office (NRO)

DCN 63/2	Composite manorial court book of the estate of the dean and chapter of Norwich Cathedral

KIM 1/9/16	Depositions concerning Litcham lings
KL/C7/4	Hall book of Lynn
KL/C17	Leet rolls of Lynn
NRS 3360, 13C6	Court rolls of Shipden
WKC 2/166 398x7	Court rolls of Runton and Beeston
Y/C 4	Court rolls of Yarmouth

Oxford, Bodleian Library (BLO)

Herefordshire Charters 7–9	Documents relating to the city of Hereford
Herefordshire Rolls 36–8	Legal writings and rental relating to the city of Hereford
Lincolnshire Charters 1	Testimonial letter of tenants of Casthorpe
Norfolk Rolls 102 and 103	Court rolls and customary of Great Cressingham
Norfolk Charters 109	Petition of the tenants of Frettenham

Oxford, Corpus Christi College (CCCO)

Bb/1–19	Court rolls of West Hendred
Ga 25/2/e, g	Court rolls of Milton
Ga 25/3/a, b, e, f	Court rolls of Milton
Ga 25/4/1	Court rolls of Milton
Ga 25/5/a, b, c, d	Court rolls of Milton
G1 Cap.8 Ev.94	Court rolls of Milton

Oxford, Magdalen College (MCO)

Beenham 40	Petition of Thomas Walyngton
Beenham 164	Petition of Thomas Walyngton
Brackley 55a	Citation for defamation, archdeaconry of Northampton
Brackley 66a	Letter from Robert Eyr concerning tenants of Brackley
Brackley 114	Inquisition into ruined building at Brackley
Brackley 209	Inquisition into ruined building at Brackley
Hilhampton 36	Exemplification of legal proceedings
Letters 31	Letter of Thomas Walyngton
Letters 32	Anonymous letter connected to Thomas Walyngton
Misc 164	Exemplification of pipe roll
Misc 275	Exemplification of Domesday
44/3–12	Various manorial documentation from Willoughby
45/1–26	Court rolls of Willoughby
140/6–16Documents	relating to a dispute between Bishop Waynflete and the city of Winchester concerning the River Itchen

Oxford, Oxfordshire History Centre (OHC)

BOR3/B2/IV/CR/2–14	Court rolls of Henley-on-Thames

Reading, Berkshire Record Office (BRO)

D/ESK/M4	Court rolls of Cookham

York, Borthwick Institute for Archives (BIA)

CCP 12/Amp 1–12	Court rolls and chapter acts of Ampleforth
DC.CP. 1401.1	Cause papers for a tithe dispute, Dean and Chapter of York Minster
DC.CP. 1491.1	Cause papers for a tithe dispute, Dean and Chapter of York Minster

York Minster Library and Archives (YMLA)

L2/3c	Visitation book of parishes of the Dean and Chapter of York Minster
M2(1)f.	Acta et Comperta, Dean and Chapter of York Minster
M2/6e	Register of the peculiar of St Leonard's Hospital, York
P1/1/4a	Court rolls of Farmanby
P1/1/4b	Court rolls of Newbald

2. Primary Sources: Published

A Calendar of the Earlier Hereford Cathedral Muniments, ed. B. G. Chales and H. D. Emanuel (6 vols; typescript, Hereford Cathedral Libraries, 1955).

Acts of Court of the Mercers' Company 1453–1527, ed. L. Lyell and F. D. Watney (Cambridge, 1936).

A Volume of English Miscellanies illustrating the History and Language of the Northern Counties of England, ed. J. Raine, Surtees Society 85 (Durham, 1890).

Bedfordshire Notes and Queries, Vol. III, ed. Frederic Augustus Blaydes (Bedford, 1893).

Beverley Town Documents, ed. A. F. Leach, Selden Society 14 (London, 1900).

Borough Customs, ed. M. Bateson, Selden Society 21 (London, 1906).

Documents relating to Law and Custom of the Sea, ed. R. G. Marsden (2 vols; London, 1915).

English Gilds, ed. J. T. Smith and L. T. Smith, Early English Text Society, original series, 40 (1870).

Heresy Trials in the Diocese of Norwich 1428–31, ed. N. Tanner, Camden Society, 4th series 20 (London, 1977).

Lex Mercatoria and Legal Pluralism: A Late Thirteenth-Century Treatise and Its Afterlife, ed. and transl., M. E. Basile, J. F. Bestor, D. R. Coquillette, and C. Donahue, Jr. (Cambridge, MA, 1998).

London Assize of Nuisance, 1301–1431: A Calendar, ed. H. M. Chew and W. Kellaway, London Record Society 10 (London, 1973).

Lower Ecclesiastical Jurisdiction in Late-Medieval England: The Courts of the Dean and Chapter of Lincoln, 1336–1349 and the Deanery of Wisbech, 1458–1484, ed. L. R. Poos, Records of Social and Economic History, new series 32 (Oxford, 2001).

Mittelenglische Originalurkunden (1405–1430), ed. H. Flasdieck (Heidelberg, 1926).

Mittelenglische Originalurkunden von der Chaucer-zeit bis zur mitte des XV. Jahrhunderts, ed. L. Morsbach (Heidelberg, 1923).

Noble Household Management and Spiritual Discipline in Fifteenth-Century Worcestershire, ed. J. P. Toomey, R. N. Swanson, and D. Guyatt, Worcestershire Historical Society, new series 24 (Worcester, 2013).

Paston Letters and Papers of the Fifteenth Century, ed. N. Davis (3 vols; Oxford, 1971–6).

Proceedings before the Justices of the Peace in the Fourteenth and Fifteenth Centuries: Edward III to Richard III, ed. B. H. Putnam (London, 1938).
Registrum Caroli Bothe, Episcopi Herefordensis, ed. A. T. Bannister, Canterbury and York Society 28 (London, 1921).
Report on the manuscripts of Lord Middleton, preserved at Wollaton hall, Nottinghamshire, ed. W. H. Stevenson, Historical Manuscripts Commission (Hereford, 1911).
Scriveners' Company Common Paper 1357–1628 with a Continuation to 1678, ed. F. W. Steer, London Record Society (London, 1968).
Select Cases Concerning the Law Merchant, 1270–1638. Vol. I: Local Courts, ed. C. Gross, Selden Society 23 (London, 1908).
Select Cases Concerning the Law Merchant. Vol. II: Central Courts, A.D. 1239–1633, ed. H. Hall, Selden Society 46 (London, 1930).
Select Cases in Manorial Courts 1250–1550, ed. L. R. Poos and L. Bonfield, Selden Society 114 (London, 1998).
Select Cases on Defamation to 1600, ed. R. H. Helmholz, Selden Society 101 (London, 1985).
Select Pleas in Manorial and Other Seignorial Courts, ed. F. W. Maitland, Selden Society 2 (London, 1888).
Select Pleas in the Court of Admiralty, Vol. I, ed. R. G. Marsden, Selden Society 6 (London, 1892).
Select Pleas of the Forest, ed. G. J. Turner, Selden Society 13 (London, 1901).
The Accounts of John Balsall, Purser of the Trinity of Bristol 1480–1, ed. T. F. Reddaway and A. A. Ruddock, Camden Miscellany 23, 4th series, 7 (London, 1969).
The Bailiff's Minute Book of Dunwich 1404–1430, ed. M. Bailey, Suffolk Records Society, 34 (Woodbridge, 1992).
The Black Book of Southampton, ed. A. B. Wallis Chapman, Southampton Record Society, 12 (3 vols; Southampton, 1912–15).
The Black Book of the Admiralty, ed. T. Twiss (4 vols; London, 1871–6).
The Commonplace Book of Robert Reynes of Acle: An Edition of Tanner MS 407, ed. C. Louis (London, 1980).
The Court Baron, being precedents for use in seignorial and other local courts, ed. F. W. Maitland and W. P. Baildon, Selden Society 4 (London, 1891).
The Court Rolls of the Manor of Ingoldmells, ed. W. O. Massingberd (London, 1902).
The Courts of the Archdeaconry of Buckingham, 1483–1523, ed. E. M. Elvey, Buckinghamshire Record Society 19 (Aylesbury, 1975).
The Domesday of Inclosures, 1517–1518, ed. I. S. Leasdam (2 vols; London, 1897).
The English Manor c.*1200–*c.*1500*, ed. M. Bailey (Manchester, 2002).
The First General Entry Book of the City of Salisbury 1387–1452, ed. D. R. Carr, Wiltshire Record Society 54 (Trowbridge, 2001).
The Honor and Forest of Pickering, ed. Robert Bell Turton, North Riding Record Society, new series, 1 (London, 1894).
The Medieval Lindsey Marsh: select documents, ed. A. E. B. Owen (Woodbridge, 1996).
The Peasants' Revolt of 1381, ed. R. B. Dobson (2nd edn; London, 1983).
The Records of the City of Norwich, ed. W. Hudson and J. Tingey (2 vols; Norwich and London, 1906–10).
The Red Paper Book of Colchester, ed. W.G. Benham (Colchester, 1902).
The Register of John Morton, Archbishop of Canterbury, 1486–1500, Volume III: Norwich Sede Vacante, *1499*, ed. C. Harper-Bill, Canterbury and York Society 89 (2000).
The Register of Thomas Myllyng, Bishop of Hereford (1474–1492), ed. A. T. Bannister, Cantilupe Society 23 (Hereford, 1919).

The York House Books 1461–1490, ed. L. C. Attreed (2 vols; Stroud, 1991).
York Civic Records, ed. A. Raine, Yorkshire Archaeological Society Record Series 98 (York, 1939).
Yorkshire Star Chamber Proceedings, ed. W. Brown, Yorkshire Archaeological Society Record Series 41 (Leeds, 1909).

3. Secondary Sources

Adams, G. B., 'Private Jurisdiction in England: A Theoretical Reconstruction', *AHR*, 23:3 (1918), 596–602.
Allen, D. (ed.), *Ipswich Borough Archives 1255–1835. A Catalogue* (Woodbridge, 2000).
Almond, R., 'The Forest as Hunting Ground', in J. Langton and G. Jones (eds), *Forests and Chases of Medieval England and Wales, c.1000 to c.1500* (Oxford, 2010), 68–80.
Almond, R., and Pollard, A. J., 'The Yeomanry of Robin Hood and Social Terminology in Fifteenth-Century England', *P&P*, 170 (2001), 52–77.
Amor, N. R., *Late Medieval Ipswich: Trade and Industry* (Woodbridge, 2011).
Appadurai, A., 'Introduction: commodities and the politics of value', in A. Appadurai (ed.), *The social life of things: Commodities in cultural perspective* (Cambridge, 1986), 3–63.
Appleby, J. C., and Dalton, P. (eds), *Outlaws in Medieval and Early Modern England: Crime, Government and Society, c.1066–c.1600* (Farnham, 2009).
Arnold, J. H., 'Lollardy and Sedition 1381–1431', *P&P*, 17 (1960), 1–44.
Arnold, J. H., *Inquisition and Power: Catharism and the Confessing Subject in Medieval Languedoc* (Philadelphia, PA, 2001).
Arnold, J. H., 'Inside and outside the medieval laity: some reflections on the history of emotions', in M. Rubin (ed.), *European Religious Cultures: Essays offered to Christopher Brooke on the occasion of his eightieth birthday* (London, 2008), 107–24.
Aston, M., 'A Kent Approver of 1440', *Bulletin of the Institute of Historical Research*, 36:93 (1963), 82–90.
Aston, M., 'The Gentlewoman and the Tapster, or, to the pub with Colin', in M. Aston and R. Horrox (eds), *Much heaving and shoving: late-medieval gentry and their concerns* (Lavenham, 2005), 121–31.
Attreed, L., 'Arbitration and the Growth of Urban Liberties in Late Medieval England', *Journal of British Studies*, 31:3 (1992), 205–35.
Attreed, L., *The King's Towns: Identity and Survival in Late Medieval Boroughs* (New York, NY, 2001).
Attreed, L., 'Urban Identity in Medieval English Towns', *Journal of Interdisciplinary History*, 32:4 (2002), 571–92.
Ault, W. O., *Private Jurisdiction in England* (New Haven, CT, 1923).
Ault, W. O., 'Manor Court and Parish Church in Fifteenth-Century England: A Study of Village By-Laws', *Speculum*, 42:1 (1967), 53–67.
Ault, W. O., *Open-Field Farming in Medieval England: A Study of Village By-Laws* (London, 1972).
Bailey, M., '*Per impetum maris*: natural disaster and economic decline in eastern England, 1275–1350', in B. M. S. Campbell (ed.), *Before the Black Death: Studies in the 'crisis' of the early fourteenth century* (Manchester, 1991), 184–208.
Bailey, M., 'Coastal Fishing off South East Suffolk in the Century After the Black Death', *Proceedings of the Suffolk Institute of Archaeology and History*, 37 (1992), 102–14.

Bailey, M., 'Manor and Leet Courts', in *The English Manor c.1200—c.1500* (Manchester, 2002), 178–84.
Bailey, M., *Medieval Suffolk: An Economic and Social History 1200–1500* (Woodbridge, 2007).
Bailey, M., *The Decline of Serfdom in Late Medieval England: From Bondage to Freedom* (Woodbridge, 2014).
Bailey, M., 'The Myth of the "Seigniorial Reaction" in England after the Black Death', in M. Kowaleski, J. Langdon, and P. R. Schofield (eds), *Peasants and Lords in the Medieval English Economy: Essays in Honour of Bruce M. S. Campbell* (Turnhout, 2015), 147–72.
Baker, J. H., 'The Law Merchant and the Common Law Before 1700', *Cambridge Law Journal*, 38:2 (1979), 295–322.
Bardsley, S., *Venomous Tongues: Speech and Gender in Late Medieval England* (Philadelphia, PA, 2006).
Barrett, T., 'Parchment, Paper, and Artisanal Research Techniques', in J. Wilcox (ed.), *Scraped, Stroked, and Bound: Materially Engaged Readings of Medieval Manuscripts* (Turnhout, 2013), 115–27.
Barrington, C., and Steiner, E. (eds), *The Letter of the Law: Legal Practice and Literary Production in Late Medieval England* (Ithaca, NY, 2002).
Barron, C., 'The London Middle English Guild Certificates', *Nottingham Medieval Studies*, 39 (1995), 108–45.
Barron, C., 'The Expansion of Education in Fifteenth-Century London', in J. Blair and B. Golding (eds), *The Cloister and the World: Essays in Medieval History in Honour of Barbara Harvey* (Oxford, 1996), 219–45.
Barron, C., *London in the Late Middle Ages: Government and People 1200–1500* (Oxford, 2004).
Bates, D., and Liddiard, R. (eds), *East Anglia and its North Sea World in the Middle Ages* (Woodbridge, 2013).
Bateson, M., 'The English and the Latin Versions of a Peterborough Court Leet, 1461', *EHR*, 19:75 (1904), 526–8.
Bäuml, F. H., 'Varieties and Consequences of Medieval Literacy and Illiteracy', *Speculum*, 55:2 (1980), 237–65.
Bazeley, M. L., 'The Forest of Dean and its Relations with the Crown During the Twelfth and Thirteenth Centuries', *The Transactions of the Bristol and Gloucestershire Archaeological Society*, 33 (1910), 153–286.
Bazeley, M. L., 'The Extent of English Forest in the Thirteenth Century', *TRHS*, 4th series 4 (1921), 140–72.
Beattie, C., '"Living as a Single Person": marital status, performance and the law in late medieval England', *Women's History Review*, 17:3 (2008), 327–40.
Beckerman, J. S., 'The Articles of Presentment of a Court Leet and Court Baron, in English, c. 1400', *Bulletin of the Institute of Historical Research*, 47 (1974), 230–4.
Beckerman, J. S., 'Adding Insult to *Iniuria*: Affronts to Honor and the Origins of Trespass', in M. S. Arnold, T. A. Green, S. A. Scully, and S. D. White (eds), *On the Laws and Customs of England: Essays in Honor of Samuel E. Thorne* (Chapel Hill, NC, 1981), 159–81.
Beckerman, J. S., 'Procedural Innovation and Institutional Change in Medieval English Manorial Courts', *L&HR*, 10:2 (1992), 197–252.
Beckerman, J. S., 'Adjudication: The Nature of Communal Judgments in a System of Customary Law', *L&HR*, 13:1 (1995), 1–22.
Bedos-Rezak, B., *When Ego was Imago: Signs of Identity in the Middle Ages* (Leiden, 2011).
Bellamy, J. G., *The Law of Treason in the Later Middle Ages* (Cambridge, 1970).

Bellamy, J. G., *Criminal Law and Society in Late Medieval and Tudor England* (Gloucester, 1984).

Benda-Beckmann, F. von, Benda-Beckmann, K. von, and Griffiths, A. (eds), *Spatializing Law: An Anthropological Geography of Law in Society* (Farnham, 2009).

Bender, B. (ed.), *Landscape: Politics and Perspectives* (Oxford, 1993).

Bennett, J., *Vibrant Matter: a political ecology of things* (Durham, NC, 2010).

Bennett, M. J., 'Education and Advancement', in R. Horrox (ed.), *Fifteenth-Century Attitudes: Perceptions of Society in Late Medieval England* (Cambridge, 1994), 76–96.

Best, S., and Marcus, S., 'Surface Reading: An Introduction', *Representations*, 108:1 (2009), 1–21.

Birrell, J., 'Peasant Craftsmen in the Medieval Forest', *Agricultural History Review*, 17:2 (1969), 91–107.

Birrell, J., 'The Medieval English Forest', *Journal of Forest History*, 24:2 (1980), 78–85.

Birrell, J., 'Who Poached the King's Deer? A Study in Thirteenth Century Crime', *Midland History*, 7 (1982), 9–25.

Birrell, J., 'Common Rights in the Medieval Forest: Disputes and Conflicts in the Thirteenth Century', *P&P*, 11 (1987), 22–49.

Birrell, J., 'Deer and Deer Farming in Medieval England', *Agricultural History Review*, 40:2 (1992), 112–26.

Birrell, J., 'Peasant deer poachers in the medieval forest', in R. Britnell and J. Hatcher (eds), *Progress and problems in medieval England: Essays in Honour of Edward Miller* (Cambridge, 1996), 68–88.

Blake, J. B., 'The medieval coal trade of North East England: some fourteenth-century evidence', *Northern History*, 2 (1967), 1–26.

Blanchard, I., 'The Miner and Agricultural Community in Late Medieval England', *Agricultural History Review*, 20 (1970), 96–106.

Blanchard, I., 'Rejoinder: Stannator Fabulosus', *Agricultural History Review*, 22 (1974), 65–7.

Blatcher, M., *The Court of King's Bench 1450–1550: A Study in Self-help* (London, 1978).

Blomley, N. K., *Law, Space, and the Geographies of Power* (New York, NY, 1994).

Blomley, N. K., 'Making Private Property: Enclosure, Common Right and the Work of Hedges', *Rural History*, 18:1 (2007), 1–21.

Blomley, N. K., 'Simplification is complicated: property, nature, and the rivers of law', *Environment and Planning A*, 40 (2008), 1825–42.

Blomley, N. K., *Rights of Passage: Sidewalks and the Regulation of Public Flow* (Abingdon, 2011).

Boisseuil, D., Chastang, P., Feller L., and Morsel, J. (eds), *Écritures de l'espace social: Melanges d'histoire medieval offerts à Monique Bourin* (Paris, 2010).

Bonfield, L., 'The Nature of Customary Law in the Manor Courts of Medieval England', *Comparative Studies in Society and History*, 31:3 (1989), 514–34.

Bossy, J. (ed.), *Disputes and Settlements: Law and Human Relations in the West* (Cambridge, 1983).

Bourdieu, P., *Outline of a Theory of Practice*, transl. Richard Nice (Cambridge, 1977).

Bourin, M., and Boisellier, S. (eds), *L'espace rural au Moyen Âge, Portugal, Espagne, France (XIIe–XIVe siècle): Mélanges en l'honneur de Robert Durand* (Rennes, 2002).

Braddick, M. J., *State Formation in Early Modern England, c. 1550–1700* (Cambridge, 2000).

Brand, P., 'The languages of the law in later medieval England', in D. A. Trotter (ed.), *Multilingualism in Later Medieval Britain* (Cambridge, 2000), 63–76.

Braverman, I., 'Hidden in Plain View: Legal Geography from a Visual Perspective', *Law, Culture and the Humanities*, 7:2 (2010), 173–86.

Brennan, G., 'Language and nationality: the role of policy towards Celtic languages in the consolidation of Tudor power', *Nations and Nationalism*, 7:3 (2001), 317–38.

Brewer, J., and Styles, J. (eds), *An Ungovernable People: The English and their law in the seventeenth and eighteenth centuries* (London, 1980).

Bridbury, A. R., 'English Provincial Towns in the Later Middle Ages', *Economic History Review*, 34:1 (1981), 1–24.

Briggs, C. D., 'Manor Court Procedures, Debt Litigation Levels, and Rural Credit Provision in England, c. 1290–c.1380', *L&HR*, 24:3 (2006), 519–58.

Briggs, C. D., 'The availability of credit in the English countryside, 1400–1480', *Agricultural History Review*, 56:1 (2008), 1–24.

Briggs, C. D., 'Seigniorial control of villagers' litigation beyond the manor in later medieval England', *Historical Research*, 81:213 (2008), 399–422.

Briggs, C. F., 'Literacy, reading, and writing in the medieval West', *Journal of Medieval History*, 26 (2000) , 397–420.

Britnell, R. H., *Growth and decline in Colchester, 1300–1525* (Cambridge, 1986).

Britnell, R. H., 'Uses of French Language in Medieval English Towns', in J. Wogan-Browne (ed.), *Language and Culture in Medieval Britain: The French of England c.1100–c.1500* (York, 2009), 81–9.

Britton, E., *The Community of the Vill: A Study in the History of the Family and Village Life in Fourteenth-Century England* (Toronto, 1977).

Brooks, C. W., *Law, Politics and Society in Early Modern England* (Cambridge, 2008).

Brooks, N., 'The Organization and Achievements of the Peasants of Kent and Essex in 1381', in H. Mayr-Harting and R. I. Moore (eds), *Studies in medieval history presented to R. H. C. Davis*, (London, 1985), 247–70.

Brown, M. P., 'The Role of the Wax Tablet in Medieval Literacy: A reconsideration in light of a recent find from York', *The British Library Journal*, 20:1 (1994), 1–16.

Brundage, J. A., *Medieval Canon Law* (New York, NY, 1995).

Brundage, J. A., *The Medieval Origins of the Legal Profession* (Chicago, IL, 2008).

Burgess, G., Knights, M., et al., 'Commonwealth: the Social, Cultural, and Conceptual Contexts of an Early Modern Keyword', *Historical Journal*, 54:3 (2011), 659–87.

Burwash, D., *English Merchant Shipping 1460–1540* (Newton Abbot, 1969).

Butcher, A., 'Textual Production and Vernacular Behaviour: Locating a Fifteenth-Century Administrative Book', in E. Salter and H. Wicker (eds), *Vernacularity in England and Wales, c. 1300–1550* (Turnhout, 2011), 295–323.

Butcher, D., *Lowestoft, 1550–1750: Development and Change in a Suffolk Coastal Town* (Woodbridge, 2008).

Butcher, D., *Medieval Lowestoft: The Origins and Growth of a Suffolk Coastal Community* (Woodbridge, 2016).

Caenegem, R. C. van, 'Reflexions on Rational and Irrational Modes of Proof in Medieval Europe', *Tijdschrift voor Rechtsgeschiedenis*, 58 (1990), 263–79.

Cam, H., *The Hundred and the Hundred Rolls: an outline of local government* (London, 1936).

Cam, H., *Liberties and Communities in Medieval England: Collected Studies in Local Administration and Topography* (Cambridge, 1944).

Cam, H., *Law-Finders and Law-Makers in Medieval England: Collected Studies in Legal and Constitutional History* (London, 1962).

Campbell, B. M. S., 'A Fair Field Once Full of Folk: Agrarian Change in an Era of Population Decline, 1348–1500', *The Agricultural History Review*, 41:1 (1993), 60–70.

Campbell, B. M. S., 'The Agrarian Problem in the Early Fourteenth Century', *P&P*, 188 (2005), 3–70.

Campbell, B. M. S., 'Nature as a historical protagonist: environment and society in pre-industrial England', *Economic History Review*, 63:2 (2010), 281–314.

Campbell, B. M. S., *The Great Transition: Climate, Disease, and Society in the Late-Medieval World* (Cambridge, 2016).

Cantor, L. M., 'Forests, Chases, Parks and Warrens', in L. M. Cantor (ed.) *The English Medieval Landscape* (London, 1982), 56–85.

Cantor, L. M., *The Medieval Parks of England: A Gazetteer* (Loughborough, 1983).

Carpenter, C., 'Law, Justice and Landowners in Late Medieval England', *L&HR*, 1:2 (1983), 205–37.

Carpenter, C., *Locality and Polity: A Study of Warwickshire Landed Society, 1401–1499* (Cambridge, 1992).

Carpenter, C., 'Gentry and Community in Medieval England', *Journal of British Studies*, 33 (1994), 340–80.

Carpenter, C., 'Political and Geographical Space: the Geopolitics of medieval England', in B. Kümin (ed.), *Political Space in Pre-Industrial Europe* (Farnham and Burlington, VT, 2009), 117–34.

Carrel, H., 'Disputing legal privilege: civic relations with the Church in late medieval England', *Journal of Medieval History*, 35 (2009), 279–96.

Carrel, H., 'The ideology of punishment in late medieval English towns', *Social History*, 34:3 (2009), 301–20.

Cartmill, M., *A View to a Death in the Morning: Hunting and Nature through History* (Cambridge, MA, 1993).

Carus-Wilson, E. M., and Coleman, O., *England's Export Trade 1275–1547* (Oxford, 1963).

Catto, J., 'Written English: The Making of the Language 1370–1400', *P&P*, 179 (2003), 24–59.

Cavill, P. R., *The English Parliaments of Henry VII 1485–1504* (Oxford, 2009).

Cheyette, F. L., 'Custom, Case Law, and Medieval "Constitutionalism": A Re-Examination', *Political Science Quarterly*, 78:3 (1963), 362–90.

Childs, W., 'Irish Merchants and Seamen in Late-Medieval England', *Irish Historical Studies*, 32:125 (2000), 22–43.

Clanchy, M. T., 'Remembering the Past and the Good Old Law', *History*, 55 (1970), 165–76.

Clanchy, M. T., 'Law, Government, and Society in Medieval England', *History*, 60 (1974), 72–8.

Clanchy, M. T., *From Memory to Written Record: England 1066–1307* (2nd edn; Oxford, 1993).

Clark, E., 'Medieval Labor Law and English Local Courts', *American Journal of Legal History*, 27:4 (1983), 330–53.

Clark, P. *The English Alehouse: A Social History 1200–1830* (New York, NY, 1983).

Cockburn, J. S., and Green, T. A. (eds), *Twelve Good Men and True: The Criminal Trial Jury in England, 1200–1800* (Princeton, NJ, 1988).

Cohen, E., *The Crossroads of Justice: Law and Culture in Late Medieval France* (Leiden, 1993).

Coleman, O., 'Trade and Prosperity in the Fifteenth Century: Some Aspects of the Trade of Southampton', *Economic History Review*, 16:1 (1963), 9–22.

Cooper, A., 'The Rise and Fall of the Anglo-Saxon Law of the Highway', in S. Morrilo (ed.), *The Haskins Society Journal: Studies in Medieval History*, 12 (Woodbridge, 2002), 39–69.

Cosgrove, D. E., *Social Formation and Symbolic Landscape* (London, 1984).

Cottle, B., *The Triumph of English 1350–1400* (London, 1969).

Crane, S., 'Ritual Aspects of the Hunt *à Force*', in B. A. Hanawalt and L. J. Kiser (eds), *Engaging with Nature: Essays on the Natural World in Medieval and Early Modern Europe* (Notre Dame, IN, 2008), 63–84.

Craun, E. D. (ed.), *The Hands of the Tongue: Essays on Deviant Speech* (Kalamazoo, MI, 2007).

Creighton, O. H., *Designs Upon the Land: Elite Landscapes of the Middle Ages* (Woodbridge, 2009).

Crook, D. 'The Records of Forest Eyres in the Public Record Office, 1179 to 1670', *Journal of the Society of Archivists*, 17:2 (1996), 183–93.

Crowley, D. A., 'The Later History of Frankpledge', *Bulletin of the Institute of Historical Research*, 48:117 (1975), 1–15.

Cushway, G., *Edward III and the War at Sea: The English Navy, 1327–1377* (Woodbridge, 2011).

Da Rold, O., 'Materials', in A. Gillespie and D. Wakelin (eds), *The Production of Books in England 1350–1500* (Cambridge, 2011), 12–33.

Davies, R., 'The Peoples of Britain and Ireland, 1100–1400: I Identities', *Transactions of the Royal Historical Society*, 6th series, 4 (1994), 1–20.

Davies, R., 'The Peoples of Britain and Ireland, 1100–1400: IV Language and Historical Mythology', *Transactions of the Royal Historical Society*, 6th series, 7 (1997), 1–24.

Davies, W., 'Judges and judging: truth and justice in northern Iberia on the eve of the millennium', *Journal of Medieval History*, 36 (2010), 193–203.

Davies, W., and Fouracre, P. (eds), *The Settlement of Disputes in Early Medieval Europe* (Cambridge, 1986).

Davis, J., 'Baking for the common good: a reassessment of the assize of bread in Medieval England', *Economic History Review*, 57:3 (2004), 465–502.

Davis, J., 'The Cross and the Pillory: Symbolic Structures of Commercial Space in Medieval English Towns', in S. Shrich and J. Oberste (eds), *Stätische Räume im Mittelalter* (Regensburg, 2009), 241–59.

Davis, J., *Medieval Market Morality: Life, Law and Ethics in the English Marketplace, 1200–1500* (Cambridge, 2012).

Day, J., 'The great bullion famine of the fifteenth century', *P&P*, 79 (1978), 3–54.

Delaney, D., *Law and Nature* (Cambridge, 2003).

DeWindt, A. R., 'Redefining the Peasant Community in Medieval England: The Regional Perspective', *Journal of British Studies*, 26:2 (1987), 163–207.

DeWindt, A. R., 'Local Government in a Small Town: A Medieval Leet Jury and Its Constituents', *Albion: A Quarterly Journal Concerned with British Studies*, 23:4 (1991), 627–54.

DeWindt, E. B., *Land and People in Holywell-cum-Needingworth: Structures of Tenure and Patterns of Social Organization in an East Midlands Village, 1252–1457* (Toronto, 1972).

Dodd, G., 'The Rise of English, the Decline of French: Supplications to the English Crown, c. 1420–1450', *Speculum*, 86:1 (2011), 117–50.

Dodd, G., 'The Spread of English in the Records of Central Government, 1400–1430', in E. Salter and H. Wicker (eds), *Vernacularity in England and Wales, c. 1300–1550* (Turnhout, 2011), 225–66.

Dodds, B., 'Estimating arable output using Durham Priory tithe receipts, 1341–1450', *Economic History Review*, 67:2 (2004), 245–85.

Dodds, B., *Peasants and Production in the Medieval North-East: The Evidence from Tithes, 1270–1536* (Woodbridge, 2007).

Doe, N., *Fundamental Authority in Late Medieval English Law* (Cambridge, 1990).

Doig, J. A., 'Political Propaganda and Royal Proclamations in Late Medieval England', *Historical Research*, 71:176 (1998), 253–80.

Donahue, Jr. C., 'Roman Canon Law in the Medieval English Church: Stubbs vs. Maitland Re-Examined after 75 Years in the Light of Some Records from the Church Courts', *Michigan Law Review*, 72:4 (1974), 647–716.

Donahue, Jr. C., 'Proof by Witnesses in the Church Courts of Medieval England: An Imperfect Reception of the Learned Law', in M. S. Arnold, T. A. Green, S.A. Scully, and S. D. White (eds), *On the Laws and Customs of England: Essays in Honor of Samuel E. Thorne* (Chapel Hill, NC, 1981), 127–58.

Donahue, Jr. C. (ed.), *The Records of the Medieval Ecclesiastical Courts, pt. 2: England*, Reports of the Working Group on Church Court Records (Berlin, 1994).

Donahue, Jr. C., 'Medieval and Early Modern *Lex mercatoria*: An Attempt at the *probatio diabolica*', *Chicago Journal of International Law*, 5:1 (2004), 21–42.

Doyle, A. I., 'The Work of a Late Fifteenth-Century English Scribe, William Ebesham', *Bulletin of the John Rylands Library*, 39:2 (1957), 298–325.

Draper, G., 'Writing English, French and Latin in the Fifteenth Century: A Regional Perspective', in L. Clark (ed.), *Fifteenth-Century VII: Conflicts, Consequences and the Crown in the Late Middle Ages* (Woodbridge, 2007), 213–26.

Dresch, P., and Scheele, J. (eds), *Legalism: Rules and Categories* (Oxford, 2015).

Dresch, P., and Skoda, H. (eds), *Legalism: Anthropology and History* (Oxford, 2012).

Drury, J. L., 'Durham palatinate forest law and administration, especially in Weardale up to 1440', *Archaeologica Aeliana*, 5th series, 6 (1978), 87–105.

DuBoulay, F. R. H., *An Age of Ambition: English Society in the late Middle Ages* (London, 1970).

Dumolyn, J., and Haemers, J., '"A Bad Chicken was Brooding": Subversive Speech in Late Medieval Flanders', *P&P*, 214 (2012), 45–86.

Dumolyn, J., Haemers, J., Herrer, H. R. O., and Challet, V. (eds), *The Voices of the People in Late Medieval Europe: Communication and Popular Politics* (Turnhout, 2014).

Duncumb, J., *Collections towards the History and Antiquities of the County of Hereford* (2nd edn; 8 vols; Cardiff, 1996).

Dyer, C., *Lords and Peasants in a Changing Society: The Estates of the Bishopric of Worcester, 680–1540* (Cambridge, 1980).

Dyer, C., 'The English Medieval Village Community and Its Decline', *Journal of British Studies*, 33:4 (1994), 407–29.

Dyer, C., *Standards of Living in the Later Middle Ages* (Cambridge, 1998).

Dyer, C., 'Small places with large consequences: the importance of small towns in England, 1000–1540', *Historical Research*, 75 (2002), 1–24.

Dyer, C., 'The Political Life of the Fifteenth-Century English Village', in L. Clark and C. Carpenter (eds), *The Fifteenth Century IV: Political Culture in Late Medieval Britain* (Woodbridge, 2004), 135–57.

Dyer, C., *An Age of Transition? Economy and Society in England in the Later Middle Ages* (Oxford, 2005).

Dyer, C., 'Villeins, Bondmen, Neifs, and Serfs: New Serfdom in England, *c.* 1200–1600', in P. Freedman and M. Bourin (eds), *Forms of Servitude in Northern and Central Europe: Decline, Resistance, and Expansion* (Turnhout, 2005), 419–35.

Dyer, C., 'Conflict in the landscape: the enclosure movement in England, 1220–1349', *Landscape History*, 28:1 (2006), 21–33.

Dyer, C., 'The Agrarian Problem, 1440–1520', in J. Whittle (ed.), *Landlords and Tenants in Britain, 1440–1660: Tawney's Agrarian Problem Revisited* (Woodbridge, 2013), 19–34.

Dyer, C., 'England's Economy in the Fifteenth Century', in L. Clark (ed.), *The Fifteenth Century XIII: Exploring the Evidence: Commemoration, Administration and the Economy* (Woodbridge, 2014), 201–25.

Dyer, C., and Penn, S. A. C., 'Wages and Earnings in Late Medieval England: Evidence from the Enforcement of the Labour Laws', *Economic History Review*, 43:3 (1990), 356–76.

Dymond, D., 'God's Disputed Acre', *Journal of Ecclesiastical History*, 50:3 (1999), 463–97.

Edwards, L. F., 'Law as Social History', in M. D. Dubber and C. Tomlins (eds), *The Oxford Handbook of Legal History* (Oxford, 2018), 119–34.

Eisel, J. C., 'The Castle Mills, Hereford', *Transactions of the Woolhope Field Club*, 50:1 (2000), 58–67.

Evans, R., Taylor, A., Watson, N., and Wogan-Browne, J. (eds), *The idea of the vernacular: An anthology of Middle English literary theory, 1280–1520* (University Park, PA, 1999).

Everitt, A., 'Country, County and Town: Patterns of Regional Evolution in England', *Transactions of the Royal Historical Society*, 5th series, 29 (1979), 79–108.

Ewick, P., and Silbey, S. S., 'Conformity, Contestation, and Resistance: An Account of Legal Consciousness', *New England Law Review*, 26 (1992), 323–68.

Faith, R., 'The "Great Rumour" of 1377 and Peasant Ideology', in R. H. Hilton and T. H. Aston (eds), *The English Rising of 1381* (Cambridge, 1984), 43–73.

Falk Moore, S., 'Law and Social Change: The Semi-Autonomous Social Field as an Appropriate Subject of Study', *Law & Society Review*, 7:4 (1973), 719–46.

Fenster T., and Smail, D. L. (eds), *Fama: The Politics of Talk and Reputation in Medieval Europe* (Ithaca, NY, 2003).

Field, R., 'Migration in the Later Middle Ages: The Case of the Hampton Lovett Villeins', *Midland History*, 8 (1983), 28–48.

Fisher, J. H., *The Emergence of Standard English* (Lexington, KY, 1996).

Fleming, P., 'Conflict and urban government in later medieval England: St Augustine's Abbey and Bristol', *Urban History*, 27:3 (2000), 325–43.

Fletcher, C., 'Langue et nation en Angleterre à la fin du Moyen Âge', *Révue française d'histoire des idées politiques*, 36 (2012), 233–52.

Fletcher, C., 'News, Noise, and the Nature of Politics in Late Medieval English Provincial Towns', *Journal of British Studies*, 56 (2017), 250–72.

Foard, G., 'Medieval Woodland, Agriculture and Industry in Rockingham Forest, Northamptonshire', *Medieval Archaeology*, 45:1 (2001), 41–95.

Forrest, I., *The Detection of Heresy in Late Medieval England* (Oxford, 2005).

Forrest, I., 'Defamation, Heresy, and Late Medieval Social Life', in L. Clark, M. Jurkowski, and C. Richmond (eds), *Image, Text, and Church, 1380–1600: Essays for Margaret Aston* (Toronto, 2009), 142–61.

Forrest, I., 'The Politics of Burial in Late Medieval Hereford', *EHR*, 125: 516 (2010), 1110–38.

Forrest, I., 'The archive of the official of Stow and the "machinery" of church government in the late thirteenth century', *Historical Research*, 84:223 (2011), 1–13.

Forrest, I., 'The Transformation of Visitation in Thirteenth-Century England', *P&P*, 221 (2013), 3–38.

Forrest, I., 'The Summoner', in S. Rigby and A. Minnis (eds), *Historians on Chaucer: The 'General Prologue' to the Canterbury Tales* (Oxford, 2014), 421–42.

Forrest, I., 'The Survival of Medieval Visitation Records', *Archives (The Journal of the British Records Association)*, 38:125 (2017), 1–10.

Forrest, I., *Trustworthy Men: How Inequality and Faith Made the Medieval Church* (Princeton, NJ, 2018).

Forrest, I., and Challet, V., 'The masses', in C. Fletcher, J-P. Genet, and J. Watts (eds), *Government and Political Life in England and France, c.1300–c.1500* (Cambridge, 2015), 279–316.

Forrest, I., and Haour, A., 'Trust in Long-Distance Relationships, 1000–1600 CE', *P&P*, 238, supplement 'The Global Middle Ages' (2018), 191–214.

Fowler, R. C., 'The Abbey of Beeleigh by Maldon', in W. Page (ed.), *VCH Essex, Volume II* (London, 1907).

Fox, H., *The Evolution of the Fishing Village: Landscape and Society along the South Devon Coast, 1086–1550* (Oxford, 2001).

Fox, H., 'Two Devon Estuaries in the Middle Ages: Fisheries, Ports, Fortifications and Places of Worship', *Landscapes*, 8:1 (2007), 39–68.

Fox, H., *Dartmoor's Alluring Uplands: Transhumance and Pastoral Management in the Middle Ages*, ed. M. Tompkins and C. Dyer (Exeter, 2012).

Fraher, R. M., 'Conviction According to Conscience: The Medieval Jurists' Debate concerning Judicial Discretion and the Law of Proof', *L&HR*, 7:1 (1989), 23–88.

Franklin, S., *Writing, Society and Culture in Early Rus, c.950–1300* (Cambridge, 2002).

Frankot, E., 'Medieval Maritime Law from Oléron to Wisby: Jurisdictions in the Law of the Sea', in J. Pan-Montojo and F. Pedersen (eds), *Communities in European history: representations, jurisdictions, conflicts* (Pisa, 2007), 151–72.

Frankot, E., *Of Laws of Ships and Shipmen: Medieval Maritime Law and its Practice in Urban Northern Europe* (Edinburgh, 2012).

French, K. L., *The People of the Parish: Community Life in a Late Medieval English Diocese* (Philadelphia, PA, 2001).

Friel, I., *The good ship: ships, shipbuilding and technology in England 1200–1520* (London, 1995).

Friel, I., 'Oars, sails and guns: The English and War at Sea, *c*.1200–*c*.1500', in J. B. Hattendorf and R. W. Unger (eds), *War at Sea in the Middle Ages and Renaissance* (Woodbridge, 2003), 69–79.

Fryde, E. B., *Peasants and Landlords in Later Medieval England,* c.*1380–1525* (New York, NY, 1996).

Fudge, J. D., *Cargoes, Embargoes, and Emissaries: The Commercial and Political Interaction of England and the German Hanse 1450–1510* (Toronto, 1995).

Gardiner, T., *An Historical Account of Dunwich* (London, 1754).

Garrett-Goodyear, Harold, 'The Tudor Revival of Quo Warranto and Local Contributions to State Building', in M. S. Arnold, T. A. Green, S. A. Scully, and S. D. White (eds), *On the Laws and Customs of England: Essays in Honor of Samuel E. Thorne* (Chapel Hill, NC, 1981), 231–95.

Garrett-Goodyear, Harold, 'Common Law and Manor Courts: Lords, Copyholders and Doing Justice in Early Tudor England', in J. Whittle (ed.), *Landlords and Tenants in Britain, 1440–1660: Tawney's Agrarian Problem Revisited* (Woodbridge, 2013), 35–51.

Geertz, C., *Local Knowledge: Further Essays in Interpretive Anthropology* (New York, NY, 1983).

Gerstenberger, H. 'Men Apart: The Concept of "Total Institution" and the Analysis of Seafaring', *International Journal of Maritime History*, 8:1 (1996), 173–82.

Getzler, J., *A History of Water Rights at Common Law* (Oxford, 2004).

Giles, K., 'Seeing and Believing: Visuality and Space in Pre-Modern England', *World Archaeology*, 39:1 (2007), 105–21.

Given-Wilson, C., 'The Problem of Labour in the Context of English Government, c. 1350–1450', in J. Bothwell, P. J. P. Goldberg and W. M. Ormrod (eds), *The Problem of Labour in Fourteenth Century England* (York, 2000), 85–100.

Goddard, R., 'Small Boroughs and the Manorial Economy: Enterprise Zones or Urban Failures?', *P&P*, 210 (2011), 3–31.

Goddard, R., 'Medieval business networks: St Mary's guild and the borough court in later medieval Nottingham', *Urban History*, 40:1 (2013), 3–27.

Goheen, R. B., 'Peasant Politics? Village Community and the Crown in Fifteenth-Century England', *AHR*, 96:1 (1991), 42–62.

Goldberg, P. J. P., *Women, Work, and Life-Cycle in a Medieval Economy: York and Yorkshire* c.*1300–1520* (Oxford, 1992).

Goldberg, P. J. P., 'Pigs and Prostitutes: Streetwalking in Comparative Perspective', in K. J. Lewis, N. J. Menuge, and K. M. Phillips (eds), *Young Medieval Women* (New York, NY, 1999), 172–93.

Goldberg, P. J. P., *Communal Discord, Child Abduction, and Rape in the Later Middle Ages* (Basingstoke, 2008).

Gordon, R. W., 'Critical Legal Histories', *Stanford Law Review* 36 (1984), 57–125.

Gordon, R. W., '"Critical Legal Histories Revisited": A Response', *Law & Social Inquiry*, 37:1 (2012), 200–15.

Grant, R., *The Royal Forests of England* (Stroud, 1991).

Green, R. F., *A Crisis of Truth: Literature and Law in Ricardian England* (Philadelphia, PA, 1999).

Green, R. F., 'The Early History of the Scriveners' Company Common Paper and its So-Called "Oaths"', in S. Horobin and L. R. Mooney (eds), *Middle English Texts in Transition: A Festschrift dedicated to Toshiyuki Takamiya on his 70th birthday* (Woodbridge, 2014), 1–20.

Green, T. A., *Verdict According to Conscience: Perspectives on the English Criminal Trial Jury, 1200–1800* (Chicago, IL, 1985).

Greiner, C., and Sakdapolrak, P., 'Translocality: Concepts, Applications and Emerging Research Perspectives', *Geography Compass*, 7:5 (2013), 373–84.

Griffiths, P., Fox, A., and Hindle, S. (eds), *The Experience of Authority in Early Modern England* (Basingstoke, 1996).

Groebner, V., *Who Are You? Identification, Deception, and Surveillance in Early Modern Europe*, transl. Mark Kyburz and John Peck (New York, NY, 2007).

Gross, C., 'The Court of Piepowder', *The Quarterly Journal of Economics*, 20:2 (1906), 231–49.

Hall, D., 'The drainage of arable land in medieval England', in H. Cook and T. Williamson (eds), *Water Management in the English Landscape: Field, Marsh and Meadow* (Edinburgh, 1999), 28–40.

Hallam, H. E., *Settlement and Society: a study of the early agrarian history of south Lincolnshire* (Cambridge, 1965).

Hammond, M. H., 'Assemblies and Writing of Administrative Documents in the Central Medieval Kingdom of the Scots', in M. Mostert and P. S. Barnwell (eds), *Medieval Legal Process: Physical, Spoken and Written Performance in the Middle Ages* (Turnhout, 2011), 123–46.

Hanawalt, B. A., 'The Host, the Law, and the Ambiguous Space of Medieval London Taverns', in B. Hanawalt and D. Wallace (eds), *Medieval Crime and Social Control* (Minneapolis, MN, 1999), 204–23.

Hanawalt, B. A., and Kobialka, M. (eds), *Medieval Practices of Space* (Minneapolis, MN, 2000).

Harding, A., *The Law Courts of Medieval England* (London, 1973).

Harding, V., 'Space, Property, and Propriety in Urban England', *Journal of Interdisciplinary History*, 32:4 (2002), 549–69.

Harriss, G. H., 'Political Society and the Growth of Government in Late Medieval England', *P&P*, 138 (1993), 28–57.

Hartrich, E., 'Charters and Inter-Urban Networks: England, 1439–1440', *EHR*, 132:555 (2017), 219–49.

Hartrich, E., 'Rebellion and the Law in Fifteenth-Century English Towns', in J. Firnhaber-Baker with D. Schoenaers (eds), *The Routledge History Handbook of Medieval Revolt* (London, 2017), 189–207.

Hartrich, E., *Politics and the Urban Sector in Fifteenth-Century England, 1413–1471* (Oxford, 2019).

Harvey, I. M. W., *Jack Cade's Rebellion of 1450* (Oxford, 1991).

Harvey, I. M. W., 'Was there a popular politics in fifteenth-century England?', in R. H. Britnell and A. J. Pollard (eds), *The McFarlane Legacy: Studies in Late Medieval Politics and Society* (Stroud, 1996), 155–74.

Harvey, I. M. W., 'Poaching and Sedition in Fifteenth-Century England', in R. Evans (ed.), *Lordship and Learning: Studies in Memory of Trevor Aston* (Woodbridge, 2004), 169–82.

Harvey, P. D. A. (ed.), *The Peasant Land Market in Medieval England* (Oxford, 1984).

Harvey, P. D. A., 'English Estate Records, 1250–1330', in R. H. Britnell (ed.), *Pragmatic Literacy, East and West, 1200–1300* (Woodbridge, 1997), 107–18.

Haskett, T. S., 'County Lawyers? The Composers of English Chancery Bills', in P. Birks (ed.), *The Life of the Law: Proceedings of the Tenth British Legal History Conference* (London, 1993), 9–23.

Haskett, T. S., 'The Medieval English Court of Chancery', *L&HR*, 14 (1996), 245–313.

Hastings, M., *The Court of Common Pleas in Fifteenth-Century England: A study of legal administration and procedure* (2nd edn; London, 1971).

Hatcher, J., 'Myths, Miners, and Agricultural Communities', *Agricultural History Review*, 22 (1974), 54–61.

Hatcher, J., 'England in the Aftermath of the Black Death', *P&P*, 144 (1996), 3–35.

Hatcher, J., 'The great slump of the mid-fifteenth century', in J. Hatcher and R. Britnell (eds), *Progress and problems in medieval England: Essays in Honour of Edward Miller* (Cambridge, 1996), 237–72.

Hatcher, J., 'Unreal Wages: Long-Run Living Standards and the "Golden Age" of the Fifteenth Century', in B. Dodds and C. D. Liddy (eds), *Commercial Activity, Markets and Entrepreneurs in the Middle Ages: Essays in Honour of Richard Britnell* (Woodbridge, 2011), 1–24.

Hay, D., Linebaugh, P., Rule, J. G., Thompson, E. P., and Winslow, C. (eds), *Albion's Fatal Tree: Crime and Society in Eighteenth-Century England* (London, 1975).

Heath, P. 'North Sea Fishing in the Fifteenth Century', *Northern History*, 3 (1968), 53–69.

Heebøll-Holm, T. K., 'Law, order and plunder at sea: a comparison of England and France in the fourteenth century', *Continuity and Change*, 32:1 (2017), 37–58.

Helmholz, R. H., 'Crime, Compurgation and the Courts of the Medieval Church', *L&HR*, 1:1 (1983), 1–26.

Helmholz, R. H., 'Harboring Sexual Offenders: Ecclesiastical Courts and Controlling Misbehavior', *Journal of British Studies*, 37:3 (1998), 258–68.

Helmholz, R. H., *The Ius Commune in England: Four Studies* (Oxford, 2001).

Helmholz, R. H., 'Local Ecclesiastical Courts in England', in W. Hartmann and K. Pennington (eds), *The History of Courts and Procedure in Medieval Canon Law* (Washington, DC, 2016), 344–91.

Herrer, H. R. O., Challet, V., Dumolyn, J., and Ruiz, M. A. C. (eds), *La Comunidad Medieval Como Esfera Pública* (Seville, 2014).

Herrup, C., 'Crime, Law and Society. A Review Article', *Comparative Studies in Society and History*, 27:1 (1985), 159–70.
Hill, F., *Medieval Lincoln* (Cambridge, 1965).
Hilton, R. H., *The Decline of Serfdom in Medieval England* (2nd edn; London, 1983).
Hilton, R. H., 'Small Town Society in England before the Black Death', *P&P*, 105 (1984), 53–78.
Hindle, B. P., 'Roads and Tracks', in L. Cantor (ed.) *The English Medieval Landscape* (London, 1982), 193–217.
Hindle, S., *The State and Social Change in Early Modern England, c. 1550–1640* (Basingstoke, 2000).
Hindle, S., 'Beating the Bounds of the Parish: Order, Memory, and Identity in the English Local Community, c. 1500–1700', in K. E. Spierling and M. J. Halvorson (eds), *Defining Community in Early Modern Europe* (Aldershot, 2008), 205–27.
Holder, J., and Harrison, C. (eds), *Law and Geography* (Oxford, 2002).
Holford, M. L., 'Pro patriotis: "Country", "Countrymen" and Local Solidarities in Late-Medieval England', *Parergon*, 23:1 (2006), 47–70.
Holford, M. L., and Stringer, K. J., *Border Liberties and Loyalties: North-East England, c.1200–c.1400* (Edinburgh, 2010).
Holt, J. C., *Robin Hood* (rev. edn; London, 1989).
Homans, G. C., *English Villagers of the Thirteenth Century* (Cambridge, MA, 1941).
Hooke, D., 'Pre-Conquest Woodland: Its Distribution and Usage', *Agricultural History Review*, 37:2 (1989), 113–29.
Hooton, J., *The Glaven Ports: A Maritime History of Blakeney, Cley and Wiveton in North Norfolk* (Blakeney, 1996).
Houston, R., 'People, Space, and Law in Late Medieval and Early Modern Britain and Ireland', *P&P*, 230 (2016), 47–89.
Hoyle, R. W., 'Thomas Lord Darcy and the Rothwell Tenants, c.1526–1534, *The Yorkshire Archaeological Journal*, 63 (1991), 85–107.
Hudson, J. (ed.), *The History of English Law: Centenary Essays on 'Pollock and Maitland'*, Proceedings of the British Academy, 89 (Oxford, 1996).
Hudson, J., *F. W. Maitland and the Englishness of English Law* (London, 2007).
Hulbert, J. R., 'English in Manorial Documents of the Thirteenth and Fourteenth Centuries', *Modern Philology*, 34:1 (1936), 37–61.
Hunnisett, R. F., *The Medieval Coroner* (Cambridge, 1961).
Hutton, R. H., *The Rise and Fall of Merry England: The Ritual Year 1400–1700* (Oxford, 2001).
Hyams, P. R., The Origins of a Peasant Land Market in England', *The Economic History Review*, 23:1 (1970), 18–31.
Hyams, P. R., 'Trial by Ordeal: The Key to Proof in the Early Common Law', in M. S. Arnold, T. A. Green, S. A. Scully, and S. D. White (eds), *On the Laws and Customs of England: Essays in Honor of Samuel E. Thorne* (Chapel Hill, NC, 1981), 90–126.
Hyams, P. R., 'What did Edwardian Villagers Understand by "Law"?', in Z. Razi and R. Smith (eds), *Medieval Society and the Manor Court* (Oxford, 1996), 69–100.
Hyams, P. R., *Rancor and Reconciliation in Medieval England* (Ithaca, NY, 2003).
Ingham, R., 'Mixing Languages on the Manor', *Medium Ævum*, 78:1 (2009), 80–98.
Ingold, T., 'Materials against materiality', *Archaeological Dialogues*, 14:1 (2007), 1–16.
Ingold, T., 'Toward an Ecology of Materials', *Annual Review of Anthropology*, 41 (2012), 427–42.
Ingram, M., '"Scolding women cucked or washed": a crisis in gender relations in early modern England?', in G. Walker and J. Kermode (eds), *Women, Crime, and the Courts in Early Modern England* (London, 1994), 48–80.

Ives, E. W., *The Common Lawyers of Pre-Reformation England* (Cambridge, 1983).

James, S., '"Langagis, whose reules ben not writen": Pecock and the Uses of the Vernacular', in E. Salter and H. Wicker (eds), *Vernacularity in England and Wales, c. 1300–1550* (Turnhout, 2011), 101–17.

Jewell, H. M., *English Local Administration in the Middle Ages* (Newton Abbot, 1972).

Johnson, T., 'The Preconstruction of Witness Testimony: Law and Social Discourse in England before the Reformation', *L&HR*, 32:1 (2014), 127–47.

Johnson, T., 'Medieval Law and Materiality: Shipwreck, Finders, and Property on the Suffolk Coast, *c.*1380–1410', *AHR*, 120:2 (2015), 406–32.

Johnson, T., 'The economics of shipwreck in late-medieval East Anglia', in J. Bowen and A. Brown (eds), *Custom and Commercialisation in Rural England, c.1350–1750: Revisiting Tawney and Postan* (Hertford, 2016), 121–38.

Johnson, T., 'The Redistribution of Forest Law and Administration in the Later Middle Ages', in L. Clark (ed.), *The Fifteenth Century XV: Writing, Records and Rhetoric* (Woodbridge, 2017), 93–108.

Johnson, T., 'The Tree and the Rod: Jurisdiction in Late-Medieval England', *P&P*, 237 (2017), 13–51.

Johnson, T., 'Legal Ephemera in the Ecclesiastical Courts of Late-Medieval England', *Open Library of Humanities*, 5:1 (2019), 1–27.

Johnson, T., 'News and Networks', in C. Symes (ed.), *A Cultural History of Media in the Middle Ages* (forthcoming).

Jones, K., *Gender and Petty Crime in Late Medieval England: The Local Courts in Kent, 1460–1560* (Woodbridge, 2006).

Jones, R., and Page, M., 'Characterizing rural settlement and landscape: Whittlewood Forest in the middle ages', *Medieval Archaeology*, 47 (2003), 53–83.

Jones, W. R., 'The Court of the Verge: The Jurisdiction of the Steward and Marshal of the Household in Later Medieval England', *Journal of British Studies*, 10:1 (1970), 1–29.

Jordan, J., 'Rethinking *Disputes and Settlements*: How Historians Can Use Legal Anthropology', in S. Cummins and L. Kounine (eds), *Cultures of Conflict Resolution in Early Modern Europe* (Farnham, 2016), 17–50.

Jørgensen, D., 'Cooperative Sanitation: Managing Streets and Gutters in Late Medieval England and Scandinavia', *Technology and Culture*, 49:3 (2008), 547–67.

Joyce, P., 'What is the Social in Social History?', *P&P*, 206 (2010), 213–48.

Justice, S., *Writing and Rebellion: England in 1381* (Berkeley, CA, 1994).

Justice, S., 'Inquisition, Speech, and Writing: A Case from Late-Medieval Norwich', *Representations*, 48 (1994), 1–29.

Kaeuper, R. W., *War, Justice, and Public Order: England and France in the Later Middle Ages* (Oxford, 1988).

Kane, B., 'Custom, Memory and Knowledge in the Medieval English Church Courts', in R. Hayes and W. Sheils (eds), *Clergy, Church and Society in England and Wales, 1200–1800* (York, 2014), 61–81.

Kane, B., *Popular Memory and Gender in Medieval England: Men, Women and Testimony in the Church Courts, c. 1200–1500* (Woodbridge, 2019).

Karn, N., 'Information and its retrieval', in J. Crick and E. Van Houts (eds), *A Social History of England, 900–1200* (Cambridge, 2011), 373–80.

Karras, R. M., Kaye, J., and Matter, E. A. (eds), *Law and the Illicit in Medieval Europe* (Philadelphia, PA, 2008).

Kelleher, M. A., 'Law and the Maiden: *Inquisitio, fama*, and the testimony of children in Medieval Catalonia', *Viator*, 37 (2006), 351–67.

Kermode, J., 'The Greater towns, 1300–1540', in D. M. Palliser (ed.), *The Cambridge Urban History of Britain, Volume 1: 600–1540* (Cambridge, 2000), 441–65.

Kerridge, E., 'The Returns of the Inquisitions of Depopulation', *EHR*, 70:275 (1955), 212–28.

Kim, K., *Aliens in Medieval Law: The Origins of Modern Citizenship* (Cambridge, 2000).

Kimball, E. G., 'Commissions of the Peace for Urban Jurisdictions in England, 1327–1485', *Proceedings of the American Philosophical Society*, 121:6 (1977), 448–74.

Kingsford, C. L., *Prejudice and Promise in XVth Century England: The Ford Lectures 1923–4* (Oxford, 1925).

Kirby, D., and Hinkkanen, M.-L, *The Baltic and the North Seas* (London, 2000).

Kleineke, H., 'Civic Ritual, Space and Conflict in Fifteenth-Century Exeter', in F. Andrews (ed.), *Ritual and Space in the Middle Ages: Proceedings of the 2009 Harlaxton Symposium* (Donington, 2011), 165–78.

Kosto, A. J., *Making Agreements in Medieval Catalonia: Power, Order, and the Written Word, 1000–1200* (Cambridge, 2001).

Kowaleski, M., 'The history of urban families in medieval England', *Journal of Medieval History*, 14 (1988), 47–63.

Kowaleski, M., *Local markets and regional trade in medieval Exeter* (Cambridge, 1995).

Kowaleski, M., 'Port towns: England and Wales 1300–1540', in D. M. Palliser (ed.), *The Cambridge Urban History of Britain* (Cambridge, 2000), 467–94.

Kowaleski, M., 'The Commercialization of the Sea Fisheries in Medieval England and Wales', *International Journal of Maritime History*, 15 (2003), 177–231.

Kowaleski, M., 'Working at Sea: Maritime Recruitment and Remuneration in Medieval England', in S. Cavaciocchi (ed.), *Ricchezza del mare, ricchezza dal mare. Secoli XIII–XVIII* (2 vols; Florence, 2006), ii. 907–36.

Kowaleski, M., '"Alien" Encounters in the Maritime World of Medieval England', *Medieval Encounters*, 13 (2007), 96–121.

Kowaleski, M., 'The French of England: A Maritime lingua franca?', in J. Wogan-Browne (ed.), *Language and Culture in Medieval Britain: The French of England c.1100–c.1500* (York, 2009), 103–17.

Kowaleski, M., 'The Seasonality of Fishing in Medieval Britain', in B. G. Scott (ed.), *Ecologies and Economies in Medieval and Early Modern Europe: Studies in environmental history for Richard C. Hoffman* (Leiden, 2010), 117–48.

Kowaleski, M., 'The Shipmaster as Entrepreneur in Medieval England', in B. Dodds and C. D. Liddy (eds), *Commercial Activity, Markets and Entrepreneurs in the Middle Ages: Essays in Honour of Richard Britnell* (Woodbridge, 2011), 165–82.

Kowaleski, M., 'The Demography of Maritime Communities in Late Medieval England', in M. Bailey and S. H. Rigby (eds), *Town and Countryside in the Age of the Black Death: Essays in Honour of John Hatcher* (Turnhout, 2012), 87–118.

Kowaleski, M., 'Peasants and the Sea in Medieval England', in M. Kowaleski, J. Langdon, and P. R. Schofield (eds), *Peasants and Lords in the Medieval English Economy: Essays in Honour of Bruce M. S. Campbell* (Turnhout, 2015) 353–76.

Kuehn, T. *Law, Family, and Women: Toward a Legal Anthropology of Renaissance Italy* (Chicago, IL, 1994).

Kümin, B. A., *The Shaping of a Community: The rise and reformation of the English parish, c.1400–1560* (Aldershot, 1996).

Kümin, B. A., *Drinking Matters: Public Houses and Social Exchange in Early Modern Central Europe* (Basingstoke, 2007).

Kümin, B. A., 'Introduction', in B. Kümin (ed.), *Political Space in Pre-Industrial Europe* (Farnham and Burlington, VT, 2009), 5–15.

Kümin, B., and Tlusty, B. A. (eds), *The World of the Tavern: Public Houses in Early Modern Europe* (Aldershot, 2002).

Kwakkel, E., 'Commercial organization and economic innovation', in A. Gillespie and D. Wakelin (eds), *The Production of Books in England 1350–1500* (Cambridge, 2011), 173–91.

Kwakkel, E., 'Decoding the material book: cultural residue in medieval manuscripts', in M. Johnston and M. Van Dussen (eds), *The Medieval Manuscript Book: Cultural Approaches* (Cambridge, 2015), 60–76.

Lacey, H., 'Pragmatic Literacy and Political Consciousness in Later Medieval England', *Cahiers électroniques d'histoire textuelle du LaMOP*, 5 [issue: L'écriture pragmatique. Un concept d'histoire médiévale à l'échelle européenne] (2012), 38–70.

Laing, L. H., 'Historic Origins of Admiralty Jurisdiction in England', *Michigan Law Review*, 45:2 (1946), 163–82.

Lambert, B., 'A matter of trust: the royal regulation of England's French residents during wartime, 1294–1377', *Historical Research*, 89:244 (2016), 208–26.

Lambert, B., and Ormrod, W. M., 'Friendly Foreigners: International Warfare, Resident Aliens and the Early History of Denization in England, c.1250–c.1400', *EHR*, 130:542 (2015), 1–24.

Lambert, T., *Law and Order in Anglo-Saxon England* (Oxford, 2017).

Lander, J. R., *English Justices of the Peace, 1461–1509* (Gloucester, 1989).

Langton, J., 'Medieval Forests and Chases: Another Realm?', in J. Langton and G. Jones (eds), *Forests and Chases of Medieval England and Wales,* c.*1000 to* c.*1500* (Oxford, 2010), 14–35.

Langton, J., 'Forest fences: enclosures in a pre-enclosure landscape', *Landscape History*, 35:1 (2014), 5–30.

Langton, J., and Jones, G., 'Deconstructing and reconstructing the Forests: Some Preliminary Matters', in J. Langton and G. Jones (eds), *Forests and Chases of Medieval England and Wales,* c.*1000 to* c.*1500* (Oxford, 2010), 1–13.

Larson, P. L. 'Village Voice or Village Oligarchy? The Jurors of the Durham Halmote Court, 1349 to 1424', *L&HR*, 28:3 (2010), 675–709.

Latham, R. E., Revised Medieval Latin Word-List: From British and Irish Sources (Oxford, 1980).

Latour, B., *We Have Never Been Modern*, transl. Catherine Porter (Cambridge, MA, 1993).

Latour, B., Reassembling the Social: An Introduction to Actor-Network-Theory (Oxford, 2005).

Latour, B., *The Making of Law: An Ethnography of the Conseil d'État*, transl. Marina Brilman and Alain Pottage (Cambridge, 2010).

Le Roy Ladurie, E., *Montaillou: Cathars and Catholics in a French Village 1294–1324*, transl. Barbara Bray (new edn; New York, NY, 2002).

Liddy, C., 'Urban Enclosure Riots: Risings of The Commons in English Towns, 1480–1525', *P&P*, 226 (2015), 41–77.

Liddy, C., *Contesting the City: The Politics of Citizenship in English Towns, 1250–1530* (Oxford, 2017).

Liddy, C., 'Cultures of Surveillance in Late Medieval English Towns: The monitoring of speech and the fear of revolt', in J. Firnhaber-Baker with D. Schoenaers (eds), *The Routledge History Handbook of Medieval Revolt* (London, 2017), 311–29.

Lilley, K. D., 'Decline or decay? Urban landscapes in late-medieval England', in T. R. Slater (ed.), *Towns in Decline AD100–1600* (Aldershot, 2000), 235–65.

Lobel, M. D., *Historic Towns: Maps and Plans of Towns and Cities in the British Isles with Historical Commentaries, from Earliest Times to c.1800* (2 vols; London, 1969).

Lyall, R. J., 'Materials: the paper revolution', in J. Griffiths and D. Pearsall (eds), *Book Production and Publishing in Britain* (Cambridge, 1989), 11–29.

McClure, P., 'Patterns of Migration in the Late Middle Ages: The Evidence of English Place-Name Surnames', *Economic History Review*, 32:2 (1979), 167–82.

McDonagh, B., 'Making and Breaking Property: Negotiating Enclosure and Common Rights in Sixteenth-Century England', *History Workshop Journal*, 76 (2013), 32–56.

Machan, T. W., *English in the Middle Ages* (Oxford, 2003).

McHardy, A. K., 'Church Courts and Criminous Clerks in the Later Middle Ages', in M. J. Franklin and C. Harper-Bill (eds), *Medieval Ecclesiastical Studies in honour of Dorothy M. Owen* (Woodbridge, 1995), 165–83.

McIntosh, M. K., 'Local Change and Community Control in England, 1465–1500', *Huntington Library Quarterly*, 49:3 (1986), 219–42.

McIntosh, M. K., *Autonomy and Community: The Royal Manor of Havering, 1200–1500* (Cambridge, 1986).

McIntosh, M. K., 'Finding a Language for Misconduct: Jurors in Fifteenth-Century Local Courts', in B. A. Hanawalt and D. Wallace (eds), *Bodies and Disciplines: Intersections of Literature and History in Fifteenth-Century England* (Minneapolis, MN, 1996), 87–122.

McIntosh, M. K., *Controlling Misbehavior in England, 1370–1600* (Cambridge, 1998).

Macnair, M., 'Vicinage and the Antecedents of the Jury', *L&HR*, 17:3 (1999), 537–99.

McRae, A., 'To Know One's Own: Estate Surveying and the Representation of the Land in Early Modern England', *Huntington Library Quarterly*, 56:4 (1993), 333–57.

McRee, B. R., 'Religious Gilds and the Regulation of Behavior in Late Medieval Towns', in J. Rosenthal and C. Richmond (eds), *People, Politics and Community in the Later Middle Ages* (Gloucester, 1987), 108–22.

McRee, B. R., 'The guilds of *homo prudens* in late medieval England', *Continuity and Change*, 7:2 (1992), 163–93.

McRee, B. R., 'Peacemaking and Its Limits in Late Medieval Norwich', *EHR*, 109:433 (1994), 831–66.

McSheffrey, S., 'Jurors, Respectable Masculinity, and Christian Morality: A Comment on Marjorie McIntosh's *Controlling Misbehavior*', *Journal of British Studies*, 37:3 (1998), 269–78.

McSheffrey, S., 'Place, Space, and Situation: Public and Private in the Making of Marriage in Late-Medieval London', *Speculum*, 79:4 (2004), 960–90.

McSheffrey, S., *Marriage, Sex, and Civic Culture in Late Medieval London* (Philadelphia, PA, 2006).

McSheffrey, S., 'Detective Fiction in the Archives: Court Records and the Uses of Law in Late Medieval England', *History Workshop Journal*, 65 (2008), 65–78.

McSheffrey, S., 'Sanctuary and the Legal Topography of Pre-Reformation London', *L&HR*, 27:3 (2009), 483–514.

Maddern, P. C., *Violence and Social Order: East Anglia 1422–1442* (Oxford, 1992).

Maddern, P. C. 'Imagining the Unchanging Land: East Anglians Represent their Landscape, 1350–1500', in C. Harper-Bill (ed.), *Medieval East Anglia* (Norwich, 2005), 52–67.

Maddicott, J. R., 'The County Community and the Making of Public Opinion in Fourteenth-Century England', *Transactions of the Royal Historical Society*, 28 (1978), 27–43.

Maddicott, J. R., 'The Origins of the Hundred Years War', in N. Saul (ed.), *England in Europe, 1066–1453* (New York, NY, 1994), 133–43.

Manning, R. B., *Hunters and Poachers: A Social and Cultural History of Unlawful Hunting in England, 1485–1640* (Oxford, 1993).

Marsden, R. G., 'The Vice-Admirals of the Coast', *EHR*, 22:87 (1907), 468–77.

Marvin, W. P., *Hunting Law and Ritual in Medieval English Literature* (Cambridge, 2006).
Masschaele, J., 'The Public Spaces of the Marketplace in Medieval England', *Speculum*, 77:2 (2002), 383–421.
Masschaele, J., *Jury, State and Society in Medieval England* (New York, NY, 2008).
Melikan, R., 'Shippers, salvors, and sovereigns: Competing interests in the medieval law of Shipwreck', *The Journal of Legal History*, 11:2 (1990), 163–82.
Melve, L., 'Mapping Public Debates along the Oral–Literate Continuum (1100–1300)', in S. Rankovic, L. Melve, and E. Mundal (eds), *Along the Oral–Written Continuum: Types of Texts, Relations and their Implications* (Turnhout, 2010), 73–100.
Mennicken, A., and Miller, P., 'Accounting, Territorialization and Power', *Foucault Studies*, 13 (2012), 4–24.
Middleton-Stewart, J., '"Down to the sea in ships": decline and fall on the Suffolk coast', in C. Rawcliffe, R. Virgoe, and R. Wilson (eds), *Counties and Communities: Essays on East Anglian History Presented to Hassell Smith* (Norwich, 1996), 69–83.
Mileson, S. A., *Parks in Medieval England* (Oxford, 2009).
Mileson, S. A., 'Openness and Closure in the Later Medieval Village', *P&P*, 234 (2017), 3–37.
Milsom, S. F. C., 'Law and Fact in Legal Development', *University of Toronto Law Journal*, 17:1 (1967), 1–19.
Milsom, S. F. C., *Historical Foundations of the Common Law* (2nd edn; London, 1981).
Mollat, M., *La Vie Quotidienne Des Gens de Mer en Atlantique IXe–XVIe siècle* (Paris, 1983).
Moorhouse, S., 'The Medieval Parks of Yorkshire: Function, Contents and Chronology', in R. Liddiard (ed.), *The Medieval Park: New Perspectives* (Macclesfield, 2007), 99–127.
Moran, J. A. H., *The Growth of English Schooling 1340–1548: Learning, Literacy, and Laicization in Pre-Reformation York Diocese* (Princeton, NJ, 1985).
Morris, W. A., *The Frankpledge System* (London, 1910).
Mostert, M., and Barnwell, P. S., *Medieval Legal Process: Physical, Spoken and Written Performance in the Middle Ages* (Turnhout, 2011).
Müller, L., *White Magic: The Age of Paper*, transl. Jessica Spengler (Cambridge, 2014).
Müller, M., 'Social Control and the Hue and Cry in Two Fourteenth Century Villages', *Journal of Medieval History*, 31 (2005), 29–53.
Müller, M., 'A Divided Class? Peasants and Peasant Communities in Later Medieval England', *P&P*, supplement 2 (2007), 115–31.
Murray, K. M. E., *The Constitutional History of the Cinque Ports* (Manchester, 1935).
Musson, A., *Public Order and Law Enforcement: The Local Administration of Criminal Justice 1294–1350* (Woodbridge, 1996).
Musson, A., *Medieval Law in Context: The growth of legal consciousness from Magna Carta to the Peasants' Revolt* (Manchester, 2001).
Musson, A., 'Sub-Keepers and Constables: The Role of Local Officials in Keeping the Peace in Fourteenth-Century England', *EHR*, 117:470 (2002), 1–24.
Musson, A. (ed.), *Boundaries of the Law: Geography, Gender and Jurisdiction in Medieval and Early Modern Europe* (Aldershot, 2005).
Musson, A., and Ormrod, W. M., *The Evolution of English Justice: Law, Politics and Society in the Fourteenth Century* (Basingstoke, 1999).
Nader, L. 'The anthropological study of law', *American Anthropologist*, 67:6 (1965), 3–32.
Neal, D. G., *The Masculine Self in Late-Medieval England* (Chicago, IL, 2008).
Neuman de Vegvar, C., 'Converting the Anglo-Saxon Landscape: Crosses and their Audiences', in A. Minnis and J. Roberts (eds), *Text, Image, Interpretation: Studies in Anglo-Saxon Literature and its Insular Context in Honour of Éamonn Ó Carragáin* (Turnhout, 2007), 407–29.

Neville, C. J., 'Common Knowledge of the Common Law in Later Medieval England', *Canadian Journal of History*, 29:3 (1994), 462–78.

Nightingale, P., 'Money and credit in the economy of late medieval England', in D. Wood (ed.), *Medieval Money Matters* (Oxford, 2004), 51–71.

Olson, S., 'Jurors of the Village Court: Local Leadership before and after the Plague at Ellington, Huntingdonshire', *Journal of British Studies*, 30 (1991), 237–56.

Orme, N., 'Access and Exclusion: Exeter Cathedral, 1300–1540', in P. Horden (ed.), *Freedom of Movement in the Middle Ages: Proceedings of the 2003 Harlaxton Symposium* (Donington, 2007), 267–86.

Ormrod, W. M., 'The Peasants' Revolt and the Government of England', *Journal of British Studies*, 29:1 (1990), 1–30.

Ormrod, W. M., *Political Life in Medieval England, 1300–1450* (Basingstoke, 1995).

Ormrod, W. M., 'The Use of English: Language, Law, and Political Culture in Fourteenth-Century England', *Speculum*, 78:3 (2003), 750–87.

Ormrod, W. M., Dodd, G., and Musson, A. (eds), *Medieval Petitions: Grace and Grievance* (York, 2009).

Ormrod, W. M., McDonald, N., and Taylor, C. (eds), *Resident Aliens in Later Medieval England* (Turnhout, 2017).

Otter, C., 'Locating matter: the place of materiality in urban history', in T. Bennett and P. Joyce (eds), *Material Powers: Cultural studies, history and the material turn* (London, 2010), 38–59.

Owen, A. E. B., 'A Scrivener's Notebook from Bury St Edmunds', *Archives*, 14:61 (1979), 16–22.

Owen, D., *The Medieval Canon Law: Teaching, Literature and Transmission* (Cambridge, 1990).

Pajic, M., and Lambert, B., 'Immigration and the Common Profit: Native Cloth Workers, Flemish Exiles, and Royal Policy in Fourteenth-Century London', *Journal of British Studies*, 55:4 (2016), 633–57.

Palliser, D. M., 'Urban Decay Revisited', in J. A. F. Thomson (ed.), *Towns and Townspeople in the Fifteenth Century* (Gloucester, 1988), 1–21.

Palmer, R. C., *The County Courts of Medieval England, 1150–1350* (Princeton, NJ, 1982).

Palmer, R. C., *English Law in the Age of the Black Death, 1348–1381: A Transformation of Governance and Law* (Chapel Hill, NC, 1993).

Parker, R., *Men of Dunwich* (St. Albans, 1980).

Parkes, M. B., 'The literacy of the laity', in *Scribes, scripts, and readers: studies in the communication, presentation, and dissemination of medieval texts* (London, 1991), 275–97.

Peake, H. J. E., 'Kintbury', in W. Page and P. H. Ditchfield (eds), *VCH Berkshire: Volume 4* (London, 1924), 205–17.

Petit-Dutaillis, C., *Studies and notes supplementary to Stubbs' Constitutional history*, transl. W. T. Waugh (3 vols; Manchester, 1908–15).

Pitcaithly, M., 'Piracy and Anglo-Hanseatic Relations, 1385–1420', in R. Gorski (ed.), *Roles of the Sea in Medieval England* (Woodbridge, 2012), 125–45.

Platt, C., *The English Medieval Town* (London, 1976).

Pollard, A. J., *North-Eastern England During the Wars of the Roses: Lay Society, War, and Politics 1450–1500* (Oxford, 1990).

Pollock, F., and Maitland, F. W., *The History of English Law before the time of Edward I* (2nd edn; 2 vols; Cambridge, 1968).

Poos, L. R., *A Rural Society after the Black Death: Essex 1350–1525* (Cambridge, 1991).

Poos, L. R., 'The Heavy-Handed Marriage Counsellor: Regulating Marriage in Some Later-Medieval English Local Ecclesiastical-Court Jurisdictions', *The American Journal of Legal History*, 39:3 (1995), 291–309.

Post, J. B., 'Crime in later medieval England: some historiographical limitations', *Continuity and Change*, 2:2 (1987), 211–24.

Postan, M. M., 'Revisions in Economic History: IX.—The Fifteenth Century', *The Economic History Review*, 9:2 (1939), 160–67.

Postles, D., 'Micro-spaces: church porches in pre-modern England', *Journal of Historical Geography*, 33 (2007), 749–69.

Pottage, A., 'The Materiality of What?', *Journal of Law and Society*, 39:1 (2012), 167–83.

Powell, E., 'Settlement of Disputes by Arbitration in Fifteenth-Century England', *L&HR*, 2:1 (1984), 21–43.

Powell, E., *Kingship, Law, and Society: Criminal Justice in the Reign of Henry V* (Oxford, 1989).

Power, M., *The Audit Society: Rituals of Verification* (Oxford, 1997).

Prescott, A., 'Writing about Rebellion: Using the Records of the Peasants' Revolt of 1381', *History Workshop Journal*, 45 (1998), 1–27.

Prestwich, M. (ed.), *Liberties and Identities in the Medieval British Isles* (Woodbridge, 2008).

Putnam, B. H., *The Enforcement of the Statutes of Labourers During the First Decade after the Black Death, 1349–1359* (New York, NY, 1908).

Rackham, O., *Ancient Woodland: Its History, Vegetation and Uses in England* (London, 1980).

Raftis, J. A., *Tenure and Mobility: Studies in the Social History of the Medieval English Village* (Toronto, 1964).

Ramsay, N., 'Forgery and the rise of the London Scriveners' Company', in R. Myers and M. Harris (eds), *Fakes and frauds: varieties of deception in print and manuscript* (Winchester, 1989), 99–108.

Ramsay, N., 'Scriveners and Notaries as Legal Intermediaries in Later Medieval England', in J. Kermode (ed.), *Enterprise and Individuals in Fifteenth-Century England* (Stroud, 1991), 118–31.

Rawcliffe, C., *Urban Bodies: Communal Health in Late Medieval English Towns and Cities* (Woodbridge, 2013).

Razi, Z., 'The Toronto School's Reconstitution of Medieval Peasant Society: A Critical View', *P&P*, 85 (1979), 141–57.

Razi, Z., *Life, marriage and death in a medieval parish: Economy, society and demography in Halesowen 1270–1400* (Cambridge, 1980).

Razi, Z., and Smith, R. (eds), *Medieval Society and the Manor Court* (Oxford, 1996).

Rees Jones, S. (ed.), *The Government of Medieval York: Essays in commemoration of the 1396 royal charter* (York, 1997).

Rexroth, F., *Deviance and Power in Late-Medieval London*, transl. P. E. Selwyn (Cambridge, 2007).

Richardson, H. G., 'An Oxford Teacher of the Fifteenth Century', *Bulletin of the John Rylands Library*, 23:2 (1939), 436–57.

Richardson, M., 'The *Dictamen* and its Influence on Fifteenth-Century English Prose', *Rhetorica: A Journal of the History of Rhetoric*, 2:3 (1984), 207–26.

Richardson, M., 'The Fading Influence of the Medieval *Ars Dictaminis* in England After 1400', *Rhetorica: A Journal of the History of Rhetoric*, 19:2 (2001), 225–47.

Richmond, C., *John Hopton: A Fifteenth Century Suffolk Gentleman* (Cambridge, 1981).

Richmond, C., 'Hand and Mouth: Information gathering and use in England in the later middle ages', *Journal of Historical Sociology*, 1:3 (1988), 233–52.

Richmond, C., *The Paston Family in the Fifteenth Century: Ending* (Manchester, 2000).

Richter, J. G., 'Education and association: the bureaucrat in the reign of Henry VI', *Journal of Medieval History*, 12 (1986), 81–9.

Riddy, F., 'Authority and Intimacy in the Late Medieval Urban Home', in M. C. Erler and M. Kowaleski (eds), *Gendering the Master Narrative: Women and Power in the Middle Ages* (Ithaca, NY, 2003), 212–28.

Rigby, S. H., 'Urban "Oligarchy" in Late Medieval England', in J. A. F. Thomson (ed.), *Towns and Townspeople in the Fifteenth Century* (Gloucester, 1988), 62–86.

Rigby, S. H., *Medieval Grimsby: Growth and Decline* (Hull, 1993).

Roberts, S., and Comaroff, S., *Rules and Processes: The Cultural Logic of Dispute in an African Context* (Chicago, IL, 1981).

Robinson, P., 'The format of books: books, booklets and rolls', in N. J. Morgan and R. M. Thomson (eds), *The Cambridge History of the Book in Britain, Volume 2, 1100–1400* (Cambridge, 2008), 41–54.

Rodger, N. A. M., 'The Naval Service of the Cinque Ports', *EHR*, 111:442 (1996), 636–51.

Rodger, N. A. M., *The Safeguard of the Sea: A Naval History of Britain, Volume One 660–1649* (London, 1997).

Rogers, K. H., 'Warminster Hundred', in E. Crittall (ed.), *VCH Wiltshire, Volume 8: Warminster, Westbury and Whorwellsdown Hundreds* (London, 1965), 1–5.

Rollison, D., *A Commonwealth of the People: Popular Politics and England's Long Social Revolution, 1066–1649* (Cambridge, 2010).

Roodenburg, H., and Spierenburg, P. (eds), *Social Control in Europe, Volume 1, 1500–1800* (Columbus, OH, 2004).

Rose, S., 'The Value of the Cinque Ports to the Crown, 1200–1500', in R. Gorski (ed.), *Roles of the Sea in Medieval England* (Woodbridge, 2012), 41–57.

Rosenwein, B. H. (ed.), *Anger's Past: The Social Uses of an Emotion in the Middle Ages* (Ithaca, NY, 1998).

Rosenwein, B. H., *Negotiating Space: Power, Restraint, and Privileges of Immunity in Early Medieval Europe* (Manchester, 1999).

Rosenwein, B. H., 'Worrying about Emotions in History', *AHR*, 107:3 (2002), 821–45.

Ross, C., 'Rumour, Propaganda and Popular Opinion during the Wars of the Roses', in R. A. Griffiths (ed.), *Patronage, the Crown and the Provinces in Later Medieval England* (Gloucester, 1981), 15–32.

Rosser, G., 'Going to the Fraternity Feast: Community and Social Relations in Late Medieval England', *Journal of British Studies*, 33:4 (1994), 430–46.

Rosser, G., 'Sanctuary and Social Negotiation in Medieval England', in J. Blair and B. Golding (eds), *The Cloister and the World: Essays in Medieval History in Honour of Barbara Harvey* (Oxford, 1996), 57–79.

Rosser, G., 'Conflict and Political Community in the Medieval Town: Disputes between Clergy and Laity in Hereford', in T. R. Slater and G. Rosser (eds), *The Church in the Medieval Town* (Aldershot, 1998), 20–42.

Rosser, G., *The Art of Solidarity: Guilds in England 1250–1550* (Oxford, 2015).

Rosser, G., and Dennison, P., 'Urban culture and the Church 1300–1540', in D. M. Palliser (ed.), *The Cambridge Urban History of Britain, Volume 1: 600–1540* (Cambridge, 2000), 335–69.

Rothwell, W., 'English and French in England after 1362', *English Studies*, 82:6 (2001), 539–59.

Rothwell, W., 'Sugar and Spice and All Things Nice: From Oriental Bazar to English Cloister in Anglo-French', *The Modern Language Review*, 100, supplement (2005), 38–50.

Rowley, T. 'Medieval Field Systems', in L. M. Cantor (ed.) *The English Medieval Landscape* (London, 1982), 25–55.

Ruddick, A., *English Identity and Political Culture in the Fourteenth Century* (Cambridge, 2013).

Ruddock, A. A., 'Alien Merchants in Southampton in the Later Middle Ages', *EHR*, 61:239 (1946), 1–17.

Runyan, T. J., 'The Rolls of Oleron and the Admiralty Court in Fourteenth Century England', *American Journal of Legal History*, 19:2 (1975), 95–111.

Sabapathy, J., *Officers and Accountability in Medieval England 1170–1300* (Oxford, 2014).

Sagui, S., 'Mid-level Officials in Fifteenth-Century Norwich', in L. Clark and C. Rawcliffe (eds), *The Fifteenth Century XII: Society in an Age of Plague* (Woodbridge, 2013), 101–21.

Sandall, S., 'Custom, common right and commercialisation in the Forest of Dean, c.1605–1640', in J. Bowen and A. Brown (eds), *Custom and Commercialisation in English Rural Society, c.1350–c.1750: Revisiting Tawney and Postan* (Hertford, 2016), 161–79.

Sarat, A., and Felstiner, W. L. F., 'Lawyers and Legal Consciousness: Law Talk in the Divorce Lawyer's Office', *Yale Law Journal*, 98 (1989), 1663–87.

Saul, A., 'The Herring Industry at Great Yarmouth, *c.* 1280–*c.* 1400', *Norfolk Archaeology*, 38 (1981), 33–43.

Sayers, W., 'Some International Nautical Etymologies', *Mariner's Mirror*, 88:4 (2002), 405–22.

Scammell, G. V., 'English Merchant Shipping at the End of the Middle Ages: Some East Coast Evidence', *The Economic History Review*, n.s., 13:3 (1961), 327–41.

Scammell, J. 'The Rural Chapter in England from the Eleventh to the Fourteenth Century', *EHR*, 86:338 (1971), 1–21.

Scase, W., '"Strange and Wonderful Bills": Bill-Casting and Political Discourse in Late Medieval England', in, R. Copeland, D. A. Lawton, and W. Scase (eds), *New Medieval Literatures*, 2 (Oxford, 1998), 225–47.

Scase, W., *Literature and Complaint in England, 1272–1553* (Oxford, 2007).

Scheiber, H. N., 'American Constitutional History and the New Legal History: Complementary Themes in Two Modes', *The Journal of American History*, 68: 2 (1981), 337–50.

Schlag, P. 'The dedifferentiation problem', *Continental Philosophy Review*, 42 (2009), 35–62.

Schofield, B., 'Wreck Rolls of Leiston Abbey', in J. C. Davies (ed.), *Studies Presented to Sir Hilary Jenkinson* (London, 1957), 361–71.

Schofield, J., and Stell, G., 'The built environment 1300–1540', in D. M. Palliser (ed.), *The Cambridge Urban History of Britain, Volume 1: 600–1540* (Cambridge, 2000), 371–93.

Schofield, P. R., 'Peasants and the Manor Court: Gossip and Litigation in a Suffolk Village at the Close of the Thirteenth Century', *P&P*, 159 (1998), 3–42.

Schofield, P. R., *Peasant and Community in Medieval England 1200–1500* (Basingstoke, 2003).

Scott, J. C., *Weapons of the Weak: Everyday Forms of Peasant Resistance* (New Haven, CT, 1985).

Scott, J. C., *Domination and the Arts of Resistance: Hidden Transcripts* (New Haven, CT, 1990).

Seipp, D. J., 'The Concept of Property in the Early Common Law', *L&HR*, 12:1 (1994), 29–91.

Seipp, D. J., *An Index and Paraphrase of Printed Year Book Reports, 1268–1535* (online database: http://www.bu.edu/law/faculty-scholarship/legal-history-the-year-books/, accessed March 2019).

Shapin, S., and Schaffer, S., *Leviathan and the Air-Pump: Hobbes, Boyle, and the Experimental Life* (new edn; Princeton, NJ, 2011).

Sharpe, J. A., 'The History of Crime in Late Medieval and Early Modern England', *Social History*, 7:2 (1982), 187–203.

Shaw, D. G., *The Creation of a Community: The City of Wells in the Middle Ages* (Oxford, 1993).

Shaw, D. G., *Necessary Conjunctions: The Social Self in Medieval England* (Basingstoke, 2005).

Sheppard, A., 'Poverty, Labour and the Language of Social Description in Early Modern England', *P&P*, 201 (2008), 51–95.

Sheppard, A., *Accounting for Oneself: Worth, Status and the Social Order in Early Modern England* (Oxford, 2015).

Sherborne, J. W., 'The Hundred Years War: the English navy: shipping and manpower 1369–1389', *P&P*, 37 (1967), 163–75.

Shoesmith, R., and Crosskey, R., 'Go to Gaol... In Hereford', *Transactions of the Woolhope Field Club* 48:1 (1994), 97–139.

Silbey, S. S., 'After Legal Consciousness', *Annual Review of Law and Social Science*, 1 (2005), 323–68.

Skeel, C. A. J., *The Council in the Marches of Wales: A Study in Local Government during the Sixteenth and Seventeenth Centuries* (London, 1904).

Skelton, R. A., and Harvey, P. D. A., *Local Maps and Plans from Medieval England* (Oxford, 1986).

Smail, D. L., *Imaginary Cartographies: Possession and Identity in Late Medieval Marseille* (Ithaca, NY, 2000).

Smail, D. L., 'Hatred as a social institution in late-medieval society', *Speculum* 76:1 (2001), 90–126.

Smail, D. L., *The Consumption of Justice: Emotions, Publicity, and Legal Culture in Marseille, 1264–1423* (Ithaca, NY, 2003).

Smail, D. L., *Legal Plunder: Households and Debt Collection in Late Medieval Europe* (Cambridge, MA, 2016).

Smith, A. T., 'Archaeologies of Sovereignty', *Annual Review of Anthropology*, 40 (2011), 415–32.

Smith, D. M., *Guide to Bishops' Registers of England and Wales: A Survey from the Middle Ages to the Abolition of Episcopacy in 1646* (London, 1981).

Smith, R. M., 'Some Thoughts on "Hereditary" and "Proprietary" Rights in Land under Customary Law in Thirteenth and Fourteenth Century England', *L&HR*, 1:1 (1983), 95–128.

Sobecki, S. E., *Unwritten Verities: The Making of England's Vernacular Legal Culture, 1463–1549* (Notre Dame, IN, 2016).

Somerset, F., and Watson, N. (eds), *The Vulgar Tongue: Medieval and Postmedieval Vernacularity* (University Park, PA, 2003).

Sousa Santos, B. de, 'Law: A Map of Misreading. Toward a Postmodern Conception of Law', *Journal of Law and Society*, 14:3 (1987), 279–302.

Steinberg, P. E., *The Social Construction of the Ocean* (Cambridge, 2001).

Strohm, P., *England's Empty Throne: Usurpation and the Language of Legitimation 1399–1422* (New Haven, CT, 1998).

Summerson, H., 'The Enforcement of the Statute of Winchester, 1285–1327', *Journal of Legal History*, 13:3 (1992), 232–50.

Sutherland, D. W., *Quo Warranto Proceedings in the Reign of Edward I* (Oxford, 1963).

Swanson, H., 'The Illusion of Economic Structure: Craft Guilds in Late Medieval English Towns', *P&P*, 121 (1988), 29–48.

Swanson, R. N., 'Universis Christi Fidelibus: the Church and its Records', in R. H. Britnell (ed.), *Pragmatic Literacy, East and West, 1200–1300* (Woodbridge, 1997), 147–64.

Swanson, R. N., 'Peculiar Practices: The Jurisdictional Jigsaw of the Pre-Reformation Church', *Midland History*, 26 (2001), 69–95.

Swanson, R. N., '"...et examinatus dicit...": Oral and Personal History in the Records of English Ecclesiastical Courts', in M. Goodich (ed.), *Voices from the Bench: Narratives of Lesser Folk in Medieval Trial* (Basingstoke, 2006), 203–26.

Swanson, R. N., and Lepine, D., 'The Later Middle Ages, 1268–1535', in G. Aylmer and J. Tiller (ed.), *Hereford Cathedral: A History* (London, 2000), 48–86.

Sweetinburgh, S., 'Strategies of inheritance among Kentish fishing communities in the later Middle Ages', *History of the Family*, 11 (2006), 93–105.

Sykes, N., 'Animal Bones and Animal Parks', in R. Liddiard (ed.), *The Medieval Park: New Perspectives* (Macclesfield, 2007), 49–62.

Sykes, N., 'Taking Sides: The Social Life of Venison in Medieval England', in A. Pluskowski (ed.), *Breaking and Shaping Beastly Bodies: Animals as Material Culture in the Middle Ages* (Oxford, 2007), 149–60.

Symes, C., 'Out in the Open, in Arras: Sightlines, Soundscapes, and the Shaping of a Medieval Public Sphere', in C. Goodson, A. E. Lester, and C. Symes (eds), *Cities, Texts and Social Networks, 400–1500: Experiences and Perceptions of Medieval Urban Space* (Farnham, 2010), 279–303.

Tait, J., *The Medieval English Borough* (Manchester, 1936).

Tamanaha, B. Z., 'Understanding Legal Pluralism: Past to Present, Local to Global', *Sydney Law Review*, 375 (2008), 375–411.

Tanner, N., *The Church in Late Medieval Norwich, 1370–1532* (Toronto, 1984).

Tanner, N., and Watson, S., 'Least of the laity: the minimum requirements for a medieval Christian', *Journal of Medieval History*, 32 (2006), 395–423.

Taylor, C., 'Ravensdale Park, Derbyshire, and medieval deer coursing', *Landscape History*, 26:1 (2004), 37–57.

Teetor, P. R., 'England's Earliest Treatise on the Law Merchant: the Essay on Lex Mercatoria from The Little Red Book of Bristol (Circa 1280 AD)', *The American Journal of Legal History*, 6:2 (1962), 178–210.

Thiébaux, M., 'Hunting in the Middle Ages', *Speculum*, 42:2 (1967), 260–74.

Thomas, A., and Boucher, A. (eds), *Hereford City Excavations, Volume 4: Further Sites and Evolving Interpretations* (Logaston, 2002).

Thomas, R., 'Chasing the Ideal? Ritualism, Pragmatism and the Later Medieval Hunt in England', in A. Pluskowski (ed.), *Breaking and Shaping Beastly Bodies: Animals as Material Culture in the Middle Ages* (Oxford, 2007), 125–48.

Thompson, A. H., *The English Clergy and their Organization in the Later Middle Ages* (Oxford, 1947).

Thompson, E. P., *Customs in Common: Studies in Traditional Popular Culture* (London, 1991).

Thomson, J. A. F., 'Scots in England in the Fifteenth Century', *Scottish Historical Review*, 79:207 (2000), 1–16.

Tomlins, C., 'Historicism and Materiality in Legal Theory', in M. Del Mar and M. Lobban (eds), *Law, Theory and History: New Essays on a Neglected Dialogue* (Oxford, 2016), 57–83.

Tompkins, M., '"Let's Kill All the Lawyers": Did Fifteenth-Century Peasants Employ Lawyers when they Conveyed Customary Land?', in L. Clark (ed.), *The Fifteenth Century VI: Identity and Insurgency in the Late Middle Ages* (Woodbridge, 2006), 73–87.

Trentmann, F., 'Materiality in the Future of History: Things, Practices, and Politics', *Journal of British Studies*, 48:2 (2009), 283–307.

Trotter, D., 'Oceano vox: You never know where a ship comes from. On multilingualism and language-mixing in medieval Britain', in K. Braunmüller and G. Ferraresi (eds), *Aspects of Multilingualism in European Language History* (Amsterdam, 2003), 15–34.

Tuck, J. A., 'The Cambridge Parliament, 1388', *EHR*, 84:331 (1969), 225–43.

Tucker, P., 'London's Courts of Law in the Fifteenth Century: The Litigants' Perspective', in C. Brooks and M. Lobban (eds), *Communities and Courts in Britain, 1150–1900* (London, 1997), 25–41.

Tucker, P., *Law Courts and Lawyers in the City of London, 1300–1550* (Cambridge, 2007).

Valverde, M., 'Seeing Like a City: The Dialectic of Modern and Premodern Ways of Seeing in Urban Governance', *Law & Society Review*, 45:2 (2011), 277–312.

Van de Noort, R., *North Sea Archaeologies: A Maritime Biography, 10,000 BC to AD 1500* (Oxford, 2011).

Vismann, C., *Files: Law and Media Technology*, transl. G. Winthrop-Young (Stanford, CA, 2008).

Vivo, F. de, *Information and Communication in Venice: Rethinking Early Modern Politics* (Cambridge, 2007).

Waddell, B., 'Governing England Through the Manor Courts, 1550–1850', *The Historical Journal*, 55:2 (2012), 279–315.

Wakelin, D., 'Writing the Words', in A. Gillespie and D. Wakelin (eds), *The Production of Books in England 1350–1500* (Cambridge, 2011), 34–58.

Walford, W. S., and Way, A., 'Examples of medieval seals', *Archaeological Journal*, 11 (1854), 367–80.

Walker, S., 'Rumour, Sedition and Popular Protest in the Reign of Henry IV', *P&P*, 166 (2000), 31–65.

Walsham, A., *The Reformation of the Landscape: Religion, Identity, and Memory in early Modern Britain and Ireland* (Oxford, 2011).

Ward, R., *The World of the Medieval Shipmaster: Law, Business and the Sea, c.1350–c.1450* (Woodbridge, 2009).

Watkins, A., 'Cattle Grazing in the Forest of Arden in the Later Middle Ages', *Agricultural History Review*, 37:1 (1989), 12–25.

Watkins, A., 'Landowners and Their Estates in the Forest of Arden in the Fifteenth Century', *Agricultural History Review*, 45:1 (1997), 18–33.

Watts, J. L., 'Conclusion', in J. L. Watts (ed.), *The End of the Middle Ages? England in the Fifteenth and Sixteenth Centuries* (Stroud, 1998), 263–70.

Watts, J. L., 'The Pressure of the Public on Later Medieval Politics', in L. Clark and C. Carpenter (eds), *The Fifteenth Century IV: Political Culture in Late-Medieval England* (Woodbridge, 2004), 159–80.

Watts, J. L., 'Public or Plebs: The Changing Meaning of "the Commons", 1381–1549', in H. Pryce and J. L. Watts (eds), *Power and Identity in the Middle Ages: Essays in Memory of Rees Davies* (Oxford, 2007), 242–60.

Watts, J. L., *The Making of Polities: Europe, 1300–1500* (Cambridge, 2009).

Way, A., 'Notices of the king's seals for passes given to Labourers and Servants, in accordance with the Statute passed at the Parliament of Cambridge, Sept. 12 Richard II. A. D. 1388', in *Antiquarian Communications: being papers presented at the meetings of the Cambridge Antiquarian Society* (London, 1859), 280–6.

Weber, J. K., 'The king's peace: a comparative study', *Journal of Legal History*, 10:2 (1989), 135–60.

Westervelt, T., 'Manifestoes for Rebellion in Late-Fifteenth-Century England', in B. Thompson and J. L. Watts (eds), *Political Society in Later Medieval England: A Festschrift for Christine Carpenter* (Woodbridge, 2015), 184–98.

Whittle, J., *The Development of Agrarian Capitalism in Norfolk, 1440–1580* (Oxford, 2000).

Whyte, N., *Inhabiting the Landscape: Place, Custom and Memory, 1500–1800* (Oxford, 2009).

Wicker, H., 'The Politics of Vernacular Speech: Cases of Treasonable Language, *c.*1440–1453', in E. Salter and H. Wicker (eds), *Vernacularity in England and Wales,* c. *1300–1550* (Turnhout, 2011), 171–97.

Wickham, C., 'European Forests in the Early Middle Ages: Landscape and Land Clearance', *Settimane di Studio del Centro Italiano di Studi Sull'alto Medioevo*, 37:2 (1990), 479–545.

Wickham, C., *Courts and Conflict in Twelfth-Century Tuscany* (Oxford, 2003).

Williamson, T., *Shaping Medieval Landscapes: Settlement, Society, Environment* (Macclesfield, 2003).

Wilson, K., 'The household inventory as urban "theatre" in late medieval Burgundy', *Social History*, 40:3 (2015), 335–59.

Winchester, A. J. L., *Landscape and Society in Medieval Cumbria* (Edinburgh, 1987).

Winchester, A. J. L., 'Dividing Lines in a Moorland Landscape: Territorial Boundaries in Upland England', *Landscapes*, 2:2 (2000), 16–32.

Winchester, A. J. L., 'Vaccaries and Agistment: Upland Medieval Forests as Grazing Grounds', in J. Langton and G. Jones (eds), *Forests and Chases of Medieval England and Wales,* c.*1000 to* c.*1500* (Oxford, 2010), 109–24.

Winters, C. L. 'The Portsoken Presentments: An Analysis of a London Ward in the 15th Century', *Transactions of the London and Middlesex Archaeological Society*, 56 (2005), 97–161.

Wood, A., *The Politics of Social Conflict: The Peak Country, 1520–1770* (Cambridge, 1999).

Wood, A., *The Memory of the People: Custom and Popular Senses of the Past in Early Modern England* (Cambridge, 2013).

Wood, A., 'The Deep Roots of Albion's Fatal Tree: The Tudor State and the Monopoly of Violence', *History*, 99:336 (2014), 403–17.

Woods, P., 'The Parsonage, or Rectory Manor of Godalming, and a Fourteenth-Century Custumal Thereof', *Surrey Archaeological Collections*, 22 (1909), 12–36.

Wright, E. C., 'Common Law in the Thirteenth-Century English Royal Forest', *Speculum*, 3:2 (1928), 166–91.

Wright, L., 'Mixed-Language Accounts as Sources for Linguistic Analysis', in J. A. Jefferson and A. Putter (eds), *Multilingualism in Medieval Britain (c.1066–1520)* (Turnhout, 2013), 123–36.

Wrightson, K., 'The "Decline of Neighbourliness" Revisited', in N. L. Jones and D. Woolf (eds), *Local Identities in Late Medieval and Early Modern England* (Basingstoke, 2007), 19–49.

Wunderli, R., *London Church Courts and Society on the Eve of the Reformation* (Cambridge, MA, 1981).

Wunderli, R., 'Pre-Reformation London Summoners and the Murder of Richard Hunne', *Journal of Ecclesiastical History*, 33:2 (1982), 209–24.

Yates, M., 'The market in freehold land, 1300–1509: the evidence of feet of fines', *Economic History Review*, 66:2 (2013), 579–600.

Young, C. R., 'The Forest Eyre in England during the Thirteenth Century', *American Journal of Legal History*, 18:4 (1974), 321–31.

Young, C. R., *The Royal Forests of Medieval England* (Philadelphia, PA, 1979).

Unpublished PhD dissertations

Bevan, K., 'Clerks and Scriveners: Legal Literacy and Access to Justice in Late Medieval England', unpublished PhD thesis, University of Exeter (2013).

Dick, B. D., '"Framing Piracy": restitution at sea in the later Middle Ages', unpublished PhD thesis, University of Glasgow (2010).

Frankot, E., 'Medieval Maritime Law and its Practice in the Towns of Northern Europe: a Comparison by the example of Shipwreck, Jettison and Ship Collision', unpublished PhD thesis, University of Aberdeen (2004).

Simpson, P., 'Custom and Conflict: Disputes over Tithe in the Diocese of Canterbury, 1501–1600', unpublished PhD thesis, University of Kent (1997).

Tompkins, M., 'Peasant Society in a Midlands Manor, Great Horwood 1400–1600', unpublished PhD thesis, University of Leicester (2006).

Index

For the benefit of digital users, indexed terms that span two pages (e.g., 52–53) may, on occasion, appear on only one of those pages.